T0323571

THE CELYS AND THEIR WORLD

THE CELYS AND THEIR WORLD

An English merchant family
of the fifteenth century

ALISON HANHAM

Reader in History, Massey University

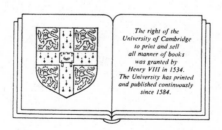

The right of the
University of Cambridge
to print and sell
all manner of books
was granted by
Henry VIII in 1534.
The University has printed
and published continuously
since 1584.

CAMBRIDGE UNIVERSITY PRESS

Cambridge

London   New York   New Rochelle

Melbourne   Sydney

PUBLISHED BY THE PRESS SYNDICATE OF THE UNIVERSITY OF CAMBRIDGE
The Pitt Building, Trumpington Street, Cambridge, United Kingdom

CAMBRIDGE UNIVERSITY PRESS
The Edinburgh Building, Cambridge CB2 2RU, UK
40 West 20th Street, New York NY 10011–4211, USA
477 Williamstown Road, Port Melbourne, VIC 3207, Australia
Ruiz de Alarcón 13, 28014 Madrid, Spain
Dock House, The Waterfront, Cape Town 8001, South Africa

http://www.cambridge.org

First published 1985
First paperback edition 2002

A catalogue record for this book is available from the British Library

Library of Congress catalogue card number: 85-4179

ISBN 0 521 30447 4 hardback
ISBN 0 521 52012 6 paperback

CONTENTS

FIGURES AND TABLES

PREFACE

Some time after March 1490, Richard Cely the younger, landed pro-
prietor, ship-owner and wool-merchant, sued the widow of his brother
George for debt. Richard and George had been trading partners from
1476 until George's death in June 1489, and as evidence in the suit, which
was subsequently prosecuted by Richard's widow, a mass of account
books and other papers were delivered into the Court of Chancery.
Commercial experts were appointed to investigate the respective claims,
and clerks sorted through the material and drew up statements of
account. But after this had been done, only some business ledgers were
returned to the heirs, and everything else was retained by the court.
When the Public Record Office was established the surviving documents,
in varying states of decay, were rescued from storage in the Tower of
London and eventually properly conserved and catalogued among the
national collections.

George Cely had kept papers indiscriminately. There are now two
volumes containing some 242 letters (a few more became separated and
are bound up in other volumes of 'Ancient Correspondence'),[1] while
nine files in the class of 'Chancery Miscellanea' now contain about 232
separate accounts and memoranda by or relating to the family.[2] There
are large chronological gaps in the surviving material, but these losses
are partly compensated for the historian by the fact that George kept
documents of the most personal or trivial kind, and the Chancery officials
failed to return even those that had no conceivable bearing on the
finances of the partnership. For variety of content, the Cely papers are
therefore among the most interesting, as well as the most disorganized,
of the English family collections that have come down to us from the

[1] Public Record Office, Ancient Correspondence S.C.1 vols 53 and 59, and 51/2, 60/94,
63/309.
[2] Public Record Office, Chancery Miscellanea C.47/37 Files 10–16, 20 and 21. The last
file was in process of arrangement at the time of writing.

fifteenth century. With all their deficiencies, they also constitute much the biggest surviving archive of a medieval English firm.

A selection of the letters, with a few other documents, was published in 1900.[3] Subsequently, a further bundle was discovered, containing some of the most lively items of the collection.[4] A complete edition, in the Celys' rather idiosyncratic spelling, appeared as an Early English Text Society volume in 1975.[5] The letters have therefore been known to scholars for a much shorter time than the far more extensive Paston collection, and have received less general attention.

The Celys' business papers have been studied chiefly for the information they give about the export trade in raw wool, although they have also been quarried for evidence on such subjects as shipping, numismatics, credit instruments and the salt trade. But thanks to George Cely's unmethodical habits, his papers contain far more than the routine records of a business firm. There is certainly much about the business of a stapler, and a series of full accounts for the rigging, provisioning and voyages of a trading ship. But here too may be found catering bills for dinner parties, funeral feasts and a wedding, accounts for daily household expenditure, lists of family silver plate, a love letter, the casual record of a cosy hour or two spent with a mistress in Calais, details of music lessons, a challenge from the married men to the bachelors of the Staple for a contest in archery, a note about the rumours current shortly before Richard III ascended the throne, items galore to be shopped for at the marts in Flanders and Brabant, and news of the horses, hounds and hawks which provided sport.

The aim of this work is to present this large amount of varied material in coherent form, and at the same time to make accessible as much information from it as possible. Deficiencies in the evidence mean that no orthodox biographical study of the Celys can be attempted. Rather, they have been left, as far as feasible, to speak for themselves, in copious extracts from their papers. In these, spelling and punctuation have been freely modernized, but the original syntax and vocabulary are preserved, with explanations where necessary inserted in square brackets. Square brackets have also been used where matter had to be supplied in the

³ Henry Elliot Malden, ed., *The Cely Papers: Selections from the Correspondence and Memoranda of the Cely Family, Merchants of the Staple, A.D. 1475–1488* (Royal Historical Society, Camden Third Ser. 1, 1900). Two of these letters had previously appeared, with some other material, in Henry Hall, 'The English Staple', *The Gentleman's Magazine*, CCLV (Sept. 1883), 255–75.
⁴ P.R.O. S.C.1 vol. 59. One was published in C. L. Kingsford, *Prejudice and Promise in Fifteenth-Century England* (Oxford, 1925), and four others in Laetitia Lyell, *A Mediaeval Post-Bag* (1934).
⁵ Alison Hanham, ed., *The Cely Letters, 1472–1488* (Early English Text Society No. 273, Oxford, 1975).

interests of sense. But in the innumerable places where words or letters have been lost through damage to the manuscripts, editorial reconstructions are offered without notice. (They are duly marked in the Early English Text Society edition of the letters.) Roman numerals have generally been replaced by arabic, and sums of money are given in modern form. As a rule, place-names and Christian names have also been modernized and anglicized, and some attempt has been made to standardize spellings of surnames, especially foreign ones. Thus Gysbryght or Gysbreth Van Wynesbragg, Wynbarow, Wynsbarge, Whenysbarge, Wynesberghe, etc. is rendered as 'Ghijsbrecht Van Wijnsberg'.

The nature of the material has dictated the peculiar organization of the book. The correspondence, and some of the other papers, lent themselves to a chronological narrative, although there are some major gaps where a whole series of letters are missing. Some of the accounts and memoranda deal with neatly defined topics, such as the expenses of housekeeping or the operation of the ship *Margaret Cely*. These subjects were best given chapters of their own, but could still find a roughly chronological place in the account of the activities of Richard and George Cely after the death of their father. There remained much material which was, in general, of more interest to the specialist in economic history than the student of social history. The great importance of the Celys' papers for the history of the English wool trade is that they elucidate many financial and technical details of the staplers' dealings at this particular period. Some of their evidence has long been known, thanks mainly to the pioneering work of the late Professor Eileen Power. But details have been misunderstood, and some aspects have not been fully investigated. In a work based on the totality of the Celys' papers it was essential to give a comprehensive account of their activities as staplers, but impossible to do so without interrupting the narrative of events. The solution chosen was to break the story at the death of Richard Cely senior in January 1482, and insert a section of five chapters concerned with the details of trade and organization. The reader who is more interested in the 'social history' aspect of the Celys' lives may wish to skip this central section, and to take the story up again at Chapter 10. But the final chapter again concerns financial affairs, because it was a quarrel over money that brought the family papers into Chancery.

ACKNOWLEDGMENTS

It is impossible to name all the people to whom I have turned for advice on different aspects of my work on the Cely papers over the past thirty years. But I owe special debts of gratitude to the late Miss Susie I. Tucker of the English Department of Bristol University, who, all unaware of the extent of the subsidiary material, first suggested that I undertake an edition of the Celys' letters and supervised the resulting dissertation; to my former husband, Dr H. J. Hanham, for his unstinted support and encouragement, and to Professor Norman Davis, who has saved me from many errors. The late Professor E. M. Carus-Wilson displayed most kindly tolerance towards a student of language who, blundering rudely into the field of economic history, appealed to her for guidance.

Professors Philip Grierson and John H. Munro corresponded at length about their subjects of speciality and generously shared materials with me. Professor J. D. Gould, while disclaiming expertise in the area, graciously agreed to read a draft of Chapter 7, and made helpful comments. My own university has, happily, a special concern with sheep and wool, and Mr W. R. Regnault, of the Wool Department, helped to elucidate some puzzles about fifteenth-century practice. In addition, I should like to acknowledge the very useful criticisms that I have received at various times from the editors and advisory readers of the *Bulletin of the Institute of Historical Research* and *Speculum*, and from the anonymous readers who commented on the typescript of this book for the Cambridge University Press.

For access to Richard Hill's commonplace book (Balliol College, Oxford, MS 354) I am indebted to the kindness of Mr E. V. Quinn.

Reference to the courteous assistance of the officers of the Public Record Office in Chancery Lane is almost axiomatic, but special thanks are due to Miss M. Condon and Dr E. M. Hallam-Smith who in 1980 arranged for me to see and transcribe some previously unknown Cely manuscripts which were still in the process of conservation and cataloguing. Nearly all of them produced valuable new information. Study-leave in that year was supported by Massey University, which also made grants towards the purchase of photocopied materials.

Modern-spelling quotations from the Cely letters are based on the text published by the Early English Text Society in 1975, and given here with the permission of the Society, which holds the copyright in the edition.

ABBREVIATIONS

A.C.M.	*Acts of Court of the Mercers' Company, 1453–1527*, ed. Laetitia Lyell (Cambridge, 1936).
B.I.H.R.	*Bulletin of the Institute of Historical Research.*
Cal. Papal Letters	*Calendar of Entries in the Papal Registers relating to Great Britain and Ireland. Papal Letters 1471–1484* (1955), *1484–1492* (1960).
Campbell, *Materials*	*Materials for a History of the Reign of Henry VII*, ed. W. Campbell (Rolls Series, 1873–7).
C.C.R.	*Calendar of Close Rolls.*
Cely Papers	*The Cely Papers: Selections from the Correspondence and Memoranda of the Cely Family, Merchants of the Staple, A.D. 1475–1488*, ed. H. E. Malden (Camden 3rd Ser. 1, 1900).
C.L.	*The Cely Letters, 1472–1488*, ed. Alison Hanham, Early English Text Society 273 (Oxford, 1975).
cl.	clove (wool weight).
Cots.	Cotswold (wool or fell).
C.P.R.	*Calendar of Patent Rolls.*
di.	*dimidium*, half.
'Discourse'	'A Discourse of Weights and Merchandise', British Library MS. Cotton Vespasian E. ix, fos. 86–108v.
E.E.T.S.	Early English Text Society.
E.R.O.	Essex Record Office. Barrett Lennard papers, D/DL T1.
Fl., Flem.	Flemish; *groot* money of Flanders.
Foedera	*Foedera, Conventiones, literae et cuiusque generis acta publica...*, ed. Thomas Rymer, 3rd edn, 10 vols. (The Hague, 1739–45.)

gr.

(1) *groot* money of account of Flanders or Calais. (2) denier(s) of this system.

MS. *Harleian 433*

British Library MS. Harleian 433, ed. Rosemary Horrox and P. W. Hammond, vols. I & II (1979–80).

ob.

obolus, halfpenny.

O.E.D.

Oxford English Dictionary.

P.C.C.

(Registers of wills proved in) the Prerogative Court of Canterbury.

P.R.O.

Public Record Office, London.

C.1 Early Chancery Proceedings.

C.47 Chancery Miscellanea. Cely material in this class (Bundle 37) is referred to by File and folio or document number.

C.76 Treaty Rolls.

E.122 Exchequer King's Remembrancer Customs Accounts.

Prob. Wills and inventories from P.C.C.

S.C.1 Ancient Correspondence.

S.P. State Papers.

qr

quadrans, farthing or quarter.

Rot. Parl.

Rotuli Parliamentorum..., Great Britain, Record Commissioners (1767–77).

s

sack-weight. ss two sack-weights.

stg.

sterling money of account, of England or Calais.

st. ta.

sterling table, money of account in Calais.

PART I

THE CELYS AND THEIR CIRCLE, 1474–82

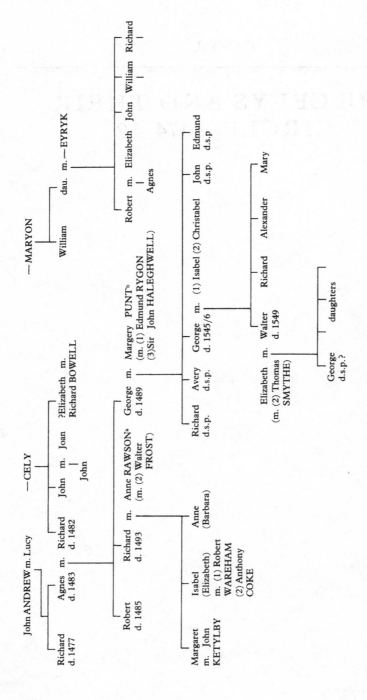

THE CELY FAMILY

a. For Anne and her family, see Ch. 10, p. 269 and Postscript.
b. For Margery, see Ch. 12 and Postscript.

THE CELY FAMILY AND
THEIR BACKGROUND

Sometime around the mid-fifteenth century the three Cely boys, Robert, Richard and George, were born to an established wool-merchant, Richard Cely senior, and his wife Agnes. The elder Richard was a worshipful citizen of London, proud to be designated 'merchant of the Fellowship of the Staple at Calais'. He was, it seems, in a minority among the larger exporters of raw wool, in that the wool trade constituted his main business interest. Many of the leading staplers of the period were also merchant adventurers, importing and exporting a variety of other goods in addition to their trade at the Calais wool staple, the only authorized point at which good quality English wool might be sold abroad. But although Richard was not one of the richest or most influential men in City politics, by the time that the Cely papers begin, about 1473, he was a man of substance, with a town-house in a desirable area of London, an estate in Essex, and other land in Oxfordshire and Northamptonshire, and was enjoying the seniority in his Company which past office-holding and long continuance conferred.

There can be little doubt that merchants (that is, men engaged in wholesale trade) thought of themselves as forming a distinct class in society, however shifting the outer edges of the stratum, however realistic might be their hopes of marrying daughters into a higher class and of making their sons into landed gentlemen, well-beneficed clergy, or rich and influential lawyers, and however close the threat of the sickness, unlucky venture or political reversal which could overturn a man's fortunes and send him and his children into penury. Poets, preachers, legislators, civic authorities and the heads of his own Company reinforced the merchant's view of himself as a person of dignity, and one distinct from other orders of men. The table of precedence in the commonplace book of the early sixteenth-century merchant Richard Hill even put the merchant immediately after masters in chancery, parsons of churches and secular priests, and before 'gentlemen', artificers and 'a yeoman of good

3

name'.[1] And citizens of London took pride in the claim that within the city their mayor ranked next to the king himself. William Gregory, himself mayor in 1451, recounted with relish the story of how one of his successors, invited to the feast for the Sergeants of the Coif, found that the Earl of Worcester had been given the place of honour. The mayor promptly walked out, with most of his aldermen. And such were his resources that when an emissary of the rejected hosts arrived at the mayor's quarters, he found in progress a far more magnificent banquet. It included swan, added Gregory importantly.[2]

But one has only to read Peter Laslett's *The World We Have Lost* to perceive that the fifteenth-century merchant had a life-style which barely touches the world there depicted.[3] This is because, as its title suggests, the book reconstructs those aspects of a pre-industrial society which provide the greatest contrast to the twentieth-century picture. In so far as it is true to say that a 'middle-class culture' permeates western civilization today, the fact is that our links with the past extend through the Celys and their fellow citizens, not through the squirearchy of the Pastons and Stonors, endlessly preoccupied with their rights over lands and tenants, and not through the yeomen, husbandmen, and agrarian labourers from whom most of us genetically descend.

For many ambitious young men who had no claim to the landed estates of the gentry proper, a successful career in some branch of overseas trade was as much a high road to fortune in the fifteenth century as it had been in distant Anglo-Saxon times, when a merchant who made three trading voyages with his own ship and acquired certain other signs of secure respectability was held to have earned the status of a *thegn*.[4] In the fourteenth and fifteenth centuries manuals circulated which promised to turn the hopeful purchaser into a flourishing businessman. Then, as now, there was a receptive market for such sage advice as

who some ever useth to buy any chaffer, he ought ever to buy it so that he may have reasonable winning thereof toward his living. And it is better a man 'to rue sold than to rear hold', that is to say, rather take a little loss than to lose all. For chaffer is ever more fresher when it is new, and more pleasant to see, than it is when it is old. And there is an old proverb that men say, 'Light winning make an heavy purse', and 'Many small make a great'. For he that hath money may renew his ware every day when he will.[5]

[1] Balliol College, Oxford, MS. 354, fo. 203v.
[2] James Gairdner, ed., *The Historical Collections of a Citizen of London in the Fifteenth Century* (Camden Soc., 1876), p. 222.
[3] Peter Laslett, *The World We Have Lost* (2nd edn, London, 1971).
[4] Dorothy Whitelock, *The Beginnings of English Society* (Harmondsworth, 1952), p. 86.
[5] 'A Discourse of Weights and Merchandise' (commonly miscalled 'The Number of Weights'), B.L. MS. Cotton Vespasian E. IX, fo. 97v.

The writer of this offered a 'get-rich-quick' formula built around the key-words 'where, what, when, be ware and [in]quisitive' which at least one American business consultant was still employing, in essence, five centuries later.[6]

Such works reflected a buoyant mood in the later fifteenth century, created, it may be, by widening opportunities, a higher standard of living for many people, and greater availability of schooling. But it was all very well to claim that 'there be many poor beginners that prove to thrifty men [i.e. attain prosperity]' provided they remembered to buy penny wares, 'as purses, knives, girdles, glasses, hats', for no more than 8*d* the dozen, halfpenny ware for 4*d*, and farthing ware for 2*d*, and to sell them at a mark-up of 2*d* in the shilling.[7] This advice applied to men 'who march with foot-packs' and other chapmen, who were, however, specifically excluded from apprenticeship in the London Mercers' Company and any share in the privilege and prestige of its members.[8] Young men without capital or connections had little real chance of breaking into the higher ranks of the commercial world.

If entry to these upper echelons of trade was not easy to achieve in one generation, it remains true that those who held that fortunate position were always to some extent 'self-made'. It would therefore be interesting to know the antecedents of Richard Cely senior. But the first certain documentary reference to him occurs in October 1449, when he was among the London staplers named in a list of those who had lent Henry VI 2,000 marks 'for the wages of Henry, Viscount Boucer' (Bourgchier) and others of the Calais garrison, in return for the remission of subsidy dues on some shipments of wool and fell.[9] In 1455 he was one of five leading staplers who, together with the mayor of the Staple, made an indenture with the victualler of Calais, Sir John Cheyne, in the same matter.[10] How he had come to enter the wool trade is not known. Possibly he belonged to a collateral branch of the family of Cely or Sely who had had some prominence in London merchant life throughout the fourteenth and early fifteenth centuries, and subsequently sank in the social scale. In 1459 the main line of that family was represented, in legitimate descent, by Simon Sely, son of John Sely, brewer of London. John's father, who had been heir to certain 'livelihood' in London and Bristol,

---

[6] Obituary notice of William J. Reilly, Director of the National Institute for Straight Thinking, *New York Times*, 19 Nov. 1970.

[7] 'Discourse', fos. 97v–98.

[8] Laetitia Lyell, ed., *Acts of Court of the Mercers' Company, 1453–1527* (Cambridge, 1936), p. xi.

[9] *Calendar of Patent Rolls, 1446–52*, p. 315; *Rotuli Parliamentorum*, v, 208. He may also be the Richard Cely given seisin of a tenement and wharves in Thames St in June 1440: Hustings Roll 169 (59).

[10] *C.P.R., 1452–61*, p. 106; *Rot. Parl.* v, 295.

killed a miller in youth and moved about from place to place under the names of John Bartholomew or John Saly. He took up with one Denise Craneford and was finally compelled to marry her, 'thereto right loath, because she was in manner an idiot and had nor knew no worldly reason'. The proof of imbecility adduced by one of her grandsons was that 'she would call a *noble* a *nubbyll*'.[11]

But the name Cely or Sely (from Old English *sælig* 'blessed') was not uncommon in fifteenth-century England. It is just as likely that Richard, or his immediate forebears, had come to London from some provincial town where the family had settled for a time after succeeding in the process of emancipation and amassment of a little land and capital in their original village, on the pattern which had become familiar in England over the preceding century or two, when 'villein' families who were lucky enough to escape plagues and famines might take advantage of shortages of labour, gradual relaxations in manorial controls and the new availability of land after a fall in population, and attain the new status of 'yeoman'. Some of the more fortunate and enterprising of these set up, in time, as merchants in a town like Leicester, Coventry, Hull, York, Bristol or London itself, as did the Wyggeston, Wyxston or Wigston family whose background is traced in W. G. Hoskins's *The Midland Peasant*.[12] William Wyggeston, who became a substantial merchant and philanthropist in Leicester, was, like the Celys, a member of the Company of the Staple. But the only reference in the Celys' papers to a member of the previous generation is the incidental information that Robert Cely's wife, who died in 1479, was buried in London beside his grandmother.[13] Paternal or maternal? If paternal, had Richard's father been buried in some country place whence the rest of the family migrated to London? All that can be said on the question is the negative observation that there are no pronounced provincial features in the language or spelling of Richard or his brother John Cely, who was a woolman and also a merchant of the Staple.[14]

Richard and John may have had a sister named Elizabeth. In 1480 John mentions to his nephew George Cely that

there was in time past a variance and a jar between Richard Bowell and my master your father for a duty [debt] that he should owe to my said master your father.

[11] Philip E. Jones, ed., *Calendar of Plea and Memoranda Rolls, 1458–82* (Cambridge, 1961), pp. 4–7. For a list of others of the family, and assorted unconnected Celys, see Sylvia Thrupp, *The Merchant Class of Medieval London* (Michigan, 1948), p. 365.
[12] W. G. Hoskins, *The Midland Peasant : The Economic and Social History of a Leicestershire Village* (1957).
[13] *C.L.* 58.
[14] Guildhall (London) MS. 9171/8 fo. 10v (17 Oct. 1490) is the will of a John Cely, skinner of London, but there is nothing to connect him with our family.

And it is so now by my labour I have made my sister and my master your father accorded and agreed for that matter, and a part is forgiven, and the t'other part ye and my cousin Richard your brother shall have to part between you.[15]

'My sister' could mean the sister of John's wife, but this seems unlikely in view of the arrangement to allow Richard and George to share the money. The probable implication is that the sister was the widow of Richard Bowell. Bowell was a stapler who had been in a partnership of sorts with Richard Cely and John Felde in 1449, when the loan was made to Henry VI, and had died in 1478. His will gives us the name of his wife, Elizabeth.[16]

There are two particular puzzles about the immediate family. John Stow, in his *Survey of London* (1598), describes a memorial in the Celys' parish church of St Olave, Hart Street, to 'Richard Cely and Robert Cely, fellmongers, principal builders and benefactors of this church'.[17] No dates are furnished. Richard Cely is presumably the father of Robert, Richard and George, who bequeathed money for making the steeple and an altar in the church, whose merchant mark was carved in two of the corbels of the nave, and whose tomb was erected by his son Richard.[18] But who was Robert? His impecunious son Robert? A member of the earlier generation? Or did Stow simplify a partially obliterated inscription which had included Richard's wife Agnes and son Richard, who were also buried in this tomb?[19]

The other 'unattached' member of the household is the William Cely who spent his short adult life as the family's faithful and deferential factor at Calais. He received no bequest in the will of Agnes Cely, who left money to John's wife and son (a student at Oxford),[20] nor is he ever addressed by a member of the family in terms that would suggest close relationship. He was probably a rather distant dependant, who shared, however, a godfather with Richard Cely junior. 'Cousins' of Richard and George, a term used loosely in a society where relationships within a wide network were carefully nurtured, were Thomas Blackham, fishmonger of London, Robert Coldale of Rainham, John Maynard, and the lawyer William Cottillard or Cutlerd.

[15] *C.L.* 88.   [16] Prerogative Court of Canterbury, 33 Wattys.

[17] John Stow, *The Survey of London*, ed. C. L. Kingsford (Oxford, 1908), I, 132.

[18] The mark on two of the stone corbels is reproduced in Alfred Povah, *The Annals of the Parishes of St Olave Hart Street and Allhallows Staining in the City of London* (1894), p. 27.

[19] Richard junior requested burial there in his will, P.C.C. 25 Dogett and Essex Record Office D/DL T1 528.

[20] P.C.C. 8 Logge. Her nephew, later called 'Master' John Cely, does not appear in A. B. Emden, *A Biographical Register of the University of Oxford to A.D. 1500* (Oxford, 1957).

The two elder Cely boys may have been named after close relatives. 'George' was still an uncommon name in England, despite the fact that it belonged to her patron saint.[21] It was, however, favoured by the Neville family at this time, and was borne by the Duke of Clarence, younger brother of Edward IV, and given to one of the king's own children, George of Windsor. A very odd feature of letters to George Cely from his father is the sudden switch in 1479 from 'thee' on 15 April to 'you' on 30 April. I have conjectured that George had attained his majority in the interim: was he perhaps born on St George's Day, 23 April?

The date at which Richard Cely senior married has not been ascertained. His wife was Agnes, daughter of John and Lucy Andrew of Adderbury, Oxfordshire. Her elder brother, Richard Andrew, had made his way in the world along one of the other main roads which lay open to an able young man: a career in the church. He served as chancellor to Archbishop Chichele and official of the court of Canterbury, and had become a clerk in royal government employ by 1433. From 1442 to 1455 he was secretary to Henry VI. Along the way he picked up a handsome collection of benefices and offices, and was rewarded for his services by being obtruded on the chapter of York Minster as Dean of York in 1452. Possibly only the replacement of Henry by Edward IV prevented further promotion to a bishopric. Andrew did, however, have the minor distinction of becoming the first warden both of Sion College and of All Souls, Oxford.[22]

Although there is no direct evidence in the Cely papers that they had much to do with this rather grand relative, property deeds show that it was from him that Richard Cely senior acquired his country estate, Bretts Place, in Aveley, Essex, in July 1462, and other properties in Aveley, Rainham and Upminster.[23] Almost certainly it was through the same connection that he obtained his house in Mark Lane, London. Andrew himself held the Essex properties as heir of Isabel, widow of Robert Arnold, a well-to-do London grocer.[24] It may also be that Andrew had

[21] E. G. Withycombe, *The Oxford Dictionary of English Christian Names* (3rd edn, Oxford, 1977), p. 129.
[22] J. Otway-Ruthven, *The King's Secretary and the Signet Office in the Fifteenth Century* (Cambridge, 1939), pp. 172–3; J. Raine, ed., *Testamenta Eboracensia*, III (Surtees Soc. XLV, 1865), pp. 232–7.
[23] E.R.O. D/DL T1 441, 442. At his death in 1477 Andrew bequeathed Richard Cely senior all the bed-hangings and utensils that he had left at Bretts Place, except the best feather bed, best brass pot and 2 muslin pillows, which were to go to Henry Fyfeld. His younger sister Agnes had a pair of sheets of 'Reynez' cloth.
[24] Andrew is described as Isabel's 'cousin and heir' in D/DL T1 441, but the properties bequeathed her by her husband were all sold after her death in accordance with his will: D/DL T1 420. Robert Arnold (sheriff of London in 1426) was granted Bretts

taken an interest in the education of his nephew Richard. In 1481 Richard paid visits to 'mine old acquaintance' in Leicester, where Andrew became Dean of Newarke College in 1450, and in York, where Andrew had lived as a residentiary canon for at least eighteen years.[25] This is hardly conclusive. But two slightly more substantial pieces of evidence suggest that Richard might have been singled out in his youth to spend some time in the north in his uncle's household. These are Richard's handwriting, which is more formal and bookish than the hands of his brothers and other merchants of the time, and the surprising existence of some northern linguistic traits in his letters, features that are entirely absent from the writings of other members of the family. For example, in his earlier letters he often uses *qw-* or *qwh-* for *wh-*, as in *qwher* or *qwerfor* 'where', 'wherefore', or *qwhych* 'which', and *at* (a Scandinavian form in origin) for the familiar southern English *that*.

William Maryon, member of the London Grocers' Company, merchant of the Staple, and fellow parishioner of the Celys, was an intimate and self-effacing friend of the whole family. He had property in Watford, and may have been a relation of the Richard Maryon, glover of Watford, who appears in documents of 1455–67.[26] William mentioned no house in London in his will of 1493,[27] and his close involvement with the Celys almost suggests that he spent much of his time in their household. His relations with the family went a long way back: he had stood godfather to Richard Cely junior (and also to William Cely, the apprentice and factor). Later he was godfather to Richard's youngest daughter. Any wife and children that Maryon may have had of his own predeceased him. His nephew, no doubt a sister's son, was Robert Eyryk or Herrick, girdler, a godson of George Cely. The Eyryks, Erykes or Herricks were another family from Wigston, Leicestershire.[28] Robert's brother John was also a citizen of London and a skinner, but John's will of 1494 left money to a third brother, William, who was still living in Wigston with his children. A married sister had moved to Coventry.[29] To complete the

in 1410 (D/DL T1 316) and Andrew had obtained it by March 1454. Robert and Isabel Arnold enfeoffed the tenement in Mark Lane in May 1424: Hustings Roll 153 (6).

[25] *C.L.* 117. But 'Alison Michael' of York was an acquaintance of both George and Richard. Alison was given one of Agnes Cely's gowns when she visited London with her husband, Michael Koke, in 1482: *C.L.* 165. For Andrew's residence see Barrie Dobson, 'The Residentiary Canons of York in the Fifteenth Century', *Journal of Ecclesiastical History*, xxx (1979), 145–74.

[26] *Calendar of Close Rolls, 1454–61*, 50, *C.C.R., 1461–8*, 210, 442.

[27] P.C.C. 19 Vox.

[28] Hoskins, *The Midland Peasant*, passim. The name appears in the earliest records, from c. 1250.

[29] P.C.C. 14 Vox. There was another brother, Richard, 'upholder' of London: *C.L.* 154; R. Sharpe, ed., *Calendar of Letter-Books Preserved among the Archives of the Corporation of the City of London at the Guildhall: Letter-Book L* (1912), pp. 150, 182, 304.

circle of Cely–Maryon–Eyryk connections, Agnes Cely, mother of Richard and George, was godmother of Agnes Eyryk, daughter of that Robert Eyryk who was George's godson and Maryon's nephew. Such ties were no matter of mere ecclesiastical convention, but entailed recognized social obligations between godparent and child, and also cemented relations between godparent and natural parents. Parents-in-god took on a spiritual relationship and could not intermarry. Equally, the system could be used to extend the network of family connections, and it would be interesting to know what other godparents had been chosen for the Cely boys.

While it is uncertain what contact the Celys had with Dean Richard Andrew in the 1470s, their letters contain plenty of references to their immediate patron, Sir John Weston, who became prior of the English branch of the semi-military Order of St John of Jerusalem in 1476, at the age of forty-five.[30] As prior, Sir John ranked as the premier baron of England and had a more or less automatic place in the king's Council. He was especially the friend and 'good lord' of Richard junior, who often stayed in Sir John's household in the Order's London priory at Clerkenwell, or on various of their country estates. The Knights of St John had much property in Essex, including the area about the Celys' country house at Aveley. At other times Richard stayed at Temple Balsall, Warwicks., at the preceptory at Melchbourne, Beds., or at Sutton.[31] When, in 1479, he had been at Sutton from 10 April to 22 May, Richard complained rather boastfully that he 'could not get from my lord of St John's, not past three days together'.[32] In 1480 Sir John took Richard with him when he was an ambassador to the court of France, and shortly before that Richard accompanied him to Gravesend in a formal party of welcome to the king's sister, Margaret, Dowager Duchess of Burgundy, who was visiting England on diplomatic business.

A more practical favour was the protection extended by Sir John, which proved valuable when Richard and George were accused of poaching in the royal forest of Essex. Their position as appreciative 'clients' of Sir John was symbolized by the wearing of gowns of his livery, and the title 'my lord' invariably used to and of him by all the family. In return for his patronage, George executed commissions at the marts in Brabant for Sir John and members of his entourage, buying such

---

[30] *Calendar of Entries in the Papal Registers Relating to Great Britain and Ireland: Papal Letters 1484–1499* (1960), p. 19.
[31] Balsall had become a personal holding of the prior in 1476: David Knowles and R. Neville Hadcock, *Medieval Religious Houses, England and Wales* (2nd edn, 1971), p. 301. 'Sutton' is presumably Sutton-at-Hone, Kent, but the order had another estate named Sutton in Essex.
[32] *C.L.* 55.

things as saddles and spurs, furs or hose-cloth. Richard Cely senior was happy to lend Sir John money when he made a visit to Rhodes in 1481–2, and anxiously reminded George, in June 1480, to send Sir John any news that was current at Calais:

I think ye might write much more nor ye do, for my lord of St Johns send to me for tiding every week. For the which my lord take it for a great pleasure for to have such tiding as ye hear in [those] parts. For the which ye may no less do but write much the more of tiding, for my lord's sake. For in good faith, he is a courteous lord to me and to you and Richard Cely.[33]

At Calais, where 'one heard from all the world',[34] George was not only in touch with events in France and the low countries, but could be expected to glean news from still further afield. And if not at Calais, then at Bruges, where the Venetian and Florentine merchants would be sure to have tidings about the situation of Rhodes in 1481.[35]

While Sir John was abroad George sent him details of the current expedition against Scotland in 1482, and any other news, some of it a little stale:

Right worshipful sir and mine essingular good lord, after all due recommendation pretending, I recommend me unto your good lordship in the most lowliest wise that I can.

Furthermore, pleaseth it your lordship to understand that I have received an letter from your lordship, bearing date at Naples the last day of November [1481]...We understand, my lord, by your said letter of your royal receiving at Naples, and of your great presents, which was to us glad tidings and great rejoicing to hear of, etc.

Pleaseth it your lordship to understand that the Duke of Albany is comen into England, and he is sworn to the king's good grace. And the king has sent him into Scotland with 60,000 men in three battles [battalions], and many lords of England with him, Jesu be his good speed. Within an month there has been with[in] 44 towns and villages burnt in Scotland, and many lords taken and slain. Dumfries is burnt. Also, my lord the king's eldest daughter save one [i.e. the princess Mary] is dead now late. The young Duchess of Burgundy is dead, and that land is in great rumour. Of other tidings I can none write.[36]

This was only a draft copy; a conclusion to match the honorific opening would have been added.

Unhappily, all but one of Sir John's letters describing his voyage have disappeared. It may, however, have been Sir John who conveyed some very hot news about disturbing events and rumours in June 1483, as the

---

[33] C.L. 90.
[34] Norman Davis, ed., *Paston Letters and Papers of the Fifteenth Century*, I (Oxford, 1971), p. 494.
[35] C.L. 114.   [36] C.L. 178.

Duke of Gloucester made his moves to capture his nephew's throne.[37] A few curious markings, both in George's letter just quoted and in the note concerning the happenings in 1483, suggest that in their exchange of information the two were in the habit of replacing certain key words or phrases by ciphers. But George was a dilatory correspondent. In early 1488, when Sir John was kept in Calais by the fear of pirates, and sent a message by William Cely regretting this because he 'longed sore' to see Richard and George in London, he also said tactfully that

he marvel that ye write him no letters. He saith [he] had no word from your masterships since he departed out of England, wherefore he feareth him ye should take some displeasure with him or with some of his.[38]

Such courtesies of intercourse were carefully kept on both sides. Sir John addresses George as 'worshipful cousin' and commends himself 'to my father and yours, and your mother'.[39] Describing Richard senior as 'my father' was a matter of politeness to an older man. There may have been some relationship, but 'cousin' in this case was probably also a mere courtly form of address. 'Worshipful' (once abbreviated by John Cely to 'wursall')[40] was, on the other hand, a standard appellation for a merchant. Even Sir Ralph Hastings, brother of William, Lord Hastings, one-time Captain of Calais and Lord Chamberlain, may address George as 'right worshipful sir'. Otherwise he starts a letter, 'my full trusty friend', and signs 'your true loving Rauff Hastings'.[41] Robert Radcliffe, gentleman porter of Calais, who gave himself airs and signed 'le filz Sir John Radclyff, Robert', opens merely with 'brother George', addressing him as a fellow stapler. The address on the outside is 'to my right trusty brother George Cely, merchant of the Staple'.[42] 'Trusty' tended to mean that the writer wanted the recipient to do something for him.

There is a clear distinction between the opening of Richard senior's letters to his sons – almost invariably 'I greet you' (or earlier, 'thee') 'well, and...' – and George's opening to his father, 'right reverend and worshipful father'. George is addressed by his godson, Robert Eyryk, 'right reverend and worshipful sir', and the servant Joyce Parmenter begins 'right worshipful master'. But William Maryon, an older man, writes similarly to George, 'right reverend sir and my special good friend', or 'right worshipful and reverend sir', and George's wife Margery uses a similar form. To an important personage, epistolary openings might be much more flowery: 'Honourable and worshipful sir,

---

[37] *C.L.* 200.
[38] *C.L.* 240.
[39] *C.L.* 129.
[40] *C.L.* 88.
[41] *C.L.* 232, 245.
[42] *C.L.* 42, and similarly ('Brother George Sely') 65.

after all humble and due reverence had as appertaineth...'.[43] But in short notes to friends and servants or apprentices there was much less formality: 'brother Cely' or 'brother George' from other staplers, 'well-beloved, I greet you well' (Richard junior to the servant Joyce), 'William Cely, we greet you well, and...', 'Hugh, I pray you...'.

While 'sir' was used of a knight or a priest, it had no specially deferential connotations in ordinary employment. William Cely uses it to his masters Richard and George, but Richard uses it to his younger brother George. Staplers call each other 'sir', as well as the 'brother' which indicated membership in the same Company, or 'fellow George'. Roland Thornburgh of the Order of St John addresses Richard junior simply as 'bedfellow'.[44] 'Master', however, indicated a certain status. In drawing up bills for her lodgers at Calais, Agnes Burnell distinguished between 'master Cely', which apparently meant Richard senior, and 'Richard Cely' and 'George Cely'.[45] George's infant son was 'master Richard' to the factor Nicholas Best.[46]

In writing, at least, Christian names seldom appear on their own, except when applied to children and servants. Even when the abbreviation 'Will' is used, it is accompanied by the surname ('Will Cely', 'Will Maryon') in the letters. And in George's personal memoranda, he always refers to 'my brother Richard', not 'Richard'. William Cely writes of 'John Dalton' but of 'Joyce', and of 'Margery', the woman of the cookshop in Calais who had children by George. Male servants are 'Hankin', 'Harry my boy', or given their surname only, as 'Kay' (John Kay), 'Luntley' or 'Speryng'. Maidservants are 'Alison', 'Margaret', 'Joan', and Richard had a shameful encounter with 'Em'.[47] George, however, calls a higher-class mistress 'my lady Clare', presumably another example, like 'reverend' and 'worshipful', of a supposedly honorific title used more generally.[48] Robert Coldale wrote of his wife as 'my dame',[49] and husbands might use 'dame', 'wife' or 'spouse' in speaking to their wives. Women probably said 'sir', 'husband', or 'spouse'. Endearments seem to have become common form rather later, during the sixteenth century.

Servants like Joyce Parmenter were addressed strictly as 'ye' not 'thou', and 'ye' was also used between husband and wife, or parents and adult children. Richard senior's change from 'thee' to 'you' in his opening greeting to George therefore marks a very definite alteration.

[43] *C.L.* 16.
[44] *C.L.* 123.
[45] File 16 fos. 11–16.
[46] File 16 fo. 36.
[47] *C.L.* 169 and below, Ch. 10, p. 269.
[48] For Clare see Ch. 2, pp. 49–50.
[49] *C.L.* 60.

Between adults, 'thee' and 'thou' were instantly recognized as insulting in intent. One priest bitterly offended another in 1491 by saying to him, 'Avaunt, churl!' and 'I would prove thee a churl of condition' (that is, a bondman by birth), while two Buckinghamshire ladies also used the familiar pronoun in an exchange of 'thou art a strong whore!'.[50] There is a well-known example of a trade of insults in the Paston letters, displayed in both syntax and gesture when the family chaplain failed to doff his hat to the son of the house, and the dialogue went, 'Cover thy head?' 'So shall I, for thee!' 'Shalt thou so, knave?'[51]

An educated person in the fifteenth century was taught how to write letters in proper form, with introductory greeting, good wishes for the health and well-being of the correspondent, and perhaps deprecatory reference to one's own, followed by news to be conveyed and the main purpose of the letter, all finished with a polite and pious conclusion. The same phraseology, with minor variations to individual choice, can be found in all the collections of contemporary letters. Possibly specimens circulated, just as examples of more formal documents, such as letters of payment, of attorney, or of protection to confer immunity from creditors, were copied and passed round, to be printed in due course in a compilation like Richard Arnold's collection of material issued in 1502.[52] Epistolary formulae persisted well into the next century, but correspondents of the Celys' class gradually became more skilful in the use of the written language, experimented more freely, expressed themselves more easily, and drew more readily on richer resources of vocabulary.

Formal politeness to one's elders and superiors was inculcated by precept and ceremonial, and as a rule it was duly observed. This does not mean that any unnatural degree of respect coloured private attitudes. George Cely probably toned down one letter which conveyed criticism of his father before he actually sent it. His final phrase in his uncompleted draft, 'in the reverence of God see better to the packing of your wool that shall come', probably struck him as much too disrespectful.[53] Possibly, too, he remembered his brother Richard's plea a month or so before, in begging George to write home more frequently and so avoid family upsets: in the interest of averting 'discomforts', 'let us endeavour

---

[50] E. M. Elvey, ed., *The Courts of the Archdeaconry of Buckinghamshire, 1483–1523* (Bucks. Record Soc. XIX, 1975), nos. 148, 296.

[51] *Paston L.*, I, no. 129.

[52] Published at Antwerp as *The Names of the Baylifs Custos Mairs and Sherefs of the Cite of London...wyth odur dyvers maters good and necessary for euery citezen to vndirstond and knowe*. An edition by F. Douce was pub. in 1811 under the title of *The Customs of London, otherwise called Arnold's Chronicle*. Cited henceforth as Richard Arnold.

[53] *C.L.* 93.

us to please'.[54] 'Ye know [our father's] condition of old', said Richard when a row was occasioned about the number of horses which George kept at Calais, as tactlessly, or maliciously, reported to old Richard at a time when he was already 'pensive and heavy'.[55] Both parents were agitated by the prospect of war with France, with its attendant risk to George, and his brother warned that if by some disaster George engaged in the fighting and was taken prisoner or killed, it would spell immediate death to father and mother. 'We must tender their age, and have an eye to our own weal.' George had had a chance to give Richard advice on the proper management of a father in September 1476, again with self-interest mingled in his part-kindly, part-patronizing attitude to the old man:

Brother, our father is now at Calais, and is worshipful, and so taken. And for our honesties let us see that all thing about him be honest and cleanly [i.e. dignified and fitting]. He is not now at Aveley, and the more worshipful as he is at Calais, the better beloved shall we be, and the more set by these acts [by] the world. Brother, I understand he hath no mo to wait upon him but you. Do your duty, and at my coming to Calais I shall do mine. I think every hour three till [I] come to Calais: I hope to be with you shortly. I pray recommend me to our father.[56]

Plenty of young people have been nervous of exposing their parents to the criticism of their peer-group. Although 'cleanly' had little of its modern meaning, George does seem to imply that by this time of his life their father was happiest when leading a relaxed existence in the obscurity of the country, and that care must be taken lest he lower their prestige at Calais. Did the brothers always treat him with proper 'worship' in the privacy of their own home?

Perhaps it is over-subtle to see some element of parody of his father's tedious instructions in George's very dutiful and detailed rehearsal of how he dealt with a routine shipment of fells, probably in April of the previous year.[57] He carefully does all the arithmetic and informs his father (what the latter surely knew already) how many fells made the equivalent of a sarpler of fleece-wool. It is very likely that George had been scolded for failing to send proper reports on his business activities. Their father was certainly ready to upbraid his sons, especially for their slackness in writing home, and he had no great opinion of their business acumen or application. But he reveals great affection and solicitude for George at a time when George was ill in Bruges, promising to meet all necessary costs of doctors and diet, and begging George not to over-exert

[54] *C.L.* 84.
[55] *C.L.* 111 and Ch. 3, pp. 69–70.
[56] *C.L.* 4.
[57] *C.L.* 247.

himself and to 'be as merry as ye can'.[58] Richard junior's report of a conversation with his father in June 1481 also gives a pleasant picture of amicable relations. It was necessary that his father should be kept informed of the brothers' matrimonial schemes, which would depend on his financial assistance, but Richard was also frank about George's more private and personal affairs:

Sir, our father and I communed together in the new orchard on Friday last, and 'a asked me many questions of you. And I told him all as it was, and he was right sorry for the death of the [illegitimate] child. And I told him of the good will that the Wigstons and Daltons owes to you, and how I liked the young gentlewoman. And he commanded me to write to you, and he would gladly that it were brought about, and that ye laboured it betimes. And I have told our father of Chester's daughter, how that I would fain be there. And our father was right glad of this communication.[59]

Consequently, if Richard senior comes across predominantly in his letters as a testy old fuss-pot, this is not the whole picture. And his criticisms of his sons were often well justified. Robert, possibly the eldest, was a gambler and wastrel, prone to sulks and self-pity, and old Richard's trust in Thomas Kesten, who acted as factor in the late 1460s and early 1470s, also turned out to be misplaced.[60] George was far more reliable than these two, but easy-going and fonder of sport and pleasant company than of his counting-house and ledgers. Richard, who could taste the life of a leisured gentleman in the company of the Knights of St John, took rather little part in the family business while his father was alive. As Richard senior indicated himself on occasion, it was difficult to manage a business which involved activity in both London and Calais, besides travel to the wool-buying centres in the Cotswolds or Northamptonshire, and there was also his land in the country to look after. A constant watch had to be kept on prices of wool in the country, and on the exchange rates prevailing at London and in Flanders and Brabant. Instalments kept falling due for past purchases of wool, for the repayment of exchange loans and for the 'custom and subsidy' tax payable on all wool exported to Calais. The 'tidings' which his sons were so remiss about sending from Calais would concern matters which could seriously affect Richard's decisions about future trade. If his wool failed to sell promptly at Calais (perhaps because the Staple Company had imposed some credit restriction on customers, or because fighting in Flanders discouraged these from travelling to Calais to buy), there would be less money to collect at the seasonal marts in Brabant where instalments were paid. If the Duke of Burgundy had enhanced the valuation of his coinage by the time of the

---

[58] *C.L.* 73 and Ch. 2, pp. 55ff.　　　　　[59] *C.L.* 117.
[60] For Robert and Thomas see Ch. 4.

mart, less money could be lent there to English merchants who would repay in London, and to meet his own commitments in England, Richard might have to borrow for future repayment in Bruges or Antwerp or Bergen-op-Zoom. 'In good faith', he wrote in 1478, 'for lack of money I forgo many good bargains of fell, for the which I am right sorry. But I pray thee have this matter in mind, and let me understand what ready money I have at Bruges of mine in hand, that I may charge thee and I may do any good therewith, as I feel well I shall.'[61]

There was always the further risk that customers or borrowers might fail to pay up on time, and even that a consignment of wool might be lost through shipwreck or piracy. There were minor concerns as well. For instance, it was necessary to know the numbers of all bales of wool sold at Calais: when Numbers 1, 3 and 4, say, were safely on their way to a customer in Ghent, those numbers could be reallocated to new bales awaiting shipment at London. Small wonder that old Richard's letters to Calais are full of demands for information. And the economic historian may share Richard's frustrations when his son, on a buying-trip for wool in the Cotswolds, is too busy telling George about his new hawk to bother mentioning the current price of wool there.

For the businessman, as for most people in the fifteenth century, the 'wheel of Fortune' was a meaningful symbol that was seldom out of mind. It so happens that, of the various people whose careers are outlined in this book, a high proportion died in debt or outright poverty. If modern estimates are right, the mere raising of three sons to maturity was something of a feat on the part of Richard and Agnes.[62] The strong probability is that they had lost more children in infancy. By the same estimates, the Cely family did unusually well to produce, from three sons of Richard senior, one grandson, the sole survivor from among the five sons born to George Cely and his wife, while in turn this George of the third generation left three grown-up sons and at least one daughter at his death in 1545 or 6, at the age of fifty-nine.[63] If Richard Cely senior can be assumed to have been born around 1420, the three generations

---

[61] *C.L.* 27.

[62] Sylvia Thrupp said that 'the average number of children in a merchant family may be estimated with confidence at no more than two': *Merchant Class*, p. 44. In his demographic studies *Epidemic Disease in Fifteenth-Century England* (New Brunswick, N.J., 1978) and *Bury St Edmunds and the Urban Crisis 1290–1539* (Princeton, N.J., 1982) Robert S. Gottfried claims that even for gentlemen and wealthy merchants the survival of sons was far below replacement level.

[63] 'In Bury, London, and indeed virtually every other provincial town 75 percent of all families failed to produce male heirs for even three successive generations', Gottfried, *Bury St Edmunds*, p. 248. I have not fully investigated the history of George Cely's grandsons.

spanned some 120 years. Richard senior would then be about sixty when he died, an old man in his sons' estimation, in January 1482. His son George, however, may have been barely thirty-one at the time of his death in June 1489, at which date George, the third of his five children, was not yet two. (The fifth son was born posthumously.)

Ambition and insecurity have often been selected as characteristics of fifteenth-century society at large, and of the merchant community in particular. As far as ambition is concerned, there was certainly a general conviction among the laity that the proper secular aim of a merchant was to 'thrive', by due application to his trade, by a prudent life-style, by making an advantageous marriage, and by investing in land to provide security for old age, or for a widow and children. It seems doubtful whether 'ambition' soared beyond these realistic goals in the case of the Celys. Neither they nor their immediate circle of friends show much interest in seeking the civic office which conferred superior status in the urban community.[64] Those staplers like the Celys who were not in the livery of a major city company would not normally stand a good chance of attaining high rank in city government, and it comes as a surprise to learn that Richard senior was 'sore called upon' to stand for sheriff after the death of William Wiking in 1481. It is less surprising that Richard Chawry gained election, as 'better known'.[65] Indeed, it was probably our Richard Cely who had earlier obtained exemption for life from holding a variety of offices, including those of mayor, bailiff, sheriff, escheator, or juryman.[66] It was more difficult to avoid a share in the routine administration of the Staple company. Richard senior was one of the two Constables at Calais in 1461 and again in 1474, and while George was recommended to tarry in Bruges in 1478 to avoid being chosen one of the 'collectors' at Calais, who had onerous duties when large shipments of wool arrived, he did serve a term as one of the local treasurers.[67]

The open enjoyment of one's achievements was socially acceptable to a greater extent than in modern England, but at the same time, stress was laid on seemly behaviour; the 'merchantlike' bearing which gave the bourgeoisie their claim to be 'worshipful, and so taken'. The mercers upheld such standards of decorum when they required that before they accepted a certain young man as a shop-keeper he should 'dispose him sadly and mannerly' in his array and style of hair-cut, and not 'go like

----

[64] Thomas Granger, a stapler who resided in Calais in the earlier part of his business career, nevertheless became an alderman of London later.

[65] *C.L.* 133.

[66] *C.P.R. 1452–61*, p. 106. These offices would have seriously restricted the movements of a stapler who expected to spend much of his time in Calais.

[67] *C.L.* 25, 44.

a gallant or a man of court'.[68] Behaviour was not, of course, always as sober as the ideal. On one occasion city sellers were reprimanded for grabbing the sleeves of passing gentlemen, and the expected influx of visitors for a Great Council in 1488 caused the authorities to warn traders not to take advantage of provincials by selling wares excessively dear, and not, by 'words of rebuke in mocking or scoffing', to engage in acrimonious dispute with any customers who, in their ignorance of London prices, made insultingly low offers.[69]

And although a show of respect for office-holders was part of the standard of conduct, it was sometimes difficult to achieve for men accustomed to deference themselves. John Pickering, 'governor' of the English 'nation' of merchant adventurers in the low countries, became carried away on a wave of mingled self-importance and resentment against the wardens of the Mercers' Company in London, and his behaviour was reported in terms of the deepest disgust by the clerk of the company:

of late, open in the street, nothing remembering of duty, his obedience [or] oath, ne fearing th'obloquy of the people, but as a man shameless, without cause given, [he] reproved and miscalled Roger Bourgchire, one of the wardens, etc.

[And, being summoned before the assembly of the company], the said Pickering, all haughty and royal [and] full of pride, disdained to stand bare head, but boldly did his cap on his head, and so told his tale ['said his piece']. And for his excuse, simple matters and causes alleged, and much thereof not of this matter aforesaid. But praised and avaunsed his deeds, 'which never man did like to him' (as he said), 'ne never bared head[70] that hath nor could do like to him', with more. Two times he said these words: 'that no warden ne none that ever sat in this place hath done th'honour and worship to this place that he hath done', with much more language multiplied and in vain spoken.[71]

But even Pickering was forced to submit humbly to the corporate discipline of his company and apologize in the end.

Tempers flared into violence at times. John Shelley, a mercer and at one time a neighbour of the Celys in Mark Lane, was a man of uncontrolled emotions, who certainly enjoyed uncomfortable relations with his brother Thomas. In a commonly quoted incident, he incurred the censure of the mercers for arresting and suing Thomas without licence of the company – a serious breach of their privileges. Furthermore, he

ungoodly and unworshipfully quarrelled with the said Thomas, calling [him] 'false harlot', 'knave' and 'drivel', and said that he was never his true begotten

[68] *A.C.M.*, p. 121.
[70] Or 'bore head'?
[69] Ibid., pp. 107, 183–4.
[71] *A.C.M.*, pp. 148–9.

brother, but as one found and changed at the Land's End, with much other more ungoodly and inconvenient ['unfitting'] language.

The dislike was mutual, and Thomas gave as good as he got:

Thomas Shelley in likewise had fully ungoodly words and language spoken and said to his brother John Shelley, in reviling the said John, to their both's great dishonour, contrary to the good old rules and customs of our fellowship. As in calling his said brother 'whore's son', with more in great derision and scorn, japed and mocked his said brother of his sheriffhood, calling him 'boy sheriff'. And said he was full unable and unworthy to occupy th'office of shrievalty. And also said that 'by mean of my lady [i.e. John's wife] he was made sheriff'.[72]

In August 1468 open violence, said to be unprecedented, broke out between John Shelley and William Pratt in the mercers' hall. John called William 'false', and William responded with 'carl', whereupon John broke William's head with his dagger. On this occasion, significantly enough, there was a fraternal alliance between the two Shelleys, because 'Thomas Shelley, in that him was, would have smitten [i.e. did his best to smite] the said William'. They were all fined, and both parties were bound over in sums of £200.[73] Such incidents did not, however, prevent a man from attaining to high office in the company or the city. Within its province, a merchant's Company fulfilled a paternal role in enforcing 'right order' and 'good governance' on members. Serious breaches of order were, perhaps, infrequent enough to be greeted with astonishment as well as pain.

Standards of sober conduct were, therefore, upheld with reasonable success. The display of wealth was not discouraged, but the limits were set for the amount of show that was permitted, more by public opinion than by such unenforceable legislation as Henry VIII's proclamation which sought to specify the number of main dishes which members of various ranks and income-groups might enjoy at a single meal.[74] In business, some competition and individual drive was, of course, necessary, although the scope for rivalry was greatly restricted, in the Staple Company especially, by rules of sale and a rigid system of fixed prices. One must remember, too, that 'ambition' was far from ranking as the virtue that it became in the industrial societies of more modern times. Ambition when it took the form of *superbia* or *surquidry* – thrusting beyond one's proper sphere – was regarded as a moral and social sin, which was likely to be punished by the sort of downfall that is consequent

---

[72] Ibid., pp. 85–6.   [73] Ibid., pp. 60–1.

[74] Paul L. Hughes and James F. Larkin, eds, *Tudor Royal Proclamations*, I (New Haven and London, 1964), No. 81 (1517). This form of sumptuary regulation was nothing new.

upon over-reaching oneself. The opposite virtue of moderation is perhaps reflected in the habit of understatement. For instance, persons mildly described as 'not content' or 'not courteous' might well be verging upon violence, and 'something other than good' meant, in Flemish as well as English, 'a disaster'.

If a sense of personal insecurity did indeed permeate English society in the 1470s and 80s, it is not necessary to seek its tap-root in childhood familial experiences, a practice of early apprenticeship, sibling rivalry occasioned by the lack of fixed hereditary succession, or even the uncertainties of trade or the recurrent epidemics of the time.[75] A rapid survey of some of the more notable events during the lifetimes of Richard Cely senior and his sons will readily suggest that they could have felt their world to be unstable, though it was arguably no more so than in previous centuries. If Richard senior were born about 1420 he would have heard many tales as a child about the great English victories at Harfleur and Agincourt, and of how Henry V had conquered half France and won the reversion of the French crown, claimed by English kings since the time of Edward III. Over the succeeding thirty years an angry and bewildered nation saw these gains lost one by one, amid squabbles among the English commanders and the highest magnates in the Council. From 1450 to 1461 the world went on wheels, as the saying was, with a struggle for power between the factions of Lancaster and York, the increasingly feeble King Henry a pawn in the middle; pitched battles in which now one side and now the other carried the day, and little stability even when the Yorkists put Edward IV on the throne early in 1461. Edward's lack of effective control was demonstrated finally in 1470, when his forces proved insufficient to counter an insurrection led by his own cousin and leading supporter, the Earl of Warwick, and his own brother, George of Clarence. Edward was forced to take refuge in the low countries, while Henry VI was brought out, dusted off and reinstated as king. Edward's

---

[75] Various conditions which led to social mobility combined with a degree of individual stress are discussed in Thrupp, *Merchant Class*, pp. 311ff. The statement by an Italian visitor in 1497 that when English children reach the age of 7 or at most 9 years the parents bind them apprentice to others for a further 7 to 9 years, so that they never return to their homes to share the paternal inheritance, is described as a 'perceptive' explanation of the solitary drive of the 15th century Englishman by Alan Macfarlane, *The Origins of English Individualism: Property and Social Transition* (Oxford, 1978), p. 175. The Italian, however, seems to have confused apprenticehood with the custom of putting children into other families for their social education and advancement. Neither the mercers in 1501 nor the staplers by 1565 would allow a boy to be apprenticed before he reached the age of 16. Moreover, few merchants' sons were formally apprenticed at all (Thrupp, *Merchant Class*, pp. 44, 207), and among staplers, at least, family solidarity was often reinforced when brothers, or father and sons, joined together either as joint partners or as principal and factors.

return the next year resulted in two resounding victories at Barnet and Tewkesbury. Possibly the Cely family was in residence in London when, shortly after Tewkesbury, the city itself was attacked by a body led by the Bastard of Fauconberg, one of the Neville clan.[76] Their determined assault was eventually repulsed by the citizens, with the spirited support of a small group of lords, notably Anthony, Earl Rivers. The invaders were said to have barges waiting in the Thames to carry off the anticipated loot, and the ruins of houses on London Bridge, burnt during the attack, were still to be seen some fifteen years later. The affair vividly recalled to the citizens the sacking of London property which had taken place during the Peasants' Revolt of 1381, and the more recent alarms during Cade's Rebellion in 1450. Doubtless it helped reinforce the desire for 'good government' in the sense of rulers who were capable of preventing riot and lawlessness.

The Yorkist military triumph of 1471 was taken by many as clear indication that Edward's reign had divine sanction, though it was less certain that the death of Henry VI, which occurred so conveniently at this point, had been God-directed. A sufficient number of trouble-makers, like Warwick himself, had been killed in the fighting to put Edward more securely in control, and he was now able to devote energy to instituting firmer measures and to placing the monarchy on a better financial footing than it had enjoyed for decades. Not that the alarms and excursions were over. A great national war effort was organized to take advantage of an alliance with Charles the Bold of Burgundy against Louis XI of France, partly in revenge for French support of Warwick and the Lancastrians, partly to rally the country against an outside enemy and so encourage unity at home, and partly for the proclaimed purpose of reclaiming the lost English conquests (and enhancing the prestige of Edward IV). These high aims were nullified, to the advantage of England, when Louis and Edward met in 1475 at the head of their armies, and tamely signed a treaty which gave Edward a pension in place of his ancestral 'rights' in France. Conditions in England now became more stable, but were hardly devoid of all excitement.

The Duke of Clarence, a prime example of unbridled ambition, was a potential source of civil disturbance until his enormities became too much and he was executed at the beginning of 1478. The queen, Elizabeth Woodville, and her relations feuded with others at court, quarrels which were kept in check by the king, but which had a serious consequence upon his death in 1483. Relations with France grew increasingly strained, and both Calais and London prepared defences against possible attack in 1481.[77] In 1482 a war against Scotland saw

[76] W. Fulman, ed., *Rerum Anglicarum Scriptorum Veterum*, I (Oxford, 1684), p. 556.
[77] Below, Ch. 3, pp. 72–3.

striking successes, including the capitulation of Edinburgh, but produced no gains apart from the cession of Berwick on Tweed to England, an acquisition which was criticized as costing far more than it was worth.[78] And in December, a shattering blow was struck at Edward's tottering diplomatic structure when France and Burgundy signed an alliance, the Treaty of Arras. At the time of Edward's sudden death in April 1483 there was a lively expectation of renewed war against France and Scotland, both of which had repudiated marriage alliances with England, together with other treaty obligations.

The rapid and startling chain of events which saw the coronation of the young Edward V first postponed from 3 May to 22 June, and then abandoned in favour of the coronation of his uncle Richard of Gloucester on 6 July – events which included a number of executions of the king's relations and friends, including that of Lord Hastings, the Captain of Calais, on 13 June – can have done little to counteract any tendency among the population to suffer from a sense of uncertainty.[79] The Cely letters, when they survive at all, are silent about subsequent events in England, not least because there was a censorship in operation, especially at the time of the Buckingham revolt and an abortive landing by supporters of Henry Tudor in October 1483. They do not, therefore, mention the death of Richard's only son about April 1484, widespread stories next year that the king had poisoned his wife and intended to marry his niece, or his dramatic and bizarre denial of them at a public 'news conference' in London. Nor is any Cely comment extant on Richard's directions to take some of the staplers' wool and sell it for his own profit, in January 1485.[80] When Henry Tudor became king after Bosworth his hold on the throne was scarcely more secure than Richard's had been, and the interesting rumours at Calais which are discreetly hinted at in the occasional letter may well have concerned some of the plots that were fomented against Henry on the continent.

In point of fact it would be difficult to prove that the fifteenth-century Londoner suffered more from tension and anxiety than his forebears, or his successors. The chief effect of chronic political instability may have been a pragmatic lowering of expectations. One cannot generalize too far about responses. When there was an invasion scare in 1481, Richard junior seems to have been more elated than disturbed at the prospect of defending London, and hastily advised his brother that there would be good profits to be made on imported armour.[81] For the young Pastons,

---

[78] Ed. Fulman, p. 563.

[79] Inter alia, evidence adduced by Christopher Coleman from the Black Book of the Exchequer seems to clinch the traditional dating of the execution: C. H. D. Coleman, 'The Execution of Hastings: A Neglected Source', *Bulletin of the Institute of Historical Research*, LIII (1980), 244–7.

[80] Below, Ch. 11, p. 300.   [81] *C.L.* 114.

the death of Charles the Bold meant prospects of advantageous employment: 'the world is all quavering [simmering]. It will reboil somewhere, so that I deem young men shall be cherished.'[82] There were always opportunists. One minor result of the Battle of Bosworth was that a seller of stolen goods could assert that they had been found abandoned on the field of conflict.[83]

It has been said that, 'to judge from [the Celys'] correspondence, one might be forgiven for believing that the Wars of the Roses never took place at all'.[84] One sufficiently compelling reason for the absence of comment is simply that there is no coincidence of dates. But more generally, the Paston Letters may have led historians to expect more open reference to political events than they are justified in seeking from most writers. The Pastons were already embroiled in court politics, and could therefore allow themselves some degree of frankness. But in an age of governmental despotism moderated chiefly by incompetency, most people felt it wise to refrain from written comment on domestic politics, in letters which might easily fall into the wrong hands. Even the Bishop of St David's, writing to a clerical correspondent, lapsed discreetly into Latin when he added to his praises of the new king Richard some slight aspersions on his court circle.[85] 'Marvellous talk' was best repeated orally, by some trusted messenger. Even so, informers were plentiful, and loose speech could be misconstrued.

Henry VII and his government were no readier to encourage criticism than his predecessor Richard, or than Edward IV, whose 'great estates' took 'great grudge and displeasure' against the mercers for their 'yll langwage' against recent Acts of Parliament in 1478.[86] In 1488, when the 'lord Cordes' had taken Gravelines and marched through the English Pale close to Calais, there was, to Henry's displeasure, 'much speaking' and 'large talking' among the common people because the king was thought to have neglected the defences of Calais. The mayor of London was instructed to deny these stories of royal inertia, and to order the citizens, 'on the peril that may fall, [not to] speak or talk of any the king's matters otherwise than according to his honour and pleasure'.[87] In May of the next year, when the king went north to put down an insurrection in Yorkshire, there was another optimistic attempt to quell idle rumour:

[82] *Paston L.*, I, no. 302.
[83] W. Campbell, ed., *Materials for a History of the Reign of Henry VII* (Rolls Ser., 1873–7), I, 252.
[84] Charles Ross, *Richard III* (1981), p. xxxvi.
[85] Cf. Alison Hanham, *Richard III and his Early Historians, 1483–1535* (Oxford, 1975), pp. 49–50.
[86] *A.C.M.*, p. 106.			[87] Ibid., p. 182.

the citizens of London were to be 'well avised in reporting or telling of tales or tidings [except] such as be sure and true'.[88]

At any time, the merest tavern squabble might be blown up by some informer into a suspicion of treasonable talk. In 1491 a drunken and inconsequential argument in York about the burial of Richard III was somehow distorted into seditious criticism of Henry VII or the late Earl of Northumberland.[89] Even more wildly, but at a time when the English were very unpopular, the English merchant Richard Arnold was reported to the local authorities of Bergen-op-Zoom in 1488 for slandering Maximilian, and imprisoned on suspicion of being a spy.[90] Anthony Bastard of Glymes and John Busshman gave testimony that what had really happened was

that at the free Passe [Easter] mart of this said town of Barrow last past, Richard Arnold...and one Anthony, hosted at the 'Lion' in Middelburgh, Lombard, sitting at table with the said Anthony Bastard in his house called the 'Horse Shoe' in this said town, had many words and arguments the one against the other, touching the valour and puissance of the realm of England and the country of Italy, in praising and enhancing everyich ['each one boasting'] of the puissance, valour and bounty of his country.

Wherein finally they chafed themself both ['became so heated'] in such wise that the said Richard, among other, said these words: 'If Englishmen were not, the Lombards should have nothing to eat but salads and cheese.' And after, they lied each other hotly ['vehemently accused each other of lying'], in such wise that Anthony Lombard rose from the table, saying to the said Richard that 'he would do him a turn', with many other hot words.

Presumably, he then laid the information against Arnold. The witnesses deposed, however, with a plethora of negatives, that

at that time nor never tofore nor never after they never heard that the said Richard had spoken or said any manner of word touching the King of Romans, that were or might in any wise turn to the prejudice or dishonour of his royal majesty or any of his servants. Moreover, the same Anthony Bastard of Glymes said and declared that often times he hath heard the said Richard speak and commune touching the King of Romans and the King of England, praying to God that he would save them both of his grace, and saying that as long as they were friends this country and the country of England should have wealth and prosperity.

People therefore watched their step by habit, if they were wise, and it would be absurd to suppose that they took no interest in domestic politics. Nor should one exaggerate the extent to which the 'Wars of the

---

[88] Ibid., p. 190. [89] For example, Hanham, *Richard III*, pp. 63–4.
[90] Richard Arnold (1811), pp. 230–2.

Roses' were matter for nobility and gentry, in which the commercial classes played no active part. The wearing of livery was by no means confined to 'indentured retainers', nor was 'clientage' exclusively a matter of territorial lordship. It went without saying that even young businessmen were well equipped with personal armour and weapons, and trained in their use, and it is not hard to imagine that if Sir John Weston had had occasion to fight on one side or another, as his predecessor Prior Langstrother had fought for the Lancastrians at Tewkesbury in 1471, his ties with the Cely family could have drawn Richard and George into the conflict. Similarly, George's parents had some cause for fearing that George, well-armed and well-mounted, might be swept into battle against the French in 1480, along with his acquaintances among the excitable young gentlemen of the Calais garrison.

On a different level, dynastic rivalries at the top created team supporters among humbler members of the merchant fraternity. Mercers and their servants had to be ordered not to shout rude things at the victors of Bosworth as they entered London,[91] and rival factions among the English seriously alarmed the town government of Bruges in 1493, when it was proclaimed

that it had come to the notice of the captain and *Wit* of the town that certain persons sojourning in Bruges as merchants have sought occasion to pick quarrels with others, so that these feel so menaced that they dare not walk the streets or engage in their business. To such an extent that they proposed to leave the town, the which should result in great damage, harm and disadvantage ['ten grooten quetse scade ende achterdeele'] to them and to this city.

Consequently, it was strictly ordered that all foreigners, whether merchants or otherwise, of whatever nation, but especially of the English nation, should behave peaceably within the town, holding peaceful communication with one another, as befits merchants in a city of commerce such as this is, without wearing any badges, whether secretly or openly, of white roses or red roses, whereby any strife, division or faction might arise between them, and without in any way miscalling or upbraiding or injuring each other in words or deeds. And it is forbidden to carry any weapons on pain of death or other punishment at the discretion of the *schepens*.[92]

The Celys themselves had an enemy named Brandon, probably William Brandon the younger who was a neighbour in Essex, where he held land in right of his wife.[93] At least twice Brandon tried to have them

---

[91] *A.C.M.*, p. 291.

[92] Translated from L. Gilliodts-van Severen, ed., *Inventaire des Archives de la Ville de Bruges: Inventaire des Chartes* (Bruges, 1871–85), VI, pp. 369–70.

[93] She was co-heiress of Sir Maurice Bruyn, who had demised Bretts Place to Richard Andrew, according to E.R.O. D/DL T1 443.

prosecuted for offences of which, by their own account, they were innocent, and involvement in other of his activities cost the vicar of Aveley his benefice in 1478.[94] But to offset the impression made by such troubles, and by many other contemporary examples of lawlessness, one should remember how popular the courts were as a means of redress. Brandon preferred false accusations against the Celys to direct attack, and when Lord Howard had a dispute with the merchant adventurers in 1472 his initial threat, if he were not reasonably compensated, was to sue at law for his dues. It was only his last position, if he could not prevail in the courts, that he would seize the merchants' goods, 'wheresoever he could have them, within Thames or without, at Calais or elsewhere'.[95] While not admitting his claims, the merchants, 'for the rest and peace, and to have his good love and lordship (which by reason shall more prevail us than his wrath)', eventually persuaded him to accept £13 6s 8d instead of the £120 he wanted. It was wiser, of course, to avoid prosecution if possible, and the Celys ensured that the cases which Brandon instituted against them never came to trial. (Brandon himself was not so fortunate, and spent some time in the Fleet prison.) But in the more settled periods of fifteenth-century England at any rate, there was a certain expectation that justice was obtainable from the law, and there was also some confidence that due forms would be observed and that the possession of 'evidences' (title deeds and the like) should guarantee the peaceable enjoyment of one's property.

The Celys give no indication that they had the lively interest in religious questions which the Reformation debates would soon instil in so many sixteenth-century English men and women. As far as one can discern, their observances were conventional, reasonably punctilious, and matter-of-fact. They made special devotions when in trouble, as during George's sickness in 1479, when his parents went on daily pilgrimage to a local shrine.[96] And they took it for granted that the deity had a benevolent interest in their everyday affairs, crediting their opportune withdrawal of money from Bruges bankers to divine prompting.[97] There is no sign of the morbid emotionalism on the subject of death which has sometimes been ascribed to the period. Indeed, it is fair to say that not death but poverty inspires eloquence in their correspondents. If it was an outbreak of bubonic plague that struck England in 1478–9, or in 1487, there is equally no evidence that it aroused quite the widespread horror and panic that we are inclined to associate with what we think of as 'the Black Death'. Men took what precautions they could – in 1487 George Cely

[94] Below, Ch. 2.
[96] *C.L.* 74.
[95] *A.C.M.*, pp. 63–5.
[97] *C.L.* 133.

deputed a servant to transact business in the city, 'the plague has been such that we dare not come there ourself'[98] – but on the whole they went on with their avocations much as usual, and there is no reference at all to 'the great sickness' or 'the death' in the extant minutes of the Mercers' Company for 1478–9. It is easy, moreover, for us to be dazzled by the mortality figures and overlook the fact that the victims of bubonic (if not pneumonic) plague often had some expectation of recovery. His parents' prayers and the ministrations of a physician in Bruges, jointly or severally, obtained George's cure in 1479.

Undoubtedly people relished literary and pictorial intimations of mortality, as witnessed by the number of 'Vado mori' and 'Timor mortis' verses transcribed into collections like Richard Hill's commonplace book. This does not necessarily mean that they devoted a great deal of their time to contemplation of their latter end. The occasional shiver could sharpen one's enjoyment of the good things of life, and a twinge of repentance help to assuage the vague guilt that arose from such satisfactions. The well-to-do in the later middle ages put a great deal of money into chantries and 'obits' or memorial services, but less, it may be, from excessive dread of hell than as a sensible piece of extra insurance, especially when premiums were payable by their heirs.[99] And it was certainly not because they were miserable on earth. Many feared that having it so good in this life could reduce their chances of bliss in the next without special provision.

In fact, of course, for most people life was neither unrelentingly hard nor unremittingly 'merry'. Conditions in England were unsettling enough at the Celys' time, but for the staplers and merchant adventurers in the late 1470s and 1480s the real source of worry was the state of Flanders and the rest of the low countries, which directly affected their trade. The death of Charles the Bold in battle against the Swiss in January 1477 introduced a further measure of turbulence in his dominions which lasted, with little intermission, for the rest of the Celys' period. The expressions 'queasy' and 'casual' (uncertain and risky) aptly indicate the staplers' considered view of the wider world in which they had to operate. In the final analysis, there is not much doubt that if Richard and George's partnership as wool-merchants collapsed at the end, the chief reason was their dependence on trade with Bruges.

But amid the changes and chances of the outside world, a merchant enjoyed a degree of inner assurance, deriving from his perception of himself as a man of substance, with an honoured place in secular and

---

[98] *C.L.* 231.
[99] There was the added secular benefit, especially for the childless, of keeping one's name alive. William Maryon, for instance, endowed an annual 'obit' for 60 years.

religious life. So long as he continued to thrive, he was an accepted member of the social circle provided by the 'fellowship' of his occupational associates, and he was supported by the protectionist policies of his Company. The Celys, indeed, give the impression that they were basically more self-assured and secure than the Pastons or the Stonors, and far more so than Lord and Lady Lisle, whose voluminous correspondence from the sixteenth century has now achieved welcome publication.[100] By comparison with these people of higher social rank, the Celys also have an engaging quality of naivety. It may be significant that the unaffected naturalness in their letters is matched most closely in the correspondence of the Johnson family in the 1540s and 50s.[101] The Johnson brothers were also wool-staplers who wrote informally and without literary pretension. Perhaps the social model to which these businessmen (and their wives) conformed was less restricting than the circumscribed social role accepted by their contemporaries who sought to make, or keep, a place in the world of the royal court and the household of great lords.[102]

In the case of both the Johnsons and the Celys, the personality revealed by most of the writers is one with which we can feel thoroughly comfortable. In the end, what gives the Cely correspondence its greatest appeal is that we get to know members of the family so well, and find them so human. An editor naturally becomes biased towards his own subjects. But most commentators have expressed dislike of the hard and pushing Pastons. The Plumpton letters are extremely dull, and William and Elizabeth Stonor do not come across in their correspondence as full-bodied individuals. Even Eileen Power's hero Thomas Betson may strike one, on critical acquaintance, as a glib, insinuating and often malicious young man.[103] Despite their affection for each other, the colourless Lord Lisle and his forceful lady have a certain stiffness, and are too preoccupied with keeping up their position to hold great personal attraction. Not only do the Celys give us an entrée into the viewpoint and life-style of plainer and more ordinary men, but they turn out to be pleasant people to know.

[100] Muriel St Clare Byrne, ed., *The Lisle Letters* (6 vols., Chicago and London, 1981).

[101] Barbara Winchester, ed., 'The Johnson Letters, 1542–1552' (unpub. Ph.D. thesis, University of London, 1953), and idem, *Tudor Family Portrait* (1955).

[102] But surely no-one who has read the letters of any of these people can share Alan Macfarlane's surprise at finding 'a self-awareness and confidence in the late fifteenth century': *Origins of English Individualism*, p. 174.

[103] Eileen Power, *Medieval People* (1924); C. L. Kingsford, ed., *The Stonor Letters and Papers* (Camden, 3rd ser., 2 vols., 1919). Assessments of Betson's 'honest charm' and 'sincerity' should be weighed against his attempt to oust another member of the household from favour: *Stonor L.* no. 213.

'JAPES AND SAD MATTERS', 1472–9

The affectionate relationship between the brothers Richard and George gives human warmth and colour to the family correspondence in its early years. Since George was the unsystematic hoarder who preserved these letters, his own side of the correspondence is poorly represented. So while the flavour of Richard's personality comes over directly from his letters to an intimate friend and brother, in the letters we see George chiefly through the eyes of his family and acquaintances, and he makes an appearance in his own right more often in his accounts and memoranda.

That Richard was the elder of the two is clear from his position as his father's chief executor and from the inheritance pattern of his parents' properties. It could not be guessed from the brothers' own correspondence, which was carried on in terms of complete equality. They also shared equally in the partnership which they began in 1476,[1] and carried on until George's death in June 1489. But most of the extant letters from Richard to George were written between 1476 and 1482, because after the death of their father both brothers lived for most of the time in London or close to each other in Essex, and the correspondence then comes from William Cely, managing the Calais end of the business.

The handwriting of the brothers is a good indication of the differences in their temperaments and personality.[2] Richard's is spacious and handsome, a little showy, with long slanted tails to his *y*s, his open-topped *g*s and his *h*s, so that the page presents a pattern of heavy horizontals and lighter diagonal lines. Later his hand degenerated badly, and came to resemble his father's, which has the same prominent descenders, though many of the letters are formed in an older fashion. George's hand is quite

---

[1] File 10 fo. 10v. Although George and Richard had equal shares in the fells shipped, only Richard's name appears in the London particular customs account for 1478–9: P.R.O. E.122 73/40.

[2] Specimens of handwriting are shown in the plates to the E.E.T.S. edition of the letters.

different, ornamental in its own style, but smaller, rounded, less even, much flourished and much more cursive. Richard's writing hints, both at a more formal education and at a certain precision in his temperament, a certain hardness, and an elegance which speaks a concern for appearances. It may be that he was rather conventional, and his correspondence suggests that he relied on others for advice before taking decisions. George's writing is more relaxed, softer, as it were, and curlier. It also displays greater individuality and self-reliance. Although George can sound pompous in his letters, and he certainly shared his father's love of giving advice, there is an openness about his nature that is appealing. In a group of people, few of whom write with any stylistic artifice, George in especial gives the impression that he wrote as he spoke. Somehow one feels that he talked rather loudly, perhaps to mask some inner uncertainties, since he was easily upset by criticism. He was clearly good-natured, generous and popular. Thanks to George for his 'good cheer' and hospitality are something more than formal politeness, and there is real warmth in messages like John Dalton's 'we would fain have you here again',[3] or 'God knows we have a great miss of you: I had liefer than the best gown that I have that you might abiden still here with us...It is of mirth the cause I would have you for.'[4]

As a concomitant of his easy-going ways, George was evidently inclined to be lazy, and his business methods were often casual, especially once his father's stern gaze had been removed. The economic historian must greatly regret the absence of any fully balanced profit and loss accounts for George's wool sales. On the other hand, there are some endearingly human touches in the private notes which George wrote to himself, such as one about a bowl with a medallion in the bottom, which he had mislaid: 'I must call to mine remembrance an mazer without band, having an "breusyll" in the bottom. I deem I took it to John Veneke [the goldsmith] twelve month agone.'[5] He also paid lip-service at least to precepts of diligence and sobriety, and once jotted down this little jingle:

> To sorrow in the morning
> And over eve spend thy good:
> If he sorrowed in the evening
> As he in the morning could
> Many should go on horseback
> That now goes on foot.[6]

[3] C.L. 180.
[4] C.L. 44.
[5] File 20 no. 11 fo. 2v (1488). A 'breusyll' seems to be a boss or medallion.
[6] File 12 fo. 32v (1481).

As the baby of the family, George was petted by his mother and her maids. When George was at Calais in April 1482 the widowed Agnes 'send[s] you God's blessing and hers, and so she doth, in good faith, every day sith ye departed',[7] and in May Richard reported 'our mother sends you her blessing, and ye must purvey for her a pot of green ginger. Ye are often in her mind: she says to her maids, "at your coming home many things shall be mend among them".'[8] It is to Richard's credit that he does not seem to have resented his brother's favoured position, though it seems a little hard that when Richard wanted a riding gown his mother told him to borrow one of George's and George would have a new one in exchange.[9]

As it happens, George was buying clothes for himself on his first appearance in the papers, when he was perhaps sixteen or younger and not yet a full member of the Staple Company. One of the earliest items among the accounts is a paper pamphlet with George's signature on the cover, and the heading on the first page: 'Memorandum that these beth parcels following that I, George Cely, hath laid out of mine own money, anno '74.'[10] The date has been altered from [14]72, and the first page may in fact date from that earlier year. In London George had bought himself two pairs of hose and a doublet cloth at 8s 6d. He went on to list purchases at Antwerp: $2\frac{7}{8}$ yards of medley at 11s 6d, half a yard of tawny 'to make me a jacket' at 2s, a yard of tawny chamlet 'for to line my cape' at 4s, and the cheaper lining for his gown, which cost 2s 9d. Chamlet was a warm luxury fabric, something like cashmere. 'Making of all this gear' cost 2s 6d. George also bought a hat and hatband for 2s 4d, a puncheon (dagger) for 18d and a 'George' of silver – a small image of the saint – for 12d. Other purchases of three daggers, two hatbands, two leather pouches and six velvet pouches – all items which made popular gifts – were probably intended as presents.

More clothing was bought in the following years. At London, George acquired a hat (16d), a tippet (16d), a hat lace (4d), a doublet (10s), a cape or cap (1s), three ribbons (16d) and an 'aglar' (*aguillier*, 'needle-case'?) at 4d. At Calais he then bought a stomacher for 2s, another pair of hose for 3s 11d, and two bonnets for 5s. In October 1475 he paid 4s 4d to Piers Taylor for making a silk doublet. There followed $5\frac{1}{2}$ Flemish ells of linen cloth to make him 'schortys' (shirts) at 5s $\frac{1}{2}d$, one English yard of fine linen for a 'nyght kercher' (2s), and $3\frac{1}{4}$ Flemish ells of black satin of Bruges making, total 13s, purpose unspecified, and another $3\frac{1}{4}$ ells of russet satin at Bruges at 11s 8d. He seems to have been particularly fond of russet. The same year two 'points' or ribbons to tie his hat cost

[7] *C.L.* 151.   [8] *C.L.* 169.
[9] *C.L.* 40.   [10] File 11 fos. 1–7v.

12*d* and a night-cap 18*d*. Nelkin (Daniel) was paid 10*s* 'for making of 3 tippets and 2 pouches and 2 stomachers and a hatband and 2 points'. In addition there were rings and an *agnus dei* of gold and 'pautenarys' of silver, presumably meaning the metal frames for purses. At the Sinxen (Whitsun) mart at Antwerp in 1476 George bought, among other things, another hatband, which cost a whole 5*s*, a hoop ring for 20*s*, more hose and a dagger for 3*s* 4*d*. At Bruges he bought another russet gown (16*s*), a pair of boots (2*s* 6*d*), a pair of spurs (6*d*), and nine ells of buckram at 5*d* the ell.

Far more unusual are the items in the three pages of this pamphlet which are headed 'Memorandum that here after follows by diverse parcels what Thomas Rede, harper at Calais, hath had of me [in 1474].'[11] George in fact took lessons from Thomas Rede over a few months in 1474 and again in October 1475. The entries of his payments suggest that the young fifteenth-century merchant was as much devoted to music for private entertainment as his better-known Elizabethan counterparts. No doubt George was not the only stapler to patronize Rede, and evenings of singing and dancing must have been a feature of life in the town, which had a reputation for being 'merry'.[12] The account for these music lessons must be given in full. Rede taught not only the harp and lute, for which George learnt a horn-pipe or rustic dance-tune among other types, but he was also a dancing- and singing-master. It is not clear whether George learnt to sing the songs he mentions, or merely their instrumental accompaniments, which were suited to a range of voices.

Item, the 10 day of March anno [1474], paid for 6 dances and mine fingering on the harp 9*s*

Item, the 14 day of June it cost me to the said Thomas for to learn to dance. 6*s* 8*d*

Item, paid for my bill of footing [a paper setting out the steps] 4*d*

Item, lent to the said Thomas upon an harp 9*s*

Item, paid the 3rd day of September for dancing . . . 2*s*

Item, the 22 day of October I paid unto the said Thomas for to learn to harp 20 dances 7*s*

Item, the first day of November I paid to the said Thomas for to learn 14 dances and an hornpipe on the lute . . . 4*s* 10*d*

Item, the 14 day of November paid to the said Thomas for a bill for to learn to tune the lute 3*s* 6*d*

Item, the 25 day of December paid to the said Thomas for to learn 'O Freshest Flower', 'Toujours', 'O Rosa Bella' . . . 3*s* 6*d*

Sum page   45*s* 6*d* [*sic*]

---

[11] Ibid., fos. 3–4.   [12] *Paston L.* no. 275.

Item, the 17 day of December paid to Thomas Rede for mine
fingering and for mine tasting ['playing'] of the harp, and for
'Mine Heart's Lust', and 'O Freshest Flower' two ways   5*s*
Item, paid a plack [groat] a week at diverse times   .   .   .   3*s* 4*d*

Item, in October anno '75 paid by me, George Cely, unto Thomas
Rede, harper, for learning me 'Of Such Complain' three ways,
and for to amend all my dances again 3*s* 4*d*
Item, paid by me, George Cely, unto the said Thomas Rede for
to teach me to set my harp another way, and for to teach me
all my dances that same way 4*s*
Item, unto the said Thomas for to learn me an song is called 'Go
Heart Hurt with Adversity' 20*d*
Item, paid by me unto Thomas Rede for an little fingering on the
lute 16*d*
Item, paid to Thomas Rede for 'My Dely Woe', and for my bill
of footing of base dances 5*s* 4*d*
Item, paid unto the said Thomas Rede for stringing of an double
harp and for bray [resin], pinning and dressing   .   .   3*s* 4*d*

The 'fingering' for different instruments, like the 'bill of footing', would
be written instructions or diagrams. With the prices charged by Rede
can be compared the 3*s* 4*d* which a week's board and lodging cost a
stapler in Calais.

'O Rosa Bella' is probably John Dunstable's famous song, and
'Toujours' might be the 'Toujours Bien' of Martini. The words of 'Go,
Heart' are printed by Rossell Hope Robbins:

> Go, heart hurt with adversity
> And let my lady thy wounds see.
> And say her this, as I say thee:
> 'Farewell my joy and welcome pain,
> Till I see my lady again.'[13]

'Mine Heart's Lust' is 'Mine heart's lust, star of my comfort',[14] and 'Of
Such Complain' is reminiscent of

> Thus I complain my grievous heaviness
> To you that knoweth the truth of mine intent.
> Alas, why should ye be merciless?
> So much beauty as God hath you sent!

[13] Rossell Hope Robbins, ed., *Secular Lyrics of the Fourteenth and Fifteenth Centuries*
(Oxford, 1952), no. 155.
[14] Carleton Brown and R. H. Robbins, *Index of Middle English Verse* (Index Soc., II, New
York, 1943), no. 2183.

Ye may my pain release –
Do as ye list
I hold me content.[15]

The other songs – 'O Freshest Flower' and 'My Daily (or 'Duly', 'sorrowful') Woe' – have not been identified.

It may possibly be significant that there was a gap in the music lessons between December 1474 and October 1475: did his father keep George out of Calais while Edward IV was preparing for war with France and then marching, at the head of a large English army, from Calais down through Picardy to St Quentin and along the Somme to Picquigny? At all events, there was probably little trade done at that time. In the end, at Picquigny the kings of England and France agreed to settle for peace. Some thought it shameful that the English should take gold not lives, but Edward's willingness to be bought off greatly benefited his own finances and the country's economy.

The staplers' interests were more immediately bound up with the Burgundian netherlands than with France, and their concern then lay with the negotiations for a new treaty to safeguard their commerce with the subjects of Duke Charles. Delegations laboured over the long series of complaints by netherlands merchants, statements of practice by the Staple, and promises of redress or indignant rebuttals. Had the English broken their agreement on exchange rates? Must customers meet the requirement to take a proportion of old wool along with new? And what were the ethical grounds on which the English made such a demand? Gradually the details were hammered out, although the new Intercourse was not finally concluded until July 1478.

Meanwhile, 1476 saw increased trade after a lull in 1475. In June Thomas Betson was in Calais, preparing to attend the Sinxen mart at Antwerp and finishing a long letter to his child fiancée, 'when every man was gone to his dinner and the clock smote noon' and the fellowship of the lodging became increasingly impatient and shouted to him in turn, 'Come down! Come down!', 'To dinner!', 'At once!'.[16] George Cely spent much of his time in Calais also, learning the business of a stapler by performance and with guidance from his father's old associate, Thomas Kesten.[17] Although he set up in formal partnership with his brother Richard in 1476, their own trade was initially confined to buying and selling a small number of wool-fells (wool-bearing skins). The greatest part of George's activity was carried on as factor for his father,

[15] *Secular Lyrics*, no. 154.
[16] P.R.O. S.C.1 46/255. This is the form indicated by Betson's own punctuation, which Kingsford disregarded in his edition, *Stonor L.* no. 166.
[17] For Kesten, see Ch. 4.

and the papers afford glimpses of him receiving shipments, arranging for the payment of incidental expenses and for the custom and subsidy dues which were payable partly in Calais and partly at London. He also negotiated sales to customers, sorted and listed the multifarious coins he received from them, and travelled to the marts at Antwerp or Bergen-op-Zoom to collect deferred instalments of the price and to make over any surplus Flemish money by exchange loans with English merchant adventurers. For such services he drew an annual salary, which amounted to £22 10s Flemish in 1477–8.[18]

'Brotherhood' was no empty term among the Fellowship of the Staple. Because the younger men among the active staplers shuttled back and forth between Calais and their homes in England, those in residence at Calais or attending a given mart often transacted business for their absent fellows. Thus John Spenser, perhaps in 1476, left money with George and asked him to 'make it over' with the London grocer and stapler, Thomas Abraham.[19] He also thanked him warmly for

the great cheer and welfare that I had with you at many and diverse times. Also of your great labour and business sith my departure, the which at my power I shall deserve at such time as that ye and I meet together.

George similarly handled Robert Cely's financial business when Robert was away from Calais, and was entrusted with William Maryon's negotiations over some fells of disputed ownership in September–November 1476.[20] Towards the end of September that year both Richard Cely senior and his sons Robert and Richard were at Calais, lodging with Thomas Kesten, while George was at the Bammis (autumn) mart at Antwerp. Even with so many of the family in Calais, business must have been pressing, as his father wanted George back there.[21] George for his part evidently feared that his elder brothers might not be treating their father with the state due to their standing in the town, and urged Richard to ensure that the old gentleman appeared suitably 'worshipful'.

The comparative tranquillity of trade was to be shattered at the beginning of 1477. On 26 January Richard senior had heard stories which proved all too accurate:

I have great marvel that ye write not to me no letters of such tidings as ye have at Calais, the which is much speech of at London. For the which I cannot write to thee nothing for lack of understanding how it stand in the parts of the Duke of Burgundy's lands and the King of France. For here is strange speaking, for the which I pray thee be wise and be not o'er hasty in sale and delivering of good

---

[18] File 21 no. 1 (fo. 2).
[19] *C.L.* 10.
[20] *C.L.* 5–9 and Ch. 4, pp. 94–7.
[21] *C.L.* 4.

into Flanders, for I fear me sore of war, and ['if'] the Duke be dead, as it is said, and the King of France entered into Picardy, as men say. For the which I pray thee see well to.[22]

Charles the Bold – or rather, 'the Rash', as people were soon dubbing him – had indeed been killed in battle at Nancy on 5 January 1477,[23] and Louis XI of France had lost little time before he set out to secure his hold on the French fiefs that Charles had ruled. The efforts of Charles and his immediate predecessors to wield a collection of territories into a unified state had left a legacy of discontent, especially in the ancient county of Flanders, where the great cloth-making towns resented ducal interference in their affairs. While French troops made rapid headway in Burgundy proper and the area of the Somme, the young Duchess Mary was forced to accede to demands by the States General, which diminished her powers and restored the old privileges of the towns, thus undoing much of her father's work. She held out, however, against plans to marry her to the young dauphin of France, and her wedding to the Archduke Maximilian of Austria took place by proxy on 21 April 1477.

A French presence close to Calais aroused great alarm among the English, and developments were anxiously watched. On 14 April John Paston II had written home from Calais:

As for tidings here, the French king hath gotten many of the towns of the Duke's of Burgundy, as St Quentin, Abbeville, Motrell [Mortel]. And now of late he hath gotten Bethune and Hedynge [Henin?] with the castle there, which is one of the royalest castles of the world. And on Sunday at even [13 April] the Admiral of France laid siege at Boulogne, and this day it is said that the French king shall come thither. And this night it is said that there was a vision seen about the walls of Boulogne, as it had been a woman with a marvellous light: men deem that Our Lady there will show herself a lover to that town. God forfend that it were French, it were worth £40,000 that it were English.[24]

'We in these parts [in England] be in great dread lest the French king with some assaults should in any wise disturb you of your soft, sweet and sure sleeps', wrote the facetious John Pympe, who pictured Paston and his fellows labouring with mattocks and pickaxes about Calais 'to overturn your sandhills, as we hear say ye do right worshipfully', with what energy they had left from their encounters with 'the frows of Bruges with their high caps'.[25]

---

[22] *C.L.* 11.

[23] In 1486 the 'second continuator of the Crowland Chronicle' seems to refer to this soubriquet in saying that Charles acted 'nimis animose, ne temerarie dicam': Fulman, *Rerum Anglicarum...*, p. 561.

[24] *Paston L.* no. 305. Boulogne had a miraculous statue of the Virgin.

[25] Ibid., no. 774.

The soft sleep of the staplers was already disturbed by the effects of war on commerce. In May Richard senior wrote anxiously to George:

I understand there come no merchants to Calais for to buy wool nor fells, for the which is right heaviness for the merchants of the Staple. For the which I fear me every man will find the mean for the sale and deliver his wool and fells into sure men's hands by the mean of sale to merchants strangers, the which have repaired to Calais afore this time. For the which I would ye had communication with such merchants as ye have found sure men and good men, for to aventure some of my wool and fell in their hands by the mean of sale at long days. For I feel men shall do so at this season.[26]

It is very unlikely, however, that wool-buyers came to Calais in any great numbers that summer. Edmund Bedingfield described to Sir John Paston on 17 August how the French were then besieging St Omer, 'and they of the town skirmish with them every day'.[27] It was said that if the King of France could not capture St Omer he would march his army to Flanders through the Calais Pale. Lord Hastings had therefore closed all the passages except Newnham Bridge, 'which is watched, and the turnpike shut every night'. Maximilian had now arrived in Ghent, but Bedingfield had small opinion of his resources in men or money, 'wherefore I fear me sore that Flanders will be lost. And if St Omers be won all is gone, in my conceit ['judgment'].' French propaganda assiduously worked on such fears, and it was perhaps at this time that a song which had not formed part of George's repertoire became current. It ran, roughly translated from the French:

> Arouse yourselves, Burgundians and Picards,
> Be sure you arm yourselves with good big clubs!
>   For now it's spring,
>   'To war!' we sing;
> We're off to give the enemy a thump, a thump.
>
> There speaks a man who never had to fight.
> I swear, my love, that it's a sorry business.
> Many a man-at-arms and gentle knight
> Has lost his life, likewise his cloak and hat, and hat.
>
> Where is the Austrian duke? In the Pays Bas:
> He's in low Flanders with his brave Picards
> Who beg him night and day to lead them far
> Into High Burgundy, on conquest bent, on conquest bent.

[26] *C.L.* 12.   [27] *Paston L.*, no. 777.

Farewell to Besançon! Salins, we must away!
Farewell to Beaune, that city of good wine!
The Picards drank it up: Flemings shall pay
Eight groats a pint, or else we'll thrash 'em!
We'll thrash 'em.[28]

The rumours which circulated so readily in Calais were not always confined to the larger events on the international scene. Early in February 1478 old Richard was greatly agitated to receive a letter from the lieutenant of the Staple. Some leading personage of Calais – possibly Thomas Prout, a former mayor of the Staple – had heard that Richard was spreading malicious stories about him and his family.[29] The informant seems to have been the Celys' relative Thomas Blackham, who accused not Richard himself but his wife Agnes, after a quarrel with her. On receiving the complaint, Richard 'had her in sharp examination', and was satisfied that there was no truth in the allegation. Had he found otherwise, he implies that he would have administered the proper marital beating: 'I would have had corrected her that she should have remembered it during her life'. So he sat down with a friend who was gifted in the art of concocting elaborate and legal-sounding phrases, and together, with much cogitation and crossing-out, they produced exculpatory letters to send to the lieutenant and the victim of the slander, protesting innocence in the face of the 'sinister suggestions and sayings' made against the Celys, and swearing Richard's 'faithful love' and service. Naturally, but unhappily for us, the drafts of these letters do not rehearse the matter complained of.

George was in England at this period, and it was the turn of his friend John Dalton to transact business for him in Calais. Sales were hampered by a current regulation that purchasers must pay cash down. Jois Frank, a frequent customer, wanted all the 'old' wool that George had left, and proposed to pay for half 'in hand, the t'other at Sinxen mart next. And I told him he should give me ready money or ['ere'] he went out of Calais, or else he should have no wool of me at this time. And so we departed.'[30] Dalton possibly misdated this letter 24 March instead of 14 March, because George had been back on the continent for some time when his brother Richard sent him an informal budget of news on 26 March 1478. His long letter, 'as well of japes as sad ['serious'] matters', pleasantly reflects some of a young man's interests, and consequently has been much quoted.

---

[28] Translated from Ottaviano Petrucci, *Canti B. Numero Cinquanta*, ed. Helen Hewitt (Chicago and London, 1967), no. 9.
[29] *C.L.* 16, 17.   [30] *C.L.* 18.

Right reverent and heartily well-beloved brother, I recommend me unto you, and I thank you for the great cost that ye did on me at your departing. Furthermore informing you, at the making of this our father and mother were in good health, thanked be God, and sends you their blessings. Also our father has received from you two letters and the reckoning of the sale of his Cotswold fells, the which he does well understand, etc. Sir, your horse fares well and is in good plight, but yet I cannot sell him. I shall do my best thereto, and there come a lucky [i.e. promising] man.

Sir, I pray ye remember me, for ye know my necessity [for money], it is great now, that knows God.

Sir, here is Richard Prowde, the bringer of this letter, that sent you and me the venison, has made labour to our father and me to write to you to be good master and friend to him, in helping him to some good service at Calais till he be better acquainted there.

Sir, I have been at Aveley almost ever sin' ye departed, and my lord of St John's lay at B[rother] Pasmer's three days, and I was there with him, and I brought him from our father two great lampreys, and he took them thankfully. And every night I had three of his gentlemen home to lie with me, and I made them good cheer. And sin' that time I had the vicar of Aveley and the priest of Aveley and the priest of Berwick [Essex] with me three nights, and dined and supped and lay with me. And they be good shooters and mannerly fellows, all three, and will be ready to do for me at all times. They are countrymen, born in Wales in mine uncle's parish at Gresford.

Sir, the 22 day of March I saw three as great harts in our wheat as ever I saw in my life, about noon-days, and the same day at even I heard a pheasant cock crow. Our whelps wax fair, and Hector is a fair hound, and a fat. His sore is whole.

Sir, I write to you of all things, as well of japes as sad matters, like as I promised you at our departing, etc. Now a letter from you to me were great comfort.[31]

The long drawn out negotiations for the Treaty of Intercourse between England and the Dukes of Burgundy were nearing their end, and the staplers awaited results. In particular they hoped that money would soon be stabilized in the netherlands: inflated valuation of the coinage meant a loss on exchange loans to England:

Sir, our father would that ye would send him writing how that ye hear of our ambassadors, and what answer they have of the Duke [of Burgundy]. Our father says he cannot write to you till he hear what they have done. 'A trusts to your wisdom that ye will do at the next mart with that 'at is grown [i.e. make over your profits by exchange], to the least loss that may be.[32]

This letter notably reveals young Richard's lofty attitude to the local clergy, three of whom came from a parish of which Richard's maternal uncle, Richard Andrew, had been rector. No doubt it was through Andrew's influence that they had obtained ecclesiastical positions in

[31] *C.L.* 19.   [32] Ibid.

another area in which he had interests. While Dean Andrew exercised that kind of patronage, and Sir John Weston extended his 'good lordship' towards the Celys, the Celys were in their own position to practise 'good mastership' towards their young neighbour Richard Prowd, who was eager to solicit their help in finding some suitable position at Calais. The other aspect of such clientage comes out in Richard's remark that the priests whose company he had cultivated would be ready to 'do' for him at need. A country gentleman, even at the Celys' relatively humble level, was well advised to build up an affinity of well-wishers in his neighbourhood. Equally, one needed to be cautious in the choice of associates, as Richard's next letter explained. It would be advisable, he thought, to steer clear of the Fulbornes, one of whom was then completing his apprenticeship to Richard senior.

Sir, I understand that Thomas Fulborn has bought fells, and he will write to you to do for him, and 'at his fells may be shipped in your name. Sir, me think the kindred is cumbrous, and therefore it were better for you not to deal with them, howbeit I find him courteous. But sir, I understand that our brother Robert and ye and I are sued at Westminster for an affra*y* 'at was made between Fulborn, Petyt, Maudyslay and the gentleman and his men at Mile End in Easter week, and are like (without good help) to be indicted, howbeit we were not there. But I trust to God to find the mean to scrape you and me with.[33]

By whatever 'mean', Richard finally succeeded in quashing the indictment, it would seem, although not before two panels of jurors had been selected to hear the case. Sir John Weston's influence probably helped, and he was making much of Richard: 'Sir, he has given me a long gown-cloth of his livery, and he would be wroth and I come into Essex and be not with him daily at Meandry[ville, i.e. Norton Mandeville?].' In December of the same year, 1478, John Houghton, who had been vicar of Aveley since 1464 and was one of those entertained by Richard in March, was forced to resign as a result of getting mixed up in some local feud between William Brandon (the 'gentleman' of Richard's earlier letter?), and the Deyncourt family of Aveley. Richard reported to George on 15 December, 'Sir, Brandon is in the Fleet still, and shall be till he 'gree with Dankowrt. And he says that the vicar of Aveley was causer of his coming to Dankort's, wherefore he shall lose his vicarage.'[34] It is not entirely clear whether this Brandon was the same as the 'young William Brandon' who, according to John Paston II, writing on 25 August 1478,

---

[33] *C.L.* 25.
[34] *C.L.* 43. Houghton resigned in Dec. 1478: Richard Newcourt, *Repertorium Ecclesiasticum Parochiale Londinense* (1708–10), II, 23.

is in ward and arrested for that he should have by force ravished and swived an old gentlewoman. And yet was not therewith eased, but swived her eldest daughter and then would have swived the other sister both. Wherefore men say foul of him, that he would eat the hen and all her chickens. And some say that the king intendeth to sit upon him, and men say he is like to be hanged, for he hath wedded a widow.[35]

Marrying a widow was not normally a capital offence, but if she was a tenant-in-chief of the crown, royal permission for the marriage was necessary in law.[36] The Brandon of the Paston letters was no friend to that family, and John may, of course, have been repeating mere malicious rumour in all this.

Richard could not spend all his time playing small-scale lord of the manor, with its attendant risks; he was soon required to assist his father at London, where there was a large purchase of wool to attend to. In July Richard saw to the shipment of a total of 48 bales of wool and 8,500 fells. When the wool fleet was ready to leave, old Richard dispatched him together with William Cely to Calais, to help George there. William's passage on one of the ships cost 20*d*.[37] They arrived on 2 August, and boarded along with George, who was now in the lodgings kept by Agnes Burnell, the widow of a former stapler. George and Richard paid 40*d* Flem. per week, while William, in inferior accommodation, was charged 32*d*.[38] Prospects for trade looked bright: the commercial intercourse between England and Maximilian was concluded at Bruges on 12 July, a day after a year's truce had been arranged between Maximilian and Louis XI.[39] 'Jesu for his great mercy send a good peace in the Duke of Burgundy's lands', prayed old Richard on 17 June, 'for else will be no good merchants [to]ward.'[40]

George had already had plenty to do with preparing to receive shipments, not only for his father but also for John Cely, William Maryon and members of the Dalton family. On top of that, on 24 July John Dalton had written from Leicester asking George to pay the freight on 28 sarplers of wool belonging to Thomas Wigston,[41] and there were fells of Robert Cely's as well as 2,968 belonging to Richard and George jointly, which were worth £133 stg.[42] In addition, George had to make frequent trips into Flanders, mainly to Bruges. His hostess's bill shows that he

---

[35] *Paston L.*, no. 312.
[36] William Brandon the younger had married Elizabeth, widow of Thomas Tyrrell, senior, and co-heiress of Maurice Bruyn. By her he held the manor of South Ockendon, and so was a neighbour of the Celys: E.R.O. D/DL T1 500; *C.P.R. 1476–85*, pp. 523–4, 530, 550.
[37] File 11 fo. 25.   [38] File 16 fos. 15–16.
[39] Cora L. Scofield, *The Life and Reign of Edward the Fourth* (1923), II, pp. 234–5.
[40] *C.L.* 24.   [41] *C.L.* 28.   [42] File 15 fo. 12.

had a month in Calais between 18 June and 18 July, then ten days in Flanders, just over three weeks in Calais from 29 July to 21 August, nine days in Flanders, and then under three weeks in Calais again until 18 September, when he set off for the Bammis mart at Antwerp. He returned to Calais only on 15 October.[43] Richard's main function during the sixteen weeks between 2 August and 23 November was to take charge during George's absences. Business was interspersed with relaxations. Over those sixteen weeks Richard entertained five guests at Agnes Burnell's, and George seventeen, at 4*d* a head. Twice Richard paid a 'winelaw' (wine bill) for George, at a reasonable 5*d* or 6*d* each time.[44]

It may have been about the middle of August that George arranged a jolly outing to Boulogne. His subsequent account runs:

Robert Cely, William Maryon, John Lynd, Richard Cely, George Cely, Charles Vyllarys, Raffe Lymyngton and Richard A'Wode, William Cely and Tom.
Sum, 10 persons.

First to Boulogne ward	8*d*
Homeward	7*d*
Item, at Boulogne for the dinner, unto the cook	5*s* 3*d*
Item, for the wine at that dinner	4*s*
Item, there as we lay all night, for wine, beds and horse	4*s* 10*d*
Item, given the minstrel	4*d*
Sum page	15*s* 8*d* Flem.
Item, paid by me for their cart	9*s*
Sum total	24*s* 7*d*
Received of Richard Wode	2*s* 4*d*
Due to him to pay	6*d*
Item, received of my cousin Maryon	2*s* 10*d* Flem.
William Cely 12*d*, William Maryon 8*d*, Richard Cely 7*d*	
George 7*d*	2*s* 10*d* Flem.
Item, 11 bear the 15*s* 8*d*	18*d* a man
Item, 7 bear to the wain	16*d* a man.[45]

'Tom' may have been William Maryon's boy, since Maryon paid an extra 8*d*. The eleventh man in the reckoning seems to be a figment of George's imagination, perhaps still heated by the wine and minstrelsy. It was a specially good dinner (unless prices at Boulogne were particularly high), costing 6*d* a head whereas Agnes Burnell in Calais catered for dinner guests at 4*d*. But one wonders whether the ostensible purpose of the outing was perhaps a pilgrimage to Our Lady of Boulogne for her feast-day on 15 August.

[43] File 16 fo. 16.   [44] File 11 fos. 28v, 37.
[45] File 16 fo. 19.

The day before George set off for Flanders on 21 August he and Richard enjoyed some sport pure and simple, playing for the unmarried staplers against the married men. The challenge which ended up among George's papers was issued on 17 August:

And it would please you for your disport and pleasure, upon Thursday next coming to meet with us [on] the East side of this town, in a place called 'the Pane', ye shall find a pair of pricks ['marks'], of length betwix the one and the other thirteen score tailor yards mete out ['measured'] with a line.

There we underwritten shall meet with as many of your order and shoot with you at the same pricks, for a dinner or a supper, price 12*d* a man. And we pray you of your goodly answer within twenty-four hours.

Written at Calais the 17 day of August, anno Jesu '78.

Ready to disport with you, wedded men:

Rob Adlyn	John Ekyngton
Philip Williamson	Seman Grantham
Thomas Sharpe	William Bondeman
John Dyars	Richard Wylowly
Rob Besten	Thomas Layne
John Wryght	Rob Knyght

To our well-beloved good brother Thomas Wryght and all other bachelors being freemen of the Staple, be this delivered.[46]

The recipient, Thomas Wright, was later to meet a violent end, being murdered at Benfleet.[47]

Luckily for George Cely, he had sent his father a long business-like letter on 13 August,[48] because on the same day that the married staplers issued their challenge, old Richard in London had penned an angry epistle:

I greet thee well, and I marvel much what is the cause that ye send me no letter from Calais, neither thy brother nor thyself. For the which I think right strange, in so much as I am so charged for this good late shipped it were great comfort for me to hear how ye do, and in what case my good is in at Calais – my fell, the bacons for to be depart ['separated'], and make all single fell, and sort Cotswold on themself, and London summer fell of themself, winter in like wise. There is none excuse but ye may write at all times, as other men do to their masters and friends. I write no more, but Jesu keep you.[49]

One can almost hear Richard's furious grunt as he finally paused to draw breath. 'Bacons' were a particular quality of wool-fell, but their exact nature is obscure.

While George was busy in Bruges exchanging Utrecht gulden and

[46] *C.L.* 29. [47] P.R.O. C.1 104/21.
[48] Acknowledged by his father on 25 August: *C.L.* 31.
[49] *C.L.* 30.

postulates for other gold coins, encashing letters of payment, buying fine linen cloth for William Maryon and perhaps obtaining a couple of hawks to be sent back to England with William Cely,[50] Richard found routine jobs at Calais a trifle boring. Probably he was trying out his pen when he wrote some *m*s and then 'amen dyco Amen dyco nobis Amen dyco nobys amen dico wobys' ('amen I say to us... amen I say to you').[51] More to the point, he noted a loan to William Byfeld of 13*s* 4*d* in pence, and on the other side of the page drew up a proper account of expenditures out of the 43*s* 4*d* which George had left with him on 20 August. Unfortunately, the account does not indicate whether the bachelors or the married men lost the archery match and paid for the dinner. On another occasion Richard headed a piece of paper: 'Jesu 1478. These been parcels i-following that I, Richard Cely', but was attacked by another fit of boredom and drifted into practising the word 'This', which led him into 'This is my last Will. In Die nomine, amen. Lego animam meam Deo et omnia bona mea a Georgea [*sic*] Cely, fratrem meum bene delectum.'[52] The 'will' was left as a jape for George upon his return.

Life was not all idleness, however. Richard had to pay for the awarding of the wool and for cartage, for pack-needles and the repacking of one sarpler, and for 'setting' fells. He also bought a pound of candle, paid 4*d* to a deputy who would substitute for old Richard in the watch mounted at Staple Hall, met one armourer's bill of 2*s* 4*d* and another of 12*d* for a dagger, and paid Clays Marchant 22*d* for services on behalf of two horses named Sorrel and Shy.[53] There was some chasing round in search of George's black gown. George thought he had left it at 'Redhode's', but it was found at William Bondman's, where Richard collected it and put it in George's chest.[54] A more onerous burden was imposed by the disgraceful behaviour of his brother Robert, who had to be bailed out from the consequences of his accumulated debts. George was always a good deal more soft-hearted towards Robert than Richard was inclined to be. Perhaps the troubles with Robert sharpened Richard's haggling prowess when, in September, he tried unsuccessfully to strike a bargain with some merchants of Rouen over some of his father's Cotswold wool, and also parlayed with some Hollanders – 'the hardest men that ever I spake with' – who would not meet his terms for the sale of fells.[55] There was a piece of excitement to relate to George at that time:

Sir, I pray ye recommend me to William Robards that is lodged with us when he is in Calais, and say to him that we know now that he left a great fardel in his woolhouse in Show Street, the which by a thief or thieves was opened, and

[50] File 11 fo. 33.   [51] Ibid., fo. 28.
[52] Ibid., fo. 36.   [53] Ibid., fos. 28v, 37.
[54] *C.L.* 32.   [55] *C.L.* 34.

a casket taken out and broken, and that 'at was in it borne away, and what 'a had more I wot not. A servant of the fellbinders yeed ['went'] into the yard to ease him, and saw the window open, and looked in, and saw canvas, linen cloth, bankers, knives, with other stuff, and marvelled, and come to the lieutenant and telled him. And so the lieutenant and fellowship went thither, and there it was packed together and had into the Staple, else we trow it had be gone the same night.[56]

Old Richard was probably more relieved than not at Richard's failure to make any sale in September, for on 10 October he wrote to tell George that it would be better to hold off for a while, until money in Flanders had been effectively revalued.[57] He rescinded this ten days later, in despair at hearing no news of reform, and summoned Richard back home:

I will ye come home with Will Maryon, for there shall be no business at Calais this mart time. I suppose George thy brother goeth to this Cold mart. I pray you see a fair weather or ye take your passage, for any haste, for the which I trust to God Will Maryon and ye will see that weather and wind be fair.[58]

Maryon returned on 5 November, landing in the Downs at 3 o'clock on the afternoon of the same day – 'sore afeared for the great mist', said old Richard – and reaching London at noon on the 6th.[59] Richard junior had lingered in Calais, alarmed by his mother's reports of death at London, but Maryon sent a reassuring message that

my master your father and my mistress your mother would fain that Richard Cely were here at home, for (blessed be God) here is no such death as was spoken of at Calais. Sir, they would in no wise that Richard Cely should take passage but at a morrow tide and a fair set weather, as I suppose my master the lieutenant and other of the fellowship that be i-purposed for to come over will do.[60]

Richard senior also wrote that his wife's fears were exaggerated, but there was great mortality in 'the West Country'.[61]

On 23 November Maryon wrote to Richard directly, assuring him that the epidemic was over:

Right reverent sir, I recommend me unto you. Furthermore, please it you to wit that my master your father and my mistress your mother, your brother Robert and all fareth well, blessed be God, and as for any death here, thanked be God, sith I came home here hath been none. And therefore my mistress your mother looketh for you daily. But yet she would not that ye should come, not till my master the lieutenant Robert Tate come, and that ye take a morrow tide and a light moon, for any haste.

[56] Ibid.   [57] *C.L.* 36.
[58] *C.L.* 37.   [59] *C.L.* 38–9.
[60] *C.L.* 39.   [61] *C.L.* 38.

Sir, I have spoken unto my mistress your mother for a gown cloth to make you a riding gown for to come home in, and she bid you that ye should borrow one of George Cely your brother, and he shall have another therefor against Easter, of cloth [dyed] in grain, she saith...

Also, sir, ye shall understand that my Lord of St John's bedfellow was here with my mistress your mother now late, within these three days, and he said that my Lord sent him hither for to wit whether that ye were i-comen home or none, for he saith my Lord thinketh long for you.[62]

There was nothing at all improper in the fact that the Prior shared his bed with a companion of the same sex; it was indeed rare for anyone to sleep alone.

Richard finally went home some time before 15 December, when he wrote a bread-and-butter letter to George:

Right well beloved brother George, I recommend me heartily unto you, thanking you of the great kindness that ye showed to me at my being with you at Calais, and for your russet gown furred with black lamb that I had in the ship with me, for I trow I had been lost for cold but for it. Sir, I delivered the same gown to John Lambe, woolpacker, to convey it to you again, and he hit me so to do [literally, 'struck hands on the promise']. Sir, our father and mother is, and we all be, in good health, thanked be God, and are right glad that ye purpose you to be with them this Christmas.

And as for death, here is none, thanked be God. I heard of none sin' I come to London. We look for you every fair wind, I pray God send you well hither and in safety...

Sir, I should 'a sent an hat by John Lambe to Twesylton, but he was gone ere I came to London. No more to you, but I pray you to recommend me to mine hostess and all good friends, a' by name.

Writ at London the 15 day of December.

Sir, our mother and I pray ye to convey some of your 'powd garnetts' [pomegranates] hither.[63]

Evidently George, with his present of exotic fruits, was home in time for Christmas, because the next letter in the collection was written to him by John Dalton in Calais, on 12 February 1479. Dalton was, he said, pining for George's company:

God knows we have a great miss of you: I had liefer than the best gown that I have that you might abiden still here with us ['stay permanently', or was George changing his lodgings?]. Ye shall understand more at your coming – it is of mirth the cause I would have you for....I pray you as goodly as you may, and in as short space, your business done in England, to speed you toward us.[64]

What merriment was afoot among the younger staplers?

[62] *C.L.* 40.   [63] *C.L.* 43.
[64] *C.L.* 44.

George was back in Calais within a month of this letter, 'welcome unto my friends', who had heard that he was dead.[65] For all other news to tell his father, trade was very slack: 'there is now none merchants at Calais, nor was but few this month'. Robert Cely had preceded him to Calais, and by 27 March was in trouble again and applying to George for help. Richard junior, asked for advice, could only remind George how unreliable their brother was. Like most correspondents, he added news of George's horses:

Sir, your horse is in good plight, and he halted ['limped'] sore sin' ye departed, but we have made bathe this for him, and so he is whole he will play with a straw.[66]

'To play with a straw' was a standard image of friskiness, also used by Chaucer.

Robert, and the horses, were not the only worry. Thomas Kesten was heavily in debt to Richard senior and ways had to be devised to get payment from him. Moreover, rumours in Calais about death at London had proved amply justified. By May 1479 Agnes and Richard senior, with the ever-present William Maryon, had taken refuge in their country house of Bretts Place, Aveley, and Richard junior was with Sir John Weston at Sutton, 'all merry', said Richard senior. 'The sickness is sore in London, wherefore much people of the city is into the country for fear of the sickness.'[67] But Richard senior continued to go up to London when business called him there, and other trading went on:

Your brother Richard hath sold his sorrel horse for four mark and lent [the purchaser] the money till Michaelmas, and I have his other horse to cart, and I shall pay for him as he cost at York, and so the horse is well sold. And as for your horse, is no sale at London. The horse is fair, God save him and St Loy, wherefore God send you a chapman for him, and ready money in hand.

Richard the younger, briefly at Bretts Place on 26 May, wrote to thank George for two letters. Their father had been to the Cotswolds to pack his wool, but Richard did not accompany him 'because of death'. Instead,

Please it you to understand of my passing of time sin' ye departed. Till Teneber Wednesday [the Wednesday before Easter, 7 April] I was at Aveley, and I departed from London on Easter Eve. And I could not get from my lord of St Johns not past three days together sin' Easter Eve. Three days afore the writing of this I departed from my lord, and come to see my father and my mother, and the morrow after this I purpose by [the] grace of God to go again.

Sir, our father and mother is in good health and merry in Essex, thanked be

[65] *C.L.* 45. [66] *C.L.* 47.
[67] *C.L.* 52. Richard had already written on 30 April (no. 50) that 'the sickness is great at London, God for his mercy cease it'.

God, and here has been Cowldall and his wife, and diver of my lord's meinie [entourage], and dined with our father and were merry.

Sir, I had your horse into Kent to show, and there was none that bade me to no purpose. Browmer proffered five mark for him, and that was the most. Oats be dear – I buy none in Essex nor Kent under 2s 8d. Your horse had a sore eye, but it mends well. I pray ye send me writing how I shall be demeaned with him.

My lord recommends him to you and prays you to remember his cloth for hosen, for he purpose to make none till it come. Sir, he prays you to purvey him of a piece of Holland cloth of 30 English ells or more, of a 14d the ell. Gladman with all my lord's servants recommends them to you. Sir, I pray ye send me word whether they die at Calais or not.

As touching the matter in your letter of the poor woman, I saw her never since, but as I come by her father's door I saw the maid stand with her mother. Me think she is little and young, wherefore I spake no more of the matter. I pray you send me word how ye do in those matters, and what your proffer was, and with whom. And there shall be nothing be done here but ye shall have knowledge.[68]

The foregoing epistle was written at intervals. It was 'the morrow after this' when Richard concluded, because Sir John's servants had arrived to carry him off again: 'at the writing of this, here was Gladman and Tomson to fetch me'.

'Those matters' which Richard mentioned so discreetly were probably amatory. It seems to have been about this time that George received a 'proffer' from a French-speaking admirer whom he later refers to as 'my Lady Clare'. The letter she sent him, possibly written for her by a professional scribe, translates awkwardly from her rather stiff French:

Specially beloved, I recommend myself to you, George Cely. Know that I am very well, and I pray God it is the same with you. If it please you to know, I have loved you a long time, but I dared not tell you so. Know that I send you a token, and I pray you to have me in remembrance, and I pray you to send me a token of remembrance, just as I do to you, for love. And I let you know that my heart is set on no man but you, but I think your love is by no means on me. But I pray you to send me a letter as soon as you can, for my heart will never be at ease until I see a letter come from you, by the token that I told you at table that I would send you a letter. I know nothing further to write to you at present, except God have George Cely and Clare in his keeping.

All Clare's heart is yours, George Cely; ever in my heart.

Know that I send a token to Bietremiu [Bartholomew] your servant, and I commend me to him. I promised it to him when he was over here.[69]

The address, 'This letter be given to George Cely', is written in Flemish.

The reference to George's servant being 'over here' or 'in these parts' [pardecha], and indeed the fact that Clare found it necessary to write at

[68] C.L. 55.   [69] C.L. 54.

all, suggest that she may have lived in Bruges or perhaps Gravelines or
Dunkirk at the time. If so, George evidently installed her in a house in
Calais, where he kept some of his wool in the garrets. There is one unique
testimony to the relations between the two, found on the back of a
business letter from John Dalton which George was keeping for future
reference.[70] This betrays an engaging picture of George and a French-
speaking lady, presumably Clare, sitting together in relaxed mood,
perhaps one evening. Clare proposed to teach George a song, the words
of which he copied, as best he could, on the piece of paper which lay to
hand. By accident, he also wrote down her offer to do the writing: *Je
nott* ('I will write'), he started, and then crossed it out. The song, in
George's inimitable spelling, went:

Je boy Avous mademoy selle	I drink to you, mademoiselle.
Je vous plage mounsenyueur	I pledge you, sir.
Poirsse ke vous l estes si belle	Because you are so pretty
Je boy, etc.	I drink (etc.)
Je sens lamor rensson estyn selle	I feel love in its spark
Ke me persse par me le kowre	Which pierces me through the heart
Je boy a [vous, etc.]	I drink [to you, etc.]
Je voue plege mounsenywr.	I pledge you, sir.

Clare interrupted the recording process at one point to interject *Je suis
sûre* ('I am certain...'), which George also wrote (as 'je ssue sseur') and
then cancelled. With much laughter, one imagines, and much further
interruption, she then proceeded to teach George a few useful French
words and phrases, while George jotted them down higgledy-piggledy
on the paper, together with the English translations:

de dauns within *de horsse* without *Bosonye* busy
shaunte sing *vn shaunssoune* an song
lere read *un shen* an dog *shoutt* hot *ffrett* cold.

Finally, *Je le vous hay de kaunt je raye*, 'I have said you when I go', that
is *je le vous ai dit quand j'irai*, 'I've told you already when I'm going.'
At that point Clare was overcome by bashfulness: *Je swy hountesse*,
George wrote, and translated it 'shamed'. It must have been the lady
who spoke, because George's rendering, 'hountesse', reproduces the
feminine form *honteuse* not the masculine *honteux*. In her role as teacher
Clare then pointed out that George's translation was incomplete, so he
repeated *Je swy hountesse* and put beside it 'I am shamed'. Perhaps
he then repeated the conduct which Clare purported to find so
embarrassing.

   In his business dealings George probably had little need to write

[70] *C.L.* 49.

French, and so rendered it phonetically when he found himself called upon to do so, to the extent of putting *lamor rensson* for *l'amour en son*....But it seems unlikely that he was quite so ignorant of the spoken language as this document would suggest. Evidently he could communicate with Clare to their mutual satisfaction. He might have got someone else to read her letter to him, but he also had dealings with the French-speaking Wauterin Tabary of Gravelines.

George's consolations at Calais made it less necessary to envy the easy life which Richard was leading in England. Sir John Weston never seemed to tire of Richard's company, and his father was sufficiently flattered by the attention to raise no objection to the recurrent loss of Richard's services. The next we hear of Richard is on 22 July in a letter from Maryon to George: Richard is in Warwickshire with Sir John, 'at a town there that calleth Baltyssall [Temple Balsall] beside Coventry':

It is not past a fourteen days sith he departed thitherward. Sir, ye shall understand that my lord himself came to my master's place in Essex for to desire of your father and of your mother that your brother Richard might ride with him into that country. Sir, ye shall understand that we look for him here again within this three weeks.[71]

Maryon's letter had also conveyed the news of deaths in Robert Cely's household, including that of his wife.

George had much business to do at the mart in Antwerp that Whitsun, and his family and friends were heaping him with commissions. John Dalton wanted some elaborate girdles matched at Bruges for Sir John Scott's wife:

Brother George, I recommend me unto you, and ye shall receive by the bringer hereof two corses, one harnessed [with metal ornamentation], and another unharnessed. And of that that is unharnessed, I would you bought six of them. It cost 3s or 40d, I wot not whether. Though they be not past two of a colour or three it skills [matters] not – blue, or tawny, or green, or violet. Also I would you bought four such as has the harness upon it, and the harness set on as it is. It cost but 2s, the corse and the harness together. Though they [are] other colours as is afore written it skills not. Also I pray you if you may not buy them that you will desire Ralph Lemington to do it for me, for it shall be for my Lady Scott.[72]

Richard Cely senior needed 500 or 600 ells of Barrois canvas to pack wool, Sir John Weston was waiting for the cloth to make new hose, there was a feather-bed and cloth for William Maryon, who had also sent a signet

---

[71] *C.L.* 58.
[72] *C.L.* 51. The 'harness' of such girdles might consist of silver or silver-gilt bars and ornamental buckles: Richard Arnold, p. 116.

ring to be remade,[73] and detailed instructions came from Richard senior about the purchase of two silver salt-cellars with covers, to weigh about ten or eleven troy ounces, and a Calais cart to replace his old one:

see the cart body be good ash, and axled ready for [to] go to work, for I have great need thereto. I suppose it will cost a 6s or 7s, cloots [cleats], linch-pins and all. Pray John Parker for [to] help you, or Thomas Granger, for I trow ye can but little skill ['have little knowledge'] of such ware.[74]

Richard's emissary with the last request was John Roosse, who had his own reasons for wanting to see George:

Item, letting you wit that my chief coming to Calais was to 'a spoken with you, for I had brought for you a gentle little ambling horse, the which I purpose to have home again without I meet with some good merchant for him. Master George, I trust verily in you to have a goshawk of you, as you promised me at London. And sir, if it please you that I shall have one, when that you will write for me to come for her I will come. And if you will that I bring an ambling horse with me I will, and write me your intent of what price, and I trust to God to please you.[75]

Roosse was not the only Englishman for whom the word 'Flanders' connoted 'hawks'. In the previous year these coveted objects had been the subject of a charming letter to George from the vicar of Watford, William Maryon's home town:

Reverent and worshipful sir, after due recommendation I recommend me unto you. Furthermore, I pray you to remember me in this season for a goshawk or a tiercel, the which liketh you best, for I wot well I shall have none but it come from you. Wherefore I pray you, though I be far from you in sight let me be nigh to you in heart, as I shall deserve it unto you in time coming. Also I pray you to send me a bill of your welfare, and the price, and it shall be content, by the grace of God, who have you in his keeping.

By your chaplain, the Vicar of Watford.[76]

The vicar duly got his hawk, and was delighted with it, according to Maryon. 'As for the Vicar 'is hawk of Watford, it proveth well: it hath i-caught this same year upon a 60 fenanys ['fen birds'? 'pheasants'?] and mallards, and the vicar saith he will not give him, not for 12 nobles, to no man.'[77] But much to old Richard's dismay, another hawk which Richard junior had given to Sir John Weston had died 'for default of good keeping', and old Richard bitterly regretted that the other had been given away to such an insignificant person as the vicar. Sir John himself was much embarrassed by its loss, according again to Maryon:

---

[73] *C.L.* 58; File 12 fo. 10; File 14 fo. 44v.
[74] *C.L.* 56.   [75] *C.L.* 57.
[76] *C.L.* 33. I have not been able to identify the vicar.   [77] *C.L.* 40.

I understand that my Lord said that he had liefer 'a lost 20 mark than the hawk should 'a be so i-lost in his keeping, and therefore my master your father would that Richard Cely should bring over another goshawk with him, if ye could buy any at Calais for 8 or 9s, and he would pay for the said hawk himself for the pleasure of my Lord. And my master and my mistress saith unto me that they repented them 20 times that they had not kept still the hawk that William Cely brought fro Calais.[78]

John Roosse had to wait for the hawk he wanted in June 1479, and it seems that George did not ship his father's cart until the following year, although he went over to England himself and spent August with the family in Essex. While they were there their father, who had again braved the reigning sickness to do business in London, wrote in excitement to tell them of a great battle, of which the news had just reached Thomas Blackham in a letter from Calais:

the which is of a battle done on Saturday last past beside Tyrwyn [Thérouanne] by the Duke of Burgundy and the French king, the which battle began on Saturday at 4 of the clock at afternoon and last[ed] till night, and much blood shed of both parties. And the Duke of Burgundy hath the field, and the worship. The Duke of Burgundy hath get much ordnance of French king's, and hath slain 5,000 or 6,000 Frenchmen.[79]

This victory was little more than a flash in the pan for Maximilian, however, and doubtless the casualty figures were exaggerated.

Despite the presence of 'the sickness', which was by now raging in Calais as well, George soon had to leave the comparative safety of the Essex countryside in order to attend the Antwerp mart in September, pursued by more requests. Robert Coldale wrote from Bretts Place, where he was again visiting Richard Cely senior,

Praying you to send me half a dozen cushions and eight yards of bankers [coverings for benches] according [matching] thereto, of English yards, verdure the colour. And a fur of budge-shanks [astrakhan] for my dame, and a fur of calaber [squirrel] for myself, if it be good cheaper there. And a dozen ells English of Holland cloth, the [one] to have 12 the ell, and the t'other 16½ the ell [i.e. to cost 16½d], and write to my cousin Richard what all draws to, and I shall content him, with God's grace, who have you in his keeping.
At your father's place on St Matthew day,
    Your R. Coldale.
I pray you budge for collar and sleeves for my wife.[80]

George subsequently had to ask for further instructions about the furnishings, and Richard explained in November:

[78] *C.L.* 39.   [79] *C.L.* 59.
[80] *C.L.* 60.

As for the bankers, they pray you that ye will buy them with flowers and no silk, with 6 cushions of the same work of the bankers. They must be in 2 pieces, the t'one 5 English yards and the other 6, and the cushions unstuffed, of the same work.[81]

John Roosse was still after his hawks and wrote eagerly to George, by then at the mart:

My master your brother Richard informed me that you had a hawk in Calais, as you told him. He said that you pointed [intended] [it] for me, and that caused me to come over sea. And therefore, sir, I beseech you, and you have any, to let me have her as she is worth. And if you have none here, that you would buy one there with you now, and send her to Calais. Or else, and you will that I come to you, I pray you let me have word by the next man that come between. For sin' I am come so far, I will have one, and it cost me more than she is worth by large money. Sir, I will not depart from Calais till I have word from you, and that I beseech you it may be shortly, for here I have nothing to do but to wait on an answer hereof from you. Sir, if it please you to do this for me you shall have my service as I am true Christian man, as long as ever I live.[82]

George had indeed succeeded in obtaining some hawks, probably through the good offices of Wauterin Tabary, who wrote to him in French (at the lodgings of Robert Radcliffe, Gentleman Porter of Calais, by which he may mean the 'Star' at Bruges?).

Please to know that I send you this bearer to escort the man with the hawks, and I have promised him three stoters [groats]. And give the falconer a pour-boire [*ung pot de vin*] at your pleasure, for his expenses. And it is only for love of you that the said hawks came hither, because since your departure they were sought by the gentleman of Monsieur de Bèvres, and also by Monsieur the Lieutenant. No more for the present, but God have you in his blessed keeping. And pay the said bearer the said three stoters.

Be it given to Master George Silait, dwelling with Monsieur Master Porter.[83]

Roosse's enthusiasm had waned, however, by the time that George wanted to take him up on his offer of assistance. Thomas Granger wrote to George at the 'Star', apparently on 20 October:

Like it you to wit how I have done your errand unto John Ros, and I have desired him to come to Bruges unto you, and ye should have paid for his costs and have rewarded him so that he should have hold him right well pleased. And sir, he answered me again and said how that he would do also much for you as lay in his power to do, but for certain, and he should win thereby 40s, he might not come unto you at this time.[84]

---

[81] *C.L.* 74.
[82] *C.L.* 61 (22 September).
[83] *C.L.* 62.
[84] *C.L.* 64.

Roosse himself wrote his excuses to George, pleading pressure of business, although he had previously said that he had nothing to detain him in Calais:

Letting you wit that Thomas Granger informed me that you would that I should come to Bruges to you, for to help to convey your hawks into England. Sir, I beseech you to pardon me, for by my troth, and I might get 40s thereby, I may not, my business is so at this time. But and your hawks come to Calais or I depart from thence, I will help to convey them there as it please you. And if it will please you, that I may have one or two of them at a reasonable price, and assign me in England to whom that you will that I shall pay, at the price that you do set of them. And yet I bought a mewed hawk in Calais sin' I came: she cost me 40s and more, the which I have sent into England. And yet I will have a couple of yours, and you will. And therefore and it please you that I shall have any of them, or and you will that I shall help to carry them into England, let them be sent to Calais shortly, for I will into England shortly.[85]

Possibly Roosse had already heard what he reported to Richard senior on his return to London, that George was 'sore sick at Bruges',[86] and this was one reason for his reluctance to go there. Ironically, George may have caught the widespread infection of the time just as its virulence was abating at Calais.

George himself wrote home on 23 October, telling the family of his sickness but reassuring them. William Maryon replied on 8 November:

Evermore desiring to hear of your welfare, for it hath be said unto us here that ye hath be sore sick, but I trust to God ye be now amended. My master your father and my mistress your mother hath been right heavy for you. After time that they heard that ye were sick there could nothing make them merry, not till it were All Hallowen Even that my master had writing from you.

Also my mistress your mother and your brother Richard, they have had a little fit of sickness, too, but now I thank God they be amended and all whole, and so I trust to God ye be also.[87]

Maryon, like everyone else, had jobs for George to do at the Cold mart next month.

George had written again on 1 November, to say that he was improving, but William the falconer had fallen ill in Bruges as well, and some of the hawks had died. It must have been difficult to find people to take letters to England, because this one did not reach London until 11 November. At George's request, William Cely was then dispatched to assist him and to take his place in riding to the mart. He carried two affectionate letters to George in Bruges. Richard senior wrote:

[85] *C.L.* 63.   [86] *C.L.* 67.
[87] *C.L.* 70.

I greet you well, and your mother and I desire for to hear of your recuring [recovery] and amending, as I trust in God ye shall right well. Be as merry as ye can and spare for no cost of such thing as may be good for you, in good meat [and] drink. And [for] your physicians, do by their counsel and please them at my cost. And take no great labour in riding till ye be strong.

And for that cause I send Will Cely to you, for to do for you with the oversight of some good man, for I will not that ye labour to the mart. Keep yourself well in any wise. I have liefer my money be not received till another time, rather nor ye shall labour yourself and not whole...Will Cely shall wait on you and tend to as long as shall please you, and I trust to God ye shall come home to London or ['before'] Christmas.[88]

Richard junior wrote no less lovingly, amid his own preoccupations.

Brother, I have received from you a letter written at Bruges upon All Hallowen Day, whereby I understand of your great sickness, thanking God of your amendment, trusting the worst be past. Sir, I have been right sick in Essex afore Hallowentide, I thank God and good diet I am quit thereof now. And in that season Meg [a hawk] took a sickness whereof she died at London. And when I come to London, among all my gowns my best black gown was gnawen with rattons ['rats'] about the skirts. And in the next money that I received for our father, was £30, whereof I lost 20s in gold, a' my soul I wot not where. Thus I write to you of my pain and grief, as ye have done unto me of yours. I pray you to come home at this Christmas, and by the grace of Jesu we shall be merry after all this tribulation and vexation of sickness....

Sir, I am sorry that ye have been so cumbered with William Falconer, but it help not. And as for the hawks that be dead, all our evil go with them. When William is mended I pray you send him home. My Lord of St Johns has written me a letter wherein he recommends him to you, and desires me to come with my hawk, for there is much fowl about him. I long sore for William Falconer.

Sir, our father and mother sends to you William Cely to wait upon you and to go and ride at your commandment, according to your writing. Sir, our father and mother is right heavy for you, and goes a' [on] pilgrimage daily for you...and we pray you be merry and take a good heart to you. Our father and mother desire you not to labour nowhere till ye be whole. Sir, I pray you of your goodly answer shortly. I had but this letter from you sin' we departed. I go nowhere ne ride till I have an answer from you.[89]

The expected reply was penned on 21 November, and George gave the letter to William Falconer, who was thought well enough by then to start out for Calais on his way home with the surviving hawks. But George subsequently had a letter from one John Goldson of Calais, written on 30 November:

Certifying you that your man with your hawks come sore sick to Calais. And so my hostess keeped him a day and a night, and then we hired two women in the

[88] *C.L.* 73.   [89] *C.L.* 74.

town, and they keeped him at another house in the town. And so he is dead and departed to God, God have mercy on his soul. And I and my hostess have buried him, and he had his mass and dirge and all his rites, as a Christian man should have.

Item, as for your two hawks, I have let a man keep them that can good skill of hawks, and they like ['do'] well. And sir, look what I may do for you here and it shall be ready to my power... By your servant, John Goldson.[90]

George himself was still far from well. He had been moved for better care to the house of 'Master Jacob the Physician' in Bruges, where William Cely addressed a letter on 7 December.[91] Perhaps Master Jacob shared some of the expertise of the fictitious Bruges physician 'Maximian', who was credited in a phrase-book issued by Caxton with everything save the ability to cure lightning-struck postilions.[92] Not only did he have the not-very-helpful power to tell from his patient's urine whether he was suffering from headache, sore eyes, earache or toothache, but he could also cure afflictions of

dropsy, bloody flux, phthisic, mormal, feet, nails, fever quartain and tertian, of the jaundice (whereof God keep us!), and of all that that may grieve us. He giveth counsel for the gout, and for other sicknesses. He hath many good herbs.

Contemporary medicine put emphasis upon the curative properties of 'good diet', which meant (one suspects) plenty of animal protein. But people put most of their faith in preventative measures. At one period of 'reigning sickness' – perhaps 1479, perhaps 1467 – Edward IV daily consumed a concoction of various herbs.[93] Most of them were harmless, but there was a component of wood-sorrel (*Oxalis acetosella*), perhaps capable of producing oxalic acid poisoning if ingested in sufficiently large quantity. Almost the same recipe, labelled 'for the pestilence', appears in Richard Hill's commonplace book in the next century.[94] Both versions say that the medicine is efficacious if taken before any skin-eruption ('any purple', or in the later copy 'the marks'), appears.

On 9 December, Richard Cely junior, 'marvelling greatly' that he had heard no word from George since William Cely had left nearly a month before, expressed somewhat selfish reasons for wanting George home, an event that he expected daily.

[90] *C.L.* 75.
[91] *C.L.* 77.
[92] Henry Bradley, ed., *Caxton's Dialogues in French and English* (E.E.T.S. e.s. LXXIX, 1900), pp. 41–2. The work was a redaction from an earlier French–Flemish text-book.
[93] *Notes and Queries*, 5th ser. IX (1878), p. 343: 'the medicine that the king's grace useth every day for the reigning sickness that now reigneth... and by the grace of God it hath holpen this year 71 persons'.
[94] Balliol MS. 354 fo. 143v. Oxalic acid is cumulative in effect and highly toxic in concentrated form.

Sir, my Lord has written to me to come see him this Christmas. I purpose to go to him three days afore Christmas, and be there four days, and come again. And ye come not to London four days afore Christmas I pray you send me my ring by some trusty man. Our mother looks for the case for the pen[s?] that ye took measure of. I pray Jesu send you hither in safety ever I go to Balsall, for then I shall be better beseen than I am like.[95]

On 12 December, having now heard the sad news of the falconer's death and received two very overdue letters from George, one written at Antwerp in October and the other, of 21 November, given to the ill-fated falconer to deliver, Richard wrote more consolingly:

There is a clause in your letter that ye wrote last, trusting to God that we shall be so merry at our meeting that all sorrows shall be forgotten. I trust the same. I pray you labour yourself not too sore till ye find yourself strong, and then 'at ye will come hitherward. I would write to you of many things, but I trust to tell you them merrily by mouth.[96]

He added a cheering postscript:

There was never more game about us than there is now. I trust ye will not tarry long at Calais at your coming if there be any sure passage.

In 1479 death or serious illness struck members of the three English families who furnish us with major collections of letters. Of the Pastons, Agnes, Sir John and William died within a few weeks of each other. Of the Stonors, Elizabeth died in late 1479 or very early 1480 and her son-in-law Thomas Betson was desperately ill for a time in September–October 1479. George Cely fell sick in October, and Robert's wife and six other members of his household had died in July. There is no proof that all these people suffered from the same disease, and Agnes Paston in particular was already advanced in years. But a recent study of the epidemics of fifteenth-century England has suggested that this year saw the most virulent 'death' of the period.[97]

Its chronology has not been securely established, partly because those modern writers who have investigated the subject have relied too greatly on statements by various sixteenth-century chroniclers, whose dating (by regnal or mayoral years) has been misunderstood.[98] The most accurate

---

[95] *C.L.* 78. Richard also wanted French gloves to give as presents.　　　[96] *C.L.* 81.

[97] Gottfried, *Epidemic Disease in Fifteenth-Century England.*

[98] Gottfried (*Epidemic Disease*, pp. 144–5) says that 'the literary sources give useful dates for [the epidemic's] onset and conclusion', but adds, curiously, that 'the earliest reliable record[s] of its presence come from Southwell in Nottinghamshire in the summer, and from East Anglia in the late summer' [of 1479], and deduces that it reached London only in the autumn of 1479. He overlooked both the record of the postponement of

description was given by Robert Fabyan, who stated that a great mortality and death in London and many other parts of the realm began in the latter end of September 1478 and continued in 1479 until the beginning of November.[99] The Cely letters do not contradict this, if the writers who discounted any danger in London in November 1478 were implying that deaths had occurred in significant numbers earlier in the autumn.[100] Evidently there was a remission in the capital during the winter of 1478–9, followed by a renewed outbreak in the spring. On 9 April 1479 the Council ordered postponement of King's Bench and other court sittings, on account of the outbreak of pestilence at London,[101] and the wills registered in the Prerogative Court of Canterbury seem to indicate that among the privileged class there represented the highest peak of mortality was reached in the first quarter of 1479.[102] What evidence that there is does not suggest that the sickness was highly contagious, and the heavy mortality in Robert's family may indicate that, in the words of an early seventeenth-century tract, Robert and his wife were persons 'such as do not greatly regard clean and sweet keeping'.[103] Richard junior and his mother may possibly have had the same sickness in Essex in October, and another presumable victim was the Tournai merchant Philip Celyer, who died in London about 25 September.[104] In Calais, where they died 'sore' by July, a maid-servant of Thomas Kesten died but his wife and children 'stood'.[105] In Calais the worst was said to be over by 20 October 1479, when the mortality was not one-quarter what it had been,[106] and on 6 November it was reported that no-one had died there 'these three days'.[107] Deaths certainly continued beyond that date in London, where Sir John Paston died on 15 November. He had written on 29 October:

London courts in April 1479 and those Cely letters published by Malden. For other datings see J. F. D. Shrewsbury, *The History of Bubonic Plague in the British Isles* (Cambridge, 1970), pp. 148–9, and Charles Creighton, *A History of Epidemics in Britain*, I (2nd edn, London, 1965), 287.

[99] Robert Fabyan, *The New Chronicles of England and France* [1516], ed. H. Ellis (1811), p. 666. Shrewsbury thought Fabyan meant Sept. 1479 to Nov. 1480; Gottfried apparently took him to mean Sept.–Oct. 1479, but himself writes of 'the epidemic of 1479–80', e.g. *Bury St Edmunds and the Urban Crisis*, p. 63 and 'Population, Plague and the Sweating Sickness: Demographic Movements in late Fifteenth-Century England', *Journal of British Studies*, XVII (Fall, 1977), p. 13.

[100] Davis's suggested date of 1478 for *Paston L.* no. 772 would fit this well enough: on 4 Nov. it was said that at Caister and Mautby 'there died none since Michaelmas', but deaths were still occurring in other places in Norfolk.

[101] *C.C.R. 1476–85*, 503.

[102] Gottfried, *Epidemic Disease*, graph 4.1.3, 3.

[103] James Bamford (1603), quoted Creighton, I, 490.

[104] Below, Ch. 8, pp. 208–9.

[105] *C.L. 58*, 76.   [106] *C.L. 64.*   [107] *C.L. 66.*

I have been here at London a fortnight, whereof the first four days I was in such fear of the sickness, and also found my chamber and stuff not so clean as I deemed, which troubled me sore.[108]

Early in December his brother reported from London that 'the sickness is well ceased here', though his fears of it were by no means at an end.[109]

What was the disease that reached epidemic proportions in 1478–9? In seeking an answer we are not helped by the linguistic evidence: official notices referred to 'pestilence' in April 1479, but all contemporary letter-writers speak only of 'the death' or 'the sickness'. And the ordinary person of the period evidently had a very limited medical vocabulary. Nowadays everyone has picked up from medical science a host of terms, together with a ready knowledge of the major symptoms that differentiate the commoner afflictions. In the fifteenth century it was legal rather than medical terminology that came trippingly off the tongue of any educated layman. It was, exceptionally, the sweating sickness of 1485 which, as a new and frightening disease, was explicitly named as the cause of death in many contemporary reports. Modern writers have consequently been left to assume that it was bubonic plague which caused the high mortality of the fifteen months between September 1478 and November 1479. The seasonal pattern of the epidemic, with its winter remissions, would seem to support this diagnosis, while at the same time it rules out influenza quite decisively and argues against typhus. It is most unlikely that it was plague in its pneumonic form that attacked victims like George Cely and Thomas Betson, because it is generally agreed that without modern treatment pneumonic plague is almost invariably fatal.

If George Cely and Thomas Betson contracted bubonic plague, in the form in which it was by then endemic in the British Isles, it is a curious fact that the Celys and other writers reserve the word 'plague' for the later scourge that killed people in London and Calais between spring and autumn in 1487.[110] In that year Richard advised George to return with his wife to Essex, 'for I understand they die sore in London',[111] and George sent his servant Nicholas Best to transact business in the city: 'the plague has been such that we dare not come there ourself'.[112] Happily, Nicholas survived. Edmund Paston, too, writing at a date put

---

[108] *Paston L.*, no. 315.
[109] Ibid., no. 384.
[110] 'Plague' did not necessarily bear its restricted modern meaning at the time. Gottfried's impression (*Epidemic Disease*, pp. 42, 50) that an epidemic in 1467 was actually called 'a pestilence of plague' rested on a miscopying and mistranslation of the phrase *pestilencie plaga*, 'a plague of pestilence', in *Rot. Parl.* v, 618. Unfortunately, Gottfried was unaware of this 1487 epidemic and writes of 'the absence of plague in the 1480s' ('Population, Plague and the Sweating Sickness', p. 35).
[111] *C.L.* 233.   [112] *C.L.* 231.

between June 1487 and February 1493, but very likely referring to the same outbreak as the Celys, described how families were taking refuge 'for fear of the plague' in Norfolk, and because 'the plague reigneth at Ormesby'.[113] On 12 September 1487 William Cely wrote that 'almighty God visiteth sore here in Calais and the marches with this great plague of sickness that reigneth'.[114] Did some mere change of fashionable nomenclature occur between 1479 and 1487, or do the distinct differences in terminology mean that the 'visitation' or 'scourge' of 1487 was perceived as different from the 'sickness' of 1478–9?

Although George eventually recovered in 1479, his natural defences may have been weakened by his prolonged illness. He was 'right sore sick' a second time in Bruges in May 1482,[115] and ill once more in England in September 1483,[116] while it may have been an infection contracted at Calais that killed him in June 1489, when he had, perhaps, recently turned thirty-one. Thomas Betson died, possibly still younger, of the sweating sickness in September 1485.[117]

[113] *Paston L.*, no. 400. [114] *C.L.* 234.
[115] *C.L.* 170–4. [116] File 20 no. 7.
[117] The cause of death is stated in P.R.O. C.1 82/102. Betson's will of 12 June 1483 (P.C.C. 24 Logge) has a codicil made on 25 Sept. 1485. Probate was granted on 12 May 1486. The date of the codicil shows that those later chroniclers who put the beginning of the outbreak of sweating sickness on 27 Sept. were incorrect (Gottfried, 'Population, Plague and the Sweating Sickness', pp. 18–19). Moreover, the mayor of London, Thomas Hill, had died of the sweat on 23 Sept.: Sharpe, *Letter Book L*, p. 226.

ALARMS AND
TRIBULATIONS, 1480–1

Much of the extant material from the Celys' papers in 1480 concerns the routine business of buying and selling wool and fell. The widespread 'death' in 1479 had perhaps interfered with trade that year, and although Richard Cely senior had braved infection and bought 27 sarplers of wool in the Cotswolds in April 1479, he kept them in store in England until they were finally shipped to Calais on 23 March 1480.[1] Part of the consignment, which old Richard had described as carefully classed or 'good packing', was quickly sold, but when George attended the Antwerp mart in June he received bitter complaints from the buyer, who said that a large proportion of the wool was wrongly designated.[2] By that time Richard had shipped 17 sarplers of new stock,[3] which George endeavoured to keep back until he had sold more of the defective shipment. This was still unsold by November, however, and the wool in the remaining 20 sarplers had to be reclassed and repacked, at the same time as 11 more sarplers had reached Calais with the autumn fleet.[4]

For both Cely brothers 1480 was a year of travel. George had a full round of seasonal marts to visit. Richard was assigned to the buying and packing of wool in the Cotswolds in the earlier part of the year, and then accompanied Sir John Weston's party on a number of official occasions, including an embassy to France. As the year wore on it also brought conflict in the wider political area and family tensions for the Celys.

To start with, Robert, who had lost wife and child in the epidemic of the previous year, got himself into a matrimonial tangle from which, as the next chapter describes, he had to be extricated by his exasperated father. Old Richard increasingly resented time spent away from his country estate in Essex, and now sent Richard junior to deal with his woolmen. Richard went off to the Cotswolds on 8 April to pack 29 sarplers, and was due to go again, to his mother's old home of Adderbury,

---

[1] *C.L.* 50, 82. [2] *C.L.* 93.
[3] *C.L.* 89. [4] *C.L.* 104.

Oxfordshire, on 1 May.[5] George, back in Calais to receive the March shipment of wool, had got off on the wrong footing by writing to his brother and not his father. Richard begged him to be more careful and to keep in mind their resolve to content the old man and avoid unpleasantness: 'I pray you write, but for ['if only for'] hope in us to awere [avert] discomforts for ever, and therefore let us endeavour us to please, as Jesu give us grace to do.' George had, however, sent 'tidings' for Sir John Weston, always avid for news from abroad. In return Richard remembered to give George the sort of information he wanted himself. His horse Ball was 'in good plight. He mourned till he had fellowship, and the smith has given him a drink for the cough [which Richard spells 'kow'], and I have sent him to Aveley by [the servant John] Lontelay till I come again.'[6]

When George wrote on 13 May he was able to report the sale of some of the wool shipped in March, which encouraged his father to send part of his new purchase of 29 sarplers.[7] Most of them were 'bought of Will Midwinter of Northleach...the which is fair wool, as the wool-packer Will Breten saith to me. And also the three sarplers of the rector's is fair wool – much finer wool nor was the year before, the which I shipped afore Easter last past.'[8] Richard senior wrote thus on 22 May, mentioning also that Richard junior, accompanied by William Cely, had just left again for Northleach, this time to select new stocks of wool-fells. George must make over money at the mart at the best rates he could, because Richard, with the enthusiasm of inexperience, was likely to buy heavily. The triumphant tone with which George drafted a letter about the state of his father's supposedly 'well packed' wool of 1479 suggests that he was tempted to requite past denigration of this sort. 'I trow ye can but little skill of such ware', his father had said, bluntly if quite truly, when asking George to buy a cart the year before.[9] Their uncle John Cely had just settled another family quarrel, a long-standing 'variance and jar' between old Richard and his sister about a debt from Richard Bowell.[10] It is clear that old Richard was not the most conciliatory or long-suffering of men. And autocratic tendencies were nurtured by an age which expected a man to thrash his elderly wife for gossipping indiscreetly and to rule children with the rod.

That June was a busy time for both sides of the family. Seventeen bales of wool had been sent off in the woolfleet, laded in four separate ships

---

[5] *C.L.* 83–4.
[6] *C.L.* 83. Through a mistranscription in Malden's edition, the horse was made to mourn until he 'had set ship'.   [7] *C.L.* 87.
[8] Ibid.   [9] *C.L.* 56.   [10] *C.L.* 88.

and carefully detailed by William Cely.[11] As George had much to do at Antwerp, Thomas Granger acted as his attorney at Calais, and was left an inventory of George's stocks there, with a request to sell as much as possible:

First, sir, an ye can, sell 456 winter London [fells] of my father's Richard Cely his. They be praised at 12 nobles 20*d* [per 100], and they be old fells. They lie in the nether chamber over my lady Clare....

Item, there is an 149 Cots. fells of William Maryon's that is the end of an sort, praised at 14 nobles. They lie in the upper garret....

There lies in an stable there as Thomas Kesten dwelleth now, 525 summer fells London praised at 16½ nobles....

Thomas, I pray you sell some of mine good Cots. wool that came at Easter, and ye can. And as for that 'at came since, I pray you let it alone till I come, but if John Vandyrhay of Mechelen come, for he must have all the middle wool that I have: I have money in my hands of his'n that I brought with me from there. That wool that came last is not awarded yet, and ye shall know the t'other by the numbers, for all that wool that is numbered aboven 27 came last.

Sir, if there come any wool or fell to Calais from my father or brother or W. Maryon, house the wool in Proud's woolhouse, and hire some of the garrets over the said woolhouse if any fells come. I deem there will come none till I come from the mart again....

Sir, if any wools of my father's comes, I pray you let the freight be paid and send me writing of the coming thereof, as ye will I shall do you pleasure in time coming, and whereto I am bound.[12]

A letter from Robin Good, old Richard's 'child' or young serving-man, gave George news of activities at home:

Right reverent and worshipful master, after due recommendation I lowly recommend me unto you, desiring evermore to hear of your welfare, the [which] almighty Jesu preserve it to his pleasure and to your most heart's desire, etc. ['Etc.' is used by most writers of the time as a kind of full-stop.]

Doing your mastership to understanden, at the making of this letter my master and my mistress, my master Richard Cely and William Maryon and all our household be in good heal[th], thanked be God, etc. If it please your mastership to understand, my master and my mistress and all our household be in Essex. They be busy at making of hay now. As for my master Richard, is much at my lord of St John's [who was spending the summer in Essex, at Berwick], and some time with my master, etc.

No more unto you at this time, but the Holy Trinity have you in his keeping. Writ at London the 24 day of June in haste, per your servant, Robert Good.[13]

Richard junior had bought 1,800 fells for himself and George, and when George arranged exchange loans at the mart he had to ensure that

---

[11] *C.L.* 89.   [12] *C.L.* 92.   [13] *C.L.* 94.

money would be available in England to meet instalments of £20 due to William Midwinter at Bartholomew Tide and All Hallows: 'Sir, I pray you have these days in remembrance: my poor honesty lies there upon', Richard admonished him.[14] But in addition to such proper business of a stapler, good-natured George was, as usual, required to act as general provider for a whole circle of family and acquaintances, all promising to pay later 'as the goods cost'. Maryon still wanted three *stics* (ells) of fine linen cloth at 20*d* the *stic*, and also a fur for his gown and a covering for a book. Richard needed a doublet, and a man named Savage also asked for a doublet-cloth.[15] For Sir John Weston, George had to buy three saddles, at 6*s* each, a pair of gilt spurs with matching rowels and hooks, which totalled 8*s*, two pairs of stirrups (4*s*), and three pairs of hose-cloths. Harold Staunton required some body-armour consisting of a pair of gussets, a fauld (apron-like protection) of fine steel and a standard (mailed collar).[16] George's itemized expenditure on these and other purchases comes to £10 10*s* 1½*d* Flem.[17] A group of friends wanted feathers: 'Lyllborn' or Littleborn four 'single' feathers, Harry Grisley a thick black one, which cost a whole 8*s*, and Richard Primrose 'an hoystyrs ruyffe', which is George's way of spelling an ostrich 'ruff', the familiar curled tail-feather. Perhaps it was unobtainable, as no price is given. On one occasion Hastings Pursuivant provided ten ostrich feathers for Edward IV, at a cost of 10*s* each.[18]

Other items requested but not priced in George's shopping lists were quarrels for Edmund Bedingfield's cross-bow, a 'covyrlyd' (bed-covers were enormous, and this contained 30 ells or 22½ yards) and ten stics of banker for 'Trowtyn', and two great chafing-dishes for Sir Richard Tunstall. But Maryon got his fur, costing 25*s* Flem., and the tailor Vincent was paid 23*s* 3*d* for Richard's doublet. A chest, bought for the stapler Robert Burdon and perhaps carved or otherwise ornamented, cost 9*s*.[19] For himself or his father George bought a pair of stirrups, two horse-harness, two saddles (one new and one mended), a pair of stirrup-leathers and a girth, four caps (two costing 4*s* and two 2*s* 6*d*, which George then totalled to 7*s* 6*d*!), and some cloth. This included 1½ ells of black sarsenet for 5*s* 3*d* and 1½ ells of 'schangeawell', i.e. 'changeable': material dyed with an effect like that of shot-silk, for 8*s* 9*d*. In 1480 Edward IV had in his wardrobe some green changeable velvet and 'sarsenets changeables'.[20] Interestingly enough, it was at Antwerp and

[14] *C.L.* 91.
[15] File 15 fo. 41v.
[16] File 15 fo. 51.
[17] File 15 fo. 52v.
[18] Sir Nicholas Harris Nicolas, ed., *Privy Purse Expenses of Elizabeth of York, Wardrobe Accounts of Edward IV* (1830), p. 119.
[19] File 20 no. 3.
[20] *Privy Purse Expenses*, p. 116.

not in England that George bought $8\frac{3}{4}$ ells of worsted (for £1 0s 8d), and $2\frac{3}{8}$ ells of woollen cloth (at 5s the ell).

On 30 June Richard junior wrote to say that George should come home, since their father did not propose to ship more wool until shortly before Michaelmas.[21] There was also some cause for worry: 'our father has been diseased sore. I trust it be but an access [attack of ague or fever], but I would fain that ye were here till he be better mended.' By 5 July he was 'all whole and right merry', except when considering the latest 'childish dealing' of his son Robert.[22] George, however, was now told not to be 'over-hasty in coming into England', but to sell some of that unlucky March shipment. Their father 'dare not send no more to Calais till he hear of the sale of the foresaid'. While George was stuck in Calais, no doubt cursing his father and his father's carelessness in the wool-packing, Richard was looking forward to his next day's expedition to Gravesend with Sir John 'to bring in my lady Marget', the king's sister, widow of Charles the Bold, who was coming on a visit to England.

To add to George's troubles, it became clear that he would have to repack the 20 sarplers of defective wool, and he learnt that he must deal single-handed with the autumn shipment, for, wrote his father on 1 September,

I have no man for to send with the ships, for Will Cely is fore ['gone'] with Richard Cely with my lord of St John's into France, God be their speed. For the which I trust to you for the receiving of my wool and fell, and also for your fell and Will Maryon's fell. I suppose ye have not much ado at this mart. For the which I pray you send me writing of your going to this mart or not. For and ye be at Calais at the landing of my wool and fell I will be well pleased and ye may so do.[23]

But he added cautiously, 'and ye hear of war, send me writing shortly, for I will not be the first that shall ship'.

Simultaneously with this letter, perhaps, George had a brief message from his brother Richard, written from Dover and telling him to meet Sir John's party next day at Boulogne. 'And I pray you to bring with you your cross [a colloquial expression for money], and £5 or £6 Flemish for me, and at our meeting I will tell you more.'[24] Sir John's secretary, Edward Plumpton, enclosed a note which George was to give Plumpton's 'brother Nowell', who seems to have been a member of the Calais garrison at the time.[25]

No more was heard from George for about three weeks, or shortly

[21] *C.L.* 95.   [22] *C.L.* 96.
[23] *C.L.* 98.   [24] *C.L.* 99.
[25] For Plumpton's employment with Sir John Weston, see *Stonor L.* no. 329 (1483). George lent 20s to 'Nowell, soldier of Calais' in Feb. 1482: File 10 fo. 8v.

before 25 September, when his father sent the detailed list of his new shipments. He had by now decided to send Robin Good to help, grudgingly enough.

I will ye see shar[p]ly to him, and when the ships be discharged send him home by water to London, for I have great miss of Richard Cely and Will Cely at this time. In good faith, I may not deal with wool and fell and my husbandry in the country both, but I may have help. I was never so weary of dealing with word as I am at this time, and sith that my lord of St Johns came to Boulogne I had no writing from you but one letter now late, for the which I understood not verily [whether] ye were in France or at the mart. I had so many saying ['heard so many reports'] of men that came from Calais, and no letters, for the which I was greatly astonied, and great letting ['hindrance'] in my business. For the which I pray thee write and send by sure men, that I may understand my dealing.

Also ye write not to me of the rest of my fell, whether they be refuse or nay, and what sum of fell there be, for I wot [not what] fell the rest should be.[26]

On 13 October old Richard wrote more briefly but just as trenchantly:

I send to you writing of my shipping at London at this time by Robert Good my child, the which I might not well 'a missed him and Will Cely both, for the which your mother and I were not so served this 20 year. For the which I purpose me to more ease, by the grace of God.[27]

It is possible that George preferred his father to remain in ignorance of whether he was 'in France or at the mart', in view of his irascibility at the time. No. 105 of the *Cely Letters* is a copy, made by William Cely, of the instructions that George left with Thomas Granger while he was away from Calais. The original, in George's hand, has now turned up, and notes of expenditure by Thomas and William Granger throw more light on George's movements.[28] Evidently the memorandum, together with £20 for expenses, was given to Granger on 8 September, and George then promised to send William Cely back to Calais 'in all the haste that I can'. Both George and William must have been absent between that date and 11 October, because William Granger saw to the rehousing of wool and gave money for petty costs to George's servant, John Kay. It might appear that George was at Calais on 16 October, because his father was somewhat mollified to receive a letter of that date reporting a sale of wool to Jan Van Der Heyden.[29] In point of fact, however, that sale took place nearly a month earlier, on 18 September, and so may have been made by Granger.[30] One wonders whether the letter was really written at Calais, or whether George was misleading his

[26] *C.L.* 104.
[28] File 20 no. 2.
[30] File 12 fo. 3.

[27] *C.L.* 106.
[29] *C.L.* 107.

father about his whereabouts. William Cely, on the other hand, was certainly at Calais on 17 October. He had also written to Richard senior, and from that time he and Robin Good were dealing with the shipments of wool as they arrived.[31] Robin went back to England on 3 November, William paying 3s for his passage. There is no evidence of George's own presence in Calais until 12 November. At some point he must have attended the Bammis mart, which ran from 27 August to perhaps 7 October that year, and it was presumably to George at the mart that Thomas Granger dispatched William Cely with £5 21d in various coins, George's casket and its key, and two obligations of Clays Alwinson of Leiden which had been in the safe-keeping of Randolf, the Staple clerk.[32] But George was clearly conscious of some dereliction of duty when he wrote to his father on 16 November, 'now I have seen that 'at I desired long to see, I took this season ['opportunity' or *cession*, 'break from work'?], which time I would that I had lain sick in my bed if ye be displeased therewith'.[33] The most likely explanation is that after doing his business at the mart George had joined Richard and Sir John in France, and returned with them to Calais only in early November.

Richard was back in London on 15 November, and wrote thanking George for 'the great cost and cheer that ye did to me and my fellows at our last being with you at Calais'. He included a lamentably laconic reference to a visit to the royal court. The Celys' correspondents are never regaled with the kind of descriptive detail thought necessary in a later and more literary age.

Sir, we had a fair passage, and the Saturday after our departing we came to the king to Eltham, to whom my lord was right welcome. And there we tarried till the king's daughter was christened, whose name is Bridget. And the same night right late we came to London. And here I found our father, brother Robert and my godfather Maryon, and they are merry. Our mother is in Essex, I see her not yet.... Sir, I would write more to you, but I depart into Essex this same day to fetch our mother.[34]

Next day George at last began on the task of repacking the wool, of which he must have been heartily sick by that time.

The English embassy had done nothing to achieve better relations with 'the spider', Louis XI, and there was much talk of war with France.[35]

---

[31] File 12 fos. 4–5.   [32] File 20 no. 2; *C.L.* 105.
[33] *C.L.* 109. Thomas Betson appears to use 'season' in the sense of 'vacation' in *Stonor L.* no. 205.
[34] *C.L.* 108.
[35] For the embassy and its reception, see Scofield, *Edward IV*, II, 291–9.

On 29 October old Richard had advised George to purchase a safe-conduct before crossing the sea,[36] and in his letter of 16 November George wanted his brother to find out from Sir John how the king had taken the ambassadors' answer from Louis, 'that I might understand by writing whether the king purposeth to have war with France or no'.[37] There were abortive plans for a conference between Louis and Maximilian, at which Maximilian wanted England to be represented, a proposal very unwelcome to Louis.[38] George reported prematurely:

Of tidings I can none write you for certain as yet, but 'at mine old lady [the dowager Duchess Margaret] is coming from Binche to St Omers, and the ambassadors both of England and France. I cannot say what world we shall have: some of the duke's council would have war and some peace – the very ground must come out of England [i.e. the English must provide the basis for a settlement?]. The French king has furnished his garrisons upon the fronts already. My lady purposeth to lie at St Omers and the French embassy shall lie at Thérouanne, three leagues thence.[39]

In fact no meeting took place, and 'the world' remained very unsettled.

Anxiety about the situation, and a mixture of bravado and guilt on George's part, helped to exacerbate a three-cornered family row at this point. It was occasioned by George's inability to resist a bargain in horse-flesh. Already in June Richard junior had warned him that there were no bidders for the two horses, the black and the grey, which he had left at London, and 'they stand you to great cost daily'.[40] As for his own horse and hawk, Richard had added virtuously, 'I purpose never to have past one at once'. Now in November trouble was sparked off when the lad Robin Good told old Richard that George had five horses at Calais. Richard junior assured his father that there were only three, and that Py No. 1 had been sold to Sir Humphrey Talbot. Meanwhile, however, William Maryon had written George a letter, as an old friend of the family, which George took as a piece of unwarranted interference. He wrote resentfully to his father:

As touching other clauses in your said letter, I understand them right well. And as for Robin, ye understand by this how well he has done none thing but put ye to cost, etc. As touching me, both by your said letter and by my cousin Maryon's, I am sorry, and I cannot be merry till that I have been with you. And I would 'a been with you shortly, saving my business is such that I cannot, as ye know. . . . I have been long hence, as ye know, nevertheless and my deputies had done their duties, I might so 'a been for that season right well. . . . I am in good way of my

<hr />

[36] *C.L.* 107.
[38] Scofield, *Edward IV*, II, 299.
[40] *C.L.* 91.

[37] *C.L.* 109.
[39] *C.L.* 109.

business now, yet was there right little done thereto when [William Cely] departed.[41]

Maryon's apologetic letter to George explains more:

I...understand that ye have received a letter fro me written at London the 9 day of November, in the which letter I wrote a clause of your horse, the which I understand ye take it sore at your stomach. Sir, in good faith I am sorry therefor, for and I had wist that ye would 'a take it so sore, I would not 'a written so unto you, not and I should 'a get thereby 20 nobles. But ye shall understand what caused me so for to write unto you.

Sir, ye wrote unto my master that ye supposed by likelihood it should be war. And if it so be it should be war, there should be great riding and mickle ado about Calais. And if ye be well horsed, I fear me that such soldiers as ye be acquainted withal should cause you for to put your body in aventure. And if there come anything to you otherwise than good, in good faith a great part of my master's joy in this world were i-do ['would be done away with']. Sir, this caused me, in good faith, for to write so unto you as I did, for I know well and ye have no good horse they will not desire you out of the town. Sir, in good faith my master your father neither my mistress your mother knew nothing of my writing. And, in good faith, ye shall understand that I wrote not so unto you for no spite, neither for no evil will that I have to you, but for great love. For, in good faith, saving my master your father and your brother Richard, in good faith there is no man in England I would do so much for, and that ye should know and ye had need. And that caused me to be so bold to write so to you, the which I would it had be undo the whiles ye take it so as ye do.[42]

George, who may well have felt his elders' argument somewhat specious, had also complained to his brother Richard that 'they' had him in jealousy, which Richard denied, saying soothingly that their father had said nothing more about the horses at all. Richard recommended George to sell 'the blind horse' for whatever he would fetch, but 'as for two or three horse, is not much as ye be purveyed'.[43] Evidently Robin's report of five horses had been quite true.

Richard echoed Maryon's explanation of their parents' fears that George's friendship with the hot-blooded young gentlemen soldiers of Calais could prove dangerous:

they think as ye are horsed and acquainted that and any war be ['if war occurs'] ye should be desired forth with other. And, as fortune of war is, ye to be taken or slain, the least of both were one death both to father and mother. We must tender their age, and have an eye to our own weal.

Maryon had taken it upon himself to write because their father had been so depressed and worried: 'he saw our father pensive and heavy at Robin Good's coming home, and afore, as ye know his condition of old'.

---

[41] *C.L.* 109.   [42] *C.L.* 110.   [43] *C.L.* 111.

George had also to forego his Christmas holiday this year. It was mutually agreed that he should remain in Calais, partly because the weather was stormy and the channel crossing risky: William Cely had had to pay 2*s* 'for tiling of master George's house that the wind had blowed down' in October.[44] Partly also the staplers expected to make sales between Christmas and Candlemas, at which time the Staple exchange rate was to be altered, to the disadvantage of the foreign buyers.[45] Richard was reassuring about the political situation: 'as for war between us and France, I can think ye shall have none. There goes over embassy shortly – what they are I cannot tell.'[46] George for his part had heard confused stories at Calais about dissension between the Burgundian and German elements in Maximilian's army:

As of any tidings here, I can none write you as yet. There is (but I cannot have the truth thereof) there has been an variance between the duke's men of war and his Almains, and there is many of his Almains slain, and therefore he takes great displeasure. There is diverse of his gentlemen stolen away therefor, and some are comen to Calais, and one of them is sent to our sovereign lord the king. And some been run Frenchmen ['have turned French'], when that the French king has gotten lately diverse of the best men of war the duke had, whereof he makes him now bold.[47]

During the winter George was able to sell a few sarplers of his father's accumulated wool stocks, and transacted business at the Cold mart at Bergen-op-Zoom, where he also made more purchases.[48] In February he went to Bruges to collect money from customers and 'to get me as many "Carowlis" groats as I can'.[49] Beforehand he wrote himself a memorandum:

Things to b.

Item, must buy hanging for my house
4 lb fenugreek for my horse
4 shirts
Hill his pouch
2 small 'cansticks' [candlesticks]
An table cloth
6 napkins and 2 towels
A fox fur for Littlebere.

About the same time he bought, among other things, a 'mall' [trunk] and a chest for 5*s* each, a pisspot for 12*d*, six cushions, costing 19*s* 6*d*, the hanging for three beds, two towels and a napkin, costing together 33*s*,

---

[44] File 12 fo. 5.
[45] *C.L.* 111–12.
[46] *C.L.* 111.
[47] *C.L.* 112.
[48] File 15 fo. 34; File 12 fo. 20 (24 Jan.).
[49] File 12 fo. 22v.

and a quilt for 3s 6d. His house may have been one leased in Calais, or the second family tenement in Mark Lane, London. In early 1482 he owed quit-rents at Calais of 26s 8d Flem. to Robert Bingham and of 53s 4d Flem. to Robert Knight.[50]

Meantime, the French king's 'boldness', especially his refusal to pay any advance dowry for the Princess Elizabeth and his encouragement of the Scots, increased a breach with England that had been widening steadily since 1479. The situation now created great excitement in London. On 26 January 1481 Richard had written to George:

The king has commanded my lord Rivers, my lord chamberlain [Hastings] and my lord of St John's to go to the Tower and see his ordnance and to admit ['appoint'] gunners and see that all things be made ready. [Sir John Weston was, after all, prior of a military Order.] And as for horse, my lord Rivers sends daily about to enquire for. Sir, gentle horse are worth much money here: I would avise you to bring over all your trotting horse and Joyce to keep them. I heard you say that your harness waxed too little for you. [George had been putting on weight!] And ye bring it [it will] be well sold. Sir, I have a pair of as fair briganders [plated body-armour] as any in London. I pray you buy me a fair and sure bicocket [casque], a standard [collar], a pair [of] sleeves as ye have, and a fauld [apron] of mail, and then I trust to Jesu that I am well harnessed to keep London with.

Sir, as for tidings I can write none but there came ambassadors out of Scotland. The king would not let them come no nearer, but sent their answer to Newcastle. We say here that my lord chamberlain comes to Calais shortly....

Sir, I would avise you to bring not past two or three horse with you, but and ye could convey a barrel or an hogshead full of sure faulds, flankards and some standards of mail well-bought, there would be done good over them. And I pray you bring the piece for doublet cloths that I wrote to you for afore Christmas, such as Hayne's is of. I have a gown cloth of musterdevillers of my lord's livery for you again[st] ye come.[51]

Calais (much more vulnerable than London) in turn caught the war fever, and, threatened by French and Scottish men-of-war in the channel, prepared for possible attack by pulling down the houses outside the walls. William Cely sent the news on 13 May to George, who was in Bruges:

Item, sir, please it you to wit that on the 12 day of May there was two Frenchmen chased an English ship afore Calais, and [the ships of] Fetherston and John Davy and Thomas Overton lay in Calais road, but themself were a-land. And as soon as they saw them they got boats and yeed aboard, and so did master marshal [Sir Humphrey Talbot] and Sir Thomas Everingham and master Nesfield, with diverse soldiers of Calais. And rescued the English ship, and took the Frenchmen and brought one of them into Calais haven. The t'other was so great she might

[50] File 12 fo. 17.   [51] *C.L.* 114.

not come in, but [they] brought the master and the captain to my lord [Hastings], and they say there is Scots amongst them. And they say that Fetherston and his fellows be gone with the bigger Frenchman into England.

Item, sir, it is said here that after this day, the 12 day of May, there shall no man keep no lodging of guests, strangers nor Englishmen, without the gates of Calais, except two houses assigned, that is [the] Searcher's house and the water bailiff's. And every man that hath housing without the gates is warned to remove his house as shortly as he can into the town, and set it there where him please that he hath ground. And if he do not so, stand at his own aventure at such time that shall come to be plucked shortly down, or else burned for the shorter work. And betwixt this and that time, none of them be so hardy, except the two places afore rehearsed, to lodge no man over an night, pain of treason.[52]

Prohibitions on the inhabitants of Calais sleeping outside the town walls had evidently become a dead letter. Staplers often did so when landing shipments, and in October 1480 William Cely had paid 5*d* 'for our supper of Robin and me one night, lying without the gates in landing of fells', while Robin was paid 'for a night that Harry and he had lain without the gates: they say their supper and their bed cost them 7*d*'. On 3 November William paid 2*d* 'for lying without the gates a night with Robert Good when he yeed to his passage'.[53] A further precaution against treachery was later taken, with the expulsion of 500 'Dutch' people (probably mainly Flemings and Brabanters) in November 1481.[54] George, however, obtained permission from the marshal and deputy lieutenant to keep his foreign servants. The town was sufficiently well supplied to be able to furnish armaments for the fleet being prepared to attack Scotland in May. On the same day that William described the activities at Calais, the captain of the *Michael of the Tower* collected numerous guns and other 'stuff and habiliments of war', including some large pieces named 'the Great Edward of Calais', 'the Little Edward', the great brazen gun, 'the Messenger' and 'the Fowler of Chester'.[55]

As for George's military array of horses, he may now have kept to the limit of three, which were indeed quite necessary, as Richard had admitted, since George would have to mount his servants as well as himself. He continued to buy and sell them, however. On 30 June 1481 he paid 'for my Bayard' 52 gulden at 3*s* 4*d* apiece, making £8 6*s* 8*d* Flem., and 'halver money' (meaning the payment known as 'halter money')?, of 22½*d*, together with 4*s* 2*d* 'to Thomas for his labour'.[56] In December 1481 he paid 37*s* 6*d* Flem. 'to boot ['to make up the difference'] between Roan and this bay horse that I have bought'.[57] The new bay horse was perhaps the one named 'Sorrel', for which John Dalton paid early in 1482

[52] *C.L.* 115.   [53] File 12 fo. 5.   [54] *C.L.* 134.
[55] Scofield, *Edward IV*, II, 314.   [56] File 12 fo. 24.   [57] File 12 fo. 32.

for 'certain stuff' for his malander (an eruption behind the knee), a horse rein and a load of hay.[58] A carter was also paid to take away dung and to bring gravel to the stable. Straw cost 8*d* and four rasers one bushel of oats 8*s* 10*d* Flem. There is an undated memorandum of payments to Twissulton for the keep of a horse for twenty-nine days at 4*d* Flem. per day.[59] In addition George paid for a load of hay (3*s* 4*d*), a load of straw (17*d*), and seven rasers three bushels of oats at 12*s* 7*d*.

In England there were matters to be settled in connection with the death of Sir William Plumpton, which had occurred in October 1480, apparently because Dean Richard Andrew, the Celys' maternal uncle, had been one of his feoffees.[60] In May 1481 Richard junior went up to York, together with (Edward?) Plumpton, to see his uncle's executors. He enjoyed 'great cheer' among his old acquaintances in the north, and wrote on his return to London to thank George for lending him his Flemish servant, Joyce Parmenter, 'for he has done to me good service in this journey, and I have delivered to him 9*s* to bring him to you'.[61] On the way north Richard met Roger Wigston (a leading stapler), 'on this side Northampton',

and he desired me to do so much as drink with his wife at Leicester. And after that I met with William Dalton, and he gave me a token to his mother. And at Leicester I met with Ralph Dalton, and he brought me to his mother, and there I delivered my token. And she prayed me to come to breakfast on the morrow, and so I did, and Plumpton both, and there we had a great welfare. And there was Friar Este, and I pray you thank them for me.... Dalton's mother commends her to you, and thanks you for the knives that ye sent to her.... Sir, I send you by Joyce a purse such as was given me at York, and I pray you buy for Alison Michael a mantle of fine black shanks, for I have money therefor. And she commends her to you.

Richard had a particular reason for wishing to visit the Dalton family: he had to make an inspection on George's behalf.

Sir, and ye be remembered, we talked together in our bed of Dalton's sister, and ye feared the conditions of father and brethren, but ye need not. I saw her, and she was at breakfast with her mother and us. She is as goodly a young woman, as fair, as well-bodied and as sad ['serious-minded'] as I see any this seven year, and a good height. [Were the males of the family dwarfish?] I pray God that it may be imprinted in your mind to set your heart there.

The match met with the approbation of Richard senior, who told George to work to bring it about:

---

[58] File 12 fo. 17v.   [59] File 16 fo. 21.
[60] T. Stapleton, ed., *The Plumpton Correspondence* (Camden Soc., 1839), p. lxxvii.
[61] *C.L.* 117.

the which matter in especial I will be well pleased to hear more of. For the which ye may have in your mind and good remembrance for to move and labour at Calais at this time.[62]

But George perhaps failed to set his heart in the right quarter, as nothing came of the proposal. If George's age has been correctly guessed he would be just twenty-three at this time. Although he did not in fact marry till three years later, it seems that his family did not consider him unduly young to think of matrimony. Nor was there any question of the sons waiting until their father died.

Richard's next news concerned Sir John Weston's coming visit to Rhodes. This stronghold of the Knights of St John had been under attack by the Turks, and Weston had been trying to get permission from Edward IV to travel there, unsuccessfully at first.[63] George was now asked to obtain foreign currency for him, and when his party finally left on 3 August, Richard accompanied them to Calais.[64] A letter from one of Sir John's household, left disconsolately behind in England, was addressed to George, but seems more probably intended for Richard.

Bedfellow, I commend me to you, and I thank you heartily of the good lodging that ye found us at Dartford. I had forgotten to have spoken with you that, and ye might, for to 'a provided for me a fur of budge, one of the finest that ye can find in Bruges. I trust by the counsel of my cousin your brother and you that, and there be any fine in Bruges, that ye will find it. And at your coming ye shall be truly paid therefor, whatsomever it cost. And I pray as heartily as [I] can that, as soon as ye may, that ye haste you homeward, for here is a heavy household, considering that my lord and his fellowship is departed.

No more to you at this time, but almighty God have you in his keeping. At St John's [Clerkenwell], the 4th day of August.

I pray you let master William, my lord's chaplain, understand privily that the parson of the church within Newgate, that is in my lord's gift, is deceased this hour.

By your bedfellow, Sir Roland Thornburght.[65]

A priest named William Ball succeeded to the vacant living of St Audoen's.[66] Was he 'master William', profiting by this early notice? But the patrons who made the presentation, in name at least, were the king's secretary Oliver King and Thomas Rogers.

While Richard and George were in Bruges together, George thought to close his accounts with the money-changers William Roelandts or Roelens and Nicholas De May, to his great relief when the news of their

---

[62] *C.L.* 116. Evidently there was no thought that Miss Dalton might transmit the physical conditions of her father and brothers to her own offspring.

[63] *C.L.* 114.   [64] *C.L.* 122.   [65] *C.L.* 123.

[66] G. L. Hennessy, *Novum Repertorium Ecclesiasticum Parochiale Londinense* (1898), pp. 97–8.

bankruptcies broke some time later.[67] Business was brisk at Calais, and George had recommended his father to buy plenty of wool for the coming year, advice heeded by other merchants as well, for his father remarked that 'wool in Cotswold is at great price...and great riding for wool in Cotswold as was any year this seven year'.[68] It was possibly in 1481 that a letter in the Stonor collection, which the editor dated only *post* 1477, commented that 'bought sheep was never so dear with us...we pay four mark for a score', i.e. 2s 8d a head.[69] When George bought Romneys some years later they cost him only 9d a head.[70]

Since only 16 sarplers and a poke of Cely wool had been shipped in May 1481,[71] once George had had it awarded as to quality he felt free to take time off with a holiday at home. There was news to be told then 'by mouth', though Thomas Granger, who took his letter of 5 August to his father, could also enlarge on the 'many things' of interest which it was better not to commit to paper.[72] This discretion leaves curiosity unsatisfied. It was John Dalton's turn again to be entrusted with affairs at Calais in George's absence, and Dalton sold six sarplers of the wool that had been shipped in September 1480.[73] He added a postscript to his letter of 22 September: 'also, sir, I forget not your hawks, but here comes none. But the first that I may get for money I shall send you, with God's grace.'

When George and Joyce had returned to Calais after their visit to England, Richard junior was soon occupied with the shipping of fells. He had good cause to miss Sir John Weston, not only for his company but also because a new neighbourly persecution befell him. On 24 October he gave George the news that 'I am going to labour to Sir Thomas Montgomery, for our father and ye and I are indicted for slaying [a hart] and certain hind calves.'[74] On 5 November he retailed the details of the charge, from which George had now been dropped. The pestiferous Brandon had again been making mischief.

It was so that by the means of Brandon our father and I were indicted for slaying of an hart that was driven into Kent, the which we never see nor knew of. And this day I have been with master Montgomery, and given him the value of a pipe wine to have us out of the book ever it be showed the king. And so he has promised me, and to be good master to our father and us in the matter between Brandon and us. John Frost, forester, brought me to his mastership, and acquainted me with a gentleman of his, whose name is Ramston, that is a nigh man to master Montgomery. And so I must inform him my matters at all times, and he will show them to his master.[75]

[67] *C.L.* 133. [68] *C.L.* 122. [69] *Stonor L.* no. 196.
[70] File 20 no. 8 (April 1484). In 1488 he bought 51 ewes at 1s 8d each: File 20 no. 11.
[71] *C.L.* 116. [72] *C.L.* 124. [73] *C.L.* 125.
[74] *C.L.* 127. [75] *C.L.* 133.

Further lobbying occurred: 'Plumar' (Robert Plummer?) promised to take Richard to the Earl of Essex, to whom Richard should show a document which Sir John Weston had given him at Berwick, Essex. 'I understand that my said lord [of Essex] says that he never gave Brandon no power.'[76] On 22 November Richard sent still more detail.

As for our matter that our father and I and Lontlay were indicted for, was by Brandon's surmise [false accusation] that we should drive an hart over Thames, the which was slain at Dartford, and that we should slay two hind calves. And all this he did himself, with much more, and is indicted himself for the death of two harts and certain calves.

It is so that Sir Thomas Montgomery is coming to Calais-ward, and so he will to St Omers for to fetch my lady. I pray you, at his coming wait upon him and thank him for us, for he has been our special good master in this matter, and has promised me to continue, and laboured sore for us. And through his labour I am come in 'quaintance of diverse worshipful men that will do much for us for his sake. I gave him of our father's purse an 100s, and Ramston, a gentleman of his, 3s 4d. I pray you make him good cheer, for he has been good solicitor for us, and he brings you a letter from me. And we would be right glad and ye might be ready to come in company of my lady with master Montgomery, for he purpose to be here afore Christmas.

And as for our foresaid matter, we have our supersedeas for all three. And our father is fully agreed that ye shall have over at your departing again, Hector and son for the Lieutenant of Gravelines, in recompense of your bitch, for he will keep no more greyhounds. 'A will be 'greable to keep a hawk and spaniels.[77]

As H. E. Malden pointed out, spaniels could not be accused of coursing deer.[78]

The supersedeas was issued by the Earl of Essex as master of the royal forest. It was a costly business, Richard lamented in his next letter, 'but and Sir Thomas Montgomery had not been our good master it would 'a cost much more. And my lord of Essex has confirmed and subserved under his signet the same writing that my lord of St John's gave me.'[79] The accounts mention two toppets of figs given to Sir Thomas, costing 2s 2d (1 lb cost about 1d) – also a 'prest' or loan to William Brandon, of 26s 8d.[80]

The bitch which was now to be 'recompensed' by other hounds had earlier died, as Richard told George on 5 November: 'a great infortune is fallen on your bitch, for she had 14 fair whelps, and after that she had whelped she would never eat meat, and so she is dead and all her whelps'. He added, 'but I trust to purvey against your coming as fair and as good to please that gentleman', possibly meaning that he hoped to taunt Brandon with the display of another greyhound.[81] He had already told

[76] *C.L.* 134.
[79] *C.L.* 137.
[77] *C.L.* 136.
[80] File 10 fo. 19v.
[78] *Cely Papers*, p. xlvii.
[81] *C.L.* 133.

Joyce about the bitch's death on 16 October, coupling the news with a
report on the health of George's horse Py the second.[82] It was one of the
jobs of the younger men to attend to the animals, and Joyce was probably
more attached to the bitch than George was. Eileen Power's picture of
George riding ten miles in gloomy silence after hearing the news is purely
fanciful.[83]

George had succeeded in obtaining a hawk, and Richard looked
forward to sport with her:

I understand that ye have a fair hawk. I am right glad of her, for I trust to God
she shall make you and me right great sport. If I were sure at what passage ye
would send her I would fetch her at Dover and keep her till ye come....I
understand ye purpose to be with us afore Christmas, and thereof we be right
glad. And we shall make merry whether Brandon will or not, by the grace of God.
And as for Py, is as hearty as ever I saw him, and in reasonable good plight and
whole. William Cely do his part well in keeping of him.[84]

The hawk duly arrived, and was named Meg, like the one that had died
'of the cray and cramp' in 1479.

Please it you to understand this same day I received a letter from you by [John]
Kay, and the fairest sore [unmewed] hawk this day within all England, the which
shall be as well kept till ye come, by the grace of God. And I have your box with
salve – it shall be well kept till ye come. And I am right glad of your appointment
and purpose to be here at St Thomas tide [29 December]....

Sir, I have received my lord's hobby [a pony], and I shall have the hawk, and
I have a good keeper of mine own purveyance, but I purpose to have him and
that hawk to Melchbourne, and leave your Meg with Watkin falconer at Bushey,
or else to have her with me into Cotswold....

I have delivered Kay 2s according to your writing, and 6d more because he
says [he] was robbed by the way of 3s, but the thieves gave him 8d again.[85]

Richard was about to go to the Cotswolds to buy wool, and anxiously
awaited £10 in Carolus groats which George had promised him. 'But it
come within these 12 days I am half shamed else by my promise, and
therefore I pray you, for God sake, remember my poor honesty.' His next
three letters are a mixture of hawks and Carolus groats, Burgundian coin
which were probably needed to repay an exchange loan in London, not
to spend in the country. 'I pray you remember the £10 that ye purveyed
at the last mart and send it at the next passage, for I had been in Cotswold
ever this, but for tarrying on that money', he begged on 22 November.[86]
'The fairest sore hawk within all England' had proved a disappointment
and was already sold. 'As for your hawk, I could not keep her, my

[82] *C.L.* 126.   [83] *Medieval People*, p. 153.
[84] *C.L.* 133.   [85] *C.L.* 134.
[86] *C.L.* 136.

business was so great. I have sold her for 7 nobles, but one noble is put on your will at your coming. She was not half enseamed. I would avise you to bring another with you, and ye may get her good cheap.' 'Enseaming' was the process by which a hawk was rid of superfluous fat before she was flown at game. She would be fed meat 'washed' with the juices of such things as garlic, parsley root or hissop. Instead of the disappointing Meg, Richard proposed to take to Adderbury the hawk and keeper which he had borrowed from Sir John Weston without his father's knowledge.

On 28 November, having waited fourteen days in London and sent George three letters, 'all 3 sounding one matter', Richard finally had one letter back – but no money.

And this same day I depart into Cotswold – I may tarry no longer – and there rides with me William Cely upon Py your horse, and I have with me my falconer with my lord's hawk, that none of our house ken of. I saw her never fly yet. The falconer and hawk shall be with our father and us at my coming home.[87]

There is a cramped note at the bottom of the page: 'not merry in heart'. He was probably mourning the lack of George's £10, but may have been referring to his father.

Regrettably, George's mind was less on Carolus groats than on a complaisant Calais cook named Margery, who had borne him one child earlier in the year. (What had become of 'lady Clare'?) John Dalton and Joyce Parmenter both sent him messages the following January, 1482. Dalton said tactfully

also, sir, where as we ate the good puddings, the woman of the house that made them, as I understand she is with child with my brother that had the Irish skene [dagger] of me.[88]

Joyce sent the same news: 'also I let you wit, there ye go and eat puddings, the woman is with child, as I understand'.[89] Dalton's discreet identification of the father was wholly unnecessary: Richard junior had told their father about the death of the previous child. We know that Margery was the mother, because in August 1482 William Cely passed on to George the message that 'Margery commendeth her unto your mastership, and she telleth me she should have raiment, as a gown and other things, against her churching, *as she had the t'other time*, whereof she prays you of an answer'.[90] Sixteen days after that, William wrote further, 'please it your mastership to be informed that Margery's daughter is passed to God. It was buried this same day, on whose soul

[87] *C.L.* 137.   [88] *C.L.* 141.
[89] *C.L.* 142.   [90] *C.L.* 181.

Jesu have mercy. Sir, I understand it had a great pang [convulsion?]. What sickness it was I cannot say.'[91]

George did get home for the Christmas season in 1481, after putting in an appearance at the Cold mart in December. He reminded himself beforehand to buy his mother's 'grenger' ('green' or preserved stem ginger), a quartern of saffron and 600 ells of Barrois canvas, and to collect six pipes of woad from a cog ship at Bergen-op-Zoom.[92] At the mart he made a large number of purchases, including black cat fur for his blue riding gown (9s), eight skins of white 'harersse' ['hairy'?] fells (2s 8d), a jacket cloth for 6s and a gown cloth for 9s, hose for his servant Hankin, botteaux and shoes for himself, his pouch, and two long-bows (2s 4d). From Calais he sent Richard junior a basket of miscellaneous goods in Harry Lawson's ship.[93] The contents were 140 quarrels, seven great pouches, an Almain [German] dagger, a standard, fauld and flankard (the pieces of armour that Richard had asked for in January), a box with more salve for his hawk, Hankin's livery gown, hose and doublet, 'white stammel [coarse woollen or linsey-woolsey cloth] for an petticoat for my mother', and cords for windlasses (for cross-bows).

Another aide-memoire preceded his passage to England:

Ever I go into England now afore Christmas, anno '81.
Item, I must take my letters of master lieutenant.
I must clear my books.
John Dalton mine attorney.
I must see my [wool] houses
And clear with Andrew Hawes.[94]

Andrew Hawes had previously sold George two woolhouses in Calais, and subsequently sold him a woolhouse with a yard to the north of it, adjoining George's stable, and two tenantries adjoining the houses previously bought, which ran north of 'the corner house against the east watch house' to Trinity Lane.[95]

It may have been this year that George took to England an important letter, probably containing information for William Lord Hastings. The day after he had left the Cold mart, William Dalton sent after him with this note:

Brother George, I recommend me unto you, praying that ye will deliver this letter to my lord, for I have writ that ye shall bring it him, though ye yeed to Windsor to him. I think he will thank you.[96]

[91] *C.L.* 188.
[92] File 12 fo. 32.
[93] File 12 fo. 31v.
[94] File 12 fo. 28.
[95] File 15 fo. 47.
[96] *C.L.* 138.

During George's absence in England, John Dalton faithfully kept a long account of his transactions on his behalf, while George's host at Bruges, Adrian in the 'Skapslaw' ('Sheep's Hoof'), received various substantial sums from George's customers and held them until his return.[97] Dalton paid Joyce 13s 4d on his wages (£2 13s 4d per annum if they were paid quarterly), saw to the sweeping of George's chimney (8d), and the 'cleansing of the aumbry' (food-cupboard) and disposal of the 'broken victuals' carelessly left there, which cost 2s 2d. He and Joyce also had to cope with a piece of destructive spite by one Bottrell, who broke into one of George's fell-houses, whose ownership he apparently disputed, and threw dung over its contents. The pair of them invited Robert Turney, John Ekington, John Elderbeck, Charles Villiers and William Hill to a breakfast, which cost 2s 6d, so as to have their witness to the damage.[98] Joyce's account runs

I let you wit that Bottrell hath broke up a window of the west side of your woolhouse, and there he hath cast in horse dung upon your fells. I did make a man with a dung fork in his hand to cast the dung aside. Bottrell came in and took the fork fro him and beat him well and unthriftily.[99]

Dalton spoke afterwards to Bottrell, 'and he is uncourteous in his saying' (probably meiosis for 'cursed me roundly'), so Dalton proposed to report him to the lieutenant.[100]

By the time that Joyce wrote, the news of old Richard's death had reached Calais. John Dalton's next letter carried messages of sympathetic exhortation.

I have received two letters from you, by the which letter I understand of your great heaviness of your father, on whose soul God have mercy.... Also, sir, sin[ce] it is so as it is of my master your father, in the reverence of God take it patiently, and hurt not yourself, for that God will have done, no man may be [against].... Sir, I pray you that I may be recommended unto your brother Richard Cely, and each of you cheer other, in the reverence of Our Lady, who preserve you.[101]

The decease of their father meant new responsibilities and a change in life-style for both brothers. Their further history is taken up again in Part III, Chapter 10. The next chapter (Chapter 4) deals with the careers of Robert Cely and Thomas Kesten, together with an account of Richard Heron's long feud with the staplers, which Sir John Weston helped to settle on his travels abroad in 1481. This is followed by Part II (Chapters 5 to 9), which fills in some of the background details to the Celys' trade in wool.

[97] File 12 fols. 11–18.
[99] *C.L.* 142.
[101] *C.L.* 141.
[98] File 12 fo. 14.
[100] *C.L.* 140.

TWO BLACK SHEEP AND A NUISANCE

If Robert Cely was really the eldest of the family, he did nothing to sustain the dignity and responsibilities of that position, and in time his brothers found themselves acting as nursemaids for Robert. Possibly he suffered from ill-health, certainly he compounded his troubles by weakness of character and a reluctance to accept advice.

Robert seems to have been a full member of the Staple Fellowship by 1474 or 5, when Thomas Kesten sold six sarplers of wool for him. He was married – young, perhaps, by the usual standards of merchants of the time – by July 1474, when his father sent him a scolding letter:

I understand nothing of receiving of wool, of no good rules of the Place [the staple headquarters], neither in a sale nor in other wise, for the which ye be slow in writing....And say to George Cely I had no word from him of your coming to Calais, and your wife think ye should have writ to her. Ye forget yourself, what is for to do. Sloth is a great thing, and doth little good [betimes], there as good business doth ease.[1]

Since George was also at Calais for much of his time, he and Robert saw a good deal of each other, and in George's memoranda of this date, 'my brother' may refer to Robert and not, as it does later, to Richard. George noted that on 24 July 1474 he borrowed 9s from Robert, and he paid for a pair of spurs which Robert had bought from the stapler Ralph Lemington.[2] In 1476 the two of them went together to the Sinxen mart at Antwerp, and George bought 'my sister' (Robert's wife) a girdle for 10s. He also bought one or other of his brothers a hawk for 16s and paid for the making of a ring and hose for him.[3] In October a postscript to a letter from Richard to George conveyed messages for Robert: 'It is telled me our gear is in Thames. And my sister his wife is in good health, but William his 'prentice is sore sick.'[4]

[1] C.L. 2.
[2] File 11 fo. 6v.
[3] File 11 fo. 7v.
[4] C.L. 8.

A year later, in November 1477, a querulous letter from Robert in London to George at Calais reflects the difficulties inherent in the situation of a merchant operating on credit and with small capital:

Right well-beloved brother, I recommend me heartily to you. Furthermore please it you to wit that I have received fro you a letter writ at Calais the 30 day of October, in the which letter were closed four letters of payment, whereof two been direct[ed] to Richard Twigge, mercer of London, both letters containing £52. Item, also two letters of payment direct to John Cowlard, mercer, containing both £20. The days been long. I care for nothing save but for my fellmen of Bermondsey Street, for they will be needy and call fast on me for money ere March be past.

Brother George, I pray you speak sharply to John Raunnse of Guines for the farm of St Tricat, for William the parson's man is at London and calleth fast on me for money. And also I understand that ye have lent to the Place for me £20. I must prest ['lend'] here at London £10, and our father £20. It is a shrewd work, God amend it.[5]

Robert was by no means the only stapler to feel hard-pressed at such times. In July 1478 Thomas Betson, having shipped 2,448 fells to Calais, owed £6 in customs dues at London, £2 to the porters and others, and £4 to 'Whyte of Broadway', the supplier, 'and so God save my soul, I have it not'.[6]

Robert concluded his letter to George with an item of family news:

Item, brother, as upon the Sunday afore the date of this letter my brother Richard Cely and I were at Paul's Cross to hear the sermon, and there we heard first word that our uncle the Dean of York is passed to God.

The importance of the occasion was marked by the fact that, as Robert noted with pride,

the preacher prayed for him by name. And there sat that time five bishops at Paul's Cross.[7]

Richard and Robert had amicably walked over to St Paul's for Sunday entertainment in hearing a sermon in the November of 1477. But by the following March a coolness had sprung up. Robert's man came to ask Richard for the chest which his master had left with him when he went over to Calais, but Richard denied having it:

Sir, I pray ye say to [Robert] I had none, nor he delivered me none: ye were at his departing as well as I. William Cely tells me that he was with our brother at his departing from Botton's, and there he saw a little chest in his chamber,

---

[5] *C.L.* 15 (19 Nov.).   [6] *Stonor L.* no. 224.
[7] *C.L.* 15. The Sunday before the date of this letter was 16 Nov. Dean Andrew's will (*Testamenta Eboracensia*, III, p. 232) was proved on 5 Nov., so the news of his death was slow to reach the Celys in this indirect way.

and our brother locked his books therein and sent you the key by William Cely, but he leaved the chest at Botton's.[8]

Robert, who seems to have taken offence readily and would then lapse into a sulk, had not bothered to say goodbye when he left London. The social courtesies of family life were breaking down on both sides, and Richard added huffily to George, 'Sir, and he had bid me farewell I would 'a prayed you to 'a commended me to him.'

Despite the fact that both Robert and George were on the continent at Easter 1478, they were accused along with their brother Richard of taking part in an affray at Mile End.[9] Whatever Robert's precise whereabouts at that time, he was not paying William Eston a debt for £5 that fell due at the Easter mart, because George had to discharge it at the Whitsun mart.[10] Shortly before that Robert had written to him from London:

Brother George, the cause necessary of my writing to you at this time is this. Forsooth, there is great shipping now at London of fells and wools to Calais-ward, God be their speed, and I cannot ship no fells before the feast of Whitsuntide, but soon after I hope to God to do.

I am not well entreated, for I have not money by me to pay the 16s 8d [customs dues] of the sarpler after the rate, for of the [e]xecutors of Cowlarde I have no comfort of payment. And as for Richard Twigge, is not courteous in his dealing, for he hath paid me by 20s and by 40s lewd [paltry] payment. And when I would have £10 I could not have it at my need but I must give him 8d for a gallon of wine. And yet he keep in his hand 20s sterling, the which ye should have of Wyytte his man ['which he alleges that you received from White']. I pray you send me word whether it be so or not, for much sorrow and anger have I had with him for receiving of my money. I pray you deliver him no more of my money: he saith you little worship, that you should owe his man 20s and abate it of my duty. [I.e. 'he pays you small respect when he claims that you owe his man 20s. And then he goes and deducts it from what he owes to me!'] I pray you tell it him.[11]

Cowlard and Twigge owed Robert money on the exchange bills which George had sent over in 1477.

Robert was back in Calais in August 1478, and all three brothers joined in the trip to Boulogne, probably for the festival of Our Lady on 15 August.[12] In the big July shipping Robert had 4,800 fells.[13] And his social standing was sufficiently good for him to have been named one of the feoffees for property in 'Woderof Lane', St Olave's parish, London, in January.[14] Nevertheless, serious financial trouble now threatened him.

[8] *C.L.* 19.
[9] *C.L.* 25.
[10] File 11 fo. 39v.
[11] *C.L.* 21 (5 May 1478).
[12] File 16 fo. 19.
[13] File 11 fo. 26.
[14] Hustings Roll 207 (23).

In August, when George had gone to Bruges, Richard wrote to him from Calais:

Sir, I have spoken with Thomas Adam, and I told him that I purposed to stop Robert from his passage [back to England], and he has desired me to spare Robert, for and I [ar]rest him there is no man that will help him out of prison. And so he, Thomas, has promised me in his brother's name that his brother shall agree with me at London. Harry Whayt delivered to the said Robert a 30s to pay his hostess, and he has played it at dice, every farthing. And so Thomas is fain to go to Master Lieutenant [of the Staple] to pray him to pay Robert's costs to London. Sir, in this matter I will do my best for you.[15]

There is nothing to show what was at issue between Robert and William Adam, but Robert's habit of living on credit is demonstrated in a bill for his board with Agnes Burnell. He owed a total of 26s 2d, 'whereof is paid by the mean of a counter – 13s 4d. Rest due to me, Agnes Burnell, – 12s 10d.'[16] Presumably the counter was a token coin used in reckoning money and delivered as a kind of I.O.U.

Eventually it was George who paid the costs of shipping Robert back home in disgrace in September 1478, when he gave him a rial (valued at 14s Flem.), 'for costs from Calais to London'.[17] Robert showed some becoming gratitude, writing from London on 6 October:

Brother, please it you to wit that I received from you by William Cely a letter, the which I have well understand, and of the praisement of my fells, God send them good sale. And brother, God thank you for the good will and good love ye show and have showed to me at my last being at Calais. And there be any thing that I can do for you in England, I will do it with all my heart and it lie in my power, the which knoweth God, who have you in his keeping, amen.... Item, brother, I send to you herewith your indenture.[18]

Indentures were made when a stapler appointed an attorney to act for him at Calais. They listed unsold stocks of wool and fell, obligations due at future date, and any ready cash handed over.[19]

The scapegrace had meanwhile acquired a fresh responsibility. 'Your brother Robert Cely and his wife fareth well, blessed be God, and she is great with child', reported William Maryon on 8 November.[20] But Robert was soon back in Calais, and the responsibility which he represented to his family was by no means at an end. George had to lend him various sums, such as twenty-four Carolus groats and 20s in halfpence in March 1479.[21] Richard junior had a great deal to say on the subject of Robert when he wrote to George on 9 April. Nobody seems

[15] *C.L.* 32.   [16] File 16 fo. 13.
[17] File 21 no. 1 (fo. 1v).   [18] *C.L.* 35.
[19] George made one with William Cely in July 1482: File 20 no. 5.
[20] *C.L.* 39.   [21] File 11 fo. 54.

to have liked Robert's wife very much, and she and her family were quick in turn to criticize the Celys. Richard wrote:

Right reverent and well-beloved brother, I recommend me unto you as heartily as I can devise or think. Informing you that I have received a letter from you written at Calais the 27 day of March, by the which I do well understand the demeaning of our brother Robert, and of his need, and how ye have holpen him, and how ye be like to help him more, and ye write to me for counsel.

Sir, me thinks it well done to lend him now at his need, so that ['provided that'] ye may stand sure.... We hear say that our brother has written for his wife, and she has excused her that there be so many Fleming and Frenchmen upon the sea that she dare not come. Sir, there was a man with my godfather, and asked him for our brother Robert, and said he was sorry of his loss ['to have missed him']. The cause of his asking for him was for he is our brother Robert's surety for £15 that our brother must pay at mart, beside £10 that is [due] to William Eston. What is more, God know. We hear say that his wife has sent to him for money.

Ye writ to me a clause in your letter, 'the more is done for him, the more is he beholden', but me thinketh the more comfort that she have of him, and the more help he have of you, the less will she set by ['esteem'] us. Be well ware how that ye do, 'it is better to pity than be pitied'. I avise you to lend him no money, ne do nothing with him but afore record ['before witnesses']. Ye know the unsteadfastness of him well enough. I cannot think how ye shall stand sure of that ye have lent him, but if ye can get part of his fells transport by the court ['transferred to your ownership'], and yet it will be said by her friends that ye have undone him.

We be informed that our brother Robert's child [servant] is gone to Calais again. We marvel in so much as he brought letters that he desired none again. Sir, I write the plainer to you for our father saw your letter ere it come to my hands, and was reasonably well pleased therewith, so that ye stand sure.[22]

There is much more emphasis on self-interest here than any affection for Robert. Robert for his part was learning the harsh truth that when a man allowed his money to slide away 'through great well-fare in household or fresh array or play [at] dice' his friends would rather give him a 'scorn' than a penny 'to refresh himself with'.[23] Much as he needed his family's help, Robert hardly did much to invite it: in May Richard told George, 'Sir, our brother Robert is come to London, and our father sent to him to wit if ye sent any writings by him, and he answered that he was not sure betrist [trusted]'. Richard added maliciously, 'wherefore I long to hear of his dealing in paying you, and of his departing from you'.[24]

As we have seen, tragedy of an all too familiar kind struck Robert in July, although it has also been observed that neither he nor the rest of

----

[22] *C.L.* 47.   [23] 'Discourse', fo. 101v.
[24] *C.L.* 55.

the family were on particularly good terms with his wife. In writing to George, William Maryon was at first more occupied with the favour shown by Sir John Weston towards Richard junior, but went on to report on the progress of the 'death' then rife in London, and broke the news, almost as an afterthought, that 'your brother Robert hath i-buried out of his house here at London by a [about] six persons, and the 19 day of July he buried his wife. She died at Stratford and buried at London by your grandam, and he shall come and dwell again in his house in Mart [Mark] Lane.'[25] Robert may have had other property, but he was a parishioner of St Olave, Hart St, and had given the church a 'vernicle', a cloth with the image of Christ's face which had supposedly been imprinted on St Veronica's handkerchief.[26] Which house belonged to Robert among the tenements crowded into the few hundred feet of Mark Lane which fell within St Olave's parish? He might have lived on the east side, opposite his father, or held the house three doors away from old Richard, which his father had acquired in 1474 and which subsequently went to George.

The next that we hear of Robert is eight months later, in a letter from Richard to George written on 7 April 1480.[27] Robert had by then become betrothed to a lady named Joan Hart, and, having quarrelled with her, now declared that the marriage was off and that he proposed to take refuge in Calais:

Sir, there is a division fallen between our brother Robert and she that should 'a be his wife, and he has given her over. And he purpose to absent himself and come to Calais shortly.

Calais did not prove to be far enough. Evidently Joan sued for breach of promise in the church court, which had jurisdiction over matrimonial affairs, and since Calais was within the province of the Archbishop of Canterbury, Robert fled to Bruges. On 3 May Richard senior wrote:

I feel Robert Cely is at Bruges [where George was also], for fear of fighting at Calais into bishop's court for the lewd ['disgraceful'] matter of Joan Harthe, the which is much ado for at London.[28]

Neither family was willing to support the couple:

The friends of her hath spoke with me for that matter, but all they will not grant a groat for [to] give them, wherefore I have said to them I will not give them a penny of my good.

In these circumstances, Joan was thought to be willing to give Robert up in return for everything Robert had given her, as well as the return

[25] *C.L.* 58.   [26] *C.L.* 5.
[27] *C.L.* 83.   [28] *C.L.* 85.

of all her gifts to him: 'I understand she will fall off for to have all the gets that Robert hath delivered her, and to have all Robert Cely hath of hers, and I understand Sir John the priest hath promised for to make this end ['bring this about'].' Robert as usual would not listen to advice: doubtless his father's in particular tended to be unpalatable, and there was no direct communication between them.

And Robert Cely were wise and well-advised, all this will be laid apart well now, for [he] is undo[ne] and he wed her. But I may not say, wherefore I have writ a letter of this matter to Will Maryon more clearly. For the which I pray you give him good counsel and send me writing, for I may do nought. But privily keep these matters privy, and let me understand his intent, and after that I shall write more to you.

Nevertheless, before Robert could change his mind again his father had succeeded in extricating him from the whole affair. Richard junior told George twelve days later:

Sir, it is so by great labour that the woman that our brother Robert was tangled with, she has made him a quittance. And she has all her own good that was brought to our brother's again, and all the good that our brother leaved with her, save a girdle of gold with the buckle and pendant silver and gilt, and a little gold ring with a little diamond, and a tippet of damask. She has all other things that he leaved with her, and will have.

Sir, our father and mother would that ye paid for his board at Calais and deliver him 5s or more in his purse, and ye to take a bill of his hand of as much money as ye lay out for him. And we would that he would come to Aveley and be there till the matter be better eased. Our father thinks he needs not to be large of spending, remembering all thing.

Sir, I pray you let him not see this letter ne tell him not of this end ['conclusion'] but of the quittance. And hie him to Aveley in as great haste as ye can.... It is not for him to come in London yet.[29]

George paid £4 for Robert, returnable on 4 June. 'I pray God send us good payment', commented Richard sourly.[30] Significantly, Robert got no share at this time in some family money which came the way of Richard and George, owed to their father by an aunt.[31] On 30 June Richard was able to tell George, 'Sir, I have received at the day well and truly the £4 sterling of our brother Robert.'[32] Alas, Robert's unaccustomed financial standing did not last long, and on 5 July their father 'understands of our brother Robert's childish dealing', evidently from the mercer William Burwell, who had been to see old Richard on business.[33] The final letter from Robert in the collection

---

[29] *C.L.* 86.   [30] *C.L.* 91.
[31] *C.L.* 88.   [32] *C.L.* 95.
[33] *C.L.* 96.

indicates that his 'childish dealing' consisted in borrowing money from Burwell which he had no hope of repaying. George was the obvious person to apply to. Robert wrote:

As for our brother Richard, is departed with my Lord of St John's with the ambassadors into France, whereof I suppose you understand right well. And I am at London, and have been greatly diseased almost ever sin' you departed fro Aveley, and most part have kept my bed, for I have been so sick and sore that I go with a staff. I thank God I am now daily amending.

Item, brother George, the cause of my writing is this, and I pray you heartily of your good brotherhood that ye will do so much for me to see that William Borwell, mercer of London, be content of his bill of £14 15s, and what money you lay out for me I will content you here for. And I had not have had that money of William Borwell at that time, I had lost all my plate. Wherefore, good brother, remember me, and I shall deserve it to you, with the grace of God, who have you and all us in his blessed keeping, amen. Writ at London the 6 day of September [1480].[34]

'With great pain', he added pathetically. George has scribbled on the letter a partially illegible Latin invocation of the Lord.

The only further references to Robert in the letters are the occasional assurance that 'your brother Robert and all the household fareth well', or that Robert sends his regards when George is in Calais in September 1484.[35] Robert must have left the Fellowship of the Staple, but it is not clear whether he is referred to in a grant of 1481 which mentions Richard Sely fellmonger and Robert Sele fishmonger.[36] The implications are that by 1482 Robert was living with his mother. In the absence of Richard senior's will, we do not know what provision, if any, he made for Robert. But Agnes Cely at any rate retained an affection for her son. In her will, made on 28 January 1483, she left Robert 'my white standing cup with a little foot', two silver goblets, 'my maser with a bow (?) in the bottom and with four torets [rings] upon the same', and 100 marks (£66 13s 4d) to be delivered by her executors (Richard, George and William Maryon) over the following ten years, ten marks each year.[37] If Robert wished, his trustees could use the 100 marks as a trading capital for his benefit, provided that he got at least 10 marks annually together with any extra profits. In addition, her lands and tenements in the town and parish of Barton in Northamptonshire were to remain in the hands of her existing feoffees to the use of Robert during his lifetime. Thereafter they were to go to Richard and his heirs. The residuary legatees were Richard and George.

Various payments to Robert, or on Robert's behalf, are entered in the

[34] *C.L.* 102.   [35] *C.L.* 223.
[36] *C.C.R. 1476–85*, p. 213.   [37] 8 Logge. Torets were rings for hanging.

auditors' later statements of Richard and George's affairs, so it seems that they expended part of Robert's small annuity from their mother on goods and services for him.[38] There is no way of knowing whether they in fact employed the capital in trade. Already in March 1482 Richard had paid for shoes, boots and slippers purchased for his mother and Robert from a cordwainer in 'Blanke Chapell' [Blanchappleton, to the north of Mark Lane]. In the same year he bought Robert a pair of botteaux at 10*d*. In November he gave Robert 5*s* and in December refurbished his winter wardrobe: 'paid for the said Robert for furring of his gown with otter – 16*d*, for one doublet of leather for him – 16*d*, canvas for the same – 4*d*, and for making of two gowns – 8*d* and 12*d*'. Early in 1483 Robert received 10*s* to buy another gown, and at Bartholomew Tide in August Richard gave him 4*s*. 'Setting of his hanger' [dagger suspended from a belt] cost 12*d*, and making a long gown, 8*d*. At some date unspecified (perhaps at Agnes's month mind) Robert got 4*d* 'for the pardoner' – the only reference to such a person in the papers – and had 3*s* to spend. There is one curious entry which reflects badly on Robert's honesty: 'Item, the said Richard paid to More baker's wife for his brother Robert Cely that he had taken – 3*s* 11*d*'.[39]

George's contributions were 20*s* given to Robert 'when he rode toward Barton', and 45*s* paid to him on 27 August 1484.[40] This last may have been travel money for the pilgrimage which Robert was about to undertake to Santiago (St James of Compostella), because on 28 and 31 August 'Denham of Lee' was paid a total of £11 1*s* 'in full payment of the viage of the said Robert Cely to Saint James'. Did he possibly sail in one of the ships of Southwold – the *James* or the *Trinity* – for which Harry Joye had obtained a licence for the voyage to Compostella in May 1484?[41] It would be delightful to have some details of Robert's journey, but nothing more is related. Presumably the £11 was the return fare, paid in advance. Robert must have left some time after 20 September.[42] The considerable hardships of the voyage may have had fatal effects on a weak constitution, or perhaps Robert caught cold more prosaically in the London winter after his return. In January 1485 Richard paid a mason 8*d* to mend Robert's chimney (where, one wonders, was he living now that his mother was dead and both his brothers married?).[43] On Candlemas Eve (1 February) Robert was given 6*s* 8*d* for his surgeon, for

---

[38] Richard's payments are given in File 10 fols. 16–17v.
[39] File 10 fo. 17, an entry from Richard's 'Russet Book B., fo. 3'. Other entries on that page had referred to 1486 (10 fo. 15).
[40] File 10 fo. 35.
[41] Rosemary Horrox and P. W. Hammond, eds., *British Library Manuscript Harleian 433*, II (1980), 135.
[42] *C.L.* 223.
[43] File 10 fo. 17.

coals and in money, while Wellys his physician was paid 20*d*.[44] On Ash Wednesday (17 February) wood and 'other gear' cost 3*s* 4*d*. Robert died three days later, on 20 February. Richard noted the payment to a waxchandler of 35*s* 2*d* 'for certain torches and other wax', probably for Robert's funeral and month mind. A general statement of payments for Robert gives a sum of £3 18*s* 7*d* from 9 January 1485 (perhaps the date when he returned from pilgrimage) to his death on 20 February, and of £11 19*s* 1½*d* subsequent to 'the day of his departing to God'.[45] He 'legated' £3 to the church of St Olave, which Richard duly paid the parson and churchwardens. Did the monument to 'Richard Cely and Robert Cely, principal builders of this church' really couple poor Robert with his canny father? It seems unlikely. But whether it happened by accident or design, perhaps it was appropriate that Robert should be associated with the church to which he seems to have been more devoted than his more successful brothers.

Thomas Kesten or Kesteven, one-time crony and attorney of Richard Cely senior, also died in poverty, as far as one can tell. He was a plausible man, with an engaging manner, but he had a poor sense of morality in business matters, and cannot have set Robert and George a good example. He had already been in trouble over an exchange loan deal made in 1468. The exchange may have been made on behalf of Richard Cely, but Richard's name did not figure in the subsequent proceedings. What happened was that in October 1468 Kesten arranged at Calais to lend William Kylton, factor and attorney of John Hayward, haberdasher of London, the equivalent of £100 stg., to be repaid in England in equal parts on 31 January and 31 March 1469.[46] He gave Kylton half the amount in ready money and an obligation in which one Ebalt Hughson or Yowet Huetson of Leiden was bound to Kesten himself in an equivalent of £50 stg. payable at the Cold mart at Bergen-op-Zoom at the feast of St Martin (11 November), 1468. Kesten swore that the obligation was 'as good as ready money', but according to Kylton's later evidence, it was agreed that if he could not receive the money for it at due date, the obligation might be returned to Kesten, and Kylton and Hayward need pay only £50 in England.

On this understanding, Kylton gave Kesten two letters of payment for £50 each. But indeed when he attended the Cold mart he could not obtain any money on Hughson's obligation, 'for the said person...was gone and

[44] This may have been the John Welles, physician of London *c.* 1480, of whom no further details are recorded in C. H. Talbot and E. A. Hammond, *The Medical Practitioners in Medieval England* (1965), p. 423.
[45] File 10 fo. 17.   [46] P.R.O. C.1 49/57.

avoided long time afore'. He therefore returned the obligation to Kesten at Calais and wrote to his principal in London to pay only the first £50 due.

Later (on 1 May 1469?) Hayward met Kesten in London and told him that neither he nor his attorney would pay the other £50, to which Kesten allegedly replied 'that him needed not to complain' for so far neither he nor Kylton had suffered any hurt, nor would they bear any loss in the future. The first was true enough, but in fact Kesten then sued Kylton for non-payment in the Staple court at Calais before the mayor of the Staple (John Prout), and the constables John Gudryk and Thomas Stevenson.[47]

In court much damaging evidence was produced to show that Kesten was well aware when he delivered Hughson's obligation to Kylton that, as Kylton's petition in Chancery later put it, 'the person therein bounden was voided and of no value to content or pay the same'. Clays Mast, merchant of Leiden, aged sixty and more, was present in Calais and gave a first-hand account, but more evidence was collected from witnesses who were summoned by Richard Wither, acting with Hayward, before the 'Scoute, burgomasters, skepens and council of the town of Leiden'.[48] Their depositions were presented in a document under the town seal, which was translated into English for the benefit of the Staple court. They give a lively picture of the background events.

The first witnesses were Floris Harmalyn and Roelef Stope, who took their oath 'as right is, with uphoven ['raised'] hands and fingers stretched out'. This was so that they could not nullify their oath by crossing their fingers, the practice that still survives among children. Floris and Roelef deposed that they had met Ebalt Hughson on his return from a 'rese' or buying-trip to Calais, and asked him 'what tidings he brought from thence, and how his rese was brought about'. Ebalt replied that he had bought four sacks of wool from Thomas Kesten, and two sacks from Alan Redeman or Redmayne. When they persisted in asking how he had managed to be in Calais, Ebalt said 'that he had been there like a pilgrim, and he said there [at Calais] that he had been on pilgrimage at St James, and he had scallops upon his hat'. The point of this was that pilgrims, as everyone knew, were exempt from prosecution for offences like debt. Ebalt also confessed that on the road out of Calais, as he was returning to Leiden and Kesten was on his way to Bruges, they happened to meet the mercer Robert Twigge, who was returning from a visit to Leiden. Something which Twigge then told Kesten caused Kesten to change his plans abruptly, so that instead of going to Bruges he accompanied Ebalt home to Leiden.

[47] P.R.O. C.47/25/10 no. 2.
[48] Wither was another haberdasher and merchant adventurer, e.g. *A.C.M.*, p. 157.

At Leiden, Twigge's story was confirmed. Kesten lodged there with the Clays Mast whose evidence was subsequently heard in Calais. Ebalt, Clays said, came to him secretly to ask what Kesten was doing there, and whether or not Ebalt's name had been mentioned between them. Ebalt admitted buying wool from Kesten and Redeman, and later promised Kesten, in front of Clays, that if Kesten would not be 'importunus' or 'impetuosus super ipsum [i.e. hassle him]', he would pay him at due date. In fact, when the unlucky Kesten had told Clays about the sale and asked his advice, Clays had replied that it was

a weak work of Ebalt Hughson, and it is me loath that ye have thus faren with Ebalt Hughson, and [I counsel] you that ye seek the way that ye best can or may, for I fear me that ye shall have nought thereof.

Further evidence pointed to Kesten's fraud in passing on that obligation, once he had been warned that he had no hope of collecting his dues. Ebalt's financial affairs were well-known in his home town. Gerijt de Breede had advised Kesten to 'make him quit' of the obligation, and Boppe Janszon and Peter John Martynzon testified that they had been at Bammis mart in Antwerp in the autumn of 1468, and there in the 'Oak' they had made a treaty between Ebalt and his other creditor, Alan Redeman, whereby Ebalt gave Alan £5 Flemish in part payment, 'and Alan Redeman would gladly have had more money at that time of the said Ebalt Hughson if he could have gotten it'. Gerijt Lam further deposed that Alan Redeman and Thomas Kesten 'wist well' after their investigations that 'Ebalt was a light man, and had no good to nigh or to lay hand upon'.

Nevertheless, William Kylton lost the case at Calais, and was sent to prison in the custody of the constables of the Staple for not paying the £50 claimed by Kesten within eight days, as ordered by the court. One can only suppose that the court ruled on the matter of non-payment of a debt duly acknowledged by Kylton's letter of payment, and treated the evidence about Ebalt's obligation as irrelevant to the suit before it. It was, of course, never wise to accept such an assignment of debt. But it is hardly surprising that Kylton appealed to the Court of Chancery, asking for a writ of certiorari to be sent to the mayor of the Staple together with one of corpus cum causa to the constables, returnable in Chancery. Kesten's proceedings had scarcely been equitable.

Despite all this, Richard Cely senior continued to employ Kesten as factor until at least 1476. Probably George learnt much of his trade from Kesten, and one pamphlet containing a record of sales was written by both men between November 1473 and August 1475.[49] With both George and Robert Cely Kesten had a particular tie: he refers to them

[49] File 11 fos. 13–17.

both as 'my goss.' or 'my gossip' – a 'god-sib' or relative in God,
implying either a shared godchild or that one of the parties had stood
godparent to the other's infant.[50]

Although Richard junior, and probably other members of the family
as well, were 'at host' with Kesten in Calais in September 1476,[51] from
that year to 1484 it is the steady downhill path of Thomas Kesten's career
that is charted in the Cely correspondence. Already on 27 September
1476 George was writing from Antwerp mart to Richard junior to say
that he had been able to receive only £70 Flem. on a bill of Kesten's hand
for £121 6s 6d, although 'Thomas Kesten hath promised me to deliver
me the rest, and more too'.[52] The Celys were not the only people to
suffer from Kesten. 'Also there is an variance betwixt Kesten and John
Vandyrhay for nine sarplers wool.' George had seen the wool when he
was at Malines, and could confirm that it was 'ill wool' and that it was
its poor quality that had caused the quarrel between Kesten and Van Der
Heyden. 'In our father's duty he hath paid me truly, and he can none
farther go but to me, and the matter is such I trow I cannot ease him.'
It is not clear from this whether it was Kesten or Van Der Heyden who
had paid what he owed Richard Cely.[53] It is to be hoped that the defective
nine sarplers belonged to Kesten himself. George might be his only hope
of support, but in such a case there was little that he could do to smooth
matters over.

At the same time, creditors in England had arrested fells of Kesten's
and various parties were now engaging in a squabble among themselves
for possession. William Maryon had won the first round, and shipped
in the *George of London* 3,850 fells, 'the which fells were Thomas
Kesten's, and they were arrested by Thomas Adam for the sum of £60'.[54]
Maryon wrote to George

Sir, ye shall understand that Thomas Kesten hath i-written unto me that I should
find the way and the mean to save the court harmless here [i.e. find sureties in
the case], and take the fells for mine own, that I should be sure of that sum in
discharging of the sureties, and also in party of payment of such goods as he is
owing unto me, as ye know well. And therefore, sir, I pray you that ye will receive
them as mine own proper good – and so it is. And also I pray you that ye will
pay the freight and all other costs thereof.

The implication is that, as another creditor alleged, Maryon was in
collusion with Kesten to 'colour' the fells by shipping them in his own
name and hand them over to Kesten in return for part of the proceeds

---

[50] *C.L.* 6 and 76.   [51] *C.L.* 4.
[52] Ibid.
[53] 8 sarplers of wool of R. Cely sen. had been sold to Van Der Heyden in Oct. 1475: File
11 fo. 16v.   [54] *C.L.* 5.

of sale. At some date in 1476 Kesten made a counterclaim against the Adams and, like Maryon, asked for George's assistance:

Good and special friend, I beseech you to recommend me unto my master your father, and to my goss. Robert Cely, and to your brother and my good friend Richard Cely. Item, and I have written to my wife to take an action, by and with the advice of you as my special friend, upon Thomas Adam the elder's goods, upon a reckoning for £50 Flem., and upon the goods of William Adam for the sum of £40 Flem., and I pray you to deliver my wife the 40s that I deliver you.

Item, I pray you to be good friend to my wife in helping her in all such thing as she hath to do, as in that 'at may be for the pleasure of my master your father and your and my friends, and Jesus keep you, amen.[55]

It was not just the principals who were involved in a quarrel of this sort. The various people who had stood surety for them, and for the due payment of customs and subsidy on the disputed fells, took their own active interest in the affair, while the Celys endeavoured to arrange a settlement in William Maryon's favour. Richard junior wrote from London to George:

Like it you to wit the cause of Thomas Miller's coming is to see how he may be discharged, for he is surety for £60 for the fells that my godfather shipped last, like as he will inform you at his coming. And as for the t'other two [Thomas and William Adam, or their sureties?], dare not show their heads. And as for Thomas Miller, will do nothing in this matter but as my father and ye will avise him.[56]

The correspondence includes the copy in George's hand and distinctive spelling of a letter, perhaps from Thomas Miller, which puts one man's side of the case engagingly, if not with total clarity.

Sir, and it please your mastership, this man [yet another of Kesten's creditors?] has said for himself as well as he can. I beseech ye give me leave to say for myself, etc.

Sir, and it pleaseth your mastership, there beth diverse of my masters here that thinks that 'at I do is for none other but to defraud this man, thinking that these fells were shipped by colour in the name of William Maryon. Sir, I will not say the contrary but ['I will not deny that'] they were Thomas Kesten's fells, but I will do it good as an Christian man owe to do. William Maryon had never i-dealt with them but for such duty [debt] as was betwixt Thomas Kesten and him. And moreover William Maryon standeth charged by the mean of these fells to save the sureties that beth bound unto Thomas Adam and William Adam harmless. And moreover, sir, I do it good, the king having his custom and these sureties saved harmless according. The rest will not serve William Maryon by £20. I trust to God your cousin will not that William Maryon's good should pay Thomas Kesten's debts....

[55] *C.L.* 6.   [56] *C.L.* 8.

I beseech your mastership, and my masters all, ye will minister your law unto me so that I shall not need to seek none other ways.[57]

It seems that once the fells were at Calais, Kesten claimed them as his own again. In Maryon's interest, pressure was put on Kesten to come to an acceptable accommodation, which involved much to-ing and fro-ing. Richard reported to George:

My godfather understand that ye have sent to Thomas Kesten for the letter that he wrote. And ye have that letter then he prays you that ye would take the letter that is closed in this letter (if ye think it be best so for to do), and ride to Bruges to Thomas Kesten, and desire him to make another letter better than this is, after your intent, according to the letter that is in my letter 'at I wrote to my father....And if so be that Thomas Kesten make it danger so to write ['is difficult about writing thus'], my godfather would that ye should entreat him ['offer him inducements'], and give unto him ten or twelve pounds, or more and ['if'] ye see that it would make all the remnant sure....My godfather is heavy, and will be till he hear better tidings.[58]

In a damaged passage, Richard was apparently telling George to pretend that he did not know the contents of the various letters. George was evidently unsuccessful in moving Kesten, even by bribery, and Maryon wrote on 5 November:

ye shall understand that I have received a letter from you, written at Calais the second day of November, and another letter i-closed in your letter, of Thomas Kesten's hand, written at Bruges. The which both letters I have well understand, and how that Thomas Kesten is disposed for to put me clean away from the fells the which I shipped last at London, that I should have no preferment by them in the nighing of my money.[59]

Richard Cely senior was then called in to help. Maryon continued:

I understand by your writing that Thomas Kesten will come unto Calais shortly. And when that he cometh, sir, I pray you heartily that my master your father and ye will labour unto Thomas Kesten, if ye think it best so for to do. Seeing Thomas Adam i-served and Thomas Miller i-discharged, then I would that Thomas Kesten and you might accord and agree together for the foresaid fell (Thomas Adam i-served), that ye might have of the said fells a 2,000 [in] party of payment of the money, [and] as for the rest of the money, [as ye] and he can agree, and I will hold me pleased.

And if that Thomas Kesten will not be agreeable unto this bargain, he be neither God's man neither man's, but the devil's.

On 28 November George had 17,040 winter fells counted and appraised at 13½ nobles a hundred, and of these 1,208 were delivered to Thomas

Adam in 'contentacion' of £54 6s 3¾d stg.[60] At this rate, the 2,000 which Maryon wanted would have had a value of £90 stg., which was indeed only part of what Kesten owed him.

Old Richard Cely had already done much to help Kesten, for it emerges later that he had arrested Kesten's silver plate, that prime moveable asset of the merchant class, and returned it on a promise of payment. But Kesten was always long on promises and short on fulfilment. On 26 January 1477 George was told by his father to

say to Thomas Kesten that he promised to me that the 10s of [the] sarpler should be paid to John Tate [the treasurer of the Staple], the which is not paid. For the which I have great calling for the payment there, and Will Maryon and Robert Cely for their part, for the which I am not well pleased with Kesten for that matter. Wherefore write me answer what he saith.[61]

Richard also wanted to know what arrangement ('pointment') Kesten had reached with his other creditors:

And also [tell me] what pointment [he] maketh with Byfylde and all other men there as he is entreated to. And say to Thomas Kesten I trust to him that he will have in remembrance his promise made to me when I delivered him plate, that I shall be pleased with some payment of him with ['like'] other men. And he will do so, I shall be his good friend, and that he shall well understand in time to come, for the which I will be glad for to do for him, and [he] will himself.

These assurances of useful patronage wrung no money out of Kesten. The next news of him comes twenty-one months later when, on 6 November 1478, old Richard reiterates his complaints:

I pray you speak to Thomas Kesten. Say to him I look that he will keep the promise he made to me at such time as I delivered to him his plate and all such stuff as I had arrest. I was the first that released my action and delivered the good the which I had in ward to himself.[62]

Other men, he grumbles, were contented by a general agreement and 'set in a way' to recover their money, 'but I am not spoke with nor entreat like the promise made to me at that time by Thomas Kesten. For the which, and Thomas Kesten will set me in worse case of assurety nor he do t'other men, he keep not his faithful promise.' Kesten would do well to remember that Richard could put in a good word for him, if he had some inducement to do so:

I hear much thing said by ['about'] him, for the which, and I were entreat for assurety of a comfort of payment, I could do and say for him, the which would be for his profit and worship. I understand that well by diverse men that I speak

---

[60] File 16 fo. 6.   [61] *C.L.* 11.   [62] *C.L.* 38.

with and [who] spere ['ask'] of me the guiding and the disposition of Thomas Kesten. For the which I will ye read all this clause to him. It be for his worship to remember this matter.

George's reply to his father came predictably.

Pleaseth it you to understand that my brother and I have spoken with Thomas Kesten, and he saith unto us, as my brother can inform you: 'a cannot keep the promise that 'a made unto you, wherefore I understand by him that he will take my brother an letter whereby ye shall see his intent more clearly. He saith well, as my brother can inform you. God give him grace to [do] thereafter.[63]

Either Kesten's plausible speech, or just a desperate clutch at a straw, persuaded Richard to make a new agreement with him, intended to clear off the debt over a period of years. Negotiations started in March 1479. George wrote to his father:

Pleaseth it you to understand that I have had communication with Thomas Kesten, and he with me. And Thomas Kesten, when I come unto Calais, he axed me if I had brought him any writing from you. He said unto me that he sent writing by my cousin Maryon and by me whereof he had weened I had brought him an answer. I said unto him again that at my coming over sea your business was such ye might not have none leisure to write unto him, wherefore ye commanded me to say unto him that ye will write unto him and to me shortly of an answer of theke [those] letters, and how that ye would that I should be demeaned in that case, etc. It will be well done if ye should.[64]

His father outlined the arrangement to George on 15 April.[65] Kesten owed no less than £400 stg., which was to be repaid over eight years. During this time Kesten was to deliver Richard an annual £100 worth of wool and fell at Calais, at Staple valuation, all costs and taxes paid. Richard was to pay £50 cash for these goods, so making a clear £50 annually on the deal. It is noteworthy that he was to get no interest, even on such long-term repayment. But

and Thomas Kesten will keep this bargain well and truly I will be a friend to him or this be all at a end, 'at he shall well find me a good friend. I think long after writing of comfort from you, the which I pray God send.

There is nothing to show for sure whether or not Richard did obtain any wool under this deal, but an obscure note by George, headed 'Thomas Kesten, anno '81, 29 day of June', runs 'Item, paid at Calais for three sarplers wool – £5 Flemish. And I must abate – £20 Flemish.'[66]

William Maryon had remained, surprisingly, on good terms with Kesten and evidently found his lodgings comfortable enough: 'I pray

[63] *C.L.* 41.
[65] *C.L.* 48.
[64] *C.L.* 46.
[66] File 12 fo. 24.

you that ye will recommend me unto mine host Thomas Kesten and to his wife, and to William Byfeld and to Thomas Granger' he ended a letter to George or Richard.[67] But some time in 1479 he begged George to sell his refuse fells (300 of them, apart from 40 black ones), 'for I know well that Thomas Kesten is loath for to sell them, for I wist him never for to sell none of mine but if that I were there myself'.[68]

Although Kesten and his wife were still running a boarding-house, the Celys had long since transferred their patronage to the widow Burnell. Towards the end of 1479 the Kestens moved to smaller premises, and Thomas wrote to George in Bruges to tell him so. He reveals incidentally some of the quality which must have attracted Richard Cely senior in better days.

Reverent and worshipful sir and my special friend and gossip, I recommend me unto you heartily, desiring to hear of your welfare, the which Jesu send you to his pleasure and to your heart's ease and will. I understand that you have been sore sick and now well revived, in the which Jesu comfort you and make you strong, for his mercy, etc.

Sir, informing you that in this town there hath been great death, and yet I thank God my children and wife stand, but my maid is dead, etc.

Sir, informing you that I am removed and have taken me a less lodging, and Bondman dwelleth in my house. And if you list to have your horse still there, or what he can or may do, I hope you shall find him good and gentle, etc. Sir, in my little lodging that I am now in I have a fair stable and a fair room and chamber for all my good masters and friends, if it please any of them to see me in my poverty. A little further from the market it is.

And if there be anything that I can or may for you, I am and shall be at your commandment. And Jesu keep you. Written at Calais the 30 day of November, per your own to his poor power, T. Kesten.[69]

The letter bears a handsome seal: Kesten liked to do things in style. George made use of his stable to house some of his fells in 1480: 'there lies in an stable there as Thomas Kesten dwelleth now, 525 summer fells London'.[70]

To do justice to Kesten, he had debtors of his own. There were, for instance, claims and counterclaims between him and another stapler, William Brierley. In February 1482, just after the death of old Richard, Kesten turned up in London. He had obtained a letter of protection against prosecution for debt, but was leading a hole and corner existence in the capital, and asked George to meet him furtively:

Please it you to understand that I am late comen to London, and for diverse causes and matters, also well again William Brerely as other, I would speak with you.

[67] *C.L.* 39 (8 Nov. 1478).
[68] *C.L.* 69. In Nov. William confided 'the charge and guiding' of his fells to Thomas Granger: *C.L.* 70.   [69] *C.L.* 76.   [70] *C.L.* 92.

And I do come to you to my heavy mistress [the widowed Agnes Cely] I should renew her heaviness and not else. And also I dare not well be seen in London. I thank God and the king I might, but I will not – and I may do otherwise – put my protection in ure ['use'] in London, for it should be a great noise thereof.

Wherefore I beseech you to do so much to come to St Laurence Pulteney before 2 of the clock at afternoon, and else the next morn in the morning at 7 of the clock at the furthest. There I shall wait upon you justly ['punctually'], by the grace of Jesu.

Written in London the Wednesday the 13 day of February, the day after the keeping, as I understand, of your father my good master's month's mind. Beseeching you to keep this letter close till I have spoken with you.[71]

Perhaps at this meeting Kesten gave George an undated letter from Brierley which shows Kesten for once in the role of creditor. In it Brierley told him

Sir, I am for you right heavy, for I have had understanding from Fitzjohn that he had of you £60 gr. Flemish. God knoweth I am therefore right sorry, that ever he should take any money of him that was my friend, and to pay him that is not my friend. But sir, sin' that it is so, I beseech you of a little patience. And sir, I trust to God...that I shall content every man, with a respite, and there shall no man lose one penny by me....Wherefore, good brother, I pray you cast not me all away, for I trust in Our Lord ye shall not lose one penny by me, to sell all that I have unto my shirt.[72]

A week later Kesten wrote again to George, asking for some details in a memorandum about his affairs that he had once given old Richard. These were required by Brierley's former attorney, William Segon. If George could find them,

I pray you let me have knowledge from you by your child, to the same place there [I] spake with you, any day this four days, in the morning from 7 of the clock till 8 of the clock.[73]

On 14 March Kesten wrote to George at Calais with a proposal which George was too kind-hearted to refuse:

I doubt me that it will be much after Our Lady day ere I come home, wherefore I send you a bill of William Brierley's hand of all the stuff that he hath of mine for the sum of £6 5s, the which is worth as much more. The which I beseech you to take into your hands, and I promise you as I am Christian man to discharge it shortly, and else you to have it at the same price. I had liefer you had a profit by me rather than he....

[71] *C.L.* 143.
[72] P.R.O. S.C.1 51/2. Lord Lisle has been mistakenly credited with the first use of the expression about selling everything down to one's shirt: *Lisle Letters*, I, 72.
[73] *C.L.* 144.

All the said things been in a great bag and sealed by me, all save three pieces: two gowns, one fur is out. I beseech you to be my good friend and gossip now in this matter, and in all other, and I shall owe you my service my life during, that knoweth Jesu, who keep you.... Per Thomas Kesten, your own servant.[74]

It is most unlikely that Kesten ever redeemed his promise, and these pledges, for the inventory is still among the Cely papers and they are listed among George's assets in the Chancery accounts.[75] They had been appraised by the town appraisers of Calais, sergeants John Whete and Saunder Wynde, on 12 December 1481, and Kesten had pledged them to Brierley for house-rent up to 'Our Lady day in Lenten next coming', i.e. 25 March 1482. The parcel included four table cloths, between 6 and 9 stics long and 2 or 3 stics wide (the stic being the Flemish ell of 27 inches). They were priced at between 8 and 12 groot the stic.[76] There were also six washing towels, which were three-quarters to one stic in width, but sometimes much longer than the table cloths: one was 15 stics ($11\frac{1}{4}$ yards) by 1 stic, and worth 7s 6gr., and another was $19\frac{1}{4}$ stics (over 14 yards) by $\frac{3}{4}$. There was also a pair of ill-matched sheets, one $2\frac{1}{2}$ breadths wide and the other 2 breadths, priced at 6s 8gr the pair, another worn sheet, worth only 20d, and a worn 'head sheet' of 2 breadths worth 2s 8gr. A fur of otter (worn) was priced at 13s 4d, and there were some women's garments, presumably belonging to Kesten's wife: 'a woman's gown of green, worn, with a train', price 13s 4d, a woman's gown of murry, furred with miniver, with a train, price 16s 8d, and a 'fine woman's smock petticoat' lumped in with a broken sheet. The whole was appraised, not at £6 5s as Kesten claimed, but at £5 8s 6d gr.

George accepted the pawn, and on his behalf John Dalton paid William Brierley's wife £6 5s for it. The arbiters' clerk who drew up the final accounts between Richard and George after the latter's death duly charged George with 'two parcels avouched in the book of Calais, foliis [*sic*] 93 for the basins of silver by him, the said George, remaining – sum £17 13s $4\frac{3}{4}$d stg.' (were these also pledges of Kesten's?), and in folio 119, 'one bag with gowns and furs...sum £4 16s $1\frac{1}{2}$d stg.'[77]

Kesten struggled on silently, as far as the Cely papers are concerned, until Richard and George received a last piteous epistle from him, which seems to be dated 1484.[78] One cannot help feeling that this fifteenth-century Micawber derived a certain mournful satisfaction from its composition. Kesten could say, not only well but also long for himself.

---

[74] *C.L.* 145. [75] File 12 fo. 29; File 10 fo. 21v.
[76] The appraisers appear to have used *groot* or *gr.*, not *Fl.*, for Calais currency: cf. Ch. 7 p. 184.
[77] File 10 fo. 21v. The conversion was made at the rate of 26s Flem. for 20s stg.
[78] *C.L.* 219.

I think in the poverty the which I must continue in all my life (the which is to my great grief a great shortening of my life days) I am not alone in sorrow...for I see daily kings, princes and other estates, from the highest degree to the lowest, witty ['clever'] and rich, that both hath failed them. Wherefore in this world ye may see men now high, now low; now rich, now poor; now alive, now dead. He that hath his life and hath no goods is worst at ease that ever had ought.

So, masters, it is so with me that I must (of fine force and poverty and not of will) take one of two ways, of the which neither been good. One is, if I may have of you for your part longer respite, I to pay you also soon as I can or may, I living a very poor life. As I might be able to keep an house, I to be bounden, upon my faith and troth and as I am a Christian, to pay you and every man also soon as I can. If you or any other will have my service, I to do them service better cheap than any man. And they that will board with me to scape by that mean.

Evidently his wife was now dead, for Kesten went on, optimistically, to propound a standard remedy for misfortune:

And if God and you, my good masters, would help me with your good word and will upon a good marriage, I might the sooner help both you and other, whereupon is one of my most trust. The which marriage to my profit I cannot obtain, nor credence, till I may be at my liberty and I doing somewhat in the world, either for myself or some other men. The which I dare not, nor other men will not trust me, till I go at large to the most men's consents that I am in way to content my creditors.

Wherefore I beseech you for your part, that I may have your surety and promise in writing: I to go untroubled for you or any for you, the term of three year. And as I deal with you in that time to the uttermost of my power, so you to deal with me further. If ever God or the world will show me the world with any favour, it will be in that time. And as I can stand in case ['when I am on my feet'], you shall see me deal with you and with every man that you shall be pleased. And after I can able myself in the said term of three year, I the more straitly to assure you to the uttermost of my power for your payments.

And if it will please you, at the reverence of Jesu, to grant me this (and the rather that I have been an old servant and intend to owe you all my service my life during, and I and all mine to pray for you), I beseech you to pity me. Though I did not always well, I had hoped it should not have comen to so evil conclusion.

Masters, if it will please you to grant me the said respite, then (as aboven said) I will abide in this country. And not, then I must of fine force take the t'other way. That is, to depart out of this country, there and thither as I shall never be able to content you, nor none other. The which I would be loath to do, both for mine own poor name and for my children's, as Jesu defend. And I come in prison, should ne'er come out, I doubt me.

Beseeching you of your good answer to Calais, 'at I may know your will in this, as my greatest sum that I am indebted. Hoping of your good wills: the remnant I hope to have shortly....

Written at Calais, the 17 day of May, with full heavy heart, I keeping my house ['staying indoors'], etc. Per your own both servant and bedeman, Thomas Kesten.

It is unfortunate that the beginning of this letter is damaged, because it alludes, for the first time, to the fact that Kesten had been, with John Prout and Richard Stokes, one of the staplers who had redeemed Edward IV's jewels from Thomas Portinari, after Portinari had advanced the king money on them during his exile in Bruges in 1470–1.[79] Presumably they had in fact acted on behalf of the Staple company as a whole, since the Staple gave them obligations for £2,700 and was itself recouped by grants from the customs. Kesten does not explain what went wrong, in his brief and damaged reference to the enterprise which

John Prout, then mayor of the Staple, and Richard Stokes took upon us...the which we took in hand at the writing and instance of the Earl of W[orcester, Treasurer of] England, of whom we had writing to have saved us harmless, but in con[clusion he was beheaded upon?] the Tower Hill at London, and as he died, died our succour, by the mean [...] undone by the same. And you understand the circumstance of my hurt [...] as Richard Stokes as by the principal, you or any man would pity me.

Worcester was beheaded in October 1470 during the short 'readeption' of Henry VI and the House of Lancaster, but it is not clear how Kesten was 'undone' thereby, or how Stokes had injured him.[80] Ready as the historian may be to pity Kesten, he could wish for a better understanding of 'the circumstance of my hurt'.

While Thomas Kesten had come to grief over the redemption of the Yorkist king's valuables, incurring losses (by his own account) when the Lancastrians summarily executed the Yorkist Treasurer, John Tiptoft, Earl of Worcester, during their brief return to power in 1470–1, the Fellowship of the Staple suffered long annoyance from another stapler, Richard Heron, who had inadvertently backed the wrong side at an earlier stage in the struggle between the rival parties, and whose patron, the Lancastrian Treasurer, was executed by the Yorkists.

Heron had been sworn a member of the Staple Company about 1447.[81]

[79] *C.C.R. 1468–76*, pp. 287–8, 341, etc.

[80] Stokes's sale of goods to Hugh Brice, Hugh Brown and Robert Fitzherbert, including the contents of his dwelling in London, in Jan. 1475 may have been meant to frustrate creditors: *Plea and Memoranda Rolls, 1458–82*, pp. 89, 172.

[81] *Cal. Entries Papal Registers: Papal Letters 1471–1484* (1955), p. 229. In this account of Heron's dealings I have tried to produce a coherent story from a variety of sources, notably W. I. Haward, 'The Financial Transactions between the Lancastrian Government and the Merchants of the Staple', in Eileen Power and M. Postan, eds., *Studies in English Trade in the Fifteenth Century* (1933), pp. 318–21; I. S. Leadam and J. F. Baldwin, eds., *Select Cases before the King's Council, 1243–1482* (Selden Soc.,

In 1459 he shipped a very large quantity of wool to Calais – 500 sarplers. With other stocks already there, he put the value of his holdings at over 24,000 marks of silver. According to his later story, he proposed to sell the wool to meet his debts and to finance a pilgrimage to Rome. He had arranged to deposit the proceeds with the stapler William Johnson and to leave Calais on his journey when, in October 1459, a group of staplers led by the lieutenant, John Prout, seized his wool and clapped him in prison.[82] Prout acted 'by the commandment, stirring, procuring and assent' of the mayor (John Thirsk), John Walden, John Tate, Roger Knight, William Holt, Richard Cely and William Broun of Stamford.[83] The wool was subsequently sold in Flanders, Heron said, by Prout, John Bingham, John Batt, Nicholas (or Anthony) James and Richard Whetehill.[84]

There is some reason to doubt that Heron was planning to go on pilgrimage. And while he maintained that his wool was taken because his large supply made him unpopular with the other staplers, their subsequent case was that Heron was known to be acting as agent for James Butler, Earl of Wiltshire, the Lancastrian Treasurer of England. There was no essential disagreement about the background to the seizure. At this time the Earl of Warwick had been officially but ineffectively ousted as Captain of Calais in favour of the Duke of Somerset. After the 'rout of Ludford' on 12–13 October, Warwick, Salisbury and the Earl of March (the future Edward IV) made their way to Calais, there to consolidate their forces for a renewed struggle against the ruling Lancastrian clique. The staplers in Calais greatly feared that Somerset would take the town, and contributed Heron's goods to its defence, 'not from love of the said earls', but because a Yorkist victory was their only hope of recovering the £30,000 which Warwick already owed them.

After nine months of imprisonment, Heron escaped in the night and managed to have Walden, Tate and another stapler, Philip Hardbene, arrested in Bruges and brought before the court of the mayor and échevins.[85] Warwick, however, persuaded the Duke of Burgundy to stop the case. Heron's complaint to the king's Council in England had brought him no redress before his principal, the Earl of Wiltshire, was executed after the Yorkist victory at Towton in early 1461. The Yorkist government now in power was scarcely likely to admit any liability for

1918), pp. cxiv–cxvi, 110–14, 121–9, and H. G. Richardson, 'Illustrations of English History in the Medieval Registers of the Parlement of Paris', *Trans. Royal Hist. Soc.* (1927), pp. 67–8. In many respects statements in earlier writings were corrected or enlarged from *Cal. Papal Letters*.

[82] *Cal. Papal Letters*, p. 230.   [83] *Select Cases*, p. 112.
[84] *Cal. Papal Letters*, p. 231.   [85] *Rot. Parl.* VI, 182.

goods seized as a prize of political war. Heron, however, did not give up easily, and he had enough money, or credit, to engage in a persistent and expensive course of litigation over the next twenty years, with the Fellowship of the Staple as his target.

Having failed in Flanders, Heron next appealed to the *parlement* of Paris, in its function as appeal court for cases heard in the courts of vassals of the king of France. There was a hearing in July 1461, taken up with discussion about the rights of jurisdiction over English subjects.[86] Heron then obtained a letter from the exiled Henry VI, written in Edinburgh on 9 December 1462, which requested the *parlement* to adjudicate in the matter.[87] But even Henry's reinstatement as king of England, with French help, in 1470, did not further Heron's cause, because the Lancastrians did not retain power for long, and Heron is said to have lurked in sanctuary for twelve years.[88] After the rapprochement between Louis XI and Edward IV in 1475, the *parlement* conceded that the jurisdiction in Heron's case belonged to Edward. The latter had every reason to support the staplers, with whom he had a comfortable financial arrangement, and no interest in encouraging Richard Heron's claims against them. Heron was therefore ordered by proclamation to cease his suits.

The French *parlement* still remained his best recourse. At some point it seems that the Staple offered to settle for one-quarter the value of his confiscated wool.[89] Heron stood out for the entire value of his wool and other goods, amounting to 24,000 marks of silver for wool, and 14,158 marks and 32,000 écus for goods taken in the dominions of the Duke of Burgundy.[90] In addition he claimed four-fold costs, damages and interest.

He then turned to Rome. His justification was now the ingenious claim to papal protection as a pilgrim at the time of his dispossession at Calais. This move was not calculated to please Edward IV, who was a king as jealous as any of his royal authority, and Edward's procurator at Rome must have been instructed to oppose Heron. For a time, though, success seemed to be within Heron's grasp. In June 1477 he was appointed honorary esquire and domestic member of the papal household,[91] and in October the same year he obtained judgment from the papal court that the staplers must pay him under threat of excommunication.[92] The pope further declared it lawful for Heron to arrest staplers, their sureties or

---

[86] Richardson, 'Illustrations', p. 67.
[87] Ibid., facsimile facing p. 68.
[88] *Cal. Papal Letters*, p. 233: 'the said merchants never ceasing to plot against his life all the time'.   [89] Ibid. p. 234.
[90] Ibid.   [91] Ibid., p. 209.
[92] Ibid., pp. 227–35.

their ships and sell their goods, until he had recovered a sum of 2,000 écus previously granted him by the *parlement*.

This disastrous outcome for the staplers was vigorously protested by Edward IV, who 'took it sore' (*egre ferebat*) that the pope should usurp royal rights of justice over a layman, and also expressed disbelief in the pious purposes of Heron's trading. As a result, in November 1479 the pope in his turn relinquished jurisdiction and revoked his previous letters to the staplers.[93] He regretted that in accordance with his previous decision, Heron had employed letters against two hapless staplers, minor members of the Company and in no way responsible for the original action, who had happened to visit Italy. Uncrushed by this defeat, Heron prepared an appeal against the annulment. It was at this juncture that Sir John Weston, Prior of the Hospitallers in England, king's councillor and friend of the Cely family, visited Rome en route to his Order's stronghold of Rhodes, under threat of attack by the Turks. The staplers had requested him to do what he could for them in the matter of Richard Heron – on the cheap, as he naively indicated when he wrote to George Cely to report.

By his own account, Sir John and his entourage had made a great impression in Rome:

Worshipful cousin, with due recommendations premised, it is so I came to Rome the 15 day of October, and was right welcome, with every nobleman saying they saw not this hundred year so likely ['handsome'] a fellowship, for so many and in that array, come out of England. The Pope's Holiness made me great cheer, and would 'a sent me home again and absolved me of all manner obediences or commandment made to me, or might be made. But I desired his Holiness 'at I might do my voyage since I was so far forth. And so his Holiness sends me as his ambassador with matters of great importance. I trust to be the sooner at home, by God's grace.

Cousin, as touching the matter of the Staple and Richard Herron, the king's proctor and I has done in that matter as much as might be done to fulfil the king's intent and the weal of the merchants of the Staple. For I take God to record, and the bringer of this (a friar), 'at I did in this as much as I would have done and they had given me a great good. As they shall see all the remedies and demands 'at the said Herron makes, I send them by the said friar. I promise you he is greatly favoured, and he would 'a made a foul work, and remedy had not soon be found....

At Rome, the 27 day of October 1481, by your cousin Sir John Weston, Prior of Sancti Johannis.[94]

The document forwarded by Sir John evidently set out Heron's claims ('remedies and demands') for a new hearing. A transcript of these was certainly obtained by the king's Council in England, which issued a full

---

[93] Ibid., pp. 252–3.   [94] *C.L.* 129.

rejoinder and final repudiation of Heron's demands in February 1482. The appeal had been annulled and revoked in Rome on 11 January. This seems to have been the end of that particular affair. In *The Yorkist Age* P. M. Kendall has given a remarkable account of Heron's subsequent impudent adventurings on the international scene before he died at Speyer in August 1485.[95] But these did not concern the merchants of the Staple.

[95] Paul Murray Kendall, *The Yorkist Age: Daily Life During the Wars of the Roses* (New York, 1962), pp. 325–7.

PART II

THE WOOL TRADE

THE TRADE IN
FLEECE-WOOL

Those starting out in the wool-merchant's business, and many small or part-time staplers like William Maryon and John Cely, might deal almost exclusively in fells, that is the wool-bearing skins of slaughtered sheep. But about 72 percent of old Richard's trade was in shorn fleece-wool, and when Richard and George inherited his business they increased this proportion to some 81 percent. One essential in the training of a stapler, whether he dealt in fells or fleece-wool, was the ability to judge the quality of a fleece and to distinguish wools from different areas of England. The original author of one section in that compendium of earnest advice, the 'Discourse of Weights and Merchandise', had observed caustically:

If a man buy Yorkshire wool [as] Burford wool or Leominster wool, he should know what he bought ere it were all uttered [i.e. 'his customers would let him know about it before it was all off his hands']. Therefore there is an old proverb: 'he is no wise merchant that buy the cat in the sack', that is to say, he that buyeth a ring and seeith it not, he trusteth another better than himself, which is against all manner wisdom.[1]

This obvious counsel was not always heeded. A case heard at Bruges in 1449 concerned the sale of six bales of English wool called *Jorcxwouts wulle* (wool from the Yorkshire wolds). Colard of Bruges had sold them to Louis Vinceguerre, who sold them to Jean Feye, who then sold them to a merchant of Bergen-op-Zoom. At Bergen the wool was inspected and it was found that it was not after all of the quality called *Jorcxwouts* but only *Jorcxkiers* (Yorkshire), and the various buyers in the chain of sale each claimed compensation.[2]

As far as the Celys were concerned, Yorkshire wool of any variety

[1] 'Discourse', fo. 96v.
[2] L. Gilliodts-van Severen, ed., *Cartulaire de l'ancienne Estaple de Bruges* (Bruges, 1904), no. 882.

would not be worth the costs of export. Nor, on the other hand, did they deal in the most expensive growths, those of Herefordshire and Shropshire, known as Leominster and March wools. Sometimes they bought the low- to medium-cost wools of Kesteven ('Kesten'), Lindsey or Holland (Lincolnshire).[3] But by far their biggest trade was in Cotswold ('Cots.') wool. Eileen Power was under a misapprehension when she stated that 'the term "Cotes." or "Cotswold" was used as a technical term to denote wool of the finest quality'.[4] It is clear, however, that in the late fifteenth century the wool of the Cotswold region was regarded as the standard Staple quality. The 'Discourse' bases its average price for exported wool on a sack of Cotswold bought for £8,[5] and about 1496 when the Staple's customers wanted all prices uniformly reduced, they took the prices of good and middle Cotswold wool as their typical example.[6]

The Celys' biggest supplier by far was William Midwinter, of Northleach, Gloucestershire. Midwinter was a 'brogger', 'woolman' or middleman, who collected from the local growers. Other suppliers of their Cotswold wool were John Peyrs or Perys, Jenkin Taylor of Farmington, and John Bush, succeeded by his widow Alice Bush, who subsequently married William Midwinter. Thomas Bush also worked for Midwinter.[7] Richard Cely senior is also recorded as buying tithe wool from the rector of Abingdon, possibly grown at Westwell, which amounted to three sarplers in 1479.[8] Contemporary estimates put the average production of shorn wool at between 1½ and 2 lb per animal, so that three sarplers would hold the fleeces of 1,400 sheep or more. In one sample of Richard's coarser-grade, 'middle' Cotswold wool, 48 fleeces weighed 89¼ lb avdp. by the time that the buyer inspected them in Ghent and found them damaged by moths and decay.[9]

[3] Eileen Power's impression that they bought wool in Lancashire (*Studies in English Trade*, p. 52) must derive from a wrong identification of Preston, Glos.

[4] *Studies in English Trade*, p. 49, following C. L. Kingsford, *Prejudice and Promise in Fifteenth-Century England* (1925), p. 126. But there is no convincing evidence cited.

[5] 'Discourse', fo. 107v.

[6] T. Rymer, ed., *Foedera, conventiones, literae et cuiusque generis acta publica...*(3rd edn, 10 vols., The Hague, 1739–45), v (4), 113 and Gilliodts-van Severen, *Cartulaire de l'Estaple*, no. 1300 (19 Aug. 1497).

[7] John Cely additionally 'gathered' wool, buying from the growers in small quantities, 'by the tod and sack and half sack': *C.L.* 67.

[8] *C.L.* 40, 85, 87.

[9] File 15 fo. 10 (below, Ch. 8, p. 204). In 1442 it took, on average, 53 lb avdp. of English Lindsey wool to make one of the 'fine black' cloths of Louvain: John Munro, 'Industrial Protectionism in Medieval Flanders', *The Medieval City*, ed. H. A. Miskimin, David Herlihy, A. L. Udovitch (New Haven and London, 1977), Table 13.2 and notes, with figures recalculated to make due allowance for Calais weights. For English cloths, see E. M. Carus-Wilson, *Medieval Merchant Venturers* (2nd edn, 1967), p. 250 n. 2.

What was the Cotswold wool like? Nobody now knows for sure: K. G. Ponting has stated pungently: 'Unfortunately, all that is known about the most famous of mediaeval breeds, the Cotswold, is that it cannot have remotely resembled the present Cotswold which is derived from Bakewell's improved Leicester breed.'[10] It can be deduced, however, that the fifteenth-century product was a relatively short-stapled fine wool, suited to the fulling process used in the manufacture of the high-grade woollen cloth of medieval Italy and Flanders. The right length was important. On one occasion one of the Celys' best customers rejected some of their Cotswold wool on the grounds that the staple was too short.[11] The fells contemptuously dismissed on another occasion as 'rabbit stuff' must also have been very soft and fine as well as short in the staple.[12] By contrast, a Cely consignment in 1480 was too coarse for its type. The buyers, De Scermere and company, classed it as no better than 'middle young Cots.' They had intended it for their own drapery, but 'now there is no man will draper none of [those] sarplers at Ghent nor at Bruges', and De Scermere thought he would have to put the wool on sale at Antwerp mart to find what buyer he could.[13] George Cely had to agree that it was the coarsest Cotswold wool that he had handled. English merchants termed such wool 'gruff', a word they had borrowed from Flemish *groof* 'coarse'.

For most growths, classing the wool seems to have involved no more than categorizing the fleeces as either 'good' (or 'fine' or 'A grade') or 'middle'. For Cotswold wool a greater distinction was made between the four grades of good, middle, good young and middle young. There was probably no 'skirting' of the fleeces, although the sheep were very likely 'dagged' and 'crutched' before the shearing proper took place. The discoloured and matted wool obtained by these operations – that from belly and britch – was known as 'clift wool', i.e. wool from the *cleft* of the back legs, and was packed and sold separately.[14] A Staple ordinance of 1478 distinguished only these two general categories of wool under the designations 'end wool' and 'clift wool',[15] and William Cely made the same distinction when he observed in 1484 that he wanted some

[10] K. G. Ponting, *The Wool Trade, Past and Present* (Manchester and London, 1961), p. 18.
[11] *C.L.* 125.
[12] 'Cony ware': File 15 fo. 3.
[13] *C.L.* 93.
[14] It was known in Flanders and Brabant as *geclijte wolle* or *la cliture*, words probably cognate with modern Dutch *klit* 'to tangle': G. de Poerck, *La draperie médiévale en Flandre et en Artois* (Bruges, 1951), III, 189 translates *geclijte wolle* as 'laine enmêlée'.
[15] Power, *Studies in English Trade*, p. 68; N. W. Posthumus, ed., *Bronnen tot de Geschiedenis van de Leidsche Textielnijverheid* (2 vols., The Hague, 1910–11), I, no. 613. 'End wool' was the wound fleece.

customers to help him away with his clift wool, and got the reply that
'now they would buy as much end wool as they might, and no clift wool,
but when they came next again they would help me away with all the
clift wool'.[16] Clift wool is very probably the *lana lavata* or *laine lavée*
('washed wool') mentioned in various documents as distinct from the
superior *lana non lavata* of the fleece washed on the sheep before shearing
and sold 'in the grease'.[17]

Any attempt to break a fleece in order to separate the highest quality
wool from the inferior portions would have come under the prohibitions
against 'clacking and barding'. But there was a permitted category of
'refuse wool', which no doubt covered short trimmings, sweepings,
'sweat-locks' and similar broken pieces produced in shearing or packing,
which were known in Calais by the Flemish term 'breckling'. 'The lock',
as in 'wound in the lock', referred to the fleece-wool proper, particularly
the best wool on the shoulders. Then, as now, the fleeces were rolled up
so as to display this portion, and a wool-packer of the Johnsons referred
to some fleeces as 'not worthy of the lock'.[18] But *locks* in the plural meant
then, as it does now, the short trimmings. Even these were saleable,
though after 1565 locks of March wool were the only ones that might
be exported to the Staple.[19]

It was probably the grower who carried out the preliminary sorting
of his clip. In 1545 John Johnson instructed his wife:

when ye do pack any wool, in any wise let it be as fair handled for ['to avoid']
breaking the fleeces as is possible, and remember that there be three sorts made
in the packing...to wit, one of th'end wool (which is that is wound in the lock),
another of the fairest of the clift wool, and the third of the darkest colour of the
clift wool.[20]

The professional gatherers like Midwinter would buy this roughly
packed wool from the growers by the stone of 14 lb or the tod of 28 lb,
pricing it at so many shillings and pence per stone or tod.[21] The variety
of weights was rather confusing. Richard Hill entered an explanation in
his commonplace book:

[16] *C.L.* 218.
[17] *Foedera*, v (3), 90. The distinction is between *laine lavée* and *les toisons* in a citation
in Georges Espinas, *La draperie dans la Flandre française au moyen âge*, II (Paris, 1923),
p. 60. 'Cleefwulle' was said in 1545 to be not worth the cost of carriage to the customer
unless the merchants had properly washed and cleaned 'les clockes ['clags'] de deriere
et lachterslach': Georg Schanz, ed., *Englische Handelspolitik gegen Ende des Mittelalters*,
II (Leipzig, 1881), no. 48.
[18] Winchester, 'Johnson Letters', no. 309.
[19] E. E. Rich, ed., *The Ordinance Book of the Merchants of the Staple* (Cambridge, 1937),
p. 146.
[20] 'Johnson Letters', no. 207.
[21] It is clear from *C.L.* 192 that Midwinter did not pay in advance for his purchases.

wool is weighed by [avoirdupois] but not reckoned [so], for wool is bought by the sack, by the nail [or *clove*, of 7 lb avdp.], by the stone or by the tod. But in the country amongst the husbands it is most used to be bought by the stone and by the tod. And between gatherers of the country and merchants it is most used to be bought by the sack.[22]

'Sack' refers to a weight, not to the bale itself.

Midwinter and his colleagues, having taken delivery of consignments from the grower after the June shearing, kept them in pile in their store-houses at Northleach, Chipping Norton, Chipping Campden and other wool centres of the Cotswolds until the staplers came, perhaps in November, often the following April or May, to 'cast a sort', that is, examine samples. This skilled work was generally the province of a senior member of the Cely family. If he found the quality satisfactory and could agree on the price, he drew up an indenture with the woolman for the purchase of so many sack-weights or bales ('sarplers') to be delivered in London or another authorized port, paying the same price for both good wool and the middle or second-grade fleeces in the clip. Often the agreement stipulated that 'refuse wool' was to be retained by the middleman. But in April 1476, for instance, Thomas Betson and William Stonor shipped 30 sarplers fine Cotswold, ten sarplers middle Cotswold, six sarplers fine young Cotswold, three sarplers middle young Cotswold, and one sarpler refuse.[23]

Between middleman and stapler the wool was generally priced at so many marks per sack-weight of 52 nails or cloves (364 lb avdp.). A particularly detailed agreement survives among the Stonor papers, dated 12 September 1478.[24] By this Robert Warner of Watlington, Oxfordshire, woolman, agreed to supply John Elys, mercer of London, with 25 sacks young Cotswold, namely 20 sacks fine wool and the remaining five sacks middle, to be delivered by 2 February, together with an extra 50 fleeces of fine wool and 25 nails, also of fine wool, for a price of £140 or about £5 9s per sack-weight. A typical Cely indenture runs:

Jesu 1476

This bill witness that Richard Cely, merchant of the Staple of Calais, have full bought and bargain with John Bush of Norlache [Northleach] 40 sack of good Cotswold wool, good wool and middle wool of the same price: the sack of both good and middle 13 mark 20d [£8 15s]. The refuse wool for [to] be cast to John Bush by the wool packer at the packing of the said wool at Northleach, and I for to receive the foresaid wool at the Lead Hall at the king's beam, and the days of payment after writ.

[22] Balliol MS. 354, fo. 182v. See also 'Discourse', fo. 87.
[23] *Stonor L.* no. 163.
[24] 'Supplementary Stonor Letters', pp. 12–13.

After the weight and receiving of the foresaid wool and the reckoning made, the 3rd penny at weight, the t'other 3rd penny the last day of May next coming, the t'other 3rd penny the 26 day of August coming a year, anno '77. The date writ at London the 28 day of August the year above said.[25]

The wool so purchased had to be repacked into bales before delivery, and the Celys liked to superintend this process themselves: 'good packing', i.e. careful classing, was the criterion of a reputable stapler.[26] Sometimes the growers had been very inefficient. Otwell Johnson complained in 1544 about a packer in the country who had marked three sarplers as 'Cotswold' and one as the cheaper Berkshire. When the wool came to be 'packed to rights' in smaller bales it made 12 'pockets' and a 'blot' (incomplete sack), no fewer than seven being A. Berkshire, three middle Cots. and only 2½ A. Cots.[27] And the next letter referred to a sarpler of wool belonging to a client which had originally been 'packed in horse-packs in her house, and I promise you there was a tod and more of refuse wool in the same, and it was very ill-rivered ['badly washed'] wool for that country as ever I saw'.[28]

The final 'packing to rights' was carried out by an officially appointed packer, sometimes known as a wool-winder. William Breten was one well-known packer who often acted for the Celys. In May 1482 Richard junior told George:

I have been in Cotswold this three weeks and packed with William Midwinter 22 sarplers and a poke, whereof be 4 middle. William Breten says it is the fairest wool that he saw this year. And I packed 4 sarplers at Campden of the same bargain, whereof are 2 good, 2 middle. There will be in all, with blots, upon 27 or 28 sarplers wool.[29]

Besides Breten, the Celys mention Robert Lynne – once paid 58s 10d for packing wool and his horse-hire – and John Gerard.[30] A specialist 'packer of clift wools' named Peryman makes an incidental appearance in a letter of 1487.[31]

The 'oath of the wool-packers' in the 1565 Ordinances of the Staple gives an indication of their responsibilities.

Ye swear, etc., ye shall be obedient to the mayor and constables of the Staple of England...and truly and indifferently serve the merchants as well denizens as strangers in all things touching your said occupation. You shall without fraud,

---

[25] File 11 fo. 19.
[26] In the 14th century the expression was also used of wool that had been 'clacked and barded'. In applying it to the 'inwinding' of foreign matter, Power (*Studies in English Trade*, p. 56) misrepresented *Rot. Parl.* III, 270.
[27] 'Johnson Letters', no. 44.
[28] Ibid., no. 45.   [29] *C.L.* 165.
[30] File 10 fo. 29.   [31] *C.L.* 235.

collusion or deceit make your packing of wools truly, indifferently and sufficiently, so that you shall not pack or wrap or cause to be packed or wrapped in the fleeces of the wool, earth, stones, dung or sand. And ye shall truly name all manner of wools by you packed of the country where they were grown after the nature of the said wools and not of any other country, in any manner of wise. And that you shall write or cause to be written with open great letters upon every sarpler, poke or pocket of good March wools, these words 'Good March'. And upon the sarplers of middle March wools shall write or cause to be written 'Middle March', and upon all sarplers of good wools of Cotswold, 'Good Cotswold'.... And also ye shall write or cause to be written upon all and singular sarplers aforesaid your own surname in such wise that the name of the wools nor your surname may not be put out without breaking of the said sarplers, pokes or pockets.[32]

The packer was not always as careful as he might have been, however. Because it enabled him to criticize his father, George Cely betrays a certain glee in reporting the dissatisfaction of his customer De Scermere in 1480:

He swears unto me largely that he has had of yours in time past better middle young Cots. than this wool was. They lay unto me great unkindness that I deal with them under this manner. They say unto me that ye might 'an taken out of this 6 sarplers and the poke, 2 sarplers middle young.... I had much work at Calais ever I could have it awarded for Cots., and much sticking was against it amongst the Fellowship [of the Staple]. In the reverence of God, see better to the packing of your wool that shall come, or else your wool is like to lose that name that it has had ever affore in time past. I never wist you send coarser wool to Calais for the country than this last was.[33]

'Our father was at the packing thereof himself', commented his brother.[34]

At packing, the wool was pressed into the huge canvas sarplers for which the staplers were constantly buying canvas produced in Bar ('Barras canvas'), Normandy or the low countries. In November 1479 Richard Cely senior had bought 97 sacks of wool, 'for the which I shall hope much canvas, for the which, and ye can buy for me four or five hundred [ells] of Burgundy canvas or Barras canvas of good breadth, as broad as Normandy canvas, and three dozen [lb of] packthread of Calais thread, it were good for me'.[35] The following June he sent a further detailed demand for 500 or 600 ells of canvas to be bought at the mart, 'of a good breadth, not ell-broad, half-quarter less. And not of the smallest, but pretty round ['good thick'] canvas for to packing in wool.'[36] 'Pretty' was almost a trade description of canvas, and the Johnsons also

[32] *Ordinance Book*, pp. 129–30. [33] *C.L.* 93.
[34] *C.L.* 95. [35] *C.L.* 67.
[36] *C.L.* 90.

use the expression. It was reckoned that it took 12 (English?) ells of canvas to cover a sarpler, at a cost of about 4s. The covering might be called 'sarpler', like the bale itself.

At the Celys' time, the bale or sarpler usually held between 2 and 2¾ sack-weights of wool. Rarely, an overweight sarpler tipped the scales at 3 sack-weights. The weight was therefore somewhere between 728 and 1,000 (or, exceptionally, 1,092) lb avdp.[37] The modern New Zealand wool-bale, by contrast, is much the same size as the fourteenth-century one, holding a maximum of 400 lb. It measures 40 × 27 × 27 inches, and the older jute covering, which weighed 9 lb, would take about 4.8 square English ells, or 8 square Flemish ells. The weight of the medieval canvas wrappings is indicated by the allowance of 28 lb given for tare and tret at buying. Bales smaller than the sarpler were called 'pokes' (weighing about 1½ sacks) and 'pockets', weighing one sack or less.[38] A 'blot', named from a Flemish word meaning 'bare' or 'lacking', would be made up in weight before sale.

The bale when packed was tied with 'ears' at each corner, and bore the stapler's merchant-mark, the number within each 'sort' or purchase, and lettering to indicate the region of growth and the quality. 'End wool' had to be marked at the top of the sarpler and 'clift wool' along the side, in such a way that the labelling could not be removed or torn.[39] There were inevitably cases of dishonest merchants altering the lettering. In 1448 the Englishman Thomas Stevenson was accused at Bruges of changing the D. on some bales to an L., 'which designated a superior quality of wool'.[40] William Cely knew from the markings that a certain sarpler contained middle not fine Cotswold, 'as upon the sarplers maketh mention, both by the M. and by the paternosters on the "koyttys"'.[41] M. stood for 'middle', but the paternosters on the quoits (leaden seals?) are mysterious.

When John Cely acted as wool-gatherer for his brother or nephews, he charged 5s per sack-weight (about 12s 6d per sarpler). It is impossible to estimate the cost to Richard senior or his sons of their own trips into the Cotswolds to buy and pack wool, but Richard junior recorded payment of 10s for the hire of three horses for eight days at 12d a horse

---

[37] Unhappily, the *O.E.D.*'s definition of a sarpler as containing 80 tods or 2,240 lb (i.e. over 6 sack-weights) has been widely and erroneously repeated with reference to the 15th and 16th centuries.

[38] It would be interesting to know what kind of wool John Hosyer (and once Hugh Clopton) shipped, exceptionally for the period, in small pockets of *c.* 26 cloves in 1488: P.R.O. E.122 78/5.

[39] *Foedera*, v (3), 91.

[40] Gilliodts-van Severen, *Cartulaire de l'Estaple*, no. 866.

[41] *C.L.* 221.

for the first day and 4*d* each thereafter, in expenses over the purchase of '20 sarplers of the first wool that William Breten packed with my father when Alice Bush was widow'.[42] Costs of £11 12*s* odd are claimed for riding into Lincolnshire to buy and pack £94 10*s* worth of wool from Edmund Clerke of 'Ashoby' (Aswarby?),[43] and the two servants Nicholas Best and John Roberts were paid 50*s* for their costs in going into the Cotswolds to pack wool on one occasion, but there are no details about the length of their stay or the amount of wool packed.[44]

While small quantities of wool may well have been transported between grower and middleman by pack-horse, the great sarplers of the late fifteenth century were far too large and heavy to be carried on horse-back: the 'Discourse' says that 280 lb is 'a reasonable horse-load'.[45] The accounts make it clear that the wool travelled to London or other port by wagon. The size of a load seems to have been variable, but an average was perhaps two sarplers at an average cost, at the Celys' time, of 18*s* 9*d* a load.[46] The Johnsons also reckoned about six sack-weights to a wagon, but one letter of theirs mentions that a wagon drawn by four mares would carry 'thirty hundredweight', i.e. about nine sack-weights.[47] Some of the Celys' carters came from Northamptonshire and others from Gloucestershire itself, while three are specified as from 'Isylton' (Islington, just out of London).[48]

On delivery at London the wool was weighed in the presence of seller and buyer, who shared the cost of weighing, which totalled about 9½*d* per sarpler. The buyer was allowed a rebate of four cloves (28 lb) in the sarpler for the weight of the canvas and the turn of the scale, or 'canvas and draught'.[49] He might pay the price in three instalments, giving cash in hand for one-third of the price and obtaining credit of anything between eight months and a year for the final payment, but arrangements varied. In an undated purchase by Richard senior from John Peyrs (of late 1479 or early 1480?) the whole price was paid in two instalments, one on 24 August and the other on 30 September.[50]

In January 1479 Richard made another indenture with Peyrs for the immediate delivery of wool, for which he paid a deposit.

Item, the 18 day of January I, Richard Cely, merchant of the Staple, have bought of John Perys, woolman of Northleach, 14 sack of good Cotswold wool, as good wool as Will Midwinter's...wool is. The good wool and the middle of the same 14 sack, price the sack of both good wool and middle wool, 11 mark [changed

[42] File 20 no. 4.
[43] File 10 fo. 29.
[44] Ibid., fo. 35.
[45] 'Discourse', fo. 87.
[46] This works out at about 2 percent of average buying price in 1476–82.
[47] 'Johnson Letters', no. 54.
[48] File 10 fo. 29.
[49] File 15 fo. 9.
[50] Ibid.

to 11½ marks]. The refuse wool for to be cast to John Perys by the wool packer at the packing of the foresaid wool at Northleach, and the said wool for to be weigh at the Lead Hall at the king's beam and the reckoning made and the wool received. And I have delivered to John Perys in hand £20 in party of payment. The rest: at the weighing a part, the last day of May a part, the last day of September the rest (the last payment) next come.[51]

Richard junior subsequently noted: 'Item, paid to John Peyrs the 22 day of January in part of payment above said – £6.' Peyrs in fact supplied three sarplers and a poke of his own wool at 11 marks per sack-weight and two sarplers and a poke of Alice Bush's at 11½ marks.[52] Richard junior wrote down the number and weight of each sarpler and the immediate petty costs, and his father entered the rebates and net amounts payable:

> John Peyrs.
> A poke – No. 4 – s di. 8 cloves [1½ sacks 8 cloves]
> No. 3. . . ss 25 cl. [2 sacks 25 cloves]
> No. 2. . . ss di. 3 cl.
> No. 1. . . ss di. 8 cl.
> Rebate of every cloth [i.e. sarpler] 4 cl.
> Sum clear – £66 9s 2d.

> Alice Bush: 2 sarplers a poke.
> No. 7. . . s 1 cl.
> No. 6. . . ss di.
> No. 5. . . ss di. 9 cl.
> Sum clear – 6 s[acks], 2 cl[oves] less [i.e. 5 sacks 50 cloves].
> Argent – £45 14s.

Item, I paid for half the weight of 5 sarplers 2 pokes. . .	2s 7d
Item, paid to the porters of Leadenhall	7d
Item, paid to John Reyd for carriage of 6 cloths from Leadenhall and a load from waterside	14d
Item, paid to John Peyrs	£5.

Another set of documents records a later purchase from William Midwinter in February 1487. George noted among memoranda that on 15 February

We made an bargain with William Midwinter of Northleach for 50 sacks wool, good and middle, of Cotswold. The refuse to be cast out by the wool-packer. The said William must have for every sack 14 mark. To be paid at Myssomer [Midsummer] next – £100, and at Midsummer come twelve month le rest of the same wool. Item, gave her [sic] for the God's penny – 4d.[53]

The total price in the event was £450 17s 4d.

[51] File 11 fo. 51.   [52] Ibid., fo. 56.   [53] File 20 no. 17.

Midwinter himself listed the sarplers with their numbers and weights as delivered to George on 15 June 1487.[54] There were 19 sarplers and one poke (containing 1½ sacks 10 cloves), of which three or four sarplers and the poke contained middle wool. According to George's corresponding list, the wool was weighed with Midwinter at the Leadenhall on 20 June.[55] The total gross weight was 49½ sacks seven cloves, net with rebate 48 sacks five cloves, but George also noted 'here is of fleeces out of the sarplers – 11 cloves'. Some sarplers may have been overweight and 'gelded'. On 22 June Midwinter was paid £40, but the whole of the £100 due on 24 June was not finally paid off until 22 August.[56] The wool was shipped to Calais in July.[57]

Along with his own wool, Midwinter had also weighed to George 13 sarplers from Jenkin Taylor. George describes three of these as middle. One other sarpler of Taylor's wool, No. 24, supposedly of good Cots., was later picked out at Calais as the sample by which to award the sort, and found to include 60 'very gruff' fleeces of middle wool. William Cely and the packer at Calais then secretly exchanged it with No. 8, of Midwinter's wool, which was 'fair wool enough'.[58] The outcome was satisfactory – for the seller, that is – 'item, sir, your wool is awarded by the sarpler that I cast out last'.[59]

There are ten records of the Celys' bargains with suppliers in the accounts, nine of which indicate the price to be paid. Other buying prices for fleece-wool are occasionally mentioned in the letters, as when Richard senior commented in July 1474 that at Kettering wool was selling for 28d a stone, i.e. £3 0s 8d per sack-weight.[60] Jane Stonor, sometime before November 1475, sold 140 fleeces (of Cotswold wool?) for £2 6s 8d.[61] Depending on the average weight of her fleeces, this suggests a price (to grower) of between £3 and £4 per sack-weight. A bill of sale in the Stonor collection shows that in January 1476 two London mercers bought nine sarplers of good Cotswold and two middle at nine marks (£6) the sack, and two further sarplers of middle (young?) at six marks (£4).[62] But in August 1476 the Celys had to pay 13 marks 20d (£8 15s) for Cotswold wool,[63] and by November Thomas Betson was being asked 13½ marks (£9), which he considered would allow him insufficient profit: 'little getting should be therein'.[64]

There is no indication of how much Richard Cely paid for the 19 sarplers and a poke 'of John Bush' gathering', which he had at London

[54] Ibid., no. 23.
[55] File 14 fo. 13.
[56] File 15 fo. 55.
[57] File 14 fos. 17–18, File 10 fo. 30.
[58] *C.L.* 234.
[59] *C.L.* 235.
[60] *C.L.* 2.
[61] *Stonor L.*, no. 157.
[62] Ibid., no. 159.
[63] File 11 fo. 19.
[64] *Stonor L.*, no. 175.

in May 1478, when more of the same purchase was already on sale at Calais.[65] But in October 1478 he reported that 'the price of wool is rise in Cotswold a mark in a sack in short time',[66] and on 24 November he paid 12 marks (£8) per sack.[67] Prices had fallen somewhat in January 1479, when John Peyrs charged 11 marks (£7 6s 8d) and Alice Bush 11½ marks (£7 13s 4d).[68] In late 1479 or early 1480 Peyrs had raised his price to 11½ marks and Midwinter was again charging 12.[69] In July 1481 Cotswold wool was once more 'at great price', but much sought-after, and Richard was willing to pay the 13 marks (£8 13s 4d) being asked.[70] The price continued to rise, so that in September 1482 Midwinter, who had expected to buy from the growers at 13s 8d a tod (£8 17s 8d per sack-weight), found himself paying 14s or 14s 6d (£9 2s to £9 8s 6d per sack-weight).[71] The next and final prices quoted in the papers are 14 or 14½ marks (£9 6s 8d and £9 13s 4d) in 1486 and 1487, price to middleman.[72] On the limited information available, the average (but far from consistent) price paid by the Celys in 1476 to 1482 was £8 per sack-weight, rising to £9 10s in 1486–7. It is important to note that this price is for net, not gross weight. The price actually paid for every sarpler of packed wool was around 3 percent lower.

If it is difficult to establish the buying price of the Celys' wool in most of their transactions, a certain amount of guesswork is also required in calculating their incidental expenses. From scattered references in their papers it is possible to obtain a detailed picture of the operations involved, but these are not always costed helpfully. Some of the Chancery auditors' accounts summarize expenses from lost originals but fail to state the quantity of wool concerned.[73] There is one reference to payments for 'canvas and carriage and other costs' on the 32 sarplers and a poke bought in 1487, which amount to an average 15s 10d per sarpler paid in England, but what did 'other costs' include?[74] The list in the 'Discourse' of 'the costs that runneth upon a sack wool of Cotswold or ['before'] it be sold', which in fact are calculated not by sack-weight but for a sarpler smaller than the Cely average and weighing about two sack-weights, appears to be reliable for the most part, but some charges had altered by the Celys' time, and other of their expenses are omitted.[75]

[65] C.L. 20.
[66] C.L. 37.
[67] File 11 fo. 50.
[68] Ibid. fo. 56; pp. 119–20 above.
[69] File 15 fo. 9.
[70] C.L. 122.
[71] C.L. 192.
[72] File 20 no. 14 fo. 2v; File 14 fo. 13.
[73] See especially File 10 fos. 12–13v, 29, 35–6.
[74] File 10 fo. 13v.
[75] We do not know when this list was compiled. Like the prices of wools at Calais, also listed, the information must have been out-of-date when copied into the extant MS. This is written on paper with a variety of the 'hand-and-flower' watermark. Similar paper appears in the Cely collection no earlier than 1487.

The list runs:

First, carriage to London or to [South]hampton, every sarpler. 8s
(The sack, 4s)
Item, for packing in the country, every sarpler 12d
Item, for 'schetynge and servyng at the corde' . . . .[15d]
Item, for the costs in riding 4d
Item, every sarpler 12 ells canvas at 4d the ell . . . 4s
Item, for sewing and painting 4d
Item, for packthread 1d
Item, for porters 6d
Item, for hostelage at the quay 2d

. . .

Item, for the cocket 2d
Item, for petty custom 4d
Item, for the 'bollett' [billet?] to the scrivener . . . . 2d.[76]

The price of 'schetynge and servyng at the corde' is left blank. The sum total given later (which confuses sarplers with sack-weights) suggests that the reading should be 1s 3d. The entry parallels one reference in the Cely accounts to 'the server at cord'.[77] Apparently the payment was for 'shutting' (closing) and roping the sarpler at the 'accord' or final agreement with the seller.[78] In George's account the 'server' was paid 2s, but this might represent 1d for each of the 24 sarplers then involved. The 'sewing and painting' of the 'Discourse' occurs in Cely accounts as 'gauging and painting' at 4d per sarpler, which seems more probable. In addition, the chalker was paid ¼d for every bale. Where the 'Discourse' estimates carriage at 8s per sarpler, carriage of the Celys' larger sarplers from the Cotswolds cost them 9s or 10s per piece. There were also payments to the porters of the Leadenhall who carried the wools there and 'inhoused' them and to the porters of the wool quay where the wool was customed and shipped, and carters were paid an average of 4d per sarpler for transporting the bales between Leadenhall, the buyer's own wool-store, and the quays.

The 'Discourse', which is dealing with wool exported to Venice, has a further item in its list: 'for the weigher at the custom, every sarpler 53s 4d.' Either this is a complete miscopying, or a mistake for the custom and subsidy dues per *sack-weight* payable by an alien merchant. The weigher's clerk was paid 1d per sack-weight in the Cely accounts. Further payments of 'indenture money' and of 'entry money' or 'cocket

[76] 'Discourse', fo. 107v.
[77] File 20 no. 4.
[78] *O.E.D.* s.v. Serve v.¹ 54 (b) 'wrap (a rope, bandage) round an object'.

silver' were made to the customers at the waterside.[79] Both the Celys and the Johnsons in the sixteenth century paid a further small fee for each ship in which they laded wools – 3*d* or 4*d* per ship in the Celys' case – and at both dates there was an 'imposition' towards the expenses of the Staple company, which came to 4*d* per sarpler for the Celys. Another expense which the 'Discourse' omits is the half-share of the costs when the wool was weighed at the Leadenhall between supplier and merchant. The merchant's share was usually accounted at 4¾*d* per sarpler, paid to weighers like Robert Cobold. There is an undated fragment among the Cely papers, written most unusually in 'commercial' French:

Richard Cely doit pour le poiser de 32 sarplers achat de Boysch [Bush] – 12*s* 8*d*.
Item, pour 20 sarplers achat de Alysche Boysche – sum 7*s* 11*d*.
Sum totall – 20*s* 7*d*.[80]

The sarplers were evidently weighed a second time at the quay just before shipment, by the official customs-house weighers such as Jeffrey Kent.

Total ascertainable petty costs in England for the Celys come to perhaps 18*s* per sarpler (around 7*s* 2*d* per sack-weight). There might well be further extraordinary expenses, and this sum does not include the cost of premises for storing the wool. Richard Cely senior kept 27 sarplers in store between May 1479 and March 1480, and in late 1480 he had more wool unpacked and 'in pile' at London, which was not shipped until May 1481.[81] There is one reference to a delayed consignment of nine sarplers 'standing' at Leadenhall for 11 weeks in September–December at 1½*d* each per week,[82] and sometimes a sarpler had to be reweighed if, for instance, it was overweight and needed to be gelded or reduced in size, which might cost 5*d*. The porters of Leadenhall were paid 10*s* 8*d* for 'winding and streking' repacked wool in 1486, and a breakfast for them on one occasion cost 4*d*.[83]

Since the 'Discourse' was dealing with wool exported to Venice it did not estimate a stapler's further expenditure at Calais. The freight charge, equivalent to about 5*s* 4*d* stg. per sarpler (6*s* 8*d* Flem., rising later to 8*s* Flem. or more), and petty costs at Calais bring the Celys' total of incidental expenses up to at least 25*s* stg. per sarpler, and perhaps more realistically as much as 27*s* (about 10*s* per sack-weight on average). This excludes such things as wages and travel costs of themselves and their servants. A memorandum of *c.* 1527, hostile to the staplers, contemplates costs which amount, when an error over the cost of canvas is corrected,

[79] E.g. File 10 fo. 36.   [80] File 16 fo. 1.
[81] *C.L.* 104, 107, 111.   [82] File 10 fo. 29.
[83] File 21 no. 3; File 20 no. 14; File 10 fo. 29.

to about 21s per sarpler.[84] In view of the figures just quoted, it seems likely that the writer was weighting his case against the staplers by under-estimating costs.

Other costs have, however, been over-estimated by modern writers. The rebate to the English buyer of four cloves in the sarpler meant that, depending on the size of the sarplers in his sort, instead of the nominal £8 per sack-weight of Cotswold wool which is the average of quoted prices in the period 1476–82, the buyer would in fact pay about £7 15s per sack-weight of the packed wool. Secondly, during its storage period in London, between its first weighing at Leadenhall and its second weighing by the customs officials, the wool normally dried out somewhat, so that it lost weight, possibly to the extent of one clove in the sack-weight.[85] By the time that it was customed, the wool might therefore weigh some 2 percent less. Thirdly, when the wool was weighed for customs purposes, the officials routinely allowed a rebate for the canvas covering of two cloves per sack-weight. This amounted to about 3.5 percent of the gross weight of a typical Cely shipment. From a comparison of the Celys' shipments customed on 26 September 1483 and the corresponding list of sarplers and weights in the Cely papers, it is clear that the customs men recorded the net weight of the wool, silently deducting the rebate.[86] It appears that this rebate was sometimes calculated on the weight of the individual sarpler, as must be the case in two of the surviving particular accounts.[87] But sometimes a slightly more generous allowance was given because the customers calculated by the total weight of a merchant's fleece-wool in each ship, which is the basis of calculation in Cely lists for 1480 and 1484.[88] That practice varied is indicated by George's uncertainty over the deductions to be made on his shipment of April 1486.[89] He first took individual sarpler weights as a basis, producing a total of 83¼ sacks customable weight, but altered the figures in one list when the clerks, calculating on the basis of weight per

---

[84] Schanz, *Englische Handelspolitik*, II, no. 130.

[85] On average there was a loss, but a proportion of the wool would always absorb some moisture and gain weight.

[86] Gross weight was 32 sacks 14 cloves, customed at 31 sacks 5 cloves: P.R.O. E.122 78/2 and File 10 fo. 30 (4 Oct. 1483). E. M. Carus-Wilson and Olive Coleman (*England's Export Trade 1275–1547* (Oxford, 1963), pp. 20, 26) were unaware that a rebate was given. They stated that 'precisely the same quantities' appear in G. Cely's record of freight payments in July 1478 and in the corresponding customs account, E.122 73/40, but 'two sarplers' in the former is hardly as precise as '4½ ss 11 cl. in 2 sarplers' in the latter. The one small variation they observed, in number of fells, was a miswriting of George's.

[87] E.122 73/40, 78/5.

[88] C.L. 104 and File 20 no. 9. The particular account (E.122 78/2) does not give individual weights.

[89] File 10 fo. 30, File 13 fos. 22–23v, File 21 fos. 8–9v.

ship, produced a total (including one apparent mistake in the Celys' favour) of 82½ sacks 22 cloves.[90] The real gross weight of the consignment was 86 sacks 11 cloves.

In calculating the amount which customs and subsidy added to buying price, one must take into account the loss of weight which typically occurred between the time that the packed bales were weighed at Leadenhall and payment agreed between stapler and supplier, and the later weighing by customs officers just before shipment. If the loss amounted to one clove per sack-weight, net, for every 52 cloves of wool originally purchased there were now only 51, and tax, at £2 for 52 cloves at this period, came to only £1 19s on each sack-weight of the initial purchase, or 24.5 percent of an average purchase price of £8 per sack-weight. If young Cotswold wool, bought at £5 9s per sack-weight, lost the same amount of weight, tax could add as much as 36 percent. By 1486, when buying price for mature Cotswold wool had risen to 14 or 14½ marks per sack-weight, the percentage of custom and subsidy over purchase price for that grade went down to an average of 21 percent. Equivalent rates on fells were 33.3 percent of the buying price of the 1,016 Cotswold fells sold by Richard and George in 1480, and 25 percent in 1487.

It is impossible to estimate the amount which custom and subsidy added to buying price over the total range of wool exports by denizens. Any attempt to do so would require an unacceptable amount of guesswork about such things as the proportion of lower-cost wools shipped, and the domestic price of fells. The average tax-rate on the Celys' combined purchases of Cotswold and Kesteven wool and Cotswold fells in 1472–82 was perhaps in the region of 26 percent of buying price. This estimate includes fleece-wool in the proportion of 7 percent Kesteven to 93 percent Cotswold. Even so, the price paid for London fell is not known. Chapter 9 will touch on the further matter of the hidden and largely incalculable increases in effective duty produced by the government's manipulation of exchange rates at Calais.

The relation of custom and subsidy to selling price at Calais can be calculated with rather more accuracy than can the relation to purchase price in England. We must now ignore the weight-loss between purchase and shipment which had to be considered in the previous reckoning, and take shipped weight as the basis on which to estimate the proportionate value of the tax. The minimum rebate of two cloves per sack-weight

[90] File 21 fos. 8–9v. For example, in the *Christopher Fynkell* 2 sarplers weighed respectively 2½ sacks 12 cl. and 2½ sacks 14 cl. Taken individually, they earned rebate of 10 cl. in all (2 cl. per sack-weight and 1 cl. for each complete half-sack). Taken together, they weighed 5½ sacks and so attracted 11 cl. rebate.

Table 1. *Custom and subsidy as percentage of price of wools at Calais*

Quality of wool	1472–82	1483–97*
Good Leominster	7.7%	7.5%
Good March	10.2%	9.8%
Good Cotswold	13.4%	12.7%
Middle Cotswold	19.6%	18.2%
Good Kesteven	20.4%	18.8%
Middle Kesteven	29.9%	26.8%

* A temporary increase of customs rebate in 1484 is disregarded. For this, see Ch. 11.

means that for every 52 cloves by gross shipped weight, custom and subsidy came to a maximum of £1 18s 5½d. Between shipment and sale at Calais the wool probably lost at least one clove more, so that by the time of sale there were only 51 English cloves for every 52 at customing, or 1.1333 Calais sack-weights.[91] There is nowhere any suggestion that the buyer at Calais got any deduction for tare and tret.[92] Custom and subsidy dues estimated on the basis described are shown as percentages of selling price on a sample range of wools in Table 1.[93]

If one assumes that middle wools made up 24 percent of the total consignments of each sort, in the earlier period custom and subsidy would amount to 14.6 percent of the weighted average selling price for good and middle Cots. combined, reducing to 13.8 percent after 1482, and to 22.2 percent on a consignment of both grades of Kesteven wool, reducing to 20.4 percent after 1482. Tax on fells ranged between 16 percent and 20 percent of average selling price in the earlier period. It amounted to 18 percent on Cotswold fells in 1483–5 and to 14.9 percent in 1487, but there are no selling prices for London fell in this second period. At 1483 selling prices, custom and subsidy could amount to 14.5 percent of the value of a consignment in the proportion of 76 sacks of good Cotswold, 24 sacks middle Cotswold wool and 6,000 Cotswold fells.

Between them, tax and usual incidental costs may have amounted to about £6 per sarpler of fleece-wool (about £2 8s per English sack-

[91] For Calais weight, see below, p. 133. A loss of 1 cl. in 48 seems to be assumed in the ordinances of 1565: *Ordinance Book*, pp. 146–7, quoted below, p. 141.

[92] 'In Calais...the canvas which is about all the sarpler is sold [as] wool': Schanz, *Englis he Handelspolitik*, II, no. 130.

[93] M. M. Postan (*Medieval Trade and Finance* (Cambridge, 1973), p. 109) calculated that 'total customs payments...exceeded 20 per cent of the value of good quality wool in Calais'. But this computation added to the standard 40s per sack-weight a fictitious 6s 8d extra 'for customs charged at Calais'.

weight).[94] In 1472–82 this meant a total increase of about 31 percent on the average buying price of good and middle Cotswold wool, and in 1486–7 about 26 percent. Good Cots. sold at a sufficiently high price at Calais to absorb these charges. So too did good young Cots., despite costs which might add some 45 percent to its buying price in England. Middle Cots., on the other hand, composing nearly 24 percent of the Celys' total stock of mature Cotswold wool, was bought at the same price in England and incurred the same costs as good Cots., but sold at a price that can have realized little or no profit. The taxation system must, in addition, have encouraged competition among English buyers for the best-quality wools, and penalized those staplers who, with smaller resources or based in the north-east of England, preferred to deal in the cheaper varieties. The lower tax-rate on top-quality wools may not necessarily have meant, as Lloyd assumed, that the foreign manufacturers 'would get far more value for their money in buying the best than in buying mediocre wools'.[95] It looks as though, at the Celys' time, the stapler made his profits on the best grades, at the expense of the foreign customer.[96]

After allowing a slightly more generous estimate for petty costs than has been adopted here (bringing up the average estimated costs to £2 9s 3d per sack-weight), I have elsewhere suggested that a sack-weight of good Cotswold wool bought at £8 might hypothetically have brought a net profit of 38.4 percent, whereas a sack of middle Cots. could incur a loss of 5 percent.[97] But various vicissitudes could easily affect the profitability of a particular consignment. In the very few cases where actual Cely transactions can be costed with any exactitude, profit of 28.6 percent can be postulated on one consignment containing 13 sarplers good Cots. and four sarplers middle. On sales in 1483–5 which included small amounts of good Kesteven, middle young Cots. and refuse wool, overall net profit may be estimated at only 18.8 percent, or 19.7 percent when sales of fells are added.[98] Exchange rates are necessarily left out

---

[94] Transport charges accounted for nearly 6 percent of the total cost of fleece-wool, but could be as high as 10 percent for fells.

[95] T. H. Lloyd, *The Movement of Wool Prices in Medieval England* (*Economic History Review*, supplement VI, Cambridge, 1973), p. 12. To speak of 'mediocre' wools may be a little misleading. A type unsuited to one manufacturer may be the best for another, and some customers preferred middle wools.

[96] Between the compilation of the undated price list in the 'Discourse' and *c.* 1473, the price of fine March wool at Calais had risen by 5 marks, that of fine Cots. by 1 mark, and of fine Berks. by ½ mark. Other varieties were all reduced by amounts between 1½ marks and 3¼ marks.

[97] Alison Hanham, 'Profits on English Wool Exports, 1472 to 1544', *B.I.H.R.*, LV (1982), 139–47. A sarpler of middle young Cots., total cost £19 4s, might well sell at Calais for only £18 7s.

[98] If Betson had bought Cots. wool, to include an average proportion of middle, at the £9 quoted in Nov. 1476 (above, p. 121), his 'little getting' might perhaps have come to just under 17 percent net profit.

of account in these calculations. How they might influence the stapler's ultimate receipts in extreme circumstances is demonstrated in Ch. 7.

In most years there were three main shippings of wool to Calais, in spring (March–April), summer (between June and early August), and autumn (September or early October). A further shipping might be held in winter. Most staplers no doubt shared George's opinion that it was unwise to ship 'in dead of winter': 'it is long lying, foul weather and jeopardous for storms', although, as he also said on that occasion, the wool might sell very quickly when stocks at Calais were depleted at that season and the spring fleet was not due for another three or four months.[99]

One can readily picture the scene at the customs house and wool quays as the carts trundled along the narrow streets with their loads of wool, while groups of staplers or their servants, anxious to get their sarplers customed, waited their turn at the weighing-beam and fumed as the tellers laboriously counted over their fells, and as the shouts of porters almost drowned the voice of the weigher as he called out the weights of each bale. Then the porters would struggle down to the waterside with their burdens, and the ships' masters assert their authority over the lading of their vessels, while apprentices wrote down the number and weight of each sarpler in each ship and made a note of the exact position of the fells:

In the *Thomas of New Hythe*...one pack half a hundred [and] fourteen fells and a little fardel of fells that is allowed for three fells with the customer, and the said fells lieth next be aft the mast, lowest under the fells of Thomas Betson, and the little fardel lieth just ['next'] to the mast upperest of my master's fells.[100]

No doubt these moments of bustle were interspersed with numbing periods of inaction in the way so familiar to any traveller. The wool-fleet left with unaccustomed speed in the summer of 1480, when the cockets (customs certificates) were made on 31 May and the ships left on 2 June.[101] At the autumn shipping, by contrast, the wool was apparently all customed by 14 September but bad weather meant that the ships did not leave until a month later, on 13 October.[102]

The staplers usually divided their wool among the ships of the fleet, placing an average of two sarplers in each vessel, which might typically carry consignments for anywhere between one and fifteen merchants.[103]

---

[99] *C.L.* 109.
[100] *C.L.* 132, Oct. 1481.
[101] *C.L.* 90.
[102] *C.L.* 104, 106, 109.
[103] E.122 73/40. Exceptionally, John Tame entrusted an end-of-season shipment of 7 sarplers 1 poke to the *James of London* in Aug. 1488: E.122 78/5 fo. 26v.

There are no specific details in the Cely papers about how the fleets were organized, how the ships were collected, the times arranged, and so on. But the Staple had officials, called 'pointers', who were entrusted with this task, and the merchants paid an imposition on their shipments which went towards the general expenses. Freight charges were paid to the ships' masters in person.[104] The Ordinances of the Staple give some details from 1565, when there were only two general shippings, the first beginning on or after 20 March and the second on or after 15 July.

Yearly, the first day of March or the first day of June, or at such time as the shipping shall begin, shall be assigned by the said company at every port where the Staple merchandise shall be shipped, four, three or two persons free of the company, which shall provide and appoint sufficient number of ships and bottoms meet for the sure and safe convoy of the wools and wool fells to be shipped...and shall by all means search and try whether the same ships and bottoms be tight or no, and well ballasted, and shall take order for shipping the goods of every brother. Without the ships to be poisered above the hatches, or any goods laden before the mast, except it shall seem otherwise good to the pointers to be otherwise ordered to their discretions....And [they] shall levy by impositions upon every sarpler of wools and wool fells equally taxed all such charges as shall be expended during the shipping time.[105]

Shipments to Calais at the Celys' time took place not only from London but also from Boston, Hull, Ipswich and Sandwich. One fragmentary Cely account, perhaps of 1475 or 1476, refers to shipments from Ipswich,[106] but the rest of their surviving accounts concern exports from London. Because so many of the ships bore names like the *Mary of Malling*, the *Mary of Brekellyssay* [Brightlingsea], *Thomas of Rainham*, or *Trinity of Milton*, H. E. Malden, the first editor of a selection from the Cely papers, assumed that the wool was shipped from the tiny harbours of Essex and the Medway region, and drew an appealing but incorrect picture of pack-horses trotting with their loads of wool along the old Pilgrims' Way.[107] In fact, as has been shown, the sarplers travelled by cart, and the ships crowded in at the old and new wool quays at the Thames-side heart of London. There were 41 ships in the large fleet of July 1478, carrying in all 1,160¾ sacks of fleece-wool by customs estimate and 268,227 fells. The smaller fleet of May 1479 consisted of 14 vessels.[108] The 'woollers', which Elizabeth Stonor refers to generically as 'hoys',[109] were a miscellaneous collection. After they had bought a

---

[104] E.g. File 11 fos. 22–7: 'Item, paid the 4th day of August [1478] unto James Hollond, master in the *Blythe of London*, for the freight of 2 sarplers, le sarpler 6s 8d. Sum – 13s 4d. Primage – 2d', etc.

[105] *Ordinance Book*, pp. 144–5.

[106] File 15 fo. 40.

[107] *Cely Papers*, pp. xxxvi–xxxviii.

[108] Power, *Studies in English Trade*, p. 42.

[109] *Stonor L.*, no. 204.

Breton ship of their own, Richard and George sent her to Calais with their fells in April 1486. She carried 3,400 fells besides chests and other goods.[110] In November 1481, 4,298 fells of Richard and George and William Maryon made up the total carried by the *Mary of Rainham*.[111] Some ships must have been much larger than this, while others which made the channel crossing were mere 'crayers', like the small vessel which carried George's 'chambering' (chamber-hangings) to England and returned to Calais with wool in the autumn of 1482.[112] The names of some of the ships which made up a wool-fleet show that, like the *Margaret Cely*, they were owned by merchants of standing: for example the *Christopher Fynkell*, the *Jelyan Chamber* or *Christopher Grene*. A few vessels were owner-operated, but these may have been exceptional.

The wool-fleet included an armed escort for protection against pirates, and in April 1486 the *Margaret Cely* undertook this duty of 'wafting' and carried 28 soldiers, who were paid 6s 8d each. The costs of the military escort were met from the 'conduct money' paid by the shippers at sums which varied, at different periods, from 10d Flem. to 3s 4d Flem. per sarpler. It appears from George's account of money paid the Staple in 1478 that this charge was deductible from the custom and subsidy dues.[113]

Soldiers were no protection against storms in the unpredictable English channel and ships might easily become separated from the convoy. In November 1481 George reported that seven ships had not yet arrived, and two of them were 'spent' (crippled by the loss of masts and tackle); 'I trust to God', replied his brother on the 28th, 'that the *Christopher of Rainham* be come to Calais by this.'[114] The next autumn three ships were behind. Two were still in Sandwich haven. The third had reached Ostend, but her master had thrown all the wool overboard.[115] There was further anxiety at Calais in early December 1483. By 5 December the Boston fleet had arrived safely, except for the *Battle*, 'which is yet behind, and she hath in an hundred sarplers wool and fell, and they hear nothing of her here yet: I pray God send her well hither'.[116] In April 1470, however, it was deliberate action on the part of a ship's master that gave the Earl of Warwick eight sarplers belonging to Richard Cely senior.[117]

Even when the ships reached Calais haven in safety (when, remarked

[110] See Ch. 14 pp. 367–8 and File 21 fos. 7, 9v.
[111] *C.L.* 133.
[112] *C.L.* 198. In the fleet of July 1478 the *Christopher of Bradwell* carried 22½ sack-weights, while the *Jesus of London* carried 90, and had a capacity of at least 103.
[113] File 11 fo. 21. [114] *C.L.* 137.
[115] *C.L.* 198. [116] *C.L.* 204.
[117] P.R.O. C.1 79/69; Ch. 13 p. 343.

George, 'the venture is borne', i.e. the risks at an end),[118] their cargoes might have suffered. At the least, coverings could be torn as the sarplers were hoisted out of the ships by crane: William reported thankfully that the wool which reached Calais in August 1482 'is dry and none hurt with none burning, save four or five sarplers be rent with hising ['hoisting'] out of the ship',[119] and by 23 August he could say that all the wool was housed dry, and 'ye have none that is sore broken'.[120] Wet wool had to be washed free of salt and laid out to dry again. A number of sarplers were drenched with sea-water in 1483, so that some of William Maryon's wool was 'shot out' (rejected), even after repacking.[121] Repacking a sarpler in 1478 cost 16d Flem.[122]

On arrival at Calais the ships were unloaded speedily, though Thomas Henham must have acted with special efficiency to get 51 sarplers unloaded and housed between the arrival of the fleet on 11 April 1476 and Easter Saturday (13 April).[123] Each stapler's consignment was registered by the Staple collectors, who levied an imposition of 1d in the £ on sales value. The wool had also to be 'awarded' or certified as correctly described. In August 1478 Richard junior, left in charge at Calais while George attended the mart, paid 3s 4d Flem. 'for warding 48 cloths ['sarplers'] wool'.[124] He also paid 7s 11d to the headman of the carters for transporting them. Sometimes the awarding was done on a sample chosen by the lieutenant of the Staple from each man's sort. The chosen sarpler was said to be 'cast out' for the purpose, and in the Cely collection there is a narrow strip of paper with the memorandum 'Item, of the 20 sarplers was No. 17 cast out. Of 17 sarplers was [No.] 37 cast out.'[125] Sometimes the awarding was done by the Calais wool-packers. In August 1481 'your wool is anwarded for good Cots. by William Bretten and Harry John. There was none sarpler cast out, but seen in the show [to buyers].'[126] The packers, however, were not always above suspicion, and their collusion might frustrate efforts to prevent fraud by the merchants, as occurred when the lieutenant happened to pick that inferior specimen of wool supplied by Jenkin Taylor in 1487. William Cely reported:

Sir, I cannot have your wool yet awarded, for I have do cast out a sarpler the which is pointed by the lieutenant to be casten out to ward the sort by, as the ordinance is now made that the lieutenant shall point the warding sarplers of every man's wool. The which sarpler that I have casten out is No. 24, and therein

---

[118] *C.L.* 22.   [119] *C.L.* 184.
[120] *C.L.* 186.   [121] *C.L.* 205.
[122] File 11 fo. 28v.   [123] *Stonor L.*, no. 163.
[124] File 11 fo. 28v.   [125] File 16 fo. 4.
[126] *C.L.* 124.

is found by William Smith, packer, a 60 middle fleeces, and it is a very gruff wool. And so I have caused William Smith privily to cast out another sarpler, No. 8, and packed up the wool of the first sarpler in the sarpler of No. 8 ... and therefore I must understand how many be of that sort and the number[s] of them, for they must be packed again. It is a very red leyr ['colour'], and great fleeces.[127]

Such privy dealing was not only very dishonest, but extraordinarily inconvenient for the historian who attempts to trace the movements of the Celys' numbered sarplers.

Besides such occasional switches of content, once they had reached Calais all sarplers of wool underwent an invisible alteration. In England they had weighed so many sack-weights of 52 cloves (or nails); now their weight was calculated by the Calais sack of 90 cloves, reckoned as the equivalent of half an English clove, so that the Calais sack-weight weighed only 45 English cloves, or 315 lb avdp. as against 364 lb avdp. in England. Richard Hill's commonplace book, for example, notes

This is the weight of the nail wool at Calais, and how many nail goeth to the sack.

In primis, 14 ounce maketh a pound, and 4 lb maketh a nail, and 90 nail maketh a sack of Calais weight.

And so the sack of England is more than the sack at Calais by 7 English nails, the which is 14 Calais nails. And so 2 Calais nails maketh but 1 English nails.[128]

The inhabitants of Calais had opted to keep their old customs when the town became English territory in the fourteenth century. Most places held tenaciously to their local weights: the sack-weights of Bruges and Antwerp differed again, both from Calais weight (which coincided, however, with that of St Omer), and from each other, but this did not concern the English staplers of the Celys' time.

The difference in weights between England and Calais certainly gave the staplers an advantage which more than compensated for the normal losses through the drying-out of their wool. Some of the Staple's customers purported to see in the discrepancy between English and Calais weights an example of English unscrupulous trading practice: in 1545 there was a complaint that

the staplers of Calais get their wool in England at small cost and by great weights. At Calais the said staplers reverse the situation, and contrary-wise resell their wool to the merchants of these parts at a great price and by small weights.[129]

The practice that caused more objection, however, was the Staple regulation that one sarpler of old wool must be bought with every three

---

[127] *C.L.* 234.   [128] Balliol MS. 354, fo. 183.
[129] Schanz, *Englische Handelspolitik*, I, no. 48, my translation.

sarplers of new. This system of selling 'free out', otherwise 'the benefit of old wools' or 'the preference of old wools', which the customers called 'a custom, or rather corruption',[130] was of long standing, and was enforced still more rigidly in the restrictive ordinances of the dwindled company in 1565.

The system occasioned much debate during the course of the negotiations leading to the commercial treaty of 1478. It was alleged at one point that the benefit meant not only that the buyers were forced to take a proportion of old wool in their purchases but that they were also charged higher prices for the old and had to pay cash in hand ('pecunia prompta et numerata').[131] This may have been so at some earlier period, but the Staple's denials were true in 1476.[132] The discussion does not seem to have attacked the root problem of slow turnover at Calais, or to have touched on the means of encouraging a more even flow of supplies or of inducing the customers to buy older stock more readily. Instead, the delegates fell into an academic argument more notable for ingenuity than logic or relevance.[133] The Burgundians said that it was all very well to compel the purchaser of spices to take old stock along with new, because of the exigencies of supply from a distance, but that wool was a native commodity in England, so that the English could choose what they would buy, and so should their customers at Calais. The English responded that wool was entirely different from spice. Spice manifestly kept a long time, so that (they said) stale spice was often sold mixed with fresh and few people noticed the difference. It was, however, the natural propensity of wool to decay, and therefore it was only right to use human endeavour to ensure that when two qualities, both perfectly good, had to be offered for sale at the same time the customers could not take all the new stock and leave the old, which would then deteriorate to the point where it had to be sold unreasonably cheaply.

The technical distinction between 'old' and 'new' wool was so well understood by the staplers that it is very difficult to discover exactly what was meant by 'old wool'. Evidently the term implied more than 'wool shorn in the previous season', because the definition could be changed at need. In 1476, when large stocks had built up at Calais, the system was put into partial suspension, so that the only 'old' wool and fells were those already in Calais unsold, and for the next two years this older stock would be given preference over all later shipments. It was decreed that

---

[130] *Foedera*, v (3), 90.   [131] Ibid., 92.

[132] But on occasion old wool might be sold on different terms from new. In April or May 1478 (*C.L.* 22), old wool was offered for payment half in hand, half at Whitsun, whereas new enjoyed the much better terms of one-third cash down and the other two-thirds in six and twelve months.

[133] *Foedera*, v (3), 90–1.

only those wools which were taken to Calais in or before February last past, and remained unsold by 6 April last, should be termed and reputed 'old wools'. Any brought to Calais since the said February, or which shall be brought between then and 6 April 1478, shall never be considered old wool ['semper reputabuntur lanae non veteres'], and the same with fells, so that none of these [later shipments] shall in any wise have preferment in the show for sale, or attract any of the privileges or benefits conferred by the customs, rules or ordinances hitherto in effect in the Staple, over or with the afore-designated 'old wools' or 'old' fells. However, even those wools or fells which became old (according to this ordinance) on 6 April last, shall have no privilege or benefit or advantage over new wools, saving only that they are to be preferred in sale according to this ratio, namely one sarpler of old (according to this definition) to three of new wool, and the same ratio is to be kept for any fells which can be designated 'old'.[134]

The delegates for the other side said vainly that if they must comply with such unreasonable rules they would prefer the ratio of one sarpler of old wool to every five of new.[135] The English did agree, however, that even after April 1478 no old wool would have preference except as it competed on the market with new ['concurrat in venditione'].

Unhappily, none of this explains the normal criterion for 'old' wools as distinct from 'new'. Were they those shipped before February in any one year? Those unsold by 6 April?

Another answer to the question of what constituted 'new' and 'old' is suggested by a letter from George in November 1480.[136] There had been 'great ado' at Calais and the wool laded at London by 25 September but not shipped until 13 October was considered by some people to be 'but new wool' 'because the dockets bare not date of the 14 day of September'. George added that 'there is direction taken that it shall neither be new nor old, but it shall have that licence that it shall pass without old wool, upon itself', that is, it would not require old wool to 'free it out'. The implication here would seem to be that the new year's rate started in October, or perhaps more exactly with the custom's year at Michaelmas, 29 September. Alternatively, the new rate may have been put into operation at the beginning of the exchequer year on 6 April, so that any remaining stocks of wool shipped before the previous October became 'old' at that date. In any case, it is not correct to say that at the Celys' time new wool was that of the spring shipment only.[137] This was so in 1565, when only two annual shipments were contemplated and when stringent precautions were taken against the shipment of any 'new' wools at the June shipping. The 'new' wool of the March shipment would, of course, have been shorn some nine months before, as George's

[134] Ibid., 91.   [135] Ibid., 92.
[136] *C.L.* 109.   [137] *Ordinance Book*, p. 164n.

set of accounts for buying and shipping Midwinter's wool in 1487 makes plain.[138]

The Celys' customers are not themselves on record as protesting against the requirement to take a proportion of old wool with their new. The rule may not have been enforced when there was no great imbalance at Calais. But in 1477 John Van Der Heyden duly ordered three new sarplers and one old,[139] and in April 1482 William Cely said, 'as for wool, I can sell here none without I had old wool, for [the Hollanders] can have no old wool but where they buy new wool'.[140] In other words, they were restricted to dealing with staplers who could supply both. The next month the staplers in Calais were ordered to give in an inventory of all their stocks, specifying how much was new and how much old.[141] In January 1484 William Kennett bought two sarplers from the Celys and wanted more, 'as much as he can get old wool for'.[142] Presumably he was going to free out the Cely wool with old wool from another stapler.

If wool changed its reputed age in an illogical fashion, and underwent a striking alteration in its official weight, money was equally affected by the rarified atmosphere of Calais. The employment of special tariffs and exchange rates will be discussed in Chapter 7. Suffice it to say here that the price of wool to the customer (see Table 2, p. 146) was invariably expressed in marks sterling per Calais sack-weight (fells being priced in nobles stg. per 100), but the total price of the purchase was then converted into its equivalent in Flemish pounds at an exchange rate dictated by the Staple. The result was, in effect, to produce a money of account described during negotiations for the Treaty of Intercourse of 1478 as 'librae quibus emuntur lanae': 'the pounds by which wools are bought', or 'wool-pounds'.[143]

Sometimes the Staple tried to insist that all sales should be made for cash down. More usually, at this period, the terms of payment were negotiable. Indeed, it was stated in 1478 that 'the method of payment is not laid down, but is such as the seller and buyer can agree together'.[144] At that date the system in common use was for the third penny to be paid in cash at Calais for end wool, £7 or £8 stg. (or its equivalent) for every sarpler of clift wool, and at least £1 stg. (or its equivalent) in hand for every hundred fells.[145] When, in 1482, the Staple tried to demand the whole payment in cash at sale it still made an exception for the favoured merchants of Delft and Leiden.[146] Often it was difficult enough

[138] Above, pp. 120–1. [139] *C.L.* 14. [140] *C.L.* 156.
[141] *C.L.* 170. [142] *C.L.* 206. [143] *Foedera*, V (3), 92.
[144] Ibid.
[145] Power, *Studies in English Trade*, p. 68; Posthumus, *Bronnen*, I, 615.
[146] *C.L.* 189.

to get the buyers to produce even so much as one-third at the time of sale, since they were very reluctant to carry gold with them in a period of unrest. William Cely explained in February 1484:

Sir, as for the £73 10s stg. which I should 'a received in hand, I have received thereof but £20 10s stg. in 'neming' groats and crowns, and the rest is £53 stg., which I lent them by a bill of their hand to pay at Passe [Easter], for they brought but little money hither with them because of troubling by the way with soldiers of Maximilianus. But the men are sure enough: they have bought here above 16,000 fells at this time.[147]

'"Lent" the buyers so much of their first instalment until the next mart' is a common entry in the records of sales.

Analysis of the Celys' sales where terms are stated (other than those to John De Lopez for payment in England), shows that in 45.8 percent there was a cash-down payment at Calais varying between half and the whole of the total price. In another 41.7 percent there was a down payment of one-third or less. Typically, but by no means always, this was accompanied by a bill of hand payable at the next mart for the balance of the first half of the total, and two obligations payable at later marts for the remaining half. In a further 12.5 percent of examples, credit was extended for the entire debt.

It might be supposed that when instalments of the purchase price were deferred for up to eighteen months, and occasionally still longer, these deferred payments would carry an interest charge. Older historians did suppose this, and asserted that the rate of exchange in credit sales was adjusted to allow for concealed interest.[148] But the supposition is erroneous. In the vast majority of cases the credit payments were made at the same rate of exchange as the initial down-payment. In some instances, certainly, a different rate of exchange, and one seemingly more favourable to the purchaser, is quoted for the deferred instalments. For example, in October 1478 some wool was sold at a total price of £1,120 8s 9d stg.[149] One-third was to be paid in hand at the prevailing Calais rate of 25s 4d Flem. per £ stg., and the remaining two-thirds were payable at a rate of 24s Flem. on 20 April and 20 October 1479. But this was an unusual arrangement, made in the expectation of the calling-down of Flemish money. In July Thomas Howlake had sold wool for Stonor and Betson on similar terms. He then expected that very shortly 'the Flemish golds shall be set down and have course like as they had in the

[147] *C.L.* 209.
[148] E.g. Power, *Studies in English Trade*, p. 65. See Alison Hanham, 'Foreign Exchange and the English Wool Merchant in the Late 15th Century', *B.I.H.R.*, XLVI (1973), 165–6.   [149] File 11 fo. 31r–v.

Sinxen mart a year [ago]'.[150] It is quite wrong to deduce from these examples that the staplers engaged in the usurious practice of 'selling time'. All that they were doing was to adjust the terms of future payments which they expected to be made in a currency that had strengthened against the £ stg. As it happened, the currency reform of 1478 was unsuccessful, and the instalments paid in 1479 had therefore been calculated at a rate of exchange which meant a loss to the staplers.

A selection of bills of sale from the Cely papers will illustrate variations in exchange rates for the Calais 'wool-pound' and the terms of credit which might be allowed.[151]

Jesu 1473 [1474 new style]

Item, the 24 day of January sold by me, Thomas Kesten, for and in the name of my...master to Peter Wan De Ratthe of Bruges, 3 sarplers fine Cots. poising ['weighing'] 8 sack 34 cl[oves], price le sack 19 mark. Argent – £106 2s 4d stg., the which to be received at 23s Flem. for the £ stg.

Sum . . . . £122 7d Flem.
Item, sold to the same 1 sarpler of middle of the same, poise ss. 61 cl., price le sack 13 mark. Argent – £23 4s 1⅔d stg. The which to be received at 22s 8d. Flem. for the £ stg.
The which amounts . . . . £26 6s Flem.
Sum total de both . . . . £148 6s 7d Flem.
Whereof by covenant is to be received at this Candlemas [2 February] the third penny . . . . £49 8s 10½d Flem.
Item, there is lent him to pay at 8 months another payment, the last day of September next . . . . £49 8s 10½d Flem.
Item, there is lent him to pay at 8 months after that the 3rd payment, that is the last day of May anno '75 . . . . . . £49 8s 10d Flem.

[8 August 1475]

Item, I, the said Thomas Kesten, have sold for and in the name of my said master to Barbell, the widow of Gerede Benowth, and Aleamus De Bollonye, 4 sarplers of good Cots., price le sack 19 mark, poising 10 sack 36 cl. Argent – £131 14s 7d stg. The which amounts as 22s 8d Flem. the £ stg. . £149 5s 11d Flem.
Of the which, received in hand £8 of the sarpler, the which amounts . £32.
Item, lent to the said to be [paid] the 3 day of May anno '76 the half rest, amounting £58 12s 11½d Flem.
Item, lent to the same to be paid the 3 day of February anno '76 [i.e. 1477 n.s.], the sum of £58 12s 11½d Flem.

Jesu 1475

Item, the 24 day of October sold by me George Cely for and in the name of my father Richard Cely un[to] John Vandyrhay [Van Der Heyden], merchant of Mechelen, 8 sarplers wool. Two fine Cotswold, price le sack 19 mark, 21s 4d

---

[150] *Stonor L.*, no. 223.   [151] File 11 fos. 15–17.

Flem. for my £ stg. Item, sold unto the said merchant 4 sarplers middle Cots., price le sack 13 mark, and 21*s* 4*d* for my £ stg. Item, sold unto the said merchant 2 sarplers middle young Cots., price le sack 10 mark, 21*s* 4*d* Flem. for my £ stg. The number and poise hereafter appeareth, etc.

Fine Cots.

No. 9 – ss di[midium] 32 cl.
No. 1 – ss di. 33 cl.
Argent . . . .
Item, it amounts in Flem. after 21*s* 4*d* for my £ stg.

Sum in sacks:
5½ sack 20 cl.
. £72 9*s* 8*d* stg.
£77 6*s* 4*d* Flem.

Middle Cots., 13 mark.

No. 30 – ss 55 cl.
No. 27 – ss 60 cl.
No. 44 – ss di. 32 cl.
No. 16 – ss di. 33 cl.
Argent . . . .
Item, it amounts in Flem. after 21*s* 4*d* for le £ stg. .

Sum – 11 sack.

. £95 6*s* 8*d* stg.
. £101 13*s* 10*d* Flem.

Middle young Cots., 10 mark.

No. 45 – ss di. 32 cl.
No. 46 – ss 21 cl.
Argent . . . .
Item, it amounts after 21*s* 4*d* for le £ stg.
Sum total in Flem. . . . .

Sum – 5 sack 8 cl.
. £33 18*s* 6*d* stg.
£36 3*s* 10*d* Flem.
. . . £215 4*s*.

Item, the 3rd penny received in hand and the remainder at Sinxen anno '76 and at Bammis next after . . . . £71 14*s* 8*d*.

Item, lent unto the said merchant by his oblige till Sinxen '76 . . . . £71 14*s* 8*d* Flem.

Item, lent unto the said John Vandyrhay the rest to pay at Bammis '76 . . . . £71 14*s* 8*d* Flem.

The difference between the exchange rate of 22*s* 8*d* in the first 1475 sale and 21*s* 4*d* in the other clearly does not reflect the difference in length of credit, since the widow Benowth (alias Berneught) paid the higher rate for only six months credit, and Van Der Heyden obtained twelve months credit and a lower exchange rate. Moreover, in January 1474 Kesten sold fine Cots. to Peter 'Wan De Ratthe' of Bruges at 23*s* Flem. per £ stg. and middle at 22*s* 8*d* Flem., final payment for both sales due 16 months later.

More rarely, an account reveals some of the petty costs that might be involved. In some years expenses were increased by 'losses' on Flemish coin which was tariffed at Calais at a lower rate. This was notably so in 1478, when Stonor's factor looked for the time 'that the merchants might come to Calais with the money to be paid without loss'.[152] Early in 1478 John Dalton made a sale on behalf of Richard Cely senior:

[152] *Stonor L.*, no. 223.

Vendez the 14 day of March, 1 sarpler good Cotswold at 19 mark to Daniel Van The Rayde, old wool.

No. 32 . . . . 1 sack di. 18 cl.
Argent . . . . . . £21 10s 8d stg. – £25 16s 9d gr[oot].
Paid to William Marchall, treasurer, as may appear by a bill to the same, 11 crowns at 4s 10gr. wherein is lost in every piece 6d . . . . 58s [8gr.]

Item, for turning of your wool, 12gr. Lost 1½d.
Sum . . . . 13½gr.
Item, costs done in seeking of the sarpler wool which Daniel had . . . . 8gr.
Item, for bringing to the weigh-house of the same . . . . . 2gr.
Item, to the broker – 12gr. Item, a fordel – 2gr.
Item, given Daniel again – 10gr. Item, spent upon the bargain making – 4gr. Sum . . . . 2s 6gr.
Wherein is lost 4gr. . . . . 2s 10gr.
Sum . . . . £3 2s 7½gr.
[Net] · . . . . £22 14s 2gr.[153]

A 'fordel' (from the Flemish word meaning 'advantage'?) may have been a small bonus payment.

Somewhere about the following October George Cely drew up this account:

Item, paid by me into the Place for the imposition of the penny of the £ of the sale of 31 sarpler good Cots. sold unto John De [Lopez?], Cornelis Van Dorne and their fellows, amounting 88 sack 41 cl. Argent – £1,031. The imposition amounts – £4 5s 11d Flem.

The loss on this amounted to 10s 9d, so that George calculated the real total at £4 16s 8d Flem. He continued:

Item, paid by me unto Robert Knyght for the brocage of the same, 12d of le sarpler – 31s. [Loss 3s 10½d]. Item, paid by me unto the porters for the duty of the same – 5s 2d. Item, for 22 overweights – 4d the overweight, that is 7s 4d. Sum – 12s 6d. [Loss 18¾d]. Item, there were 3 cloths that weighed too heavy, wherefore I paid unto the king's clerks 4d of an cloth, sum – 12d, and I paid unto the porters to have them from the weigh-house and to the weigh-house again – 12d. Item, to a man to geld them – 6d.
Sum . . . . 2s 6d. [Loss 3¾d].
Item, paid by me for the fordel of the same . . . . . 4d.[154]

Evidently an 'overweight' did not necessarily 'weigh too heavy'. The porters probably made their own terms. A sarpler which exceeded the Staple's maximum weight, however, would incur a fine and require to

---

[153] File 11 fo. 46r–v.   [154] File 16 fo. 20v.

be 'gelded' or have the surplus wool removed. The ordinances of 1565 laid down that the pockets in which wool was shipped by that date must weigh no more than 12 tods (48 cloves or 336 lb) when customed in England.[155] Any pocket which proved, after shipment to the Staple, to weigh more than one sack four cloves (i.e. 47 English cloves or 329 lb) was to forfeit the first clove of the surplus weight or its value at full price, and a further 12d was payable for each clove over that. The stapler himself was forbidden to 'geld or augment any pocket by putting in or taking out any wools, either in the weigh-house or in any other place after the same shall be shipped' on penalty of 20d 'for every pocket so augmented, gelded or diminished'. But the possibility that sarplers might be officially reduced at the point of sale at Calais further bedevils efforts to establish the Celys' exact profits on any transaction.

A large part of the Celys' stocks of fleece-wool would be sold to a few substantial customers, perhaps as many as 31 sarplers at a time, as in the last sale quoted. The rest might find lesser buyers, who typically took between one and six sarplers each. At an earlier period, when the execrated 'partition ordinances' had been in force, proceeds from the sales of each variety of wool at Calais were divided between all the staplers who had exported that particular variety, and commentators all assume that this system disadvantaged the smaller dealer, who would have to wait for his money until his wealthy competitors had disposed of their much larger consignments.[156] This aspect of the situation may have been exaggerated, since the major English exporters probably had established clients among the Flemish clothiers, just as the Celys relied on John De Lopez and his partners for the bulk of their sales. It seems at least as likely that the top men sold a part of their wool quickly, to the benefit of the smaller exporters, as that the lesser men saw their immediate gains disappearing into the pockets of rich staplers whose stocks were hanging fire. It is clear, at any rate, that a first partition would be made before all the year's stock was sold.[157] The system may, however, have discouraged merchants from specializing, as the Celys did, in only one or two varieties. The small dealer, who could not afford to wait long

---

[155] *Ordinance Book*, pp. 146–7.
[156] E.g. Power, *Studies in English Trade*, pp. 85–6. For the system of partition, see T. H. Lloyd, *The English Wool Trade in the Middle Ages* (Cambridge, 1977), Ch. 8. Whatever leading staplers may have felt about partition and the associated 'bullion ordinances' at the time, in May 1549 Anthony Cave was much disturbed about an agreement 'to make a rate and apportion' every man at Calais, which would concentrate trade in the hands of the rich and 'will bring us again to the order of partition'. Cave had a copy of 'the articles of the partition' once used at Calais and claimed that in 14 years (1429–43?) the system had diminished the Staple trade by half and lost the king more than £40,000 in customs dues: 'Johnson Letters', no. 617.
[157] E.g. *Foedera*, V (3), 90.

for his full returns, would have been well advised to diversify into a range of the cheaper wools. Many of these disappeared from the Calais market once the restrictive ordinances had been lifted. Other such varieties appear to have suffered a marked reduction in value when, after partition was abandoned, they met free competition from the better-quality, medium-priced wools like Cotswold, Berkshire and Lindsey.

The other legacy of the partition system, and the objection which may well have lain behind the criticisms of the customers, seems to have been the maintenance of fixed and rigidly observed prices at Calais. Despite some contradictory statements made in the negotiations for the 1478 treaty, it was not until some time in the sixteenth century that price-fixing was partially abandoned again.[158]

Notes of sale in the Cely papers furnish an almost complete range of the selling prices at Calais for the variety of wools in which the Celys dealt, namely the various grades of Cotswold wool, good and middle Kesteven and good and middle North Holland. The exceptions are 'clift' wool, good young Cots. and the Lindsey wool of which they are known to have had a small quantity at one time. A list of wool prices in the 'Discourse of Weights and Merchandise', headed 'these be the prices set at Calais upon wool of diverse countries in England',[159] has been widely assumed to date from the period about 1475. Comparison with prices in the Cely and Stonor papers shows this to be impossible. The mistake arose because the contents of the manuscript were supposed to be homogeneous and it was not recognized that the work is a mere compilation from diverse sources, and one written, moreover, by a less-than-skilful copyist. As matters stand, the date of this schedule must remain very doubtful. One feature which sets it off from late fifteenth-century price-lists is its lack of any distinction between 'good' and 'middle' wools.[160]

The Cely papers demonstrate that Staple prices were increased by one mark sterling per Calais sack-weight in late 1482 or early 1483. This price rise evidently occurred across the board. During the negotiations for a new commercial treaty in 1495–6 the Staple's netherlands customers demanded the removal of this increment, which they described as a

---

[158] William Cely's use of the expression 'at the price of the Place' in *C.L.* 209 and 234 refers to agreements with John De Lopez and need not imply that price-cutting occurred at Calais. By contrast, Andrew Halyburton in the 1490s sold Scottish wool on a free market in Bruges and other centres. He also gave regular rebates to the buyers: Cosmo Innes, ed., *The Ledger of Andrew Halyburton, Conservator of the Privileges of the Scotch Nation in the Netherlands, 1492–1503* (Edinburgh, 1867), passim.

[159] 'Discourse', fos. 106v–107; printed from an inaccurate transcript in A. R. Myers, ed., *English Historical Documents*, IV (1969), no. 590.

[160] 'Cotswold fine' is specified, but not other grades. Its price for Lindsey wool is the one quoted in 1442 in Munro, 'Industrial Protectionism', cited above, Ch. 5, n. 9.

'novelty'.[161] The staplers strongly resisted their claim. But pending an investigation of the matter by representatives of the king and the Archduke Philip, and without prejudice to the outcome, the English eventually conceded in 1497 that of every three sacks sold to a customer, two should be new wool, and these would enjoy the reduction of one mark per sack-weight. The third should be of old wool, and all old wool would keep the customary price.[162] The reduction was to apply to all [new] wool, whether good or middle, the examples given being that wool which customarily sold for 20 marks (i.e. good Cots.) would now cost 19 marks, and that sold for 14 marks (i.e. middle Cots.) would now be sold for 13 marks.[163] In the event a different compromise was reached, and the Treaty of Intercourse finally agreed in April 1499 contained the provision that all wool prices at Calais would be immediately lowered by half a mark, the new rates to remain in force for twelve years or until the death of one or other of the signatory princes, if this (as God forfend) occurred earlier. Provided always that they might be raised temporarily if any great death of sheep occurred in England.[164]

Two extant documents offer versions of the schedule thus introduced. One, headed 'the prices of wools in Calais', occurs in Richard Hill's commonplace book.[165] It is undated, but might have been copied as early as 1503. The inclusion of prices for single cloves of each quality, using the wool merchants' distinctive symbols for fractions of a penny, suggests that Hill's source was a list compiled by a practising stapler. Wools are listed in ascending order of value, from middle Lindsey March at $8\frac{1}{4}$ marks to A. Leominster at $33\frac{1}{2}$ marks.

The second price-schedule was discovered by John Munro in Brussels.[166] Headed 'prijs vander Ingelsche wulle ghemaect ende gheordonneert anno IIII^c XCIX te Calis', this copy was in fact written in 1523. This time the wools are listed in two columns, one for fine grades and the other for middle and refuse wools. The arrangement is basically by descending order of value within each column, but a number of items are out of place. 'Clijt [clift] wool' is twice inserted, without price but following the two grades of fine young Cots. and middle young Cots. I suspect that the first entry was a mistake, and that the original schedule bracketed middle young Cots., refuse Cots. and clift wools together.[167]

[161] *Foedera*, v (4), 113.
[162] Previously the agreed proportion was 3 new to 1 old, with no difference in price.
[163] *Foedera*, v (4), 113. [164] Ibid., 136. The treaty was formally ratified in May 1499.
[165] Balliol MS. 354, fo. 184.
[166] Algemeen Rijksarchief, Rekenkamer no. 1158, fo. 22b; J. H. Munro, 'Wool-Price Schedules and the Qualities of English Wools in the Later Middle Ages, c. 1270–1499', *Textile History*, IX (1978), Table 9 and pp. 154–5. I am grateful to Prof. Munro for generously sending me a copy of his transcript of this schedule.
[167] Although the two kinds were sold separately, clift wool seems to have been classed with

Where there is agreement between these two lists, or where their prices can be compared with a quotation in the Cely papers, it is possible to deduce the prices that had obtained in the two earlier periods, *c.* 1472–82 and 1483–97. But there are a few discrepancies between the two sixteenth-century versions, and neither appears to give a complete range of growths and grades. Hill omits the wools of Surrey and Norfolk, 'clift wool', and the refuse wool of Leominster and the Cotswolds (but includes refuse March). The Flemish version omits good and middle Lindsey March (the last being the cheapest item in Hill's list), and gives an improbable price, of $9\frac{1}{2}$ marks, for refuse Cotswold. The two disagree on the price of middle Leominster, which Hill puts at 22 marks. The Flemish list has instead a (miscopied?) 'Neder Luaster' at $23\frac{1}{2}$ marks. On the price of Kentish wool the two differ irreconcilably. Hill places it with middle young Cots. and refuse Cots. at $10\frac{1}{2}$ marks. The other list prices it at $11\frac{1}{2}$ marks, just above the fine wools of Surrey and Norfolk, which it prices at 11 marks, although the price of Surrey wool has been corrected to 11 from $11\frac{1}{2}$ marks.

A third source appears to rank, but does not price, the wools exported to the Staple in 1506.[168] This list was drawn up in answer, once again, to complaints from the buyers, who alleged that the cheaper qualities were no longer being sold under their own names but were mixed with better and more expensive wools. It is remarked that formerly 36 or 38 varieties of wool were available at Calais, but now there are only 10 or 12 qualities and growths (*lanarum conditiones et differentias*). It has therefore been agreed that the merchants will export the wools of 13 areas, under their right designations, making a total of 29 (*recte* 30?) grades. These were to be as follows:

Good wools of 'Lempster', Middle Leominster
Good wools of March, Middle March, 'Pejores' March
Good wools of Cotswold, Middle Cotswold, 'Pejores' Cotswold
Good wools of Berkshire, Middle Berkshire
Good young Cotswold, Middle young Cotswold
Good Lindsey, Middle Lindsey
Good 'Kesten', Middle Kesteven
Good Rutland, Middle Rutland
Good Holland, Middle Holland
Good Low Lindsey, Middle Low Lindsey
Good North Holland [Middle North Holland?]
Good Norfolk, Middle Norfolk

refuse wool: *Studies in English Trade*, pp. 367–8 (n. 60). It was stated, however, in the 1478 negotiations that *lana lavata* bore no fixed price at the Staple: *Foedera*, v (3), 90.
[168] Printed in *Foedera*, v (4), 225.

Good Kent, Middle Kent
Good Lindsey Marsh, Middle Lindsey Marsh

In the main, the ranking here agrees with that in the two schedules previously discussed. The list confirms, incidentally, that 'young' wool was exported only from the Cotswolds, and that the only refuse (and clift?) wools exported – *lanae pejores* – came from the Hereford–Shropshire and Cotswold areas.

Unfortunately, the 1506 list raises some new problems. In the first place, the Celys sold North Holland wool at 12 marks in 1482, which suggests that no distinction was made between it and the 'Holland' wool priced at 12½ marks in 1499. North Holland does not have a separate entry in the two 1499 schedules. Secondly, Low Lindsey is placed well down in the 1506 list, between Kesteven and Holland/Rutland, whereas the other two schedules place it with middle Cotswold, above these two groups. Finally, Lindsey March or Marsh is put below Kent, whereas Hill values it at 1½ marks above. Hill may be right, because it appears that most middle grade wools were reduced by about 32 percent below the equivalent fine grade. If Hill is right in pricing middle Lindsey March at 8¼ marks, this would agree with his price of 12 marks for fine. It seems also that, to judge by the two priced lists, while middle Lindsey March wool was sold, the middle wools of Kent and Norfolk were not of exportable quality in 1499. On the relative ranking of Kent and Norfolk, the 1506 list, by putting Kent lower, supports Hill's value against the higher Flemish estimate. The Flemish schedule stands alone in suggesting that Surrey ('Sudree') wool figured in exports of the time.

In view of various doubts about the Flemish schedule's accuracy, and its late date, Hill's list has been adopted in constructing Table 2, with the proviso that the prices for Kent and fine Lindsey March wool are not certain. The price of Norfolk and Surrey wool is taken from the Flemish schedule. Table 2 gives prices for the complete range of wools reported to be sold at Calais between *c.* 1472 and 1499. Those which have had to be deduced appear in italics. For further explanation of Richard Hill's symbols in the 'price per Calais clove' column, see Chapter 7.[169] No wool-stapler himself, Hill evidently misread the abbreviation 'cl.' ('clove') as 'ob.', which he wrote throughout. It must be remembered that while all prices are expressed in 'sterling', this was the sterling of Calais, which was not always the equivalent of sterling in England.[170]

It has been pointed out that middle wools cost the stapler the same as the equivalent fine growth, and incurred export tax and incidental costs amounting to about £2 8s per English sack-weight. In the case of middle

---

[169] Pp. 166–7.   [170] See Ch. 7 p. 175.

Table 2. *Sale prices of wools at Calais, in Calais sterling*

	1472–82		1483–97		1499–1511		
	marks per sack-weight	pounds per sack-weight	marks per sack-weight	pounds per sack-weight	marks per sack-weight	pounds per sack-weight	per Calais clove[a]
A Leominster	*33*	*22.00*	*34*	*22.66*	33½	22.33	4ˢ 11ᵈ o ø
A March	*25*	*16.66*	*26*	*17.33*	25½	17.00	3ˢ 9ᵈ o
M Leominster	21½	*14.33*	22½	*15.00*	22	14.66	3ˢ 3ᵈ ø
A Cotswold	*19*	*12.66*	*20*	*13.33*	19½	13.00	2ˢ 10ᵈ o o
A Berkshire	*17*	*11.33*	*18*	*12.00*	17½	11.66	2ˢ 7ᵈ ø
M March, Refuse } Leominster	*16*	*10.66*	*17*	*11.33*	16½	11.00	2ˢ 5ᵈ o
A Young Cots.	*15*	*10.00*	*16*	*10.66*	15½	10.33	2ˢ 3ᵈ o ø ø
A Lindsey } M Cotswold	*13*½	*9.00*	*14*½	*9.66*	14	9.33	2ˢ 0 o ø ø
Low Lindsey	13	8.66	14	9.33	13½	9.00	2ˢ
A Kesteven	12½	8.33	13½	9.00	13	8.66	23ᵈ ø
M Berkshire A Holland A Rutland Refuse March	12	8.00	13	8.66	12½	8.33	22ᵈ ø ø
A Lindsey March	11½	7.66	12½	8.33	12	8.00	21ᵈ o
Surrey } Norfolk	—	—	—	—	11	7.33	—
M Young Cots. Refuse Cots. A Kent?	10	6.66	11	7.33	10½	7.00	18ᵈ o o
M Lindsey	9	6.00	10	6.66	9½	6.33	16ᵈ o o o ø
M Kesteven	8½	5.66	9½	6.33	9	6.00	16ᵈ
M Holland } M Rutland	8	5.33	9	6.00	8½	5.66	15ᵈ ø
M Lindsey March	7¾	5.16	8¾	5.83	8¼	5.50	14ᵈ o o

^{a} o = ⅓d, ø = ⅑d.

Lindsey March wool this was the equivalent, at different dates, of between 39.3 percent and 41.8 percent of the price which might be realized at Calais on 52 cloves originally purchased in England, when a loss of weight has been allowed for. It is hardly possible that with such costs any worthwhile profit was obtained on the lowest-priced wools, and it is not surprising that they were not finding their way to the Staple – at least under their own designations – in 1506. Significantly, in 1565 the

Company's ordinance which forbade staplers to sell in England any wool which could be exported to the Staple, made an exception for middle Lindsey and middle Kesteven, along with refuse wools.[171] In fact, middle Kesteven, at £7 13*s* per Calais sack-weight, is the cheapest wool in the list of prices in the *Ordinance Book* of that year.[172] Neither middle Lindsey nor middle Young Cotswold is mentioned.

[171] *Ordinance Book*, p. 151.
[172] Ibid., p. 168: £24 per 'sarpler' of three pockets.

WOOL-FELLS

The part played by fells – the wool-bearing skins – in the wool trade as a whole has been somewhat under-estimated by students. This neglect no doubt reflects the fact that fells formed a relatively small proportion of the total English wool export. But, equally, contemporary documents reveal little about fells by comparison with the amount of information available on fleece-wool. For example, there is no schedule of prices to be put beside those which survive for wool.[1] It has recently been implied that the sale of fells at Calais was concentrated in the hands of a few 'specialists', while the great majority of staplers dealt almost exclusively in fleece-wool.[2] It is true that, as far as the few surviving particular port books go to show, some men had a decided preference for fleece-wool, while a very much smaller number concentrated their trade on fells. Among the latter were several members of the Skinners' Company, notably (in 1488) Roger Grantoft, John Pelet and John Pasmer, a merchant adventurer who had joined the Staple company three years earlier.[3] Thomas Granger, George Cely's host, belongs in this category. But the vast majority of established staplers, like the Celys and later the Johnsons, habitually sold both kinds of ware, and even Granger and William Maryon occasionally added a few sacks of fleece-wool to their consignments of fells. An individual's shipments could vary widely from one shipping to another, and the proportions of fleece-wool and fell shipped to Calais also varied considerably.[4] On average, however, fells

[1] It seems, however, that scales of price formerly existed. In the later sixteenth century staplers said that they observed the rates laid down in 'the Intercourse': *Ordinance Book*, p. 62.

[2] G. D. Ramsay, 'A Saint in the City: Thomas More at Mercers' Hall, London', *English Historical Review*, XCVII (1982), 274–6.

[3] The skinner William Wiking, however, shipped more fleece-wool than fells in 1478.

[4] In the customs years Michaelmas 1485 to Michaelmas 1500, when the mean annual rate was 24.6 percent of staplers' shipments, fells once made up as little as 10 percent of the total, and once as much as 35 percent: figs. taken from Peter Ramsey, 'Overseas Trade in the Reign of Henry VII: the Evidence of Customs Accounts', *Econ. Hist. Rev.*, 2nd ser. VI (1953–4), 181.

formed about 26 percent of staplers' total shipments between 1470 and 1500. Of the shipments made, first by Richard Cely senior alone and then by Richard and George at the period when they dealt in both commodities, fells composed on average 20 percent. (This figure is based on comparison with the gross weight of fleece-wool at shipment. It would be marginally higher if the customed weight were taken.) Fells accounted for about 18 percent of the value of their sales.

Fells were naturally much heavier than shorn wool, so that carting and freight charges were correspondingly higher, and it may seem surprising that they were considered a profitable export. By and large, they also decayed more readily than fleece-wool. Nevertheless, they found a ready sale among netherlands buyers, and the wool from such skins is still well-regarded. Before manufacture into cloth it has to be removed from the skin by a process of dissolving the keratin so that the wool will separate easily. This would have been done by 'sweating', a process in which the skins are hung in a close, warm and humid atmosphere until natural bacterial action has loosened the wool. It can then be plucked out by hand or pushed gently off with a blade.[5] The wool thus obtained is, of course, rather longer than shorn wool, and the denuded skins can be sold for leather (especially to glove-makers) or for manufacture as parchment. The merchants of Leiden were especially good customers for English fells, and Power estimated that they bought about half the total number of fells sold by the Staple in the later fifteenth century.[6] Their rivals from Delft accounted for much of the rest.

The fells bought by the Celys and their associates came into four broad categories: Cotswold fells, 'country' fells (Warwickshire is once mentioned, but the term may have implied a mixture from various areas), summer Londons and winter Londons. Occasionally Cotswold fells were also subdivided into summer and winter. Country fells were inferior to Cotswold: some of the Celys' Cotswolds were once appraised as 'country' but kept the higher price of Cotswolds,[7] and in 1481 Richard junior

---

[5] When bayes began to be made in England it was said that one cloth contained 20 to 25 lb wool 'pulled off from the fells': *Ordinance Book*, p. 68. A seventeenth-century fellmonger's two 'pulling chambers' are mentioned in David Dymond and Alec Betterton, *Lavenham: 700 Years of Textile Making* (Woodbridge, Suffolk, 1982), p. 99.

[6] *Studies in English Trade*, p. 61. Leiden was regularly rendered as 'Leyth' by fifteenth- and sixteenth-century Englishmen, and Deryke Hobynson and Co. who bought fells from Thomas Heritage in 1534 were not Scotsmen from Leith engaged in illicit trade (N. W. Alcock, *Warwickshire Grazier and London Skinner, 1532–1555* (British Academy: Records of Social and Econ. Hist. n.s. IV, Oxford, 1981), pp. 5, 112, 119), but Dutch merchants buying legally at Calais for Calais coin.

[7] *C.L.* 46. 'Country fells' were apparently what the Dutch sources call 'contergary' and 'noerde conterhary': Posthumus, *Bronnen*, II, 102. In 1545 there were complaints about an English practice called 'contergarynge', whereby winter, autumn and summer fells, fine and gruff, long and short, big and small, were sold mixed up together: H. J. Smit,

warned George to keep a pack of Warwickshire fells separate from a Cotswold consignment 'for hurting of the t'other sort'.[8] 'Summer' fells were valued above winter ones, presumably because the quality of the fleece deteriorates late in the season and breaks develop. John Johnson indicates the desirable characteristics in describing some fells bought in 1546: 'although they have no great head of summers, yet they (being well set and large patrons) be good fells'.[9]

There is no specific information in the Cely papers about the purchase of those skins that came from the London butchers, which were evidently bought through a middleman – the fellman or fellmonger. The term 'fellmonger' has caused some minor confusion among economic historians. Properly, it applied to the middleman who bought and sold wool-bearing sheepskins, whether or not these subsequently went for export. They were not skinners or tanners, and presumably played no part in any process of separating the wool from the skin, or in the preparation and sale of leather.[10] They were also distinct from 'woolmen', who had a separate craft organization in London,[11] although country woolmen like William Midwinter often sold fells as well as shorn wool. By no means all fellmongers were merchants of the Staple, but some staplers, like the Celys, held formal membership in the minor London Fellmongers' Company.[12] Many fellmongers, in the occupational sense of the term, lived south of the Thames. In November 1477 Robert Cely was worried about paying 'my fellmen of "Barmessay Strette" [Bermondsey High Street], for they will be needy and call fast on me for money ere March be past'.[13] Possibly the 'Londons' had a particular attraction for merchants like William Maryon who dealt in fells only as a side-line. There was no need to travel out of town to buy them, and there would be minimal carriage costs. Richard and George preferred to handle Cotswold fells, especially after their father's death. Many of these were supplied by William Midwinter. Other consignments, often only a few hundred at a time, came from smaller suppliers whose names are

---

ed., *Bronnen tot de Geschiedenis van den Handel met Engeland, Schotland en Ierland* (The Hague, 1928–42), I (2), no. 755.

[8] *C.L.* 133.

[9] P.R.O. S.P. 46/5 fo. 117.

[10] Skinners, however, dealt in lambskins.

[11] Balliol MS. 354, fo. 107v; *A.C.M.* p. 188.

[12] R. Cely sen., his sons and Robert Eyryk were all 'citizen and fellmonger' in documents, but the wool-packer Henry John was *lanarius*. There can be little doubt that 'Thomas Granger, fellmonger' was the Celys' friend and fellow-stapler and distinct from the tallow-chandler of the same name, now identified as Sir Thomas More's grandfather: Ramsay, 'Saint in the City', p. 274.

[13] *C.L.* 15. A John Wylcok, fellmonger of Southwark in 1480, appears in *C.C.R. 1476–85*, 739.

otherwise unfamiliar: William Spyer of Chipping Campden, Margaret Garnes and Margaret Pynner of Chipping Norton, Richard Coolys of Preston, Glos., and Robert Wolsten.[14] George noted in 1488 a present from one seller: 'Item, Tom Barbar sent my sister[-in-law] an fell and my wife another.'[15]

On the face of it, it may seem a little puzzling that large numbers of good-quality sheepskins came from a great wool-growing area like the Cotswold district. One might suppose that shearing would be preferable to slaughter. But presumably the flocks were regularly culled, producing fells from the rams and older ewes.[16] On occasion they were simply the skins of animals found dead from natural causes. Richard Cely junior remarked in November 1480 that 'there is like to be many fells, for sheep begins to die fast in diverse country [districts]'.[17] After any such disaster the quantity of fells sent to Calais might rise dramatically relative to the sacks of fleece-wool. Skin-wool from diseased sheep might not be of the highest quality, and could indeed be classed as 'morling', which was not of Calais standard. All the same, the Cotswold fells usually sold at Calais at a price midway between that for an equivalent amount of middle mature Cotswold and fine young Cotswold fleece-wool, and if all went well could yield a respectable net profit of about 25 to 27 percent. If disease meant a glut, shortages produced keen competition. There is an entertaining description in the Johnson letters of how eight or ten buyers converged on Oundle in April 1546, so that all the incoming fells were snapped up, at a great price, 'at the town's end' before they could reach the market-place.[18] The following March the foreign buyers were equally anxious to obtain stocks: 'the Hollanders of Haarlem I perceive attend ['await'] the fleet at Calais [and] purpose to prevent ['forestall'] the Leideners. If they can bring their purpose to pass they do wisely, howbeit I think the Leideners be as wily as they'.[19]

Fells made a good introduction to the trade for the beginner, because he had to learn to distinguish the various kinds and qualities by comparing and handling them. Old Richard sent Richard junior to look at fells in the Cotswolds in May 1480 'for his lering', that is, to learn, and commented wryly that George had better send him money at the best rate he could get, 'for I fear me Richard Cely will charge me with fell in Cotswold and ['if'] he like the parcel well'.[20] In 1478 he had given

---

[14] File 10 fo. 12.   [15] File 14 fo. 42.

[16] Archaeologists have deduced from a few middens that sheep might be killed for eating at an advanced age: Colin Platt, *Medieval England: A Social History and Archaeology from the Conquest to AD 1600* (London and Henley, 1978), p. 187. The 'great Martinmas butchery of beasts' may be more modern myth than fact.

[17] *C.L.* 111.   [18] 'Johnson Letters', no. 333.

[19] S.P. 46/5 fo. 125.   [20] *C.L.* 87.

Richard £30 to buy a thousand fells for George and himself, and Richard
told George triumphantly that he had bought 1,200 at £3 per hundred
and sent them to London in three cart-loads at 20s a load, 'there is not
money enough for another load'.[21] Later, in June 1488, Richard listed
other deliveries of fells, with the names of the wainmen and what they
were paid (20s in almost all cases). John Tobe, John Hyll and John
Whellar each brought 3½ hundred odd, and William Tayllar, 'Morresse'
Tayllar, Edward Manros, John Hawckys, William Bawel and John
Barttelott each brought 4 hundred odd.[22]

How does it come about that in 1478 Richard senior specified the
purchase of a thousand fells whereas Richard junior bought 1,200? This
was one of the first things the apprentice had to learn: that fells were sold
in England by the 'long hundred' (or 'great tale') of six-score, not our
familiar hundred of five-score. As Richard Hill noted, 'this is the general
rule of the reckoning of fells in England. In primis, six-score fells goeth
to the C, and 10 dozen maketh an C.'[23] Consequently, when the supplier
counted out 'one thousand' fells at £3 per hundred, he meant £3 for 120
fells, and the seller's 'thousand' by long hundreds made 1,200 fells for
subsequent sale at Calais by the short hundred of five-score. Such
discrepancies in weights and measures were not at all unusual and indeed
lingered in some cases until Napoleon's metric system finally conquered
Britain in the 1970s. Until then, a hundredweight (cwt) of 112 lb or 8
stone was still in use, for instance in the domestic coal trade. In the
fifteenth century, purchase in England by the long hundred was so much
taken for granted that it is not made clear in the Cely accounts which
'hundred' is used in calculating the subsequent petty costs of carriage
by wain and storing, but the Johnson papers in the next century show
that the long hundred was still the unit for these purposes. But for
customs purposes, in calculating freight charges and for selling at Calais,
the modern hundred of five-score was used. Hill duly noted that fells
were customed by the sack, 'that is to wit, 2 C and 40 fells maketh a sack,
after 5 score to the C'.[24]

Before shipment, the fells were counted by the 'teller' of the customs
house. They paid duty at the same rate as fleece-wool, that is £2 per
sack-weight, which was reckoned, as Hill said, as the equivalent of 240
fells. Since fells were not wrapped or weighed there was no rebate
allowed for tare and tret. Elaborate tables existed for calculating the tax
payable on the odd number of fells in a consignment, which had to be

---

[21] *C.L.* 25.
[22] File 15 fo. 56.
[23] Balliol MS. 354, fo. 183.
[24] Ibid., fo. 183v. I was regrettably misled on this point earlier, e.g. *C.L.* p. 297.

done in a cumbersome but relatively accurate manner.[25] To be exact, customs (at 6*s* 8*d* per 240) should be reckoned separately from subsidy (33*s* 4*d* per 240), and connoisseurs of medieval arithmetic may like to know that, for instance, the custom on one fell (0.333*d*) was expressed as 'qr. iij di. qr. of qr.', i.e. one farthing plus three half-quarters ($\frac{3}{8}$) of a farthing, in other words $\frac{3}{32}d$. The subsidy on one fell came to $1d + \frac{1}{2}d + \frac{1}{8}d + \frac{1}{32}d$ ('1*d* ob. di.qr. & di.qr. of a qr.'), and on nine fells it is rendered as '14*d* ob. qr. di.qr. di.qr. of qr.', the equivalent of 14.90625*d*.[26] Such clumsy modes of expression were often necessary in a system in which halves and quarters were the only fractional units in use. Nevertheless, fractions in a total of 240 units costed in shillings and pence were relatively simple to deal with by comparison with the difficulties in costing fleece-wool.

Although calculating the dues and prices was somewhat easier with fells than with fleece-wool, the stapler still had to bear in mind two other conversions. The native merchant did not pay his whole custom and subsidy in London at the time of shipment, indeed would-be merchants were told that 'the custom of wool and the subsidy of wool be all one, except that the custom is paid in hand and the subsidy is paid at days' (i.e. by deferred payment).[27] In fact at the Celys' time the distinction between custom and subsidy seems to be completely blurred, and the proportion of dues that was payable in England, some time after the receipt of the goods at Calais, was often defined as, say, a mark or 10*s* on the sarpler. When dealing with fells the stapler therefore had to have an equivalent for the sarpler of fleece-wool as well as his reckoning of 240 fells to the sack-weight, and 500 was the accepted equivalent for a sarpler – a calculation which must have dated back to a period when sarplers of fleece-wool were smaller. This conversion was apparently used only in calculating a proportion of customs dues and for the 'conduct-money' paid for the escort of the fleet. In calculating freight charges the fells were counted by the 'pack' of 400 fells (roughly equivalent to a cart-load), which paid the same as a sarpler of wool.

George Cely gives these details in a letter to his father, probably of April 1475:

Pleaseth it you to understand I have received, according unto your writing, of William Wylsson, master in the *George of London*, 3,100 fells, the which I have sorted according to your intent. There be of your winter Cots. 1,465 fells, and there be of your summer London 910 fells, and there be of your winter London 725 fells. Sum – 3,100 fells.

[25] Balliol MS. 354, fo. 184; 'Discourse' fos. 104v–105.
[26] The true amount is 15*d*.
[27] 'Discourse', fo. 104.

Item, paid by me unto William Wyllson for freight of the said fells, for every pack 6s 4d [Flem.], whereof were 7 packs 300 fells. Sum total freight – 49s 1d, and for primage [payment for loading and unloading a vessel], of every one pack, 2d, sum – 16d. Sum total – 50s 5d.

Also pleaseth it you to understand that by the 23 day of April next coming we must bear into the Place half your custom in ready money, and of the t'other half I must make an bill payable the last day of June next come, and must make here another bill payable at London the last day of May of the 10s of the sarpler, which shall be sent unto John Tate. Pleaseth it you to understand the custom of your 3,100 fells amounts to £25 [16s] 8d stg., whereof ye must abate to pay at London, of 6 sarplers and 100 fells (every 500 fells is an sarpler, and ye must pay 10s of le sarpler), sum – £3 2s stg.[28]

Nearly all these fells were sold on 24 April 1476 to two groups of Leideners.[29]

The consignment of each merchant in a ship was labelled with his mark and sometimes with a symbol to indicate provenance, for instance 'C' for winter Londons and 'O' for summer fells. The piles were separated from each other by a layer of reed or thin cords or something similar, and the recipient was sent careful descriptions, which might be carried by the ship's master:

By the grace of God ye shall receive of the *Mary Grace of London*, John Lokyngton master, 6 packs fell which lieth next the mast afterward lowest, and next above them lieth 5 packs fell of Thomas Granger. Of the 6 packs fell beth ['are'] 538 cast (small tale) winter fells of London marked with ink – the mark is a C – and certain summer fells – the mark is of them a O – which 6 packs ye must receive and pay the freight.[30]

At the same shipping in October 1481 there were, among other Cely consignments, seven packs of Cotswold fells stowed behind the mast in the *Mary of London*: six 'under holl [hull]', 'and a pack lies uppermost upon Dalton's, behind the mast'.[31] In the *Christopher of Rainham* were 7½ packs aft the mast, and under them '200 fells of Wetherfeld's, William Lynd's man of Northampton, and the partition is made with small cords',[32] and also 'a fardel of pelts, marked with ink my godfather Maryon's mark, and with chalk my master [Richard Cely senior's] mark, and part of them be my master's and part my godfather Maryon's, and my master's be marked with a C [for 'Cely']'. In the *Thomas of Maidstone* were six packs of Cotswolds mixed with summer Londons marked 'O', five 'next before the mast under hatches, no man above them', and one pack in the stern sheet, or, as Richard junior put it, 'behind even next

---

[28] *C.L.* 247.
[30] *C.L.* 128.
[32] *C.L.* 131.

[29] File 11 fo. 17v.
[31] *C.L.* 133.

the mast, in a pile as broad as two fells be long'.[33] In the *Mary Grace* the partition between the Celys' fells and those of Thomas Granger was made with reed.[34] But fells were packed more carelessly in 1486 in the *Mary of Deptford*, 'John Greves or Creusse' master, where Richard and George had 500 fells 'after mast amongst sarplers'.[35]

A merchant often divided his shipment among several ships to minimize the risks of loss, but in August 1488 Richard and George lost their entire joint consignment of 5,250 fells through the alleged negligence of the master and owner of the *Clement of Southwold*, John Goodman.[36] An incidental reference suggests that customs dues were exacted even on 'drowned' fells: 'Sir, and it please your mastership I put an case. [Supposing that] these fells had been drowned by the way or taken with enemies, who should 'a been called upon for custom and subsidy?' asked a stapler when disputing the ownership of a consignment in 1476.[37]

On the arrival of the wool-fleet at Calais the fells were located and claimed by their owner or his factor, unloaded under the supervision of the 'headman of carts', who charged 1d per hundred for his services, and transferred to the storage places arranged. The wise merchant had a boy to follow the carts to prevent loss: 'I have Robert Rover to follow the carts, and he followeth every cart', said William Cely, reporting his progress in landing and housing a consignment in August 1482.[38] The housing was performed under the supervision of the headman of fellbinders, who also charged 1d per hundred. During the season Calais was full of raw wool, and its distinctive musky-sweet smell must have permeated the town. All spare room was used for storage. At Michaelmas 1478 George paid a quarter's rent for 'the wool house in the Duke's Inn, which goeth for 7 nobles by the year', and another sum of 7s for seven weeks' rent of 'the great hall in the Duke's Inn'.[39] These premises belonged to the Duchy of Lancaster. At the same date he housed 880 fells of William Dalton's, paying for two weeks at 8d the week.[40] Space may have been at a premium at the time: in late 1481 John Dalton rented for George 'a house behind Godfrey's' (Godfrey the hackney-man?), paying 4d a week for a total of 15 weeks.[41] At other times George had a fell-house by St Nicholas' church and another 'by Our Lady church'.[42] The Johnsons in the sixteenth century refer to fells at Calais 'at Mistress

[33] *C.L.* 131, 133.   [34] *C.L.* 131.
[35] File 13 fo. 23v.   [36] File 14 fo. 15 and 10 fo. 30.
[37] *C.L.* 7. Once the loss had been formally proved, the owner was allowed to ship the same quantity from the same port without payment of subsidy: *Rot. Parl.* VI, 239.
[38] *C.L.* 184.   [39] File 21 no. 1 (fo. 1v).
[40] File 15 fo. 46. Richard and George rented a fell-chamber from the Trinity Guild for the two years ending 10 Aug. 1480 at 33s 4d p.a.: File 10 fo. 7.
[41] File 12 fo. 17v.   [42] *C.L.* 182, 44, File 12 fo. 5.

Baynam's herring-hang' and at the school-house behind William Stevens.[43] Even the garrets in the dwelling-houses might be stuffed with fell, and there was a fellchamber 'over my Lady Clare', George's French-speaking mistress.[44]

Once the fells were 'forehoused' (a term probably adapted from Flemish), the factor had to count them carefully, inspect them for damage and sort them into categories. 'Sort Cotswold of themself and London summer fell of themself, winter in likewise', instructed Richard senior.[45] In August 1482 William duly reported

As for your fells, I have searched them and told them over, and ye have all your tale, and there is none of them that is hurt with burning. But there is an 200 rent with the landing and the housing, which shall be made as shortly as I can.[46]

William had already given the news that the newly landed fells 'rise reasonable fair yet'. The wool, that is, was acquiring 'loft'. 'They were hot in the ship and began to sweat, but none of them that I have landed that be perished.'[47] Sweating meant, of course, that the hair became detached from the skin prematurely. Burning was also an ever-present hazard, presumably due to 'spontaneous combustion'. Any damaged fells that were not too far gone were 'made' or mended:

Sir, I understand there remain behind which be made and sore brent [burnt], 225 [of my] fells, the which ye will do your best to put away ['dispose of in sale'] with your fells, for the which, sir, I thank you heartily. Also, sir, I understand that I shall lose clear of my brent fells, the which will never be made, sum – 132 fells. Sir, I thank God, as the case requireth, that I lose no more

wrote William Maryon resignedly to George in April 1482.[48] 'Making' involved sewing up tears, probably cutting away spoilt portions, and often patching with pelts bought specially at a cost of 8*d* to 13*d* a dozen, or more in times of exceptional demand. This is one of those practices for which the medieval merchants must have had a good reason, but one no longer clear to us. Possibly the pelt was regarded primarily as backing for the fleece: one of the Johnson letters refers to a shipment of fells, from which 'I daresay there cannot be 40 fells made, for nothing is left of the pelts: only the wool remaineth'.[49] Both men and women were hired to do the work of mending, at 6*d* and 5*d* a day respectively. In early 1482 there were so many fells to be 'made' that the supply of pelts at Calais was exhausted, and staplers were sending to St Omer, Bruges and Sandwich to obtain them. Repairing the Celys' consignment took two

[43] 'Johnson Letters', p. 355.   [44] *C.L.* 105.
[45] *C.L.* 30.   [46] *C.L.* 186.
[47] *C.L.* 184.   [48] *C.L.* 149.
[49] 'Johnson Letters', no. 549.

people eleven and a half days, with some extra assistance, and used 19.7 skeins of thread weighing 1 lb each and costing 5*d* per lb.[50] Tenpence worth of thread sufficed for 400 'broken' fells out of 4,033 in another account.[51] 'Making' was usually reckoned to cost 2*s* or 3*s* per hundred in labour charges. The operation does not seem to have greatly affected the selling price.

In November 1480 over 1,000 fells had to be made out of one Cely consignment of 5,400.[52] Exceptionally, the process was carried out in England in 1483 when, 'because of the trouble upon the sea and here in England', a consignment of 6,780 of the Celys' fells was unloaded again at London, on 26 March, and found to have been damaged by burning in the ships while they waited permission to sail.[53] 'Diverse labourers' had to be paid 32*s* 6*d* for 'bearing, drying and mending' them, and the mending required 3*s* 4*d* worth of pelts and 18*d* worth of packthread. These fells were reshipped early in June, shortly before more 'trouble' erupted in England with Richard III's climb to the throne. They again suffered burning on this second shipment, and William Cely described them as 'sore blemished' when he managed to sell 2,500 of them in March 1484.[54]

The 'ordinance for the fellbinders' in the sixteenth-century Staple ordinances illustrates the duties of these officials:

The fellbinders of this estaple shall house and cause to be housed all and singular the company's fells of the said estaple well and safely at th'arrival of every fleet, and search every man's mark, and tell out to the merchant stranger according to the broker's bill. They shall have and perceive to their uses for their labours as hereafter ensueth.

Imprimis, for sorting of every thousand fells in the ship, 3*d*.

Item, for telling of every 1,000 fells out of the ship, 3*d*.

Item, for housing of every 1,000 fells, 2*s* 1*d*, and so after th'afferant ['pro rata'].

Item, for sorting of every 1,000 fells in the house, 3*d*.

Item, for setting of every thousand fells, 4*d*.

Item, for casting over of every thousand fells, 2*d*.

Item, for piling of every 1,000 fells, 3*d*.

Item, for making of one hundred burnt fells, 4*s* 2*d*.

Item, for serving ['binding'] of 100 rent fells, 2*s* 2*d*.

Item, for telling of every 1,000 fells to the Hollanders or other merchant strangers, 2*d*.

Also, the said fellbinders or any of them shall not remove any fells from one house to another without especial licence of the heads of this estaple for the time being.[55]

---

[50] *C.L.* 140, File 12 fo. 17.

[51] File 16 fo. 2.

[52] *C.L.* 104, 109, File 12 fo. 4.

[53] File 10 fos. 30, 36.

[54] *C.L.* 212.

[55] *Ordinance Book*, pp. 126–7.

It is not clear what 'setting' (at 2*d* per 1,000 at the Celys' time) involved, although it formed a regular chore, especially after fells had been housed or moved. It often goes with 'casting': 'for casting and setting of your 5,659 pells – 20*d*', or with 'telling': 'for setting and telling of your fells afore the commissioners – 8*d*'.[56]

One of the fifteenth-century 'headmen' of fellbinders made out this bill:

Parcels wrought for Master George Cely

First, for searching of 4,033 fells in the lower chamber · · ·	8*d*
Item, for making of 400 broken fells in the same chamber, 2*s* the 100. Sum · · · · · · · · · · · ·	8*s*
Item, for thread to the same · · · · · · · ·	10*d*
Item, for setting of the same · · · · · · · ·	8*d*
Item, for telling of the same · · · · · · · ·	4*d*.

Parcels wrought for Master Cely, above in the garret

First, for making of 105 fells · · · · · · · · ·	2*s*
Item, for thread · · · · · · · · · ·	2*d*
Item, for setting of the same garret · · · · · · ·	6*d*
Item, for removing of 1,100 fells from Duke's Inn to the same house · · · · · · · · · · · ·	16½*d*.[57]

Before sale, fleece-wool had to be 'awarded'. Fells were similarly '[ap]praised' or valued by the official 'praisers' of the Staple, whose services cost 4*d* per thousand fells. In the case of fells, 'praising' meant that a minimum market price was put on each lot, but seller and buyer were free to bargain over the exact price and the seller could hope to realize more than the praiser's estimate. A typical case is a sale to Peter Johnson of Delft, in which Cotswold fells 'praised at 14 nobles [per 100] sold for 14 nobles 5*s*'.[58] But old fells were liable to deterioration: 'the longer that I keep them the worse will the fells be', observed William Maryon.[59] The praisers might then be invited to reassess the value: 'these be all the old fells that I have. It is said that many of them beth refuse. When the praisers hath seen them, as they award it I am pleased. If the price be too much they to set it lower: I will be content because I would have them gone', instructed George in 1480.[60] At another time 500 old fells of William Dalton were inspected by the praisers 'and awarded good for the praisement', so that they kept their original valuation.[61] While awaiting sale the fells had to be 'cast' periodically: either looked over and sorted for damage, or perhaps turned to keep the skins dry. William

[56] File 14 fo. 44.
[58] *C.L.* 44.
[60] *C.L.* 105.
[57] File 16 fo. 2.
[59] *C.L.* 58.
[61] File 15 fo. 46.

Maryon reminded George once that his fells at Calais must be 'scast hoft ynow', i.e. cast often enough, 'for else they will take harm', and when George was away in October 1480 he left the key of his fellchamber so that his servant John Kay could cast the fells.[62]

The arrival of buyers – mainly 'Hollanders' from Delft and Leiden – was eagerly awaited. 'Doing you to wit ['letting you know'] that there be no Hollanders come unto the day that this bill ['letter'] was made, and then there came one cart', wrote George's servant Joyce on 30 January 1482.[63] In May there were many Hollanders at Calais, all from Leiden except for a solitary merchant of Delft, who inspected the Celys' fells, but, said William Cely sorrowfully, 'he looked but lightly on them'.[64] The spurned sellers muttered that illicit bargains had been made in advance: 'we say they wist where to abide or they came at Calais, for they saw not, all the fellowships of them, but three or four men's fells or they were sped'. That is, 'they knew where to go before they reached Calais, for they were all supplied from the stocks of only three or four staplers'. And William added significantly, 'John Dalton hath sold...10,000 fells'.

The valued custom of the fell-buyers from Delft and Leiden could earn them special terms from the Staple, and in 1482 they were allowed to buy on credit when other merchants had to pay the full price cash down.[65] Not that they were always popular with the staplers. Richard junior attempted to do business with Hollanders in September 1478, but 'they be the hardest men that ever I spake with'. 'I was in hand with them for our fells, and set the Cotswold at 14 nobles 20*d* or not ['take it or leave it'], and country at 13 nobles 40*d* or not, and then they would [refuse] a certain [proportion], and I would not, and what they will do I wot not yet.'[66] It seems unlikely that the sale went through, but Richard accounted for the payment of 8*d* 'for setting of fells when the Hollanders had cast them'.[67]

'Casting' in this sense, or the right of the buyer to 'shoot out' or 'refuse a certain' number of fells in a sort, was a bone of contention, and in 1545 merchants were still divided over whether to 'give casting out to men [of] Haarlem'.[68] It had been agreed, however, in 1471 that the Leideners might reject 'gruff' or rotten fells or winter fells misclassed among summer ones, but must accept the unexplained 'bacons', whose peculiarity may have been exceptionally thick or fatty skin. Customers evidently tested their strength: if they tore them they must either retain them or

[62] *C.L.* 58, 92.   [63] *C.L.* 142.
[64] *C.L.* 167.   [65] *C.L.* 189.
[66] *C.L.* 34.   [67] File 11 fo. 37v.
[68] 'Johnson Letters', p. 374.

pay their value.[69] Clays Peterson and William Arndson of Delft 'cast out' 80 refuse fells from a sort of 3,230 in 1484,[70] but if the customers tried to pick over the goods unreasonably the staplers sometimes insisted on arbitration. In February 1479 John Dalton, acting for the Celys, sold 3,971 fells to another company of Delft merchants. The merchants said scornfully that 500 of their fells were 'cony ware' (rabbit ware), not Cotswold fells.[71] Dalton called in John Ekington, John Elderbeck and some other senior staplers to inspect the rejects, which cost him 3s 4d Flem. 'for seeing of a 500 fells, the which the Hollanders had shot out', and a further 12d was 'spent upon [the arbiters] at wine'. The same merchants refused 200 fells of William Maryon's, and in that case at least the Hollanders were apparently forced to accept them after the praisers had adjudicated. The foreign merchants were not slow to point out that in such disputes the English were their own arbiters.

When buyer and seller reached an agreement on number and price, the sale was recorded by the Staple treasurer at Calais and the fells were 'told out' to the buyer by one of the Staple brokers, who were paid 'brogage' of 4d per hundred. Robert Solle, John Whorme and Harry Skepwith are named as brokers in 1479.[72] The seller paid something 'at the bargain making', perhaps 7d or 10d, and, as with fleece-wool, he also paid a 'fordel'. Sometimes it is 'a fordel at table' – perhaps the table of coinage valuations in Staple Hall which had to be consulted when payment was made, but once 'a fordel at table made by the Fellowship' [of the Staple] cost as much as 2s.[73] Dalton's account of his sale in 1479 ran:

Vendez the 4th day of February unto Peter Johnson of Delft and his fellowship, of your father Richard Cely's, 3,971 Cotswold fells praised at 14 nobles, sold for 14½. Upon every 100, 25s 4d Flem. for a pound sterling [down payment].

Sum of sterling money thereof . . . . . . £39 10s stg.
Sum thereof in Flemish money . . . . . . £50 6d Flem.
Rest. . . . . . £152 10s 4d stg. after 24s [Flem. per £ stg.]
Sum thereof in Flemish money . . . . . . £183 5d Flem.
£333 11d Flem.

. . .

Paid to Robert Solle for brogage of
3,971 pells of Richard Cely's the elder, of every 100, 4d.
Sum . . . . 13s 4d.

[69] Posthumus, *Bronnen*, I, p. 489.   [70] *C.L.* 209.
[71] File 15 fos. 2–3. In *Cely Papers*, p. 172, the word is given as 'Conyswaye', which Malden took to be a place-name and identified tentatively with Kingsey, Bucks. This is impossible, both linguistically and geographically.
[72] File 15 fo. 3, File 12 fo. 15v.
[73] File 12 fo. 15v.

Item, for telling out of the same 4*d*. Item, spent at bargain
making, 9*d*. Item, a fordel at table, 4*d*. Lost in the money
after 8*d* on every £1, 5*d*. Sum . . . . . . 15*s* 2*d* Flem.[74]

It appears that sometimes a good customer was given a bonus of a few
extra fells, or else a slight discount. In February 1474 Thomas Kesten
sold for Richard Cely 1,932 winter Cots. fells, 'to the which sale is given
to the hundred one pell and kerke' in addition to the 1,932.[75] And in
February 1482 John Dalton sold for William Maryon 1,266 fells at a total
of £76 16*s* Flem., less 6*s* Flem. 'given of the same for kerke pells'.[76] But
'kerke' is mysterious unless it means a levy for church purposes.

Like fleece-wool, fells might take some time to find a buyer. Out of
5,400 sent to Calais in July 1482, 2,000 were eventually sold in March
or April 1484.[77] But Richard and George had little trouble in selling 1,016
of the fells which Richard had bought with their father's gift of £30 in
1478. On 23 November George wrote to his father 'I have lately made
an sale unto men of Deffe [Delft] of my brother's Richard Cely his Cots.
fells, 1,016 sold at 14 nobles 20*d*', which was 20*d* per hundred above the
praisement.[78] The total price came to £48 5*s* 2*d* stg. Of this, the buyers,
Peter Arndson and Cornelius Williamson, paid 20*s* stg. per hundred in
hand, making £13 6*s* Flem. at the Staple's exchange rate of 25*s* 4*d* Flem.
to the £ stg. The rest, £37 15*s* 2*d* 'two farthings' stg., was to be paid
at 24*s* Flem. in two instalments, at the Easter and Whitsun marts. Total
price in Flemish money of account was £58 12*s* 3*d* Flem.[79] The total cost
to Richard and George could have been £38 8*s* 10*d* stg., made up of
purchase price £25 8*s*, carriage of three loads £3, customs and subsidy
£8 9*s* 4*d*, freight 16*s* 8*d*, and various petty costs amounting to 14*s*. The
last includes 9*s* 10*d* Flem., which need not be reduced to sterling because
the Celys would have lost on the exchange when they presented their
obligations for the delayed payments at the marts. The net profit on the
transaction, by these estimates, comes to 25.5 percent. In general, costs
may be reckoned as adding a minimum of £1 4*s* 5*d* per 100 to purchase
price, allowing for no mending or costs of storage.

It is, however, very difficult to give a general estimate of costs and
profits in the fell trade. In the first place, the Cely papers contain very
few quotations for purchase prices in England, and after 1485 a selling
price at Calais is cited only once. The numbers of fells exported have
often to be taken from summarized shipping lists in the papers, which
do not specify types. There was, however, a range of qualities, selling
prices varied accordingly, and prices at Calais seem to have been

---

[74] File 15 fos. 2v–3.
[75] File 11 fo. 15v.
[76] File 12 fo. 12v.
[77] *C.L.* 214.
[78] *C.L.* 41.
[79] File 11 fo. 31v, File 15 fo. 26.

negotiable to some extent. At times special exchange rates were also in operation for transactions with buyers from Delft and Leiden. Incidental costs also varied more than was the case with fleece-wool. Not all petty costs were calculated according to the number of fells involved, notably in the payment at bargain making, which seems in any case to have varied from time to time. In some, but not all, cases, there might be extra expenses in rehousing, reappraising, or casting and setting after inspection by buyers. Finally, there is not enough specific detail to be able to give any average figure for the number of fells which might have to be 'made' after damage, eventually sold at reduced price, or written off entirely as 'refuse'. Of 780 fells purchased in England in 1487, 10 percent proved unsaleable.

Although average profit cannot be calculated, some prices can be given. In 1478 the buying price for Cotswold fells is quoted as £3 for 120.[80] In both May 1480 and May 1482 the price was still £3 for the bulk of Richard junior's purchases, but William Midwinter was charging £3 3s 4d, possibly because his fells were 'cast', i.e. selected ones.[81] In June 1487 Midwinter delivered 195 fells at £2 3s 4d for 120, and 780 at £4 6s 8d for 120.[82] In June 1488 the price was £4.[83]

Over the period 1476 to 1482, selling prices show a fairly wide range for each category of fells, depending partly, no doubt, on age, condition and demand. Prices quoted for winter Cots. range from 11½ nobles (£3 16s 8d) per 100 to 13 nobles 5s (£4 11s 8d); for unspecified 'Cots.' between 13 nobles 5s and 14½ nobles (£4 16s 8d); for winter London between 13 nobles (£4 6s 8d) and 13½ nobles (£4 10s). Summer Londons are once quoted at 13 nobles (for old fells?), otherwise they range between 16 nobles (£5 6s 8d) and 17½ nobles (£5 16s 8d). The mean figures are:

Winter Cotswold. 12.6 nobles (£4 4s), the equivalent of £8 14s per Calais sack-weight of fleece-wool (on the basis of the conventional 240 fells per English sack-weight), which would approximate to the price of middle Cotswold wool at that date.[84]

Cotswold. 14.2 nobles (£4 14s 8d) or £9 16s per sack-weight, putting it a little below the value of fine young Cotswold wool.

Winter London. 13.3 nobles (£4 9s), or £9 4s per sack-weight, between fine young and middle Cotswold.

Summer London. 15.9 nobles (£5 6s), or £11 per sack-weight: half-a-mark below the value of fine Berkshire wool.

From 1482 onwards, 'Cots.' fells are sold in almost all the surviving Cely accounts. In 1483–4 the selling price is routinely 14 nobles (£4 13s 4d),

---

[80] C.L. 25.   [81] C.L. 91, 165.   [82] File 14 fo. 13v.

[83] File 15 fo. 56v.   [84] For values of fleece-wool, see Table 2, p. 146.

or slightly more than middle Cots. wool then fetched.[85] This had risen to 16 nobles 5s (£5 11s 8d) in one sale recorded in September 1487, which would put the value just below that of fine Berkshire.[86] But in June 1484 Simon Gijsbrechtson of Rotterdam bought 250 'refuse pells of Cotswold' at 10 nobles Flemish the hundred (£2 4s stg. at the current rate of exchange).[87] At £4 12s per sack-weight, these rejects were cheaper than any fleece-wool then sold at Calais.

As some indication of the Celys' share in the total market at Calais, over the season July 1478 to May 1479, 104 individuals or partnerships shipped from London a total of 8,170 'sacks' of wool and fell, by customed weight.[88] Richard Cely senior had 1.7 percent of this total, which is about the average of the family's share of exports from London during the period 1478–88. When the fells belonging to Richard junior and Robert are included, the family's total shipment of 172 sack-weights (2 percent) puts them eleventh in the list of shippers in 1478–9, above the partnership of William Stonor and Thomas Betson, who came fifteenth. The highest amount shipped by an individual in the ten-month period was the 264.8 sacks owned by Robert Fleming, which gave him 3.2 percent of the total at that time.

Over the period 1478–88, the Celys' mean annual export was about 95 'sack-weights' of wool and fell. The size of their shipments fluctuated greatly, however. They apparently sent no stocks to Calais in 1479, and shipments were well down in 1485 and 1488. But they sent large shipments in 1478, 1480 and 1484. In these swings they followed, but exaggerated, the general pattern of staplers' exports from the port of London.

It may be noted that shipments cannot be correlated with purchases in England in any given year. For example, wool shipped by Richard Cely senior in March 1480 was from the 1478 clip, and another shipment of 16 sarplers in May 1481 was of wool shorn in 1479. Between March 1480 and May 1481 the Celys shipped a total of 70 sarplers and 2 pokes of fleece-wool to Calais. The last of this was sold in February 1482, and their next consignment of stock was shipped in July 1482. In the meantime, they had the November 1481 supply of fells to sell. The absence of exports in 1479 meant, similarly, that all income that year derived from their sales of stock shipped in 1478 or earlier. A small shipment did not necessarily mean rapid turnover. Much of the 1485 clip remained unsold at Calais in February 1487, when it was decreed that wool shorn in 1486 should not be put on sale until stocks were cleared.[89]

---

[85] File 10 fo. 31. [86] *C.L.* 234. [87] File 12 fo. 40.
[88] E.122 73/40. [89] *C.L.* 227.

MONETARY MATTERS

The staplers and their customers in the low countries both accounted in terms of pounds, shillings and pence (librae, solidi and denarii), the centuries-old system accommodating two schemes, one based on the unit of a dozen (twelve pence in the shilling), and the other on the unit of twenty (shillings to the pound). The duodecimal unit fitted neatly into its own 'hundred' of six-score, used for certain commodities in Britain, but not into the 'small tale' hundred of five-score, by which other goods were commonly sold, for example fells at Calais or cloth when priced by the hundred ells. The great advantage of the duodecimal unit was that, unlike the score or the hundred of five-score, it was readily divisible by three. Some of this advantage of a duodecimal shilling was lost in England, because its constituent unit, the penny, was divisible in practice only into a half (the halfpenny, in Latin *obolus*, abbreviated *ob.*), and a quarter (the farthing, Latin *quadrans*). The difficulties caused by this were demonstrated in Chapter 6, when calculations of the custom and subsidy due on fells were examined. In the low countries, on the other hand, the penny was subdivided conveniently into 24 mites, or three units of account named in Flemish the *engelsc* or *ingelsche* and in French *esterlin*, 'sterling'.

The awkwardness of the twenty-shilling pound was mitigated by the existence of another ancient unit, the *mark*, which expressed two-thirds of a pound, whether weight or money. In monetary terms the mark therefore represented 13s 4d, half a mark was 6s 8d, a quarter of a mark was one-sixth of a £ or 3s 4d, and one-eighth of a mark 1s 8d. Pounds, shillings and marks were money of account ('imaginary money'), and had no direct counterpart in coin of the period. The silver coins current in England were the groat of fourpence, the half groat, the penny, and its fractions of halfpenny and farthing. The English gold coinage consisted, from 1465, of three varieties of *noble* and various fractions thereof. These were the 'old noble', showing the king standing in a ship and struck from

1412 to 1464, originally with a value of 6s 8d, but revalued in 1464 to
8s 4d sterling; the *rial, royal* or *rose noble*, with a value of 10s (half a £),
and the *angel noble* depicting St Michael, which was first minted in 1465
with a value of 6s 8d. The angel therefore represented half a mark, and
for the English the word *noble* without any specification could indicate
6s 8d in money of account.

When reckoning sums of money, the Celys and their fellows had
recourse to a counting board, wax-covered 'tables', or simply to a scheme
of lines and dots which reproduced the lay-out of a counting board.[1]
Counters were part of a merchant's equipment, and George shipped 'a
pair of tables' when he moved belongings from his Calais lodgings to
England in 1482.[2] With the use of a board, the dual character of the
£ s d system was less cumbrous than it could be in mental arithmetic,
because the board copied the abacus system, units being moved over to
the next column as they added up. The method is used in a problem given
in the treatise 'A Good Informacion of Agryme' copied by Richard Hill:

2d a day, what 365 days?
For every 1d per day lay me [i.e. place counters to represent] a £ and half £, a
groat and a penny. Answer: £2, 2 half-pounds, 2 groats and 2 pence = £3 10d.[3]

Or, it is added, you can reckon the sum 'in agrym', that is by modern
arithmetical methods.

With a counting board, too, the semi-representational character of
roman numerals gave them a positive advantage over arabic numerals.
Thus .iij. is plainly more than .ij., and .iiij^{xx}. immediately indicated 'four
score' for people who thought more in concrete or pictorial terms than
in abstracts. Roman numerals are also less subject to misreading than the
rather formless arabic ones of the fifteenth and sixteenth centuries. In
the early sixteenth century Richard Hill copied parts of a work on
'algorism' and often used its arabic figures in his own notes, but kept
roman numerals where they occurred in other material, and in the 1540s
the Johnsons, too, used both systems haphazardly. The Celys were
presumably acquainted with 'algorism' and its use of the zero, which was
already widely taught in England at their time, but did not themselves
employ it. William Rogers, however, sometimes used arabic symbols in
auditing their accounts for the Chancery arbiters.

The 'second dialogue of accounting by counters' printed in *The
Earliest Arithmetics in English* does not venture into the subject of
fractions: 'as for broken number', says the author, 'I will not trouble

---

[1] See, for example, J. M. Pullan, *The History of the Abacus* (2nd edn, 1970).
[2] File 16 fo. 23.
[3] Balliol MS. 354, fo. 188v.

your wit with it, till you have practised [whole number] so well that you be full perfect'.[4] It was the lack of any modern method of reckoning, or writing, fractions that created the greatest difficulty for merchants. The wool merchant met the problem in particularly acute form when he had to calculate the price of his fleece-wool. Because the Calais sack-weight contained 90 cloves or nails, and an individual sarpler seldom held an exact number of sack-weights, the price of a sarpler could involve fractions of thirds and ninths of a penny sterling. A third might be called 'one part', but there does not seem to have been any symbol for it in ordinary use. The staplers' solution was to adopt the Flemish accounting unit of the *engelsc*, representing $\frac{1}{3}d$. In Flanders the engelsc was the relic of an earlier monetary system which had had a penny modelled on the English sterling penny. The coin itself had long since been replaced by the heavier penny *groot* (French *gros*), worth three times as much. But the engelsc and the system to which it had belonged lingered on as a money of account in Flanders, and indeed at the end of the fifteenth century wool at Bruges was still being priced in 'fictional' marks engelsc or esterlin, which translated into the marks groot or *gros monnaie de Flandre* of the standard system when divided by three.[5] This directly concerns us no more than it concerned the Celys, but is a good example of the conservatism, and localism, of the period. The Bruges 'wool mark' was a special money of account used in buying and selling a specific commodity. The 'wax mark' was another such, which translated into a most awkward equivalent of somewhere around 17.875 Flemish pence.[6] This use of special units of account for specific wares makes it easier to understand the way in which manipulations of the exchange rate at Calais produced a 'wool pound' for sales by the Staple.

The Flemish *engelsc*, then, called by the staplers an 'english', provided the means to express thirds of a penny, and a further device, the *point*, was employed to represent one-third of an *english* ($\frac{1}{9}d$ or $0.111d$). The english was depicted as a small open circle, like a small zero, and the point as a large solid dot or roughly diamond-shaped figure, here represented by ø. Thus a merchant who was faced with calculating the price of a sarpler which weighed two sacks three cloves Calais weight and sold at 12 marks per sack-weight, would first multiply the two sacks by £8. Then, rather than reckoning the price of the three cloves as $\frac{3}{90} \times 8$ (£0.266

[4] Robert Steele, ed., *The Earliest Arithmetics in English* (E.E.T.S. e.s. 118, 1922), p. 63.
[5] *Ledger of Andrew Halyburton*, passim; Alison Hanham, 'A Medieval Scots Merchant's Handbook', *Scottish Hist. Rev.*, L (1971), 115–16.
[6] Ibid., p. 119 and n. 3; see also Michail P. Lesnikov, ed., *Die Handelsbucher des hansischen Kaufmannes Veckinchusen* (Berlin, 1973), pp. 251–2.

or 5.333*s*), he said, in effect, that one clove cost $\frac{1}{90} \times$ 1,920*d* = 21.333*d*, or in his terms, 21*d* and one english. Three cloves therefore cost 63*d* and 3 english, i.e. 64*d* or 5*s* 4*d*, and total price of the sarpler was £16 5*s* 4*d*. There is an example in a sale note by William Cely of 1484:

> Sold...to Simon Gyesbryghtson of Rotterdam...8 cloves middle Kettering wool, price after 9 mark half sterling [£6 6*s* 8*d*] the sack – the nail amounting 16*d* o o ster. Sum argent – 11*s* 3*d* ster.[7]

Most wool merchants must have kept their own ready-reckoning tables to show price per clove according to price per sack-weight. At least three examples of such tables still exist. One, calculated for Bruges wool weights in marks engelsc, is in a Scottish merchant's handbook.[8] Two sets, which calculate both English and Calais cloves in terms of sterling money, are in English compilations. Those in the 'Discourse of Weights and Merchandise' are unusable because the copyist did not observe the difference between english and points.[9] With greater care Richard Hill incorporated similar tables into his commonplace book and when he came to enter a list of the wool prices operative at Calais from 1499 he wrote down price per clove alongside the price per sack-weight (see Table 2, Chapter 5), e.g.

A. Cottes 19 mark d*imidium*   clove 2*s* 10*d* o o
A. Young Cottes 15 mark d*imidium*   clove 2*s* 3*d* ø ø[10]

Corrected, the 'Discourse''s reckonings for its four top prices run:

Sack at												Clove
17 mark	.	.	.	.	.	.	.	.	.	.	.	2*s* 6*d* ø ø
18 mark	.	.	.	.	.	.	.	.	.	.	.	2*s* 8*d*
19 mark	.	.	.	.	.	.	.	.	.	.	.	2*s* 9*d* o o o
20 mark	.	.	.	.	.	.	.	.	.	.	.	2*s* 11*d* o o ø[11]

There was also a general rule:

> Imprimis, ye must take for every 20*s* [in the price per sack-weight] 2*d* 2 english; of every 10*s*, 1*d* 1 english; of every 6*s* 8*d*, o o ø ø; of every 5*s*, o o; of every 3*s* 4*d*, o ø; of every 20*d*, ø ø, and so forth.[12]

Or more succinctly:

> Look how many pounds the sack wool cost, and so many 2*d* and 2 english amounteth the clove or the nail. Also look how many mark the sack wool cost, and so many pence 2 english and 1 point amounteth the clove.[13]

---

[7] File 12 fo. 40. William must mean 'Kesteven' not 'Kettering'.
[8] Ed. Hanham, *Scottish Hist. Rev.*, 1971.   [9] 'Discourse', fo. 106r–v.
[10] Balliol MS. 354, fos. 182v–184.   [11] 'Discourse', fo. 106v.
[12] Balliol MS. 354, fo. 183v.   [13] 'Discourse', fo. 106.

A different set of fractions was required in dealing with the sarpler in England, where the sack-weight was calculated as containing 52 cloves of 7 lb each. ('Man that will be a wool merchant, he must know how and by what manner of weights it is bought and sold', as the 'Discourse' justly warned.)[14] At some unknown date some merchant must have had the bright idea of adapting the english of Calais and Flanders to represent the denominator needed for prices in England – the relevant fraction was not this time one-third but one-thirteenth (0.0769d). The point was also taken over, this time not as a third of an english but as a quarter, or 0.019d. As Richard Hill's source explained:

To know what every nail standeth you in, after what price so ever ye buy it [by], ye must reckon after 13 english [to the penny], which been made thus: .o. And every english is 4 points and [they] been made thus: ø ø ø. And then depart 13 .o. in four. And so 3 o o o ø maketh [a] quarter penny of silver, and so ye may reckon up into what sum ye will.[15]

In other words, rather than lay down a whole string of 13 english, one converted every 6 english and 2 points into $\frac{1}{2}d$, and 3 english and 1 point into $\frac{1}{4}d$.

Hill's book gave an example and proof:

As thus: ye buy a sack of wool for 5 or 6 pounds. Then ye must divide the pounds into marks, and look how many marks ye buy the sack wool for, so many 3d o draweth the nail to. As thus: a sack wool cost 13s 4d, and the 52nd part of a mark is after the rate 3d o, so it followeth that this reckoning is true.

Or, in the similar words of the 'Discourse':

To reckon justly [exactly] ye must look how many £ your sack wool cost, and ye must divide the pounds into marks. As [many marks as] the sack cost, so many 3d o draweth the nail or the clove. For like as the clove is the 52nd part of a sack wool, so is 3[d] o the 52nd part of a mark, i.e. 13s 4d, and so this rule is true.[16]

Thus at a price of 12 marks (£8) per sack-weight in England, one clove cost 3s $\frac{3}{4}d$ o o ø.

The rule for buying fells, where there were usually 10 dozen to the long hundred of six-score, was that for however many shillings the dozen cost, one fell cost that number of pence. Equally, of course, from the price per dozen you could find price per long hundred by multiplying the shillings by 10.[17]

---

14 Ibid., fo. 102.
15 Balliol MS. 354, fo. 182v.
16 'Discourse', fo. 103r–v.
17 Ibid., fos. 103v, 104; Balliol MS. 354, fo. 183.

An interesting scrap of paper among previously unsorted 'Chancery Miscellanea' in the Public Record Office probably represents an exercise by some apprentice who was learning his way among these mysteries.[18] He had been given a series of calculations to perform, starting with the buying price of six sarplers of wool at $11\frac{1}{2}$ marks per English sack-weight, a feat that he managed with some initial inaccuracy. The results are recorded in a typical mixture of English, French and Latin.

[Sarpler No.]								[Weight]
1	.	.	.	.	.	.	.	ss [i.e. 2 sacks] 14 [cloves]
2	.	.	.	.	.	.	.	ss di*midium* 2
3	.	.	.	.	.	.	.	ss 22
4	.	.	.	.	.	.	.	ss di.2
5	.	.	.	.	.	.	.	ss 24
6	.	.	.	.	.	.	.	ss 21

Summa ponderis 14 sacc & di*midium* 17 *cloves* [corrected later to 7 cloves]. La sacc 11 m*arke* di*midium*. *Summa* d'argent £113 13*s* 6*d*.

He then worked out the cost of 12 sacks 22 cloves at the same price, producing an incorrect total of £91 4*s* 10*d* instead of £95 4*s* 10*d*, and followed this with the note:

Memorandum that the naile is 7 lb., and 52 naile is a ss. At 11 marcz *et* di*midium* the nayle is 2*s* 11*d* q^r & di. q^r.

Finally he worked out that at $11\frac{1}{2}$ marks per sack the tod (4 cloves or $\frac{1}{13}$ sack) cost 11*s* $9\frac{1}{2}d$ (in fact with strict accuracy it would be 11*s* $9\frac{7}{13}d$ or 11*s* $9\frac{1}{2}d$ ø ø), and that a rebate of 4 tods would amount to 47*s* 2*d* in value.

The next arithmetical skill that the apprentice had to acquire was the ability to convert a sum in sterling into its Flemish equivalent at a given rate of exchange. The recommended technique was to express the English noble of 6*s* 8*d* stg. or 80*d* ('the certain') in the equivalent number of shillings and pence Flemish. Then to find, say, the equivalent of £4 stg. at 24*s* Flem. per £ stg., otherwise 8*s* Flem. for 6*s* 8*d* stg., you would multiply the sterling sum by 'the Flemish noble in pence' (8*s* × 12*d* = 96*d*), and divide by the 80*d* in 'the English noble', producing £4 16*s* Flem. In the other direction, of course, one multiplied by 80 and divided by the requisite number of Flemish pence. Or as Richard Hill's book puts it:

For to bring Flemish money into sterling money, and sterling money into Fl. money.

To bring ster. money into Fl. money bring all your ster. money into pence and multiply it with the Fl. noble in pence and divide it with the sterling noble

[18] File 20 no. 41.

in pence, etc. And if ye will have your Fl. money be turned into ster. money, your noble must be the multiplier and the Fl. noble the devisor, and this is a general rule, etc.[19]

Hill then demonstrates the series of exercises needed to find the sterling equivalent of £49 10s Flem. at 10s 6d Flem. for 6s 8d stg., and vice versa.

This conversion was a very necessary exercise to master. Not only must it be performed in order to calculate how much the stapler's customers must pay in Flemish money for wool priced officially in sterling, but one currency had to be converted to the other in the exchange loans by which money was commonly transferred between London and the low countries and vice versa. In the loan transactions the rate was commonly expressed in the same way, as so much per noble.

'Bringing one money into another' was not the merchant's only monetary problem. Little sterling coin circulated at Calais at this date, when the mint there had been closed, and the legal tender was the same mixture of coin as circulated in Flanders and the other netherlands dominions of the Duke of Burgundy. This was manifold and various, and by no means confined to coin minted for the dukes themselves.[20] In addition, therefore, to the ducal gold coins such as the *Andreas gulden* or florin of the cross of St Andrew, *leeuw* ('lion'), *rider* and old Burgundian noble, the Celys and their customers might employ French crowns (the old crown, or *écu à la couronne*, struck before 1475, and the new crown, or *écu au soleil*), English angels and *rials*, Venetian and Hungarian ducats, Rhenish gulden of the Rhineland Electors, *Utrechts* of the bishop of that city, and many other gold coins of varying degrees of debasement. As the 'Discourse' warned:

It is right necessary a merchant to know the valure of the gold in [Flanders], for there be many diverse pieces of gold and diverse coins and many diverse names of them. And if a man know not the valure of them he may lightly ['easily'] be beguiled and lose money in them, etc.[21]

Silver coins seem to have been more manageable, the preferred ones being the *Carolus* groats, struck by Duke Charles betwee 1467 and 1474 and often purchased at a premium, or the double *briquets* (double *patards*

[19] Balliol MS. 354, fo. 187.
[20] The coins used by the Celys were identified and discussed by Philip Grierson, 'Coinage in the Cely Papers', repr. in Grierson, *Later Medieval Numismatics (11th–16th centuries): Selected Studies* (1979). See also John H. Munro, 'Money and Coinage of the Age of Erasmus', in R. A. B. Mynors, D. F. S. Thomson and W. Ferguson, eds., *Collected Works of Erasmus*, I (Toronto, 1974), 312–32.
[21] 'Discourse', fo. 100.

or *doppel vuurijzer*) struck between 1474 and 1485.[22] The second of these were mysteriously known to the Celys and their friends as *nymhekyn, nymhegyn, nemhegen, nymeryn, nymyng* or *nemyng, lemyng, lymon* or *lymmyn* groats. In default of any better explanation of this name I have only been able to suggest that the various forms are corruptions of Middle Dutch *limegnon* or *lemignon*, 'match', in reference to the badge on the coins which furnished the other names of *briquet* and *vuurijzer*, the flint and steel used with a tinder-box.

Coins might be hard to distinguish and sometimes had to be sorted into 'good' and 'evil' specimens. In August 1475 the young George was given 60 old groats and an old noble to pay costs on fells of John Ross. The noble was valued at 9s 8d Flem. and the groats were identified as Carolus groats at 5d Flem., making an alleged total of 34s 8d Flem., but George noted 'There is eight of the said groats I trow be but new groats', or briquets.[23] And in 1484 he drew up an account for his brother Richard of money in England:

Item, the[re] is told ['counted'] of good groats	£15
Item, of bad groats	£9
Item, of pence with an half rial	£30
Item, 2 rials	20s
Item, in [pence?]	22d
Sum	£55 22d
And ye made it but	£54 2s 2d.
Item, I paid Pasmer in groats	£10
Item, of good groats	£6
Item, of evil groats	£4 13s
Item, in pence	£9 4s 5d
Item, in pence	£10[24]

The pile of weights, amounting to 32 ounces, and the pair of balances which Richard and George left in their counter at Calais in 1482 were perhaps for weighing coins.[25] For large sums, pence and groats might pass by weight not number ('tale').

Unlike modern currencies, coins of the time bore no inscription of value. The English sterling coinage maintained a fixed relation to the £ stg. money of account (e.g. 1 rial = 10s, 1 groat = 4d) during the years covered by the Cely papers. Not so the currency of the Burgundian netherlands, where the authorities notably failed to fulfil their aspiration

[22] The 'Calais groats' in some late fifteenth- and sixteenth-century English documents appear to be Carolus groats in reality, e.g. File 10 fo. 8v.
[23] File 11 fo. 6.
[24] File 20 no. 44.
[25] File 12 fo. 33v.

'de avoir et entretenir bonne monnoye ferme et durable',[26] and valuations fluctuated quite wildly between 1474 and 1490. Here *fiat* valuations of the wide variety of coins that were accepted as legal tender were adjusted from time to time by official promulgations issued by the dukes. A number of these promulgations survive. Sometimes their prices were a belated attempt to catch up with movements in the market. At other times the authorities tried to call down the coins (i.e. reduce valuations), with very limited success. Valuations, whether ducal or at a more pragmatic market level, were proclaimed at the start of each of the major seasonal marts in Flanders and Brabant, and all coin received in payment was supposed to be accepted at the valuation imposed by the ruling tariff, 'according to the ordinance and proclamation made thereof, and as men give at the exchange at the places where the marts are held'.[27] Consequently, when the stapler received deferred payments from a customer at one of the marts, or specie in exchange for a draft on a money-changer-cum-banker at Bruges or Antwerp, or when he 'made money over' to London from a mart, he had of necessity to take or give coins at their current mart valuation.

In Calais, however, the English were not bound by any ducal tariffs. Calais had its own tariff, in which valuations were set by the king's council. Although these valuations ('money current in Calais' or 'Calais table money') were usually expressed in terms of the 'Flemish' money of account in which goods were priced in the town, coinage values in Calais did not necessarily coincide with values in force in Flanders. One example of how values might differ is found in a note written by George when he was about to attend the Cold mart (in 1476?): 'I must give Roger Grantoffte in Andreus "gyldornus" at 4s 4d Flem., £10, and I must receive of him Rhenish "geldornus" at 3s 10d Flem. for the same sum – £10.'[28] At ducal valuation, Rhenish gulden were usually worth 2d Flem. less than the Andrew. They were certainly not worth 6d less. George was pricing the Andrew at mart valuation, but the Rhenish (for use in Calais?) at the Calais tariff. Some people used 'Fl[emish]' for the former and 'gr[oot]' for the latter. From a later period differing valuations for English coin are demonstrated when, in November or December 1539, Lady Lisle sent a sum in two English coins to Dunkirk in settlement of a debt. Her correspondent wrote back that the 'rozinbos' (rose nobles or rials?) had recently been called down from 21 to 20s, and the 'stoter' had also been reduced. She added 'Madam, I . . . beg you to send no more

[26] Quoted by Peter Spufford, *Monetary Problems and Policies in the Burgundian Nether-lands, 1433–1496* (Leiden, 1970), p. 139 n. 1.
[27] Posthumus, *Bronnen*, II, no. 577.
[28] File 15 fo. 45.

money for the time being, because the money is worth much more at Calais than it is here.'[29] At the Celys' time, money – that is, coin – was usually 'worth less' at Calais than in Flanders, in Flemish terms. In 1478, when Maximilian had not yet fulfilled his promise to call down the coinage and reduce valuations by 12½ percent, there was a difference of 2s 6d Flem. in the £ between money at Calais and in neighbouring Bruges. In September 1478 George left Richard at Calais 'in ready money in pence – £3 10s [Flem., valuation at Calais]. Item, it amounts as money goeth in Flanders – £3 18s 9d Flem.'[30]

While the valuation of coins was linked with an exchange rate between the two moneys of account, in a sense the two things moved in opposite directions at Calais: what contemporaries saw as a lower exchange rate for the £ Flem., i.e. fewer Flemish shillings for the £ stg. at Calais, also meant that a lower valuation was placed on the coins in which payment was made, so that, for instance, the Andrew bought only 4s Flem. worth of goods instead of 4s 4d worth. Thus whether the Staple customer saw the exchange rate at Calais as favourable or unfavourable could depend on whether he thought in term of moneys of account or coinage. Already before September 1476 numerous 'diets' had fruitlessly discussed the vexing question of 'the variety, true estimation, due price and fixed value' of the coinage employed by the merchants.[31] The netherlanders had vainly (and unreasonably) attempted to get the Calais exchange rate reduced to a level which corresponded to the rate set by Duke Charles upon the coins back in October 1474. They complained that there had been 'ordained a fixed price or fixed value' for 'the pounds by which wools are bought', namely for every £ the price of 22s 8d Flem., but the staplers were disregarding this agreement and insisting on receiving 24s Flem. for every £1 Calais.[32] The matter was left unresolved in the treaty that was signed in July 1478, because the English put the onus of monetary reform on the duke, replying

that it was true that [in 1474?] the price of 22s 8d had been fixed for the pounds by which wools were bought, [and] that when the enhancements of the coinage current in the duke's dominions had been duly reformed, as agreed in the article about coinage in the present diet, they would wholly observe it and punish any transgressors. But otherwise they could not keep to the price of 22s 8d, since it was necessary to ordain the price of the pound of Calais in accordance with the value of the currency in the duke's dominions, and its enhancement or reduction.[33]

So far from reducing 'the price of the Calais pound', in September 1478 the authorities there raised it further, to 25s 4d Flem., a rate which

[29] *Lisle Letters*, no. 1588. [30] File 15 fo. 39. [31] *Foedera*, v (3), 72.
[32] Ibid., p. 92. [33] Ibid.

corresponded to the coinage tariff earlier established by ducal decree in Flanders in November 1477. This price of 25s 4d for two rials had already been agreed as the exchange rate at Calais to be given in sales of wool to the Leiden merchants who had long been paying 24s Flem.[34] The duke's attempt to strengthen the £ Flem. in a monetary ordinance of 12 October 1478, which would have reintroduced the same rate of 25s 4d, had small effect,[35] and on 18 December a further conference had to be set for 12 January 1479 because the monetary question was proving so thorny.[36]

Rates at Calais were thus controlled by government policy, which was sometimes influenced by agreements made in the course of trade negotiations. Eileen Power believed that wool prices were held steady for long periods by variations in what she supposed to be charges 'for the sale of time' in payment.[37] In fact, prices appeared consistent only because they were expressed in Calais pounds 'sterling'. In practice, the price varied according to the exchange rate at which it was converted into 'Flemish' money, and the valuation placed upon the coins used in payment. The staplers at this period actually subsidized their wool prices, to the extent that they might use a devalued pound and sell on credit terms which sometimes cost them dear.

The current table of coinage valuations in Calais was displayed in the lower hall of 'the Place' or Staple Hall. There is a description in the Johnson papers of how a stapler could get his own back on customers who had incurred disfavour, by staging an elaborate inspection of their proffered coin and ostentatiously comparing it with the specifications laid down by the table.

Do ye take such moneys as they will pay you, writing [down] the contents of every sort, and then peruse them according to the table in rating their prices, weight and fineness. And so doing you shall gird the Hollanders well enough – as much to their displeasure as the taking of our fells against our wills.[38]

The Calais table rated all coin acceptable at Calais, both English and foreign, on a scale corresponding to a designated exchange rate between the two moneys of account, Flemish and English. In 1487, for example, the table specified 'the course of all manner of coins of gold and silver, as well of the realm of England as of all other parts', which it duly rated and valued. Every coin so listed was 'to have course within the said town

---

[34] Posthumus, *Bronnen*, I, no. 501.

[35] H. Enno van Gelder and Marcel Hoc, *Les monnaies des Pays-Bas bourguignons et espagnols, 1434–1713* (Amsterdam, 1960), p. 24.

[36] *Foedera*, v (3), 97.　　　　　　　　　　[37] *Studies in English Trade*, p. 65.

[38] 'Johnson Letters', no. 472 (1547).

[of Calais] and marches, for every 20*s* sterling, 30*s* Flemish, and 30*s* Flemish for every 20*s*, and not above'.[39] Since the ordained exchange rate for money of account at Calais frequently differed from that in operation at London, Bruges or Antwerp, in effect a £ Calais (known as 'sterling table' or *st.ta.*) was created which was often undervalued in relation to the £ sterling of England, or 'mere sterling'. Thus in a document thought to date from 1535 it was reckoned that the king profited by 'the 13th penny' or 7.5 percent from the fact that wages of the garrison at Calais were paid 'by sterling table, whereof 21*s* 6*d* doth make a pound [mere] sterling'.[40] Every £1 in wages paid at Calais was therefore at that date worth only about 18*s* 7*d* mere sterling. But later, during the 'great debasement' period in England, the position was reversed. £1 sterling table at Calais was worth 21*s* mere sterling in August 1544, rising to 23*s* 4*d* mere stg. about August 1546 as the £ mere stg. steadily weakened against the £ Flem. on the international exchange.[41] The effect was that the £ Calais was held at 28*s* Flem. 'money current in Flanders' although the £ mere stg. had fallen to 24*s* Flem.

The Calais exchange rate and table valuations had to be strictly observed by everyone in the buying or selling of merchandise or victuals, payment of house-rent, and all other business in the town.[42] Accordingly, when in 1504 Henry VII indented with Sir Hugh Conway to act as treasurer of Calais the wages of his retinue were specified in 'sterling after the rate of the table of Calais', which then corresponded, as it had in 1487, to 30*s* Flem. per £1 Calais.[43] And thus the wage-bill for the garrisons of Calais and the neighbouring castles in 1500 was estimated at £9,920 13*s* 4*d* 'sterling table'.[44]

In dealings at Calais, 'sterling', confusingly, could therefore include money minted abroad. It is so defined in the proclamation announcing the trade treaty with the Duke of Burgundy in May 1499, which laid it down that

The merchants and subjects of the said archduke shall make their payments to the merchants of the Staple of Calais...in good sterling money [the Latin text of the treaty said more exactly 'good money to the value of sterling'], after the rate of a table made, which remaineth in the hall of the said Staple, except it be

[39] *Tudor Royal Proc.*, I, 553–4.
[40] *Lisle Letters*, II, p. 566. 'Sterling table' is defined as a weight by the editor, through a misreading of *O.E.D.* s.v. Sterling sb. 2b.   [41] S.P. 46/5 fo. 182r.
[42] Or so it was stated in 1487 (*Tudor Royal Proc.*, I, 553). The Staple seems usually to have had some licence as far as exchange rate was concerned. Thus from March 1481 to *c*. April 1482 staplers sold at 26*s* Flem. per £ stg., but valued coins received at Calais on a scale of 26*s* 8*d* per £.   [43] *C.C.R. 1500–1509*, no. 359.
[44] J. G. Nichols, ed., *A Chronicle of Calais in the Reigns of Henry VII and Henry VIII to the Year 1540* (Camden Soc., 1846), p. 5.

otherwise agreed between the said parties [to the treaty]. And it shall be lawful
to the said merchants...to receive of their debtors all manner of coins of gold
and silver now having (or hereafter shall have) course within the lands and
lordship of the said archduke.[45]

A list of the coins which were acceptable tender at the Calais Staple in
1499 includes as 'good sterling money' not only the rial, angel and Henry
noble but also coins such as the golden fleece (to be taken for 6s stg.),
the lion (at 5s 3d stg.), the Andrew (at 3s 6d stg.), and the old and new
French crowns (at 4s 2d and 4s 3d respectively).[46]

Some of the tariffs or scales of value employed variously at Calais and
in Flanders in valuing coins at different dates between 1467 and 1487
can be reconstructed with reasonable completeness (see Table 3).
Because the Calais exchange rate was fixed at 30s Flem. per £ stg. for
a relatively long time, this scale is included, although I have found few
of the relevant quotations. Other scales are based chiefly on ducal
promulgations,[47] supplemented by prices quoted in the Cely papers and
in other, printed, documents. It will be seen that there was seldom total
consistency in the rating of any given coin at different times. Thus, two
separate scales have had to be included to correspond to a valuation of
14s Flem. for the rial. One relates to the unofficial scale in use on the
market in August 1478, as reported by George Cely.[48] The second is the
scale employed after the death of the Duchess Mary in March 1482,
which was officially adopted, with a few modifications, in an unsuccessful
attempt to call down the coinage in the ducal dominions in December
1485.[49] Market rates for particular coins could themselves vary: on one
occasion when George Cely received two rials, worth together 27s Flem.,
he also took 11 Burgundian nobles from a customer at 11s Flem. each
and paid them to a 'Lombard' at only 10s 10d Flem., while Utrecht
gulden kept the same value in both transactions.[50]

Although the first tariff given in Table 3, that introduced by Duke
Charles in October 1467, valued the rial at 10s Flem., the scale as a whole
does not correspond to an exchange rate of 20s Flem. to 20s stg., but
rather to something like 20s 9d Flem.[51]

[45] *Tudor Royal Proc.*, I, 50 and *Foedera*, V (4), 137.
[46] Munro, 'Money and Coinage of the Age of Erasmus', Appendix A.
[47] I am indebted to Prof. Grierson for details of valuations collected by him for Oct. 1467,
     Oct. 1474, Nov. 1477, July and Dec. 1482, Dec. 1485 and Sept. 1487.
[48] E.g. File 11 fo. 21r–v.
[49] Grierson, 'Coinage in the Cely Papers', table.   [50] File 15 fo. 17.
[51] The Calais 'sterling table' similarly kept English values for the rial and angel, but put
     local prices on other coin: see the 1499 list in Munro, 'Money and Coinage of the Age
     of Erasmus', Appendix A.

Table 3. *Sample scales of coinage valuations, in Flemish shillings and pence*

(For chronological alterations of scale, see Fig. 1, p. 182. Where two quotations are given they refer to the operation of the scale at different times or places.)

Rate per £ stg.	20/-	22/8	24/-	25/4	26/8	27/-	28/-	{28/- 29/-}	30/-	31/-
Rial	10/-	11/4	12/-	12/8	13/4	13/6	14/-	{14/- 14/6}	15/-	15/6
Angel	—	7/10	—	8/2	8/8	—	—	9/4	—	10/4
Old noble	8.8	{9/8 10/-}	10/4	11/-	11/-	—	12/-	12/4	—	14/-
Burgundian noble	8/4	9/4	—	10/4	10/8	{10/10 11/-}	11/8	12/-	—	13/8
Andrew	3/6	4/-	4/2	4/6	4/6	4/8	5/-	5/-	5/4	5/6
Rider	4/6	5/-	5/4	5/8	5/8	5/10	6/4	6/4	—	7/2
Lion	5/2	6/-	6/4	6/8	6/8	{7/- 6/10}	7/2	7/6	—	8/2
Philip	2/6	2/8	—	3/-	3/-	3/4	3/4	3/4	—	4/-
William	3/6	4/-	—	{4/6 4/4}	4/6	4/8	5/-	5/-	—	5/6
Old crown	4/2	{4/6 4/10}	5/2	5/2	5/4	{5/6 5/5}	5/8	5/10	6/-	6/4
New crown	—	{4/8 5/-}	5/4	5/4	5/6	5/8	5/10	6/-	—	6/6
Salute	4/4	4/10	—	6/-	5/6	—	6/2	6/2	—	7/-
Venetian ducat	4/4	5/-	5/2	5/6	5/6	6/-	6/4	6/4	—	7/2
Hungarian ducat	—	5/-	—	5/8	5/8	5/8	6/2	6/2	—	7/-
Rhenish gulden	3/5	3/10	4/-	4/4	4/4	4/6	4/10	4/8	—	5/2
Utrecht gulden	—	—	3/8	4/-	{4/- 4/2}	4/2	4/4	—	4/6	—

Variations in the price of individual coins were not solely dependent on estimations of their fine gold content. They could be affected by political policy or market pressures. The fallacy in equating precious-metal content with fiat value is shown by the fact that a coin like the old noble and the salute of Henry VI (which were no longer minted, so that there is no question of an alteration in fineness) could change their market valuation in relation to other coins in a manner which does not reflect the current mint price for the metal.[52] For example, when the rial was valued at 12s 8d Flem. in November 1477, the old noble was assigned a value of 11s Flem., a price it retained when, in 1480–1, the rial was current in Flanders at 13s 4d Flem. Many, but not all, of the coins in circulation in the low countries also failed to reflect the increased valuation of the rial, the angel and the French écus in this later schedule. The salute was actually called down. Consequently, the valuation of the rial and therefore the exchange rate for money of account cannot usually be deduced from the valuation put upon other coins. From the valuation in Calais st.ta. ascribed to the toison d'or in May 1499 compared with its valuation in the Bruges mint accounts, J. H. Munro derived an exchange rate of 27s 9d Flem. per £ Calais. When, however, the Philippus is taken as a base, the rate appears to be 29s 5d.[53] Such evidence is not sufficient to produce any certain conclusion about the parity fixed at Calais at that date. Moreover, the valuation of the rial in Flanders, if known, gives parity as estimated in Flanders between the £ Flem. and the £ mere stg., not the Calais rate for Flemish money against the £ Calais 'sterling table'.

The requirement to pay cash at Calais in specie valued at a local price by the Calais table was one among many reasons why the Staple's customers sought to make deferred payments which would be in 'money current at the mart', and probably valued on a higher scale of prices. They then got the favourable exchange rate fixed by the stapler for his sterling pounds of account, and the more generous valuation of their coin that prevailed at the mart. In September 1478 when Richard Cely junior negotiated with some merchants of Rouen who wanted good Cotswold wool at Calais, the merchants offered to buy three sarplers, two-thirds to be paid in hand at an exchange rate of 25s 4d Flem for the £ stg., and wanted six months' credit for the third part, 'money current in Flanders'.[54] Richard, preferring not to risk the future payment in coin

---

[52] For criticism of attempts by Unwin and others to equate mint equivalents with par rate, see J. D. Gould, *The Great Debasement: Currency and the Economy in Mid-Tudor England* (Oxford, 1970), pp. 93ff. The difference between gold equivalents and exchange rates is also stressed by H. Van der Wee, *The Growth of the Antwerp Market and the European Economy*, 1 (The Hague, 1963), 117–21.

[53] Munro, 'Wool-Price Schedules', p. 155, and private communication.   [54] *C.L.* 34.

which might possibly be over-valued, made the unacceptable counter-proposal of all the price cash down, part at 25s 4d per £ in the 'money current in Calais', which he explained meant in coins valued on the current scale, with the Rhenish gulden at 4s 4d Flem., and the rest of the payment at the reduced rate of 24s Flem. per £, 'with all other golds as they yeed at Cold mart [1477]', i.e. at the same 25s 4d tariff, according to the Calais rules.

Because of the frequent discrepancies between Calais and the low countries, the values that the Celys ascribe to the coins in various lists among their memoranda may depend on where the list was made, whether at Calais by local valuation or else at Bruges or one of the marts. The number of such lists in their papers testifies to the difficulties caused by a succession of enhancements and reductions, and it is unfortunate that many are undated and bear no indication of place.[55]

Coins had always to be carefully listed and priced. In August 1480 George sold fells of John Cely and William Maryon to a merchant who paid half the total in hand, at a rate of 25s 4d Flem. per £ stg., making £34 12s 6d Flem.[56] He gave George the following coins:

93 Andrews at 4s 6d Flem. each
18¼ crowns at 5s 4d
6 Venetian ducats and 2 salutes at 5s 6d
1 Rhenish gulden at 4s 4d
5 Utrecht gulden at 4s
and £8 0s 2d in double briquets at 4½d.

Altogether these came to £37 5s 8d Flem., so George then gave the buyer change in the form of 12 Guilhelmus (scilden of William VI of Holland), valued at 4s 4d, and a further 14d in small coin.

George acquired a particularly rich range of gold coins, some of which sorely tested his spelling, in the summer of 1481. There is one list of sums amounting to a total of £171 10s 10d Flem., composed of 177 Andrews at 4s 6d Flem., 5 English rials at 13s 4d Flem. and 2 quarter rials, 6 'Hongres' (Hungarian ducats) at 5s 8d, 11 new French crowns at 5s 6d, 11 old crowns at 5s 4d and one 'crown' at 5s 2d, 22 Rhenish gulden at 4s 4d, 3 'Phelypus' (écus of Philip the Good) at 3s, 5 'clembars' (*clemmergulden* of Guelders, so called because the two lions depicted seemed to be climbing a central line on their shield) at 4s 3d, 5 'lewis'

[55] There are lists in *C.L.* 56, 151, 187 and 196, and in File 11 fo. 21r–v; File 12 fos. 2, 25r–v, 39; File 13 fos. 63, 64; File 15 fos. 8, 11v, 14, 17, 18–22, 25v, 29, 31, 54; File 20 no. 2 fo. 2, no. 43.
[56] File 15 fo. 11.

(lion gulden) at 6s 8d, one 'Quellhelmus' (Guilhelmus) at 4s 6d, one unspecified coin at 2s 3d, 13 riders at 5s 8d, 3 'Bavarys' (coins struck by John of Bavaria, Count of Holland, or imitations of them) at 2s 10d, 80 postulates, from Utrecht or Liège, at 2s 8d, and two 'Arnoldus' of Duke Arnold of Guelders at 2s 10d, besides £19 9s 1d in double briquets at 4½d, £36 in double placks or patards at 2½d, and 38s 4d in groats at 2¼d.[57] At the same date he had 10 'salewes' (salutes, struck by Henry VI as king of France and depicting the angel's salutation of Mary at the Annunciation), valued at 5s 6d apiece.[58]

In July 1481 George had with him at the mart £58 8s Flem. made up of some of these coins and some others again: 28 lions, 54 Rhenish, 21 Andrews, 22 old crowns, 18 postulates, 23 Bavarius, and in addition 64 'Hettrytus' or Utrecht gulden at 4s 2d, 17 Petrus of Brabant at 3s 8d, and 11 'Borgen nobles' (Burgundian nobles) at 11s 8d.[59] Dr Peter Spufford has expressed some surprise at the numbers of Rhenish gulden, postulates and Utrecht gulden which the Celys handled, and suggested that these must have come from customers from the Rhineland and Utrecht.[60] The Rhenish and Utrecht gulden were, in fact, very popular with English merchants and circulated freely in Calais. They were probably brought by the fell-buyers from Leiden and Delft: for example the down-payment at Calais on fells sold on 1 December 1481 to Maurin Clayson and company of Leiden consisted of £78 13s 10d Flem. made up of 146 Utrechts, double briquets to the value of £26, and groats of 2¼d to the value of £21, plus a small sum in 'white money'.[61] Sometimes customers preferred to pay in small coin: John Williamson and company of Leiden once paid a bill of £7 12s Flem. almost entirely in small coin, including 'brass pence', the only gulden being three Philippus at 3s 4d and a lion at 7s 4d, and Jacob Williamson and company of Delft met a bill of £14 19s 8d in groats at 4½d or 2½d.[62] It may be that it was thought safer to carry small change rather than gold coins at a period of disturbance, and there was sometimes also less loss in the exchange on silver. In December 1478 George had 'by me in ready money' no less than £100 Flem. in 'white money', which had cost him, at that date, a premium of 10d in the pound 'the getting'.[63] By contrast, in 1474 or 1475 Gard Floo or Frow of Leiden met bills with as many as 263 Rhenish gulden and 183 Andrew gulden.[64]

What, in practice, was used as the indicator of parity of exchange or 'agreed value' between the English and Flemish pounds? In apparent

[57] File 15 fo. 20r–v.   [58] File 12 fo. 25.   [59] File 12 fo. 25v.
[60] *Monetary Problems*, p. 68; but the Celys had few if any buyers from these places.
[61] File 12 fo. 31v.   [62] *C.L.* 173, 172.   [63] File 11 fo. 49.
[64] File 15 fos. 38, 54.

contradiction of the facts cited earlier, which indicate that the price of gold was not the sole controlling factor, George Cely once appears to take the price of gold as a basis. In October 1487 he made this note:

The reckoning of fine gold.

First, 20 englishes [i.e. penny-weights] makes an ounce of gold, and an english of fine gold is worth 3s 4d Flem. And 8 ounces makes an mark weight of gold or silver. And 12 ounces makes an pound weight. And an ounce of fine gold is worth 40s stg.

At the 12 day of October anno '87 it was at Bruges £3 6s 8d Flem., that is after 33s 4d le £ Flem. for the £ stg.

The weight on this side the sea and England differs half an english in an mark weight, and so much is England the heavier weight.

The coinage in England is 8d of the £ stg.[65]

But this calculation is sufficiently elaborate to imply that it was an unfamiliar exercise: George was interested in obtaining bullion for minting in England at the time. Moreover, at that date the actual exchange rate for money at Bruges seems to have been higher than 33s 4d Flem. per £ stg. – more like 34s. A similar discrepancy is revealed in William Cely's note in December that he could not obtain an ounce of fine gold for £3 12s Flem., which would make an exchange equivalent of 36s Flem. per £. At the same date the rial was valued at 20s Flem. in Bruges and the effective exchange rate was 40s Flem. per £ stg.[66]

In usual practice it seems inescapable that the Flemish mart valuation of a specific gold coin was the base in commercial dealings. There is some suggestion that the English might take the value assigned to the Rhenish gulden as indicative of the general scale of coinage valuations in operation at a given time, as when Richard junior specified payment in 'Ryans' at 4s 4d Flem. 'with all other golds as they yeed at Cold mart'.[67] If admitted at all to official ducal promulgations, the *Rijns gulden* were usually valued at 2d Flem. below the Burgundian Andrew. But it has been shown that in official tables neither the Andrew nor the other popular Burgundian gold coin, the lion, related consistently to the valuation of the English rial. Nor do the official Burgundian prices of the English angel or old noble. Burgundian values of the rial, on the other hand, correspond exactly to recorded exchange rates between the Flemish and English pounds as money of account. It is therefore significant that in the agreement with Leiden of 14 May 1478 the exchange rate in sales to Leiden merchants was specifically defined as 25s 4d Flem. for two rials (*duo regalia anglicana*).[68]

Figure 1 tentatively plots the movement of the exchange rate for two rials (£1 mere stg.) on the market at Bruges between October 1474 and

[65] File 13 fo. 30v.   [66] *C.L.* 238.
[67] *C.L.* 34.   [68] Posthumus, *Bronnen*, I, no. 501.

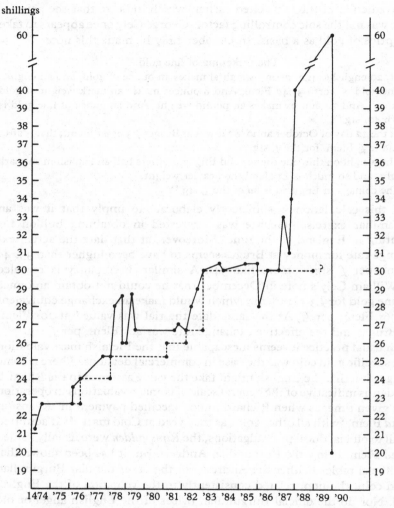

Figure I : Exchange rates in Flemish shillings per English pound. ———,
Exchange rate at Bruges; ------, exchange rate at Calais.

December 1489, together with a number of official revaluations which
had no practical effect, for comparison with the rate in force at Calais
(for £1 Calais stg.). Flemish valuations are taken as far as possible from
official promulgations and reported mart values, supplemented by some
imprecise deductions from the rates quoted in exchange loans and by

calculations based on Van der Wee's table of gold equivalents for the Brabançon groat.[69] The latter, being based on mint accounts, does not adequately reflect movements in market valuation. Nor can it be used to give anything more than an approximate indication of the exchange rate for the rial.[70] Consequently, figures derived from Van der Wee have been used only where no alternative was available, that is, for some points after December 1487.

Ducal promulgations have been found from October 1467, October 1474, November 1477, mid-1482, April 1485, December 1485, ?20 April 1487, September 1487, and December 1489. Some of these acknowledged enhancements which had already taken place in the market. At other times, notably in October 1478 and December 1485, there was an abortive calling-down of prices. The ducal valuations of 1487 were evidently ignored in Flanders, and in 1489 the price of the rial rose steadily at Bruges until it apparently reached over 30s Flem.[71] A draconian reassessment on 14 December then attempted to bring coin values down to a scale on which the rial was valued at 10s Flem. or less. Values soon rose again, but more slowly.

It will be observed that the exchange rate of 'money current in Calais' was adjusted from time to time to bring it closer to the exchange rate in Flanders, but contact was rapidly lost again. The Cely papers unluckily contain no evidence to show Calais rate after 1487. It again stood at 30s Flem. in 1504: had this figure been maintained over the preceding 17 years?

There were undoubtedly some changes in rates in Flanders which are not indicated in the outline of Fig. 1. On 10 May 1482, and again on 6 June 1484, the Staple complained to the authorities of Leiden about breaches of a common tariff for coins,[72] and in Calais itself the English widely disregarded the ordained rate of 30s Flem. per £ in 1487, so that a royal proclamation had to reassert it in July or August of that year.[73] At times the rial attracted a premium which presumably did not affect the exchange rate for money of account. In 1482 Leiden claimed that it was the English themselves who failed to observe the tariff at the mart:

[69] Van der Wee, *Growth of the Antwerp Market*, I, Table xv, pp. 127–8.
[70] Mint prices for silver are also misleading. On that basis, Munro postulates a rate of 23s 6d for the Calais £ stg. in 1475. The real rate was 22s 8d. (John H. Munro, 'The Medieval Scarlet', *Cloth and Clothing in Medieval Europe*, ed. N. B. Harte and K. G. Ponting, 1983, Tables 3.1 and 3.16.)
[71] In Brabant at the Cold mart of 1488–9 the crown stood at 10s Flem. It rose to 11s at the Easter mart 1489, and to 12s at the Sinxen mart of Antwerp: Posthumus, *Bronnen*, II, p. 69 n.
[72] Posthumus, *Bronnen*, II, nos. 554, 575.
[73] *Tudor Royal Proc.*, I, 553–4.

As it is told us, they demand from our merchants, and others, cash payment in rials, stoters, and some other coins at higher and greater price than that for which they are current. And they not only take them so in payment; what is more, they buy them with small coin. And if there has been a breach, it has occurred by this means, as we understand the matter.[74]

A clear infringement of Calais regulations is betrayed by George's note that in November 1486 he received from John De Lopez and Gomez De Soria 'in sterling money, Carols at 6*d* le piece, and 2*s* le £ to get them – £10 Flemish'.[75] Apparently the Carolus groats were valued at Calais at 6*d* Flem. on the official exchange rate of 30*s* Flem. per £ stg., but had in fact to be obtained at a premium of 10 percent, or an effective exchange rate of 32*s* Flem. per £.

To summarize conclusions in this complicated and often confusing area: at this date when there was an English coin which bore a constant sterling value of 10*s*, the exchange between the £s Flemish and English as money of account was necessarily equated with the number of *solidi* and *denarii* Flemish money of account to be given for two rials. The number of shillings and pence in this transaction could, of course, vary according to whether the rials were exchanged in England, Calais, or the Duke of Burgundy's dominions. The staplers might bargain with their customers about the exchange rate at which their deferred payments were to be converted from sterling to Flemish money of account when the term fell due at the mart, and there were similar negotiations about the sums which the staplers were to produce for the payment of the garrison's wages (see Ch. 9). In some circumstances the stapler might be conducting transactions which variously involved four different calculations of 'parity' between the two moneys of account. The further adjustments to be made in exchange loans will be discussed below.

   In his own day-to-day activities in Calais, for example purchases of clothing or foodstuffs, or the payment of rent, petty costs on his wool, and dues to the Staple, the English merchant accounted in 'Flemish' money of account and paid in a mixture of coins, both English and foreign. This Calais 'Flemish' money may conveniently be termed 'Flemish table money of Calais' or *Fl.ta.* by analogy with 'sterling table money', although I am not aware that the former expression was in fact used. When John Johnson wished to distinguish between the 'Flemish' moneys of account at Calais and Antwerp, he seems to have used *groot* for the one and *Flemish* for the second.[76] The inhabitant of Calais who

---

[74] Posthumus, *Bronnen*, II, no. 555.   [75] File 20 no. 20.
[76] S.P. 46/5 fo. 182. Unfortunately, in present usage both terms can imply the monetary system of Flanders.

was paying his rent, or his servants' wages, or the freight charges on his last shipment of wool, or buying fish for dinner, or a new horse, was not immediately concerned about the relation between his currency and its valuation in England or Flanders. This question might only arise when he arranged a deal with his netherlands customers, or became acutely aware that the coins he was using had cost him much more at Bruges than they were worth at Calais, or that the government was not allowing him the current Calais price when he paid taxes. He might often be aware that it was more profitable to pay in one sort of coin rather than another – if the recipient could be persuaded to accept it. It goes without saying that there had to be a conventional value placed upon the coins in use, and those permitted to circulate in Calais were tabled – possibly in both 'Flemish' and sterling terms – on a board on public display. Currency at this official valuation was thus known, perhaps at the Celys' time and certainly by 1500, as 'Calais table money' or 'sterling table' (st.ta.). During the period 1472–89 the valuations of the coins on the scale which I have dubbed 'Flemish table' sometimes tallied with current valuations in Flanders and Brabant. At other times, however, the two estimates diverged and the coins bore a higher valuation in Flemish money of account in Flanders than in Calais.

On the Calais sterling table, the rial always bore its face value of 10s stg.[77] Its equivalent value in 'Flemish table money of account' at any given time produced the exchange rate in 'Flemish table money' for the £ sterling table, or what the Staple's customers thought of as the 'wool pound' of Calais. This £ st.ta. was also the unit commonly employed in calculating the wage bill for the Calais garrison. The fact that the £ st.ta. might be worth less than the £ mere sterling of England becomes important when one attempts to estimate a stapler's total profit on sales, the advantage which the government derived from paying its soldiers at one artificial exchange rate, while it was taxing its subjects at another, or the financial concessions which the Staple made to certain customers. But it does not enter directly into discussion of the stapler's ordinary financial transactions with his clients in the low countries.

The ideal of maintaining complete 'equality of estimation' between the currency systems of England and Flanders was never achieved. At best, and only for very brief periods between 1472 and 1489, the government of Calais and the Duke managed to hold the same exchange rate between their respective pounds and to give the same values to their common coinage. The advantage to the merchants of both sides was obvious. The staplers could bring back to Calais the money received from their customers at the marts 'without loss', whereas at other times they found

[77] 'Face value' in the technical, not literal, sense.

themselves forced to accept deferred payments which were made at the marts in over-priced coin. Their customers, for their part, no longer came to Calais with money for a down-payment on wool purchases, only to discover that their coins were worth much less there. When that situation existed, it was not entirely redressed by the fact that a lower exchange rate in Calais meant that they had to pay fewer pounds, Flemish money of account, for wool priced in pounds sterling table, than would be the case if the conversion was made at the parity between the £ Flem. and the £ mere stg. which prevailed in their own country. But hopes of keeping an equilibrium in 1482 were nullified when the death of the Duchess Mary destroyed the political stability of the ducal dominions, and with it, for the time being, any stability that the ducal monetary system had achieved. By October 1482 George, at the Bammis mart in Antwerp, was receiving rials at 14s 6d Flem., making 29s for the £ stg. At Calais they were rated at 13s 4d Flem. The Andrew was assessed at 5s at the mart and 4s 6d at Calais, the rider at 6s 4d instead of 5s 8d, and the salute at 6s 2d instead of 5s 6d.[78]

Occasionally the buyer of wool at Calais paid the whole price for his purchase cash down. More often, he paid part in hand and might give a promissory note ('bill of his hand'), either a sight bill or a short-term bill, for a further proportion of the price, and two obligations payable at future dates, possibly at the next two marts. A sale of fells by William Cely in 1485 illustrates this particular pattern of four instalments.[79] Exceptionally, it fails to convert the sums due into Flemish money.

Memorandum, the 5 day of August anno '85 sold by me William Cely in the name of my masters Richard and George Cely to Jacob Williamzon [etc.] of Delft:– 5,150 Cots. fells, price le 100, 14 nobles sterling. Argent . . . . . £240 6s 8d stg.

Whereof I have received in hand in Flemish pence & Philippus placks, sum . . . . £53 6s 8d stg.

Item, I have lent them by a bill of their hands to pay in Calais within the space of 6 weeks, sum . . . . . £66 16s 8d stg.

Item, lent them by an obligation payable in Cold mart next coming, sum . . . . £60 20d stg.

Item, lent them by another obligation payable in Passe mart next following, other . . . . £60 20d stg.

[78] *C.L.* 187, 196. In May there had been rumours that a royal exchange would be set up in Bruges, to establish 'the money' at 24s Flem. per £ stg. for English merchants: *C.L.* 165.

[79] File 20 no. 12.

One typical informal 'bill of hand' from an unidentified debtor who signs perhaps 'Nutry' or 'Nutin' runs:

Jorge Cely, je vous prometz payer a votre volente ou au porteur de cestes, six livres dixhuit solz huit deniers gros monne de Flandres, en moy rendant cestes. Signe de mon saign manuel, le 25 de May, '79.[80]

The obligation, colloquially known as an 'oblige', was more formal. The formula ran:

Noverint universi me [A.B. de C.], mercatorem, teneri et firmiter obligari [D.E.] in [X] libris bone et legalis monete...ad quam quidem solucionem...faciendam obligo me, heredes et executores meos [etc.].

Or, in translation,

Be it known to all by these present writings that I, John Benyngton, citizen and grocer of London, am bound and straitly obliged to Richard Cely and George Cely, merchants of the Staple of Calais, in £13 6s 8d money of England, to pay to the said Richard and George or either of them or their acknowledged attorney or executors on the 23 August which shall be in 1487. And I bind me, my heirs and executors to make this payment faithfully by the present writing. In witness whereof I have set my seal to this. Given 4 February A.D. 1485 [/6], and the first year of the reign of King Henry VII.

Per me John Benyngton.[81]

When one of the Celys or their factor came to collect payment on such an obligation from a foreign customer, the debt might be met either in coin 'money current in Flanders' or else with a draft on a wisseler [Flemish *wisselaer*] – a money-changer-cum-banker – at Antwerp or Bruges. For example, at the Antwerp Bammis mart in September–October 1478 George received from Jan Van Der Heyden £13 Flem. 'in ready money' and £80 Flem. by assignment on Jacob De Bloke, the Antwerp money-changer, who paid him in double briquets.[82] John De Scermere of Ghent made two payments in ready money of £31 7s 3d Flem. and £3 9s 6d Flem., and 'writ me upon Collard De May [of Bruges]' £20 10s 6d Flem. (Sometimes the expression used is 'set upon' a wisseler.) John De Lopez and his fellows similarly gave George a draft on Collard De May for £112 1s Flem. George's total receipts at this mart came to £543 0s 11d Flem., of which £232 odd was in the form of drafts on wisselers, mostly in Bruges.

At the next mart, the Cold mart at Bergen-op-Zoom in December 1478, George was furnished with obligations to a total of £697 7s 1d Flem., comprising the following sums:

---

[80] File 11 fo. 55. [81] File 13 fo. 19. [82] File 11 fo. 33v.

£54 8s for Lois De Moy
£13 11s 1d for De Scermere, payable 1 December
£49 for the same, payable 20 December
£107 6s 6d for De Lopez and Van Dorne, payable 27 December, and
£473 1s 6d for the same, payable at sight.[83]

Lois De Moy 'set' him upon John Newenton, wisseler at Bruges, and subsequently George received £20 in Flemish pence and 'an bill of £30 to pay at my pleasure'. The remaining £4 8s is unaccounted for.[84] He failed to collect on the other bills, because, as he noted on 24 December before returning to England, 'I could not occupy [the money] at that season'.[85]

When, in April or May 1479, George did present his bills, De Lopez paid him the one sum of £107 6s 6d in Carolus groats, and, in exchange for the sight bill, wrote him £473 1s 6d on Collard De May.[86] De Scermere, for his part, paid the sum of £13 11s 1d in ready money and George received most of his other £49 from 'Absylond' or Absolom De Vynt. Out of this he paid £20 to 'Peter, Collard Ast his fellow' in exchange for 'Garlis' (i.e. Carolus) groats.[87] George also collected cash from the wisselers Newenton, De May and William Roelandts. The £78 15s which he obtained from the last two had been deposited to George's account by John Dalton out of the receipts from a sale of fells which he had made on the Celys' behalf.[88] At another time George noted that he had 'standing upon Collarde De May, westlar of Bruges, that Collet set me upon – £19 10s 4d Flem.'.[89] He took £130 'out of the wisselers' hands' at Bruges a month or two before De May and Roelandts went bankrupt in 1481.[90] Like Dalton, George made use of Bruges banking facilities when he wished to transfer money from the mart for staplers at Calais in June 1478:

Item, I writ William Dalton pour John Dalton upon Collard De
May . . . . £22 Flem.

Item, I writ Thomas Morcroft of Roger Grantoft's money upon
John Newenton . . . . £20 Flem.

Item, written John Spenser upon John Newenton . . . £8 Flem.[91]

These drafts on wisselers were often cashed, because the staplers needed money to meet their custom and subsidy dues payable at Calais,

[83] File 11 fos. 41v–42.
[84] Possibly it remained on the books, in credit to George.
[85] File 21 no. 1 (fo. 2v).   [86] File 15 fo. 28.
[87] He had to pay a premium of 9s Flem. for these groats.
[88] File 15 fo. 5v.   [89] File 15 fo. 29v.
[90] *C.L.* 33.   [91] File 11 fo. 40.

and also had their own not inconsiderable expenses in that town. But since there was no longer a mint at Calais, there was no need to take large amounts of specie back there, so that money might be left in account with a wisseler or transferred to London by means of an exchange loan.

A typical set of transactions arose from George's sale of 1,000 fells belonging to William Maryon in 1479.[92] The buyer, Richard Starkey, gave two obligations in the name of himself and his mother, each for £18 5s 11d Flem. One was payable on 20 May and the other on 20 November. When George presented the first in May, Starkey 'wrote him upon' the wisseler next door to Jacob De Bloke in Antwerp. George then wrote £17 upon the same wisseler in favour of the English merchant William Welbeck, as part of a total of £51 10s Flem. to be 'made over' to England by means of an exchange loan with Welbeck. In all he had received £125 12s 6d Flem. on Maryon's behalf, and noted that he must take back the equivalent of £15 16s 8d stg. to Calais to pay Maryon's custom and subsidy. 'Item, the rest I must bring home with me in fine gold, or make it by exchange.'[93]

Of the £543 0s 11d Flem. which George received at the Bammis mart of 1478, he 'made over' £449 14s Flem., and out of that amount, £109 11s 6d Flem. was paid to the borrowers in the form of drafts on wisselers. Sample transactions may be quoted from George's account. Richard senior had told George to deal with 'Borgan's man', i.e. Gilbert Palmer, attorney for the mercer Thomas Burgoyn, 'for his payment is good to me at all times before the day'. Also 'the man of Lynn [Thomas Burwell] is good payment, and that is merry for to deal with such men. Take good men and do the better to them rather.'[94] George noted:

Money made over by me.
Upon Collard De May, etc.
Item, made over by Richard Wellis, attorney of Thomas Follar, mercer of London, £30 stg. payable the last day of February next coming, at 8s 7d. Sum . . . . £38 12s 6d Flem.
Item, I made with Gylbard Pallmar, £100 stg., at 8s 8d. Sum . £130 Flem. To be paid May, June, at each time £50 stg. Sum I writ him upon Collard Day May, £50 8s 6d. I paid him in ready money £79 11s 6d Flem. Sum. . . . . £130 Flem.
Item, made by William Borwell £120 stg., at 8s 8d. Sum . £156 Flem. Where[of] I gave him John Delopis and Cornelys Vandornys bill to receive of £90 6d Flem., which he hath received of the said merchants. [N.B. at face value.] Item, I delivered unto the said William in ready money the rest, sum £65 19s 6d Flem. Sum total £156 Flem. to be paid at [blank] . £156 Flem.

. . .

[92] File 12 fo. 10v; File 15 fo. 41.   [93] File 12 fo. 42v.
[94] *C.L.* 31 (25 Aug. 1478).

Item, I made over by Robard Herryc, fellmonger, for William Maryon £10 stg. at 9s. Sum . . . . £13 10s Flem.

. . .

Item, made by me with Gylbartt Pallmar, attorney of Thomas Borgon, £50 stg., at 8s 8d. Sum paid by [me] in ready money . . £65 Flem.

. . .

[For William Maryon]

Item, I writ William Borwell upon Collard De May . £12 9s. Item, I gave him in ready money . £33 11s. Sum . . . . . . £16.

Item, I took him at Antwerp in ready money, £36. Sum. £52 Flem. This money I delivered him at 8s 8d, to pay the [blank]. It is £40 stg. and at 8s 8d it amounts unto £52 Flem.

The £36 is writ upon the other side, wherefor it is not here writ. [Entry subsequently cancelled. 'The other side' – now fo. 33v – notes that on 4 October George left Burwell an obligation of Garrad Coupar for £36 Flem. to receive for William Maryon.]

Robard Cely
John Spensar   Item, I writ William Borwell upon Jyllys Desmett for these

3 [sic] persons here against . . . . £96 Flem.

Item, I writ the said William upon Lois Syr Moy also for the same men . . . . £36 Flem.[95]

A typical 'bill of exchange', with bearer clause, was drawn up by a borrower at the Cold mart in 1478:

Be it known to all men that I, John Breten, attorney for John Breten, salter of London, hath received by exchange of John Grenerard, merchant of Cologne, £40 sterlings. The which £40 sterlings to be paid to the said John or to the bringer of this bill in the first week of Clean Lent at London after the date hereof. The which payment well and truly to be paid at the day aforesaid, and thereto we bind us, our heirs, executors and all our goods to the full payment of the sum of £40 sterlings. And if there be any default of payment by change or by rechange or any other thing that may fall, we the said John and John promise to make it good. In witness hereof I set to my seal the 22 day of December anno 1478.[96]

Breten had not in fact received £40 stg. from Grenerard, but a sum in Flemish money. Characteristically, the bill does not specify what the Flemish equivalent had been.

In attempting to estimate the rate of interest at which exchange loans were made it is first necessary to establish the prevailing market parity, because the rate at which a loan was negotiated was adjusted to allow the 'deliverer' or lender interest. When a sum was made over from the mart to London the taker was paid Flemish money calculated at a rate below

[95] File 11 fos. 34–6.
[96] P.R.O. reference unavailable at the time of writing.

the current exchange for sterling, so that the lender lent less money at the outset than he received back in England. On the other hand, when sterling was lent at London for repayment in Flemish money at the mart or in Bruges the exchange rate was set above that at parity, so that the lender received more money abroad than he had lent at home. Merchants at the time thought in those terms. They were in fact buying and selling bills, but it is not altogether appropriate to discuss their transactions in modern terminology. In particular, the practice of reselling such bills at a discount does not appear to have been common at the period. Nor, it would seem, did rate of interest vary for these merchants according to time in the standardized way that became the practice in the next century.[97]

The best bargain in the group of transactions at Bammis 1478 was made by Robert Eyryk, no doubt because as Maryon's nephew he was given a favourable rate. The rial was current for 14s Flem. at the mart, so that the exchange rate was effectively 28s Flem. per £ stg., and the equivalent of £10 stg. at market rate was £14 Flem. Eyryk was lent only £13 10s Flem., so that 10s Flem. was deducted as interest, making a discount rate of 3.6 percent. On such a basis of calculation, a comparatively high interest prevailed on exchange loans at this mart. Size of loan and standing of borrower clearly affected the charge, as well as length of loan. The loan of £38 12s 6d Flem. for five months was discounted by 8.0 percent (which would correspond to an annual interest rate of 19.3 percent), while Palmer's £130 repayable in eight and nine months allowed the Celys a discount of 7 percent, like the £52 for unstated term to Burwell. Richard senior treated this exchange rate (8s 8d Flem. per noble stg., or 26s Flem. per £) as the base, or prevailing one for loans at this particular mart.[98] Palmer's £65 Flem. for nine months was borrowed at the equivalent of 9.5 percent per annum.

By comparison, discount on loans arranged at the Sinxen mart of Antwerp in 1480 apparently ran at either 2.5 percent or 4.4 percent of the sum lent. Parity in Flanders was then 26s 8d Flem. to the £ stg., to judge by the valuation of the rial at 13s 4d Flem. George listed his loans as follows:

Item, ... I made by exchange with Robert Heryke £24 stg. at 8s 8d Flem.
Item, the same day I made an bargain with Richard Cryspe for £50 stg. at 8s 6d Flem., 3 months and 4 months.

[97] It could be stated in 1564, for instance, that the exchange at London should be 2d Flem. 'above the true value of the sterling English £ of money', while that at Antwerp 'keepeth about 4d Flem. under the exchange in Lombard St' at usance: R. H. Tawney and Eileen Power, eds., *Tudor Economic Documents* (3 vols., 1924), III, 347–8.
[98] *C.L.* 36.

Item, made with Borgon's man £100 stg., at 8s 8d Flem., at 4 months and 4
   months.
Item, I have made with Whelbeke £40 stg., 8s 6d, 3 months and 3.
Item, with William Borwell £40 stg. at 8s 6d at 4 and 4.
Item, Richard Cryspe, £50 stg., 3 and 4, at 8s 6d.
Item, Gilbert Palmer, £30, 8s 6d Flem., 6 months and 6 months.
Item, the 14 day in June delivered Robert Heryc £8 4s Flem. Item, I have
   delivered Robert Heryc in ready money in part of payment of his sum – £10
   Flem. To pay – £13 Flem.[99]

   Clearly, there were many variables in supply and demand to affect the
rates at which loan exchanges were made. In September 1480 George
was holding £91 Flem. belonging to his aunt (Mrs Elizabeth Bowell?),
who had made an agreement with the London mercer John Matthew that
Matthew should receive this amount from George at the Bammis mart
and repay her with £75 16s 8d stg. at London 'at such days as they be
agreed'.[100] If the market exchange rate was still 26s 8d Flem. this gave
her a discount of 10 percent, on an agreed rate of only 24s Flem. to the
£ stg.

Some practical effects of instability in the Flemish money market may
be illustrated from 1478, when coinage valuations in Flanders were
rapidly enhanced, not by ducal fiat but by pressures from the market
economy. In March 1478 John Dalton paid the treasurer of the Staple
at Calais 11 crowns tariffed at 4s 10d Flem. on a Calais scale which may
have corresponded to a special tax rate of about 23s 6d Flem. per £.[101]
He lost 6d Flem. in each coin, because they were valued in Flanders at
5s 4d Flem., on the scale of 25s 4d Flem. per £ introduced in November
1477. Subsequently – about October 1478 – George Cely received crowns
for 5s 10d Flem. 'money current in Flanders', i.e. on the scale of 28s
Flem. per £.[102] Similarly, in June 1478 he paid William Eston on a bill
of hand from his brother Robert for £5 stg. 'taken up at 8s 8d Flem.',
making £6 10s Flem.[103] The bill, which had fallen due the previous
Easter, had apparently specified payment with 30 Rhenish gulden. In the
meantime their mart valuation had risen from 4s 4d Flem. to 4s 6d Flem.,
so that George recorded a loss of 5s on them and accounted the payment
to Eston at £6 15s Flem. Before November Rhenish gulden had risen
further, to 4s 10d Flem. in Flanders, but were still valued at 4s 4d by
the Calais table.[104] Richard senior had good cause to warn George on 10
October that he had heard that

99 File 15 fos. 51v–52.   100 *C.L.* 100, 101.
101 File 11 fo. 46v.   102 File 11 fo. 21.
103 File 11 fo. 47.   104 File 11 fo. 21; *C.L.* 34.

the money in Flanders shall be set at a lower price shortly, for the which be well ware [to] keep no money by thee, for there shall be a great loss to all them that hath much Flemish money in hand.[105]

It may be worth concocting a fictitious case to demonstrate the effects of some of the variations that might occur in exchange rates at such a time. The situation presented will be unrealistic in two respects. First, it will be postulated that a stapler – we will call him George Cely – transferred to England all his receipts from a given sale of wool. It is most unlikely that this would in fact occur. Secondly, for purposes of comparison it is necessary to assume that all the payments in a series of transactions were made in the same gold coin – the Burgundian Andrew has been chosen. This would never have happened in reality. In the first place, cash payments were usually made in a mixture of coins and in both gold and silver, and in the second place it has been shown that many transfers took place on paper, that is through a deposit banker. Nevertheless, let us suppose that George sold £200 stg. worth of wool in early March 1478, of which £100 stg. was to be paid in hand at Calais at a rate of 24s Flem. per £, making £120 Flem. At the exchange rate of 25s 4d Flem. per £ then obtaining in Flanders, the equivalent would have been £126 13s 4d Flem., so the customer got a preferential exchange rate, offset by the valuation of his coin. If he paid in Andrew gulden, the Staple valued the coins at 4s 2d apiece instead of the 4s 6d which was the current value in Flanders, so that he had to pay not 533.33 but 576 for £120. George would lose a notional £6 13s 4d Flem. on the exchange rate for sterling, but gain £9 12s on the difference in tariff for the coins. If he 'made over' the whole of his receipts at the mart in June by exchange loans at 25s Flem. per £ and with a value of 4s 8d for the coins, he could lend £134 7s 7d Flem. and receive £107 10s stg. in London in due course.

If, however, we should suppose that he owed £12 15s 5d stg. payable at Calais as part of the custom and subsidy due on the wool, and that the Staple charged this at a special tax rate of 21s 8d Flem. per £ and valued the Andrew at 3s 8d Flem. for the purpose, George would have to pay the Staple 75.47 of his Andrews at considerable loss.[106]

We will assume further that another £50 stg. of the selling price was payable in September 1478 at a prearranged rate of 25s 4d Flem. per £ stg., making £63 6s 8d Flem. The Andrew was now valued at 5s Flem. at the mart, and George's customer need pay only 253.33. At Calais they were now rated at 4s 6d Flem., so would be worth only £57 Flem. at Calais. At the current market exchange rate of 28s Flem. per £, £50 stg. should have been worth £70 Flem., so George again lost a notional

[105] *C.L.* 36.   [106] See below, Ch. 9, pp. 226ff.

£6 13s 4d (9.5 percent) on the exchange. He could, however, have made over his £63 6s 8d Flem. at a rate of 26s Flem. to the £ stg., so obtaining £48 14s 4d stg. in England and somewhat reducing his loss on the instalment of a nominal £50 stg. Nevertheless, his father regarded this rate of exchange for loans as 'not good', in fact as representing 'a great loss for the merchants of the Staple', because it was above the rate at which they received the debts of their wool buyers.[107]

The final instalment of £63 6s 8d Flem. might have fallen due in June 1479, when the exchange rate at the mart was 26s 8d Flem. per £, so that George lost a notional £3 6s 8d Flem. But at 4s 6d Flem. each, he would now receive 281.5 Andrews, and might again have made over all his receipt at 26s Flem. per £ stg., to produce another £48 14s 4d stg.

His eventual receipts for wool sold at a nominal £200 sterling of Calais would then have been £204 18s 8d mere sterling, if we ignore any payments towards custom and subsidy. Had George deposited with a wisseler his original receipt of 576 Andrews, total value in Flanders then £129 12s Flem., and conducted all further transactions on paper (by taking drafts on a wisseler from his customer and by assigning them to his exchange-loan partners), his final receipts in England would have been £201 mere stg. In these purely artificial models, it is only the stapler's ability to make over his total receipts by interest-bearing loans which changes losses on the exchange into a small profit. Even so, the transaction was skewed in the stapler's favour by allowing him to receive as much as half of his payment cash-down at Calais. It must, however, be stressed that the circumstances of 1478–9 were unusual.

At the Bammis mart of 1478 there was probably no shortage of English merchants wishing to borrow Flemish money, even at a comparatively high rate of interest. A calling-down of the coinage by some 12.5 percent was imminent, but was delayed until 12 October, after the closure of the mart. As soon as the gap narrowed between Flemish and sterling money, they would of course have to repay more sterling for any future Flemish borrowings, though interest rates might be expected to fall as well. Meanwhile they doubtless made the most of the inflated value of the Flemish coin, buying at Antwerp for resale at home, where they possibly marked up their goods on the system of 'sterlings for groats', which meant that they charged as many English pounds for their wares as they had paid in Flemish pounds.[108] A mercer could then charge his English customers 30 percent above the amount which he had to pay the creditor in England from whom he had borrowed at the mart. For example, if he borrowed £10 Flemish at a rate of 26s Flem. per £ stg. he had to repay

£7 13s 10d stg. The wares bought for the £10 Flem. could be sold at £10 stg., giving him a profit of £2 6s 2d over and above the interest paid on the loan, which was covered by the adjustment in the Flemish–sterling exchange rate employed.

Attempts to strengthen the £ Flem. were initially unsuccessful. The following April, the lowest terms at which Gilbert Palmer would take up money at the mart were 9s 6d Flem. per noble (28s 6d Flem. per £ stg.) and a term of four or five months, an offer which George found unacceptable.[109] The current rate for loans taken up at London for repayment at the mart was then 9s 8d Flem. (29s per £), which equally represented 'great loss', to the borrower.[110] The closeness of the two rates implied that a reduction in Flemish valuations was again expected, and indeed at the Whitsun mart the exchange rate seems to have dropped to 26s 8d Flem. per £ stg. at parity.

Why did English merchant adventurers wish to borrow money at the overseas marts at all, when, as exporters, they could expect to obtain all they needed from sales at the mart to their own customers?[111] No doubt there were many, especially among the mercers, who were self-sufficient in this way. Many, too, traded in wool as well as other goods and may have had their own receipts from wool sales to invest in purchases at the mart. William Maryon, for instance, a grocer as well as a stapler, wanted his receipts from fells to be invested in madder at the Cold mart in 1479, if the price was right.[112] Otherwise, he requested George to 'give [my money] out unto some good man. And if Richard, Robert Eyryk's child, have any need of any money now at this mart, I pray you that ye will deliver unto him as much as he will have.' More often, though, Maryon had his profits from the Staple trade made over by such exchange loans. He wrote to George in April 1482:

Sir, I understand that ye were purposed... shortly to the mart ward. Sir, I pray you that ye will do for me in the letting out of my money that is grown at this time as ye do with your own.[113]

Presumably there were usually some merchant adventurers who engaged in a one-way trade only and concentrated upon buying at the marts for import into England.[114] William Burwell was one who often seems to have had spare sterling in England which he was willing to exchange for Flemish money at Antwerp or Bergen-op-Zoom. Such a

[109] *C.L.* 50.   [110] Ibid.
[111] J. L. Bolton, *The Medieval English Economy, 1150–1500* (London and Totowa, 1980), p. 304.
[112] *C.L.* 70.   [113] *C.L.* 153.
[114] It was in their capacity as buyers that the English merchants were accused of coming late to the marts in the hope of reducing prices: *Foedera*, v (3), 89.

connection between exchange loans and the purchase of goods from the mart was made explicitly by William Cely, writing from the Cold mart in December 1479. So far, he said, there had been no exchange making, for the reason that there was 'but little ware here for men to bestow their money upon. They ween ['think'] the ships shall go home half unladen.'[115] The fact that payments were made only in its closing days may also have left sellers short of money during the opening weeks of a mart. Whatever the reasons, whenever English merchant adventurers attended the marts of Flanders and Brabant there were those who were willing and even anxious to take up money from staplers who had no immediate use for their surplus funds on the continent, but would need sterling in England to pay custom and subsidy and meet debts to their woolmen. Thomas Crisp, a mercer, is one example of a trader who spoke to Richard Cely senior in London, 'for to have £40 or 50, for the which I will ye deliver to Richard Crisp his son as ye can agree in the mart', as Richard wrote to George in May 1479.[116] Mercers in fact made up a large proportion of the adventurers who dealt with the Celys. Out of some 45 English merchants mentioned as partners in exchange-loan transactions (in either direction) in the papers, at least 27, or 60 percent, can be identified as London mercers. Three others were drapers, two grocers, two fishmongers, two upholders, one a haberdasher and one an armourer. William Maryon's nephew, Robert Eyryk, is described as a girdler as well as member of the fellmongers' company, but was not apparently a stapler.

One interesting pattern of connection between the activities of mercer and stapler may be revealed incidentally in this memorandum by George Cely:

Robert Cely.

Item, the 26 day of June [1478] I sent unto my said brother by Ralph Lemington, closed in an letter, an letter of payment of Helsabethe Reche, mercer of London, containing £50 stg., payable at London the last day [of] November next. I delivered [the money] unto her attorney [at] 8s 4d. Sum it amounts . £62 10s Flem.[117]

'Helsabethe Reche' is George's way of spelling 'Elizabeth Rich', and the obvious identification is with Elizabeth née Croke, who had married the mercer Thomas Rich before 1465.[118] But three years before George negotiated this deal she had become the wife of William Stonor. If the identification is correct, George's note is significant for several reasons. First, it was not at all uncommon for a widow to carry on her husband's business, but perhaps less usual for her to continue an active part in affairs

[115] *C.L.* 77.					[116] *C.L.* 53.
[117] File 11 fo. 47.					[118] *Stonor L.*, I, xxvii.

once she had remarried, especially so under her former name. Certainly Mrs (later Lady) Stonor was a woman of forceful character who seems to have spent much of her time leading an independent life in London while her new husband was in the country. Secondly, Kingsford was probably correct in deducing that William Stonor acquired his interest in the Staple trade in wool, together with his partnership with Thomas Betson, upon his marriage to Elizabeth. After her death in late 1479 or early January 1480 the partnership seems to have been effectively dissolved.[119] In 1478, however, the situation was evidently that Elizabeth Stonor was trading in her own right as a mercer and, through her attorney, taking up money from a stapler for purchases at Antwerp, while her husband and her son-in-law exported wool as staplers (an activity in which Elizabeth took a good deal of interest),[120] and themselves lent money at Antwerp to other merchants such as William Welbeck and John Pasmer.[121]

In the opposite direction, both staplers and merchant adventurers might 'take up' money at London for repayment at the mart. In 1497 the fellowship of London merchant adventurers can be seen selling a bill on the netherlands in this way to meet the costs of convoying their ships to the Bammis mart. Their letter of payment ran:

Be it known to all men that we, Richard Laken, Thomas Eyre, Robert Drayton and Philip Ball, citizens and merchants of London, have take up by exchange of William Buttry, citizen and mercer of London, £50 sterling to be paid to the said William or to Edmund Wotton his attorney at Antwerp in this mart the first day of October next coming after the date hereof. That is to wit, for every 6s 8d sterling, 10s 2[d] groot Flemish money. And if there be any default of payment of the said £50 sterling or any part thereof at the day abovesaid, it shall be lawful to the said William or Edmund to take it up by exchange and rechange at costs and losses of us the said Richard, Thomas, Robert and Philip.

In witness hereof to this, our first and second letter of payment, we have set our seals. Given the 17th day of September anno domini 1497.

> By me Richard Laken, mercer
> By me Thomas Eyre, grocer
> By me Robert Drayton, draper
> By me Philip Ball, haberdasher.[122]

[119] On 10 March 1480 Betson surrendered a number of bills and obligations to Stonor (ibid., no. 264), and thereafter he traded on his own. For instance, he shipped fells to Calais in Nov. 1481 (*C.L.* 132), and was one of the staplers accused of trying to corner the market in 1484 (*C.L.* 220). In early 1482 he still owed Stonor £1,200 (*Stonor L.*, no. 310). He was reluctant to deal with Stonor's stock, i.e. trade in partnership with him, and Stonor's adviser recommended Stonor to press for a cash settlement.

[120] E.g. *Stonor L.*, nos. 180, 211.

[121] Ibid., no. 264.

[122] *A.C.M.*, p. 640.

Three other members of the company had taken up £40 sterling for the same purpose from the Celys' old friend and fellow stapler, John Dalton, and because £5 was still owing Dalton threatened to return that amount by rechange.[123]

The haberdasher Richard Arnold included two specimen letters of payment in his commonplace book.[124] Evidently these were copies of letters he had himself issued in connection with loans that he had taken up in England. The first runs:

Be it known to all men that I, R.A.... have received by exchange of N.A. mercer...£20 sterling. Which twenty pound sterling to be paid to the said N. or to the bringer of this bill in Sinxen next coming; for 6s 8d sterling 9s 4gr Flemish, money current in the said mart....

His alternative version apparently equates the exchange rate with a particular coinage tariff:

Be it known to all men by these presents that I, R.A..... have taken up by exchange in London the day of making hereof, of T.W., citizen and mercer of London, £64 13s 4d sterling, to be paid at Antwerp in Brabant the 13 day of June next coming after the date hereof unto T. Balde in good money of Brabant as was there proclaimed by the King of Romans in the year of our Lord 1489... Sealed with my seal. Written the 17 day of May in the year of our Lord God 1492. [The years given vary in different editions of the printed work.][125]

It would accordingly be wrong to suppose that it was always the staplers who were the deliverers of money (or 'buyers of bills') at the marts and the takers (or 'sellers') at London. They were, however, obvious partners in dealings in these two directions. Robert Cely in particular was often short of money in England and in the market for small advances there. At the Bammis mart of 1478, when George was making over money from receipts, he also paid £11 Flem. to William Eston on a bill of Robert's hand for £8 stg. taken up at London at 9s 2d Flem., and £29 14s Flem. to the mercer William Burwell for £22 stg. taken up at 9s Flem.[126] In September 1480 Robert was begging George to 'see that William Borwell... be content of his bill of £14 15s' for a loan which had saved Robert from losing all his plate.[127]

Even Richard Cely senior found it convenient to take up a sterling loan on occasion, as in May 1479 when 27 sarplers of wool had arrived from the Cotswolds and 'I look daily for the men of Cotswold for to weigh at Lead Hall, and then I must have money for them.'[128] £60 due to John Peyrs of Northleach for wool had to be paid, not to Peyrs but to the

---

[123] Ibid., p. 644.
[124] Richard Arnold (1811), p. 117.
[125] Ibid.
[126] File 11 fo. 34.
[127] C.L. 102.
[128] C.L. 52.

London mercer Richard Haynes, and was possibly deductible from the return of the Flemish money that Haynes wished to borrow at the Sinxen mart.[129] Hugh Brown and Richard Twigge were both willing to oblige with the loans required by Richard Cely at London, but in the event he made another agreement of mutual accommodation with another London mercer, John Hosyer. By this Hosyer gave him £100 stg., repayable at the mart at 9s 6d Flem. or 28s 6d per £. But George was not merely to repay the loan, he would lend Hosyer as much Flemish money again, at the same rate. Richard therefore sent him a letter of payment for £200 stg. (£285 Flem.), and on receipt of the money at the mart Hosyer would in turn give his bill for a second £100 stg. to be paid by him at London in October. When the arrangement was made, 28s 6d Flem. may have been the rate at parity. But George made other loans at this mart at rates of 25s 6d Flem. or 26s Flem., so that his father lost money by the fall in the exchange. Despite that risk, this form of reciprocal loan was not uncommon. John Spenser made exchange with Thomas Abraham, grocer of London, for £20 stg. (£25 Flem.) on 2 December (1476?).[130] Spenser had already received £10 stg. at London, and on receipt of the £25 Flem. Abraham would make a bill for the other £10 stg., to be paid within a fortnight after Candlemas (2 February). Spenser requested George Cely, who held his Flemish money, to ensure that Abraham was duly paid, 'for I have found him so courteous in his dealing that I would not for twice the valure he were disappointed at the sight of his bill'. Robert Cely specified the same procedure in an arrangement with Eston in April 1476:

Well-beloved brother, I recommend me heartily to you. Furthermore informing you that the 13 day of April the year abovesaid, I, Robert Cely, have received of William Eston, mercer of London, £12 stg., to pay at Antwerp in Sinxen mart the 24 day of June, for every noble of 6s 8d stg., 7s 10d Flemish. And I pray you to deliver to the said William Eston £12 sterling at the same rate, taking a bill of his hand to pay at London the said £12 at a day as long after the day as I took the money up before.

In witness hereof I set my seal at London the 13 day of April.
Per Robert Cely.[131]

Such a letter of payment might well be described as a 'letter missive', but only in the sense that it passed from writer to recipient just like any other piece of correspondence, and not as any technical term.[132]

Apparently these double loans were not found convenient in the

[129] *C.L.* 53.   [130] *C.L.* 10.   [131] *C.L.* 3.

[132] Postan was misled by an annotation in the Cely papers into supposing that the expression was used with special application to a letter of payment: 'Private Financial Instruments in Medieval England', *Medieval Trade and Finance*, p. 56 and n. 65.

changed conditions under which Richard and George were trading in the later 1480s. Indeed, from 1486 onwards there is far more evidence in their papers of borrowing at London than of lending at the marts. William Burwell was still ready to supply sterling in return for Flemish currency, and on 4 September 1486 he lent £20 stg. payable on 4 October at 30s 9d Flem. per £ stg.[133] George converted sums at parity of 30s Flem. per £ at that time, so interest on principal amounted to 2.5 percent per month. Other loans at London were made by the mercers Richard Crisp and John Reynold. Crisp lent £40 stg. at 31s 6d, time unspecified (interest of 5 percent on the sum), and Reynold lent £50 for 76 days at 32s 6d Flem. (8.33 percent, or 40 percent per annum). A third loan, of £90 stg., was made by the fishmongers Roger Hongate and Richard Pighels, at 32s Flem. for 66 days (6.66 percent on the sum, or 36 percent per annum).[134] Evidently, when merchants argued that interest of up to 10 percent did not contravene the church's ban on usury, they were not thinking in terms of annual rates.

But it is not altogether meaningful to describe these financial dealings in terms of percentage of interest over price at parity. In October 1487 parity at Bruges was perhaps 34s Flem. per £ stg. About the same date George repaid a loan of £50 stg. which had been taken up at London for 30 days at a rate of 35s Flem. per £.[135] The interest must be seen in the context of his other transactions as an exporter. At Calais the English government was trying to hold the old rate of 30s Flem. per £ stg., and so were effectively devaluing the sterling in which exported wool was priced. If, for example, John De Lopez owed £50 stg. for wool bought, he would pay William Cely at Calais £75 Flem., at the prescribed rate of 30s Flem. per £. If the current rate at Bruges was 34s Flem., £50 stg. taken up at London might have to be repaid at 35s Flem., making £87 10s Flem. At the same time, William might have to lend £82 10s Flem. at Bruges, at a rate of 33s, in order to make over another £50 stg. to London. If (*per impossibile*) all these sums were paid in English rials of 10s stg. at appropriate tariff, De Lopez would hand over 100 at Calais valuation of 15s Flem. each. William, however, would have to pay 102.9 of them, at a mart valuation of 17s Flem. each, in return for the borrowed £50 stg., but give only 97 to the merchant who took up £82 10s Flem. to be repaid as £50 stg. in London.

The alternative method of repaying a loan was by means of 'change and rechange'. It is possible that a reference to brokerage charges at Bruges implies that this means was sometimes used when the Celys took

133 File 13 fo. 34.
134 Ibid. and File 20 no. 38. See also Ch. 15, p. 400ff.
135 File 20 no. 24 fo. 1.

up sterling loans from Alvaro De Cisneros, for instance in repayment of a loan of £60 in April 1486, in connexion with which George noted: 'Item, the £60 sterlings that Alvard took up for us in April is returned the 5 day of June – £63 8s 2d [stg.].'[136] There is, however, no positive evidence of the practice in the papers.

There seems little doubt that many English merchants at the Celys' time greatly preferred to transfer their money across the channel by private exchange-loans between themselves. When such facilities were available the Celys left the services of 'Lombards' and other financiers to people like Sir John Weston, who needed relatively large sums in foreign currency when he journeyed to Italy, en route for Rhodes, in 1481. He then borrowed, on highly favourable terms, the Flemish equivalent of £100 stg. from Richard Cely senior, repayable in England in two years time as £105 stg., and George was asked to look round in Calais for Venetian ducats in which to pay the sum. But Sir John also made over £500 'to receive of Lombards at Bruges in Flemish money', and sent George three letters of exchange, payable within eight days of sight, which he was to deliver to Bruges.[137]

The Celys themselves are very seldom recorded as engaging in loan transactions with 'Lombards', since a distinction must be drawn between their exchange-loans and payments made on behalf of John De Lopez, which were handled by Italian or Castilian agents in London. In May 1479, when Richard Cely senior had urgently requested £50 stg., George sent him two letters of payment directed respectively to John Dominico Barthelomeo and John Spyngell, 'Lombards', both of whom promised to pay at the day.[138] (A third letter was directed to Philip Celyar of Tournai, who was expected in London, where he in fact died suddenly before discharging his debt.)[139] It is possible that the two Italians were meeting payments for De Lopez. But this was at a time when George had refused Gilbert Palmer's offer to take up money at the mart at a rate no better than parity.[140] and when his father complained about money sent over in coin which George had reckoned at an exchange rate of 25s 6d Flem. per £ [Calais?] stg.:

I have received of the bringer of [your] letter £12 stg. in Carleche groats, 12d less [i.e. £11 19s stg.]. The which £12 stg. is 6 lb weight, ½ oz. The loss is great in the mint: I shall receive but £11 18½d for the same, wherefor send me no more.[141]

'Lombards' may have provided an acceptable service in these unusual circumstances.

[136] File 16 fo. 42. [137] *C.L.* 119–22. [138] *C.L.* 56.
[139] *C.L.* 70, 71, 78. [140] *C.L.* 50. [141] Ibid. and File 11 fo. 54.

William Cely certainly had occasional recourse to foreign dealers at times during the period between 1486 and 1488 when there was an absence of obliging English merchants. The details of his transactions with Benigne Decason and Jacob Van Der Base in September 1487 were printed in H. E. Malden's edition of the *Cely Papers* and have been widely quoted as an example of the making over of money with such aliens.[142] But these two transactions appear to have been exceptional. This was a time when coinage valuations were sky-rocketing at Bruges during its revolt against Maximilian. On 12 September 1487, when William was desperate to find means to transfer receipts back to England, the [manual?] exchange on the Burse at Bruges was 33s 10½d Flem. per £ stg. 'and goeth ever the longer worse and worse'.[143] Decason took up a sum at 33s 7½d Flem. per £ stg. or only 0.7 percent discount; the loan to Van Der Base allowed perhaps 1.5 percent discount. English merchant adventurers gave better terms, even when the money market was so insecure, and William dealt with these foreigners only because no Englishmen were available at the time. (For further details of his difficulties, see Chapter 13.)

Many of the loans made at this later period were 'at usance', which meant, between Bruges and London, for 30 days. The expression, which was standard parlance among Italian bankers, makes its first appearance in the Cely papers in 1486, signalling the new short-term basis on which they had to make and accept their exchange-loans. Changing circumstances, especially the disturbed conditions in Flanders in 1486–8, meant a disruption of the familiar patterns of trade. English merchant adventurers could not be sure of their attendance at any forthcoming mart, and in April 1487 George Cely had to agree with one lender, a London mercer, that if the latter did not wish to receive repayment of his loan at the Easter or Whitsun marts, he must be given sterling again at London.[144] Long-term loans had become much too risky, for both sides. Moreover, Richard and George were now diversifying their operations and no longer had surplus cash available to lend out for long periods.

[142] *Cely Papers*, nos. 128–9: *C.L.* 234–5; cf. *Studies in English Trade*, p. 69; Bolton, *Medieval English Economy*, p. 304. Bolton regards these transactions as 'a simple transfer', but as deliverer Cely still got more, not less, sterling than market rate at Bruges would dictate.

[143] *C.L.* 234. The only acceptable coins were briquets, écus, Andrews and Rhenish gulden.

[144] File 20 no. 22 fo. 2.

CUSTOMERS AND MARTS

Because sales on credit were a normal feature of the Staple trade at this period, new customers of good standing must often have brought letters of introduction, like that which John De Scermere presented to Richard Noneley.[1] No year is given, but the letter was written by Lowis De Moy, the Celys' 'Lois De May', who masquerades in the Public Record Office Index as 'Allyn Weijlowijs de Moy', because his valedictory clause, 'By d'alhu vrij Lowys de Moy', was misread and mistaken for the whole signature. 'Lieven Huter Meere' who is mentioned in the letter may conceivably be the 'Levyn Demore' whose name is written on a Cely note of sale to De Scermere (?) in 1478.[2] Quite possibly Noneley sent De Scermere on to George Cely, so that his letter of accreditation came into the Cely collection, from which it was later separated. Translated from its original Flemish, it runs

Honoured friend, I recommend me to you and let you know that the bringer of this is a *drapier* of Ghent. Lieven Huter Meere has prayed me to help him make his acquaintance with the merchants of the Staple of Calais. I understand, moreover, that he is a good young man, and that his business at home is such as to make him a very wealthy clothier, and if he wished to buy eight or ten sarplers of wool here, he should be in good credit.

If you have some of his variety, which is middle Cotswold, I understand that he wishes to buy two or three sarplers. He will keep to his promise, and I should willingly trust his word. Know further that the bringer, whose name is Jon De Scermere, has left £32 gr. with me, which he would have brought with him to Calais mart, except that he was never at Calais before, and that he comes alone, and so dared bring nothing with him. If you have no wool of his quality, then take him to Thomas Wischaert, or to anyone else whom you think suitable.[3]

---

[1] S.C.1 51/75. The *Lisle Letters* contain a rather similar letter of introduction for a merchant of Antwerp who came to Calais in 1536, anxious to sell cloth-of-gold and silks to the Deputy and the gentlemen of the garrison: *Lisle Letters*, no. 780.

[2] File 15 fo. 8.

[3] I cannot identify 'Thomas Wischaert'.

Further, Lieven Huter Meere requests that if the three sarplers middle Cots., which I mentioned to you when you last had money from him here, are ready, that in that case you should deliver them to this young man, and discuss with him the price and how he is to pay for them.

Item, let me know whether I shall rebate Lasere Lomelyn the bettering.[4] If I do not rebate it he will pay me no money. I write no more.

At Bruges, the 29th November. By your entire friend, Lowis de Moy.

To Richard Nonneley, merchant of the Staple of Calais.

Although De Scermere became a customer of the Celys, he was particularly unfortunate in his experiences with their wool. It was he who made great complaint to the English staplers at the Sinxen mart about the six sarplers and a poke of middle Cots. that he had bought in 1480, which contained, he said, the equivalent of two sarplers of middle young Cots., which would be worth £2 stg. per sack-weight less.[5] De Scermere took no official action because he was reluctant to 'strive' with George. But it was very likely De Scermere who had already written, in September 1478, asking for betterings on two other sarplers.

Memorandum for George Cely.

That in sarpler Number 28, weighing at Calais 5 [weys or half-sacks] and 40 nails, of this mark [a sketch of the pseudo-heraldic shield which they used as a merchant-mark], there were 48 fleeces moth-eaten and rotted, which weighed 25 nails and 2 lbs. Calais weight. To deduct a third in betterings makes 8 nails and 2 lbs. And for costs of the awarders' dues and of the certificate, 5s 2d groot. Sum of the costs – £1 8s 6d gr.

Also in sarpler Number 4 of the same mark there were 54½ nails Calais. The third in betterings comes, with 20 gr. of the awarders' costs, to £2 3s 9d gr., and this sarpler weighed at Calais 5 [weys] 25 nails.

Total of both – £3 8s 3d [sic].[6]

George's note of this sale shows that the two defective sarplers were the two sarplers of 'old' wool in a total sale of five.[7] According to the ordinance of 1476 this old wool must have spent at least four years in the sack, and possibly more, before it reached sale.[8] The details of the sale may be quoted in full, since they illustrate a number of the points discussed in a previous chapter.

Item, 2 old middle Cots. and 3 new middle Cots.

No. 28 . . . ss di. 40 cl.

No. 4 . . . ss 70 cl.   Sum – 5½ sack 20 cl.

---

[4] 'Of Ic slaen wille Lasere Lomelyn de beterynghe.' A Lazare Lommelyn sued one of the Pardo family over payment on a letter of exchange from Nantes in 1468: L. Gilliodts-van Severen, ed., *Cartulaire de l'ancien Consulat d'Espagne à Bruges* (Bruges, 1901), I, 102–3.   [5] *C.L.* 90.

[6] File 15 fo. 10 (translated).   [7] File 15 fo. 8.   [8] See Ch. 5, pp. 134–5.

New:

No. 47	. .	ss 70 cl.	
No. 48	. .	sss – 3 sack	
No. 61	. .	2½ 30 cl.	Sum – 8½ sack 10 cl.

Levyn De More:

Sum total in sacks	. . . .	14 sack 30 cl.
Argent	. . . £124 5s 3d 0 ster. [Corrected to [£124] 4s 5d 0.]	
At 8s it amounts	. . . .	·£149 16s 4d Fl.
		2s

[*Recte* £149 1s 4d]

In hand, 3rd penny	·£49 13s 10d Fl.
Item, 6 months after	· £49 13s 9d Fl.
Item, 6 months after	£49 13s 9d Fl.

Item, received in white money of them, of 5d the piece, sum	£25 Fl.
Item 25 [old crowns] 5s 2d	· £6 9s 2d
Item, 4 riders, 5s 8d	22s 8d
Item, 24 old nobles, 11s	£13 4s
Item, 12 Rhenish, 4s 4d	52s
Item, 6 Andreus, 4s 6d	27s
Sum	·£28 14s 10d Fl.
	£49 [14]s 10d.

It is to be feared that after his experience in 1480 De Scermere ceased to buy from the Celys, since no further sales to him are recorded in the papers, although it must be added that no argument can safely be based on their silence.

Jan Van Der Heyden of Malines (Mechelen) also purchased a small quantity of defective wool from the Celys in 1477, and stopped 16s from his account for betterings on it.[9] But relations remained good, and sales to him are recorded between 1475 and 1481. He had put enough faith in George to order by mail in 1477. He then wrote, in translation,

Know that I greet you heartily, master 'Soersse', and confirm in my own writing that, as you are aware, we discussed the wools which you were to send me by Ryken, factor of Joes Frank, as you will also remember. And therefore I, Jan Van Der Heyden, write to you, my good friend George Seely, and let you know that you must send me four bales middle Cotswold, *schoen ghebont* ['good packing'?], as I put my faith in you. That is to say, three new and one old. And know, George, that we shall settle everything at Bergen, God willing. Send me the best, George, and write me if you wish me to do anything for you. Written at Mechelen, anno 77, 9 October. By Jan Van Der Heyden.[10]

[9] File 21 no. 1 (fo. 2).   [10] *C.L.* 14.

Such a tried and true buyer would often be given credit with little trepidation, especially when customers were scarce. In May 1477, when trade was inhibited by fighting between French and Burgundians after the death of Charles the Bold, Richard senior wrote

I understand there come no merchants to Calais for to buy wool nor fells, for the which is right heaviness for the merchants of the Staple. For the which I fear me every man will find the mean for the sale, and deliver his wool and fells into sure men's hands by the mean of sale to merchants strangers the which have repaired to Calais afore this time [i.e. 'foreign buyers who are known at Calais']. For the which I would ye had communication with such merchants as ye have found sure men and good men, for to aventure some of my wool and fell in their hands by the mean of sale at long days, for I feel men shall do so at this season.

For the which I would think that John Underhaye [Van Der Heyden] were a good man for to trust, and other men such as ye think good men. Spare not for a long day, for I fear me it will come thereto. For I understand well there be diverse men of the Fellowship of the Staple of Calais have sold wool for three year day the last payment.[11]

A year later, in May 1478, George reported to his father that the current terms for the sale of new wool were 'the third penny' cash down and two further instalments in six months and 12 months, as we saw in the sale to De Scermere. George added, 'the day ['term'] is long. I will know him right well that shall have any [wool] at that day.'[12]

William Cely, as a mere factor, was still more cautious. William Kenett of Bruges, who was well known in Calais, wanted six sarplers of Cots. wool in January 1484, 'if I would 'a respite him of two parts of the money till Easter, and he would 'a set me good surety of our Fellowship, but I would not'.[13] Everyone else, however, was allowing credit on those terms: 'here beth diverse merchants of Bruges, and they have bought much wool, and they have been in hand ['have been negotiating'] with me for your Cots. wool, but I can sell them none without they may have Passe day of payment, as they have of other men'.[14]

As mentioned earlier, the bulk of the Celys' consignments of wool was usually bought up by one or two of their established clients. At the Sinxen mart in 1480 Van Der Heyden made a (probably illegal) bargain with George for all his stock of middle wool and sealed it with a 'God's penny'.[15] But their major customer was John De Lopez of Bruges, and very probably his role was still greater than appears from the sales in his name. Bruges merchants often acted in partnership, as the fell buyers from Leiden and Delft did. One example is Barbel, the widow of Gerard Benowth, buying wool with Aleamus De Bollonye in August 1475.[16]

[11] *C.L.* 12. [12] *C.L.* 22. [13] *C.L.* 206.
[14] *C.L.* 207. [15] File 15 fo. 51v. [16] See Ch. 5, p. 138.

Peter Van De Rath and Ghijsbrecht Van Wijnsberg bought jointly at the same date, while Cornelius Van Dorne bought six sarplers ten days later, apparently on his sole account.[17] In October 1478, however, a consortium is mentioned of 'John De Lopez, Cornelis Van Dorne and their fellows', and the other 'fellows' were in fact Ghijsbrecht Van Wijnsberg and Aleamus De Bollonye.[18]

Among the Celys' minor customers for fleece-wool at various times were John Spengel, John Van De Wolpytt, the Bruges merchants Master Jacob Damast or Damaske, Lowis De Moy, William Kenett, Robert Le Gaynard, Collard Mesdaw, John Myller, Jacob Pottry, John Record, Peter and Daniel Van De Rath or Rade and Giles Van Dewle, and the Malines merchants Cornelius Cappe, John De Selonder, Jois Frank and Giles Frank, senior and junior. As we have seen, De Scermere was from Ghent. From Antwerp came Arnold Johnson, from Lille John Borgesse of 'Ryssyll', and from Courtrai Wotter Van Tylde. A company of Normans from Rouen are mentioned once.[19] The Hollanders from Leiden, Delft, 'Gowe' [Gouda] and once Rotterdam bought almost all the fells. They usually operated in fellowships, for example 'Garad Birevay, Gord Faw, Dyryc Allbrytson, Garad Van Egmond, Cornelys Mast, Garad Artson, Copman Albrondson of the town of Leythe [Leiden'],[20] or Jacob Wylliamson, Symond Isbrandson, Clays Cornellisson, Francke Gerredson, Mychell Pollson and Gyesbryght Van Deryell of Delft.[21] Once George uses the expression 'sosyys' (Latin *socius*, 'associate') for one of these fellowships.[22] Among so many names it is not surprising that there was occasional confusion, and John Dalton refers in one document to a buyer whom he called indiscriminately 'Peter Johnson' and 'John Peterson'.[23]

To counteract these lists of featureless men, one might quote the vignette of a later Staple customer, who bought wool at Calais in September 1538. The authorities, in the paranoia of the time, suspected that he had gone on to England in pursuit of some nefarious activity, and instituted secret enquiries at Calais. Their sinister stranger was identified by the treasurer of the Staple as one John De Caster, 'a man of honest conversation and of few words, and also somewhat halting ['lame'], being of a good age, and a draper of wool, dwelling in Mechelen'.[24]

On the whole the Celys seem to have enjoyed amicable relations with their customers, even the Hollanders, who were sometimes exigent. Their letters do not contain the execrations occasionally used by the

[17] File 11 fo. 18.
[18] File 11 fos. 34, 30.
[19] *C.L.* 34.
[20] File 11 fo. 17v.
[21] File 20 no. 12.
[22] File 15 fo. 15.
[23] File 12 fos. 15v, 16.
[24] *Lisle Letters*, nos. 1247–1247a.

Johnsons, who longed to call some of them 'javels' ['churls'] to their faces.[25] Possibly, however, the Celys sometimes had to write letters like this one of 1546, translated from John Johnson's Flemish.

> It behoves you to know that I have understood by letters received from Antwerp that you and your fellowship have made very sorry payment of what you owe me, whereby I have great loss. And it is very ill done of you, when you deal so shamefully with us of the Staple in your payment that you lose your credit there. I pray you let there be no default in your payment at the approaching term at the mart, since I have taken up money by exchange. And if I incur damage through default of your payment I shall proceed against you, and also let the lords of Delft know how ill you have kept your troth with me, as Our Lord knows, who defend you.[26]

As far as the record goes, Richard and George Cely had more trouble with their English exchange-loan partners than with their foreign buyers. Two obligations from John Benyngton, issued in 1486, are still among their papers.[27] They also went, apparently in 1482, to the Admiral's Court to get payment of £30 delivered by exchange to John Rose or Ross.[28] This was presumably the unreliable John Roosse who pestered George for hawks in 1479.[29] George did institute a law-suit at Bruges in 1481.[30] Clays De Moll, a prominent local 'man of the law', was engaged to represent him, and William Dalton gave the court sureties on George's behalf from a group of men from Ypres: Matthew De Cortt, Philip De Camell, George Kalcoun, and two *scepens*, Charles of Dixmude and Arthur Ubermeer, to the total amount of £367 16s 11d Flem. Dalton delivered 18s to Clays De Moll, 'to see and know whether the said persons be sufficient or no', and George then paid 20s to the 'procuraries' of Ghent to 'sue the said matter accordingly', and 26s to Clays 'to sue a reliefment of the said duty'. But no more details are given.

It was sudden death that caused some legal complications in 1479, when Richard Cely senior was owed £60 by Philip 'Seller' or Celyer of Tournai.[31] Celyer had duly come to London, where his bill was payable, but fell victim to the epidemic there. His will, dated 25 September 1479, was drawn up as he lay on his death-bed, 'afflicted with the pangs of sickness, but whole in mind' ('iacens in lecto dolore egritudinis vexatus tamen sanus mente').[32] In it he bequeathed £10 to Henry his 'famulus', and custody of all goods in England to 'John De Colonea alias Johannes

[25] S.P. 1/198 fo. 181v.
[26] S.P. 45/5 fo. 87v. (To Derek Peterson of Delft?)
[27] File 13 fos 19–20.
[28] File 10 fos. 8, 18.
[29] Ch. 2, pp. 52ff.
[30] C.L. 133 and File 12 fo. 21 (a copy taken from George's 'book bound with tanned leather').
[31] C.L. 56.
[32] P.C.C. 12 Logge.

De Cassa', citizen and cheesemonger of London. George Cely had a fardel of arras in pledge from Philip and was instructed not to part with it until the debt was paid.[33] George, himself lying ill in Bruges, probably took little interest in the matter, which was settled in due course at London. Richard junior reported to him on 9 December that Philip's factors, named Harry De Morres and John Forner, had arrived in London.[34] John had wedded Philip's daughter. The London broker John Jacoby was retained in the Celys' interest and successfully maintained that the bill had been previously 'protested', that is, that payment had been refused when it had been presented, perhaps so that Celyer could pay in London. In the upshot, the broker picked out 300 crowns, valued at 4s stg. each, from 400 offered for his inspection, and £5 was awarded for the protest and costs. At the mint the crowns fetched 4s 6d each, but there was one cloud on this silver lining: 'the broker's part will be much', said Richard ruefully.

If Celyer had purchased wool from the Celys he was exceptional in seeking to pay them in England. John De Lopez and his partners often preferred to do so, but most of their clients were happy to follow the custom of meeting deferred instalments at Bruges or one of the great seasonal marts, namely the Easter (Pasche or Pask) mart and the winter 'cold' mart at Bergen-op-Zoom ('Barrow'), and the Antwerp Whitsun (Sinxen or Pinxter) mart and Bammis mart, held around the feast-day of St Bavon of Ghent. Quite why merchants did not make still greater use of the banking facilities provided by the wisselers is matter for speculation, but probably these were too local to offer an adequate network of correspondents between the various parts of the low countries. In 1478 Leideners wished to deposit money in Bruges and give bills of exchange for wool bought at Calais, but it seems that this applied only to their initial down-payment.[35] The system whereby staplers or their factors regularly made the laborious journey to the marts at which they trusted to meet their customers and obtain satisfaction of their debts, was cumbersome. The Hollanders often arrived late. English buyers were also accused of doing so, in the hope that the locals, desperate to get home, would reduce their prices for a quick sale.[36] Bad weather, poor roads, robbers, retaliatory measures on behalf of the aggrieved merchants of particular towns, or general harassment by soldiers all posed risks which sometimes seriously reduced attendance. A wise merchant always travelled in company. George paid 3s 10d Flem. to 'our guide that rode with my brother and me' to the Sinxen mart in 1476, and in May 1478 his father begged him 'keep thee in good fellowship to the mart-ward, and

[33] *C.L.* 70, 71. [34] *C.L.* 78.
[35] *Studies in English Trade*, pp. 67–8. [36] *Foedera*, v (3), 89.

in the mart, and from the mart to Calais-ward, for there is most dread'.[37]
De Scermere, making a lone journey from Bruges to Calais, was careful
to leave his money behind, and George was told once not to 'jeopard'
himself too often by riding to Bruges since, in his father's opinion, the
world was then 'queasy, and ye are well-known': it would be safer to
send his servant Joyce.[38]

The Cold mart at Bergen was aptly named, and the least popular of
the four; 'neither healthful nor merry', in George's experience.[39] But
Bergen was a good place at which to buy woad and madder, sturgeon
or barrels of salmon or tunny. This is a sample account of George's
purchases, at Cold mart 1480:

Two ounces quarter of coral, 2s 8d le ounce	6s
Item, paid for 7 gauds [the large beads in a rosary] to the same	2s 4d
Item, paid for 25 dozen lute strings	17s
Item, paid for 3 girdles for cross-bows	20d
Item, paid for an firkin salmon	7s 6d
Item, an firkin tunny	7s 6d
Item, an pouch	14d
Item, an fur of fitchews	16s Fl,
Item, an lute	10s Fl.
Item, an dozen cords	10d
An long rope	14d
An feather bed	30s Fl.
2 pillows	3s 4d
An covering of verdure	27s 3d
Le fashion of my chain	6s
My girdle harness	7s 6d
My girdle itself	8s
3 caps	8s
3 ells satin	26s
Le making	4s
A pair hosen	4d
Laces and points	6s
2 stomachers	7s
2 pillowberes [pillow-cases]	20d

[Sum £10 4s 7d].[40]

According to the rules laid down in 1479, the Easter mart at Bergen
began on the Thursday before Easter, and the Cold mart (sometimes
called St Martin's) the Thursday before All Saints' Day, 1 November.
Nominally they each lasted one month, but two weeks' extension was

---

[37] File 11 fo. 7v; *C.L.* 23. In 1482 Joyce Parmenter accompanied George to the Bammis
mart and then took the horses back to Calais until George was ready to return. His
costs from Calais to Antwerp on the second journey were 6s 9d Flem.: *C.L.* 194, 196.
[38] *C.L.* 134 (1481).   [39] *C.L.* 111.   [40] File 12 fo. 8.

customarily permitted for the winter mart.[41] Unofficially, bad weather or the tardy arrival of merchants might cause the Cold mart to continue into January or even February. During the 'franchise' of a mart visiting merchants might travel to and fro and trade without fear of being arrested for the debts of any fellow citizens – or such was the pious hope. The usual pattern at a mart was to allow a period for travel, and then three show-days, after which selling began. Payments were made only towards the end of the period.

The Antwerp fairs were also published for a month, with 15 days' customary extension. The Sinxen mart at Antwerp began 15 days before Whitsun, the feast from which it took its dialectal name.[42] Including the extension, it would have a possible range of 25 April to 13 June, and 29 May to 10 July. This was the time to purchase linens, which were bleached in the spring and ready for market about June. The Bammis mart began the second Sunday after 15 August, and was named, as mentioned before, for the feast-day of St Baf or Bavo[n], patron saint of Ghent, on 1 October, a date which coincided with the day of St Remy, Bishop of Reims. Some commentators have confused this St Remy with another saintly namesake, and thus confused the dating of the mart. Including its extension period, its earliest opening date would be 23 August, with closure on perhaps 3 October. Its latest date of opening would be 29 August, with closure on 9 October.

Staplers like George Cely relied on meeting English merchants at the marts, with whom to make home money. 'Yet I may do no more good, neither in buying of wool nor fells nor in building, for default and lack of money. For the which I shall think long till Bammis mart come', wrote his father in July 1478.[43] But aside from such necessary business, the marts were great social and commercial occasions. Young men fresh out of England must especially have enjoyed the spectacle of all the world and its goods on display. George's purchases for himself, family or friends have been repeatedly mentioned. As the 'Discourse' says,

who some ever will use Antwerp mart and Barrow mart, he shall find merchandise there of the most part of countries in Christendom, and such as he faileth of in these marts, he shall be served thereof in Flanders.[44]

Of those goods which the 'Discourse' describes as specialities of different places in Europe, many could indeed be obtained at the netherlands

---

[41] Nelly J. M. Kerling, 'Relations of English Merchants with Bergen-op-Zoom, 1480–81', *B.I.H.R.*, XXXI (1958), 131; Gilliodts-van Severen, *Inventaire des chartes*, VI, 435 (1498).
[42] In Latin, *Penticostabilia nundina* (*A.C.M.*, p. 389). There is no connection with St John's Day, as sometimes supposed by English writers.
[43] *C.L.* 26.
[44] 'Discourse', fos. 99v–100r. 'Except such things as be banned out of the land', it adds.

marts. Of mercery there was Paris silk, either close or open and 'right fine', finer and better than the cheaper London silk; the coarse silk of Genoa called 'Cadase silk', raw silk for fletchers, 'gold of Damask, and that is all wire, and gold of Cyprus is the second, and gold of Florence and of Venice', also 'gold of Genoa that is called skein gold, for it is commonly in skeins. Also there is Cologne gold, gross gold, "Sypers" gold (these be coarse), and there is copper gold that is coarsest of all'.[45] Cloths included bustian, dorniks and bord Alexander, all kinds of buckrams, 'tartrun', and the fine lawn or 'umpill' which was sold in 'plights'. William Maryon wanted, from the Cold mart in 1479, a cloth he called 'haustar' or 'halfftar', to make sheets. It could also be obtained from Hanseatic merchants in London.[46]

To the marts came, from the Baltic area, resin, wax (either 'Poleyn' or 'Spruce'), different kinds of iron, timber (deal, 'ragalds' (from Righolt?), wainscot, claphall and bow-staves), and furs such as sable, ermine, lettys (from snow-weasels), beaver, foins (stone-marten), marten and otter ('and these be great plenty' in those parts).[47] From Portugal and Mediterranean lands were imported sweet wines like ossey, bastard and romney, olive oil, 'which is most wholesomest for man's meat and medicines, and when it is old it is good wool oil', honey, dates, figs, pomegranates and citrus fruit, besides the 'grain' which made superb dye.[48] Sugar by this time came chiefly from Madeira and the other Portuguese islands in the Atlantic. The curled 'budge', equivalent of astrakhan or 'persian lamb', and particularly suited to sober merchants and lawyers, owed its name to its origin from Bougey in North Africa, though Ireland could supply a cheaper substitute: 'black lamb, fellow to "bogy"'.[49]

Some of the goods for which Antwerp was itself most noted seem to have strayed into the 'Discourse''s list of desirable English exports to Iceland: arms and armour such as 'sallets' (head-pieces), gauntlets, long swords and daggers, linen cloth, silver buttons, amber beads, knives and points, glasses and combs.[50] Nearly all these things figured among George's purchases at one time or another, along with other examples of the art of gold- and silver-smiths, leather-ware, especially saddles and gloves, his mother's sugar-loaves and pots of green ginger, and tapestry work. The pattern in this that was favoured by many of his friends was

---

[45] Ibid., fo. 98v.

[46] *C.L.* 69, 70. In Aug. 1485 the *Mary of Middelburgh* and the *Mary of Hamburg* had pieces of 'haustre' in their cargos at London: E.122 78/3.

[47] 'Discourse', fo. 99r–v. For the identification of furs, Elspeth M. Veale, *The English Fur Trade in the Later Middle Ages* (Oxford, 1966).

[48] 'Discourse', fo. 100v.

[49] Ibid., fo. 101. [50] Ibid., fo. 99v.

'verdure', an over-all design of foliage, which might be diversified with flowers and animals. He seems to have bought nothing as grand as the 'chamber of arras of the story of Nabugodhonosour [Nebuchadnezzar]' with matching counterpane and bed-hangings which enlivened one of the rooms of Sir Walter Herbert,[51] or Sir John Fastolf's eight costers of arras

whereof one is of the siege of Phalist [Falaise Castle, 1417?], another of the shepherds and their wives, another of the morris dance, another of Jason and Lancelot, another of a battle, one of the coronation of Our Lady, another of the Assumption of Our Lady,

or his other coster of 'tapseri', depicting gentlewomen playing at cards.[52]

The compiler of the 'Discourse' perhaps took his material from a period before printed books became a noted export from the low countries. The 'book' for which William Maryon wanted a cover in 1480 and William Dalton's 'great book' shipped to England in 1482 might have been in manuscript, or just merchant's ledgers, and there is nothing to indicate whether the book, costing four crowns, that George had on order 'against St John's church' (in Antwerp?) in 1478 was in manuscript or print.[53] The same is true of his 'calendar of the planets'.[54] But the almanac made by Master John Laete which William Dalton sent in 1487 was certainly printed,[55] and so were the two volumes which one R. Shipden requested, probably about 1478. Shipden had already seen copies and now wanted his own. He wrote to George

My trusty and very trusty friend and lover, I recommend me unto you, to John Eldurbek and John Dalton, to my master Wigston first, and all other. And master, how be it that I have charged you oft and many times with many things, whereof as yet no recompense, in sooth, is made on my part, yet wot ye well that I am he which with all mine heart shall make recompense in part, with all mine heart and service.

Praying to take in patience this my request, and according to the same to buy, by the help of my brother John Dalton and friend, in the mart two little books imprinted. One is entitled or called 'Beliall', and another 'Formularium Instrumentorum'. And for the love of Jesu forget not this, as ye will have my service while I live. There is matter in the t'one that shall do you pleasure as well as me. If ye will not buy them, speak to John Dalton. And let me have ready word.

Your true lover, R. Shipden, per.[56]

Both these books still exist in a number of editions, and in several languages in the case of *Belial*. The *Formularium* was an ecclesiastical

[51] *C.P.R. 1494–1509*, p. 601.   [52] *Paston L.*, no. 64 (pp. 109, 111).
[53] File 15 fo. 41v; File 16 fo. 23; File 11 fo. 36.
[54] File 13 fo. 26 (1486).   [55] *C.L.* 228.
[56] *C.L.* 244.

legal formulary in Latin and unlikely to interest George, but no doubt – if he did obtain a copy – he enjoyed *Belial*, alias 'the Consolation of Poor Sinners', which described how Belial, procurator of Hell, sued in the Almighty's consistory court for the possession of souls. The work was calculated to appeal both to religious sentiment and the widespread fascination with the law and its processes, and was enlivened with woodcuts, for instance of a long-eared devil serving his Opponent with a writ in proper form. George is recorded as spending 53s 4d on a law-book for 'his cousin of Northampton', and this entry may conceivably refer to Shipden and the *Formularium*.[57] Not only books but also paper came from the continent, so that the Celys, writing their letters and memoranda in Calais or London, and William Caxton, printing his books in England, often used batches with the same water-mark. A ream cost George 5s Flem. in 1487.[58]

One account survives for some plate which George had made abroad: two pieces and a cover, weighing in all 75 oz. 3½ dwt. Flemish troy weight. The silver cost 4s 6d per ounce. Fashioning them, at 9s 4d each, came to 28s Flem., and George paid a further 4s for the case.[59]

Two undated bills concern purchases of cloth, also made in the netherlands, although in one of them prices per Flemish ell of 27 inches are also translated into price for the English ell of 45 inches.[60] The large quantities suggest that the goods were bought for resale in England. Besides 25 'pieces' of Holland cloth at varying prices (one 'of linen cloth called Holland' contained 31¾ Flemish ells at £3 per 100), there were 8 ells of diaper at 10d the Flemish ell, 355 ells of 'linen cloth called Flemish' at 4d the ell, Brabant cloth at 2½d, Milan fustian at 10s the half-piece, canvas at 18s the 100 Flemish ells, sheets at 10s the dozen, two dozen napkins at 12s, two 'posts' of buckram at 23s each, and 124 ells of 'werkyn' at 28s the 100. In addition, 20 books of silver (i.e. silver foil?) were bought at 16d each.

Purchases, like the books of silver, were sometimes frankly luxury items. Early in his career George bought at Antwerp mart such goods as a musk-ball, twelve silver buttons, 'mantles' (a measure of skins) of wild peltry, 'two laces to put about an man's neck of gold', and a rosary, of amber with 15 silver and gilt paternoster beads.[61] At the Bammis mart in 1475 he had three rings, an agnus dei and 'pauteners' (pouches) made. The gold in the rings and agnus came from two old nobles and two rials, in addition to more supplied by the goldsmith himself at a total cost of

---

[57] File 10 fo. 8v.
[58] File 13 fo. 31v: the equivalent of about 3s stg. at this date.
[59] File 16 fo. 29.   [60] File 16 fos. 28, 46.
[61] File 11 fo. 5.

27s 10d, which included half an ounce of silver for the pautners. For these George supplied a further 2½ oz 1 dwt costing 10s Flem. Fashioning three rings cost 5s, and making the agnus cost 7s.[62] Spanish boots, shoes for his mother and a demi-lance, or Maryon's feather-bed from Antwerp, were among rather more utilitarian items at different dates.[63]

A merchant's friends were well aware that all these enticing products were available, and shortly before mart-time the requests came pouring in. George clothed a group of six people at the Bammis mart in 1478.[64] There were four yards of material to be bought for Ralph Lemington, two and a half for John Dalton, and another three-quarters for a short gown (cloth was, in general, wider then than now), two and three-quarter yards for Richard Wood, two yards for Edward Lenallis, three for Richard Cely and six and a quarter for George himself. Compliance with such requests meant conferring a favour which would be duly noted and, one hoped, reciprocated in time to come. Harry Bryan obtained supplies of gloves and other goods through George, and in return acted as his 'good solicitor' (for a further consideration) when a matter of over-charging on exchange rates came up before the lieutenant of Calais.[65] When commissions could be executed for any person of standing, the merchants were delighted to oblige, always mindful of the pursuit of 'good lordship'. George bought silk and velvet and a gold tassel for Sir Ralph Hastings in 1486 and seems to have given him a reduction on the exchange rate, just as he sold wine very cheaply in London to Hastings and Sir Thomas Tyrrell.[66] William Adam was interested in buying a horse for 'a great gentleman, of whom you might deserve great thank',[67] and John Dalton passed on careful instructions for the purchase of girdles for Lady Scott.[68] Like most people, Robert Radcliffe, 'gentleman porter' of Calais, was careful to promise future benefit when he begged George to 'vouchsafe to take the pain' to buy him a whole list of goods at the Cold mart in 1478.[69] He wanted 60 budge skins, to cost 7d or 8d each, six sugar-loaves of three hundred-weight (troy), and 12 lb of 'raisins of Corinth', i.e. currants. 'And if ye can find any fair fur of marten tails for a long gown, I pray you buy for me.' All this would be paid for when George returned from the mart. And Radcliffe added politely, 'and if it lie in my power I shall do as much that shall be unto your pleasure', and 'brother, I am bold to desire you to do thus mickle, but I shall acquit you in taking double the pain for your sake, in anything ye desire [me] to do for you, or any friend of yours'.

[62] File 11 fo. 5v.
[63] File 11 fo. 36 (1478); File 12 fo. 10 (1479).
[64] File 11 fo. 31v.
[65] C.L. 161–2.
[66] File 13 fo. 27; File 20 no. 21; File 13 fos. 38, 44.
[67] C.L. 166.
[68] C.L. 51.
[69] C.L. 42.

It was probably in 1480 that Edmund Bedingfield, who was a man of some importance in Norfolk and was to be knighted at Richard III's coronation in 1483, sent George a lengthy list of goods to be bought at Antwerp at the Bammis mart. He gave detailed specifications.

I must pray you to take some labour for me in this mart, for to buy for me, if there be any, one [or 'worn'?] long gown of chamlet, damask or satin, that be not but of a small price of 4 noble or thereabout. I pray you buy me one, but I had liefest have chamlet, so it be black, tawny or violet, but none other colour. Furthermore, I pray you to buy for me two dozen pair of gloves for women, one dozen of the largest assize and another dozen, the one half lesser than the t'other. And also to buy me a sheaf of good quarrel ['cross-bow bolts'] for a bow of 14 lb, and a windas for both hands for a bow of 6 or 7 lb. And let the quarrel be sent to Lynn or to Boston with my gear that Bondman sends. And that my quarrel may come home that ye bought for me the last mart, which I would had be sent to Lynn or to Boston also. And else I pray you let them come hither [to Calais] and this stuff both, as soon as ye may.

And if there be any mannerly daggers or punches ['small daggers'] at the mart, that I may have some to give away. And Our Lord keep you.[70]

Both daggers and gloves were favourite presents, and might be given as New Year gifts.

Harold Staunton was one of those who commissioned George to buy armour at Antwerp: at the Sinxen mart in 1480 George noted that he was to find him a pair of 'gussets', a fauld of fine steel and a standard collar.[71] At the same time he was trying to satisfy a fashionable desire among his friends for, literally, fine feathers, for the adornment of man and horse. Naturally there were sometimes difficulties. George would have to follow his own judgment when Harry Bryan asked him to 'bespeak' 12 dozen pairs of Louvain gloves, 'two dozen mark 2, three dozen mark 4, two dozen mark 3, and four dozen mark 2'.[72] On one occasion a servant of William Paston III, having been asked to send nine yards of stuff to his master, had to enquire which of three varieties was meant, for 'I cannot discern whether ye would have frieze or cotton or plain blanket. There is of each.'[73] In 1482 George had 'chambering' made for himself in Bruges, and when it arrived in Calais William Cely reported, 'I have received it everything according to your remembrance ['memo'], save the curtains be stained but on the one side, and there is no demi-curtain, but they be all whole that ye may slit which ye think best.'[74] Evidently these were 'painted cloths', like the one that George had ordered from John Wells of Antwerp in 1478, or those sent to William Maryon in 1486.[75]

[70] *C.L.* 103.   [71] File 15 fo. 51.   [72] *C.L.* 161.
[73] *Paston L.*, no. 858.   [74] *C.L.* 189.   [75] File 11 fo. 36; File 20 no. 18 fo. 2v.

Apart from notes of transactions, the Celys give disappointingly few details about their visits to the marts. They may have stayed with designated hosts at Antwerp and Bergen, unless they enjoyed the use of a special house. There was an 'English' street at Bergen,[76] and George lodged sums of money in the town with what he terms the 'howser', apparently the *huushere* or concierge.[77] In 1488 Richard Arnold quarrelled with a Lombard, identified as being 'hosted' at the 'Lion' in Middelburgh, although the squabble took place as they drank in the 'Horse Shoe' at Bergen.[78] No doubt the staplers and their customers met at such taverns to talk business. In 1468 a settlement was arranged in the 'Oak' at Antwerp between Ebalt Hughson and one of his creditors,[79] and perhaps George and Van Der Heyden made their bargain for all George's middle wool over a tankard 'the Friday, the same day I came to Antwerp' in 1480.[80] In similar places De Scermere could have complained about Cely wares to George's fellows in his absence.[81]

Letters by John and Otwell Johnson and their associates in the sixteenth century more often give precise directions about where to find, for instance, Walter Garrwaye, servant of William Chester, lodged in the 'Golden Stork' behind the Red Port Bridge, 'the sign of the "Golden Lattice" in the Linen Cloth Market at Antwerp, called in Flemish the *Gulden Traylle*', or Peter, the cutter of stones for rings, 'who standeth in the pawnd by the old Burse' there.[82] The *pand* was a sort of covered shopping mall.

Rather more appears about George's frequent trips to Bruges. Although Bruges was at least two days' journey from Calais, the staplers regarded it as shopping and banking centre. 'Let me understand what ready money I have at Bruges', wrote Richard senior in July 1478.[83] Bruges was also a convenient place in which to meet Flemish clients and other English merchants. Even after the merchant adventurers moved their overseas headquarters from Bruges to Antwerp there was usually a large colony or 'nation' of Englishmen residing in Bruges. It is absurd, however, to suppose that when William Caxton had been stationed there as 'governor' of the mercers he was so completely cut off from life in England that his native English speech merged with Flemish. The truth is that there were a number of Flemish words and expressions current among the English merchant community at Bruges and Calais, like *overcorn* for a supplement on a bill or other additional payment, Caxton's

[76] Kerling, 'Relations of English Merchants with Bergen-op-Zoom', p. 136.
[77] *C.L.* 151.
[78] See Ch. 1, p. 25.
[79] See Ch. 4, p. 93.
[80] File 15 fo. 51v.
[81] *C.L.* 93.
[82] 'Johnson Letters', nos. 167, 224.
[83] *C.L.* 27.

own *spoil* for 'wash' (Flemish *spoelen*), *stic* meaning a length of cloth, or a piece of anything, the staplers' *shorling, forehouse, bettering, breckling, gruff* or *inship* 'lade', the terms for bales of wool: *sarpler, poke, pocket* and *blot*, and many more. Flemish was not so very different from southern English as to present great difficulty to an insular merchant, and while George may not have been fluent in French he evidently communicated readily enough with his customers from Flanders, Brabant and Holland.

Bruges, then, was almost as familiar to the staplers as Calais itself, and for the modern visitor it is their haunts in the former that are now more easily identified. The Rue Anglaise remained into the twentieth century, although the English merchants' church of St John has been demolished long since. The topography in a letter to George from Harold Staunton can be traced on Marc Gheeraerts' pictorial map of the town in the sixteenth century, where the wide thoroughfare the Vlamijnck Dam (subsequently the Rue St-Georges) runs up to the 'Oude Burse' and 'Hoedemakers Straete' is two blocks away, past the Augustinian monastery.[84] Staunton had the usual errands to be done.

Master Cely, I pray you let your man do so much for me as to go to the sign of the 'Star' next unto Flemings Dam where as daggers be made, and I pray you let him receive a dagger of him and pay therefor 2s 6gr, by the same token that I paid him 6gr in earnest. Also I pray you that he may go to the capmaker next beyond William Kenett's on the same side to Flemings Dam-ward, and let him receive of him 6 single bonnets of diverse colours as I bespake for. And I pray you let him be paid for them. And at your coming to Calais ye shall be content, with God's grace.

He concludes engagingly,

Sir, ye may say ye have a homely fellow of me, for ye have done so much for me that it lies not in me to deserve it. But ye shall have my service, and that God knows, who preserve.[85]

George was lodging at another house called the 'Star' which was much frequented by staplers, when Radcliffe sent him this message:

Brother George Sely, I commend me unto you, etc. Letting you have in knowledge that I understand by my fellow Gilbert Hussy that a flecked spaniel of mine was late at your lodging at the 'Star', the which I would be loath to forgo, and specially at this season. Praying you to help that my servant this bearer might have him delivered.

I have none other cause to send him for but only that. Saving I require [request] you, and ye see any goodly feathers, to buy for me twain, one to wear

[84] Malcolm Letts, *Bruges and its Past* (2nd edn, Bruges and London, 1926), misnumbered as p. 20.
[85] *C.L.* 97.

myself and another for an horse. And at your coming I shall content you, both for them and for that ye have laid out for me heretofore. I pray you giveth credence to Golbrond this bearer. In haste, with the hand of your brother and fellow, this Wednesday at Calais.

Le fils Sir John Radclyff, Robert.[86]

Radcliffe's spaniel is a reminder that hunting country was within easy reach of most people, even town-dwellers. Inn names change, but if this was the same as the 'Star' which stood in 'Langhestrate' in the next century, it was in the modern Rue Longue, running from the High Street to the Porte Ste Croix in the town wall.[87] We get a brief glimpse of the company at the 'Star' of 1478 when George noted

Item, the 28 day of July I lent unto Hemond Sheldon at the desire of Thomas Hotton, he being borrow [guarantee] for him (Master Ynns was by him at that time in the 'Star') – 4 Andrews – 20s.

Item, the same day and time I lent unto Thomas Unton 20s in Flemish pence, he to give me so many when he come unto Calais for them.

[And later:] Hyns have paid me the t'one half, sum – 10s.[88]

In 1482 a horse of William Bondman's was left stabled at the 'Star' while his master was in Calais.[89]

A host like Adrian De Frey, George's later landlord at Bruges, bore special responsibilities for his foreign lodgers, and relations might be close. On one occasion Adrian held £92 for George and was also sent an obligation for payment by one of his customers.[90] In 1482 Adrian sent George's chambering to Calais when it was ready, and paid for a poll-axe he had ordered.[91] After a visit to Bruges in 1486 George left 'with mine host Atryan at the "Shepys Clawe"' a little fardel with cross-bows and a long barrel with bolts, both marked with his family mark and to be sent to London by the next ship.[92] On that occasion he stayed in Bruges for 44 days, paying a supplement for his fires and 3s for the glass window in his chamber. In 1580 there were three houses named *De Schaepsclaeuwe* ('Sheep's Hoof', rendered by George and his friends variously 'Skape Slaw', 'Scape ys Clawe' or 'Shepys Clawe'), one, appropriately enough, in Wulfhaghestrate (Rue Fossé aux Loups), one 'achter Dhalle' (behind the Halle), and one in St James Street.[93]

Since letters often failed to carry any exact address, we have no indication of where in Bruges lived 'master Jacob the Vesyschon

[86] *C.L.* 65.
[87] L. Gilliodts-van Severen, ed., *Les registres des 'Zestendeelen' ou le cadastre de la ville de Bruges de l'année 1580* (Bruges, 1894).
[88] File 11 fo. 40v.   [89] *C.L.* 170.
[90] File 12 fo. 13.   [91] File 16 fo. 24.
[92] File 13 fo. 28.   [93] *Registres des Zestendeelen*, pp. 141, 227, 248.

[physician]', who cared for George in his serious illness in 1479.[94] Nor do we know what was sold by 'him of the "Two Horns"', to produce a bill for 24s; and why did George write a note running 'Belkyn and Nelkyn in the gate'?[95] In 1486, however, a 'Nellkyn' (a pet-form of Daniel) made tippets and little caps for George's two young sons and also sold him two dozen black silk points.[96] 'Satin of Bruges making' was famous and often figured on shopping-lists.

The sort of good-humoured bargaining that went on in the market-place – and the leisurely quality of commercial life – emerges from one of Caxton's dialogues in French and English, an adaptation from an earlier manual in French and Flemish.[97] The buyer starts by greeting the seller, and then says, 'Dame, what hold ye the ell of this cloth?', or more shortly, 'How much the ell?' To which she answers:

'Reason!...Ye shall have it good cheap...four shillings for the ell, if it please you.'
'It ne were no wisdom! For so much would I have good scarlet!'
'Ye have right! If ye may! ['I bet you would, if you could.'] But I have yet some which is not of the best, which I would not give for seven shillings.'
'I believe you well! But this is no such cloth of so much money, that know ye well!'
...'Sir, what is it worth?'
'Dame, it were worth to me well three shillings.'
'That is evil boden' ['a poor offer'].

Finally the buyer decides on 15 ells, and makes her cut from the other end of the bolt. ('It is all one, by my soul, but I shall do it gladly.') In the irrational way of people in phrase-books, they end by agreeing on payment of 19s for 15 ells, which are said to be two and a half ells in width.

Martin Rondelle of Bruges, armourer to Monsieur the Bastard of Burgundy in 1473, was more business-like. One of the merchants of Calais had brought him news of John Paston II, with whom he had previously had a dispute over some horse-harness, but now he had heard that Paston was in the market for a complete harness for himself. Rondelle had taken Paston's measurements when he was last in Bruges, and would gladly make it for him, at an acceptable price, if Paston will tell him what pieces he would like, and the fashion desired, when he wants it, to whom Rondelle should entrust it, and (most important) who is going to pay?[98]

It has been seen that a large number of the Celys' customers were residents of Bruges, like the William Kenett mentioned in Staunton's

[94] *C.L.* 77.   [95] File 16 fo. 24; File 11 fo. 36.   [96] File 13 fo. 27.
[97] Ed. Bradley (E.E.T.S., 1900), pp. 15–17.   [98] *Paston L.*, no. 769.

letter, and John De Lopez. De Lopez may be the 'Jean Loupes' whose name stands second in a list of people who contributed compulsory loans to the city in 1491.[99] The largest was of £266, Loupes paid £134, and the next sum was only £73. It seems possible, again, that he was the Johannes Loupes who, in 1470, had been factor and administrator of the goods of the Society of Pardo in Bruges.[100] In the 1480s the Celys' De Lopez was in partnership with Gomez De Soria, 'of whom it was said when he died that he could be spared less than twenty-five of the principal townspeople'.[101] De Soria lived in the once-famous Hotel de Mâle or 'House of the Seven Towers' in the High Street, and provided one of the houses which the town bought for the Spanish community of Bruges in 1494–5.[102] Some small part of his fortune must have come from the Celys' good Cotswold wool.

When the Staple customers visited Calais they probably put up at one of the 'free lodgings' kept by burgesses of the town, and were subject to careful supervision. According to the ordinances issued about 1540, after the Lantern Gate was shut for the night – at 3 pm in winter and 4 pm in summer – lodging keepers had to make an official report on the number of 'strangers' whom they were housing that night.[103] The men who came with their fishing boats to the herring mart, however, were regarded with still deeper suspicion, and not permitted to be on land at all during the evening hours. A shot was fired to warn them back to their ships at the due time. About 1540 it was estimated that at least 340 herring boats belonging to strangers might visit the port in the season, between the feasts of Michaelmas and St Andrew.[104] Such an influx meant that special precautions were also taken in the town. During the herring season the Lantern Gate was the only one of the four town gates to be opened, and as soon as 15 herring boats had appeared in the haven the mayor and aldermen maintained nightly patrols of the town, 'to see that good rule be kept'. The staplers kept their own watch: in 1478 George Cely paid 8d 'for my father's watch this herring time', and in October 1480 William Cely paid the same sum to 'John Ryfflyng for two watchmen that he set in the Staple Hall, one for master George, another for William Maryon'.[105] Herring time also meant that the members of

[99] Gilliodts-van Severen, *Inventaire des Chartes*, VI, 349.
[100] Idem, *Consulat d'Espagne*, I, 108–10.
[101] Letts, p. 40, quoting R. de Doppere.
[102] Gilliodts-van Severen, *Inventaire des Chartes*, VI, 398.
[103] Lisle Letters, II, pp. 659ff.; *Chronicle of Calais*, pp. 140–62. For the dating, see *Lisle Letters*, I, pp. 679–80.
[104] *Lisle Letters*, VI, p. 49.
[105] File 16 fo. 20; File 12 fo. 5.

the Council of Calais took it in turns to mount their own, more spectacular, 'banner watch', which began at 8 pm with a trumpet blown at the four corners of the market-place, after which trumpet, fife and drum proceeded to the house of the official concerned to summon him and his company.[106]

In the sixteenth century there were also a regular 'standing watch' on the walls themselves, a 'search watch', and a 'scout watch', which perambulated the outside of the town, with instructions that if overcome by any enemy they should throw their keys into the town ditch to prevent seizure. The regulations do not indicate great zeal on the part of the sentries. The search-watch patrols were enjoined not to tarry on their rounds or stop for a game of dice, and a member of the standing watch should be reported for sleeping on duty, if caught three times in one night, and so deep in slumber that he could be taken by the nose. The punishment, however, was salutary. The next market day the culprit was to be suspended in a basket from the walls, 10 or 12 feet above the water, with one loaf of bread, a pot of drink and a knife. The knife was to cut the rope when the offender finally preferred a ducking to further inactivity. The under-marshal was instructed to have a boat ready to take him up from the water, but he was then imprisoned in the mayor's prison until the next market day, when he was banished for a year and a day. The proceeding ingeniously combined retribution with free amusement for the populace.

In accordance with the position of Calais, precariously situated in the midst of foreign territory, containing a proportion of foreign-born residents and frequented by alien merchants, great care was taken to secure the means of entrance and egress. The daily openings and shuttings of the gates entailed a ceremony of the keys, performed in the presence of the master porter and an armed guard. The Lantern Gate, the principal exit, was opened for short periods twice or thrice in the morning, and again between 1 pm and 3 or 4 pm. Each of the other gates – in turn the Milk Gate, Water Gate and Boulogne Gate – was normally opened on two days of the week. In herring time or misty weather (a frequent occurrence in Calais) passage was allowed only through a wicket in the Lantern Gate. At night the keys were kept locked in a coffer at the lieutenant's bedside, and when carried abroad they were supposed to be covered with a cushion or something similar 'so that no man shall see the secrets of them'. No wonder panic might be caused by rumours that the lieutenant – Lord Hastings in 1481 or 1482 – had himself given duplicates to the French.

While they might afford protection against intruders, strict controls

[106] Ordinances of 1540, as cited above, n. 103.

could make it difficult to get out in an emergency. In January 1494 Andrew Halyburton, 'conservator' of Scottish merchants in the low countries, learnt that a Lombard was waiting at 'Gralyn' [Gravelines] to arrest the Scotsman Robert Rynd, who had just set out from Bruges for Calais. Halyburton hastily sent a man after Rynd with a message of warning, paying 12*d* 'to the barber's son to convey him by night', and 6*d* 'for drink-silver to let them out at the ports of Bruges after 10 hours in the night'.[107]

[107] *Ledger of Andrew Halyburton*, p. 39.

CALAIS AND THE STAPLE
COMPANY

The situation of Calais as an outpost of English territory – the last survival of Edward III's gains during the earlier stages of the Hundred Years' War – had two concomitants which directly affected the members of the Staple company in this period. One was the need to keep the town and its marches garrisoned and fortified against possible attack. The other was the anomalous position of its currency which, as described in a previous chapter, often diverged from the valuation of the same coins at either Bruges and Antwerp or London. The closure of the Calais mint in 1442 had meant that it was no longer possible to insist on the use of sterling coin in the town.[1] But what the government no longer reaped from the recoinage of foreign bullion it could recoup, to some extent at least, by instituting special tariffs to its own advantage.

There had been times in the past when the staplers' stocks of wool were seized to meet the demands of the unpaid soldiers in Calais, or used to provide a loan to one or other side in the quarrels between York and Lancaster. By the agreement reached with Edward IV in 1466, a convenient means was found of discharging the king's own large debt to the Staple company, while at the same time he ensured regular payment of the wages of the Calais garrison. The company now became directly responsible for finding the wages and maintaining the defences of Calais out of the customs and subsidy taxes which were levied on the exports of its members, and which had long formed a substantial part of the crown's revenues. A further proportion of these dues went to reimburse the company for its loans to the crown. Finally, after certain other fixed charges for fees and salaries were met, the king enjoyed his 'surplusage' from any remainder.[2]

Individual staplers who had contributed to a crown loan were issued with Staple 'debentures' for the amount due to them, and from time to

---

[1] For the date, see Spufford, *Monetary Problems*, p. 104.
[2] See, for instance, Power, *Studies in English Trade*, p. 75.

time a 'partition' was declared for a certain proportion of the sum outstanding.[3] Debentures or 'obligations of the Staple' changed hands readily, and they constituted assets which might be distrained upon, as when an 'arrest' was taken upon a debenture of John Alburgh: 'the sum my father took upon it amounts unto £26 10s, whereof my father's duty is, and the plaint, £16 12d stg.', noted George, who then deducted the sums he would shortly receive by two partitions.[4] About 1481 Harry Bryan entrusted George with two 'obligations of the Staple' made out in the name of Nicholas Bristol. When a partition of 15s in the £ was declared, to be payable at 26s Flem. per £ stg., various staplers at the mart offered Bryan a rate of 26s 6d.[5] Bryan was happy to allow George the proceeds, but advised him that if he had now received the full sum due the obligations must be cancelled by the Staple collectors and returned to 'the same man that owes them, for there be diverse men that has received more money of them than I. And I know not how much money that I have received of them till I see the obligations.' In fact they were by no means 'full content and paid' at that time, because they were subject to a later partition of 10s in the £, which was eventually paid at an exchange rate of only 25s Flem. but in 'money current at Calais', so that the coin was valued on a scale corresponding to 26s 8d Flem. George received payment not only on Bristol's debentures but also on one of his father's, one issued to Richard Bowell, and one in the name of William Fethyan.[6]

When a partition was declared the warrants for payment of it could often be used to offset current custom and subsidy charges. In September 1478 part of William Dalton's dues at Calais were met from a partition of 4s in the £ which was payable on two debentures, one of his own and one in the name of John Thorp, on a 'bill of 18 months and 18 months' of William Wigston's, amounting to 26s 6d stg., and on another such bill of John Thorp's, for £7 1s stg.[7]

If he did not sell his debenture to someone else, a stapler might have to wait years before he recovered his entire debt from the Staple. Richard Cely had acquired a debenture in the name of William Ede. About 1476 he received £6 4s 1d stg. from it, in the form of two partitions, one of 7s Flem. and the other of 6s 8d stg. in the £.[8] When the further partition of 4s stg. in the £ was declared in 1478 he was able to have the resultant

---

[3] Power, *Studies in English Trade*, p. 371 n. 158, quotes the case of 'a bill of debenture' issued under Staple seal in return for 'the 10th penny' on the value of merchandise at Calais. George Cely paid a levy of £7 per sarpler in Aug. 1474 or 1475: File 15 fo. 25.

[5] *C.L.* 200, 135.

[7] File 15 fo. 37.

[4] File 16 fo. 49.

[6] File 13 fo. 51.

[8] File 16 fo. 49.

19s 9d stg. deducted from his customs bill.[9] But 24s 5½d Flem. still remained unpaid when George Cely left 'William Ede's debenture' in the care of William Cely early in 1483, along with a debenture of Richard senior's on which £8 11s 6d stg. remained from an original £100 17s stg.[10] And so far from getting Nicholas Bristol's obligations cancelled in 1481, George still held them in late 1485.[11]

Bills of payment bound exporting staplers, in turn, to their payment of customs dues. This sealed but unsigned copy is among the Cely papers:

Jesu 1480

Be it known to all men that we, Richard Cely and George Cely, merchants of the Staple of Calais, oweth unto the mayor, constables and fellowship of the same Staple for custom and subsidy, £75 13s 1¼d stg., to be paid to the said mayor, constables and fellowship, or to the bringer hereof, at their pleasure.

To the which £75 13s 1¼d stg. well and truly to be paid we bind us and either of us for the other, and to make good all the costs and losses that shall happen or fall for unpayment of the said sum, be it by exchange or re-exchange or otherwise. In witness hereof we have set unto our seals the 11 day of July anno ut supra.

To this George appended the note:

Item, allowed by a warrant fro Sir William Stocker, knight and mayor of the Staple at Calais, for the 23s 4d stg. [per sarpler] paid in England

£19 16s 5d stg.

Rest. .£55 16s 5¼d stg.

Item, paid the 11th day of July by the hands of George Cely · · £55 stg.

Rest clear· ·16s 5¼d stg.[12]

Although it was the Staple company that collected the custom and subsidy dues, two questions had to be settled in consultation with the king's council. Both regularly caused 'much heaving' between the two bodies. Twice a year it must be decided what proportion of the dues should be paid at Calais rather than London, and the rate of exchange at which this proportion should be converted from sterling to Flemish money of account was also at issue. The same rate would be employed in converting the next half-year's wages for the garrison from the sterling in which they were nominally expressed to the Flemish money which was actually paid out, theoretically on 6 April and 6 October. The garrison could put forward its views on the matter as militantly as any modern

---

[9] File 11 fo. 21.   [10] File 15 fo. 37v.   [11] File 20 no. 45.

[12] File 12 fo. 1r–v. I have termed this a 'bill of payment' because it is in almost the same form as the specimen acknowledgements of debt so headed in Richard Arnold's book (1811, p. 106).

union. The rate finally decided might well be below that corresponding to 'Calais table', so that in some years the staplers found themselves paying substantially more than the 40s stg. per sack-weight of wool which they were nominally taxed. Thus early in 1475 (?) Richard Cely senior shipped 3,100 fells. The total custom and subsidy came to £25 16s 8d stg. On 31 May, 10s stg. of the 'sarpler' of 500 fells was payable to the mayor of the Staple at London, and the remaining £22 14s 8d stg. had to be paid to 'the Place' at Calais, at a rate of 21s 4d Flem. per £ stg., making £24 4s 11¾d Flem. George commented that 'the loss in Flem. amounts 30s 3¾d Flem.', since the market exchange rate, both in Flanders and Calais, was then 22s 8d Flem. per £ stg.[13] On this estimate, the special tax rate imposed represented a loss of 6 percent. The coins in which George paid one instalment in May were, however, valued on the higher, 22s 8d, scale.[14]

There were still greater losses in 1478. In April of that year the mayor of the Staple and a delegation, which included Richard Cely senior, had met in London 'with the king and his lords of his council', and agreed to pay their custom and subsidy at Calais at the prevailing Calais exchange rate of 24s Flem. per £ stg., and the wages at the same rate.[15] In June, however, Richard heard from Thomas Granger that 'the soldiers at Calais will not be pleased for [to] take for their payment 8s Flem. for the noble stg., for the which it is too great a loss for the Staple to bear after their desire'.[16] Eventually the soldiers did agree to accept the 24s exchange rate, but this was no victory for the Staple, because of the valuation placed upon some of the coins in which payment was made.

At the meeting in April the Recorder of London had been consulted on the question, and 'the answer was plainly "shall be none otherwise: the Act of Parliament is to pay them in sterling money", and so they will be paid'.[17] 'Sterling money' in this case meant 'mere sterling', not Calais table sterling, with the rial valued at 10s and foreign gold coins pro rata, so that the scale of values corresponded to an exchange rate of 20s Flem. per £ stg. George commented to his father in alarm:

I feel by your...letter it is concluded with the king and his council that we shall pay the soldier[s] sterling money. We were at loss enough afore, though it be no more. Money is still at Calais 2s 6d lower than it is in Flanders, and no sterling money, to that it is too great an loss. We must suffer it, we may not choose.

Meseemeth if it could be brought about that we might have an coin ['mint'] at Calais again, and let none other money go in the town of Calais but sterling money, then should we make better shift ['exchange'], and it should not turn

---

[13] *C.L.* 247. Tentatively dated 1476 in *C.L.*, but more probably of 1475.
[14] File 15 fo. 54v.   [15] *C.L.* 20.
[16] *C.L.* 24.   [17] *C.L.* 20.

us to so great loss. For now, as the case standeth at this time, there is no merchant
that spend an groat in the town of Calais but they lose an halfpenny, and men
of the Staple bring the money to Calais that is brought.

Ye may see what loss is in great sums. But if ['unless'] the mayor and the
fellowship seek an remedy herefor it will be for the fellowship too great an loss.[18]

No 'remedy' was forthcoming, except that a concession may have been
given over the price to be assigned to Flemish groats. The effect of the
special rates imposed on the gold coins is shown clearly in an analysis
of the payments which George made towards his father's customs dues
on the 116¾ sacks of wool (by customs reckoning) and 5,568 fells shipped
in August 1478.[19]

The total bill came to £279 18s stg. Of this, £77 18s 4d stg. was paid
at London, leaving £201 19s 8d stg. to be paid at Calais. At 24s Flem.
per £ this made £242 7s 7d Flem. Out of this total, £71 3s 0d stg. (£85
7s 9d Flem.) was met by warrants for a partition on debentures and for
repayment of £50 stg. lent by Richard the previous November. The
remaining £130 16s 8d stg. (which should have converted to £156 19s
10d Flem.) was paid as follows.

In lions valued at 5s stg. .   .   .   . £17 5s 0d stg.
    Cost in Flanders – 7s 6d Flem. each, making £25 17s 6d
    Flem.
In crowns valued at 4s   .   .   .   . £16 4s 0d stg.
    Cost in Flanders – 5s 10d Flem., making £23 12s 6d Flem.
In nine rials, one half and one quarter rial and 20d stg. [at 10s
per rial] .   .   .   . £4 19s 2d stg.
    Cost in Flanders 14s Flem. per rial, making £6 18s 10d
    Flem.
In Andrews valued at 3s 2d   .   .   .   .   .   . £14 1s 10d stg.
    Cost in Flanders 5s, making £22 5s 0d Flem.
In four half old nobles at 4s 2d   .   .   .   .   .   . 16s 8d stg.
    Cost in Flanders – 6s, making £1 4s 0d Flem.
In groats of 4d 'money current in Calais, 24s the £'   .   . £75 0s 8d stg.
    In Flanders they were at 4½d Flem., making 27s Flem. per £
    stg., but 'they cost in every £ to have them so in Flanders,
    20d, that [is] 28s 8d le [£] sterling', so making £107 11s 0d
    Flem.

Finally, George was credited with the 12 Rhenish gulden which he had
paid for conduct money, at 10d Flem. per sarpler, 'money current in
Calais at 3s 10d [stg.], and 3s 4d in white money'. As the gulden had cost
him 4s 10d Flem. when he received them at the mart, he charged the

18 *C.L.* 22.
19 File 11 fo. 21 and File 21 no. 1. Power's summary in *Studies in English Trade*, p. 77,
   is full of errors and includes a falsified total.

Flemish equivalent as £3 2s Flem. and the sterling as £2 9s 4d stg. The anomalous valuation of these coins (priced much higher than the Andrews) is due to the fact that for the conduct payments coin had been accepted at a different tariff.

George had good reason to tell his father on 23 November:

> I understand that ye be loath to pay any of your custom and subsidy in England, wherefore I have endeavoured myself that ye pay so little as ye do. But when ye see my bill closed in this letter, I deem ye will think it had been more profit that more had been paid in England. Now it cannot help, it is past, etc.[20]

George had in fact paid, by market valuation in Flanders, £190 10s 10d Flem. in place of £156 19s 10d Flem., and nearly 10 percent extra had been added to his total tax bill for the year.

When it came to paying the next half-year's wages there was again 'much heaving betwixt the king's council and us'.

> We would an taken diverse ways with them, but they will no other way but as they were paid last, saving we have brought it that they shall have two manner of golds 2d dearer in an piece than they did; that is the crown and the Rhenish gulden.[21]

By 'dearer' George meant, of course, that the valuation of these two coins was enhanced, so increasing their value in terms of sterling, to the advantage of the staplers.

Often there was a scramble among the staplers to acquire acceptable specie in which to meet their debts to the Staple. In November 1479 Ralph Lemington, who had shipped 17.87 sacks from London in September and was in charge of 113 further sacks for two other staplers,[22] wrote urgently from Calais to George in Bruges:

> Sir, I spake unto you for 'Carroldus' groats at Antwerp, and ye told me ye had at Calais upon 200 pounds. And if it please you to depart with all or part of them, how many so ever ye will, and I shall give you in every pound according as ye desire. Because that master lieutenant calleth so fast upon [us] for custom and subsidy, ye shall have in every £ 6d, etc.... If I may be sped of you, I pray you send the key of your counter to John Dalton or whom that it please you for to deliver me, and I shall make you a bill as attorney of Thomas Burton and Thomas Marshall.
>
> I pray you of answer by the next man 'at comes between, for if I be not sped of you I must go seek farther.[23]

George could be sure of repayment, because Lemington expected William Dalton to bring him £31 odd that week, and his debtors at the forthcoming Cold mart were 'fast men'.

[20] *C.L.* 41. [21] Ibid.
[22] E.122 73/40. [23] *C.L.* 72.

No further comments about the arrangements to pay the garrison occur
in the papers until May 1482, when a highly complex series of negotiations
was in train. On 2 May William Cely wrote from Calais to George, 'Sir,
as for this payment of the soldiers, we be yet at no certainty, but men
suppose it shall be sterling money' – that is, in a mixture of coin which
was again to be valued according to the London tariff.[24] The staplers
hoped, however, that they had won an important concession on the
exchange rate. For the dues on the coming shipment the rate was 'put
at the discretion of my lord' (the lieutenant of Calais), but thereafter it
was to coincide with the rate of 'money current in Calais':

Sir, master mayor and certain of the fellowship of London hath written to master
lieutenant [of the Staple] and to the fellowship at Calais that they be in a way
with the king's good grace, and hopeth for to stablish it from this payment
forward that the fellowship of the Staple shall pay for their custom and subsidy
as much for the pound stg. as they receiveth for their pound stg. [in sales], and
none otherwise.

At the same time, the king, with war on his mind, had been granted a
'surplusage' of 6,000 marks (£4,000), and William understood that in
order to raise this money, 'there shall be a commandment sent that every
man shall ship such goods as he hath by him shortly'. The king was also
demanding that all members of the Staple who were 'of ability to occupy'
should ship their wools by a certain day, or be penalized. His majesty
had been 'greatly moved and displeased' in April 1480 when he heard
a malicious story that the merchant adventurers, faced with a large bill
for arrears of subsidy, were refusing to ship to the Pask mart out of pique,
and with intent to deprive him of his custom.[25] He wanted no such
intransigence from the wool merchants.

On 5 May 1482 William reported negotiations between the lieutenant
of the Staple, Lord Hastings and the king's council over the next
six-months' wage-bill. The soldiers wanted the whole payment made at
Calais. It was decided, however, that while any stapler who wished to
pay 'sterling money' at Calais was welcome to do so, in general half the
dues should be paid at London by 31 July, and 'the t'other half to be
paid at Calais by midsummer in Flemish money at 26s 8d the £'.[26] This
compromise was reached through the good graces of Hastings: 'Sir, my
master lieutenant says he find my lord his good and gracious lord for the
Staple, etc.'

Meanwhile, George's 'good debtors' among the Calais garrison, to
whom he sometimes acted as pawnbroker,[27] begged to be excused 'till

---

[24] *C.L.* 160.   [25] *A.C.M.*, p. 136.   [26] *C.L.* 162.
[27] E.g. he lent 6s 8d to John Casse, soldier of Calais, on a 'camew' (cameo): File 10 fo.
8v.

they be paid of their wages', which had been due on 6 April. Two days later it was understood that after all there was to be no payment of dues in England, and the whole sum would be payable at Calais by Whitsuntide, 'for the soldiers hath liefer to be paid here at 26s 8d than to have in England sterling money, for they mistrust their payment there'.[28] By a typical volte-face, however, it was the previous arrangement that was adhered to, 'for diverse considerations, as for duties owing by the Place in England'.[29] These dues included the king's surplusage.

'The Place' itself was very short of money at the time. For nearly a year, since May 1481, William had been hoping to get payment on some warrants, or at least have them set against customs and subsidy.[30] On 23 April 1482 he reported that he had been, with John Dalton, to see the lieutenant about the matter, and had been promised part payment 'within five or six days'.[31] But the treasurer could not afford to pay the whole amount due. Nor could the sums be deducted from the bills of customs and subsidy, because already an excessive number of staplers had been allowed to take that course. In fact, William failed to get even this much. The lieutenant was still temporizing on 10 May:

John Dalton and I have spoken many times unto master lieutenant for payment of your warrants of 15s of the pound, and he hath driven us off many times, and desired us to forbear but six or seven days and we should have payment. But as on the 10 day of this month we spake to him again, and desired him that we might have payment of them, or else that they might be set upon your bills of custom and subsidy. And he desired us to tarry till ye come [from the mart], and then they shall be set upon your bills of custom and subsidy.[32]

The 'six or seven days' lengthened out, and on 20 May William repeated the promise and reported a new difficulty: he could not even obtain from William Bentham the Staple debentures on which a partition of 10s was owed – making £30 10s Flem. in all.[33] 'He puts me off always. But he saith I shall be first that shall be served.'[34]

When the first instalment of customs was due shortly, William again asked the lieutenant either to pay as promised or to allow the warrants to be set against customs,

and he said they may not [be], but I must pay ready money and receive ready money. And he saith now I may not be paid but of the t'one half at this time of your warrants. For he saith there is but £200 in the treasury, and every man that be behind with their warrants must be paid part-like, every man after his quantity of his principal sum, etc.

---

[28] *C.L.* 163. [29] *C.L.* 170 (26 May). [30] *C.L.* 115.
[31] *C.L.* 156. [32] *C.L.* 164. [33] File 13 fo. 51.
[34] *C.L.* 167.

Sir, he is no steadfast man, nor he oweth you no good will, though he make a fair face. For I have spoken to him for your warrants twenty times, and he giveth me at every time a contrary answer. But I shall upon him today for them again afore William Dalton.[35]

The king's surplusage was causing the Staple authorities other head-aches. The newly elected solicitor for the Staple had written in late April to the lieutenant and fellowship 'to find a mean' of paying it,[36] and at an assembly on 6 May it was agreed to allocate dues on part of the July shipment from London for this purpose. This involved back-dating part of the shipment in the customs accounts: it would be 'cocketted in afore the 6 day of April last past...and to run to the payment of the said surplusage'.[37] The remainder, together with shipments from ports other than London, was to be cocketted as exported after 6 April, and the dues all paid at Calais to meet the next half-year's wages of the garrison.

Currency valuations in Flanders were already rising again, and it is significant that George had been in trouble in April for demanding more than the exchange rate officially imposed at Calais in satisfaction of a debt from one 'old Henley'.[38] In the next round of talks, in August, the soldiers demanded to be paid exclusively in 'neming' groats at $4\frac{1}{2}d$. 'Sir', grumbled William, 'it will be a shrewd loss to receive the neming groats at $5d$ and pay it into the Place at $4\frac{1}{2}d$.'[39]

The July shipments from London and Ipswich, which were to help meet the bill, reached Calais on 16 August. On 20 August a letter from the mayor of the Staple, Sir William Stocker, was read to the Staple court, detailing the king's new requirements for the other half of his surplusage, to be raised from dues on all shipments made before 6 October.[40] The fellowship acceded to his demand that the money should be guaranteed with six obligations under Staple seal, for 500 marks each, three payable in February 1483 and the other three in August 1483. The king's attempt to force staplers to export was not very successful. Shipments during the customs year Michaelmas 1481 to Michaelmas 1482 were well down on those of the preceding 12 months: an estimated 7,258 sacks against 9,944, which would produce only £14,516. The king had customarily been entitled to a surplus only when customs and subsidy, plus rents from Calais, exceeded £15,022 4s 8d, if the Staple retained £3,000 in repayment of its loans to the crown.[41]

[35] *C.L.* 170.   [36] *C.L.* 160.
[37] *C.L.* 163.
[38] *C.L.* 162. 'Old Henley' was probably Richard Henley senior, draper of Calais: *C.C.R. 1485–1500*, no. 277 (1496).
[39] *C.L.* 182.   [40] *C.L.* 185.
[41] *Studies in English Trade*, p. 75.

Once more, the garrison's initial demands, for nothing but neming groats, were not eventually met. On 29 August William sent a full report of the final decision reached between the Staple's representatives and the council at Calais.[42] The exchange rate of 26s 8d Flem. was confirmed,

and these be the golds and white money that followeth that is appointed for the payment, as they were current afore the duchess [Mary of Burgundy] died first.

The new crown at 5s 6d   The old crown at 5s 4d
The lion at a 6s 8d   The Andreus gulden at 4s 6d
The rider at 5s 8d   The Guilhelmus at 4s
The salute at 5s 6d

And two or three other golds after the same rate.

The old noble at 11s   The rial at 13s 4d

And the neming groats at 4½d and the old single plack at 2½d.

And as for any other golds and other silver, they will none, etc.

In other words, the acceptable coins (which, interestingly, did not include Carolus groats), were to be tariffed on a scale corresponding to the 26s 8d exchange rate. But pegging the valuations of specie to those operative before the Duchess Mary died on 27 March 1482 meant that the staplers were back in the old situation of 1477–9, with a significant discrepancy between the tariff in Calais and that in the Burgundian netherlands, where the gold coins were soon current at valuations which ran between 8.75 and 12 percent higher.[43]

The staplers now achieved the aim which they had expressed in May, to 'pay for their custom and subsidy as much for the pound sterling as they receiveth for their pound sterling', but at the cost of forbidding sale on credit to most of their customers. The Staple court passed an ordinance

that we shall receive from that [court] day forward, ready money in Calais, and 26s 8d Flem. for the pound sterling – money as it was current afore the Duchess of Burgundy died – for all wool and fell that shall be sold at Calais from hence forward.[44]

Even so, a concession was made to the towns of Leiden and Delft, whose merchants need pay only half in hand, at 26s 8d Flem., money at Calais tariff 'as it was current afore the Duchess a' Burgundy died', and the rest at six months and six months, converted at 28s Flem. per £ stg., 'money as it is current at the mart' at the future date of payment.

Poor William had still not succeeded in getting his warrants paid in full:

For the money which I should 'a received out of the Place for your warrants of 15s of the £, I can have but £14 Flem. yet, for it have be spoken of in court,

[42] *C.L.* 187.   [43] *C.L.* 196.   [44] *C.L.* 189.

and there is diverse that be in case like as ye are. And the court saith they can take no direction for it till it be grown in treasury. For the which they say ye must forbear a season.[45]

It is unlikely that the arrangements of September 1482 lasted very long. The loss of William Cely's letters between October 1482 and November 1483 means that we can only deduce the course of events, but it is clear that by 15 March 1483 the prices of all wools sold at Calais had been raised by one mark per Calais sack-weight.[46] Possibly this change was introduced with effect from 2 February 1483: Candlemas was often the chosen time for alterations in the Staple's rules. According to Henry VII's proclamation to the Council of Calais in July or August 1487, the 'table' valuations for Calais currency which rated the coins on a scale of 30s Flem. to 20s stg. dated back to an ordinance of Edward IV.[47] If this is true, this rate must have been introduced at some time between September 1482 and Edward's death the following April. It may well have come into effect concurrently with the price rise for wool, and done something to lessen the blow to the Staple's customers, whose money was now valued at Calais at rates more commensurate with those obtaining in the low countries; until values rocketed again in Flanders in 1487 and caused the infringements that Henry's proclamation was intended to redress.

In November 1483 the staplers were faced with the usual bill for the Calais garrison.[48] They had already, by September, paid the wages of an extra 'crew' of soldiers, hired for the defence of Calais two months previously. For this they were to be recouped, if possible, by retaining all or part of the surplusage for that year.[49] In October the wool-fleet had been provided with an extra armed escort, under John Naseby or Narsby, possibly in command of the king's ship the *Clement*.[50] The staplers who had shipped that year held warrants for the repayment of conduct money, paid in England at 3s 4d stg. per sarpler, and for the 'prest' for Naseby's services, levied at 2s 8d per sarpler. In September Richard and George Cely had shipped 32 sacks 14 cloves of wool, calculated for tax at 31 sacks 5 cloves, and 3,250 fells, and owed £89 4s 9d stg. in custom and subsidy.[51] The 6s per sarpler owed to them as repayment of conduct and prest money should have reduced this bill by £5 14s stg.

But that autumn there was even more confusion than usual over the payment of custom and subsidy. The subsidy, incidentally, had not yet been granted to the new king by parliament. On 13 November William

[45] Ibid.
[47] *Tudor Royal Proc.*, I, 553–4.
[49] *MS. Harleian 433*, II, 15.
[51] File 10 fo. 30; E.122 78/2; *C.L.* 202.

[46] Sales recorded in File 10 fo. 31.
[48] *C.L.* 202.
[50] *C.L.* 204; *C.P.R. 1476–85*, p. 264.

Cely expected to have to pay the full sum of £89 4s 9d within 14 days, and to 'lay out' £20 of his own money for the purpose.[52] He feared that the Staple was not yet likely to pay up on the warrants for the prest money, since there was little enough cash available to meet the garrison's wages. Earlier, as he reported on 18 November, folk thought in Calais that the wool shipped in the Boston fleet would bear a great part of the wages, and those who had shipped from London would be able to postpone much of their own payment until April 1484.[53] But the Boston fleet had been delayed

wherefore the goods that came at this last shipping must bear the charges of this half-year's wages. Wherefore, sir, all the money that ye have grown [accumulated] at this day here, and [that which] shall be grown at this mart will be little enough to answer your custom and subsidy and my godfather Maryon's together.

By 5 December William had paid half the customs due, but the staplers were still uncertain whether the rest was to be paid at Calais or in London.[54] The Staple court had agreed on 2 December that 'bills of 20s of the sarpler, payable at pleasure, of the goods that came last from London, and also of that is come now from Boston, shall be sent over to answer such charges as been grown in England', and if this happened (which seemed undecided) William would send over enough money to meet them. At least the allowance of 6s on the sarpler was now to be deducted from the outstanding debt, and Richard Parker would take to the Cold mart specialities for payments due from the Celys' customers which were worth variously £45 stg. and £10 Flem.

In the event, the unpaid bills for custom and subsidy were also taken to the mart to be answered, 'for to pay the 500 mark [for the king] that was taken up by exchange in England by master Stocker and the solicitor for the Place'.[55] Richard Parker was duly paid the sums owed by the Celys' buyers, in the form of English and Carolus groats. But Harry Wayte, appointed to receive the custom and subsidy on behalf of the Staple, refused to accept the coin at the enhanced valuation current at the mart, 'for it should be a great loss to the Place, for it was not so good as 30s [Flem.] the £ [stg.]', the fixed rate at Calais,

wherefore Richard Parker wrote that I should find the means that the money should be conveyed home shortly. So I have been at Bruges and shifted the money [i.e. exchanged it for other coin], and paid your bill.

Similar difficulties with the exchange evidently lie behind the warrant which the staplers obtained at one point during Richard III's reign for

---

[52] *C.L.* 202.
[54] *C.L.* 204.
[53] *C.L.* 203.
[55] *C.L.* 205, 5 Jan. 1484.

a tally from the Exchequer for the sum of £160 for certain sums due to them, 'and so much lost by the payment of Flemish money'.[56]

William had been lucky to get his deduction of the prest money. On 17 March 1484 the staplers in Calais were praying that at the April shipping

there may be enough shipped to pay this half-year's wages that is grown at the 6 day of April next, for that must be paid all of this shipping, for here is nothing toward it. And also a great part of the prest money that was prested in October to pay the fleet with must be repaid of the same, for much of it is unpaid. But yours is repaid. Wherefore, sir, all such goods that cometh now at this shipping must pay whole custom at the [ar]rival of it.[57]

Twenty shillings on the sarpler was paid at London before the fleet left.[58] Of the remainder, William Cely had already paid part at Calais by 23 April, 'and the rest must be paid as soon as the mart is done, for the soldiers call sharply for their wages, wherefore there can be no respite given to no man'.[59] Richard III could ill afford to have dissident soldiers stationed at Calais and Guines, where he seems to have enlarged the garrison, as well as dismissing men whose loyalty was suspect.[60]

In September 1487 Richard and George still had a warrant for £55 stg., paid as their share of a loan of £2,000 made by the City of London to aid King Richard against Henry Tudor in June 1485.[61] This they used to offset against their custom and subsidy at that time. By then individual merchants were also being called upon to make personal loans of fixed sums to the crown, a practice on which the mercers commented that 'none such ill precedent aforetime hath been understood, known or seen'.[62] At George's death in June 1489 the brothers held a debenture of £25 for 'money lent the king' and a warrant for £10 lent the king 'for my lord Daubeney', for special defence measures at Calais in 1488.[63] Doubtless the lords of the Calais council, like the humbler members of the garrison, had often found the staplers a source of private loans. Their attitude to repayment is suggested by the nine months it took George Cely to receive the price of goods that he bought for Sir Ralph Hastings in 1486.[64] Compare Lord Lisle's airy message to his wife on 20 November 1538 that 'Smythe of the Staple' had lent him £60 repayable on 30 November. 'If he come to you, give him some gentle answer. And

---

[56] *MS. Harleian 433*, I, 203.

[57] *C.L.* 211.

[58] *C.L.* 214; File 20 no. 8.

[59] *C.L.* 216.

[60] *MS. Harleian 433*, II, 187–8.

[61] File 13 fo. 30; *A.C.M.*, p. 776.

[62] *A.C.M.*, p. 296. Richard and George lent £20 to the crown in July 1487, which was repaid a year later: File 10 fos. 2v, 3.

[63] File 10 fo. 3.

[64] Ch. 13, p. 345.

if he may tarry to take it off mine April payment of his custom for wool, he doth me and you great pleasure.'[65]

The primary duty of the lieutenant of Calais and his council was viewed as the defence of the town and the maintenance of good order. In these respects the Council of Calais may have served as a model for the Council of the North, as set up by Richard III. In such a vein Thomas Boyes sent on an official complaint to Lord Lisle in 1539:

The king's grace hath appointed you there to see the town well ordered, and hath given you power to punish them that are evil doers. And you take upon you in punishment of them nothing, but troubles the king's grace and his council with such matters as you should redress yourselves.[66]

The business of government, however, meant a much closer involvement in the ordinary affairs of Calais, especially its commerce, than the *Lisle Letters* reveal. At the Celys' time, when the crown employed the Staple company as paymaster and finance house, the council of Calais exercised control over matters which might be thought the exclusive commercial concern of the merchants, such as the appointment of supervisory wool-packers in 1481.[67] In 1475 there was 'much ado' over the question of the surplus stocks of wool that had accumulated at Calais. The staplers wished to keep the latest consignment off the market for the time being, but were overruled by the king's council of Calais.[68] And in May 1476 William Hastings (the lieutenant of Calais), Sir John Donne, Sir John Scott (the marshal), Sir Geoffrey Gate, Thomas Thwaytes (treasurer) and William Rosse were commissioned 'to search and oversee wools and fells at the Staple of Calais according to the ordinance'.[69] It has been seen previously that it was the council, too, which set valuations on the currency in ordinary use at Calais. The Staple acknowledged its close interaction with the council at Calais by giving honorary membership in the fellowship to leading royal officers. In his right as a stapler Hastings shipped a moderate amount of wool and fell in 1478,[70] and in March 1484 there were present at an assembly of the Staple court at Calais the lieutenant of Calais (John Lord Dynham), the marshal (Sir Humphrey Talbot), and Sir Richard Tunstall (lieutenant of the castle of Calais), 'with other of the council that be made free of the Staple now late'.[71] But when the Celys describe negotiations with the government they seldom draw any clear distinction between the king's council in

---

[65] *Lisle Letters*, no. 1280. The editor read 'well' instead of 'wool', and punctuated accordingly.
[66] Ibid., no. 1445.
[67] *C.P.R. 1476–85*, p. 277.
[68] C.L. 247.
[69] C.76/160.
[70] E.122 73/40.
[71] C.L. 212.

general and this 'Council of Calais', comprising the royal officers of the town and its neighbouring castles.

Lieutenants of Calais at the Celys' time were William Lord Hastings (to 13 June 1483), then John Lord Dynham, succeeded by John of Pontefract, bastard son of Richard III, and, early in 1486, by Giles Lord Daubeney.[72] Below the lieutenant and his subordinates, his deputy, the victualler, treasurer, comptroller, and master porter, came a host of minor officers, concerned either with the garrison – like the constables of the castles, the master and yeoman of artillery, the king's gunner, the master smith and master carpenter – or with the king's other interests in the town – the searcher, the customer and collector of the money from the weighing of wool, the customer at the Lantern Gate, the beadles of Mark, Oye and Guines, the collector and receiver of rents and farms in the town of Calais, the plumber, the sub-clerk of the works, and various other clerks and yeomen.[73] The water bailiff, who was chosen from among the aldermen of the town, had the responsibility for collecting the small customs due to the king from the ports of Calais and the adjacent New Haven, particularly 'anchorage, pontage, wharfage and head-silver'.[74]

The town was divided into 12 wards, and a survey in 1535 showed a population of just over four thousand at that date.[75] Of the municipal authority little is said in the Cely papers. When George took a lease of some property in the town he took as witnesses five burgesses (John Parker, Thomas Redewhode, Robert Soll, John Baven and Thomas Colton), and three aldermen (Alan Redeman, Richard A'Chamber and Robert Adlen).[76] In fact most, probably all, of these were fellow staplers as well. The Staple kept a jealous eye on its own privileges in the town, and on 21 February 1484 an assembly summoned nine men who were informed that they must choose between retaining their freedom of the Staple and their position as aldermen of the town, because

the Fellowship found them[selves] grieved with them, because they were sworn first unto the Staple and brought up ['raised to prosperity'] there, and since sworn unto the juridiction of the town, and observe that in many things contrary the wealth of the Place.[77]

John Chawley, Harry A'Chamber, Thomas Benett, Alan Redeman, Robert Bingham, William Muston and John Deram all chose to remain in the Fellowship, and only two – Romenett De Sall and William

[72] The Celys refer to Dynham in exactly the same terms as they use of Hastings, but Ross (*Richard III*, p. 161) says that he was never more than Deputy Lieutenant.
[73] B.L. MS. Harl. 433, fo. 337b, reproducing a list of Henry VI's time.
[74] Campbell, *Materials*, II, 434.   [75] *Lisle Letters*, I, p. 462.
[76] File 15 fo. 50.   [77] *C.L.* 208.

Fethyan – refused to forsake their aldermanship and were consequently 'crossed the Place'. Three of the staplers certainly remained active as burgesses: Henry 'Chambre', Robert Bingham and John Derham later served on a commission to oversee repairs to the walls, ditches, sewers and causeways in the marches.[78]

Rules of citizenship were even more restrictive, until Henry VIII, 'of his blessed disposition and abundant grace', allowed free marriage between 'mere English' men or women and persons born within the town and marches of Calais, and decreed their children to be 'mere English' – provided they did not move to foreign parts.[79] But during Richard III's time Harry Botfisshe, mayor and escheator of Calais, was directed to deliver to Sir Thomas Everingham certain goods forfeited to the king because one Peter Johnson had willed them 'to an alien born', contrary to the statutes.[80] The 'offices of charge' in the Staple at Calais, namely those of mayor, lieutenant, constable, treasurer and collector, could be held only by merchants usually resident in England. Staplers who were inhabitants of Calais were declared ineligible by Act of the Parliament of 1472–3.[81]

For those who could avoid tangling with Staple, town council or royal authorities, Calais could provide an escape from the rather short arms of the law in England. Robert Cely had to go further – to Bruges – to avoid prosecution in the ecclesiastical courts,[82] but if John Dighton really lingered out his days in Calais after assisting in the murder of the princes in the Tower, as a later writer asserted, he was a typical refugee.[83] When John Elderbeck's servant William was in trouble over a less serious crime in London, his friends sought likewise to ship him across the channel. According to Elderbeck's undated and damaged letter to George Cely, one John Barkway had come into possession of nine bed-coverings, evidently stolen,

and after that the said Barkway understood that there would be trouble for the same coverings, it fortuned that William my servant was lodged with him at London. And because that he was a stranger and not known, therefore the said Barkway caused the said William to make sale, wherefore he is troubled at this

---

[78] Campbell, *Materials*, I, p. 352.
[79] *Tudor Royal Proc.*, I, no. 64 (March 1512).
[80] *MS. Harleian 433*, I, 176.
[81] *Rot. Parl.*, VI, 59.
[82] *C.L.* 85.
[83] The Grafton-Hall version of More's *Richard III*: Richard S. Sylvester, ed., *The Complete Works of St Thomas More*, II (New Haven and London, 1963), p. 87 (footnotes). Since Robert Radcliffe had been 'keeper' of Henry VI at the time of his sudden death in the Tower, he may be another of those who found it discreet to accept a post overseas, as gentleman porter of Calais.

time. I beseech you, master George, be his good master, and what pointment you make him, I will abide it. The master of the [ship's name mutilated] of Ospringe hath written a letter to his cousin Christopher Collins, or in his absence to his wife, to help forth in this matter.[84]

It has been seen that the affairs of the Staple were subject to government regulation to some considerable extent. In matters such as offences against currency controls, its members came under the jurisdiction of the king's lieutenant and his council. Like other residents of the town, the staplers were also subject to the mayor and council of Calais in the normal concerns of town government. Otherwise, they formed a self-regulating company and had their own court of law to hear disputes among members. Practically, their organization was split between the Fellowship as a whole, represented by the mayor in London, and the 'Place' at Calais. It was at Calais that disputes were heard and ordinances passed, by courts which were usually presided over by the lieutenant of the company, his deputy and constables, and attended by any members who were present in Calais at the time. Many of the leading staplers were important City men whose business at Calais was commonly handled by attorneys. This must have meant, exceptionally for the period, that the younger members had their say in the company's affairs.

Even the mayor of the Staple of Calais was elected at Calais, at an assembly held on or about 25 March.[85] He was elected by ballot from three 'of the most worshipful, grave, ancient and expert of the Company'.[86] The man chosen was often a prominent member of the mercantile oligarchy of London, like Sir John Crosby, mayor in 1475,[87] Sir John Yonge, mayor 1476–7 and known as 'the good mayor' of London during his earlier tenure of that office,[88] or Sir William Stocker (mayor of the Staple in 1479–81 and again in 1484). Sir Richard Yorke (mayor 1486–7) became a citizen of London only when he was admitted to the Mercers' Company in December 1487, however.[89] The mayor conducted negotiations with the king and his council on behalf of the Staple, and generally looked after its interests in England, as when, in September 1487, George Cely was elected by the court in Calais 'one of the twenty-eight the which shall assist the mayor of the Staple now at this parliament time...and to labour certain matters for the Place, whereof is instructions sent to the mayor by writing'.[90] The Staple also had a treasurer (also termed solicitor) at London, to whom a proportion

---

[84] *C.L.* 246.
[85] *C.L.* 212.
[86] *Ordinance Book*, p. 106.
[87] C.1 59/299.
[88] Gregory's Chronicle, ed. Gairdner, *Historical Collections of a London Citizen*, p. 233.
[89] *A.C.M.*, p. 305.
[90] *C.L.* 235.

of the customs and subsidy dues were paid. This was John Tate, *c.* 1475–8, and later Richard Noneley[91] or John Thornborough.[92] 'Randolf, the Staple clerk' carried a letter to Calais in November 1481, and had been dispatched to London in June 1479, 'for great matters for the Place', as old Richard Cely suspected.[93] He had custody of some obligations issued by customers from Leiden in 1480.[94] 'Master Morgan, clerk of the Staple' is mentioned in ?1486.[95]

It was, however, the mayor's lieutenant who was stationed in Calais and bore the brunt of the administration. The Celys usually refer to him simply as 'master lieutenant', but occasionally holders of the office are identified by name. Robert Tate was appointed in May 1478,[96] John Tate was elected before October 1482 to serve the next term,[97] and Roger Wigston was chosen in March 1484, to be at Calais by 30 April.[98] Henry Kebell was lieutenant in 1485,[99] followed by Thomas Grafton.[100] All these men were substantial shippers. None of their deputies are named, and only one constable – Thomas Amerys in March 1484.[101] Richard Cely senior had served in this capacity at least twice, once in 1461 and the second time in 1474.[102] By the ordinances of 1565 ten 'assistants' were appointed annually, three to serve for the two terms between Michaelmas and Christmas and between Lady Day and St John's Day, and two to serve between Lady Day and St John's Day and between St John's Day and Michaelmas.[103] From the ten assistants one or two constables were chosen. These had to be senior men, free of the Staple for at least 12 years. The assistants had, however, to be under 60 years old.

The rules in 1565 give a vivid picture of the sitting of a Staple court.[104] The president, after taking his seat, struck a stroke with his mallet, commanding those present to be seated in order and the door to be shut. He then struck a second blow, and the clerk read out 'the doings of the court precedent' for approval. After that, the third stroke of the mallet meant that late-comers were fined 4*s*, or 5*s* after half an hour 'run up by the glass'. Those who failed to attend paid 10*s*. No sales were to take place or to be discussed while the court sat. While all qualified members were expected to attend, the elders of the company were accorded proper distinction:

such as shall have been mayor of the Staple, lieutenant, constable, mayor or alderman of any city or town or justice of the peace shall sit upon the highest

[91] File 10 fo. 9.   [92] *A.C.M.*, p. 776.   [93] *C.L.* 137, 56.
[94] *C.L.* 105.   [95] File 10 fo. 9.   [96] *C.L.* 32, 40.
[97] *C.L.* 196.   [98] *C.L.* 211.   [99] C.1 82/102.
[100] *Foedera*, v (3), 182.   [101] *C.L.* 213 (March 1484).
[102] C.47 33/8/48. On the second occasion his fellow constable was Henry Colet.
[103] *Ordinance Book*, pp. 112–14.   [104] Ibid., pp. 185–8.

benches next unto the mayor, lieutenant or constables for the time being, as they shall be in ancient ['seniority'] by bearing of office in this company. And every other brother shall take his place in degree as he hath borne office in the same....

And who so ever shall in any common matter speak in the court, he shall rise up and reverently, in quiet manner and decent terms, declare his mind. And he that will speak in any private matter, shall rise out of his place and stand before the heads for the time being, and shall declare his mind in honest and decent wise, whether it be in any request touching himself, or in speaking of any matter touching any particular brother of the company.

Only the officers and such of the company as were shippers or attorneys had a voice in the proceedings, and 'for avoiding of confusion of voices in deciding of causes and controversies' those who had no vote must sit on forms or benches set apart from the rest. It was strictly forbidden to disclose 'any secret matter showed or moved in court'. From similar fear that the common counsels might be betrayed, a stapler who married a woman born outside the realm must, unless her father was 'mere English', keep her and her children in England.[105] The Staple, like other companies, was very jealous of its rights of jurisdiction, and a chancery petition of 1486 stated that any member who took out a writ of certiorari to remove a case from the court of the mayor and constables would incur a penalty, which cannot be certainly deciphered from this badly damaged document.[106]

Various offices within the Staple administration were shared out among the younger members of the company. There were two treasurers at Calais, who probably served a quarterly term. George Cely and William Dalton acted together in this capacity in 1477 or 1478.[107] In 1481 treasurers named are John Hatfeld and Piers Schylton.[108] The collectors, also appointed quarterly, apparently supervised the collection of dues such as the impositions which were levied on the sales value of wools and fell. The 'conductors' who arranged the wool fleets and collected the 'conduct money' were senior men at London, like 'master Britten [Thomas Bretayn] and [John] Broke' in April 1483, or 'Robert Flemyng and his fellows'.[109]

What was the size of the Staple's membership? One list of staplers was made in July 1472.[110] Twenty-one names remain legible: those of John Prout, mayor, Robert Tate, William Horne, William Wykyng, Robert Byfeld, John Tate the younger, John Tate, alderman, Thomas 'Breteigne', John Lymyngton of Leicester, Philip Hardbene, John

[105] Ibid., pp. 192–3.
[106] C.1 82/102.
[107] *C.L.* 44.
[108] File 12 fos. 14v, 16.
[109] File 10 fo. 13.
[110] S.C.1 57/111.

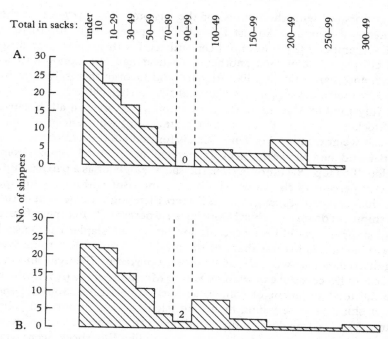

Figure 2: Proportionate share of wool export among shippers from London. (Note: a joint partnership is counted as a single shipper.) A. Shipments July 1478–May 1479 (mean 82 sacks). 104 shippers. B. Shipments March–August 1488 (mean 54.5 sacks). 92 shippers.

'Ealdebek', Thomas Grafton, John Challey, William Brereley, John Wode, John Dycons, Alan Redeman, Simon Grantham, John Ekington, Nicholas Bristall and Richard Sely. The rest of the document is damaged, but had space for some 250 names in all.

London particular port book entries for 1478–9, 1483 and 1488, together with the Cely papers, produce a random sample of at least 220 staplers active during all or part of the period 1474–89, but only 108 individuals are named as shipping from London in the port book covering the peak period July 1478 to September 1479 inclusive.[111] Fig. 2 shows the share in wool exports from London held by individual shippers or partnerships in the season running from July 1478 to May

[111] E.122 73/40. The 108 appearing in the particular port accounts were far from the total number of active staplers at the time. Eleven others were in the list of married men issuing their challenge in Aug. 1478 (Ch. 2 p. 44), and George Cely himself is not named as a shipper.

1479, compared with the figures for the customs year 1487–8 (i.e. the shipments of March to August 1488).[112] The port account for 19 June to 26 September 1483[113] has not been utilized for this purpose because the Cely papers show that another wool-fleet had left London about 5 June, and many staplers, like Richard and George themselves, must have sent their new supplies to Calais at that earlier date.

In July 1478 to May 1479, the nine shippers (11 men in all, because two Stockers and two Tates were in partnership) who sent more than 200 sack-weights of wool or fell to Calais formed 8.6 percent of the total number and had between them 25 percent of the total export from London. The top 18, shipping over 100 sacks, singly or as a partnership, had 41.7 percent of the shipments by volume. But within this group, individual percentages ranged from Robert Flemyng's 3.2 percent of the total shipment down to Richard Noneley's 1.6 percent.[114] The mean figure for all shippers would be 1 percent, so that no one stapler can be said to have had a dominating share of the market. Despite this, there was a big discrepancy between the 264.7 sacks exported by Flemyng and the 3.7 sacks of fleece-wool exported by Henry Marlond, or the 91 fell which were the total shipment of John Elderbeck at this time. Some of the smaller shippers were young men, like Richard Cely junior and John Dalton, often factors doing a little trading on their own account as well as handling shipments for senior men. Some, like Elderbeck, were well established staplers active in affairs at Calais. A third group among the minor shippers included men like William Maryon who exported regularly but never in large quantities. Among those shipping between 24 and 36 sacks were a number of city merchants like the mercers John Elys, Thomas Feldyng, Stephen Gibson, Richard Haddon and Robert Hardebene, for whom wool was a useful sideline.

In the three fleets of 1488, only four shippers (4.3 percent) had over 200 sacks, or 24.8 percent of the whole. And two of these, Robert Flemyng and the partnership of Thomas Windout and William Salford, had between them 665 sacks, or 14 percent of the total export from London. They were followed by Richard Haddon (292 sacks or 6.2 percent), Henry Cantelow and his father-in-law Nicholas Alwyn in partnership (204) and John Broke and Richard Noneley in partnership (180 sacks or 3.8 percent). If the figures for 1488 are at all typical of this later period, a handful of the richer staplers had increased their stake in a diminishing trade, but a greater proportion of all shippers had an average or above average share in the whole export. At each period recorded in these port books there was a long tail of shippers with

---

[112] E.122 78/5. [113] E.122 78/2.
[114] Ranking is necessarily by volume, not value, of shipment.

somewhere under 20 sack-weights each: 39 percent in 1478–9 and 32 percent in 1488. The vast majority of this group had under 10 sack-weights. (A few of these were men who had individual shipments in addition to stocks shipped in partnership with someone else.)

Four hundred and eighty people (including twenty-one women) figure in the list of staplers who obtained pardons in November 1505 for offences against the statute and for exporting wool without giving surety to bring back silver plate to the value of two marks for each sack (surely an example of the anachronistic demands which were used to enrich the Tudor treasury).[115] As the pardon was no doubt sued out by the mayor and fellowship on behalf of the whole company, it is reasonable to suppose that the number includes all those free of the Staple, whether they traded actively or not. The first 30 names are not in alphabetical order and probably indicate senior status. To judge by surnames, many of the families known from the Cely papers in the 1470s and 80s are represented in the 1505 list, often by several members, for example Rowland and John Lemyngton; Alan, James, Nicholas and Robert Redeman; Edward, Nicholas and William Grantham; George, Ralph and William Sybsey; the Wigstons (John, Roger and William senior and junior), or Richard, Thomas, William and Margery Tourney.

In 1478–9 John Tame came fourth in the list of larger shippers. He probably exported wool of his own growing, and also had a flourishing business as a clothier: the church of Fairford, Gloucestershire, still contains the splendid Flemish glass which he presented. It seems doubtful whether he took any personal part in selling his wool at Calais, or in Staple administration. In fifth place came Roger Wigston who, like his brother, was prominent in civic affairs in Leicester. Others among the top shippers were leading city men in London, like Robert and John Tate, William and John Stocker, William Horn, Robert Byfeld, Richard Gardener and Hugh Clopton. So just as the greater city companies included a range of people, some trading actively in their designated occupation, others merely nominal members, so the staplers were a mixed lot. For some, like the Celys, wool was the major source of income. For adventurers like the grocer John Benington or the mercer Hugh Clopton, the Staple trade was one lucrative interest among many, and for others again the occasional small shipment of fleece-wool or fells produced a little extra pocket money.

From a comparison of staplers' wool exports, chiefly in the year Michaelmas 1439 to Michaelmas 1440, with the import–export of other commodities between Michaelmas 1438 and Michaelmas 1443, H. L. Gray concluded that 'in general, the share of wool merchants in

[115] *C.P.R. 1494–1509*, pp. 447–50.

the exportation and importation of commodities other than wool in the middle of the fifteenth century was not much more than 2 per cent of the total', and 'the Staplers restricted their ventures almost entirely to shipments of wool'.[116] Eileen Power reiterated that 'the Staplers were not commonly buyers in the marts of Flanders', quoting a statement to this effect from the Rolls of Parliament, 1423.[117] Conditions changed a great deal during the course of the fifteenth century, and it would be dangerous to conclude that what has become 'a commonplace of economic history'[118] for the first part of the century holds true for the last quarter. It has been indicated that the word 'stapler' embraced a wide variety of persons. Nevertheless, of the group of 94 staplers who shipped from London in 1488, 33 Londoners are identifiable as well-known merchant adventurers, predominantly mercers (who formed at least 21 percent of the total number of shippers), drapers or grocers. These include men like the mercers Hugh Clopton, Nicholas Alwyn and Henry Cantelow, Richard Pontesbury, Richard Haddon, Thomas Grafton, Thomas Burgoyn, John Reynold, William Salford and Thomas Wyndout; the haberdasher William Welbeck, the grocer Thomas Abraham, and the salters William Horn and Richard Chawry. Such men certainly traded in commodities other than wool. Indeed, Richard and George Cely were more active as ship-owners in this particular year, when they imported a cargo of salt and jointly exported (or attempted to export) only one consignment of fells. The mixture of goods belonging to Richard Stoke in 1475 – wool, Spanish iron, wax, madder, body-armour and linen cloth – suggests that this salter and stapler engaged in a typical mixture of undertakings.[119] But it would probably be impossible to say certainly whether the adventurers who enjoyed the freedom of the Staple commonly reinvested their profits from wool in the import of other goods. Much might depend on the state of their markets, and, indeed, on whether any trade was possible in the domains of the Duke of Burgundy at a given time. If Sylvia Thrupp's estimate of 6 percent to 19 percent, and an average of 10 percent, profit from the Grocers' corporate trade has general validity,[120] it may be that, so far from investing the profits from wool in the import of other goods, a merchant was often well advised to employ his returns from importing in the more lucrative Staple trade which, it seems, was capable of producing a net profit of 20 percent,

[116] 'English Foreign Trade from 1446 to 1482', *Studies in English Trade*, pp. 15–17. He confirmed this estimate from customs accounts of 1449–50: p. 363 n. 44.
[117] 'The Wool Trade', ibid., p. 68.
[118] T. H. Lloyd, *The English Wool Trade*, p. 308. Lloyd qualified this 'commonplace' as 'no more than a useful generalization'.
[119] *Cal. Plea and Mem. Rolls, 1458–82*, p. 89.
[120] S. Thrupp, 'The Grocers of London: A Study of Distributive Trade', *Studies in English Trade*, p. 252.

and sometimes, on the best Cotswold wool, of as much as 38 to 43 percent.

One difficulty is that staplers can be hard to identify. A citizen of London would usually be designated in official documents by his company affiliation, not as 'merchant of the Staple of Calais'. To take one example at random: Robert Byfeld's will of January 1482 describes the testator as ironmonger.[121] One daughter was the wife of Richard Haddon, a mercer, and the other the wife of William Welbeck, a member of the Haberdashers' Company. The overseer of Byfeld's testament was John Benington, grocer. Byfeld (and his widow), Haddon, Welbeck and Benington all appear sooner or later in the customs records as substantial shippers of wool to Calais. Welbeck possibly acquired this interest in 1485 along with his second wife, the widow of Thomas Betson. Similarly, Thomas Heritage (*c.* 1534) was certainly a merchant of the Staple, although he described himself only as a member of the Skinners' Company.[122]

For any but important personages, who might have it conferred as a compliment or reward, the cheapest method of acquiring the freedom of the Staple was by patrimony. The Cely boys could have entered by this means, although some fathers preferred a formal apprenticeship. Richard Rawson had his sons bound apprentice to himself in the Mercers' Company.[123] According to the Staple rules in 1565, once the son of any man who had enjoyed the freedom by patrimony or apprenticehood attained the age of 16, he could claim admission, paying 50s for his hance if he were born before his father's admission, and only 40d if his birth had taken place subsequently.[124] The mercers had great difficulty in discovering the age of some boys, and decided to go on physical appearance alone.[125]

The second method of gaining the freedom was by 'redemption', or payment of an agreed sum. What was true of the mercers applied equally to the Fellowship of the Staple of Calais, 'provincial merchants, members of minor London Companies, officials and country gentlemen all found membership of the Mercers' Company desirable, and were prepared to pay largely for their privileges'.[126] John Pasmer, a London skinner and

---

[121] P.C.C. 5 Logge.

[122] 'As Thomas Heritage did not describe himself as a Merchant of the Staple, he was surely not one': N. W. Alcock, *Warwickshire Grazier and London Skinner*, p. 113 n. 70. But Alcock goes on to cite good evidence against his own view.

[123] A.C.M., p. xii. When Sir John Yonge made his will in Nov. 1481 his youngest son was the apprentice of another grocer: P.C.C. 4 Logge.

[124] *Ordinance Book*, p. 132.

[125] A.C.M., p. 382 (1510): they must be 'of reasonable stature and growing, according to the age of 16 years'. [126] Ibid., p. xii.

merchant adventurer, and possibly a relation of the Hospitaller Richard Pasmer, wrote to George in September 1484:

touching the matter whereof I communed with your mastership at your last being at London, for mine entry and admission into the right worshipful and honourable Fellowship of the Staple at Calais, I am fully appointed and condescended ['decided'] in my mind, and would be right glad to be a poor brother of the same, if it will please them to accept and admit me thereto.[127]

Since he was unable to travel to Calais himself, would George please 'break this matter' to the Fellowship, and if they agreed to accept him, would he

lay down and pay there for me to them the duty used and accustomed for such entry and admission...and so upon the said admission, that it will please them to write unto my master the mayor of the said Staple being in London, that it will please him to receive mine oath there.

The practice of taking such 'redemptioners' at a substantial fee helped to swell company numbers – and coffers, though it increased the competition in buying wool in England and had to be stopped for a period after 1565.[128]

The third method of gaining entry to the Staple was, of course, by apprenticeship. Very little is said specifically about the Celys' apprentices, whose existence was probably taken for granted and whose activities seldom required comment. The only direct statement about an apprentice of Richard Cely senior in the letters is Richard's request to George to have 'Thomas Folborne, my 'prentice' made free, since he was now within three years of his term, which was for eight years according to his indenture.[129] William, Robert's apprentice, was 'sore sick' in October 1476.[130] There is a great deal on the subject of apprenticeship in the ordinances of 1565, which probably reflect much older custom, although by that date the minimum term of apprenticehood was nine years.[131] In 1544 John Johnson took as apprentice Peter Master, who was then almost 18. There was some argument about whether the year when Peter had been 'set to his learning for to have language' at his father's keeping and finding should count as one of the statutory nine.[132] Languages were essential. A young man of Calais, recommended to Hastings for the position of clerk of the kitchen, was 'well-spoken in English, meetly well in French, and very perfect in Flemish. He can write and read.'[133]

---

[127] *C.L.* 224. For Pasmer as skinner and merchant adventurer, e.g. *A.C.M.*, pp. 194, 200.
[128] *Ordinance Book*, p. 140: for seven years from 1565.
[129] *C.L.* 13 (June 1477).
[130] *C.L.* 8.
[131] *Ordinance Book*, p. 134.
[132] S.P. 46/5 fo. 49.
[133] *Paston L.*, no. 370 (1476).

Like Thomas Folborne, Peter Master gained the freedom of the Staple part-way through his indentured term, in 1548.[134] In 1565 apprentices had to be between the ages of 16 and 24 at the time they were bound. Those who had served a full six years were permitted to ship four sarplers of wool and fell a year and were hansed, at their master's expense, before the term was complete. But anyone in this position could be disfranchised if he 'do use himself obstinately or sturdily, or do not serve his master or mistress as an apprentice ought to do'.[135]

Apprentices must be 'mulier born, that is to say of father and mother certain in matrimony' [i.e. properly married], 'mere English born, both of father and mother certain', and not the sons of any bondman.[136] Their attire was strictly regulated, on paper at least, and probably with some variation according to fashion. In 1565 it was ordered

that none apprentice shall be suffered to wear, in this Estaple or elsewhere out of his master's sight, in his shirt, hose, doublet, coat, jerkin, jacket, cloak or gown, any manner of silk unless it be one stitch of silk in his doublet, coat or cloak, or small buttons of silk to the same. And that none apprentice shall in his doublet wear any other thing than fustian, canvas or worsted, in his jacket any other thing than cloth, nor in the lining of his coat or gown any other thing than cotton, or worsted at the best. Nor shall [he] wear any shirt but with a single ruff, nor shall wear any Spanish leather or cut shoon

upon pain of fines for the first and second offence and dismissal to England for the third.[137] Apprentices must also sit at table in the places appointed unless they were invited to fill up a space by the heads of the Staple. In this case a youth so honoured must sit bareheaded 'for the reverence of his superiors' until permission was given to be covered. These restrictions, however, did not extend to apprentices who had their master's favour and only two more years to serve.[138]

Once a man had completed his apprenticeship his career might well depend on his wealth and connexions. William Cely, for example, seems never to have traded on his own account and was content to work for Richard and George. In May 1484 William wrote to say that a young man named Hugh Padley was out of his apprenticeship to William Dalton and, having left him 'with good love and leave', was anxious to take service 'if your masterships were destitute of a servant, and if his service might please you, he would do your masterships service afore all the men in the world'.[139] In time, naturally, many young 'servants' amassed enough capital to trade and prosper. Nicholas Kirkeby, a former

[134] Winchester, *Tudor Family Portrait*, p. 223.
[135] *Ordinance Book*, pp. 134, 150, 139.
[136] Ibid., p. 141.   [137] Ibid., p. 189.
[138] Ibid., p. 190.   [139] *C.L.* 218.

apprentice of Margery Cely's first husband, became a fully fledged stapler. The well-connected Thomas Betson, who had been apprenticed to the stockfishmonger, John Fenn, subsequently took service with Thomas Rich.[140] When Rich died his widow married William Stonor, and Betson, after going into partnership with Stonor as a stapler, took the classic step of marrying his old master's daughter, Katherine Rich, as soon as she was old enough. Under Betson's supervision at Calais in the 1470s were the three young men, Goddard Oxbridge, Thomas Henham and Thomas Howlake. Henham witnessed Betson's death-bed disposition of property in September 1485.[141] Howlake, whom Betson had described as Katherine's 'gentle squire' in 1476, makes brief appearances in the Celys' memoranda as a stapler, fell into debt and 'kept himself secret... in the parties beyond the sea'. By 1486 he was indebted 'in great sums of money' to Henry Kebell, lieutenant of the Staple, and attempted to satisfy Kebell with 16 sarplers of wool which he claimed from Betson's estate, but Betson's widow and her new husband, William Welbeck, counterclaimed that it was Howlake who had been indebted to Betson.[142]

Roger Egge, the free-mason who was employed to make the tomb of Richard Cely senior, did better for himself, after a shaky start to his career. Once he had completed his apprenticeship he had to borrow money from his friends and relations in order to set himself up with tools. Before he could repay them, his tools were 'inbeseld away' by another mason who had 'great disdain and envy' of his competition. A fight ensued, and in order to escape a conviction for assault by a partial jury, Egge appealed to the Chancellor from the London sheriff's court.[143]

Since the word 'servant' was used of both apprentices and serving-men, it is not always easy to distinguish between them. John Kay, for instance, whose work included casting George's fells in 1480,[144] may have been apprenticed. Later 'servants' like Nicholas Best, John Speryng, Giles Beckingham and William Rogers, who acted as general factotums for George or Richard, were probably – in the case of Giles certainly – apprentices or former apprentices.[145] None gained a bequest in the wills of George or Richard, and none appears in the staplers' list of 1505. The John Colyns there mentioned might, however, be identical with the boy who features in some of George's domestic accounts.

George was probably a kind-hearted master who enjoyed a good relationship with his pupils and servants. It is to be hoped that he found

---

[140] *Stonor L.*, I, xxviii. [141] P.C.C. 24 Logge.
[142] C.1 82/102 (1486). [143] C.1 66/165. [144] *C.L. 92.*
[145] 'Gyllys my 'prentice': File 13 fo. 5 (1486). For all these, see Ch. 14, *passim*, and for N. Best also Ch. 12 pp. 326ff.

none so difficult as the boy who inspired an unsigned and undated draft letter which appears elsewhere in the Public Record Office volumes of 'Ancient Correspondence', addressed by a fifteenth- or early sixteenth-century West Country merchant to some lubberly apprentice or son:

Jesu

Remember that at London thou receivedest 12*d* and gavest me no knowledge thereof. Also thou takest no heed for to learn to read. And as for the shop, thou wilt not come therein to learn for to serve men of ['with'] ware, but rather thou wilt lurk into corners, as thou dost when thou, upon holy days, shouldest say grace. And to read, a man were as good to bring a bear to the stake!

Wherefore I would put thee in remembrance. And if this will not be amended by this warning, it shall be amended by the token that thou sendest me my horse to Blockley [Worcs.] unshod, like as thou diddest when that thou rodest with me for wool [?], and then promisedest to me that thou wouldest amend.

And so thou dost as the fletcher [who] mend[ed] his bolt when he bit off the nock. For in two days and half thou madest a double [lined] cape, and for thou wouldest speed it to a purpose, thou tookest the great needle to the fine, and smote iron [i.e. 'went all out'], and wouldest not let [leave] thy work to serve any man in the shop.

And upon St Michael's Day thou were so busy in shooting that thou wouldest not serve a man of half a pound wax. And so I stand in as good surety of thy service in my absence as to bear powder in the wind. And so clean is blown all parcels out of thy beak that...[146]

Here mounting rage appears to have left the writer speechless. Unlike the Celys' own correspondence, this epistle does much to justify the contemporary opinion that the English were inordinately fond of proverbs. Besides containing several idioms that have not been recorded in modern reference books, it explains how 'the fletcher mended his bolt' from bad to worse. This saying was so well known that it occurs elsewhere only as a cryptic allusion.[147]

[146] S.C.1 46/271.
[147] Morris Palmer Tilley, *A Dictionary of the Proverbs in English in the 16th and 17th Centuries* (Ann Arbor, 1950), p. 634b (quoting Palsgrave), 'Hey, than wold ye mende, as the fletcher mends his bolt'.

PART III

RICHARD AND GEORGE
CELY, 1482–9

RICHARD AND GEORGE, 1482–3

The death of old Richard in January 1482 had released his sons from tutelage and opened a new chapter in their lives. It meant much immediate business for Richard junior, who was charged with making the funeral arrangements in accordance with the terms of his father's will, setting up his tomb, hiring the 'soul priest' who was paid an annual salary of ten marks (£6 13s 4d) to 'sing for the soul' of the deceased, and superintending the making of the steeple and the altar of St Stephen in St Olave's church, for which his father had made bequests. He had also to take charge of his mother's household in Mark Lane, and of Bretts Place, Aveley, of which he now became owner. There were the usual legal questions about his father's estate to be settled. In March 'John Croke of the Temple' told Agnes that he had heard the Escheator of Essex say that he had to go into Essex to hold the inquisition *post mortem* into old Richard's lands, and there was a story that George's inherited place Mallins was held of the king, so Richard had to take advice of master Molenars [Molyneux] and explain that all the properties were in the name of feoffees. He gave the escheator 40s, 'and so we be through with him for all matters and perils, but I must bring him at leisure a bill of the day a' the decease of our father, our age, and of whom our land is holden, 'at he may set it in the king's books'.[1]

Although the accounts contain the entry of 55s 4d paid for the probate of Richard's will,[2] no copy has been found. Nor, unfortunately, is the inventory which was made of his goods extant. Payments to 'Rede, freemason' for making the church steeple were spread over several years, and depending on whether various entries in the accounts have been duplicated or not, the total came to either £25, £38 or £45. Roger Egge, described as freemason and marbler, and the man who in youth had his tools stolen by a workmate, was paid a total of £8 3s 4d for the tomb, and the only recorded payment for the altar, also made to Egge, is 5s,

[1] *C.L.* 147 and File 10 fo. 25. No record survives.   [2] File 16 fo. 43.

together with 18*d* for lime and sand.[3] 'Making' could mean 'repairing', so perhaps that was all that was involved. Other bequests mentioned in the accounts are £6 13*s* 4*d* to the servants William Aldridge and Alice for their marriage, £36 11*s* 7*d* to John Cely senior, possibly owed to him for wool supplied, and to John's son John an annual £2 13*s* 4*d* towards his expenses as a student at Oxford.[4] Whether or not Richard's widow was specifically mentioned in the will, she would, by custom of the City, be comfortably provided for.

A trental of masses were said for Richard at a cost of 10*s*, and a standard sum of 6*s* 8*d* was given in alms to the church. There were further unspecified payments to poor men and women at the funeral and at 'minds' (memorial services) thereafter.[5] Two 'legends' (books of readings from scripture or saints' lives) appraised in the inventory at 26*s* 8*d* remained in St Olave's. One year later Agnes Cely's will was drawn up for her by one 'Wadecobe' at a cost of 5*s*.[6] In her case there was again a payment of 55*s* 4*d* for probate, and apparently a further 13*s* 8*d* was paid to Dr Pycknam (William Pykenham, chancellor of the Archbishop of Canterbury?) for 'probation'.[7] Her will is duly registered in the books of the Prerogative Court of Canterbury.[8] Her son Richard paid 14*s* 6*d* to Kyd, carpenter, for her chest (coffin) and 'other gear'.

A great deal of wax was bought for candles used at the various funeral ceremonies and about the tomb on subsequent occasions. Thomas Wylde, waxchandler, charged 35*s* for torches and other wax for the burial and month mind of Agnes in 1483,[9] though this was far less than the £10 5*s* 10*d* expended on wax (at 7*d* per lb) for the funeral of Joan, mother of Thomas Stonor, who died before 1425.[10] Another waxchandler named Robert Dyckkys supplied candles for the grave of Richard Cely senior, and 22*s* 2½*d* was paid 'for certain wax delivered unto their church about their father's tomb and otherwise at Easter and other times sithen in '82'.[11]

For his month mind, one sum of 33*s* 6*d* included 12*s* 6*d* for sturgeon, 2*s* 7*d* for earthen pots, and 15*s* 4*d* to the mercer Gilbert Palmer for 34 ells of Flemish cloth at 5½*d* the ell.[12] This last may have provided the 11 black gowns made at a cost of 3*s* 8*d*, perhaps to be given to selected

[3] File 10 fo. 15.
[4] Ibid. and fo. 9v. On 23 May 1485 the quarterly 13*s* 4*d* was spent on 4 yards of 'musterdevyllers' for John. At the same time, 4 yards of russet for 'Friar William' cost 8*s*: fo. 15.   [5] File 10 fo. 14v.
[6] File 10 fo. 16v.   [7] File 10 fo. 17.
[8] P.C.C. 8 Logge.   [9] File 10 fo. 17v.
[10] *Stonor L.*, no. 47.
[11] File 10 fo. 15v. Candles were still being bought in 1490, when a waxchandler was paid 41*s* 6½*d* 'for wax spent in the church': fo. 15.
[12] File 10 fos. 14, 15v, 17v.

mourners.[13] At this or another of the commemorative feasts for Richard 4*d* worth of apples were bought, a cook and turners (spit-boys) were hired for 12*d*, and 16*d* was paid to Thomas Lyn, butler. At the year's mind a total of £3 18*s* 4*d* was spent on such items as 20*d* to five priests, 10*s* for the trental of masses, 13*s* 4*d* to 'Wylchyr cook for his labour', 10*s* to the butcher, 18*d* to the milk-wife, and 6*s* 8*d* to 'Watkyn to purvey for poultry'.[14] Recorded payments for the third year's mind come to £2 4*s* 6*d*. Richard junior later claimed that he had paid in all £527 19*s* 4*d* towards his father's legacies, debts, funeral, probate and alms, a sum the equivalent of nearly five years' estimated net income from his own trading in wool.[15] Funeral expenses, excluding individual legacies but including £2 for probate of the will, for Thomas Stonor who died in 1474 came to £76 2*s* 5*d*.[16] William Maryon wanted no month mind to be held for him and specified that £12 should be spent on his funeral.[17] Ascertainable costs over Agnes Cely's funeral and month mind, which exclude fees paid to the church, were in the region of £18 13*s*. The total of her immediate monetary bequests was £75 6*s* 8*d* (excluding the value of her legacy of 100 marks to Robert).[18]

William Maryon supervised some of the catering for the funeral of Agnes, for which he was given £1 10*s* 2½*d*.[19] For her month mind there was a quantity of wild fowl supplied by Collett the poulterer at a cost of £4 4*s* 11*d*, and 'victual' bought from Croke the baker for 13*s* 4*d*. William Dygon, spicer, was paid 42*s* 3*d*. As well, there were six dishes of butter for a total of 10½*d*, 7*d* worth of eggs (this would buy probably 100), and two Banbury cheeses costing 13½*d*. Richard supplied a calf priced at 3*s* 4*d*, and George 'spent in the forest [of Waltham?] against my mother's month mind – 10*s*'.[20] It was perhaps for the same occasion that he bought at London 2 lb of dates, 2 lb of prunes and 2 lb 'R. Corans' (currants), for 19*d* in all. Wylshyre, cook, received 2*s* 10*d* 'for his labour', and sixteen 'garnish' (sets) of pewter dishes were hired at a cost of 9*s* 4*d*.[21] In 1475 one such garnish of silver which had belonged to Dame Alice Wyche consisted of two chargers or large serving plates, a dozen platters, a dozen dishes and a dozen sauce-dishes.[22] These were

---

[13] File 10 fo. 16v.

[14] File 10 fo. 14v. A dinner for the bishop's officers, apparently in connexion with probate proceedings, cost 10*s*: fo. 14.

[15] File 10 fo. 34. For estimated income, see Ch. 15, pp. 417ff.

[16] *Stonor L.*, no. 157.

[17] Will, P.C.C. 19 Vox. The mercer John Don, senior, went further, requesting 'no pompous array done at my burying nor at my month's mind, nor in lights [nor] clothing nor in no great dinners', the money to be spent rather on poor people: P.C.C. 2 Logge (1480).   [18] P.C.C. 8 Logge.   [19] File 10 fo. 16v.

[20] File 10 fo. 24, File 20 no. 36.   [21] File 10 fo. 16v.

[22] *A.C.M.*, p. 83.

all for serving food. The guests would eat off 'trenchers' of bread. At the mayor's feast given by John Wynger in London in 1504 8s worth of trencher bread was provided, in addition to 7s worth of fine 'chet' bread in 'manchets' and 4s worth of halfpenny bread.[23]

At funeral occasions a barrel of 'tyre', a variety of strong sweetened wine, seems to have been a standard item. Holding probably $31\frac{1}{2}$ wine gallons, one barrel cost 18s 10d at Richard's funeral, and another was supplied for Agnes's, at a cost of 17s 6d, in addition to $2\frac{1}{4}$ gallons of claret wine. For Agnes's month mind Stabylton of the 'Dolphin' provided three 'kinderkins' (kilderkins) and one firkin of 'good ale' – a total of 56 gallons – and five kilderkins (80 gallons) of three-halfpenny ale, costing 15s 11d in all. More ale from 'Scarlet's wife' at burial and month mind cost 13s 2d, and in all there must have been at least $233\frac{1}{2}$ gallons (about 1,061 litres). Some of this may have been distributed to poor men of the parish, as was customary.

The most vivid account of the necessary preparations for funeral celebrations is in the collection of Stonor papers and concerns the funeral of the Thomas Stonor who died in 1474.[24] A rather harassed organizer listed the various ornaments and hangings to be provided in Pyrton church, including 'for the herse ['bier'] and for the burial, black cloth to the ground with a white cloth of gold', four tapers about the herse and two tapers about the burial. Like any modern hostess, he went on to draw up menus and itemize the necessary provisions, which were evidently to be cooked and served from temporary accommodation. There was careful discrimination between the two chief classes of society (were women included?).

Meat for poor men at diriges [the dirge]. Item, after *diriges* bread and cheese for the said poor men. Item, for [priests] and gentlemen, 'sew purtenaunces' of lambs and veal ['offal', served in a broth, probably with onions], roasted mutton, two chickens in a dish.

On the morrow to breakfasts. For priests and other honest men. Item, calves' heads and sodden [stewed] beef.

At the dinner on the morrow.

For poor men. Item, umbles [tripe, etc.] to pottage, sodden beef [and] roasted veal in a dish together, and roasted pork.

The first course for priests, etc. First to pottage, browes [broth] of capons [this was changed from frumenty], capons, muttons, geese [changed from 'sodden beef and mutton, pig and veal'], custard.

The second course. The second pottage, jussell [a dish of eggs or fish-roe mixed with breadcrumbs and cooked in broth], capons, lamb, pig, veal, pigeons roasted, baked rabbits, pheasants, venison, jelly, etc.

[23] Balliol MS. 354, fo. 103v.   [24] *Stonor L.*, no. 138; C.47 37/4/9.

Item, voutes [?voidées, a 'dessert' of sweetmeats and spices eaten at the end of a meal].

Item, spices. First a pound of saunders [sandalwood, used as a red colouring], a ounce of saffron, 3 lb pepper, half a pound cloves, half a pound maces, a loaf sugar [changed from 4 lb], 3 lb raisins-currants, 3 lb dates, half a pound ginger, 1 lb cinnamon. Item, in turnsole [a plant used to produce a blue food-dye] – 4*d*. Item, in grains ['cardamom'] – 1 lb. Item, in almonds – 4 lb.

If the references to stewed and roasted meats suggest the joints of 'good plain English cooking', the impression is illusory. Such meat would be sliced or even chopped up and served in a more or less elaborate sauce, often of the sweet-and-sour ('poignant') variety. 'Custard' was a dish something like mince-pies, made with chopped veal, gravy, herbs, spices, eggs, dates and prunes, all baked in a pastry case.[25]

The memorandum continued:

Item, treen ['wooden'] vessel for poor men. Item, sitting places for the poor men. Item, pewter vessel for gentlemen. Item, a room for them according ['suitable']. Item, spoons of silver, salt-cellars for the most worshipful men, etc. [Spoons were usually provided only for the most important guests, others were expected to bring their own. The humble, of course, sat below the salt in its elaborate cellars. They had salt provided on pieces of bread, as most people did on less grand occasions.]

Item, board-cloths for gentlemen and poor men. Item, salt, etc. Item, a convenient room for the two butteries for gentlemen and poor men. Item, a convenient place for the kitchen. Item, cooks. Item, butlers. Item, a man to oversee the sad ['befitting'] purveyance of the church. Item, a porter. Item, other servants to serve, etc. Item, vessel for ale. Item, cups and bowls and pots. Item, spits, cauldrons, rakes and other necessaries for cooks. Item, wood and coals.

A further aide-memoire on the dorse of the paper included:

Item, cheeses for poor men, and more geese.
Item, remember milk, pulters [young fowl], eggs.
Item, wine for green geese.
Item, remember pigs.

A quantity of bread must also have been provided for these meals, but like the ale and any wine that was drunk, it does not figure in the surviving portion of the memorandum. The poor men were given cheese, but the menu for the better-class guests consisted almost entirely of the meat dishes which epitomized good living and good diet for contemporary people.

In some ways, funerals like this were more significant as social

---

[25] Thomas Austin, ed., *Two Fifteenth-Century Cookery Books* (E.E.T.S. o.s. 91, 1888), p. 74.

occasions than weddings. (But for George's wedding celebrations, see Ch. 12.) The giving of mourning gowns and rings to the more important guests was a way of cementing relations which might otherwise have decayed with the loss of the family's erstwhile head. A funeral and mind were also occasions for the display of the family wealth, indicated not only by the lavishness of the food and drink, but also by the amount of 'plate' on show. The expense involved therefore had some practical purpose, especially when the heirs were, like Richard and George, on the marriage market.

The Cely family certainly rallied round to provide an impressive display at the month mind for Richard on 14 February 1482.[26] Thomas Blackham lent no fewer than 35 pieces of plate, besides five dozen silver spoons. Agnes herself possessed 31 items, besides three dozen spoons,[27] Richard junior had four pieces and 15 spoons, and Robert Eyryk produced 12 pieces and a dozen spoons, while 'Jelyan Lyn' lent a further 12. It is odd that no plate of William Maryon's is mentioned, but if he contributed he may have made his own inventory. George laboriously itemized all the other pieces, with a careful description of each. To judge by his rendering of some of the Latin inscriptions, he wrote from dictation. The list is long, but extensive quotation is irresistible. The catalogue gives a tantalizing picture of the handsome examples of the silversmith's skill which a merchant family of late medieval London might possess. There is, however, nothing to match the positively late-Victorian exuberance of the gilded salt-cellar belonging to a yeoman, William Shepey, in 1447, which was made like a ragged staff standing on a battlemented base.[28] The base contained white sheep and a man and maiden beating away a wolf. A dog like a bloodhound and a bear supported the main structure, to which they were chained. The cover was similarly adorned with sheep, dog and bear, and was designed to hold a banner. Seven other banners, also of gilded silver, stood round about and in the top, 'wrought with diverse arms'. 'The which salt-cellar with the covercle, base, terrages, sheep, man, maiden, wolf, dogs, bears and banners aforesaid' weighed 12 lb troy weight. Edward IV had a rather vulgar, heavily jewelled, salt in the form of a gold elephant and castle, which was passed round leaders of the merchant community in pawn.[29]

From 'my cousin Thomas Blacham' George had borrowed:

[26] File 12 fos. 35–6.
[27] Evidently, wills are no sure guide to the amount of plate possessed by the testator: Agnes specified only four pieces in her will.
[28] Philip E. Jones, ed., *Calendar of Plea and Memoranda Rolls, 1437–1457* (Cambridge, 1954), p. 107.
[29] *Cal. Plea and Mem. Rolls, 1458–1482*, p. 51.

An standing mazer with an covering of mazer castle-wise, with an pelican in the top, gilt. ['Mazer' was maple or other wood.]

Another standing mazer with an crowned rose in the bottom [and] a painted covering of wood with an knop, gilt, with four apples.

Two great square salts parcel gilt, with an covering having a maiden's head in the top, gilt.

Two serpentines with two coverings, silver and gilt, crowned with an shield having three 'broshesse' [brushes].[30]

An salt all gilt, with an covering, ten quarters.

An goblet, parcel gilt, with an covering, standing on two men with staves in their hands, and a child in the top, gilt.

An tub gilt, covered, with an hart [or heart?] in the bottom.

An standing cup, covered, parcel gilt, with scripture about it, and about the foot is writ 'Spesse Mea in Deo Est'.

An standing cup standing on three lions, without an covering.

An standing cup gilt, with an covering having two children upon the top, silver, back to back, pounced with flames.

An standing cup, parcel gilt, with an covering blue enamelled in the top, standing upon three lions.

An little standing cup with an covering, parcel gilt, with an acorn in the top.

An standing cup gilt with an covering crowned, and the cup stands upon three hounds.

An low flat cup plain pounced in the bottom, the foot and border gilt.

Four low cups quarteraged, parcel gilt, with stars gilt in the bottom.

Six low plain standing cups, with an covering, parcel gilt, five having five months, the sixth an flower in the bottom. The covering with an knop gilt and an star underneath it.[31]

Six gilt cups, with an covering, enamelled in the bottom, with a lizard in every bottom chained, with a crown about the neck.

An flat gilt piece with an covering, pounced like an rose, with an small point in the top.

. . .

An flat piece writ under the bottom with scripture and an R. and an G. chained.

There were also 1 dozen spoons 'with the acorn gilt', 1½ dozen with 'round wreaths gilt', 1½ dozen with cut ends and 1 dozen with 'spear points' and packthread about the ends.

Agnes Cely had the following;

Six gilt cups, with an covering, with low standing feet, having none prints in the bottom. The covering with an bell knop chased with vines.

An great pottle pot of silver, parcel gilt, with an 'brosell' [medallion?] on the lid, gilt, enamelled with blue violets and daisies.

[30] A serpentine was a container made from the stone so called.
[31] Often a set of cups had one single matching cover. How were the months depicted?

An less pottle pot of silver, parcel gilt, with an brossell in the top enamelled with blue and green with an man.

An less pot, parcel gilt, with an browssell in the top gilt, enamelled with an flower, blue.

An high standing cup, with an covering, parcel gilt, with scripture about it: 'O Mater Day Men to May y' ['O mater Dei, memento mei'], and about the foot, 'Glorya Tyby Domine'.

An standing cup, with an covering, parcel gilt, standing upon three lions, and the knop above blue enamelled.

An great standing gilt cup with an covering, standing on three men blowing bagpipes.

An little standing gilt cup with an covering, standing on three lions, and in the top of the covering an crown and an cony [rabbit] therein.

Six chased bowls, parcel gilt, with a star in the bottom, having a flower called an blue-bottle [cornflower], with an covering with an rose in the gilt chase.

Two great salts with an covering, every other chase gilt, and the covering having an great knop with eighteen quarters.

An salt with an covering, parcel gilt, written R.M. within, the covering enamelled.

Two salts with an covering, parcel gilt, the knop quartered.

An nut with an covering, all gilt, and about the nut is writ 'Bene Dyctos Deus in Donys Suys'. [A 'nut' was properly a cup made from a mounted coconut shell (a rather rare curiosity), but the name was also given to a metal cup of similar shape.]

An great square salt with an covering, parcel gilt, with an small diamond point in the top.

Three plain bowls with an Andrew cross under the bottom.

An gilt tub with an covering, with hoops with an round knop in the top.

A low standing cup plain, with an star in the bottom and roses about the foot.

Agnes's three dozen spoons had gilt lions at the end, or 'diamond points' which were marked with blue thread.

Robert Eyryck's plate consisted of

Six low standing cups with an covering, all parcel gilt, with 'browssellis' in the bottoms, having knots with flowers, and the top of the covering is hollow and have none 'brewssell', and Our Lady sitting within the covering in an mantle of blue.

Two chased low standing pieces, parcel gilt, with an covering and stars in the bottom and an star about the covering, having this under the bottom: 2 9 [in arabic numerals].

Three plain low standing pieces, the feet gilt, having the same mark in the bottom.

An standing cup with an covering, all gilt, chased with vines, and an pelican standing upon an crown on the covering.

An dozen spoons with maidens' heads, gilt.

Richard Cely had

Two salts with an covering, parcel gilt, standing on three ragged staves.
An standing cup gilt, with an covering, having an star in the top.
An nut with an covering with the twelve months.
Fifteen spoons: six has acorns, and nine spear points, marked with white thread.

In addition Eyryk provided 13 napkins, marked in red with a kind of laundry mark, and Jelyan Lyn lent 20 more, bearing the same mark in blue. Was she the wife of the butler, Thomas Lyn, hired for the occasion? And were they relations of Eyryk's? Jelyan also lent a dozen spoons with spear-points, six with gilt and six with 'white' ends, all marked with red silk. Agnes Cely for her part 'delivered to the butler':

Five diaper table cloths, 8 plain table cloths, 4 diaper towels and 1 plain, 4 small plain towels, 18 fine napkins, 1 fine napkin and 41 diaper, 5 plain 'pourpains' [long cloths for carrying bread or 'wafers'], 2 diaper dappled cloths, 5 cupboard cloths, 2 other diaper cloths, a diaper cupboard cloth and 2 small diaper towels.

Diaper was patterned in the weave. The towels used by butlers, servers and carvers were very long and narrow, measuring perhaps 2–2½ yards by 12 or 18 inches.[32]

All this impressive display after the death of old Richard failed to arouse due gratitude in some of those present. Moreover, while it might be desirable to magnify the status and prospects of marriageable sons, the same sons were not anxious to lose control of the widow's share of property. Although the younger Richard was usually ready enough to pass on gossip himself, he resented any that came too close to home, and when rumour presented him with a step-father he wrote angrily to George on 24 June 1482:

Sir, it was telled Robert Eyryk at Calais that our mother should be married or in the way of marriage, into so much that they said our mother should go on procession on Corpus Christi Day in a crimson gown, and her meinie ['household'] in black. And a' my soul our mother went at that day but as she went at our father's month's mind. And therefore I would it were tried out ['ascertained'] the bringer of that to Calais. Sir, we are greatly envied, I trust to Jesu we shall be able to withstand our enemies. Sir John [Wendon, the chantry priest?] is in great trouble, and God knows full wrongfully, and part of them that we gave gowns to labours most against him. I had liefer than a good meed ['reward'] that ye were here.[33]

If the Celys' own difficulties with their neighbours in Essex were connected with that common cause of dissension, a dispute over land,

---

[32] Balliol MS. 354, fo. 103.   [33] *C.L.* 175.

no doubt Richard's death was a signal for fresh trouble. At any rate, Richard junior had already suggested, on 25 May, that a present of hawks might help to sweeten one local man, very likely William Brandon. If they bought a nest of goshawks and gave one or two away, it 'should cause us to live in great rest in Essex, for the gentleman is but strangely disposed'.[34] The expression 'strangely disposed' meant, not so much 'uncertain in temper', as 'overtly hostile'. A correspondent of John Paston in 1461 described how a group of men who were 'strangely disposed' against Paston were 'making revel' in Cotton Hall, melting lead, breaking down the drawbridge, and preparing to hold the place against him.[35] 'The gentleman' was a kind of family code-word for this particular neighbour of the Celys.

But one of the Celys' enemies, the Bottrell who had thrown dung over fells, was removed from Calais in August of that year. William Cely wrote home to say

Item, please it your masterships to wit that all they that were before in the wages of master Robert Radclyffe, porter of Calais, be put out of wages and warned to void the town by Friday next come. And as for Botterell, he shall out of prison, and all that were therein for the same matter. And they all be warned to void the town of Calais and the marches, wife, children and goods, by Friday next come, pain of death. For the which I trow Botrell will not disease you of your house no longer, etc.[36]

On 29 August he confirmed that 'Bottrell is departed out of Calais and is in England, and this day his wife goeth to him with all her stuff. And they be commanded that they shall not come within the town of Calais as long as my lord chamberlain is lieutenant of Calais.'[37] My lord chamberlain ceased, in fact, to be lieutenant of Calais nine months later, when he was executed on the orders of Richard III. Although both parties finished by opposing Richard, in the previous year Hastings had been at loggerheads with the Woodville faction, and there were mutual accusations of sedition. It seems that at one point the Woodvilles nearly succeeded in ousting Hastings from the king's favour.[38] On the other side, an informer, encouraged by Hastings, had denounced Radcliffe, Earl Rivers and the queen's eldest son, the Marquis of Dorset, to the Council of Calais early in 1482.[39] In August of that year there were stories rife about a plot to make copies of the town keys and deliver them to the

[34] *C.L.* 169.
[35] *Paston L.*, no. 648.
[36] *C.L.* 185.
[37] *C.L.* 188.
[38] The Latin version of More's *Richard III : Complete Works* (New Haven), II, 51.
[39] James Gairdner, *History of the Life and Reign of Richard the Third* (2nd edn, Cambridge, 1898), pp. 338–9, and S.C.1 44/60.

French.[40] This accounts for the expulsion of the servants of Radcliffe, the porter of Calais, and Bottrell may have been one of them, or at least got himself mixed up in the same affair. A minor feud with one of the staplers would not have been grounds for expulsion on the lieutenant's orders.

During Agnes Cely's widowhood, William Maryon acted as a kind of major domo to the household in Mark Lane. Between them, Richard and George gave him £19 3s 11½d for expenses between 24 January 1482 and 24 January 1483.[41] Richard himself paid further for necessary repairs to the house and for goods like three loads of hay 'at the garden end' and supplies of firewood. At Christmas he bought pepper, cloves, maces and dates for 7s 9d, cinnamon for 16d, and other spices for 8s, a little fish, bread and flesh, four 'kennets' (meaning?) for 6d, a pig for 4d, and two cades of herring, each containing 620, and one cade of sprats, containing 1,200, for 8s. The supply of wine and beer seems huge until one remembers that, with ale, they supplied the place of all the various beverages, including plain water, in use today. Richard bought for his mother's household a total of 81 gallons of 'romney' [sweet wine, probably from Spain]. Sixty kilderkins of beer, each holding 18 gallons and costing a total of 60s, were drunk at Bretts Place in Essex during 1482, while the same beer-brewer supplied 121 kilderkins, costing £6 6s 8d, which were used in London. This would be in addition to ale.

Clothing bought by Richard for his mother included two Paris kerchiefs costing 13s 4d and 14s, a black 'corse' (girdle) for 4s, shoes and slippers, sarsenet to line her hood, and a handsome 'harnessed' girdle bought from the goldsmith John Veneke, which cost 11s 11d and was ornamented with 3¾ ounces of silver.[42] Thirteen yards of russet were woven for her at a cost of 2s 8d. Agnes and her servants all had fur put in their gowns for winter, and cloth for her livery cost 66s 8d. Richard and George had their own livery of tawny medley – a cloth of 30 ells (37½ yards) cost them 60s. These amounts would suffice to make 10 or 11 gowns each. Although a bolt might have been kept to last more than one season, it looks as though there was a large household. Wages which are mentioned as paid to Agnes's servants are 8s to Joan Thomson, 9s to Watkin, and one payment of 3s 8d to Luntley. At another time Luntley

---

[40] N. H. Nicolas and Edward Tyrrell, eds., *A Chronicle of London from 1089–1483* (1827), p. 147.

[41] Richard's 'costs and expenses of household' from 12 Feb. 1482 to May 1484 are given in File 10 fos. 22–4.

[42] Payments on behalf of Agnes are in File 10 fos. 16–17v. Henry Punt made a bequest of a girdle studded with silver-gilt, the silver or harness ('argentum sive harnesum') to be set on red silk: P.C.C. 20 Milles.

was paid wages of 3s up to 10 March 1483. 'Joan [their] mother's maid' was buried at a cost of 5s 11d in July (1482?). She was certainly not the only woman servant, but no others are named.[43]

In September 1482 Agnes went to stay in Essex, with incidental costs of 10s 6d, while 'Venables' was paid 4s 10d for the boat-hire to Aveley. He must have carried a number of persons and a quantity of provisions and furnishings. The normal wherry fare for one person was 1d. Earlier in the year Agnes had had trouble with her leg. Although William Maryon wrote reassuringly to George on 2 April that 'my mistress your mother is in good health, so reasonably, and waxeth all strong, as of a woman of her age', he qualified this further by saying in his next letter, 'saving her leg is not yet all whole, but I trust to God it standeth in good case'.[44] Richard paid 26s 8d to 'master Norton, surgeon, for healing of his mother's sore leg'. There is also a recorded payment of 12d to her unnamed physician.[45]

It was as well for Richard that he had William Maryon to keep an eye on the household in London, because he was frequently absent on business. He was planning to pack wool in the Cotswolds on 25 March 1482, and got as far as Abingdon, where he

waited upon William Breten for to go unto Northleach, but William Breten might not attend it. And in that mean time came William Midwinter to London, and so none of them spake with other.[46]

Richard's costs for riding to Abingdon came to 11s 6d.[47] Breten was held up at Southampton, packing 'Lombards'' wool for export to Genoa in the king's ships, but promised to meet Richard at Northleach on 21 April. Accordingly, Maryon reported

Ye shall understand that the 19 day of April your brother Richard Cely departed out of London into Cotswold-ward at three of the bell at afternoon. And as he was taking his horse, writing came from you, the which was written at Calais the 15 day of April. The which writing, sir, he might not well tarry for to read, and therefore, sir, he hath borne them with him into Cotswold.[48]

Evidently Richard opened the letter and noted the date at the end. George's letters were not usually very long. Does this casual sentence indicate that reading, as well as writing, could be a slow process? Or

---

[43] Unless when Richard 'delivered to his mother 20d which she gave to heme' (File 10 fo. 16), 'heme' means 'Em'. These accounts are only a clerk's copies from original entries.   [44] *C.L.* 149, 151.

[45] File 10 fo. 16. Norton is unrecorded by Talbot and Hammond, *Medical Practitioners*, unless he is the John Northorne who was apprenticed to John Hobbes, surgeon, ante 1463: pp. 156, 174.   [46] *C.L.* 149.

[47] File 10 fo. 25.   [48] *C.L.* 153.

is it evidence for the view that reading was not usually a matter of silent and cursory perusal but would be done aloud?

Richard, having spent three weeks packing wool and buying fells, wrote himself to George on 13 May, commenting (with relief, one imagines) on the fact that George expected to send over above £500 by exchange. The news with which he was bursting, however, concerned other matters.

Sir, I write to you a process: I pray God send thereof a good end. The same day that I come to Northleach, on a Sunday before matins, from Burford, William Midwinter welcomed me. And in our communication he asked me if I were in any way of marriage. I told him nay, and he informed me that there was a young gentlewoman whose father's name is Lemryke, and her mother is dead, and she shall dispend by her mother £40 a year, as they say in that country. And her father is the greatest ruler and richest man in that country, and there have been great gentlemen to see her, and would have her, etc. And ever matins were done, William Midwinter had moved this matter to the greatest man about the gentleman Lemeryke, and he yeed and informed the foresaid of all the matter, and the young gentlewoman both. And the Saturday after, William Midwinter went to London, as all wool-gatherers were sent for by writ [in an effort to cure abuses in packing]....

When I had packed at Campden and William Midwinter departed, I came to Northleach again to make an end of packing. And on the Sunday next after [i.e. next day, 28 April], the same man that William Midwinter brake first to ['raised the matter with initially'] came [to] me and told me that he had broken to his master, according as Midwinter desired him. And he said his master was right well pleased therewith. And the same man said to me, if I would tarry May Day [Wednesday 1 May] I should have a sight of the young gentlewoman. And I said I would tarry with a good will. And the same day her father [a Justice of the Peace] should 'a sitten at Northleach for the king, but he sent one of his clerks, and rode himself to Winchcombe.

And to matins the same day come the young gentlewoman and her mother-in-law [i.e. stepmother], and I and William Bretten were saying matins when they come into church. And when matins was done they went to a kinswoman of the young gentlewoman, and I sent to them a pottle [½ gallon] of white romney. And they took it thankfully, for they had come a mile a'foot that morning. And when mass was done I come and welcomed them, and kissed them, and they thanked me for the wine, and prayed me to come to dinner with them. And I excused me, and they made me promise them to drink with them after dinner. And I sent them to dinner a gallon wine, and they sent me a heronceau roast [a roasted young heron]. And after dinner I come and drank with them, and took William Bretten with me. And we had right good communication, and the person pleased me well, as by the first communication ['on first impressions']. She is young, little, and very well-favoured and witty [intelligent], and the country speaks much good by her.

Sir, all this matter abideth the coming of her father to London, that we may understand what sum he will depart with, and how he likes me. He will be here within three weeks. I pray send me a letter how ye think by this matter.[49]

It may well be supposed that unseemly nudging and whispering went on among the two parties in the magnificent church at Northleach during those May Day services. But however well Richard and Elizabeth Limerick liked each other, her father and Richard must have failed to agree on a price, in the form of marriage settlements. Or perhaps Richard himself decided that good merchant's money was a better bargain than some rents and a father-in-law who cut a figure in the country. Piquantly, one of the Limericks later became a Tudor 'drop-out'. In 1596 Edward Hext, J.P. in Somerset, wrote to Lord Burghley about the problem of how to deal with the numbers of idle vagabonds, 'wandering suspicious persons' and suchlike in his county, and sent him a counterfeit pass employed by one young man, who could expect to inherit land worth £40 per annum from his father, a gentleman named Lymeryck who dwelt at Northleach. For two months in prison young Limerick had upheld the validity of his document 'with most execrable oaths'. Whipping failed to make respectable citizens out of such youths, 'the liberty of their wicked life is so sweet unto them'.[50]

Almost as soon as his father was dead, Richard Cely's acquaintances had noted him as a good match-making prospect. Already on 21 March he had told George that since 16 March he had been 'spoken to for a wife in two places'.[51] One of these proposals came from the Staple appraisers of fells. And within three weeks of his inspection of Elizabeth Limerick, Harry Bryan was labouring him 'sore to go and see Rawson's daughter'.

I am beholding to him for his labour, for I know well that he would I did well. And I pray you deliver him some money at this time and do well by him, for it is sure enough. I have many things in my mind, but I have no leisure to write. Ye may understand part by my letter that I sent you before this.

Sir, I understand as I ride in the country many things. One is that our brother [fellow stapler] William Dalton shall be married to one of the next kinswomen that Christopher Brown has.[52]

At this point Richard received a jolt. Three days later he wrote in shame and agitation to George, addressing him as 'my ghostly brother' and punning on 'ghostly father', which was the common term for a confessor. He confided:

[49] *C.L.* 165.
[50] Tawney and Power, eds., *Tudor Economic Documents*, II, 343.
[51] *C.L.* 146.　　　　　　　　　　　[52] *C.L.* 168.

Sir, it is so that a chance is fallen that lies upon mine honesty, but I cannot keep no counsel from you, for by policy ye and I may find the mean to save all thing clear at your coming,

or, in translation, 'an accident has occurred to discredit me, but I cannot conceal anything from you, for we may be able to make a plan to save the situation when you come home'.

It is so that Em is with child. And, as God knows, but that once that it was gotten I deserve it for mine. It was gotten on Shrove Even, and she has been sick ever sin' ye departed of the access.... No more to you, my ghostly brother, but I pray Jesu that all things may be well conveyed.

Per your brother Richard Cely and your lover.[53]

Nothing more is known of Em, and it is not clear whether Richard's liaison with her damaged his matrimonial prospects, whether he had poached on George's preserves, or whether Em was one of his mother's maids, for whom provision would have to be arranged.[54]

In fact Richard did take Harry Bryan's advice to go and see Rawson's daughter, who was named Anne. He evidently liked what he saw, since the couple were married later that year. Anne's father, who gave her 500 marks ($£333$ $6s$ $8d$) in dowry, was Richard Rawson, a Yorkshireman who became a member of the Mercers' Company of London and was an alderman of London from 1476 until his death. Three of his sons, Avery, John and Christopher, also became members of the Mercers' Company. Two younger daughters later married John Fox, mercer, and Godfrey Darrald, merchant of the Staple.[55]

On her deathbed, near the end of January 1483, Agnes Cely gave Richard and Anne his wife all the contents of the house in Mark Lane,

according to her promise made to Richard Rawson...and to Isabel his wife, before and at the time of marriage of the said Richard Cely and Anne. Which household foresaid, as appeareth by a quire thereof made, is to the value of $£45$ $4s$ $8\frac{1}{2}d$.[56]

Other '[h]ustilments of household, wearing clothes, plate, jewels and ready money specified in their father's inventory' had apparently been given away to various people by Agnes during her widowhood.[57]

In her will, dated 28 January 1482/3, Agnes had bequeathed a set of vestments to St Olave's, Hart St, and Richard's father-in-law supplied $17\frac{3}{4}$ yards 'save the nail' of 'blue cloth of gold' priced at $26s$ $8d$ the yard, 20 yards of green buckram at $6d$ the yard and 16 yards of Holland cloth

[53] *C.L.* 169.
[55] Thrupp, *Merchant Class*, p. 363.
[57] Ibid.
[54] See n. 43 above.
[56] File 10 fo. 34.

for albs, at 9*d* the yard.[58] These were made up by John Throkylton, vestment maker, who also provided a 'single suit of orphreys of needle-work', costing £13 6*s* 8*d*. These were a matching set of ornamental borders or bands. Throkylton charged 10*s* for making the vestment, while ten pieces of ribbon and two pieces of fringe weighing 15⅛ ounces cost an extra 17*s* 7½*d*. The total cost was £39 8*s* 11½*d*, which makes an interesting comparison with the valuation put upon the furnishings of the house.

Anne Rawson's dowry was added, in due course, to the trading stock which Richard and George had inherited from their father.[59] The 'good marriage' came conveniently. In May 1482 Richard had told George 'and ye will that we shall buy any wool the next year, make part of your money [in receipts from wool sales] to be paid before Bartholomew Tide [24 August]'.[60] In September there was an unpleasant shock in the form of a somewhat incoherent letter from William Midwinter, their major supplier, whose Gloucestershire accent comes through strongly in the spelling of his original.

Right reverent and worshipful sir, I recommend me unto you, desiring to hear of your welfare. Furthermore, I thank you of the great cheer that ye did me at my last being with you.

Sir, I made a bargain with you at that season, the which I would I had slept [or 'slipped'?] the whiles. For theke customers ['those suppliers'] that I trusted most for to 'a sold them, and I trusted that I should not 'a bought their wool above 13*s* 8*d* a tod, and now I cannot buy their wool under 14*s* and 14*s* and 6*d* a tod. The price is that I buy at above that I sold you right much. And to reckon the refuse, I shall lose, by my troth, a noble or 10*s* in every sack. And as my troth help me, and they must have ready money by and by ['immediately'], they that were wont to leave in my hand most part of their money, now they must needs have all their money. And now I must trust to your courtesy. And I pray you consider this well, as ye may have my service, and I must trust to you that I may have the £200 that ye said I should not have it till November: I pray as heartily as I can that ye make it ready within 14 days after Michaelmas [29 September], or else I am hotly shamed. For I made myself never so bare without money, and therefore I pray you that ye make it ready.[61]

Richard sent this letter on to George, saying 'I wot not how to answer it. And our father's tomb is a-setting up, and our eme ['uncle' – John Cely] is here for money, and this day I depart into Cotswold, and how soon they will call upon [us] for the 20*s* [duty] of the sarpler I cannot say. I am at my wits' end without your comfort.'[62] On 17 October he

---

[58] File 10 fo. 17v (1 March 1484).   [59] C.1 194/17.
[60] *C.L.* 169.   [61] *C.L.* 192.
[62] *C.L.* 195.

wrote again, having heard from George that fighting had prevented the Hollanders attending the mart at Antwerp. Under the new cares of business, he begins to sound very like his father.

I have been at Chipping Norton and set all thing in good way, and with mine eme John Cely, and he has gathered 16 sack of fair wool. And now here is come William Midwinter, but I spake not with him yet. How that I do with him I shall write to you in my next letter.... I pray God send us a merry world: it is evil for a man to charge him far nowadays, for I hear of none utterance ['sale']. If I may depart fair from the bargain with William Midwinter that ye and I made, I will do my best. Me think it will be well done, for our debtors are slow payers.[63]

The Celys, however, had to become accustomed to paying more for their Cotswold wool, and seem in fact to have shipped 31 sarplers during 1483, which was no less than usual. In late 1483 Richard and George were seriously underestimating the prices at which wine, herring and onion seed could be obtained in Calais.[64] Perhaps that rise was only a temporary one, but William Cely's host also put up his charges in December 1483.[65] The staplers' steep increase in the price of their wools at Calais in 1482 or 1483 was not an isolated phenomenon.

George for his part continued much as before for the first few months after old Richard's death. He went back to Calais on Saturday 16 March 1482,[66] and an itemized account for five days' expenditure on Lenten fare may belong to that period, in which case it refers to either 23–8 March or 30 March–4 April, Passion week.[67] George gave a series of small dinner parties. On Sunday and again on Tuesday 'master lieutenant' (of the Staple – the one who was in the habit of showing a deceptively fair face when he owed no good will?) attended. The other guests on Sunday were Robert Tourney's wife and Thomas Whode, and on Tuesday George also entertained 'the steward Gynus' (meaning the steward of Guines Castle?), 'Relkys' and Sir R. Goodman (probably a priest). On Thursday the staplers Harold Staunton, Bennet Trotter and John Elderbeck were invited. Elderbeck either was or had 'a guest at side table'. It is not clear where George lodged at Calais at this time; it may have been with Thomas Granger or with William Bondman, who had taken over Thomas Kesten's old premises, or he may have had his own house and housekeeper. At any rate, 'Allson' (Alison), presumably the cook, was

[63] *C.L.* 197.   [64] *C.L.* 202, 203.
[65] *C.L.* 204. The price index constructed by E. H. Phelps Brown and Sheila V. Hopkins bears out these indications of high prices at this time: 'Seven Centuries of the Prices of Consumables Compared with Builders' Wage Rates', *A Perspective of Wages and Prices* (1981), Appendix B, p. 29.
[66] File 10 fo. 18.   [67] File 16 fos. 17–18.

given daily sums of money to procure the variety of sea-food which featured on the menu over the Saturday to Thursday. The total cost was £2 2s 10d, to include 'an overcorn' (supplement) of a jowl of fresh salmon (1s 8d) and a piece of porpoise, treated as a fish and so permissible eating in Lent, which cost 2s 2d. Besides other provisions, George paid for two loads of wood (3s), a vat of beer (2s 3d), four bushels of wheat (8s, and 4½d for baking it into bread), soap (2d), rather oddly, seeds ('zedys') in the garden (2d), and five pounds of candle (8¾d). A cancelled entry says that Alison was lent 4s 6d for wine.

Unlike many a modern housewife who tends to think of fish as the white flaky substance that accompanies chips, the medieval cook had a knowledgeable appreciation of the different kinds available, and each was clearly enjoyed for its own distinctive qualities. Each day's menu in George's list included both white fish and shellfish of some kind, and on most days fresh herbs and spices were also bought. 'Herbs' might include a few vegetables, but these had none of their modern importance in the menu. Parsley dipped in vinegar was a favourite garnish for fish, but the closest thing to salad was probably fresh sorrel stamped with salt and served as a sauce. Sage often flavoured dishes. Cinnamon was also an important ingredient, listed separately from the other undifferentiated 'spices', perhaps because it is a bark. Sevenpence worth of 'mustard and vinegar' in Thursday's list had probably been bought earlier to serve for the whole five days, and the same may be true of the 4d worth of oil under Monday's heading. Mustard was the expected accompaniment, not for beef or ham, but for fish, especially herring. Because it was Lent, no eggs, butter or cream feature in the account. This deprivation must have imposed irksome limitations in cooking fish dishes, but the olive oil would substitute for butter or fat in frying or broiling.

Nevertheless, in a seaside place like Calais there was a good choice of material. Saturday's menu featured a carp, a bream, two eels, a cod, six plaice, whitings, three soles, a cod's head (probably for stock), two jowls of salt salmon (which was cheaper than fresh: they cost 18d in all), fourpence worth of whelks and twopence worth of mussels. The guests also had twopence worth of bread. On Sunday there were two pickerels, a 'green fish' (fresh cod), white (salted) herring, a piece of fresh salmon, a plaice and cockles. Possibly also some of Saturday's purchases had been made up into dishes for Sunday's dinner party. Monday's purchases were again comparatively small: plaice, a jowl of fresh salmon for 20d, two great eels, also 20d, whiting, half a green fish and fourpence worth of mussels. (A bushel of mussels cost 6d at London in March 1479.)[68] Tuesday, when the lieutenant again dined, featured four plaice, an eel,

[68] *Stonor L.*, no. 233.

half a green fish, whiting, oysters (a good many, since they cost 3*d*, the same as the half fish), shrimps ('shyrympis'), and cockles. Wednesday's dinner was very simple: three plaice, green fish, almonds and mussels. Almonds, like coconut in tropical countries, were used to make a cream-like sauce. On Thursday there were four plaice, green fish, whiting, eels, whelks and mussels. It is not clear when the second jowl of fresh salmon and the piece of porpoise were eaten.

In connexion with the probate proceedings, George had been instructed to draw up an inventory of his father's goods at Calais. His note survives of the number of fells which remained unsold at Calais.[69] Stored in four places (at Nicholas's, master Proud's house, Bondman's and Proud's son's), they amounted to 10,902. Richard and George themselves had 1,641. These, together with the original 11,464 of old Richard's, had been sent to Calais in November 1481.[70] Many of the fells had arrived in poor condition and John Dalton had to get them patched.[71] John Elderbeck had appraised at least 5,500 at only 13 nobles per hundred.[72]

On 10 April George drew up a statement of joint account with Richard.[73] His 'charge' of receipts amounted to £1,451 12*s* 11¾*d* Flem. (these were itemized in a book which has disappeared), and his 'discharge' of expenditure, including money already transferred to England, came to £186 17*s* 7*d*. He had £200 Flem. worth of fells, and expected to make £100 Flem. from a certain sale of North Holland (Lincs.) wool, the proceeds of which were to be shared between George and Thomas Colton.[74] George had 'entered in my book to deliver at this next mart by exchange' £663 19*s* 6*d* Flem., there were also letters of payment which had not yet fallen due, to the sum of £234 8*s* 3*d* Flem., and 'there is by me in ready money to the sum of £50 Flem.'. This left a balance of £116 7*s* 7¾*d* Flem. At the same time he had a 'charge' for William Maryon of £426 9*s* 11¾*d* Flem., and was taking to the mart obligations and letters of payment for £130 8*s* Flem., to be made over by exchange for him. More 'obligations of days to come' were worth £149 10*s* 8*d* Flem., and 'there remains by me in ready money to the sum of £141 3*s* 10¾*d* Flem.'. Cely assets of very long standing were those debentures issued to Richard senior, William Maryon, Richard Bowell, William Fethyan and Nicholas Bristol.[75]

The staplers were now caught again between a conservative exchange rate in Calais and rising rates in Flanders. While he was absent from

---

[69] File 12 fo. 33.
[70] File 12 fo. 14v.
[71] File 12 fo. 17.
[72] File 12 fos. 15, 33.
[73] File 12 fos. 38–9.
[74] File 16 fo. 50; File 12 fo. 38.
[75] File 13 fo. 51.

Calais in late April, George was reported by 'master Deputy' to the
lieutenant of the Staple, in the presence of Lord Hastings, for demanding
payment of a debt from 'poor Henley' at the rate of 28s Flem. to the £
stg., which was above the legal Calais rate of 26s 8d.[76] Harry Bryan had
been given 20s in February 'to be good solicitor to the lord chamberlain'
on behalf of George and Richard,[77] and now executed his commission
to good effect, reporting to George on 2 May:

Ascertaining you since your departing there hath been labour made against you
and your brother for the matter ye know. But my fortune was to be by my lord
when it was question, and I remembered [reminded] my lord, which had
forgotten the said matter. And so after my remembrance my lord made such a
answer as shall be to your pleasure, in so much as my lord hath promised his
singular good lordship unto you and your brother, all men reserved. And in any
thing else he can do for you or your brother, he will be your good lord.[78]

According to Richard, at this time a scheme was mooted by the English
government to set up 'wissels' at Bruges, Calais and London, which
would maintain an exchange rate of 24s Flem. to the £ stg.[79] Staplers
would be permitted to buy wares with the proceeds of their wool sales,
or else to take the money to the royal exchanges at Bruges or Calais, for
payment at London in a month's time. Richard added that (not
surprisingly), 'the mercers be not content therewith'. There is no record
of any such proposals in the extant mercers' minutes, but these are only
copies made in the sixteenth century from disordered originals.

Enhancements in the valuation of coins would not deter George and
his friends from buying goods in the low countries. In the same letter
Harry Bryan requested horse-harness for the Duke of Buckingham, his
own 12 dozen pairs of gloves, and three stics of tawny or violet satin of
Bruges. Nicholas Knyveton wanted George to buy him a bed and its
furnishings:

Brother George, I heartily pray you to do for me, as another time I shall be as
glad to do you pleasure, and if I can. To buy a bed, tester and celure and covering
thereto, and let the covering be large and the bed as it please you best. Of good
works, as ye would do for yourself, and of the strangest ['most unusual', or
'strongest'?] work. And also if ye can find a hanging of the same work and of
like price, three yards deep and 30 yards of length, I pray you to buy it according
to the same.
    See what ye may do, it shall be truly answered every penny. I pray you, master
'Jarge', do for me as I would do for you – it shall be quit, by this my writing.
    Your very friend, Nicholas Knyveton.[80]

[76] *C.L.* 162.   [77] File 10 fo. 25.
[78] *C.L.* 161.   [79] *C.L.* 165.
[80] *C.L.* 159.

At the same time George seems to have been purchasing some silver, to judge by his note on the back of Knyveton's letter: 'The goblets 34 oz. 5 dwt. Four silver 26 oz. 15 dwt.' Whether for himself or Knyveton, he also ordered from 'my stainer' a 'bed' (hangings) of four ells of green and blue buckram, with covering and six other pieces, costing almost £5 Flem.[81]

George did not relinquish his interest in horses. 'Charles' had offered £8 for Bayard in January, but Joyce held out for £9.[82] On 23 April William Cely reported to George

Sir, Bayard your horse doth well, and so does your t'other horse at Twyssullton's too. And I hear nobody that makes any do for ['shows any interest in'] him, Joyce would fain have him home into his stable. I pray you send us word how we shall be demeaned with him.[83]

On 29 April, 'your horses be all in good point, and Bayard is all whole of his "maledy", and he was never better to labour than he is now, etc. Sir, Joyce prays you to send him word when ye think ye shall be ready to come to Calais [from the mart], that he might send you lyccwll Bayarde [Little Bayard] to come home on.'[84]

On 7 May William wrote further:

Item, sir, I understand that your mastership would that John Dalton should buy the horse that he wrote to you of. Sir, he hath bought one as on St Helen Day [the Invention of the Cross on 3 May], beside Oudenbourg at a fair, and he stands in your stable. His colour is manner of a grey colour, and he is but young, for he was never broken yet. And he is almost as much as your great Bayard.[85]

William Adam was interested in buying one of George's string of mounts:

Like it you to wit that at my last being at Calais John Dalton and I had certain communication for your horse, and if I might 'a spoken with you I would 'a bought him of you, so that ye would 'a been reasonable. For he should be for a great gentleman, of whom you might deserve great thank if it be so that you think the horse would serve him. Praying you to owe me therein your good will, and send me word by the bringer hereof your disposition of answer by writing. And you shall have my service at all times.[86]

And Richard had at last succeeded in finding a buyer for Py II in England: 'sir, I have sold Py. I cannot get for him but five mark, on my faith, and yet he that has him thinks himself full beguiled.'[87]

---

[81] File 16 fo. 24.   [82] *C.L.* 142.
[83] *C.L.* 156.   [84] *C.L.* 158.
[85] *C.L.* 163.   [86] *C.L.* 166.
[87] *C.L.* 168.

The young grey horse failed to thrive at first. On 3 August, after George had returned to England, William Cely wrote

Item, sir, please it you to wit that your young horse is sore appaired since your mastership departed from Calais, for he will eat no meat yet but grass and green tares, for of hard meat [i.e. hay and grain] he will none. And he is but bare in plight: I cannot think that he may be laboured shortly. But Great Sorrel is in good plight, God save him. But I suppose he will not be sold here.[88]

Eventually the new horse was sent over to England, to Richard's charge. Richard told George on 26 September,

Informing you that I have your young horse at London, and I have spoken with the best corsers [horse-dealers] and smiths in Smithfield, and they give me counsel to let him run in a park till Hallowentide, and then take him up and sear him, and let him stand in the dead of winter [in a stable], and let [him] run the next summer, and then he shall be safe while he is hoarse....I shall seek the surest place in Essex for your young horse.[89]

'Searing' or 'firing', which had the effect of immobilizing an ailing horse, continued into the twentieth century to be a popular treatment. It is to be hoped that the horse had crossed the channel before the storms mentioned by William Cely in a letter of 30 September, in which he apologized for not sending sooner: 'for here was none passage no sooner. The wind was so contrary and the sea so troublous, passage was half-sea-over once or twice, and was fain to come to Calais again.'[90]

Richard found good pasture in Essex:

Sir, I have put your young grey horse in Thundersley Park, and there he has pasture enough, and there are but three horse going in all the park. And ye must pay the parker for his pasture 4d a week, and I have promised him a bow. And I trust that he will see well to your horse and make you sport at your coming. He is a man of master Montgomery's.[91]

Bayard was also in England by now, and was eventually sold to a man named Bexwell for £5 6s 8d.[92] The young horse was probably the 'great grey trotting horse' which George sold Richard for £10 in May the next year, the sum payable at Michaelmas 1483 and 1484.[93]

The horses at Calais, and their stables, caused some difficulties between rival claimants. On 10 May William Cely had written helplessly to George:

Sir, as for your horse that Twyssullton hath, I would 'a had him home to your stable, but Joyce says it is not best so to do till ye come, for he says John Dalton

[88] *C.L.* 179.
[89] *C.L.* 193.
[90] *C.L.* 194.
[91] *C.L.* 195.
[92] *C.L.* 197; File 10 fo. 8.
[93] File 10 fo. 3v.

will misdeem then, and take it at a great unkindness, etc. Sir, I pray you send me word how I shall be demeaned with him.[94]

No sooner had George left Calais in July than there was a conflict of claims between Joyce and Dalton, with William again put in the middle. Dalton wrote engagingly to George on 12 August:

Please it you, I asked William Cely now after your departing if you had told him what you would that he should do with your house where as your stable is, and he told me you said nothing to him thereof. Sir, if it please you that you will let it out, I pray you that I may have two of the rooms of the stable. And if it please you, ye shall have at your commandment at all times the foresaid rooms again, and with the grace of God ye shall find hay and oats for your horses at your coming.

Whether I have the foresaid house or not, ye shall not fault ['lack'] of none thing that I have ne may do for you to my utterest power. But sir, one thing I pray you of: that in case be that you will that I shall have the foresaid house, that I may know what I shall pay therefor. For without that I may pay therefor like as you may let it to another, else (I will pray you to take none displeasure), for else I will not have it. And if I have it, like as I have written you, ye shall at your coming alway have it and do therewith that shall please you, that knows God.[95]

But Joyce had told William that George had promised him the stable and the house for his own use, with a similar arrangement that George was to have his room whenever he came.[96] The outcome is not recorded.

George was, as usual, trying to buy hawks in the autumn, and on 3 September William Cely reported

Sir, as for a goshawk, I can get none here yet, for all that come to Calais, my lord chamberlain buyeth them up and they be anything worth, etc. And as for your man that ye delivered your money to for hawks, I hear not of yet, etc.[97]

In the next letter he added to this that

here hath come diverse hawks, but they be so dear that no man buyeth them but my lord. They be at four nobles, five nobles an hawk.[98]

George's contact (Wauterin Tabary?) was finally successful in his quest, and on 18 October Joyce arrived in Calais accompanied by three hawks and three men who were to take them on to England.[99] But William then sent news of an accident.

On Saturday at afternoon, betwixt 4 and 5, the falconer when none of us was by did call the least hawk, that is not reclaimed ['fully trained'], with a creance

---

[94] *C.L.* 164.
[96] *C.L.* 181.
[98] *C.L.* 190.
[95] *C.L.* 180.
[97] *C.L.* 189.
[99] *C.L.* 198.

[leash]. And the creance broke, and the hawk flew away over the walls. Then came a soldier of town, and took her up, and would 'a brought her into town again. But master porter [Robert Radcliffe] met him and took her from him. And I have been with master porter for her, and there was [Lord Hastings' brother] Sir Ralph Hastings, and I pray them to have her again. But master porter is loath to depart from her. But he said he would give me as much as she cost, and you much thank. And master Sir Ralph said afore master porter that he would not keep your hawk against your will for an £100, and so master Sir Ralph bade me that I should wait upon him this day. And he said that he would see that I had as much money as she cost, and more too, or else the hawk again.[100]

Whatever the nature of the sickness from which George had suffered in the autumn of 1479, it may have left him with a lowered resistance to infection. He was again taken ill in Bruges in May of 1482. William had dispatched Joyce to him on 20 May, with the news of some 'marvellous talk' in Calais which could not be entrusted to paper: 'other tidings have we none here but that Joyce can inform your mastership by mouth well enough'.[101] On his return to Calais Joyce brought a letter which indicated that George was now 'well mended of [his] great sickness'.[102] But George's friends at Calais were solicitous for him, and vied with each other in the offer of horses which would be comfortable for an invalid. William told George on 26 May:

we send you by Joyce an ambling horse of Thomas Hayward's for you to come to Calais on. He will be glad if he may ease you. It is but 'lyccull', and if it be not big enough ye may have William Bondman's horse. He is at Bruges at the 'Star', and William Bondman hath sent an letter to his man by Joyce to deliver you the horse to come home on.[103]

It was in fact William Dalton who sent Thomas Hayward's ambling horse with Joyce, 'because Thomas Hayward telleth me that W. Bondman horse will stumble, and this is little and easy'.[104]

Dalton had encouraging news to pass on about the progress of the English expedition against Scotland. He had been standing by when Lord Hastings had 'good tidings come of England, copy of letter sent from my lord of Gloucester and my lord of Northumberland, that late were sent to the king. The messenger that brought them, I heard him say he departed from the king at the Tower of London upon Friday last past.'[105]

On 1 June Richard wrote to George about arrangements for his return home:

[100] *C.L.* 199. [101] *C.L.* 167.
[102] *C.L.* 170. [103] Ibid.
[104] *C.L.* 171. [105] Ibid.

I understand by William Cely's letter that ye have been right sore sick. And 'a writes to me that 'a has sent to you an ambler to bring you to Calais, and that ye purpose to come shortly into England. I pray you send me an letter and I will send my hobby [pony] to Dover to meet you, and many matters abides your coming...I never longed so sore for your company. I pray Jesu bring you well hither and send you health.[106]

But before he could leave Calais George had numerous affairs to settle. Henceforth he would be resident in England and pay only occasional visits to Calais, Bruges or the marts. As a man of substance, he had to have his 'livelihood' (property) in Calais 'cleared'. William Cely explained obscurely on 4 July,

as for your livelihood, is not yet cleared, but the wards men hath seen your livelihood and entered it in their books, and within this two days your evidence [deeds] must be showed afore the commissioners. I have them still by me, for John Parker prayed me so for to do. For he said it was so best and most readiest. For when they come to that ward they shall be sent for.[107]

About the same time, George listed a number of properties, held or rented, in England: 'Byrttys' (Bretts Place), Kennington (Kenningtons in Aveley or Kennington, Berks.?), 'Menhall' (Manhall in Aveley), 'Bomstedys' (Bumpstead, also in Aveley), 'Gaynus' (Gaines), Upminster Hall, Aveley lordship and Wennington, and 'Scargellis in Dagnam [Dagenham]'.[108] Not mentioned is Mallins, Little Thurrock, the principal property which George had inherited. George headed this list with the draft of a formal note:

I am an young possessioner and late comen there unto. I must and will obey your commission, albeit I will pray you to go none farther with me than your commission holds in. I am not very ripe in my evidence: I pray you give me reasonable respite to bring them in.

This material is mixed up with memoranda about the goods which George proposed to ship to England, and 'things that longs unto my brother's chamber and mine at Calais, which shall remain'.[109] The second list gives a good picture of the chamber and its furnishings: a chest in the counter, which cost 10s Flem., a bow case (6s 8d), a case for harness which cost 8s, a great chest for gowns (12s), a little chest for sheets and linen (7s), a little chest for doublets and hose (5s), the bedstead with blue 'costerings' (hangings), tester and curtains and a settle by the bed, together valued at 20s, a feather bed (40s), a pair of blankets (9s 4d), four pairs of sheets (48s), three pillows (6s 8d), a 'coverlid vardeor' (coverlet of verdure), of considerable size as it contained 30 ells, valued at 30s, and

---

[106] *C.L.* 174. [107] *C.L.* 176.
[108] File 12 fo. 34v. [109] File 12 fos. 33–34v.

'another for everyday of blue' (10s), a quilt (5s), a press for caps (18d), and a (looking) glass (3s). There were also a tin basin, two plain towels, four pairs of sheets for servants priced at 21s, as containing 63 Flemish ells at 4d an ell – or about 17 feet each – and a piss-pot of tin. For the counter there was a standish with a glass, a low candlestick, a dust box, containing fine sand for drying one's ink after writing – often these grains can still be seen glistening on the Celys' documents where the ink has caught them – and 'a pill [pile of weights] and an pair of balance – the pill is 32 oz.', priced at 8s.

The memorandum contains the more detailed costs for the purchase of a bed and fittings, including 15 ells for tester and valance and another 11 ells of valance, three curtains and a demi-curtain containing 24 ells, 'the frame which the joiner made', costing 3s, three rods and hooks of iron, costing 4s 6d, 22 'sticks' weighing 3½ lb, and 'leyr'. The whole cost £1 12s 3d.[110] Apparently George had it sent to England, where Richard paid further to a bed-maker 'for certain fringes of silk' 24s, for green lyre 4d and 'for sewing of the said fringe and lyre upon valance – 8d'.[111] Lyre was an edging or tape made from fine thread or packthread.

George's chamber at Calais must have been a good size. Apart from all the things that he left there, he sent to England in John Harryes's ship, the *John of London*, in addition to 200 wainscot boards and 60 tiles, three chests, one pipe, one harness barrel and a cupboard.[112] Having bought two quires of paper for packing with,[113] he filled his chests with an assortment of goods. The smaller one held a miscellany consisting of two brushes, an old satin bag, a piece of fur, a glass, a box with sugar, a sugar loaf, two doublets, a pair of hose and six hats.[114] As well there were a pair of hose, a sugar loaf and a great book, belonging to William Dalton. In the great chest were a little chest, eight dripping pans, an axe, a pair of brigandines, a latten basin and 'laver' [ewer], a windlass for a cross-bow, a pair of tables [writing tablets], a cross-bow, two great glasses, a complete harness, two steel bonnets, three bits, a cranket, a dagger, three long gowns, a demi-gown, another pair of brigandines, and George's 'ssoychis' dagger. George, on occasion, spelt 'such' *soyche*, but what he meant here is matter for guesswork. It is unlikely that he meant 'fox', which he spelt in orthodox fashion.

Further, on 11 July 'Tewne the packer carried down into Zealand my chest and coffin [i.e. 'coffer'] with bows, and my two "hakke-a-bakkys"

---

[110] File 12 fo. 33v.   [111] File 10 fo. 20v.

[112] File 10 fo. 18; File 12 fo. 34v. The tiles may have been decorated floor tiles: in June 1499 Andrew Halyburton shipped 1,000 tiles for the chamber floor of the Archdeacon of St Andrews: *Ledger of Andrew Halyburton*, p. 251.

[113] File 16 fo. 48.   [114] File 16 fo. 23.

[?'packs'] covered with black leather. He had for his costs and all – 8*s* Flem.'

Not content with all these possessions, George then seems to have done a little more shopping, besides paying 24*s* for 'my bill of him at the "Two Horns"'.[115] He lists a dozen pairs of gloves (3*s* Flem.), a complete harness for £5, together with a head-piece at 20*s* and a pair of gauntlets for 2*s* 6*d*, 20 buckram bags, ten white and ten black, at 8*d* each and another 12 dozen gloves at 3*s* 4*d* the dozen. The headpiece, gauntlets, bags and gloves were for Harry Bryan, who traded as a mercer. For himself, George paid 6*s* 6*d* for the making of two shirts, and 18*d* for another two for 'my boy', and he bought a doublet of white and red damask which cost 18*s*. Finally, he paid his host at Bruges 'for my horse and me' 31*s* 9*d* Flem. Richard paid in England 4*s* 2*d* for the custom of the wainscot and 'for a bill', 25*s* 8*d* for freight of 'George's gear' in the *John of London*, 21*d* 'to John Rede for carrying seven loads of his stuff', 4*s* 2*d* for costs of a dry-fat [large container for dry goods], and 4*s* 1*d* for costs of a chest in the *Mary Daubeney*.[116]

Before leaving himself, George made an indenture with William Cely as their attorney in Calais, listing 'all deliveries and receipts'.[117] On 24 July George delivered him various bills and obligations, amounting to £433 14*s* 11*d* Flem., the bag of Thomas Kesten's pawned goods, a Staple debenture of Richard senior for £8 11*s* 6*d* stg., a warrant of William Ede's debenture for 24*s* 5½*d* Flem., a sarpler (No. 1) of good Kesteven wool and a sarpler (No. 4) of fine Lindsey wool, a poke of middle Cotswold wool (No. 44), and 2,300 fells. George returned in order to attend the Bammis mart in September, and would make further periodic visits to Calais (two such trips from England cost a total of £23 6*s* 9*d* stg. in travelling expenses),[118] but henceforth William was the firm's usual representative abroad, and the activities of George and Richard have to be uncovered mainly from accounts and memoranda.

The various items of George's goods and chattels in Calais can be compared with those listed in the inventory of possessions left by Thomas Nandyk, priest and scholar of Cambridge by profession and nigromancer by notoriety, who died in 1491.[119] Nandyk's clothing consisted of three short gowns – one murry (mulberry colour), one of blue 'sore worn', and one of tawny, 'feeble'; three russet gowns, two of them furred with black lamb and the third, an old one, furred with fox; a black gown furred with fox, a sanguine gown furred with 'grey' (squirrel), a murry gown furred

---

[115] File 16 fo. 24.   [116] File 10 fo. 18.   [117] File 20 no. 5.
[118] File 10 fo. 10v.
[119] P.R.O. Prob. 2/48. Thomas Nandik, late of Cambridge, 'nigromansier' was accused of conspiring with the Duke of Buckingham in Oct. 1483: *Rot. Parl.*, VI, 245.

with broad miniver (another variety of squirrel) and valued at 12s, a green gown lined with 'tartrum' and another, which was his best at 15s in value, lined with chamlet. Besides his 11 gowns he had a cloak of green medley, one doublet of spruce leather and five 'sore worn' of silk in various colours, one old jacket of tawny cloth and an old 'broken' one of chamlet, an old worn red mantle, a tawny riding hood, an old tawny hat, an old cap of green medley lined with velvet, a pair of boots and spurs, three pairs of old hose, and 'an old fur of calaber wombs', i.e. belly-fur of squirrels.

Bedding, worth a total of 32s 2d, consisted of a little feather bed with two bolsters and three pillows with their cases, a pair of blankets, an old 'counterpoynt' which, like George's best one, was of 'tapestry verdure', an old banker for covering a bench, containing seven yards of woollen cloth, three old broken coverlets 'of Norfolk making', five little 'costrynges' of red saye 'bastard feigned' (imitating the cloth called 'bastard'), and six little shelf cloths. Linen, worth 10s 6d in all, included four pairs of badly worn sheets and three 'broken' ones, four little plain towels, three breast kerchiefs and three handkerchiefs.

Under the heading 'latten and brass' came a bell-candlestick, two little chafers of brass, two little broken salts of pewter, and an astronomer's equipment of 'two estrolabers' (astrolabes) of latten. Already sold were a little brass pan, a pewter basin and pint pot, a fire-rake and melting ladle of iron (did Nandyk conduct experiments in alchemy?), an iron trivet, a pair of tongs, a gridiron, other candlesticks, a chafer and a pail.

As a priest and scholar Nandyk had fewer items of plate and jewellery than the Celys sported – only £5 4s 4d worth, including a silver spoon, a George, a tache (buckle or clasp), and two aglets (points for laces) of silver and gilt, a prayer-book with a clasp of silver and gilt set with pearl, various silks, crystal stones, small pearls, and a variety of boxes and girdles. His most striking articles of personal adornment were a 'bettor clee' or bittern's claw garnished with silver and gilt, which must have resembled the grouse-foot brooches beloved of modern tourists in Scotland, and his two rosaries, one containing 50 amber beads with silver and gilt 'gauds', and the other having ten great amber beads with two large tassels.

The area in which the Celys could not compete with Sir Thomas was the book department. Nandyk had the following:

A little mass book and a portews of Rome use in print, price . .	8s
Two little books of physic, price	16d
A book of physic, in secundo folio *intelectum*	3s 4d
A book of Astronomy, in secundo folio *iurisdictione* . . .	3s 4d

Seven small books, boarded 11s 8d
A little psalter, broken 12d
Item, 15 pamphlets of diverse matters, some printed, some unprinted,
    price of all . . . . 5s.

He also had 'a press for binding of books' priced at 8d, another little book of 'fesyk' sold for 2s, and two books of 'exstranymy' (astronomy), which master abbot bought for 3s 4d.

Furniture, much of it sold by the time the inventory was compiled, or in the keeping of colleagues, had included a table and form, 'a painted shelf with two fenestrales ['lattices']', valued at 4d, 'a great desk to write upon and to lay books in' (10d), two presses (cupboards) for books (2s), 'a spruce table called a counter' (3s 4d), a turned chair (6d), and 'a glass to look in' (4d). There were also three cushions of red worsted stuffed with flocks, 26 yards of painted cloth at 4d the yard and four more which cost 10d in all, and 'a Saint John unpainted'.

Among miscellaneous items were two cross-bows with winches and a little gun of brass, a handsaw, two 'persours' (awls or similar tools), two hatchets, two shovels without irons, three glasses (variety unspecified), four sheets of paper royal at 1d, a saddle and bridle with old harness, two hair brushes, two calking stones, and a lute in a case, valued at 3s 4d. There had also been sold 22½ lb of pewter at 3d per lb (perhaps comprising the plates and other utensils which are otherwise absent from the list), 37 lb of wrought lead at ¾d per lb and 18 of unwrought at ½d.

The total value of Nandyk's possessions was £18 8s 8d, of which clothing and valuables (appraised at almost equal amounts) came to £10 13s 8d. At the time of his death he owed £7 5s 4½d to various people, principally £3 18s 1d to a mercer, Robert Yarum. His modest funeral cost 27s 6d, for priests, clerks, ringing of bells, his 'leistowe' (grave), linen cloth, bread, ale, wax and other necessaries and for alms to poor people. Probate of his testament and other charges came to a further 10s.

'THE WORLD GOETH ON WHEELS', 1482–5

Before describing the Celys' domestic life in further detail, a chapter must be taken to sketch in the background of international affairs and the fortunes of the Staple trade in the years 1482 to 1485.

March 1482 had seen further negotiations dragging on between England and France: 'upon Palm Sunday the French embassy come into London, and they were worshipfully received with the mayor and all the crafts of London', but their entertainment was to little real purpose.[1] There had also occurred a disaster to one of the new English ultimate weapons: 'at afternoon [of 27 March] was the great new gun of brass shot at Mile End, 'at was made at the Tower. And it brast all to pieces.'[2] On that same day the Duchess Mary of Burgundy died as the result of a hunting accident. It was not long before the Estates of Flanders declared that her widower, Maximilian, was unacceptable as regent for his son, who was in the custody of the people of Ghent. In May there was word in England that Thérouanne had been burnt by the French and that Ghent and Bruges had made their own peace treaties with France,[3] and on 31 July William Cely sent the alarming news that

the town of Aire is given up to the Frenchmen, and another castle within a Dutch mile of St Omers, by the means of treason...and the Frenchmen purposeth to be at Gravelines, and they be not letted [prevented] within this two days and less. And there comes every day from St Omers to my lord a messenger desiring of my lord chamberlain help and rescue out of England. And my lord hath promised them that they shall lack no men nor victual, wherefore we look after here that there shall come a fellowship out of England shortly, etc.[4]

Gravelines and St Omer were most uncomfortably close to Calais. The king in fact ordered that 1,000 archers should be sent to Calais, but only for the safe custody and defence of the town and marches.[5]

[1] *C.L.* 149.   [2] *C.L.* 147.
[3] *C.L.* 169.   [4] *C.L.* 177.
[5] *C.P.R. 1476–1485*, p. 322.

William continued with the staplers' other immediate worry:

Item, sir, we fear here that there will be shrewd passage to this Bammis mart and if the Frenchmen have Gravelines – as men fear they shall have it, for they have all the passages to it [al]ready.

It was in this atmosphere of alarm that rumours circulated about a plot to open the gates of Calais to the French.

Even in Calais it was not always easy to get accurate news. On 3 August it was said that

the Duke of Burgundy [Maximilian] lieth still at Ypres with a great host. And as for the Frenchmen, it is said here they have victualled and manned the town of Aire, and the remnant be gone back again, as it is said here.[6]

On 13 August William wrote:

As for tidings, we have none here for very certain, but that the Frenchmen lieth still in garrisons upon the borders, and gathereth and increaseth daily, as it is said. And as for the Duke of Burgundy, it was said he was a' this side Ypres with a great host of men, and should 'a be at St Omers ere this time, but we hear not of him yet – some men say he is gone back again.[7]

He reported on 16 August that Maximilian was at Bruges, but his forces were in Brabant, and said to be advancing very slowly.[8]

There was, however, some first-hand information by 23 August:

on Monday last was [19 August] Robert Hobard was at Bruges, and he saith the same day he saw the Duke of Burgundy depart out of Bruges, but with ten horse, into Zealand, for they of Ghent and of Bruges will not grant him such things as he asketh for. The duke asketh nothing of them but money, and he will take such men with him to go upon the Frenchmen as pleaseth him. But the Ghentners and they of Bruges will not give him no money without he take such men as they will assign him. For the which he departed into Zealand. But I understand the Frenchmen lieth still in garrisons upon the marches, and increase daily with new men out of High France.[9]

The French continued to make headway, but Bruges and Ghent fell out between themselves. On 12 September,

we have tidings here that the Frenchmen hath gotten the city of Luik [Liège] and slain the bishop of Luik. [The common story was that the bishop, a cousin of Charles the Bold, had been murdered by the faction of the De La Marcks.] And we have tidings here now that men of the land of Luik, with the help of Brabanters, hath broken up all the *burgs* betwixt France and them, and hath besieged the town of Luik again, and likely to recover the town again, etc.

Furthermore, please it your masterships to understand that we have tidings

---

[6] *C.L.* 179.　　　　[7] *C.L.* 182.
[8] *C.L.* 183.　　　　[9] *C.L.* 186.

here that the town of Ghent and the town of Bruges be at a variance betwixt themself. In so mickle that they of Ghent hath sent to the English nation [of traders resident in the town], and to every nation in Bruges, commanding them to sit still and do their merchandise, and intermet [interfere] with no party, pain of that will come thereof.[10]

As a result of the fighting, few if any customers came to Calais that September, and no Hollanders attended the Bammis mart at Antwerp.[11] International concord was not improved by acts of piracy on all sides. The stapler Thomas Colton asked George to pay an obligation for him, 'for I look every day for tidings out of Holland for my ship and my prisoners. And brother, this payment lieth my poor honesty upon, wherefore I beseech you to remember me, as my special trust is in you above all other.'[12] Robert Eyryk was 'chased with Scots between Calais and Dover [and] scaped narrow',[13] and one ship in the wool-fleet returning with goods from Calais in September or October was rifled by Flemish pirates.[14]

News of English victories in Scotland in early August must have given a welcome boost to morale in Calais. On 16 August William had written:

This day...the wool-fleet came to Calais, both of London and Ipswich, in safety, thanked be God....Sirs, other tidings have we none here, but that came out of England, done upon the Scots. For the which my lord commanded a general procession, and at night bonfires to be made at every man's door, as was at Midsummer night, and all the guns in the bulwarks and about the walls were shot for joy.[15]

But a new crisis arose in October, when Lord Hastings's presence was required in England, where 'the king is at the Tower, and his lords in council daily'.[16] He went over accompanied by all his household entourage, and they heard in Calais that 'there was at Dover to abide him 500 men, all in white gowns, to bring him home'.[17] Miss Scofield deduced that the council meetings concerned the renewed quarrel with Scotland of that date.[18] But the fact that Edward IV prevented the English fleet from York and Hull from sailing to Bordeaux for wine that autumn may suggest that it was as much war with France that he anticipated.[19]

---

[10] *C.L.* 191.
[11] *C.L.* 194, 196, 197.
[12] *C.L.* 172.
[13] *C.L.* 175 (24 June).
[14] *C.L.* 198.
[15] *C.L.* 183.
[16] *C.L.* 197.
[17] *C.L.* 198. Does the reception accorded to Hastings indicate support for him in his quarrel with the queen's relations?
[18] Scofield, *Edward IV*, II, 352.
[19] *MS. Harleian 433*, II, 5–6. The ships got as far as Plymouth and were still there on 6 Aug. 1483.

It was not until 23 December that Louis XI struck his grievous blow at Edward by signing the Treaty of Arras and thereby detaching Maximilian from any adherence to the English camp and throwing over the marriage alliance between the dauphin and Elizabeth of York in favour of one with Margaret, daughter of Maximilian and Mary. Margaret's dowry, including Artois and the County of Burgundy, was to be handed over to France forthwith. The Celys, however, do not comment on this major reversal, because there is a lacuna in their correspondence between 20 October 1482 and 13 November 1483.

One very curious note survives on the back of a memorandum, apparently of 1482, about Nicholas Bristol's Staple partition and Harry Bryan's obligations.[20] Adorned with some of the strange marks which George employed in his correspondence with Sir John Weston, and written by George but reproducing some of Sir John's characteristic spellings, it runs:

There is great rumour [uproar] in the realm. The Scots has done great in England. Chamberlain [Lord Hastings] is deceased in trouble. The chancellor is disproved and not content. The Bishop of Ely is dead.

If the king, God save his life, were deceased, the Duke of Gloucester were in any peril, if my lord prince, wh[ich] God defend, were troubled, if my lord of Northumberland were dead or greatly troubled, if my lord Howard were slain.

De Monsieur Saint Johns.

Most of these flying rumours were untrue, but the news bears general relevance to the events of 13 June 1483, when 'the king' was the young Edward V.

Perhaps the armour which George had sent over the previous year was put to use when special watches were mounted in the City in the latter half of that June of disquiet and sudden coups. The Celys certainly made the contribution expected of them (30*s*) towards the sum presented to Richard III at his coronation on 6 July,[21] and Richard's later return to London after his visit to the north may have been the occasion when Robert Eyryk rode to meet the king, as a representative of the fellowship of fellmongers, and Richard and George gave money for his attire.[22] The auditors' accounts reveal that they prepared to defend London against attack in the Buckingham rebellion of the following October. There is no knowing whether they were relieved when the insurgents failed to reach the capital, or disappointed at the lack of action. Richard paid,

In October anno '83, the time that great watches were kept in London, for 2 bills of Normandy – 6*s*, for 4 sheaves of arrows – 8*s* 8*d*. Item, for a yard and half of

[20] *C.L.* 200.
[21] File 10 fo. 20v.
[22] File 10 fo. 25v.

black fustian – 8*d*, for 4 yards white damask – 28*s*, for white tuke – 3*s*, red velvet – 18*d*, and white woollen cloth for jackets – 3*s* 4*d*.[23]

There were also 'diverse petty costs the time of watching', amounting to 4*s* 2*d*, and 'to Smith's wife for mending – 20*d*'. In all, the alarm cost him a hefty £2 16*s*. But perhaps these handsome outfits came in useful again when, two years later, the citizens mounted new watches while the troops of Richard III and Henry Tudor battled it out in Leicestershire.[24]

George had had another of his recurrent bouts of illness while he was staying with his brother and sister-in-law in September 1483. On Monday 15 September he 'delivered to my sister Anne', 5*s*, and later,

I took my said sister when I was sick, for household, also 6*s* 8*d*. I took Cattorne [Catherine] that is sick – 12*d*. Item, to her water – 2*d*. [Was this the cost of taking a sample of urine to the doctor for diagnosis?]...Item, I sent Cattorne again – 12*d*. Item, for bread and ale at diverse times while I was sick in the household – 6*d*....Item, I sent Kattorn when my brother come home – 12*d*. Item, paid for 4 gausys [pieces of gauze, possibly used for embroidery?] – 1*d*. Item, paid for prunes and raisins of Corans at diverse times – 10*d*.[25]

'Cattorne' is unidentified. The household seems to have been at Aveley at this time, and perhaps it was after his recovery that George joined Richard in a hunting expedition and paid 16*d* for a reward and 8*d* for a bottle of wine.[26]

When the letters from William Cely start again, in November 1483, both William and Joyce had also been ill. There had been no letters between Calais and England for a month during the rising, with its accompanying government searches for treasonable correspondence abroad, and William had difficulties of his own. There were complicated triangular dealings with John De Lopez and his agent in London over wool sales, and it was impossible to fulfil George's demand for the new season's Gascon wine, or Richard's for herring. William wrote to George on 13 November

Item, sir, I understand your mastership would have a ton of good Gascon wine, both red and claret. It is reasonably good cheap, but the council of the town will suffer none pass out of town, not yet, without he be in favour to have a licence of my lord [Dynham, the new lieutenant]. Sir, I shall assay if I can get a licence for a ton, etc.

Sir, as for all other things, I shall see as well to as I can. I have been a 'lykull' diseased, but I thank God I am amended and walking. And Joyce hath been sick also, but now he is well mended, thanked be God.[27]

[23] File 10 fo. 25.   [24] *A.C.M.*, pp. 180, 289.
[25] File 20 no. 7.   [26] File 10 fo. 26.   [27] *C.L.* 201.

William's letter to Richard, apparently written on the same day, is more woeful:

As for your bill of Piers Joye, I sent it to the mart by William Hyll, and there was no man for Piers Joye, nor for Christopher Collyns neither, that would pay the bill. Nor no man in the mart could tell of no attorney that Piers Joye had there, whatsomever Piers Joye saith....

Also, sir, I understand ye will that I should deliver Joyce your £10 Flem. that is received, and the bill of £10 that is to receive. Sir, herring is at £8 a last,[28] both at Ostend and Damm, and Joyce lie sick in his bed. And also, sir, I cannot spare this money till time I have made a sale, for all shall be lykyll enough to pay your custom and subsidy, and yet I shall lay out £20 of my [own] money.[29]

On 18 November William apologized for the 'lewd and untrue English' which he had written in two letters, now lost,

for at that time my mind was not quiet, for I was sick. But howsomever I wrote, I meant well. But, sirs, whereas I wrote to your masterships that I trowed that ye might have over out of your charges here a 30 or £40 stg., sir, it cannot now be spared without God fortune you [a] sale....

I understand by your... letter that and herring were at £6 Flem. a last master Richard would have his money bestowed therein. Sir, herring is at £8 a last and above, etc. Item, sir, I understand your masterships would have a ton of good Gascon wine. Sir, yet is none sold here more than is retailed in town. They lay it all in cellars within town, and will suffer none go out, not as yet. Good Gascon wine is at £6 a ton, and so the vintners of the town buyeth.[30]

William had to commission 'Richard Parker, John Parker's son of Calais' to receive money for him in the Cold mart and make a further attempt to cash the bill of Collins and Joye for £10 Flem.[31] He was himself beset by anxiety about a possible change of lodgings, since Thomas Granger had raised his prices and William did not know whether Richard and George would pay the new rates:

here is a variance fall betwixt our host Thomas Granger and the fellowship of our lodging. For Thomas Granger promised us at his coming into our lodging that we should pay no more for our board but 3s 4d Flem. a week at the high table, and 2s 8d at the side table [rates that had been operative in 1478]. And now he saith he will have no less than 4s a week at the high table and 40d at the side table. Wherefore the fellowship here will depart into other lodgings, some to one place and some to another. William Dalton will be at Robert Torney's, and Ralph Lemington and master Brown's man of Stamford shall be at Thomas

---

[28] A last contained 12 barrels or 20 cades and held 12,400 fish. Richard Arnold's book offered the information that 'at the coast' (in England) a last should cost no more than 53s 4d stg., including salt, barrels and labour: (1811), p. 263.

[29] C.L. 202.   [30] C.L. 203.

[31] C.L. 204.

Clark's. And so all the fellowship departeth save I, wherefore I let your masterships have knowledge that ye may do as it shall like you best.

To William's pleasure, his masters said he should stay where he was until they directed otherwise. 'Sir, I am glad of the same, for I know no place in all Calais that I can be so well lodged, nor with a sadder man, étc.'[32] Financial matters were in a less satisfactory state at Calais, for the new exchange rate of 30*s* Flem. to the £ had already been overtaken by rates at the mart.[33]

On 5 January 1484 William sent news of a minor naval battle which had occurred the previous evening.

On Sunday before Twelfth Day the Breton fleet and the Frenchmen came together tofore Calais from Sluis, and that same night certain ships that was manned out of Calais, with the Carvyll off Hewe [*Carvel of Eu*], yeed amongst them, and took a thirty sails of Frenchmen. But all the Bretons be scaped, for there was none of all the other ships of Englishmen that hath done any good, without that the western men will do anything to the Bretons. For all our other ships, when they saw the fleet, they ran with the Downs, for there was Bretons and Frenchmen seven-score and sixteen sails.[34]

Despite this signal failure to live up to (or anticipate) the proud traditions of the British navy, and the escape of the Breton fleet, for which the English had been lying in wait, Sir Humphrey Talbot was rewarded for the part played by the Calais contingent with the grant of a Breton vessel, the *Michael*, which was already lying captive at Calais.[35]

There were now fears of war between England and Flanders, and relations were exacerbated by English seizures of Flemish goods. But William wrote reassuringly on 29 January:

As for war with Flanders, I trust to God we shall not need to dread it, for I understand they are not disposed to have no war against England. For there is certain Englishmen that came lately out of Flanders, and they say Flanders will have no war, wherefore there shall come out of Flanders, as they say, an embassy to the king's good grace of England. And as for the ships that were taken to Sandwich while your mastership was there, it is said here that they were fraught with Bretons' goods. We hear no tidings of theke ships from Bruges, not yet, wherefore we think here if the ships may be delivered again there shall no displeasure [arise].[36]

A letter of 10 February explains further:

Here is come to Calais, which is purposed to come into England, certain merchants of Flanders, the which certain of the goods belongeth unto that was

---

[32] *C.L.* 206.   [33] *C.L.* 205.   [34] Ibid.
[35] The signet letter to Lord Dynham to deliver the vessel is dated at Sandwich, 14 Jan. 1484: *MS. Harleian 433*, II, 75.   [36] *C.L.* 206.

taken in the ships that were brought into Sandwich haven at the season the king's good grace was there. Wherefore the said merchants hath brought a letter from the young Duke Philippus and the council of Flanders, directed unto the mayor and fellowship of the Staple at Calais, desiring them to write unto the king's good grace that he will be favourable unto his subjects, and that his good grace will see they may have restitution of their goods that is taken by his subjects. Like as he [i.e. Philip] hath done in his land of Flanders: discharged the king's subjects and made them restitution of their goods.[37]

The Flemish could, in fact, scarcely afford to go to war with the English, as they were in renewed rebellion against Maximilian, who had taken the opportunity offered by the long-expected death of Louis XI on 30 August 1483 to exert his authority by repudiating the 'Council of Regents' which had been set up in Flanders in the name of his young son. William continued on 10 February:

Item, sir, please it you to understand that the council of Flanders hath let cry in every town to be ready in harness as soon as the town bell ringeth. And also he that will take wages, to enter his name to the Regent for to withstand the Duke Maximilianus. For they fear because he hath gotten two towns of Flanders – Roubaix and Lille. But as far as we know here, they will have peace with England.

For a time Maximilian made little headway, despite his contingent of German troops. William Cely reported on 29 February:

Sir, please it your masterships to understand that the Duke Maximilianus is in Flanders with much people, and he hath certain towns in Flanders submitted unto him. And as on Tuesday the 25 day of February he was with a thousand horses at Bruges gates for to 'a comen in, but they shut the gates and would not let him come in. Then he saw that and sent a messenger to the gates, desiring that some of the rulers of the town should come to the gates and speak with him, but none would come, wherefore he returned back again unto his host. And so he lieth still within four Dutch mile of Bruges. And his desire is no more but to have six persons at his will, that is, three of Bruges, two of Ghent and one of Ypres. Wherefore the common people would have him full fain, save five or six of the heads be of a contrary opinion. But folks that came from Bruges saith that they think it shall not be long or they will let him in at Bruges.[38]

William's customers from Delft at this time 'brought but little money hither with them because of troubling by the way with soldiers of Maximilianus'. Nevertheless, these Hollanders were managing to come to Calais. While keeping a very wary eye on events in the major Flemish cities, the staplers were more immediately concerned about the French garrison in Gravelines. William gave the latest news on 17 March:

[37] *C.L.* 207. William's very assiduous references to Richard as 'the king's good grace' will be differently interpreted in different quarters.   [38] *C.L.* 209.

Here is much ado betwixt the duke Maximilianus and certain towns of Flanders. The duke hath been afore Bruges, wherefore Ghent and Bruges and other towns of Flanders be afeared of him. For they keep strait watch and ward in every town daily. And they of Bruges hath beheaded five or six of the dwellers of Bruges that took duke['s] part. But no man saith nor doth nothing to none Englishman, but that they may resort to and fro, as they have done in times past. Saving only men been afeared of Frenchmen, for they have taken two Englishmen coming from Bruges betwixt Dunkirk and Gravelines. One is John Eston, and the t'other is one James, Robert Stocker's man.[39]

The mercer John Eston was attorney for Henry Cantelow.[40]

William had previously told of a passenger ship that was intercepted by French ships as she made her way between Dover and Calais, and driven into Dunkirk haven.[41] Now he had news about one rash English entrepreneur who had made a disastrous attempt to combine piracy with passenger transport.

On Friday last past, one Richard Awrey, that was master of my lord Dennam [Dynham's] ship, yeed forth a-warfare in a ship of his own, and took in merchants and set them a-land at Dover, and at Dover took in passage to Calais-ward again. And as he came to Calais-ward, two men of war of French met with him, and fought with him, and there he was slain, and diverse more of his company. They say eight or nine persons, on whose souls Jesu have mercy. And so on Friday at afternoon the Frenchmen brought them into Dunkirk haven. And William Bryerley is in the same ship, and diverse landmen more – what they are I cannot tell yet.[42]

To everyone's relief, the wool-fleet arrived safely at Calais on 10 April, 'there be Frenchmen on the sea, but they stirred not at this season. And we know none otherwise here but we shall have war by land with France this summer.'[43] It would seem unlikely that Richard III could have afforded a foreign invasion at that point, either politically or financially. But William continued to send ominous tidings. On 14 April 'there came three passengers [passenger ships] from Dover, and there was two great ships of war of Frenchmen chased them into the haven mouth. And the passages had had but a mile to 'a run farther they had be taken. And our men of war lieth all in Cambrai [an area of the channel off Winchelsea].'[44] The news of 23 April could not be committed to paper: 'as for such newels as is here, please it you to commune with the bringer hereof and he will tell you, for I dare not write'.[45] The matter could have concerned the activities of Henry Tudor and other opponents of Richard on the

---

[39] *C.L.* 211. [40] *A.C.M.*, p. 162.

[41] *C.L.* 209. [42] *C.L.* 211.

[43] *C.L.* 214. [44] *C.L.* 215.

[45] *C.L.* 216.

continent, or was it the death of Richard's only son, the ten-year-old
Edward, which occurred at an uncertain date about the beginning of
April 1484 and might have started much talk in Calais?

At the same time William was sending coin to England by trusted
messengers: £40 stg. by Joyce, sealed in a canvas bag, and another £40
in a leather bag, carried by John Burne, draper of Calais.[46] This was a
risky and unpopular proceeding when the channel was infested with
pirates, but the English merchant adventurers were operating a 'restraint'
on trade with Maximilian's Burgundian territories. In May 1483 they
had agreed to 'appoint no shipping to this Sinxen mart, nor to any other
till we have assurance both of our adventure and also of th'entercourse
in the duke's dominions',[47] and in August 1484 they extended their
protest to complete prohibition on any trade in wares to or from the
duke's lands.[48] This affected the staplers insofar as there were few
English merchants willing to take their Flemish money in exchange loans.
The *Intercursus* made in 1478, which safeguarded the interests of both
English merchants and their Flemish and Dutch customers, had effectively lapsed and its re-negotiation was endangered by worsening
relations between England and the netherlands, marked by seizures of
goods on both sides. On 25 March 1484 there had been a move to arrest
Ghijsbrecht Van Wijnsberg at Calais as a 'pledge' for English property
that had been taken. It was pointed out

that there is an intercourse made betwixt the king of England and the land of
Flanders in Duke Philip's days, and since confirmed by Duke Charles, and since
that confirmed by Duke Maximilianus, how that any merchant of England, being
free of [the] Staple, may go safe and come safe into Flanders, both his body and
goods, at all times, without any interruption for any hurts done to any man of
Flanders by sea or land by Englishmen. And in like wise, all merchants of
Flanders or of theke parties, coming to Calais-ward to buy Staple merchandise,
shall go free and come free without any interruption in like wise.[49]

It was therefore agreed that the Staple should send two responsible
members to the Council of Flanders in Ghent to 'know whether they will
abide by that intercourse or not': an interesting example of merchants
taking the initiative in diplomatic affairs which directly concerned them.

Next day five people – the constable (Thomas Amerys), Robert Adlyn,
William Bentham, William Dalton and John Ynge – were appointed
ambassadors to attempt

to get a safeguard under the seal of Flanders that no merchant of the Staple shall
be troubled in Flanders for any malfeat done by any other Englishman to any

[46] C.L. 216.   [47] A.C.M., p. 150.
[48] Ibid., pp. 156–60.   [49] C.L. 212.

person of Flanders, without it be for trespass by him done [personally]. And in like wise my lord lieutenant of Calais shall give a safeguard to all merchants of Flanders coming to Calais to buy Staple merchandise, that no man shall do nor say to them nor their goods at Calais nor in the marches, for no malfeat done by any Fleming to any Englishman, without it be for trespass by him done.[50]

The efforts of the embassy were unsuccessful, and on 14 April,

what world we shall have with Flanders I cannot say. I fear me they will break with us, for the men that were sent by the Staple to the lords [of] Ghent to labour a safeguard for all the Fellowship of the Staple be come home again dayless ['without redress' or 'without any further meeting being fixed']. For they were answered how that Flanders hath sustained many great hurts done by Englishmen, and no restitution made them again, wherefore they can sustain no longer. And as for any safeguard, they will give none. Whereto this shall grow I cannot say.[51]

On 9 May:

As for Flanders, whether we shall have war or peace I cannot say as yet. Many folks be gone to the mart, and no man do nor saith nothing to them as yet. What they will coming from the mart, I wot ne'er. Many men fear that Flanders will not be our friends long, because Englishmen hath done them so many shrewd turns on the sea now lately.[52]

Although there were 'few men come over yet that been of any substance that taketh up any money by exchange, to regard ['worth mentioning']', it was taken as a good omen for trade at Calais that there had been a great 'vent' (sale) of wool, and a few of the leading members of the Staple had sold heavily. But William added gloomily, 'howbeit they put no doubts in Flanders, sir, it is unlikely for to be all well there long, etc.'.[53]

One English seaman and yeoman of the crown to Edward IV, who had operated sometimes as an official guard and convoyer around the coasts of Norfolk and Suffolk, sometimes as a pirate (when captain of the *Nicholas of Fowey* he had seized a Breton ship on 10 May 1483, and he had also taken two Spanish vessels, the *Mawdelyn* and the *Cropsaunt*, owned by Pedro De Salamanca),[54] had met retribution from some of his victims:

Item, sir, John Davy which was captain of the *Carvel of Eu*, he yeed a-land in Zealand at Yarmouth [i.e. Arnemuiden]. And he is taken and set in prison in

---

[50] *C.L.* 213.   [51] *C.L.* 215.
[52] *C.L.* 218.   [53] *C.L.* 220.
[54] *C.P.R. 1476–85*, pp. 317, 355. Davy was appointed captain of the king's ship *Carvelle of Ewe* with authority to take 120 mariners and soldiers, 2 June 1483: J. G. Nichols, ed., *Grants etc. from the Crown during the Reign of Edward the Fifth* (Camden Soc., 1854), pp. 67–8.

Middelburgh, and was likely for to be put to death for certain men that he robbed on the sea, of that country. But the men that wasted Zealand fleet hath been a-land at Flushing and at Camfer [Veer], and taken diverse men of the same country, and hath them to ship with them, and saith 'look how they serve John Davy, they will serve these men the same'.[55]

Happily, this act of private retaliation did not affect the staplers, and something had at last been done at government level to redress the grievances of the Flemish merchants. William could report on 3 June:

For any other news here, we have none here but good as yet, thanked be God. For all Englishmen were but courteously entreated in Flanders and in theke parties, for there was no n'other troubled but John Davy in Zealand. And yet I understand he is but courteously entreated by them. Wherefore many men thinketh here that Flanders nor theke parties intendeth none evil to none Englishmen. For Flanders is well satisfied, for that the king hath made restitution to such men that hath been in England to labour for their goods that was taken on the sea by Englishmen.[56]

'Liberties' for the merchants of both sides were eventually restored, for the time being, through the efforts of the king's commissioners, who included Hugh Clopton, a warden of the Mercers' Company.[57] By now Maximilian had become, for the English, 'Duke of Austria' instead of 'Duke of Burgundy'. The English embassy was received more cordially by the Flemish. On 8 October, when George was in Bruges on a visit, William wrote to Richard that George

purposed at his departing to 'a been again at Calais at this day or tomorrow, but I think he tarrieth to come with the ambassadors of England, for they be comen to Bruges. And they have had answer of the Duke of Austria and of the land of Brabant [of the which] we have no veray knowledge of yet. But I think it was not so very pleasant as they thought it should 'a been. Sir, they have had great cheer in Flanders, and Englishmen be cherished there as well as ever they were.[58]

Trade was in fact restored with Antwerp and the other towns, and ships were sent by the adventurers to the Cold mart of 1484–5.[59] But barely had this happened when in April 1485 the king sent a privy seal to the mayor of London, 'charging that none of his subjects shall go unto the town of Barrow [Bergen] in Brabant, nor to buy or sell with any of the

[55] *C.L.* 220.
[56] *C.L.* 221.
[57] Clopton and his associate John Salford were accused of trading in disobedience to the restraint at the same time as Clopton served as a commissioner: *A.C.M.*, pp. 161ff.
[58] *C.L.* 225.
[59] *A.C.M.*, p. 168. The restraint seems to have been abandoned on 27 Nov. 1484: ibid., p. 164. The staplers had been permitted to attend the Bammis mart to receive their debts, but were forbidden to buy wares there: *C.L.* 225.

inhabitants of the said town in no manner place, on pain of £100'.[60] A copy was also sent to the lieutenant, constables and fellows of the Staple of Calais. This effectively prevented the staplers from even collecting debts at the Easter mart.[61]

The staplers seem meanwhile to have incurred the wrath of a group of disadvantaged members of the lesser wool-working crafts of London, whether because the staplers could continue to trade while cloth exports were restricted, or because, as will be suggested shortly, they were sending wool out of the country when it was scarce at home. In October 1484 William Cely had sent up a prayer for the safe arrival of the wool-fleet, 'while the weather is fair'.[62] The wool had in fact been endangered by something other than bad weather. The scribe of the Mercers' Company left the story on record.[63] On the morning of 19 October, many 'simple-disposed persons of diverse crafts, as shearmen, fullers, tuckers, cappers and such other of like occupations' had gone to the Guildhall and demanded of the mayor 'to have the wools laid again on land which then were shipped toward Calais, with much crying and matter of grief and complaint, simple and rudely then uttered, etc.'. Aldermen Edmund Shaa and [Thomas] Breteyn were deputed to answer them, and offered to stop further lading and hold all the wool-ships in port, 'until the coming of the king to the town, at whose coming then the mayor and aldermen would help to show their grief, and beseech and pray the king's grace to see a remedy to their comfort'. But this temporizing was not good enough. 'The said persons then [were] not with that answer content and pleased, but with a great cry and shout departed from thence unto the Friar Austins, and there held their congregation [mass-meeting]'.

The mayor then sent them master William [Dunthorn], the town clerk, and John Haugh, gentleman, with the same offer. But

they in no wise would trust nor have any confidence in the said answer, saying it was all under a cloak spoken, and [for] prolonging of time. For that the wool-ships in mean time should go from the quay-side, which utterly they will restrain. And so then incontinently, without any other avisement, departed down to the wool-ships and took from them their sails and other tackle, and began to remove certain cloths [i.e. bales] of wool out of the said ships.

The mayor and aldermen, 'fearing riot and the great inconveniency which might grow by such simple and riotous persons, as God defend' (and no doubt also fearing to lose some of their own wool in many cases) then assembled in armour with a company of 'the wardens and sad

[60] *A.C.M.*, pp. 177–8.
[61] B.L. Harleian MS. 433 fo. 299b.
[62] *C.L.* 225 (8 Oct.).
[63] *A.C.M.*, pp. 159–60.

persons of the worshipful crafts of the city', and made their way to the waterside

which so hearing, the foresaid rioters with their company departed and fled, and durst not abide his coming, except a few persons, which that there and in other places in town were taken and had to prison.

To prevent any further disturbance, the aldermen then kept a nightly watch about the city, and messages were sent to all the guilds, telling them to be ready in harness if called, to see that no servants 'go into any congregation or assembly', 'that no man keep any servant but such as he will answer for, and of good guiding', and that no one should lend out his harness, but keep it by him. The mercers' clerk was not concerned to explain the grievances that lay behind the wool-workers' actions. So this attack on the wool-ships, like a later one, remains one of those incidents that we learn of by chance and in isolation. They make the study of the period both fascinating and frustrating.

The various events of 1483–4 help, however, to explain why the enrolled customs accounts show a sudden decrease in exports of wool during Richard's reign. T. H. Lloyd estimated that in the years [October] 1482 to [September] 1485 the annual average was only 5,283 sacks exported by denizens, compared to an average of 8,064 sacks in 1472–82, and 8,742 in [October] 1485 to [September] 1490.[64] There was also a drop in the export of broadcloths. 'Unfortunately', Lloyd commented, 'the commercial history of Richard III's reign still awaits exposition and no explanation can yet be offered for the decline'.

The situation was, in fact, complex. As we have seen, Richard III took the throne at a time of considerable international tension. About 26 March 1483, shortly before the death of Edward IV, a fleet of wool-ships had set out from London for Calais and turned back again, 'for fear and danger of enemies'.[65] According to the discharge of £2,353 10s 4¾d which the staplers subsequently obtained, its cargo had been customed at some 1,176¾ sacks.[66] It was June before the next shipping took place.[67] English relations with France, Brittany and the low countries were near breaking-point, and in the channel there was something like a free-for-all maritime war. Richard's government mounted attacks on Breton ships as a means of pressuring their duke,[68] and governments on all sides ordered reprisals against each other's merchants, so doing little to inhibit piracy. The

[64] T. H. Lloyd, *English Wool Trade*, pp. 281–2.
[65] File 10 fo. 36.   [66] *MS. Harleian 433*, I, 120.
[67] File 10 fos. 30, 36.   [68] Ross, *Richard III*, p. 197.

Patent Rolls add further incidents to William Cely's stories of attacks on shipping and seizures of merchants and their goods. They also give the subsequent history of Peter Hoke, merchant of Calais, who was one of the survivors when Richard Awrey's ship met French pirates as it made its way from Dover to Calais on 11 March 1484. Hoke was taken to Boulogne and there imprisoned for 13 weeks, being finally put to ransom for 250 gold crowns (£50 stg.).[69]

Such disturbed conditions did not prevent trade entirely, but equally they cannot have greatly encouraged it. Exports to the Staple were naturally sensitive to political alarms, so that they fell off markedly in, for instance, 1462, 1471 and 1477, after the death of Charles of Burgundy. The most dramatic drop under Richard III was in fact in exports of wool from the north-eastern ports, of which only Boston shipped in 1482–3 and 1484–5 (989 sacks and 883 sacks).[70] This may well have been due to a shortage of ships, combined with the lack of a sufficient armed convoy. At the same time, the staplers had to cope with the difficulties posed by the restraint of trade operated by the merchant venturers in 1483–4, which also helps, of course, to explain the fall in cloth exports. The staplers' customers in turn suffered harassment from troops, both French and Burgundian, and faced the blockade which the Flemish are reported to have mounted to prevent merchants attending the marts of Antwerp in those years.

A more specific factor in the down-turn of wool exports must have been the price-rise which occurred, probably early in 1483. The steep increase of one mark per sack in selling prices at Calais, which apparently coincided with an increase in the Calais exchange rate, representing a devaluation of the Flemish pound of account on the Calais market, would certainly have caused a slackening of demand among the Staple's customers. At the same time, domestic prices had suddenly risen in the Cotswolds. In September 1482 William Midwinter could not alter the price he had already agreed with Richard and George for his next sort, but demanded payment of £200 one month before the due date.[71] Richard, at his 'wits' end' for money, contemplated cancelling the entire bargain.[72] The increase in price to grower was probably a response to shortage, whether caused by sales to 'Lombards', or the mortality among sheep first mentioned in November 1480 and again, 'up in England', in late November 1481.[73] George had already warned in March 1482 that wool would be 'scant' at Calais that season.[74] Competition between

[69] *C.P.R. 1476–85*, p. 529.
[70] Carus-Wilson and Coleman, *England's Export Trade*, table, p. 68.
[71] *C.L.* 192.   [72] *C.L.* 195, 197.
[73] *C.L.* 108, 137.   [74] *C.L.* 148.

staplers and clothiers for depleted supplies would then explain the proclamation sent to certain counties in October 1484, forbidding anyone 'to buy or bargain any wool not shorn before the Feast of St Bartholomew [24 August], except to make cloth within the realm'.[75] That is to say, staplers were not to forestall the clothiers by entering into advance contracts for the next year's clip. Available evidence suggests that this was not normally their practice at this period, but William Cely's description of how Hugh Clopton, Thomas Grafton, Richard Pontesbury and Thomas Betson were making 'sweepstake' of the market and intended 'to begin betimes' may imply such activity.[76] An acute shortage of wool would also help explain the attack on the London wool-fleet by the wool-workers of London.

The market at Calais may well have suffered a period of stagnation in 1483. Between March and September the Celys sold only 1,200 fell (for £56 Calais sterling), and wool to a value of only £910 4s 10d.[77] William noted that there were very few customers at Calais in the autumn, and since the new prices had also applied to old stock, wool from the shipments of 1482 may have remained unsold for longer than usual. Certainly there was a build-up in stocks of fell. In March 1484 William had difficulty in disposing of his new fells, 'for there is great plenty of old fells in town: three old against one new'.[78] Nevertheless, he then encouraged Richard and George to ship more than the 20 sarplers of fleece-wool they intended, 'if ye could have good ships'.[79] He hoped to be well furnished with money from previous sales to pay the custom and subsidy, and 'also, sir, I think (as far as my simple reason give me) it is more surer shipping now than shall be hereafter, for diverse causes'. He remains silent about these reasons, but uncertain relations between England and the Council of Flanders were undoubtedly one, and it was also believed at Calais that 'we shall have war by land with France this summer'. Richard and George accordingly got 25 sarplers and two pokes (nearly 67 sack-weights) to Calais. The shipment arrived on 10 April, escaping by four days the two French men-of-war lurking in the channel.[80] As far as sales were concerned, William's optimism was justified. On 14 April 1484 he calculated that within less than 12 months (and mainly since September 1483?) he had sold more than £2,000 worth of stock, and his further sales up to October 1484 totalled £1,189 odd.[81] More generally, on 22 May 1484 he reported that staplers had been making exceptionally large sales in short time, but obtaining very little

[75] *C.P.R. 1476–85*, p. 519.
[76] *C.L.* 220.
[77] File 10 fo. 31.
[78] *C.L.* 212.
[79] *C.L.* 213.
[80] *C.L.* 215.
[81] *C.L.* 215; File 10 fo. 31.

money in hand.[82] The four men who had made a corner in the market meant to continue, 'wherefore, sir, I think they will make wool dear in Cotswold this year'.

Shipments had picked up somewhat in the customs year 1483–4, only to take another down-turn in 1484–5. Dear wool in the Cotswolds, and a long wait for any payment from previous sales, would have helped dampen activity. There was also a lack of ships for transport and convoy duty while the country was put on alert against the expected invasion by Henry Tudor; preparations were already in hand in January 1485.[83] It would be difficult to say whether King Richard's licence to his mother to ship 775½ sacks of wool in 1484 and 1485 had any significant effect on the stocks available to staplers.[84] Another deterrent to shipping has, however, lain apparently unremarked in the register of signet documents, B.L. MS. Harl. 433.[85] On 20 January 1485 an order was issued to Sir James Tyrrell and the stapler William Bondman to take from the merchants of the Staple wool-sacks to the value of £3,000 and to sell them for the king's use. If valuation was by selling price at Calais, the total may have been no more than 243 sacks of good and middle Cotswold, or about 97 sarplers, which would be the equivalent by volume of 14.7 percent of the two London shipments of 19 June and 26 September 1483, or 5 percent of the total wool export by denizens in the customs year 1484–5. The money was probably intended for the defence of Calais: Tyrrell had been appointed to take special charge of the defence of the Pale.[86] But the wording, and the order to Tyrrell himself, may well indicate that the scheme was not promoted by the merchants. Was it, indeed, one of those illegalities at which the continuator of the Crowland Chronicle hints darkly?[87]

Whatever the cause, while Richard and George apparently shipped over 55 sarplers to Calais between March and October 1484, they sent only 17.68 in the calendar year 1485.[88] Even this small amount is reached by including 11 sarplers from a shipment which is dated '15 October 1484' in a summarized account, but which should probably be dated to October 1485. In their shipment of 9 March '1484' [1485 new style] there were only six sarplers and a poke, containing 17 sacks 14 cloves. These were the remnant of a sort of which 19 sarplers had been laded on 4 October 1484, in the fleet that was attacked at London.

82 *C.L.* 220.
83 *MS. Harleian 433*, II, 187–9.
84 *C.P.R. 1476–85*, p. 441 (9 Feb. 1484).
85 *MS. Harleian 433*, II, 191.
86 Ross, *Richard III*, p. 202 n. 28.
87 Ed. Fulman, *Rerum Anglicarum...*, p. 572.
88 File 10 fo. 30.

But while wool exports undoubtedly fell off during the period between late 1482 and late 1485, some were marginally higher than the customs accounts indicate. The customs figures for shipments of fleece-wool (but not fells) always require to be increased by between 3 and 4 percent to indicate gross weight, because the allowance of two cloves per sack-weight was deducted before weights were entered on the 'cockets'.[89] George Cely's account of his shipment of nine sarplers and two pokes on 16 June 1484 shows, however, that on that occasion he enjoyed double the usual rebate: four cloves per sack-weight, or 8 percent of his total shipment customed.[90] This allowance was evidently general at Boston, Hull, Ipswich and London at that time, the customers, controllers and weighers in those ports being instructed to allow the staplers 'two nails free in every sack'.[91] This clearly meant in addition to the customary allowance. The number of sacks of fleece-wool entered in the enrolled accounts would therefore have to be increased by at least 4 percent before they became compatible with the entries for other years. It is not clear why or for how long the increased allowance was made.[92]

It will have become plain enough in the preceding pages why many staplers, Richard and George among them, welcomed the custom of the Bruges-based Spaniard, De Lopez, who had always preferred to pay for his purchases of wool at Calais by giving obligations payable by associates in London. (For example, he had bought middle Cots. wool from Richard senior in this way in November 1473.)[93] When, in May 1484, the small group of large exporters 'made sweepstake', selling on credit despite serious doubts over relations with Flanders, William Cely complacently observed that 'I trow all their money shall not be so ready to them as yours shall be to your masterships'.[94] The only illegality in payment at London lay in the fact that it contravened the technical regulations of the Staple. The wool was put on sale at Calais in accordance with the law, and all taxes on it were duly paid. Receiving the money in England obviated all the difficulty and uncertainty which a stapler faced in collecting debts at the marts and then arranging to transfer the receipts home.

But William's self-congratulation in May 1484 was preceded by six months in which he had been very coy with De Lopez and his partner Ghijsbrecht Van Wijnsberg, and reluctant to allow credit at all. Payment

[89] See Ch. 5, p. 125. In 1486 George reckoned a rebate on 86.2 sacks which amounted to either 3.4 percent or 3.8 percent, depending on which method of calculation was employed. [90] File 20 no. 9.
[91] MS. Harleian 433, I, 154, 160, 167.
[92] It no longer applied in April 1486.
[93] File 11 fo. 14v. [94] C.L. 220.

in London suited his principals, who were perpetually short of cash there, but William was mindful of the need to meet customs and subsidy dues which fell due at Calais. The Staple in turn set its face against payments at London because of its responsibility for meeting the wages of the Calais garrison in local coin. William was chary of breaking Staple regulations, and reluctant to commit himself without specific instructions from his masters. At the same time, he knew better than anyone how difficult it had become to make money over by exchange with English merchant venturers. The situation was further complicated by the propensity of Richard and George to make arrangements without notifying William, by letters which crossed each other, or failed to arrive at all, and sometimes by William's fear that De Lopez was defaulting when his agent failed to pay instalments of the debt on time.

For a month in October–November 1483 no letters passed between Calais and London because 'the search was so strait' as the agents of Richard III kept a watch on Henry Tudor and his sympathizers in England.[95] Richard and George, unaware of the situation, blamed William for being so slow in writing and accused him of 'remembering little' to speak to De Lopez for £300 due to them by Christmas. 'Sir, I have remember it as much as lay in my power to do', protested William with some acerbity, also pointing out that he had been ill at the time.[96] At the beginning of January 1484 De Lopez sent his man Willikin to Calais with money to buy more wool,

and so he would have some of your wool, with that he might have a like respite [as before] in payment of some of the money, but I would grant him none without ready money all gr. [i.e. cash down in Flemish money of Calais]. What he will do I wot ne'er.[97]

On 29 January, after hearing from Richard and George, William declared that he thought De Lopez 'means truly, howbeit he is greatly charged diverse ways', and De Lopez had convinced him that letters of exchange for the previous purchases had been sent to 'Peter Bayle' (Valladolid) in London. De Lopez valued his connexion with the Celys and

he would ye should be content and pleased afore all other. Wherefore I hope your masterships shall stand in no jeopardice of that that is betwixt your masterships and him, for he is a man that is in great credence [credit] amongst the Fellowship here now, and doth great feats [business deals]. And now Willikin his man is here, which I am sure that he will buy much wool or he go.[98]

---

[95] 'Of a month day we could have no conveyance of no letters to London by no manner man, for there was no man that yeed that would bear any letters for searching': *C.L.* 201 (13 Nov.).   [96] *C.L.* 202.

[97] *C.L.* 205.   [98] *C.L.* 206.

In late 1483 De Lopez had sent over to England letters of payment for various staplers to a total of no less than £5,000 sterling.[99]

When the further complications of the Celys' dealings with De Lopez and his associates are considered, it is no wonder that old Richard once complained of the weariness of 'dealing with word'.[100] On 10 February 1484 John's servant Willikin told William Cely that De Lopez in Bruges had written to 'Peter Bayle & Delyte' in London, 'to speak with your masterships that John De Lopez might have all your Cots. wools that remaineth here at Calais, and pay you for it in England as he hath done in times past'.[101] And Willikin reported that Peter Valladolid had written back to De Lopez to say that George and Richard had told him (Peter) that William Cely would obey their instructions. Willikin therefore begged William to sell no more wool to other customers until he heard from London. But to this William returned a dusty answer: 'I would keep none for him, but take the market as it cometh, without your masterships writeth me the contrary. For I told him he hath not deserved in paying of the last to have respite of this.' Further pressure was then applied by De Lopez's partner, Ghijsbrecht, who offered to give a bill for the whole sum, payable at pleasure wherever the Celys chose.[102]

On 16 February Richard and George had in fact written confirming the grant of the remaining wool, half to be paid at London by Easter and the rest four months after delivery of the goods.[103] This letter was delayed, because it went to Bruges by mistake. William maintained to Ghijsbrecht and Willikin that he had by now promised the wool to another man. 'But nevertheless I have taken a God's penny of them' to seal the bargain. He duly sold them six sarplers and a poke of good Cots. and sent over their letter of payment for £242 17d stg.[104] Three weeks later, when Ghijsbrecht again came to Calais and 'took show to buy wool', the lieutenant of Calais (Dynham) tried to have him arrested as a hostage for English goods which had been arrested at Nieuport in revenge for English acts of piracy. The lieutenant, a man without much political sense, it seems, was dissuaded from engaging in this long-drawn-out vendetta by the lieutenant of the Staple. The latter pointed out that, besides being contrary to the Intercourse, Ghijsbrecht's arrest should cause a great inconvenience to the Staple, for Ghijsbrecht and his fellow [De Lopez] be the men that doth greatest feat of any merchants that cometh hither...wherefore if they should be stopped there would come no more merchants hither, the which should cause a great stop.[105]

---

[99] *C.L.* 205. The first letters, for £2,000, caused some embarrassment to his agent in London, who 'knew not at that time that John Delowppys had sent over such charge as he did'.   [100] *C.L.* 104.   [101] *C.L.* 207.   [102] *C.L.* 208.
[103] *C.L.* 209.   [104] *C.L.* 210.   [105] *C.L.* 212.

He shrewdly added that

if merchants strangers might not resort hither, that men might make sale of their goods, they could make no payment unto the soldiers of their wages. And also [it] should cause men to land again such goods as they were inshipping withal

so that the king would lose his custom and subsidy. In the upshot, 'Ghijsbrecht is at his liberty, and he buyeth wool here as he hath done in times past'.

At this point correspondence had again been interrupted; Richard and George heard nothing from William because 'there hath no passage gone [between Calais and England] this fourteen days'.[106] The next we hear of De Lopez and Ghijsbrecht is on 14 April, when they want more Cely wool. Valladolid had paid another visit to Richard and George, offering to find sureties for payment.

Sir, [advised William] if the sureties be of substance and abiding then I would avise you to take them, or else not. For what world we shall have with Flanders I cannot say. I fear me they will break with us....And sir, I pray you to write me in what case Peter hath set your masterships for such [wool] that I deliver John De Lopez here....I shall deliver him no wool till I have writing from you again. Howbeit the man is good enough, were we in certainty of peace betwixt Flanders and us. But sir, if ye can be set sure of your money there, it were a good way. For there is no merchant that cometh here that payeth ready money for any new wool that he buyeth here.[107]

After giving this (rather ambiguous) encourgement, on 28 April William suddenly sounded a note of alarm:

Please it you to understand that Willikin, John De Lopez' man, come[s] over into England with this passage, wherefore I think he will commune with you for your Cots. wool. Sir, I will avise you to grant him none other wise than to pay it at Calais according to the ordinance or the wool pass the town ['before the wool leaves Calais']. For it is known well enough here that Willikin cometh over for none other thing than to make bargains with certain persons in England for such wools as they have at Calais.

And also, the dealing of diverse men in England with John De Lopez is known, wherefore there will be a great search made shortly and forfeits shall be levelled. For it is known well here that Peter Bayle & Delytt answereth at days in England for much of the wool that John De Lopez buyeth here.

But as for your dealings, knoweth none man without they search Peter Bayle's books. As I think great search shall be made, for the forfeit is levelled on some persons already, but they be not yet openly named.[108]

George took certain precautions against detection, to be described later, but the danger passed. Probably the heads of the Staple themselves were not innocent of similar dealings with De Lopez.

---

[106] Ibid. (25 March).   [107] *C.L.* 215.   [108] *C.L.* 217.

Again letters crossed. On 9 May William wrote that he had lately received two letters from London, one written on St George's Day (23 April), the other on 30 April,

and as touching John De Lopez' matter, it is so that he and Ghijsbrecht be come to Calais, and so they have bought here already above 200 sarplers end [wound] wool, and so they have spoken to me for your wool, showing how that they had writing from your masterships how that Peter De Baylle had made a bargain with you, and was through with you for all your wool. Nevertheless I said unto them again how that I had no such writing from your masterships, wherefore I had sold part of it and promised all together.[109]

On 30 April he had sold a sarpler each to Robert Le Gaynard and Collard Mesdowe of Bruges, 'and to pay as they fetch it, and to fetch it within a month'.[110] Subsequently he sold five sarplers to John De Selonder of Malines.[111] William's action disconcerted De Lopez and Ghijsbrecht, but they persevered:

with the which answer they were sorry, nevertheless they laboured still to me for [the wool], and desiring they might have it that was unsold. And they would pay here or the wool pass, according to the ordinance, as other men would do. And then I said I would not, without they would take certain of your clift wool withal. And they answered me again that now they would buy as much end wool as they might, and no clift wool, but when they came next again they would help me away with all the clift wool.[112]

And so, in conclusion, before a broker I have sold them 19 sarplers and a poke fine Cots. at the price of the Place, and to pay ready money here or it pass. So upon this I have weighed unto him already 2 sarplers.

But it was then William's turn to be frustrated:

And when I sent to him to reckon he delivered me a letter from your masterships. Which letter holdeth in like as he said unto me afore, how that your masterships be through with Peter De Baylle for your wool. But nevertheless I said unto John De Lopez I would do none other wise than according to the bargain that I made with him here. Then he answered me again, if so be that your masterships be not content to be paid for your wool in England according to the communication that Peter De Bayle had with your masterships at London, what! ['well, then'], he will pay me here according to the bargain that he had made with me here. And upon this I shall receive a bill of him for the said two sarplers wool.

William then abruptly changed his tune once more:

But sir, if so be that your masterships may be set sure for your money at the day, it were as good to receive your money there as other wise, howbeit the days are long. But he saith he shall set you the best Lombards in all London to surety.

---

[109] *C.L.* 218.   [110] *C.L.* 217; File 10 fo. 31.
[111] *C.L.* 221.
[112] *C.L.* 218. For 'end' and 'clift' wools, see Ch. 5, pp. 113–14.

Sir, all the wool that he hath bought here at this time, he must pay it in England in like wise. And as for the matter that I wrate to your masterships of the ordinance, ye shall not need put no doubts in it ['there is no need to worry about it'].[113]

Now William's principals in London reversed their decision, mysteriously unless George was still in a guilty panic about his illegal receipts. They had written instructing William to deliver no wool to De Lopez without ready money.[114] Willikin had been waiting at Calais to receive the wool promised, and was greatly taken aback to hear this. 'But now I have answered him that he nor none other man shall not have it without he bring his ready money.' It was arranged that Willikin should go to Bruges to consult his master, and that William would 'take his next merchants' if he was not back within four or five days. Richard and George had also told William to make over by exchange any money that remained by him. William replied that so far there were few substantial English merchants willing to take up much, and chided gently 'as for the substance of your money, if your mastership will, ye shall have it in England with as little aventure and in shorter space' from Valladolid.

Willikin duly returned to Calais and William weighed out to him eight more sarplers,

and so there remaineth behind ten sarplers, whereof is eight fine and two middle, which at his coming again I shall deliver unto him. Which, as he saith, shall not be long erst.... I have received a bill of his hand payable at pleasure, which I must keep by me till the rest be delivered, and then we shall have both in one reckoning. And make the bill according to the promise made betwixt your masterships and Peter Vayle & Delyt [!].[115]

By 8 October 'John De Lopez hath fet[ched] the rest of your Cots. wool, with the which he is well content.'[116] Evidently Richard and George had, in the end, accepted William's advice and agreed to payment in England. In November–December De Lopez also bought six sarplers of good Kesteven wool from them.[117] The ten original sarplers of Cots., sold, according to the bill of sale, on 10 May and 1 June 1484, came to £371 19*s* 11*d* stg.[118]

George had apparently solved the problem of possible investigations into their dealings, to his own satisfaction. It was a search of Valladolid's books that William had feared in April. In order to prevent the Staple officials connecting receipts from Valladolid in London with sales made

[113] Ibid.   [114] *C.L.* 220 (22 May).
[115] *C.L.* 221 (3 June), 'and as for your clift wool, he saith that John Delowppys will do therein that your masterships shall [be] pleased'.
[116] *C.L.* 225.   [117] File 10 fo. 31.
[118] File 12 fo. 40.

at Calais to De Lopez, George made himself a special book of sales, which covered his dealings with all his customers between March 1483 and August 1485. An annotated and emended copy of this schedule, made by the factor William Rogers for Chancery auditors after George's death, is among the papers.[119] Since De Lopez did not deal in fells, George left the record of fell sales unaltered. But in his special account book he ingeniously doctored all the sales figures for fleece-wool, so that (presumably) he could defy anyone to prove that the sales to De Lopez bore any relation to those suspicious payments in London. He did this basically by falsifying the weights of the sarplers sold, with the result that he increased the alleged prices paid. Often he inflated his supposed receipts still further by over-pricing the odd cloves in the total weight. And in an extra attempt to cover his tracks, he played a set of variations on his method. This depended essentially on the difference between the 'sack-weight' of 52 cloves of 7 lb avoirdupois by which wool was weighed in England, and the local 'sack-weight' of 90 cloves of $3\frac{1}{2}$ lb avdp. by which the wool was sold in Calais. Thus in a sale to Giles Frank, one pocket of middle Cots. weighing 35 cloves Calais 'after the rate of £9 6s 8d the sack' (the correct price) is charged at £6 5s 7d, as though the wool weighed $\frac{35}{52}$ of a sack, instead of £3 12s 7d for $\frac{35}{90}$ sack.

To take a more complicated example, in May 1484 William Cely sold De Lopez $5\frac{1}{2}$ sacks 31 cloves, by Calais weight, of good Cots. wool at 20 marks the sack, making a total price of £77 18s 6d.[120] In George's book the weight of the wool was given as 6 sacks 24 cloves Calais, which he then priced as though the 24 cloves had cost $\frac{24}{52}$ of £13 6s 8d, not $\frac{24}{90}$. He must have arrived at his alleged weight by taking the half-sack and the odd cloves in William's true weight, which make 76 Calais cloves, and then treating them as English cloves, so that he obtained a fictitious extra sack and 24 cloves. By this combined means he achieved an alleged total price of £86 3s. Usually, as in this example, it is not difficult to discover how George has treated the original weight of the purchase, though one could not work in the opposite direction and deduce true weight from false. But in another instance, the sale of the five sarplers to John De Selonder, it would be impossible to make any *prima facie* connexion between George's weight of 15 sacks 13 cloves and the true total weight of 13 sacks 41 cloves Calais without a detailed bill of sale made by William Cely.[121] William gives the weights of each sarpler: 2 ss. 65 cl., $2\frac{1}{2}$ ss. 36 cl., 2 ss. 73 cl., 2 ss. 16 cl. and $2\frac{1}{2}$ ss. 31 cl. George rightly added this up to make 11 sacks 221 cloves Calais, but then, as usual, divided the

---

[119] File 10 fo. 31. See also Alison Hanham, 'Make a Careful Examination: Some Fraudulent Accounts in the Cely Papers', *Speculum*, XLVIII (1973), 313–23.
[120] File 12 fo. 40.   [121] *C.L.* 221.

odd cloves by 52 instead of 90, to create 4¼ further sacks by English weight. This wool was middle Cots., priced at £9 6s 8d per sack: real total price was £125 11s 8d, which George inflated to £142 6s 7d.[122] The point here is that if William had only written 2⅓ ss. 20 cl. and 2½ ss. 28 cl. in place of 2 ss. 65 cl. and 2 ss. 73 cl. – using the much more usual form – George's version of the weight would have been 14½ sacks one clove, not 15 sacks 13 cloves.

The idea of falsifying accounts was clever, provided investigation was limited to England and no suspicious official examined records at Calais, or William's sale bills, to compare them with George's version. But George overdid things by the prices he imputed to his sarplers: any stapler could have recognized at once that the arithmetic was wrong if the cloves were Calais weight. George simply got carried away in the refinement of his own cleverness. It was just as well for him that the threatened searches never took place. As things were, De Lopez remained a leading customer for English wool at Calais. But an arrangement of mutual benefit in 1483–5 created different problems in subsequent years. When Bruges was isolated by civil war in the late 1480s it became difficult for her merchants to fetch their wools from Calais, and there were long periods when the Celys, dependent on a single customer for most of their sales, had a greatly reduced turnover.

The extent of De Lopez's dealings with the Staple is indicated by William Cely's report, on 25 March 1484, that during the previous year De Lopez and Ghijsbrecht had bought above £25,000 stg. worth of wool.[123] Richard and George had supplied something like 5 percent of this amount. Over the longer period of March 1483 to August 1485, De Lopez and his partners bought from the Celys at least 65 sarplers, representing £2,212 stg.[124] At the same period their other customers for fleece-wool are recorded as purchasing between them just under £662 worth.

---

[122] He could not alter the price per sack-weight, because it was fixed and perfectly known.
[123] *C.L.* 212. This sum might buy more than the total amount of fleece-wool in the two London shipments of June and Sept. 1483.
[124] File 10 fo. 31.

MARRIAGE AND HOUSEKEEPING

Matchmaking was an enormously serious business for the parties and their relations, and a favourite sport for those less directly involved in the outcome. In April 1484, shortly before the alarm about illegal payments by John De Lopez, George Cely was conducting marital negotiations in two quarters. In the small merchant community, these proceedings were watched with great interest, and at Calais William Cely, acting on instructions, sounded a friend or relative of one of George's prospects without revealing his own identity:

As touching the matter that your mastership wrote me of Thomas White, mercer, in certain, sir, I spake with him, and he dined at home with mine hostess (howbeit he knew not me). And there he showed how that that matter lay betwixt another man and you. Howbeit he said she had you more in favour than the t'other man. But, sir, ye have his good will.[1]

This is one of those letters which bear evidence of intermittent construction. Writing could be a slow and tedious business, and sometimes quite a long period would elapse between the completion of one sentence and the moment when a correspondent took up his pen to continue with the next. Such an interruption occurred at this point, and when William resumed, his earlier news had become irrelevant.

Item, sir, William Salford is come. And I spake with him and welcomed him. And he told me how that your mastership and that other gentlewoman were at a point ['concluded'] in that matter. Of the which I was right glad, and so he said he was. But he spered ['asked'] me none other questions, not yet. And sir, it is said here by many persons here how that ye be sure ['contracted'] to her. With the which, sir, I am well content and right glad thereof. And sir, all those here that knoweth you, both merchants and soldiers, commend you greatly, saying 'if that gentlewoman should be worth double that she is ye were worthy to have her'. And as for any making of search of your dealings here, I trow there is no man that maketh any. If they do, they need go no farther than the books

[1] *C.L.* 215.

in the treasury, where they may find that your sales made within less than this year amounts above £2,000 stg., where that the person that laboured for to 'a be afore you ['who was trying to best you'], he and his brother had not in this town this twelve months the one half of that.

George's success in the marriage race may have had one unfortunate consequence. Richard and George Cely and John and William Dalton were not the only brothers in partnership in the Staple. But John (whom William Cely had never much liked) receives no further mention in the papers of his former friend George, despite the fact that William Dalton remained on good terms with George and Richard. Mere chance may of course account for John's disappearance from the memoranda, but it is odd that George records no more dealings with him. Was he George's unsuccessful, and subsequently embittered, rival in 1484?

Richard Cely junior had done well for himself by capturing the first marriageable daughter of a prominent alderman, whose dowry of 500 marks compares very favourably with the 200 marks allotted to daughters of the Stonor family in 1431 and 1474.[2] George succeeded in winning, against competition, that prize of the market, a young and well-to-do widow. Margery Rygon's first husband, Edmund, had left her comfortably off at his death three months earlier.[3] A widow who did not wish to remarry sometimes took vows of celibacy – on 29 March 1482 Richard had thought it important to mention that 'Byfelde' (Robert Byfeld) had been buried on 27 March, 'and on the morrow early his wife took the mantle and the ring', so removing herself from the marriage market.[4] Her husband had bequeathed Joan 1,800 marks of dower, 'take it or leave it', and there must have been many disappointed men to contemplate the loss of such a woman.[5] Margery Rygon, however, 'that other gentlewoman' of William's letter, was young (the second wife of Edmund Rygon) and childless, and had every reason to take a second husband of her choice. Eligible members of the Staple company were especially interested in her, because Rygon, a citizen and draper of London, was probably also a stapler and left property in Calais and its marches.[6] Margery was also his chief executor, and was bequeathed the bulk of his estate, to employ at her will, for the good of Rygon's soul.

Margery's maiden name was unknown until a stray piece of paper from one of George's accounts, dated by 1484 by a Chancery auditors' clerk,

---

[2] *Stonor L.*, nos. 54, 137.
[3] Will of Edmund Rygon, P.C.C. 22 Logge (19 Jan. 1484).
[4] *C.L.* 147.
[5] Will of Robert Byfeld, ironmonger and stapler, P.C.C. 5 Logge (22 Jan. 1482).
[6] Perhaps she was the 'Mistress Regons' of a fragmentary account for household purchases, dating from Aug.–Sept. 1483: S.P. 46/123 fo. 25.

turned up among unsorted material in the Public Record Office.[7] This includes the casual item, 'Paid to Hary Pounke my wife's father – £20'. Closest approximation to this name among testators whose wills were registered by the Prerogative Court of Canterbury was one Henry Punt of Little Over, Derbyshire.[8] Punt's will, of 28 October 1489, happily settled the identification by including a bequest to his son Thomas of 'my sword and my "gesiren" formerly belonging to George Cely'. Besides his son and heir Thomas, Henry specified four surviving but unnamed daughters, who were to share a third part of his estate between them. This property consisted of a tenement in the parish of St Peter in the town of Derby, and a farm and 'hospicium' (inn?) at Little Over. His wife was Cicily, sister of Richard Salford, so that the William Salford (a London mercer and stapler) who gave William Cely the news of the match was doubtless one of Margery's maternal relations.[9]

While Margery brought George a substantial dowry, George had to satisfy her family that he was 'worthy to have her', and to make his own contribution to the marriage settlement. A decade later Richard Cely's widow alleged that George had spent all his proper share of the stock which he had inherited together with Richard, on 'jewels diverse and many rich gifts and pleasures given to one Margery Rygon, then widow, and other her friends, time of his wooing, expenses of his marriage and household, and in lands [bought] to have th'expedition of his said marriage', and that he also paid £483 13s 4d on the purchase of land and property.[10] The new-found account has an entry of £10 16s 5d stg. 'paid by me to Thomas Borgen [Burgoyn, mercer] for my jewels, praiser (?) John Elderbekke'.[11] George certainly bought his wife a (wedding?) ring, as witness a dorsal note on the back of a letter from William Cely of 10 April: 'item, delivered unto John Veneke in fine gold to make a ring for my wife, 26⅛ dwt – sum, 53s 6d'.[12] He may also have bought plate at this time, which was included in the connotation of 'jewels' at that period. And he acquired, either as a purchase or as pledge for a loan, a red spinel ('balas ruby') which had belonged to King Richard, valued at £100.[13]

George also added to his land-holdings in 1484, although it seems dubious that he spent as much as Anne Cely supposed. On 5 April 1484 he paid £6 13s 4d to 'master Brown of the Chancery' for William Newman, from whom he was buying property.[14] Richard advanced £5 6s 8d to pay Newman at various times.[15] It may also have been in 1484

[7] File 20 no. 8, dorse.   [8] P.C.C. 20 Milles.
[9] The will also mentions Henry's brother, John Punt.
[10] C.1 194/17: see Ch. 15, pp. 414–15.
[11] File 20 no. 8.   [12] *C.L.* 214.
[13] Wills of G. Cely (P.C.C. 8 Horne) and R. Cely jun. (P.C.C. 25 Dogett).
[14] File 20 no. 8, dorse.   [15] File 10 fos. 18v–19v (1483).

that Richard lent £6 to pay one 'Cossall' or 'Cessale' in part payment for 'Sacokkys', George's property at Socketts Heath, Little Thurrock, Essex.[16] In April, again, George bought 50 Romney sheep, at 9*d* a head, to stock one of his properties.[17] 'The Place' at Stratford (-at-Bow?) was bought some years later. 'Hungerford's wife' received a last instalment of £10 (borrowed from Alvaro De Cisneros, agent of De Lopez), on the price of £40, in April 1489.[18] With this price, compare the £20 (20 years' purchase) paid by the Mercers' Company in 1520 for a house near the Crutched Friars.[19]

Two further newly found accounts, together with a list of purchases made by the invaluable William Maryon, provide a comprehensive picture of the provisions for the wedding of George and Margery, which took place between 13 and 22 May 1484, probably on Tuesday 18th.[20] Total recorded costs of the celebrations (which do not mention church fees) come to £10 5*s* 6*d*. If allowance is made for wine, beer and ale missing from the accounts, the total might be £12 16*s*, to be compared with the £18 13*s* estimated to have been spent on the two occasions of Agnes Cely's funeral and month mind the year before. It would be enough for six months' normal household expenditure on food and other usual outgoings, estimated below at 10*s* per week.

George had given Maryon 40*s* on 13 May, a Thursday, 'to lay out for me for cates [purchases] to my household', and Maryon's account of expenditure, which in fact came to £2 12*s* 10*d*, is headed 'These be the parcels here following that I have laid out at the marrying of my cousin George Cely'.[21] The same day he paid for three bushels of wheatmeal at 12*d* the bushel, half a salt fish and two mackerel. On Saturday he bought plaice and mackerel, a bushel of coarse Bay salt (9*d*), a hundred oranges (13*d*) and fourpence worth of 'garlands and bows', and paid 10*d* 'at supper for fish'. Greenery, violets and garlands were among provisions bought for the late fourteenth-century May wedding detailed in *Le Menagier de Paris*.[22] Purchases on Monday 17th were beef and mutton (8*d*), a gallon of white wine (10*d*), a quarteron of parti-gold for the painter (18*d*), four cruses to hold beer (3*d*), a 'leyen' (loin) of mutton and another of 'feyell' (veal) (8*d*), and two pounds of figs (2*d*). On the same day, apparently, he also bought a quarter of a turbot (4*d*), half a 'blowyd' fish (i.e. a 'bloater' or smoked fish, for 6*d*), two plaice and a

---

[16] File 10 fo. 19v.   [17] File 20 no. 8.
[18] File 10 fo. 9.   [19] *A.C.M.*, p. 489.
[20] File 20 nos. 33–4, 39; File 12 fos. 41–3.   [21] File 12 fo. 42.
[22] Georgina E. Brereton and Janet M. Ferrier, eds., *Le Menagier de Paris* (Oxford, 1981), pp. 187, 190.

side of salt fish, and, for supper, a bret and another plaice. 'Four men that washed dishes' were paid 2*d* each, and seven gallons of raw cream, one gallon of 'sodden' (clotted) cream and eight gallons of curd cost 3*s* altogether. John Morley supplied a large quantity of 'fenegar' (vinegar), mustard and honey to the total of 8*s*.[23] On Friday 21 May Maryon paid 2*s* 9*d* for 'fyght' (his usual spelling for 'fish'), and 'for a plaice and half a salt fish the which was fetched at home' and cost 5*d*. Saturday's purchases were three plaice, a salt fish (5½*d*), a quarter turbot (6*d*), sea-bream, four mackerel and four whiting. There were more mackerel on Sunday 23rd. In addition, Maryon paid 9*d* 'for four mats for my master's pew' and 2*s* 1*d* 'unto Steven water-bearer for bearing of water'. *Le Menagier* notes that one or two water-carriers were needed for a wedding,[24] and the water would be required for cooking, washing by the guests, and the four men who did the dishes.

The high proportion of fish in these purchases is misleading, except insofar as it indicates that fish was not regarded only as a Lenten penance. The food that Maryon bought made up only part of the menus. Two further bills are from the butcher and the purveyor of poultry, probably Collett, their regular supplier. On Monday 17 May the poulterer provided one dozen chickens (18*d*), six rabbits (12*d*) and a dozen pigeons (12*d*).[25] Rabbits were a favoured delicacy at the time: in 1476 Elizabeth Stonor thanked her husband for a present of 'good venison and conies...the which is great dainties to have here in London'.[26] On Tuesday, 'to the wedding master Sely', the poulterer sent one dozen fat capons (10*s*), ten pheasants (11*s* 8*d*), four dozen and one chickens (5*s* 6*d*), 21 geese (10*s* 6*d*), one dozen herons (14*s*), two dozen and nine quails (11*s*), five dozen and two 'house pigeons' (10*s* 4*d*), one dozen 'rennys' (wrens, alas, for 2*s*), three dozen rabbits (6*s*), and sweet butter at 12*d*, one gallon of (salted?) butter at 2*s*, and four hundred (by the long hundred, so 480) eggs, which cost 2*s* 8*d*. It was reasonable enough for a poulterer to supply eggs, but the butter comes oddly into his province. Next day the remaining company made do with 18 chickens and five geese, but things looked up on Thursday, when there were another 21 chickens, four geese, 13 rabbits, a dozen pigeons, half-a-hundred eggs (4*d*), and two dishes of butter (2*d*). A dish of butter held about two pounds or something under a kilo. On Sunday 23rd there were two geese and six rabbits (the rabbits cost 10*d*). On 'Holy Serysday' – Thursday, Ascension Day – there

---

[23] A Thomas Morley was godson of Agnes Cely (P.C.C. 8 Logge). Robert Byfeld also left money for 'the exhibition and finding to school of Thomas Morley, the son of John Morley, my neighbour' (in St Dunstan-in-the-East): 5 Logge.
[24] *Le Menagier*, p. 187.
[25] File 20 nos. 33–4: 34 largely duplicates 33, but contains additional entries.
[26] *Stonor L.*, no. 172.

were one goose and six pigeons, and on Sunday 30 May again two geese and six rabbits.

One further and entirely unexpected item appears in the poulterer's bill. Along with the three dozen rabbits to be eaten at the wedding breakfast on Tuesday 18 May he supplied 'three quick [i.e. live] rabbits' for 6d. These, it would seem, were let loose among the guests as part of the festivities (a medieval equivalent of balloons?). There is a parallel in the celebrations for the marriage between Katherine of Aragon and Prince Arthur in 1501.[27] At one of the 'disguisings', held at Richmond, there was a pageant holding eight 'pleasant gallants' who cast out 'many quick conies, the which ran about the hall and made very great disports'. Subsequently eight disguised ladies loosed white doves and other birds, 'that flew about the hall, and great laughter and disport they made'.

George's bill for butcher's meat is damaged and undated, but probably covers Wednesday 19 May to Saturday 22 May.[28] Tuesday's items are almost wholly illegible. On Wednesday, to eke out the chickens and geese, there were delivered 'a hole surlyne of beffe price 16d', a quarter of 'wele' (veal) for 12d, a lamb (15d), four shoulders of mutton (16d) and three breasts of mutton (8d). On Thursday there was another sirloin of beef, this time at 10d, another quarter of veal, two breasts of veal (10d), four shoulders of mutton, four necks of mutton (12d), three breasts of mutton and 20 pounds (!) of suet at 20d. There was, of course, no meat eaten on Friday, but on Saturday there were two pieces of beef (6d), two rounds of beef (8d), two shoulders of mutton, two breasts of mutton (5d), two 'lynes' of veal (12d), one breast of veal (at 6d a breast must have contained much more of the best-quality meat than the modern term designates), and half a lamb (10d). The total butcher's bill for the four days came to £2 2s, compared with £5 10s 8d for the poultry etc. over nine days and 9s 1d for Maryon's fish. There is no mention in these accounts of the spices and herbs which must have been used in the cooking. Nor do they include much of the drink that must have been provided. Of the cost of all the foodstuffs mentioned as bought, nearly 87 percent went on meat, poultry and fish.

It would be interesting to know how many guests attended the festivities. Those celebrations superintended by 'maistre Helye' at a fourteenth-century French wedding consisted of a dinner for 40 people and a supper for 20.[29] They concluded with 'dancing, singing, wine and spicery and lighted torches'. But it looks as though George provided more than one day's entertainment for some guests. It is noteworthy that it was the groom, not the bride's family, who provided the celebrations.

[27] Leland, *Collectanea*, v (1770), p. 372. I owe this reference to the kindness of Lorraine Attreed.   [28] File 20 no. 39.   [29] *Le Menagier*, p. 184.

And did Margery, like a couple described in *Le Menagier*, continue to wear widow's weeds until the church ceremony had taken place?[30]

As a footnote to the wedding accounts, one might quote the words of a marriage vow made in 1456:

Here I take thee, Jennet, to my wedded wife. To hold and to have, at bed and at board, for fairer for lather, for better for warse, in sickness and in heal, to death us depart. And thereto I plight thee my troth.[31]

'Depart' became 'do part' when it lost its meaning of 'separate'.

In June 1484 George and his new wife and servants went into Essex on a visit to Richard and Anne, and Richard is recorded as paying a total of 6s for petty expenses, 3s for two kilderkins (32 gallons) of ale, 6s for six kilderkins (108 gallons) of beer, 2s 4d for three and a half bushels of wheat, 20d for a wether and 16d for boat-hire and other costs.[32]

When George went to Calais in September, Margery wrote him the one letter which survives from her, and which may well be in her own hand.[33] It would be pleasant to account for its present state, punctured with small holes, by supposing that George carried it around on his person while away.

Right reverent and worshipful sir, I recommend me unto you with reverence, as a spouse owe to do to her spouse, as heartily as I can, evermore desiring to hear of your welfare, the which Jesu preserve to his pleasure and your heart desire. And if it like you, sir, to send me a letter of your welfare, that I desire aldermost [most of all] to hear. And if it like you, sir, to hear of my health, at the making of this simple letter I was in good health of body, blessed be Jesu. As I trust that ye be, or I would be right sorry.

And I pray you, sir, that ye will be of good cheer, for all your goods are in safety at home, blessed be God. And as soon as ye may make an end of your business, I pray you to speed you home, for I think it a long season sin' ye depart[ed] from me, and I wot well I shall ne'er be merry to I see you again. And I pray you to send me word in haste what time that ye will be at home, if ye may.

Sir, letting you wit I sent you a heart of gold to a token by Nicklay Kerkebe. And ye shall receive in this letter a fetterlock of gold with a rib therein.[34] And I pray you, sir, to take it in worth at this time, for I knew not who should carry

---

[30] Ibid., p. 190.
[31] Cited by Stapleton, *Plumpton Correspondence*, p. lxxvii.
[32] File 10 fo. 23. The kilderkin of beer held 18 gallons, but that of ale only 16 gallons.
[33] *C.L.* 222.
[34] A tiny 'fetterlock of gold' was found in the fifteenth-century 'Fishpool hoard' near Newstead Abbey in 1966 and is now in the British Museum. It is a padlock with sliding rod attached with a chain, engraved with flowers and foliage and inscribed 'De Tout Mon Cuer': illustrated in Colin Platt, *Medieval England*, p. 184.

the letter, and therefore I sent none other thing with this letter. No more unto you at this time, but Jesu have you in his keeping.

By your wife, Margere Celye.

Nicholas Kyrkeby, 'late my servant', was mentioned in Edmund Rygon's will, together with John Crane and William Adlyngfeld, also 'late' servants. All three may have been former apprentices. The domestic servant Alice Andrew was also left a bequest.

If the three live rabbits at the wedding feast were intended as a symbol of fertility, they did their work well, for Margery was already pregnant by the time that she wrote in September. William Maryon sent George news of her on 20 September.

I understand by your writing that ye would that I should be comforter unto my mistress your wife. Sir, i' good faith I would that I could do unto her any comfort or service. But such as I may ye shall find it ready at all times, by the grace of God.

Sir, she is sad [preoccupied?] and not greatly merry, for that she is not so assisted ['is not so well provided with servants'] as she was wont to be. For now the nights beginneth to wax, and she is fearful for to go into any place in her house in the night alone. And she hath delivered Thomas her man [i.e. young boy servant] away unto his mother, and therefore she prayed you that ye would deliver you of another lad a' that side of the sea, for to be in his stead.

Sir, my mistress your wife recommend her heartily unto you, she informing you that she sent a letter unto you the last week by one Richard Carter of Derby. In the which letter she sent unto you a little lock of gold i-closed in the said letter, the which she trust to God ye have received. Also, sir, my mistress your wife prayed you heartily, as soon as ye have do your business at Calais that ye would come home, for she said she thought never so long for you as she do now.

Sir, as for your brother Richard, he departed fro London into Cotswold-ward the 13 day of September, I pray to God be his speed. No more unto you at this time, but my mistress your sister[in-law] and your brother Robert recommend them unto you.[35]

Poor loving Margery, with her stilted letter (entrusted in the end to one of her compatriots from Derby), her loneliness, her fear of the dark, and her evident fondness for the sort of ornaments which George was accused of using to help capture her initial affections. But she soon had plenty of babies to occupy her, and there seems to have been no real lack of servants about the house. In particular, one named Joan, who was 'a nigh kinswoman' to Margery, later claimed that she had been a 'long and true servant at will' to George and his wife.[36] But thanks to Maryon's kindly letter, we catch a living glimpse of one of those many wives who found themselves in strange surroundings and married to men whom

[35] *C.L.* 223. [36] C.1 368/86.

they barely knew. It is a useful corrective to the commercial terms previously employed in these pages as a reflection of the common fifteenth-century attitude to marriage.

It appears that George and Margery lived in one of the two houses that Richard Cely senior had owned in Mark Lane, London. This house was subsequently inherited (and sold) by their surviving son, also called George.[37] The property was situated on the west side of the street, immediately to the north of the boundary between the parishes of St Olave, Hart Street, and All Hallows, Barking. In 1474, when Richard acquired it from Thomas Babham, grocer, and his wife Margaret, its boundaries were: on the north a tenement belonging to the London Carthusians which was named the 'Unicorn' and in use as a brew- or ale-house, and on the south the tenement recently held by Robert Billingay, capper (who was one of the executors of Isabel Arnold), and before that by Thomas Steel, mercer.[38] This property, in All Hallows parish, was given to the Drapers' Company in 1540.[39] On the west in 1474 stood the tenement formerly of John Shelley, mercer, which then belonged to William Baron.[40] Next door to the 'Unicorn', going northwards, was a tenement which was demised in 1488 by William Smith, woolman and Margaret his wife, with Richard Muston, mercer and merchant of the Staple, to the lady Margaret Taylor, widow of Richard Wode of Coventry, grocer, and of Sir William Taylor, grocer, merchant of the Staple and alderman of London, together with Robert Tate, alderman, her son Richard Wode and Richard Cely junior.[41] Richard 'Awode' still held it in 1513.[42] Next to this, and so three doors up from George's house, Richard and Anne Cely had the house, originally belonging to Robert Arnold, which Richard Cely senior had almost certainly acquired from his brother-in-law Richard Andrew, heir of Isabel Arnold. In 1424 an enfeoffment by Robert and Isabel Arnold described this property as a tenement with house, shops, manses, cellars, solars, etc., between the tenement formerly of Eustace Glaston and now of Henry Whitebrede on the south, the tenement of William Eynsham on the north, and the tenement and garden of the abbot and convent of [St John's] Colchester on the west.[43] Richard Cely seems in fact to have rented his garden from the abbot,[44] and a further portion of the ground

---

[37] Hustings Roll 236 (11), 1513.

[38] Hustings Roll 204 (32). For Billingay and other executors of Isabel, including John Rede, woolman: E.R.O. D/DL T1 420. Isabel's co-executors of her husband's will were John Carpenter, common clerk of the city, and John Bacon, woolman.

[39] It was then 'a great messuage and 3 tenements adjoining, the northern boundary being a house of the late Sir John Dauncy': *Survey of London*, xv (pt 2, Parish of Allhallows, Barking, 1934), 21; Hustings Roll 243 (28).

[40] Hustings Roll 204 (32).

[41] Ibid., 218 (1).

[42] Ibid., 236 (11).

[43] Ibid., 153 (6).

[44] E.g. File 10 fo. 2v.

ran down beside the next house to the south. Both Cely properties adjoined the road to the east. On this side of Mark Lane there were perhaps only five or six houses which belonged to St Olave's parish. Hart Street, in which the church is situated, runs east off Mark Lane, and would have been not far north of Richard's house.

The advowson of St Olave's had passed from Isabel Arnold, widow of Robert Arnold, to Richard Cely senior and then to Richard junior.[45] Until the church was bombed in 1940 there were ceiling bosses in the nave which bore the Celys' merchant mark. It now contains no memorial to them, although the association with a later and more famous parishioner, Samuel Pepys, is well marked.

The customs house, adjoining the wool quays on the Thames, was a few hundred yards away, while Leadenhall, where stood the great beam for weighing wool when it came from the country, was reasonably convenient. The Celys lived almost literally in the shadow of the Tower of London, in an area of the city full of staplers and mercers, and probably well peopled also by the customs officials whose successors in the nineteenth century inhabited it along with all manner of merchants, warehousemen and tradespeople. Huge office blocks would now make the whole district unrecognizable to fifteenth- and early nineteenth-century denizens alike, though a *revenant* Christopher Rawson, brother of Anne Cely, could view his own brass in All Hallows.

Richard's house was typical of a fifteenth-century merchant's in having shops and cellars, used for storing wine and other domestic supplies, and perhaps also for wool and fell which was awaiting shipment. The miscellany of goods for which Richard Stoke made a bill of sale in 1475 were 'lying in his dwelling-place in the parish of All Hallows Barking'.[46] A hall, 'parlours' and chamber are mentioned in Richard Cely's accounts, and Richard, like George, set about modernizing his properties by installing new glazed windows. There would have been stables attached to the houses, and both Richard and George had gardens and yards in Mark Lane. Before his death George also acquired the reversion of two tenements and two gardens in Mincing Lane, which adjoined his brother Richard's Mark Lane property.[47] When his son George sold the Mark Lane garden to Sir John Dance in 1513 it was an oddly shaped piece of land, which extended north to south about 91½ feet on the west. It ran

[45] Newcourt, *Repertorium Ecclesiasticum Parochiale Londinense*, I, 511–12.
[46] *Cal. Plea and Mem. Rolls, 1458–82*, p. 89.
[47] Hustings Roll 217 (27), June 1488. Between tenements of the abbot of Colchester on the N., the tenement of James Dryland and various gardens formerly of John Crosse and John Croke on the S., the tenement formerly of R. Cely and others on the E. and Mincing Lane on the W.

47 feet along the house itself, as far as 'a corner post of a gable-end of the said tenement'.[48]

In the Lay Subsidy Roll of 1436 Isabel Arnold had been assessed on her properties in London and elsewhere at £26, which put her in a group of decidedly well-to-do London women.[49] Among her properties outside London were a number in Aveley, Essex, six miles north-west of Tilbury.[50] Of these, Bretts Place and another house in the village itself, next the poultry market, were acquired by Richard Andrew after her death, in 1446. In 1462 both properties passed to Richard Cely senior, who left them to his son Richard. Bretts Place, now known as Brett's Farm, still exists. The name is recorded from 1350, when it was held, perhaps, by a descendant of the John Le Brett who appears as early as 1206.[51] The house had already become a mere farmhouse, albeit a handsome one, by 1768, when Philip Morant described it:

The Manor of Bretts

The mansion house is about a mile north-west from the Church, within sight of the road leading from Aveley and Romford. It is large, encompassed with a wide moat of clear water: and though long since converted into a farm house, retains signs of its having been once a Gentleman's seat.... The lower story is of brick, with very ancient Gothic windows: the rest is of plaister, or rough cast.[52]

There is a more technical description of the house in the early 1920s, which shows that it had two storeys, with walls of plastered timber-framing and brick and slate-covered roofs.

It was built possibly in the 14th century and is of half H-shaped plan with the cross-wings extending towards the E[ast]. Alterations were made in the 16th and 17th centuries.... The reset 15th century entrance doorway has a four-centred head with trefoiled spandrels, with a square moulded frame.... The hall was divided into three bays and had curved braces to the roof-trusses forming two-centred arches.... The moat is incomplete, the n. and w. arms remain and are still filled with water, and on the e. side is a sunk wall of old brickwork which was possibly a retaining wall to the e. arm.[53]

Bretts and its surrounding land were protected from encroachment as part of a Green Belt scheme in 1936. Nothing, however, remains of George's place, Mallins, Little Thurrock, which was not far from Aveley

---

[48] Hustings Roll 236 (11). Dance or Dauncy paid £100 for the garden.
[49] Thrupp, *Merchant Class*, p. 378.
[50] E.R.O. D/DL T1 441, 444.
[51] P. H. Reaney, *The Place Names of Essex* (Cambridge, 1935), p. 122 n. 2.
[52] Philip Morant, *The History and Antiquities of the County of Essex* (1768), 1, 83.
[53] Royal Commission on the Ancient and Historical Monuments of England, *An Inventory of the Historical Monuments in Essex* (4 vols., 1916–23), IV, 6.

and a little distance north-west of Tilbury. The name of his second property, 'Sacokkys' is now preserved only in the minor name of 'Socketts Heath'.[54] In 1625 the family were still commemorated in 'Celyes Marshes' on the west side of Wennington creek in Wennington.[55]

Scattered and often uninformative references in the papers give indications of other Cely interests in land. At his death Richard senior owed 10s 'for farm of Fylpottys', and six months' rent of 'Kennington', amounting to £4 13s 4d, was due to John Swan of London.[56] Richard junior paid Swan a further 63s 4d 'for midsummer and Michaelmas farm of Kennington' in November 1482.[57] The Celys had tenants on their properties, such as a 'farmer' of Richard junior named Spenser Lighterman, to whom George once owed 41s 6d.[58] A Bartholomew Lighterman is also mentioned.[59] John Scot, who had provided Richard senior with 'fallow, corn, timber and boarding' in Essex, was paid £4 at the reckoning held at Bretts Place, and had further sums deducted from his house-rent.[60]

Like George, Richard junior extended his holdings of land. An obscure entry in the auditors' accounts notes that George lent 'old Thomas Cantlowe' 12s 'on certain evidences', i.e. deeds given as security. Richard must be charged with this sum, 'because he hath bought the land'.[61] In March 1484 Richard, with Robert Gower (rector of St Olave's) and William Maryon, acquired lands and tenements called Goseford's in Stifford and South Ockendon, and a three-acre meadow in South Ockendon between Southhouse Water on the east and a meadow called Crowescrofte on the west, formerly of John Gosford.[62] It was popularly reckoned that it took 15 years to get back an investment in land, or 'In 15 year, if thou wise be, Thou shalt again thy money see.'[63] This envisaged a return on investment of 6.666 percent per annum.

Richard paid for a variety of repairs or improvements to their different properties, including materials such as nail bought from Robert Eyryk for himself and George for 65s 8d and eight pounds of solder for 4s.[64]

---

[54] Reaney, *Place Names of Essex*, p. 173.
[55] E.R.O. D/DL T1 743.
[56] File 10 fo. 14. There were various payments due to shearmen, such as Harry Morton (14v).   [57] File 10 fo. 14v.   [58] File 10 fo. 20.
[59] Ibid. 'Lighterman' seems to be an occupational name, not a patronymic.
[60] File 10 fo. 14.
[61] File 10 fo. 3v. Thomas Cantlowe, gent., released and quitclaimed the properties in Aveley known as 'Courtes' and 'Bankes' to Richard Cely, Henry Cantlowe, mercer, and Geoffrey Cantlowe, gent., in July 1491: *C.C.R. 1485–1500*, no. 549.
[62] D/DL T1 507.
[63] 'Whoso will be ware in purchasing', Balliol MS. 354, fo. 100v.
[64] File 10 fos. 14v, 18v. William Mette, plumber, supplied another 4 lb of solder: fo. 16v.

In December 1482 Thomas Kid the carpenter received 26*s* for 'board, quartrerns and other stuff'.[65] There were several payments to plumbers for casting lead, and a dauber and his man were paid 2*s* 4*d*.[66] While his mother was alive Richard paid William Briggs for paving and paving-stone, and 'Bonke, carpenter, for undersetting the beam in the hall'.[67] 'Colby, glazier' was paid 21*s* 10*d* 'for setting up diverse windows in the parlours and chamber' (at Mark Lane?), and Robert Kevell had 4*s* 8*d* 'for lining of the place'.[68] John Winter of Havering-atte-Bower, Essex, supplied for Bretts Place 13,000 tiles, at 5*s* a load of 1,000, and 50 roof tiles, while two loads of lime cost 10*s*.[69] On George's behalf Richard paid William West, carpenter, 13*s* 4*d* in part payment for setting up a bay window and 'stulpys' (pillars).[70] He lent George 20*s* to buy carpets – for hanging on walls or covering benches or tables rather than floors – and generally paid workmen on George's properties in his brother's absence.[71] Luntley and another servant 'Lasse', had been sent to mend the hedge at Mallins in early April 1482,[72] and other hedgers were paid 20*s*, while a workman and a labourer had 11*s* 11*d*, and a plumber was paid 4*s* 'for solder delivered for George's gutters at his place' in January 1483.[73]

Another extracted account shows Richard providing for George lead at 13*s* 4*d* besides provisions such as 20 quarters of coals (five tons) at 10*s*, a quarter ox (5*s*), a wether (18*d*), a lamb (10*d*), a calf (2*s*), and a load of hay (5*s* for 18 hundredweight). A quarter of oats bought from 'Wharley' for George's horses cost 2*s* 4*d*.[74] Shoeing and 'pointing' the brothers' horses meant payments to Waterman, smith, of 15*s* 4*d*, and 11*s* 'for full payment of things had from him' over the 16 months up to September 1483. John Waterman, smith of Aveley, was a nominal feoffee of Bretts Place in 1478.[75] William Wren, shoesmith Without Aldgate received two sums of 8*s* 9*d* and 18*s* 8*d*.[76] Payments of 5*s* 4*d* to 'William Saddler' and of 8*s* 3*d* 'for leather to cover saddles' are found in an account for petty costs on wool.[77] Richard Pursevant, parker, was paid 3*s* 4*d*, probably for grazing a horse, and Edward Meryman, parker of St John's, received 30*s* at one point for the care of Richard's ambling horse.[78] There was also 'freight of a boar and a sack of hops' at 6*s* 8*d*, and beans for the boar and horses were bought for 2*s* 6*d*.[79]

It seems that Richard was in fact making most of these payments as

[65] File 10 fo. 25.
[66] Ibid.
[67] File 10 fo. 16.
[68] File 10 fo. 16v.
[69] *C.L.* 174; File 10 fo. 16.
[70] File 10 fo. 18.
[71] File 10 fos. 19v–20v.
[72] *C.L.* 150.
[73] File 10 fo. 20v.
[74] Richard Baldwin and Veere of Cranham were other suppliers: fo. 19.
[75] File 10 fo. 25; D/DL T1 480.
[76] File 10 fo. 25r–v.
[77] File 10 fo. 29.
[78] File 10 fos. 25, 1v.
[79] File 10 fo. 25.

executor of his father. Before George's marriage he paid for various items of apparel, not only for his brother but also for George's servants, beginning about March 1482 with 21s 4d paid to Peter Tailor 'for making of his brother George's gear, William Cely and Hankin's gear'.[80] At other times George had a long murry gown, 33 lamb skins bought from a skinner for 6s, and a pouch costing 11s 6d.[81] He and Richard each had a tippet-cloth of sarsenet costing 6s. Later, in 1485, they shared 11 yards of 'satin of Sypyrs' (crepe satin) at 10d a yard.[82] Richard also paid 20s for an expensive 'shapew' (hat) that George had.[83]

Of George's servants, Joyce had a gown and lining costing 4s 5d and a pair of shoes costing 6d.[84] Clays was made a 'kendal' gown, and Ambrose another gown and three pairs of shoes. The cordwainer also made a pair for 'Levyng' (Flemish Lieven?), Hankin had a cap costing 10d and 'pantofyll' (slippers or over-shoes) at 6d. All these servants were Netherlanders: in 1484 George paid to the subsidy collected from aliens in England 2s for each of three Flemish- or Dutch-born servants: Joisius Permanter (Joyce Parmenter), '— Hamerosse' (Ambrose) and 'Jacobus Van Wessyll', who must be Hankin.[85] Another Hankin, more often called 'Hayne', had left George's service by April 1482.[86] Later, a shoemaker's bill, undated but probably c. 1486, lists wares provided for some English members of George's household: Robert Wallys, Nicholas Best, 'Tom', John Adlington and John Collins.[87] These all had shoes costing 6d a pair, which was also the price of pattens and slippers 'for my mistress'. George himself had five pairs of slippers at 10d a pair, two pairs of shoes, and two 'pensons' (a sort of moccasin?) at 4d. Another pair of slippers and two pairs of George's 'boteaux' were resoled. Boteaux were distinct from 'boots': Sir William Stonor once paid 16d for a pair of long 'botews' to the knee, and 'the child of his chamber' was provided with a pair of boots costing 20d and a pair of 'botews' which cost only 8d.[88]

Besides the five Englishmen previously mentioned, John Copper occurs in George's domestic accounts of 1486–7. From the evidence, it looks as though George regularly employed four or five male servants in England, in addition to Joyce, who was more often at Calais until he drops from the papers after 1484, and to possible apprentices like Nicholas Best, who had been with him since at least November 1484.[89] Of women servants, Margaret and Jane (Joan) each make one incidental appearance in different accounts, and a nurse (a wet-nurse for one of the

[80] Ibid.
[82] File 10 fo. 25v.
[84] File 10 fo. 19v.
[86] *C.L.* 155.
[88] *Stonor L.*, no. 234.

[81] File 10 fos. 18v, 20v.
[83] File 10 fo. 19.
[85] S.P. 46/123 fo. 7.
[87] File 16 fo. 25.
[89] File 10 fo. 1.

children) received 6s 8d at Easter 1488.[90] There is still less information about Richard's household. After their mother's death and George's marriage John Luntley seems to have stayed on in Richard's employment, but he may not have lived in: one William Mylner of Eryth was paid 26s 8d for 'Luntley's farm'.[91] Other servants mentioned are John King and John Poynton, to whom 'the Monday in Whitsun week [1485]' George delivered £30 'in his lap to bear to...Richard Cely when he brought the empty bags to the said George Cely'.[92] Giles Beckingham was an apprentice of Richard's, doing business and writing accounts for him as Nicholas Best, John Speryng and William Rogers did for George.[93] Nicholas Best and John Roberts, perhaps another apprentice of Richard's, were sent to the Cotswolds to pack wool in 1486 or 1487.[94] William Aldridge, who had been left money by Richard senior towards his marriage, served Richard and George as purser for a time when they bought the ship *Margaret Cely*.

George made a number of contributions to joint household and other expenses in 1482–4. Besides 10s towards costs of his mother's month mind and 2s 6d 'spent in Kent to meet master Rasson [Richard Rawson, Anne Cely's father] to 'an brought him to Essex' in 1483, George bought 'upon the common charge' two hoop nets (16d), nine purse nets (4d), 3d worth of fish-hooks and a long line, 3 lb of gunpowder (2s 2d), 13 board-bolts, 12 arrows, bow strings and two dozen trenchers (wooden platters), and paid 3d 'for the heading of our shafts'.[95] Since it was on this occasion that Anne Cely held an old noble of George's as stake in a wager, it may have been for a bet on their comparative skill at shooting or fishing. At the top of this account there is a later addition by George, 'item, the 5th day of August I received of him that keepeth the lions, for wood – 20s'. Presumably this was the keeper of the lions in the Tower.

Between Friday 29 August and at least 15 September 1483 George contributed a total of 27s 8½d to Richard's household expenses, including about 1s 6½d for fish, 3s 5d 'to the butchery', 5d for eggs and butter, some purchased at Leadenhall, 1s 1d for bread, and about 2d for ale, 1d for soap and 10d for prunes and currants.[96] He also paid 1d 'to a man to beat down the walnuts'. These handsome and productive trees must have been favourites with fifteenth-century landholders. Was this particular tree in fact the one which appears in a corner of one Mark Lane garden in the 'Copperplate' map made about 1558?[97]

[90] File 20 no. 11 fo. iv.
[91] File 20 no. 25 (1487); File 10 fo. 14v.
[92] File 10 fo. 1.
[93] File 10 fo. 22v.
[94] File 10 fos. 9v, 35; File 16 fo. 37.
[95] File 20 no. 36.
[96] File 20 no. 7.
[97] Harry Margary and Guildhall Library, *A Collection of Early Maps of London, 1553–1667* (Lympne Castle, Kent, 1981).

Besides these payments, George 'took my sister Anne when I yeed to Aveley – 3s 4d', and gave her 5s on 15 September and 6s 8d for household purposes when he was sick. He also paid 14d for a coat-cloth for Richard Godyng, perhaps one of the servants. To Richard Cely, George paid £12 'when [Richard] rode to a fair' on 2 May 1484, £6 'when he yeed to Northfleet to buy beasts', and 50s 'when he rode to Windsor'.[98]

It would seem that George spent at least part of his time in his brother's household before he himself married. Richard and Anne probably shared the Mark Lane house with Richard's widowed mother between the time of their marriage and Agnes's death, so that they lived very briefly as an extended family. Later Richard was given allowance by the Chancery auditors for his 'costs of household' between his father's death in January 1482 and George's marriage in May 1484.[99] Excluding George's contributions and specific payments for Agnes or Robert, the total came to £138 7s 9½d over a period of 117 weeks, or £1 3s 8d per week on average. This is less than the £1 5s 7d to £1 18s per week which Sylvia Thrupp found allowed by well-to-do London merchants for total household expenses,[100] but these costs of Richard's do not include expenditure on clothing, rent-charges, or wages beyond a payment of 5s to 'Watkin', probably a falconer. There are one or two items such as a 'change of vessel' from a pewterer and the beadle's payment at Christmas, but basically purchases consisted of food, drink, firing and hay for the horses. Two dinners for important guests are specifically mentioned.

If the entries in the auditors' accounts are reliable, 33 percent of Richard's provisions bills was expended on drink: 8s worth per week. There is no suggestion at all that the Celys brewed their own ale or beer. In the household of a variable number of adults, possibly between 12 and 14 at most periods, consumption must have run to a weekly 72 gallons of beer, 21 gallons of ale and at least 2½ gallons of wine. Ale and beer together must then have been drunk at the average rate of about 13 gallons a day. This does not include the 233.5 gallons of ale bought for Agnes Celys' burial and month mind. The *Margaret Cely*'s complement each had 5½ pints (0.7 gallons) per day, and almsmen of Henry VII were allowed a ration of two pints (0.25 gallons) each at dinner.[101]

Bought usually in kilderkins of 18 imperial gallons, the beer cost on average 0.68d per gallon, but on one occasion a barrel (36 gallons) of double beer cost 3s. Ale was apparently regarded as a better-class drink, and was more expensive than beer. Bought by the barrel, this time of

---

[98] File 10 fo. 1; File 20 no. 8.
[99] File 10 fos. 22–4.
[100] Thrupp, *Merchant Class*, p. 143 and n. 130.
[101] *C.C.R. 1500–1509*, no. 390.

32 gallons, the kilderkin of 16 gallons or the firkin of eight gallons, ale usually cost 1.125*d* per gallon for so-called 'three-halfpenny ale', while 'good ale' cost about 1.6*d* per gallon. For wine, there is one entry of malvoisie (malmsey) costing 29*s* 2*d*, and five hogsheads of wine were bought at an average price of 33*s* each, making about 6*d* for the wine-gallon, which was less than imperial measure. Of the total drink-bill for the period, Richard spent 50.3 percent on beer, 29.4 percent on ale and 20.3 percent on wine.[102]

The bakers and brewers who supplied Henry VII's almsmen were to be paid within 15 days at the furthest, but the well-off householders frequently ran up much longer credit for their supplies. In July 1478 Sir William Stonor's baker and ale-brewer (who was owed £5 odd) were calling daily for money from him, and his wife was similarly plagued by 'the beer-wife' and others in October.[103] The Celys were sometimes well in arrears with the accounts with brewers, while a fragment of a domestic account drawn up by Richard senior notes 'two parcels not paid nor summed – the brewer and tailor'.[104] On 20 July 1483 Thomas Stabylyon (alias Cabylian) goodman of the 'Dollffyn', was paid £6 10*s* for nine barrels and one firkin good ale and 24 barrels of three-halfpenny ale (making 1,064 gallons), previously supplied.[105] On Christmas Eve 1483 Paul Godfrey's wife was paid £10 5*s* for 200 kilderkins of beer (3,600 gallons) used during the preceding 12 months, and in January 1485 there was a further payment of £4 to 'Paul Godfrey's wife, beer-brewer, for beer spent from Christmas anno '83 to the 4th day in May in anno '84', being 80 kilderkins (1,440 gallons).[106] Paul Godfrey, alias 'Poll beer-brewer', was one of those Dutchmen who had brought their specialized skill to England.[107] The beer bought from his wife alone during 1483 would amount to an average of 9.86 gallons a day.

Possibly the baker's bill had also run up when Thomas Baker was paid 27*s* 5*d* in December 1483. On the other hand, the bill from 'Kollett Poulterer' for 45*s* 1*d* may not have covered a long period if it included some of his higher-priced items, which could be a major component in a dinner like that given for Avery Cornburgh, which cost 10*s*. One expensive purchase about this time was half a pound of saffron for 8*s*. The price reflects the tiny amount that can be harvested from one acre of bulbs, but as a few stamens are sufficient to colour a dish, such an amount as ½ lb could last the housewife a long time. Its popularity is

---

[102] The proportions (by price) are very similar to those in a dinner for barons of the Exchequer in 1587: table 7.
[103] *Stonor L.*, nos. 222, 229. [104] File 16 fo. 45.
[105] File 10 fo. 22v. [106] File 10 fos. 22v, 23.
[107] Paul Godfrey, beer-brewer, of the Duchy of Holland, obtained letters of denization c. 1484: P.R.O. C.1 59/44; *M.S. Harleian 433*, I, 285.

attested by the frequency with which it was bought for the priests of Munden's chantry, Bridport.[108]

Although a London 'milk-wife' was paid 18*d* for products for the year's mind of Richard Cely,[109] most of the dairy products used in the household of his son Richard were 'delivered out of [Richard's] herdwicks and farms'.[110] Purchases of farm milk, butter, cheese, cream and curds from 24 February to 16 May 1483 came to 5*s* 2*d* (none would have been used in Lent during that period). 'Milk, butter and cheese spent here at London from the 9th day in June till the 28th day in October' 1483 came to 23*s* 7½*d*. There were some separate purchases of cheese: a wey of cheese (336 lb by Essex measure) cost 10*s* 8*d*, and 'a draught of cheese and a cheese' cost 5*s*. Richard's herd also furnished some meat: a cow for 6*s*, six lambs against Shrovetide at 6*s*, five lambs against Easter and after, at 6*s* 5*d*, which were accompanied by ten dishes of butter at 20*d*. Among miscellaneous items in Richard's accounts are 3*s* 4*d* to clerks and women on their church holy day (29 July), and 6*s* 2*d* 'given [at] Christmas in offering money to bakers, brewers and other' as what was later called a 'Christmas box'. In the Celys' case it perhaps served as a sweetener to tradesmen kept waiting all year for their dues. The beadle got 8*d* at Christmas.

To put beside Richard's domestic costs, we have five detailed accounts for part of George's household expenditure, made at different periods, apparently between 1486 and 1488. These are not directly comparable: they were written by Nicholas Best, chiefly at times when George was away from home, they cover periods of varying and mostly indeterminate length, and they do not give complete costs, omitting, for instance, bulk supplies of ale, beer or grain, wages, and George's own expenses. Two accounts cover an ascertainable period, one for approximately 11 weeks between 30 March and 12 June, and the other for four weeks from 23 September 1487.[111] Mean expenditure in the one was 7.4*s* and in the other 8*s* per week. It is very difficult to estimate the likely total of George's domestic expenditure from these figures, because some provisions were certainly bought by people other than Nicholas, and when he made trips to London, the only costs recorded are his own. Any addition made for bread, ale and beer must be conjectural. When such an addition is made a figure of 10*s* weekly appears possible.[112] This would be for a household

[108] K. L. Wood-Legh, ed., *A Small Household of the Fifteenth Century* (Manchester, 1956).
[109] File 10 fo. 14v.
[110] File 10 fo. 23v.
[111] File 16 fo. 32; File 14 fos. 61–2.
[112] The figure still excludes wages, rent-charges, purchases abroad (e.g. clothing), fodder and shoeing of horses, further building costs, and so on.

which included at least six adults and adolescent servants and between one and three young children. The figure of 10s can be compared with amounts quoted by Thrupp: a maximum of 6s 8d per week allowed for food, drink and hire for a young kinswoman and five servants by William Laurence, grocer, in 1476, and a weekly expenditure of 13s 7d by the widow of a mercer who had been worth nearly £1,000 in 1464. Her household contained seven children and three servants.[113]

Nicholas Best's accounts of expenditure for his master's household require some explanation before further analysis is attempted. Some of them evidently refer to residence at Mallins, while others may have been compiled in London. The first, apparently relating to September–December 1486, is in File 16 fos. 30 and 34–7. George was abroad for most of the time, but Best continued to keep the account for a period after his return on 3 December. Fos. 36–7 are a duplicate copy of the other three, apparently prepared for George, who appended a later note of other payments on 31 August 1487. Fo. 30 seems to be addressed to Margery Cely: 'when I came to you...', which in fo. 36 becomes 'when I came to my mistress'. Fo. 36, on the other hand, has an item 'delivered to your mastership'. The cataloguer in the Public Record Office, not noticing the duplication, separated fo. 30 from fos. 36–7. Fos. 31 and 32–3 are two separate accounts, probably of 1488.

File 14 fos. 61–2 is headed in Margery's name but Nicholas Best's hand, 'Received of my husband when he departed to Calais – £4'. It covers 22 September to 18 October. An old sheet of paper was utilized, which had been inscribed 'Charge de me George Cely in anno l[x]xix'. The real date of the account seems to be 1487. Judging by the days on which meat was purchased, which were presumably not Fridays, appropriate years would be 1485 and 1487, and a reference to Margery's two children rules out 1485.[114] File 14 fo. 41 is a short and incomplete account from February 1488. File 16 fos. 32–3 covers ten weeks five days between 30 March and 12 June, apparently of 1488, when Easter fell on 6 April, because the accountant bought meat at some date shortly after 2 April. File 16 fo. 31 carries no evidence of date of any sort, except that purchases of strawberries and peas suggest the months of June or July. It has also been hypothetically assigned to 1488.

Table 4 shows the proportion of expenditure on various commodities and services in Best's accounts. While amounts are shown as percentages

[113] Thrupp, *Merchant Class*, p. 143 and n.
[114] It is commonly stated that three days in every week were strictly observed as fish-days. But George's household kept only Friday as a day of abstinence, and 'flesh' was bought for the crew of the *Margaret Cely* on Wednesdays and Saturdays when she was discharging at London in Jan.–Feb. 1488 (File 14 fo. 57r and v). Dispensations may have been quite general.

Table 4. *Distribution of outlay on certain items in domestic accounts*

	1486 Sept.– Dec. %	1487 22 Sept.– 18 Oct. %	1488 Feb.– March %	1488 April– June %	?1488 c. July %	Average %
Building materials	19.8	5.0	14.2	18.4[a]	0.3	11.5
Clothing	24.2	35.6	22.7	7.3	0	18.0
Mending and shaving	4.9	4.7	3.3	1.2	3.3	3.5
Firing[b]	0.5	0	0	25.8	4.6	6.2
Soap and candle	1.4	3.2	0	0	4.9	1.9
Local travel[c]	4.4	1.3	0.8	0.2	14.5	4.2
Meat	4.5[d]	26.0[e]	6.5	7.7	14.1	11.8
Poultry[f]	5.4	1.1	0	2.8	31.4	8.1
Fish	13.7	9.1	20.7	16.3	2.6	12.5
Spices, etc.[g]	4.6	0	0.8	1.1	1.2	1.5
Fruit and vegetables[h]	3.3	0	0.8	0.5	4.1	1.7
Dairy and eggs	2.9	3.2	2.4	1.1	2.0	2.3
Drink[i]	3.3	2.0	16.4	8.6	5.3	7.1
Other[j]	7.1	8.8	11.4	9.0	11.7	9.6
100% =	£2.72	£1.60	£0.50	£3.98	£1.26	£2.01

[a] Includes payment to mason.
[b] Coal and billet, also baking bread.
[c] Includes meals away.
[d] Includes 2% for hawk's meat.
[e] Includes 0.9% for hawk.
[f] Including rabbits.
[g] Including salt, honey, vinegar.
[h] Including dried fruit and almonds.
[i] Predominantly wine.
[j] Excludes exceptional large payments, e.g. to midwife.

of the whole, they must not be taken to represent the true percentage of total household expenditure, because of the missing items. Neither can most of the totals be reduced to expenditure per week. The five accounts are treated separately in order to show the variations which occur. They relate only to certain seasons of the year (seven particular months in all), and the last column, averaging amounts over the five, bears obvious limitations as an indication of usual expenditure.

The greatest cost in these accounts was for food and drink, which made up 45 percent of averaged expenditure. As noted, that figure does not include the cost of the daily beer, ale and bread. The particular seasonal distribution of the accounts may explain the fact that on average rather more was spent on fish than on butcher's meat. Really large purchases of poultry and other birds were reserved for special occasions such as weddings. If George and Margery commonly ate quails, pigeons or mallards they were caught locally and not bought. They did however buy rabbits, at prices between 2*d* and 4*d*, and Best made single purchases of 'small birds' for 1*d*, a goose (4*d*), seven chickens for 7*d*, a hen (5*d*), an unstated quantity of 'wild fowl', also for 5*d*, and two green geese at 6*d* each. One day's purchases for an unusually lavish meal consisted of a 'seynette' (cygnet) at 4*s*, two heronceaus for 2*s* 10*d*, four rabbits (9*d*), and two bottles of wine for 11*d*.

Unusual items of meat were, on single occasions, a sausage at 1*d* and 'a pasty of mutton and a pie' for 2*d*. Bacon, if eaten, must have been home-produced: a pig, at 5*d* or 5½*d*, was sometimes bought. Fish included lampreys, at 5*d* or 6*d* each (four were bought on one occasion), a cade of sprats (1,200) at 16*d*, 'flowders' (flounder) at 1*d*, a pike and two eels for 2*s* (eels were bought quite often), and a gurnard. Oysters and 'ossey' wine together cost 1*d* for one meal. Dietary experts recommended the combination of shell-fish and a 'hot' wine such as ossey, which was thought to counteract the 'cold' quality of oysters. Elizabeth Stonor paid 4*d* for 200 oysters in March 1479.[115] There are few specific items of preserved fish in Best's accounts – ling, two stockfish and two salt fishes were bought on the same day in May 1488. Herring were purchased for ½*d* or 1*d* a time.

In November 1486 Best twice paid 1*d* for pears, and another time 3½*d* for 'wardens' (cooking pears), perhaps to be stewed in the ½*d* worth of honey bought at the same time. One summer there were two purchases of 'peascods', i.e. green garden peas, and strawberries (together costing 3½*d* or 4*d*), and one of peascods alone, for 1*d*. Such peas may have been cooked in the pod, which is how they were sold from street barrows in nineteenth-century London. Apples were bought for 1*d* in February–March 1488. In 1486 Nicholas paid 1½*d* for 'butter and parsnip roots', a vegetable sometimes supposed to have been introduced much later into England. Garlic was bought in season, for 1*d* or ½*d* a time (eight 'bunches' cost Elizabeth Stonor 2*s*), and there was one purchase of 'seeds' unspecified for 5*d*. No cabbage, leeks or onions are mentioned. They were probably home-grown, like walnuts. Dried fruit and nuts included 'small raisins' at 2½*d* per lb, several purchases of ordinary raisins and figs (1*d* per lb), and once 1 lb of almonds for 4*d*.

[115] *Stonor L.*, no. 233.

There are not many references to spices, apart from small quantities of pepper and mustard, and one pennyworth of cinnamon, but one pound of pepper was bought for 17*d* in 1486, and so was 10*d* worth of cloves and mace. Another half pound of pepper cost 9*d* in 1488. A peck of white salt at 3½*d* is the only reference to that commodity, and no sugar was bought locally. There are occasional purchases of soap: 7 lb for 5½*d* in one account. Eggs, butter and milk were bought regularly outside Lent. The absence of cheese does not mean that it was not eaten. Rather it would be bought in bulk if not made at home. Similarly, Nicholas bought little grain, which may have been supplied from the farms, just as hay was. A payment of 19*s* to Nicholas Frend of Essex for corn in October 1487 has been omitted from the table, because this may have been bought for export. In February 1488, 2*d* was twice spent, once 'for carrying up of wheat' and once 'for carrying down of rye', while 'carrying up of oats' cost 2½*d*. Payments of 3*d* to the miller indicate the grinding of grain supplies for household use. On a single occasion, in 1486, the baking of bread at 1*d* occurs. Sometimes Best enters 1*d* 'for milk and wheytt', 'whyed' or 'whyth'. He does not differentiate between the spellings for 'wheat' and 'white' and the invariable association with milk suggests (but does not prove) that he meant 'white-meat', the curd which appears in Richard's accounts. 1½*d* spent on oatmeal appears once. Horse-bread usually cost 1*d* a time, but once 3*d* was paid 'for master Prout's horse'.

Expenditure on wine was sometimes heavy, and particularly large quantities of ossey were bought in February–June 1488, especially during Lent. Did the wealthy, one wonders, regularly relieve the fast in this way? In October 1486 a pint of ossey cost 1½*d* and a bottle 4½*d*. A pint of 'wine' was also 1½*d*, a quart 2½*d*, and a pottle 5*d*. In April–June 1488 there were purchases of red wine and claret wine (a quart of claret cost 2*d*), a bowl (holding half-a-bottle?) of malvoisie at 1½*d*, and bottles were filled with 'bastard' (a sweet wine, such as muscadel) at 8*d*, with 'sweet wine' at 5*d*, and with 'wine' at 14½*d* or 15*d* for two bottles.

Naturally, when George's household ate *en famille* they did not have the elaborate service of many courses and dishes so lovingly related in contemporary descriptions of banquets. Nor, if Best's purchases accurately reflect their diet, was their food usually prepared with the variety of exotic spices and colouring matter which feature prominently in recipe collections of the period. It cannot be known whether Margery Cely herself cooked the meals.

For heating and cooking a total of 1,500 billet is mentioned, with carriage at 7½*d*. Sixteen quarters (four tons) of coals in May 1488 cost 6*s*, and a further load (5 tons?) cost 9*s*. There were periodic purchases of candle, including 'watching candle' at 1½*d* per lb. Another recurrent expense was the replacement of the rushes used as disposable floor-covering. In April–June 1488 two burdens of fresh rushes cost 3½d, but carrying away the old ones cost 4d.

Building materials included 500 tiles (2s 2d) and 10 roof tiles (5d), 500 'harth-lates' (laths of heart-wood, for 2s 3d), 2,000 sprigs (12d) and half a bushel of plaster of Paris (8d). Nail – counted by six-score to the hundred – included one thousand rove-nail for 9d,[116] three hundred 'threepenny' nail for 7½d, one hundred fourpenny for 3d, and one hundred fivepenny for 4d. (Designations were purely conventional, and by 1573 'sixpenny nail' sold in fact for 3½d per hundred.)[117] One account includes 13s 4d paid to a mason.

Miscellaneous household objects bought included a bast rope (2½d), brooms (½d), a pair of bellows (4d), a urinal (2d), a censer (5s), six glasses (7½d), four cruses (2d), a pair of 'garnedys' (hinges) for 1d, and wool oil at 2d for a pint. 'Scouring oil' was also bought. George's hawks required bells (2d) and a hawking hook (12½d), besides special purchases of meat in some accounts, for instance in 1486 a piece of beef for 1d or half an ox heart for 1d. No special provision was made for dogs, although George had bought a chain for his dog at Bruges in 1486.[118] The eighteen royal hawks of Richard III in the mews near Charing Cross were each allowed 1d a day for meat, while four hounds each had a daily allowance of 4d.[119] Best's purchases of ½ lb of 'trette' at 7½d on 20 May 1488 and another pennyworth of 'tretth' on 12 June may refer to ointment for use as a poultice, perhaps for treating animals.[120] The cost is too high for the items in question to be 'thread' (which he elsewhere spells 'threyd') or 'treat' in the sense of fine flour or bread. Trete, entrait or emplastrum was used to make 'cere-cloth' and consisted of a mixture of wax, rosin, animal fat or oil and various medicinal herbs, to be heated and spread on a dressing for wounds, bruises, etc. There were numerous recipes, including several for a famous plaster called 'Gratia Dei'.[121]

The barber was paid 4d from time to time for shaving Nicholas himself, and other frequent payments were made for clouting shoes (for instance, 'setting on of my heel clouts – 1d'), and for mending hose or doublets for Nicholas and John Collins. Nicholas once entered a charge of 1d 'for drying of my mattress couchers' (i.e. covers). He paid for a

[116] Rove-nails were clinched by a rove or rivet.
[117] Mary Prior, 'The Accounts of Thomas West of Wallingford: A 16th-century Trader on the Thames', *Oxoniensia*, XLVI (1981), 80.
[118] File 13 fo. 27.
[119] *MS. Harleian 433*, I, 158.
[120] File 16 fos. 32v, 33.
[121] E.g. Warren R. Dawson, ed., *A Leechbook or Collection of Medical Recipes of the Fifteenth Century* (1934), pp. 105–18, 270–3, 284–9.

few items of clothing, besides purchases of cloth such as half a piece of Cyprus at 3s, or 2¾ yards of 'blakelyng' for 2s 8d. 'Two red corses powdered', i.e. girdles sprinkled with ornamentation in the form of spangles or fur, were bought for 2s 8d in 1486, and Nicholas had two shirts for himself at 2s 4d, while 'Thomas' had hose and a cap for 2s 5d. In October 1487 gowns were made for 'John', Margery Cely and her two sons, Richard and Avery, then aged about two years eight months and perhaps eighteen months. Margery herself added a note to this account: 'for furring of the children's gowns – 8d. Item, for furring of two gowns for myself – 2s'. Possibly the toddlers' gowns were lined with lamb, because there is another item of 12d paid to the tawer for tawing white lambskins. In November 1486 Best had accounted for ½d 'delivered to master Richard your son', who must then have been under two. On another occasion he lent Margery ½d from the house-keeping money.

Also about 2 November 1486 2d was 'delivered to John Clerk for the ringers'. The reason is not stated, and church bells might be rung on all sorts of occasions, including births and funerals and moments of national rejoicing.[122] It was also widely held that the practice would avert damage during a thunderstorm. The vicar of West Thurrock was once paid 12d, and on September 1487 the clerk at church was paid 12d 'at my churching', and Margery made an offering of 5d.[123] This churching was the service of thanksgiving after the birth of her third child, George, the one who eventually survived his four brothers. The midwife had been paid 6s 8d and Thomas Fengraffe's wife 6s. Possibly a fourth birth is reflected in the payment recorded in the undated account in File 16 fo. 31 for Nicholas Best's boat-hire up to London with Fengraffe and his wife. In this case, John Cely was perhaps born in the summer of 1488. The fifth child, Edmund, was born after George's death in June 1489.

When the family were in Essex, Nicholas made frequent trips up to London, and expenses include the necessary payments to wherry-men and boatmen and for barge-hire. 'Roger the boatman of Grays' was paid 1d in 1486, for example, and boat-hire down to Purfleet would also cost 1d. 'Boat' was a word which gave Nicholas great difficulty, as he could not fix on one way of spelling it for long. He started with 'bod', changed to 'botth' in the copy of his account that was made for George and kept that in the next three accounts, but switched to 'botte' in File 16 fo. 31. In 1488–9 when he went to Bordeaux he changed back to 'bot(t)h'.[124] Extra horses were sometimes hired when servants were sent on errands

---

[122] It may, of course, have been delayed payment towards the celebrations for the birth of Prince Arthur on 19 Sept.
[123] These items were clearly written at Margery's dictation.
[124] File 14 fos. 49–58.

to places like 'Crowhome'. When Nicholas was in London his meals usually cost 1*d*, whether for breakfast, dinner or supper, and he paid ½*d* for a bed. One dinner at Woolwich cost him 2*d* in 1486.

It will be seen from many of the items in the foregoing description that the Celys' households, even when resident in the country, failed to live the self-sufficient life so often presented as typical of the pre-industrial world. A merchant's wife and maid-servants were clearly not expected to mend hose, to make their own clothes, their butter or the household soap or to brew their own ale, nor did the men cut and cart rushes or firewood, shave themselves, mend their shoes or catch eels. Even the hawks were dependent on others for some of their sustenance.

Besides the shoemaker's bill previously referred to, the papers contain three accounts from tradesmen in England, all undated. The first, which is torn on the right-hand side, runs:

Master George Cely

Memorandum. For dressing of a rostet [russet] gown of my [mistress?]
Item, for the dressing of a russet gown of my master the same time...
Item, for the dressing of a murry gown for Jane your maid...
Item, for dressing of a russet gown of Nicholas your man...
Item, for the dry scouring of a scarlet gown and scarlet hose...
Item, for the dressing of a green gown and dying the...
    Sum total – 4*s* 6*d*.[125]

The reference to dry-cleaning strikes a rather modern note, and in fact 'dry-scouring' is not in the *Oxford English Dictionary*.

A tailor's bill runs:

Master Jorge Sely

Item, for making of a black riding gown for yourself	.	.	.	.	10*d*
Item, for black lining to that same gown .	.	.	.	.	20*d*
Item, for making of a riding gown for John Adlington	.	.	.	8*d*
Item, for making of two black satin stomachers and fustian	.	.	8*d*[126]

A wax-chandler's is still shorter:

Item, delivered to master Jorge Sele at Candlemas: a taper of half a pound and three penny tapers and halfpenny candle, two farthing candles. Sum – 8½*d*.[127]

In addition to these, and to Nicholas Best's accounts, there is a note of expenditure, written by John Speryng, which apparently relates to hay-making in Essex in 1485 or 1486.

Item, for beer .	.	.	.	.	.	.	.	.	.	3*d*
Item, for 3 men beside Wells .	.	.	.	.	.	.	.	10*d*

[125] File 15 fo. 57.   [126] File 16 fo. 27.   [127] File 16 fo. 26.

Item, for 2 women 4*d*
Item, on Wednesday for bread. 2*d*
Item, for butter 1*d*
Item, for beer 2*d*
Item, for eggs 1*d*
Item, for beans 1*d*
Item, for a woman 2*d*
Item, on Thursday for bread 2*d*
Item, for flesh 6*d*
Item, for beer 4*d*
Item, for carrying of the hay 2*s* 10*d*
Item, for a man 3*d*
[In George Cely's hand: Sum – 10*s* 6*d*] .
Item, tithe 2*s*
Item, porycolis [borecole?] . . . . 4½*d*.[128]

It is not clear how many people were involved in the hay-making: probably the whole household turned out in addition to the extra hands. The beer would have amounted to about 13½ gallons. If 'porycoles' means cabbage or some other kind of brassica there were more vegetables bought than usual.

George himself left a number of accounts in connection with his building and farming activities, including miscellaneous notes about the payment of 20*d* to his gardener and 10*d* to the ploughman, 20*s* 'for brick to Ellis', and 19*s* 8½*d* paid 'for 23½ acres, 9½*d* the acre, nets and all'.[129] Were the nets for trapping fish, hares, or birds such as the quail for which he shipped a cage to England in 1486?[130] In 1484 he purchased 3⅛ yards of chalk, for top-dressing land, at 10*s* the yard.[131] In February 1487 he bought from Edward Downs 1,300 elm boards at 16*d* per hundred plus carriage, and paid Clark for the carriages of seven loads of piles.[132] John Dauber was employed at Mallins for 13 days at a total of 5*s* 5*d*, and for three further days at a total of 12*d*, while his man got 3*d* per day. On 10 March 1487 there were payments to Whethe (White?), John Carpenter, Robin Ilott and John Dogett, and Thomas Bettys was lent 12*d*. Thornborow was paid 15*d* for five days at tilling and 8*d* for dyking at 'Sawcokys' (Socketts), and Walker and his fellow were paid 10*s* for 12 days 'to make my watering'.[133] Also in 1487 George had 64 feet of glass put in at Mallins at a cost of 20*s* 8*d*, and one foot (costing 4*d*) at Stratford.[134]

More payments in 1488 were 2*s* 2*d* for two dressing knives and two

[128] File 20 no. 43.   [129] *C.L.* 229.
[130] File 20 no. 18.   [131] File 20 no. 8.
[132] File 13 fo. 24.   [133] File 16 fo. 38.
[134] File 16 fos. 38–9.

small knives, 6*d* for ten irons for 'piercers' (?), and 2*s* 4*d* for stock-cards for carding wool.[135] A man named Laurence was paid for carrying dung and gravel for 16 days (7*s* 2*d*), mowing brakes for twelve days (8*d*), mowing and making 'my alers gresse' (grassing alleys, for 4*s*), and five days' labour in harvest (20*d*). George's 'wood-maker' was paid a total of 15*s* on four occasions, and his reedman was 'taken upon reckoning' 16*s* 8*d* (the reed was presumably for thatching). 'Sherwell' was paid 6*s* for hay. In February 1488 George noted 'bought by me of old Wade of Bercotts, four parcels of wood wh[ich] was his father's, standing in hedgerows – price 23*s* 4*d*. Item, hereof I paid him on Saint "Volantyns" Day – 13*s* 4*d*.'[136] The only reference to livestock is a further purchase of sheep: 51 ewes bought from Thomas Chetter, drover, for £4 5*s*.[137] George made up the money from £2 received from Richard on 31 January 'of Nyghtyngale's money', £2 in new groats from William Maryon, and 6*s* 8*d* 'of my wife'. The drover was also asked to obtain payment of £6 owed to George by John Smith of Wrotham (Kent) and Combar or Tom Bar, tailor. The obligation was entrusted to him in the presence of Margery Cely and another witness, 'Roger, brother to Coke, cooper, dwelling in the same parish that Chetter dwells' and so good security for him.

George also had a mill, let for two years from 24 June 1485 to one Canon, apparently at 6*s* a week.[138] This may have been at Stratford, where William Welles, miller, rented a house from George in 1487.[139] In that year George acquired six millstones, valued at £24, partly paid for with some Gascon wine.[140] He also had a quarter share in 'Four Miln Lock' (Bromley), for repairs to which in December 1486 he had to contribute.[141] They took 29 feet of timber, four staples, spikings, a new hook and two ropes. Thomas Wells was paid 12*d* for two days' labour, and one night's labour by John Thomson cost 4*d*. John Gosse, who drew up the account, worked the lock with one man for one day at a wage of 12*d*, and for two days and one night with two men at a total of 6*s* 8*d*. Of the total cost, of 18*s* 4*d*, three-quarters was shared equally between George, the Prioress of Stratford, and one George Lees. Gosse himself perhaps had the fourth share.[142]

Finally, one very odd concomitant of landholding is revealed, imperfectly enough, in this entry in the auditors' accounts:

[135] File 21 no. 8. [136] File 20 no. 11. [137] Ibid.
[138] Ibid. [139] File 14 fo. 61. [140] File 13 fo. 42.
[141] File 13 fo. 25.
[142] The prioress presided over 'St Mary Spital', Stratford-at-Bow, 'a poor priory that...keepeth hospitality for poor men. And some sisters in the same place to keep the beds for poor men that come to the place': J. Gairdner, ed., *Historical Collections of a Citizen of London*, p. ix.

Item, the said George Cely paid of his charge for costs and expenses about th'execution of certain felons taken at St Katherine's, as it appeareth in the margin of the book marked with C, *inter recepta*. To the which costs and expenses Richard Cely, Thomas Hotoft, John Arnold, Raynold master Shaw's cousin, John Kirkeby, Richard Frith (otherwise called Granger), John Blyot, William Notte, William Shonke, William Blyot, John Chapman of Bulphan, John Rydley of Orsett, Roger Baker of Mucking, Robert Blyot of Mucking, Thomas Hoberd of Mucking, William Hoberd of West Tilbury, John Hoberd of East Tilbury, William Garlond of Stanford and John Abraham of Horndon promised to make contribution.

Which costs and expenses, beside costs made and done by the said Thomas Hotoft, William Shonke, William Notte, William Blyot, Robert Blyet, Thomas Hoberd, William Garlond and John Abraham, extend to the sum of £4 10s.[143]

Richard Cely promised the auditors to contribute his share pro rata. A number of these neighbours of the Celys in Essex sold them grain for export *c.* 1487, but there is no record in the papers of how the 'certain felons' had transgressed.

For a variety of reasons, it is impossible to make any direct comparison between the Celys' domestic expenditure and the household budgets formulated by Phelps Brown and Hopkins in their seminal study of 'Seven Centuries of the Prices of Consumables Compared with Builders' Wage Rates'.[144] They drew their specimen fifteenth-century budget from the accounts of two chantry priests in 1453–60.[145] The priests' account for the single year 1455–6 had been chosen for analysis in Tables 5 and 7 below, because in that year numbers in the household were increased from three to four.[146]

One question of interest is the proportionate amount spent variously on drink, on farinaceous material and on other food, chiefly flesh and fish. Table 5 shows the distribution in the priests' account, in Richard Cely's purchases for the visit of George and Margery to Bretts Place in 1484, in a budget averaged from pursers' accounts for two voyages of the *Margaret Cely* to Bordeaux in 1487–9, and in Speryng's account for haymaking *c.* 1486.[147]

143 File 10 fo. 7. While 'St Katherine's' would normally suggest the dock area to the east of the Tower, there was an outlying chapel of St Katherine at Tilbury, which seems a more likely locality.

144 *Economica*, n.s. XIII (1956), repr. with additions in *A Perspective of Wages and Prices* (1981), Table I, p. 14.

145 Wood-Legh, *A Small Household of the 15th Century*.

146 One major difference is that the priests spent perhaps half their disposable income on food and drink. The Celys devoted a much smaller proportion of income to ordinary household provisions.

147 See pp. 315 and 333–4, and File 14 fos. 35–40 and 49–58. In the year 1455–6 the chantry priests spent well under one-third of their food budget on cereals, not one-half as suggested by Christopher Dyer, 'English Diet in the Later Middle Ages',

Table 5. *Proportionate expenditure on drink, bread-stuff and other foods*

	Priests 1455–6 %	Richard Cely, 1484 %	Ship's crew, 1487–9 %	At haymaking %
Drink	29.0	47.4	39.0	34.0
Bread/meal	21.0	12.3	18.0	15.0
Other food	50.0	40.3	43.0	51.0
100%	183.17s	19s	19s[a]	2.2s

[a] Per week.

Table 6. *Items of expenditure as proportion of estimated budget, 1486–8*

	Shillings	Percentage of total
Building materials, etc.	4.5	8.8
Clothing	7.0	13.7
Mending and shaving	1.4	2.7
Firing	2.5	5.0
Soap and candle	0.8	1.6
Travel	1.7	3.3
Foodstuffs	19.6[a]	38.5
Beverages	9.7[b]	19.0
Other	3.8	7.4
Total	51s	100

[a] Bread and meal (estimated): 4.5s (8.8%), other foods: 15.1s (29.7%).
[b] Wine: 2.8s (5.5%), ale and beer (estimated): 6.9s (13.5%).

Unluckily, it is ale and beer and bread-stuffs which are notably absent from Nicholas Best's accounts of 1486–8. Table 6 presents selected categories of expenditure from Best's averaged accounts, including the postulated costs of these major omissions.

Where so much of a jigsaw was available, it was tempting to find a substitute for the missing pieces, and (in an exercise for which much of the evidence is defective in any case) to extrapolate costs from other sources.

Social Relations and Ideas: Essays in Honour of R. H. Hilton, ed. T. H. Aston et al. (Cambridge, 1983), p. 193. Even for the crews of the *Margaret Cely*, bread cost at most 39 percent of the total food bill.

In Richard Cely's expenses in June 1484, cereals cost 30.4 percent of the amount spent on other foods. This agrees closely with the cost of bread, wheat and baking in George Cely's account for Lenten entertaining at Calais, namely 30.8 percent of expenditure on other food.[148] It was 29.4 percent in the haymaking account. The cost of non-farinaceous food in the average of Best's accounts was 15.1s, so that bread and meal have been estimated at 4.5s, or 29.8 percent of other foods. The proportionate cost of ale and beer was more difficult to determine. It appeared very high in Richard's 1484 account, and very low in George's entertainment budget. The 33 percent of Richard's total provision bill from February 1482 to May 1484 which he spent on wine, beer and ale was therefore taken as a guide, and an appropriate amount was added to the cost of wine and the small amount of ale already included in Best's accounts. Hypothetical proportions then became: drink 33.1 percent, bread-stuffs 15.4 percent, other food 51.5 percent, which closely resembles the known proportions in the haymaking account.

Table 7 has been constructed to compare proportionate expenditure on selected items in domestic budgets with similar provisions for the *Margaret Cely* on a single Bordeaux voyage (of 1488–9) and with two accounts for entertaining guests.[149] The last two agree in the large amount spent on animal protein, and the comparatively low cost of drink. The amount spent on spices, honey, etc. in the 1587 account is inflated by the purchase of half a bushel each of white and bay salt, total cost 3s, and of a quantity of sugar, probably used for mulled wine. The priests, unlike Best, included cheese among dairy products bought. They also purchased oatmeal regularly, in addition to the weekly bread. Their wine was provided chiefly for visitors.

The priests' expenditure on this selection of items amounted to an average 46d per week, or 11½d per head, which allowed for feeding occasional workmen and visitors. The estimated budget based on an average of Best's five accounts might equal expenditure for five weeks, at 76d per week, for an undetermined number of persons. Provisions for the ship's complement, with cost of items that were bought in France inflated by an unfavourable exchange rate, can be averaged to 13.5d per man per week.

[148] Ch. 10, pp. 271–3.
[149] A single voyage was chosen, because the number of crewmen varied from voyage to voyage. For further details of the trip, see Ch. 14, pp. 389–93.

Table 7. *Proportionate estimated expenditure by N. Best on foodstuffs, drink and firing, compared with consumption of similar items by priests of Munden's Chantry, crew of 'Margaret Cely', guests in Calais, 1482, and participants of a banquet in 1587*[a]

	Priests 1455–6 %	N. Best %	Ship's crew %	Calais 1482 %	Banquet 1587 %
Butcher's meat	23.5	14.8	23.4	0	0
Poultry	0.2	10.0	0	0	5.1[b]
Fish	17.9	15.7	12.9	54.4	45.6
Subtotal 1	41.6	40.5	36.3	54.4	50.4
Spices, honey, sugar, salt, vinegar	2.5	2.0	2.0[c]	4.1	14.6
Fruit and vegetables	2.2	2.2	0.2	1.0	1.9
Dairy and eggs	1.4	2.8	0.2	0.7[d]	5.4
Bread, etc.[e]	20.5	14.0[f]	25.0	18.6	8.3
Drink	27.6	30.5[f]	33.4	14.7	9.7[g]
Subtotal 2	95.8	92.0	97.1	93.5	90.3
Firing	4.2	8.0	2.9	6.5	9.7
100% =	£9.56	£1.59	£20.15	£2.3	£6.18

[a] Giles E. Dawson and Laetitia Kennedy-Skipton, *Elizabethan Handwriting 1500–1650* (London, 1968), Facsimile 19.
[b] Capons and larks.
[c] Chiefly salt for preserving.
[d] Oil.
[e] Including flour, oatmeal, biscuits.
[f] Estimated.
[g] Beer 6s, ale 3s 4d, wine 2s 8d.

WARFARE AND TRADE,
1486–9

Another most unfortunate lacuna in the extant correspondence means that we know little about the Celys' social activities during the period between October 1484 and January 1487, save for such casual references in extracted accounts as one of their attendance at William Walgrave's marriage on 15 January 1486.[1] Their business affairs are better documented, especially for the years 1486 and 1487, which saw their important new diversification into the shipping trade. Their acquisition, early in 1486, of the Breton fishing-vessel which they renamed the *Margaret Cely*, and her subsequent operations, will have a chapter to themselves.

Besides their new commitment as ship-owners, Richard and George started 1486 with a heavy investment in wool, to compensate for their scanty shipments in the previous year. In April they exported 31 sarplers and a poke and 2,194 fells.[2] In addition, they made an exceptional deal with the Spaniard Juan Pardo. Pardo, from a family originating in Burgos, did business in Bruges and also London, where he was associated with Pedro De Salamanca, an associate in turn of Alvaro De Cisneros, who had now replaced Pedro Valladolid as the English agent of the Celys' customer, De Lopez.[3] There was a whole group of such Spanish (or rather Castilian) merchants, who are to be found in English records trading in a variety of commodities, in what appear to be ad hoc partnerships among themselves. Wendy Childs quotes evidence which shows that this was not Pardo's first purchase of wool in England.[4] She also deduced that he usually appeared in English documents as a representative of Spaniards suing in England, but in this case it seems that he became a defendant on his own account.

---

[1] File 10 fo. 1v. Another (fo. 8) was of Sir John Weston's niece.
[2] File 10 fos. 30, 32; File 13 fos. 22–3. Another 1,000 fells had been shipped on 25 Jan.
[3] Wendy Childs, *Anglo-Castilian Trade in the Later Middle Ages* (Manchester, 1978), pp. 57, 216, 229.   [4] Ibid., p. 229.

On 24 March 1486 George had received from William Midwinter a large consignment of 45 sarplers of good and middle Cotswold wool, weighing 124 sacks six cloves and priced at 14½ marks (£9 13s 4d) per sack-weight. The sort cost £1,166 6s 4d.[5] About the same time he also bought from a mercer named John Smith another five sarplers of Cotswold wool. It had probably been stored some time in the Cotswolds. George had it repacked, paying a bill of 10s 8d on 28 June to the porters of Leadenhall 'for the winding and "strekyng" of these five sarplers', and 7s on 26 August 'to the keeper of Leadenhall for the house 'at John Smethe's wool was packed in'. Over half a sack-weight of refuse wool was returned to Smith before he was paid for the remainder. With costs of repacking, weighing, and the 'repoising' of two sarplers which had to be weighed again before resale, the cost price of Smith's wool came to £9 11s 4d per sack-weight, or a total of £118 13s 1d for 12 sacks 21 cloves net.

On 30 April three sarplers of Smith's wool and nine of Midwinter's were sold, in England, to 'John Pardo, Spaniard' – in all 32 sack-weights at 15½ marks (£10 6s 8d) per sack-weight.[6] Including petty costs for the carriage and weighing of Midwinter's wool, the total cost of Pardo's wool to the Celys might have been £304 5s 8d. Price to Pardo was £330 13s 4d, giving the Celys an estimated profit of £26 7s, or 8.67 percent on a sale which included three sarplers (25 percent) of middle wool to nine of good. At a rough calculation, had this wool been exported to Calais and sold there in the usual way, it might have made a profit of something like £71 14s 6d or 19 percent, despite the greater costs of transport, handling and taxation. One can do no more than speculate on the Celys' reasons for selling at home. Possibly the transaction was part of a wider deal with the Spanish financiers of London and Bruges. Possibly Smith's wool would have been the subject of litigation if it had been sent to Calais. The obvious explanation is that the Celys needed ready cash. Both Pardo and a second purchaser of their wool in England, Thomas Crayford, paid in instalments, but they could perhaps have expected a shorter delay in returns than when stocks had to await buyers abroad. It should perhaps be added here that the Celys' first editor was mistaken in supposing that they ever smuggled wool across the channel: he misunderstood their financial dealings with De Lopez.[7]

Crayford bought the rest of Smith's wool and one sarpler of Midwinter's.[8] The remainder of Midwinter's sort was sent to Calais, despite a new attempt by a group of discontented Londoners to stop the

---

[5] File 20 no. 14.   [6] File 13 fo. 23v.
[7] *Cely Papers*, pp. xxix, xli.
[8] File 10 fo. 37. Avery Cornburgh paid £40 on behalf of Crayford in July: File 10 fo. 2.

sailing of the wool-fleet in April.[9] The Celys' shipment at that time probably constituted the bulk of the 30 sarplers of good Cots. which they sold in November to De Lopez and Gomez De Soria for £1,153 15s 6d stg.[10]

Scattered references in the Cely papers imply that in fact Pardo defaulted on part of his debt for their wool. On 22 September 1486 Alvaro De Cisneros was given Pardo's obligation for £100 stg. in part payment of a loan of £120 'taken up' by Alvaro for Richard and George on 26 August.[11] In December Richard paid Alvaro £8 'for parcel that lacked in John Pardo obligation', and 2s 6d was deducted from a payment of £50 which Alvaro made on Christmas Eve, 'for the costs of a man coming into Essex for John Pardo's bill'.[12] At one point William Cottillard was given a breakfast and money 'to have a writ of subpoena', and a payment was made 'for the writing of two obligations of John Pardo'.[13] A further reference to Pardo is found in a mutilated scrap of paper written by George:

John Pardo. Item, the 11 [or 20?] day of January 1486 [old style], my brother and I plained upon John [Par]do, Spaniard, in the mayor's court, Fox attorney [...].
Item, the entering of the plaint – 4d. I left the oblige with mine attorney.[14]

It seems likely that two journeys made to Sandwich by George's servant John Speryng in early 1487 were in connection with the same lawsuit.[15] Speryng paid 12d at Sandwich 'for 'resting of the Spaniard', 6d for entering the plaint, 4d for 'entering of attorney', and 2s 'for the 'torney in the court'. On the second visit he paid 3d 'for drinking with the officers [of the court?]'.

Speryng's journeys, which cost 18s 10d in all, involved the hire of a horse for the short ride from Gravesend to Rochester at a cost of 4d, another horse from Rochester to Canterbury at 12d, and breakfast and baiting (fodder) at Sittingbourne, where he evidently spent the night and paid 2d. Dinner at Canterbury (a meal eaten some time in the morning) cost another 2d. A horse to ride the distance of about 19 km from Canterbury to Sandwich cost 8d, and supper (and bed?) there cost 2d. After attending to the suit he retraced his steps back to Gravesend, again changing horses at Rochester, and concluding with dinner at Gravesend. A horse between Gravesend and London (where he probably stayed some time) and back again cost 18d. He then recorded 2½d spent at Dartford, and payment for breakfast at Gravesend as he set out on his second trip.

[9] *A.C.M.*, p. 292. [10] File 20 no. 38. [11] File 10 fos. 9, 39.
[12] File 10 fos. 19v, 9. [13] File 10 fo. 37. [14] File 20 no. 15.
[15] File 13 fo. 18.

This again took him through Rochester and Canterbury, with baiting at Sittingbourne and dinner at Canterbury. A horse to and from Sandwich cost him 12*d*, and he had supper for 2½*d* and paid 3*d* 'for the horse at night'. Back again at Gravesend, barge hire cost 2*d*, and he paid 3*s* 'for a wherry to go to South Sand Head'. There are no further details about the suit against Pardo, but as Alvaro does not seem to have claimed his £100 against the Celys, the matter was perhaps settled satisfactorily.

Another piece of litigation during this year was a Chancery suit relating to an incident that had occurred 16 years earlier, when 'Warwick the Kingmaker' was preparing to topple his former protégé, Edward IV.[16] Richard and George, as executors of their father, now petitioned for a writ of subpoena to Robert Vincent, formerly master of the *Trinity of Dover*. They alleged that on 28 March 1470 the *Trinity* had been one of 30 or more ships which laded wool at London for delivery at Calais. As the customers' and controllers' cockets would confirm, Richard had entrusted to Vincent the unwisely large consignment of eight sarplers of good Cotswold wool, containing 21 sacks 15 nails and valued at £250, and Vincent swore the customary oath upon a book that he would duly convey the wool and the rest of his merchandise to its destination. But he left the cocket behind him in London, deliberately (as the Celys supposed) so that when the wool reached Calais it would be forfeit to the king (or rather the Captain of Calais, Warwick?) 'for lack of the said cocket'. This ploy was frustrated in the event because none of the wools reached Calais at that shipping. As the fleet was making its way down the Thames, at Gravesend one of the sergeants at arms brought a message 'from the king' (who was not in London at the time), that the Earl of Warwick, 'then rebel to the same King Edward, lay in the narrow sea betwixt Dover and Calais with a certain number of ships of war'.[17] The king, at the particular request of Richard Cely and the other merchants concerned, therefore commanded all the masters of the wool ships to return to London. This they all did, save Robert Vincent. He, 'maliciously intending the hurt and impoverishing of Richard Cely', slipped away from the rest of the fleet, joined Warwick's ships and handed over his cargo for the comfort and aid of the earl, so that Richard neither saw his wool again, nor ever in his life received compensation from Vincent.

Robert Vincent was one of the owners and masters of ships from Dover hired in 1485–6 to transport the king's commissioners.[18] Evidently Richard and George now saw some chance of recovering the money lost.

[16] C.1 79/69.
[17] This must have been about the time (20 April) when Warwick's ships seized Flemish vessels off Calais: Charles Ross, *Edward IV* (London, 1974), p. 146.
[18] Campbell, *Materials*, I, 494.

344   *Richard and George Cely*

Richard paid 'for costs of [the] suit against Robert Vincent of Dover that sailed into Normandy with wools of their father's' a total of 17s 10d, and 'master Constable' was given 3s 4d when he was 'retained of counsel when the cocket of Vincent was delivered'.[19] But as so often, the outcome is not revealed.

In Flanders, Maximilian's mercenaries had succeeded in entering Bruges in June 1485. Ghent, whose guilds included a strong peace party, submitted shortly afterwards, and on 15 October Maximilian and his son Philip jointly concluded peace with Flanders.[20] In November Maximilian went to Germany, and returned in June next year with the title of King of the Romans, conferred in February. For a short time there was an appearance of greater stability in the low countries.

George Cely made two of his periodic visits to the continent in 1486. The only record of the first, in July, is a list of the goods 'sent by me to London in the *Margaret* [*Cely*]':[21]

First, an case for my long bows, with certain arrows in it.
Item, three long bows, two pricking shafts [arrows for target practice].
Item, an case for my harness, of estrich board [timber from the Baltic region].
Item, an fair standard [tall case] wherein is an feather-bed and an bolster. Item, in the same an pillow, an sallet [head-piece] and my fox gown; painted cloths of William Maryon's.
Item, an less joined chest of mine with four pair sheets and pillowberes [pillow-cases], and pillow and coverlet and quilt, an jacket of silk, one of blanket, an gown lining, an standish.
Item, an chest with an padlock wherein is an feather-bed and an bolster, an sword, an axe, a gobbet [piece] red saye.
Item, an harness barrel with an complete harness.
Item, long spear.
Item, an black-bill.
Item, an long iron rod.
Item, an quail cage.

Surviving portions of a pamphlet deal with George's later trip to Calais and the low countries in October–December.[22] He was 'in Flanders and the east parties' for 44 days from 16 October to 28 November. In Bruges he paid his host 'Attryan' (Adrian) 4s Flem. a day 'for me, my child [young servant] and my two horse', with an additional 3s paid 'for the glass window in my chamber at Bruges', and the usual extras 'for my fires', at 57s and 'for certain "berhegys"' (beverages) 7d. Extra horse-hire for 14 days cost 14s. When Hankin was sent back to Calais he travelled with two horses, at a cost of 10s. George's own costs at Calais, 'both going

---

[19] File 10 fos. 25v, 37.   [20] Gilliodts-van Severen, *Inventaire des Chartes*, VI, 253.
[21] File 20 no. 18 fo. 2v.   [22] File 13 fos. 26–31; File 20 no. 21.

and coming, and my lying without the gate', came to another 10s Flem., and the return journey from Calais to London cost him 19s stg.

One of the horses that Hankin took with him was probably one named 'Bless' or 'Bliss', which George had bought at Ghent and which he sold to Sir Ralph Hastings on St Andrew's Eve (29 November), for £20 Flem. Next day he sold Thomas Granger, his host at Calais, a bay horse valued at £4 16s Flem. This was partly in repayment of a loan of £4 from Granger, made on 14 October in 'nymhegyn' groats at 5d apiece.[23]. In Bruges, George also bought on Sir Ralph's commission a tassel of gold for 18s, three ells of fine satin at 10s 6d the ell, and one and three-quarter ells of black velvet at 13s the ell.[24] He was unable, however, to buy any crimson velvet for Lady Hastings under 32s the ell. Such requests to perform a service for the great were regarded as highly flattering. There was no question of making a monetary profit on the transaction, nor would George and his friends have seen anything ironic in the statement attributed to Lady Lisle, that she hated to be in debt, except to those who had shown themselves her 'very trusty and assured friends in deed'.[25]

On St Andrew's Day Sir Ralph gave George a letter of payment addressed to Sir John Dee ('sir' being probably the appellation of a priest in this case), payable at Christmas.[26] The sum in Flemish money came to £23 12s 3d, and made £14 15s stg. at the rate which George charged – 32s Flem. per £ stg., at a time when he converted Richard's debts at Calais rate of 30s Flem. per £. Hastings might well, on another occasion, thank George for his 'good and true heart'.[27] The bill was not met until 15 September 1487, when George received £9 stg. from Jeffrey Kent, perhaps the wool-weigher of that name of the London customs house, and £5 17s from Hastings' chaplain, William Fosse.[28] In May 1487 Sir Ralph had already apologized for one delay.

Right worshipful sir, I recommend me unto you as heartily as I can, etc. Letting you understand that I received a letter from you wherein ye wrote for your money. I pray you that ye take it to no displeasure, for I insure you, ever till Sir William come home I weened ye had been content of Sir John Dye. But I have sent him writing under such form that ye shall be content in all the haste possible without fault. And I pray you that ye will cause him to have a letter sent to him which shall be bound and sealed with this your letter. And after the sight of the bill I wot well ye shall not fault of your money. And at my coming I shall make such amends as ye shall hold you well content. Which time shall be right shortly, by the grace of God, who preserve you.

At Calais on the 8 day of May. 'Your luffuyng Rauff Hastyngys.'[29]

---

[23] File 20 nos. 20, 21.
[26] File 20 no. 21.
[29] *C.L.* 232.

[24] File 13 fo. 27.
[27] *C.L.* 245.

[25] *Lisle Letters*, no. 1535.
[28] File 20 no. 21.

As usual, George took the opportunity of a visit abroad to buy numerous goods for himself and his family, besides a fur for which Sir John Weston's henchman Gladman had given him 13*s* 4*d* in London.[30] He sent from Bruges to Calais 'in Leven's basket' a windlass for a cross-bow and ten pair of cords for it, a girdle for a sword, and 'my calendar of the planets'.[31] He also sent his 'baver' (armour for the lower part of the face, the 'beaver' worn by Hamlet's father) with 'Alan Redeman's servant that carries horse to Calais, and I gave him for his labour 5½*d*'. There is one instance, incidentally, of the carriage of a letter for 4*d* stg.[32] George had bought a case for his cross-bow costing 4*s* 7½*d* Flem., a case of a 'gray's skin' (badger-skin) for his quarrels, and 'an case for my windass [*sic*] for to set the bow in on horseback', five steel bows at 6*s* 8*d* each, 13 dozen 'mattresses [bolts for cross-bows] and other shafts' at 6*d* the dozen (but perhaps the 13 were a sort of baker's dozen, as George makes the total only 6*s*), five 'tellars' (stocks for cross-bows) and five stirrups (totalling 19*s* 4*d*), a saddle and a black harness (8*s* together), two white reins, two stirrup leathers and another pair of stirrups (2*s* 4*d* altogether), 'an chain for mine dog' at 8*d*, and two pouches, 'one [re]covered, another new', at 5*s*.

From the Bruges suppliers George bought three violet bonnets for Richard and himself, at 3*s* each, three black bonnets at 3*s* 4*d* each, and a red one for his servant Adlington, at 12*d*. He had himself made a short gown and a doublet of black saye, and Nelkin made, for 5*s* ½*d*, two tippets and two little caps for George's young sons, besides supplying two dozen black points of silk, for ties and laces. George also generously bought the same quantity of the black velvet that Sir Ralph Hastings had, to make frontlets for his wife Margery. A black cap and a violet cap were left 'to dress with the capper next the saddler's. I must pay for the dressing 6*d* le piece.' George collected them on his next visit, a year later. At Calais he bought six Flemish ells of white tuke at 18*d* an ell. One further expense was an unbudgeted payment of 5*s*, 'to Hankin, more than I weened to 'an paid him for nine days'. His host Adrian in the 'Sheep's Hoof' was left George's safe-conduct to keep for him, and the cross-bows and mattresses to be sent over with the next ship.

George returned home to London on 3 December 1486, and next morning delivered to Richard three 'vedemossys', i.e. evidences or deeds, two pairs of hose (11*s*), two caps (6*s* 4*d*), a pair of Spanish boots (5*s*), six pairs of gloves (2*s*), and a doublet cloth of two and three-quarter ells of black saye at 2*s* 8*d* the ell.

Opportunity offered for another deal with Spanish merchants in February 1487, and one which proved more profitable than the sale of wool to Pardo

---

[30] File 20 no. 21.   [31] File 13 fo. 26.   [32] File 10 fo. 9v.

the previous year. Richard and George were purchasing cargoes of assorted grains for their ship to take to Zealand on her spring voyages of 1486 and 1487, and in February 1487 they agreed to supply 400 or 600 quarters of wheat for Alvaro De Cisneros and 'Petter Salamon' (Pedro De Salamanca), price 7s per quarter, 'licence and all reckoned, and they must pay £4 toward the custom, and they must have 21 quarters for 20'.[33] 'Alvard' was to pay £100 the next week, on account. On 12 March George promised to make up the full 600 quarters, in return for a further cash payment of £40. The wheat was to be shipped, presumably to Spain, in 'Roderigo''s ship, along with 20 quarters of peas belonging to Richard and George, for which Roderigo was to 'bring the return in iron'. There is no further mention of the iron.

The Celys' brewer friend Harry Brazier or Vavasour supplied them with 106 quarters seven bushels of wheat at 5s 8d the quarter, nine for eight, which cost £30 in all, and another 104 quarters at 5s 10d each, nine for eight, total cost £30 6s 8d. The first lot, which 'made to the ship 117 qtr', was brought from the old wool-quay by Spenser, and 'Sanders' lighter brought from above the bridge' the second consignment, which made 116 quarters shipped weight.[34] The remainder, bought in smaller quantities and priced variously at 6s or 6s 4d the quarter, mostly with a rebate of one in nine, was delivered by the suppliers Wagstaff of Yarmouth, Hobard of West Tilbury, master John Dotten, John Blyet, Raynold master Shaw's man, Rydelay, Richard Page of Kent and Harry Baker of Hadleigh. In all there were 651 quarters 'bare' (130 tons), which at the agreed rebate of one in 21 made 620 quarters, for which Alvaro was to pay £221, inclusive of his share of the customs.

The Celys paid £170 5s 6½d for the wheat, plus payments to Randolf of 16s for measuring 413 qtr and of 5s for 138 qtr, and 'Wade of the king's house' was given 7s. The customs and other charges paid by Richard came to £9 5s 1d, and George also lists 'Speryng's costs while the ship was a-lading, and the meters, and his riding to Sandwich – 28s'.[35] This seems to be an example of George's disregard of the principles of cost accounting. Speryng's account for buying the wheat shows expenditure of only 9s 3½d.[36] George has added in the account previously described, which itemizes the costs of a journey to Sandwich for arresting a Spaniard and entering a plea against him.[37] But there is nothing to suggest that this was connected with Roderigo and his ship, or, at any rate, with Roderigo's cargo of wheat. Speryng's relevant account for 'when I was sent for the corn into Essex' covers numerous trips between London and Essex, and includes payments of 'earnest silver' to some of

[33] File 13 fo. 39; File 20 no. 17.
[34] File 14 fo. 47; File 13 fo. 39. Discrepancies were due to differences in local measures.
[35] File 13 fo. 40. [36] File 14 fo. 43. [37] File 13 fo. 18.

the suppliers of grain, 6*d* 'for breakfast and dinner and supper at [Thurrock] Grays with Hotoft and Dotten', 4*d* 'paid for Page and his meinie', 3*d* on Saturday 'for expenses upon Page and Randell', and 6*d* 'for going aboard the Spaniard at diverse times'. An entry of 2*d* for rat's bane has been cancelled, necessary as this substance may have been for the protection of the wheat. Total cost of the wheat to the Celys came to £181 7*s* 11*d*, so that they made a nominal £39 12*s* on the transaction, or a profit of 21.8 percent. In fact, however, Alvaro kept back £62 10*s* of the sum due, in repayment of £60 'taken up' from him in March, with £2 10*s* interest.

Meanwhile, the story from Calais had been resumed by William Cely in January 1487, and his letters constitute the bulk of the collection from then until March 1488. We know all too little about William. His letters to his 'masters' are dutifully deferential, save on rare occasions when Richard and George demanded the impossible and he allowed a slight note of impatience or reproof to colour his replies. He seems to have been an efficient factor, and, unlike George, he reported home regularly and often at length when there was news of events in Flanders or at Calais, or dealings with customers to fill his paper, writing an undistinguished, small, untidy and rather cramped businessman's hand.[38] But there are a few tantalizing glimpses of a personality behind the often colourless communications. William had a capacity for experiment and adaptation. He gradually abandoned some old-fashioned speech-habits under the influence of society in Calais, where the majority of merchants probably said 'them', not the old southern English 'hem', and 'their', not 'her'. He even used new-fangled expressions like 'news' for 'tidings', or 'he dares' for 'he dare', began to use 'are' – originally a northern form which was becoming more common in the south now – and to favour forms like 'they run' in place of 'they runneth'. Like the Book of Common Prayer and the King James version of the Bible, however, he seems to have regarded forms like 'he hath' as more suitable to the written and formal language than 'he has', also a northern usage which was coming into fashion.

William was also unusual among members of the family in that he was not content to keep to identical formulae of greeting and conclusion in his letters. He adopted different variations at different periods, so that his letters can be roughly dated by his usage in this respect. And he sometimes shows a turn for the vivid expression, for instance his description of the attitude of the lieutenant of the Staple: 'he is no steadfast man, nor he oweth you no good will, though he make a fair

---

[38] See *C.L.* plate 1.

face'.[39] Unless there is somewhere a cache of missing Cely letters, we shall never know what constituted the 'lewd and untrue English' in a lost letter for which William apologized.[40] He may have meant that the letter had been lacking in respect. There is no doubt that he exercised some conscious restraint in most of his correspondence with Richard and George. But, interestingly, he seems to have enjoyed a sudden surge of self-confidence at the beginning of 1487, because in a few specimens of his writing at that period the character changes markedly. It becomes larger and more expansive and decorative, resembling George's in the use of curled finals. Clearly William had one hand for the routine matters of accounts and business letters, but developed a more personal and ornamented style for other occasions.

There is nothing in the letter he wrote early in January 1487 to account for any alteration in William's circumstances, and the next, of early February, mainly concerns tidying-up operations after George's visit the previous October–December, belated, because one of George's letters had failed to reach William.[41] George had also forgotten to leave certain instructions, and William said, with pardonable self-justification, 'as for such gear as your mastership left with Adrian Deffrey [in Bruges], I have made no conveyance thereof, for I knew not that your mastership left anything with him till now'. The baver had also gone missing, but

I have enquired for it, and hath found him that hath it. The which I shall send you by Piers Batton's ship with your saddle and your other gear, and also a barrel of green fish for my master your brother and you.

Item, sir, I have remember Sir Ralph Hastings according to your writing, and he telleth me that he hath written to Sir John Dee to make you speedy payment, etc. And sir, as for Twyssullton, I have spoken unto him in like wise, and he showeth unto me that he is not as yet in that case nor ability to make you payment, wherefore he beseech your mastership to continue his good master, and to give him a sparing for a season, etc. And also I have remember William Dalton in like wise, and he telleth me that he hath written unto his man of the same, in any wise to see you content, etc.

Dalton himself replied to George, accompanying the letter with a present.

Like it you to wit that [I] purveyed at my being in Holland salmon of the Maas, of the which all is not comen. But sithen it is so that I have but one firkin comen, I send it to you by Thomas Bernard, servant with John Reynold, mercer, to deliver you. Praying you that it will please you for [to] open it, and take out thereof the one half for yourself. And that other half, that it will please you to put some piece of wood in the said firkin because of bruising of the fish that shall be left there in that other half, and that it may be sent to my Joan, and this letter

[39] *C.L.* 170. [40] *C.L.* 203. [41] *C.L.* 226, 227.

therewith. Other by cart if any go to Leicester, or else by the carriers of Derby, that they may carry it upon horseback. And that I beseech you in as goodly haste as may be, etc.

Please it you to understand that Will Cely told me that ye had no knowledge from me for payment of the £20 ye of your courtesy delivered unto William Lemster my servant, to my great marvel. Sir, ye shall be ascertained for truth, continent upon the knowledge of your courtesy and kind dealing to me of the said £20, I made £20 by exchange, and sent you the letter of payment, with a prognostication and an almanac of the making of master John Laete. [Laete was a famous almanac-maker of Antwerp.] And this I sent you all bounden and sealed together by [the stapler] William Drynklow. And sithen Will Cely told me, I delivered unto him the second letter of payment to send over unto you. Like as I have written to you in a letter sent over at Shrovetide, the which I trust ye have received.

Item, if my other salmon had comen I intended to have done other. But I pray to excuse to my good mistress that it is no better, howbeit it swam sith Candlemas.

W. Cely can tell you more than I dare write. Jesu keep you. Written at Calais the 12 day of March.[42]

The coincidence of uncommunicable news at Calais and several undelivered letters and packets suggests that government searchers were active again, not Richard's now but Henry VII's.[43] There was, however, little change in the news from the low countries. William Cely had said in February:

As for the ambassadors of the King of Romans and our king's commissioners, cannot grow to no conclusion for the intercourse betwixt them and us, no longer than till Midsummer next. For the King of Romans' commissioners hath fully answered that their master hath sent them a commandment for to conclude for no peace, no longer than Midsummer next. But they commune still of other matters for two or three days till they depart.

And sir, the King of Romans hath rescued his town of Thérouanne which the Lord Corddys laid siege to. But the Lord Corddys is fled and all his company, and the King of Romans hath new victualled the town and put in mo' men. And his army lieth still yet at St Omers, etc.[44]

Thérouanne had been taken in 1486 by Maximilian's German troops, led by 'Petty John' Salazar, the Spanish mercenary captain who had fought bravely for Richard III at Bosworth.[45] But d'Esquerdes, whose presence

[42] *C.L.* 228.
[43] The noted merchants John Colet and John Wendy were under suspicion the following Sept. of having aided the king's rebels and traitors overseas: *A.C.M.*, pp. 300–1. In April 1487 the King had issued a proclamation against 'feigned, contrived and forged tidings and tales': Sharpe, *Letter Book L*, p. 243.   [44] *C.L.* 227.
[45] Gilliodts-van Severen, *Inventaire des Chartes*, VI, 267. For Salazar see G. Wheeler and E. Nokes, *The Ricardian*, no. 36 (1972), 4–5.

so close to Calais greatly alarmed the English, had not fled far in February 1487, and later campaigns that year went disastrously for Maximilian. D'Esquerdes took St Omer in May, and regained Thérouanne in July. Maximilian was so hard-pressed for money that in June he was pawning his plate and jewels.[46]

Richard and George were largely preoccupied that summer with their affairs in England. They were busy buying grain for sale, victualling their ship, and finding money to pay William Midwinter. Some of this money was borrowed from Richard's brother-in-law Avery Rawson, and some provided by 'Alvard' De Cisneros or Farand Decordet in London, in payment for wool bought by De Lopez in Calais. There is a short series of undated notes from each brother written about this time. Richard wrote to George, probably from Essex, where he had gone on 8 March 1487:[47]

Right well-beloved brother, I recommend me unto you and to my sister. It is so that here is Dudley's man, the butcher of Eastcheap, and I have paid him all the money that I have, yet I owe him 33s 4d, which I pray you pay him. And send me a noble by Thomas Wade. The three oxen for the *Margaret* comes to 35s, that is 10s 20d [to] pay at my coming a' Wednesday [as Richard's third share].

I want a little fardel with two cradle cloths, a tin basin, with other gear. If it happed to be laid in your boat [for the crossing between London and Essex], I trust it will be safe.

I understand by Adlington 'at Midwinter is come. God rid us of him. Send me a bill of your mind, I pray you.

The cradle-cloths constitute the only indication that Richard and Anne had had children as early as this, and the baby for which they were provided may have died. William Midwinter was owed £100 at midsummer 1487 for 50 sacks of wool bought from him in February.[48]

Sometime before 12 August Richard wrote again:

Right well-beloved brother, I recommend me unto you and my sister in as hearty wise as I can. Sir, I have received a letter by Adlington – he brings you the same. I understand it right well, etc. I long sore to hear how ye have purveyed for William Midwinter.

If I had spoken with you ere ye yeed to London we might 'a made a £100 with my brother Avery. Sir, I pray you make him a bill in both our names of his money, to pay him at Bruges, as ye and he can agree, for he had never the bill 'at ye took me. Ye remember we had £40 at our coming, and I had £20 more, whereof yeed £12 and more for carriage of wool. I pray you make his bill of £60 stg.[49]

---

[46] Gilliodts-van Severen, *Inventaire des Chartes*, VI, 267.
[47] File 10 fo. 2; *C.L.* 230.
[48] File 20 no. 17.   [49] *C.L.* 233.

George then borrowed a further £40 from Avery.[50] On 22 August Midwinter was paid £50, and on 31 August various men in London were given a further £59 12*s* on his behalf.[51] At Michaelmas Midwinter was owed £95 8*s* more.

Richard had concluded, 'Sir, I would avise my sister and you to come again into Essex, for I understand they die sore in London.' Evidently George did take refuge at Mallins from Mark Lane. Either then, or earlier in the year, he sent this note to Nicholas Best:

Nicholas, I have writ to Alvard and have desired him by my letter to deliver to William Midwinter £150. See that ye endeavour you to that William Midwinter may have it shortly. The plague has been such that we dare not come there ourself. And tell him if he help us not at this time, it will scathe us the buying of 100 sack of wool at this season.

And go to Bishop and receive my nine mark of him, and as soon as William Midwinter comes, make him payment of such money as I understand ye have received of Alvard, and keep good reckoning.[52]

The news that William Cely sent from Calais on 12 September was scarcely comforting, at a time when Richard and George were borrowing heavily in England.[53] John Adlington had brought William a bill of payment from John De Lopez, probably for the last instalment on his wool purchase of November 1486. On this, William received only £300 Flem., and it was extremely difficult to find takers for exchange loans back to England. The Merchant Adventurers were again being urged to 'spare the shipping' of goods, since 'no intercourse, league nor amity is between the king our sovereign lord and the King of Romans', while the chancellor roundly rated those who traded with Maximilian's dominions as 'very supporters and maintainers of the king's enemies'.[54] On the burse at Bruges the exchange rate was now 33*s* 6*d* or 33*s* 7½*d* Flem. to the £ stg., and still rising. William was forced to deal with foreigners at bankers' rates: 'in Lombard Street ye shall hear of' their correspondents in London. To add to his troubles, 'almighty God visiteth sore here in Calais and the marches with this great plague of sickness that reigneth, I beseech [him] of his mercy to cease it'. Finding a customer for his wool was the least of his difficulties:

John Lowppys long sore after your coming, that he might make a bargain with you for your wools. He desireth to have two sarplers to prove it by till your mastership come. He saith ye shall be too far out of the way without ye 'gree

---

[50] File 20 no. 24. [51] File 14 fo. 14; File 15 fo. 55.
[52] *C.L.* 231. [53] *C.L.* 234.
[54] *A.C.M.*, pp. 299, 300. Those already engaged in business were to be out of the Burgundian dominions by 15 Nov.: p. 303.

and bargain together. Sir, it is well done that ye take your market betime, for diverse considerations, etc. Also, the market wax very slack here.[55]

Some of William's difficulties over transferring receipts were lessened when Richard and George sent him bills to meet on loans which they had taken up at London: 'as for master Lowys More, Lombard [Lodovico Moro?], is paid and I have the bill', but 'his attorney is a wrangling fellow – he would none other money but nemyng groats'.[56] Richard and George took up another £50 from 'Lewes Mowre' on 19 September, payable 'at the usance'.[57]

By 18 September two more letters, written by William at Bruges, had failed to reach their destination. 'The t'one was sent from Calais by James Jarfford, mercer [alias Yerford, stapler], the t'other by Peryman, packer of clift wools. He is lodged [in London] at the Cross Key.'[58] William was returning to Bruges, and left George's black box and £6 in Calais for him in case he came in the mean time.

As for going into Flanders, is good enough as yet, but all the jeopardy is in coming home. For and if our men of war take their fisher [fishing-boats], as I fear they will, there will be many Englishmen stopped in Flanders. And also the town of Dunkirk is not content, and that we shall well know if so be that they meet with any merchants of substance.

Dunkirk was the main stopping-point on the journey between Bruges and Calais. To provide some protection, in the absence of any effective treaty of intercourse, William needed a letter of attorney under the Staple seal, for which he required a formal letter from Richard and George, 'for your mastership hath been at Calais diverse times since I was entered your attorney. Wherefore your presence hath defeated that entry, and a letter of attorney is needful now at this time.'

On the day this was written (18 September), the Staple court at Calais had elected George 'one of the twenty-eight, the which shall assist the mayor of the Staple now at this parliament time, where some ever it be holden, and to labour certain matters for the Place'. Such sectional lobbying was an important behind-the-scenes activity at parliamentary sessions.

George had in fact left London for Essex on 22 September. He saw Richard at Bretts Place on 23 September, and reached Calais on 30 September. His costs from Mallins to Calais were 18s 7d stg. He went on to Bruges on 3 October, and was back in Calais on 14 October and home again before 29 October.[59] Part of his business at Calais was to collect debts, for instance that from John Twissulton for £3 13s 4d stg.

[55] *C.L.* 234. [56] *C.L.* 235. [57] File 20 no. 24.
[58] *C.L.* 235. [59] File 13 fos. 29–31v; File 20 no. 20.

He also took with him some money for his son Richard, but how it was to be applied is unclear. Before leaving Calais again, on 17 October he 'let to Thomas Spenser, that married James Grene's widow, my stable at Calais and the house for an year, for 20s Flem.'. He added, 'I must commune with him for his livelihood at Kingston.' At Bruges (?) he paid 4s 8d 'to Hanykyn the pursuivant to fetch my specialities at Ghent of master Jellys Jaculett'.

Naturally he made more purchases: six pairs of knives, a casket, four saddles at 5s each, six pairs of pantofles and six of pinsons, at 16d the pair, nine pairs of 'wosyn' (hose), six for himself and three for Richard, three biggins ('beguines' caps or hoods) of Flemish cloth for the children at 12d an ell, and better quality ones at 20d the ell for himself. He also bought 12 ells of a cloth called 'bayards' at 12d the ell, paying 16d in earnest-money, four black hats at 2s each, 'a sheath to my sword and the making clean', 20 mink skins at 3s each, four pairs of hose garters, two pairs of 'key-bands' at 4d a pair, four black bonnets 'for my brother and me' at 3s each, and others at 2s each for his three children. Black bonnets are hardly the modern style for infants, but even very young children were dressed as miniature adults.

More objects which were stuffed into the luggage home were a ream of paper (5s), two pairs of black spurs (13d), a javelin (14d), a piece of 'Myllen ffostyen' (Milan fustian) for 13s 8d, four ells of canvas, two pairs of shoes and another pair of pantofles for Margery Cely, and two boxes for his 'specialities'. George paid for dressing the caps left in Bruges in 1486, and 2s for the 'connyng [crafting? coining?] of my silver rings'. Among these goods it is the paper which cost notably more, in comparison with other items, than one would expect to pay today, but it is hand-made rag paper which has stood up very well to the passage of 500 years. Similarly, the velvet bought for Margery and Sir Ralph Hastings in 1486 would be of high-quality silk. The saddles, on the other hand, were perhaps cheaper when they were more common commodities.

It was probably for protection in any encounter with 'discontented' inhabitants of Dunkirk that George paid 8s 'to Watkin Tabere for riding with me to Dunkirk and for fetching of me'. He had failed to give William Cely the letter of attorney, which he wanted urgently on 29 October.[60] The general safe conduct issued to English merchants had now been annulled, for 'the English ships forfeited it when they departed out of Zealand, they being under arrest'. But as the Celys' accredited attorney, William would be able to use George's personal safe conduct, for which George had borrowed £20 Flem. from young Giles Frank in Malines in November 1486.[61]

---

[60] *C.L.* 236.   [61] File 20 no. 20.

The world is here now very casual ['uncertain'], for there is many wains laden with Englishmen's goods now arrested at Ostend and at other diverse places. And no goods may pass through as yet, no ways, for Englishmen hath taken many of their fishermen, which causeth here a great rombur [rumour: uproar or disturbance]. But we understand as many as hath singular safeconducts, their goods shall be delivered and let pass through.[62]

This was the season for the herring which would form a staple of winter diet:

As for herring, I have been at Damm diverse times. The rone [selected large fish] is at £9 10s, and yet [there is] none to get in regard ['worth mentioning'], but there is wrack enough, and £8 the last. And so there is a ship at Sluys that goeth to Calais, called *Rumbold Williamson*, wherein I have laid you four last [of] herring, three wrack and one rone. The wrack cost £8 and the rone £9. The which I trust to God shall come full well to Calais, for Sir James Tyrrell hath goods in the same ship.

Item, sir, there is a great rombur at Ghent. The chief of the town be come and fled to Bruges: I fear me Ghent will be French shortly.

George was lucky that he had not stayed on longer in Bruges on business that year. On 19 November William wrote of his own adventures.

Please it your masterships to understand that I am comen to Calais in safety, thanked be almighty God. For I was never in so great jeopardy coming out of Flanders in my life, for men a' war [soldiers] lying by the way waiting for Englishmen. And also I and my company was arrested two days at Dunkirk, but for Sir James Tyrrell's sake we were let go. [Tyrrell was one of the English ambassadors to Maximilian.] And so, sir, the world goeth marvellously in Flanders now, for it is open war betwixt Ghent and the King of Romans, etc.

Sir, as for making over of your money, since this trouble began I could not make over a penny, saving an £48 stg., whereof I shall send you the bills at the next passage.[63]

The exchange was 'right nought', and William seconded advice from John De Lopez to

bestow your money in gross wares now betimes at this Barow mart, in such wares as your masterships thinketh will be best at London. Whether it be in madder, wax or fustians, but I trow madder be best. And so be that ye will, Gomers De Sore shall buy it for your masterships, and ship it in Spanish ships in his own name. For John De Lopez and he are purposed to buy much madder to send into England. And if so be that it falleth to peace, there will be good done upon madder if it be bought betimes.

De Lopez himself was reluctant, 'for diverse causes', to collect the wool he had bought, as Giles Frank had been in February.[64]

[62] *C.L.* 236.   [63] *C.L.* 237.   [64] *C.L.* 227.

By 16 December William had been able to find only three Englishmen who would take up money, two of them the adventurers (in a derogatory as well as literal sense), John 'Flewelen' (William's Shakespearian rendering of Llewellyn), mercer, and William Warner, armourer.[65] 'Sir, I can make over no more money as yet: the world fareth marvellously now in Flanders.'[66] He went on with a note of sheer desperation:

all safeconducts given afore this day be disannulled, and they have granted and given a safeconduct general during the space of ten months to all manner merchants, of what nation or country they be of, bringing victual into Flanders, or else not. As ye shall understand more clearlier by the copy of the said safeconduct, the which is sent unto master mayor of the Staple to show unto all the Fellowship at London.

For the time being, Calais was virtually isolated.

Wherefore, sir, I know no remedy as yet to make over the rest of your money, without ye will bestow it in rated wares by the [ad]vice of John De Lopez, like as I wrote unto your masterships in my last letter by William Dalton. For there dares no man here aventure into Flanders till we know of a better surety than yet is known.

For there is great war betwixt the King of Romans and Ghent, and there may no man pass by land to Bergen, for they of Ghent take them prisoners, what manner men some ever they be. For they have taken diverse Easterlings and Cologners lately, wherefore there dares no merchants resort to nor fro. And here hath comen no merchants strangers of a good season. For the garrison of Gravelines hath stopped wools of John De Lopez, and will keep it still at Gravelines till they have their wages that the King of Romans oweth them. But all your wools remaineth in Calais still in my hands. Sir, we thinketh the world goeth on wheels in Flanders, God better it.

After writing this portion of his letter, William apparently received a letter from Richard and George, dated 27 November, by which he understood

that ye purpose not to meddle with no wares. Sir, in good faith as yet I know not how, nor with whom, to make over a penny by exchange. For there is not in theke parties, of Englishmen above three or four, which are purveyed already. And as for fine golds or fine silver, it is now too outrageous out of the way for any man to bring over. For ye shall not now get a ounce of fine gold for £3 12s gr. and above, for I have enquired for the same. For rials are worth here now in Flanders 20s Flem., and other golds after the rate of the same.

---

[65] Llewellyn was involved with Thomas Wyndout in a reprehensible gamble on futures, namely a loan repayable when and if Wyndout obtained the reversion of Thomas Shelley's wife: *A.C.M.*, pp. 130–3. William Warner and his father, according to Richard Arnold's story, bought a ship of Arnold's from the pirates who had captured her, removed her cables, anchors and tackle, and refused to sell her back to her rightful owner, unless it were a half-share for half the price they had paid to the 'rover' or pirate: Richard Arnold (1811), pp. 130ff.   [66] *C.L.* 238.

William's letter was to be carried by William Iland, a servant of Hugh Clopton, but Iland took too many risks when pirates were about: 'he took his passage in a crayer laden with goods and made sail in the night, with whom I durst not aventure the said letter at that time'.[67] One exchange loan had fallen through. William had arranged to lend £30 stg. to the mercer John Etwell, 'but when this trouble fell in Flanders he would not of it, howbeit I was through with him before for it'. John De Lopez had sent word that the Celys' money was ready for them, and he 'marvelled' that William had not sent for it. 'But sir, I know no way how to make it you over without great loss. For the exchange goeth very ill, for there is no man to take up money but strangers, the which taketh all at usance. And money goeth above 12s 8d the noble [38s Flem. per £ stg.] at usance, wherein is great loss.'

That winter Charles VIII of France took Flanders under his official protection, and with this encouragement Ghent captured Courtrai in January 1488. In the same month Maximilian convened the States General at Bruges, and arrived there himself in advance, with a small force. On 22 January William Cely reported gloomily that most of his business was

as your mastership left it, which I think ye shall not repent. For I fear me of Flanders. It standeth marvellously with Bruges, for the worshipful merchants of the town had liefer than much good they were out of the town, for they look every hour when the commons of the town shall rise and [revolt?] against the Romans' king. For they have been up once or twice already, but they have been [ap]peased by fair means. And the king lieth still in Bruges, and would have the guiding of the town, but the commons will not suffer him. And so he hath sent Philip Monsieur [Philip of Cleves] and the Bishop of Liège into Brabant for men. What shall come thereof, God knoweth. But all the lords of the land taketh the king's part.[68]

The English favoured Maximilian, not so much from any particular love of him, but because it was essential for him to establish firm authority over his dissident subjects before there could be any security for trade.

Item, sir, please it you to understand that Sir James Tyrrell hath been at Bruges, and hath spoken with the King of Romans diverse times. And the king made Sir James great cheer, and so did the town of Bruges and all other towns of Flanders that he came through, as great cheer as any man might have. And so it is thought if the King of Romans may subdue Ghent and rule Flanders (as within short space we think he shall, or else must flee his way out of the country, or be destroyed), that he will grant our sovereign lord king all things that he will lawfully desire, for to have peace with us. For the country would gladly have peace with us.

[67] *C.L.* 239.   [68] *C.L.* 240.

As it was,

as now, we nor they dare not resort to nor fro, with safe-conduct nor other wise. For Harold Staunton, Edmund Knight, Nicholas Taylor, mercer, they hath been at Bergen mart, and in their coming homeward from the mart, at Sluys they been taken prisoners, and laid in the castle of Sluys. And lieth still there and hath done this three weeks. And not likely to come shortly out without they [pay] much money for their ransom.

Richard Arnold was similarly imprisoned at Sluys after the Easter mart that year.[69]

The latest news at Calais was that

one [is] come from Bruges, and he saith there is an embassy sent from Bruges and from Ypres unto Ghent, for to make the peace betwixt the King of Romans and them. Which is thought they shall conclude. And that done, there shall an embassy come from thence into England in as possible haste as may be to make a good peace, as I trust to God shall be.

The English merchants were now being far too optimistic about affairs in Flanders. About a month later, on 15 February, William sent his next news. He had written to De Lopez, but

the season is such at Bruges now that no man there hath no leisure to go about any things pertaining [to] merchandise. For eight days long the gates of Bruges were shut, and no man suffered to come in nor out. And ever since Candlemas Even all the commoners of Bruges hath been in harness and keep the market-place. And they have set the King of Romans out of his place, and put all his men from him, and keepeth him under ward. But they say they will do him no bodily hurt. And they have taken diverse that were rulers about him, which men think they have or shall suffer death. And many of his lords be fled. And the chief rulers of Ghent be come to Bruges, and so they will plainly have peace with France, and to be under the obeisance of the King of France, if the town of Bruges would be agreeable to the same. But as yet they be not agreed amongst themself.

Wherefore they have sent into Brabant and into Holland and Zealand, that every one of these countries do send to Bruges certain wise men with full authority of their country for to commune and talk with the Ghentners and them, and that may take such ways and conclusion amongst them as they can drive by reason, most beneficial for them and their countries. But they are utterly determined that the Romans' king shall rule no longer amongst them. For already they have discharged all the old Wytt [town council] of Bruges, the which was set in by the king, and made a new Wytt. And they say that they will have the coins set down again [i.e. reduced in value]. And so they of Bruges saith all shall be well shortly. But it is unlikely. The ambassadors that should 'a comen into England beth fled to Sluys.[70]

---

[69] See Ch. 1, p. 25.   [70] *C.L.* 241.

There would be no making over of money 'till this heat be over'. Among the men in harness in the market-place were Gomez De Soria and John De Lopez. Nevertheless, De Lopez had a man at Calais ready to receive his wool as soon as he heard of a settlement at Bruges, which was expected within eight or ten days. Bruges had 'denied them of Ghent diverse of their desires', and it was hoped that their league would not last long. But amity continued for the time being. On 29 February William reported that the ambassadors of the Flemish towns had met as arranged, 'and one feasted another, and each of them swore to other they would keep the town of Bruges to the behalf of Philip Monsieur, as protector of Duke Philip';

but many men think it will not be in their power to keep it long. For they have had many great displeasures, and mo' are like for to have shortly. For there is much people comen lately out of Brabant and Zealand to Nieuport and to other towns that be Burgundian in Flanders, for to lie in garrison. And mo' shall come shortly, had the King of Romans done with his siege at Rotterdam in Holland, which he hath besieged by water and by land so strait that it must needs give up, as they say that come lately from thence.[71]

There was some more news concerning the English which could not be entrusted to writing: 'Sir, here is now marvellous dealing with many folk, and that I think ye shall understand by some men shortly, etc.' Speryng had been summoned home by the Celys, and would no doubt elaborate on this cryptic comment, but the 'by [concerning] some men' suggests that a seditious plot was afoot.

William's last extant letter was written on 12 March, still in gloom over affairs in the low countries:

Sir, as for tidings out of Flanders they continue still in mischief, like as I have written you in my last letter...save on Saturday last was beheaded at Bruges the lord 'Dugell' [the former burgomaster of Bruges, Jacob Van Dudzeele], and mo' is like to be shortly. They surmised a matter upon John De Lopez, but he hath stopped them with money. And so such men as beth of any substance in Bruges feareth this reckoning, and diverse of them stealeth daily away, and goeth to Middelburgh in Zealand. For they fear the end will be naught. Which I pray almighty Jesu amend it.[72]

Thanks to bribery, rather than his efforts to appear one with the crowd, De Lopez survived the upheavals in Bruges. But it was some time before he could collect the Celys' final consignment of wool. A letter which George accidently started on the back of some memoranda began:

1488

William Cely, we greet you well. And it is so that we have sent to you diverse letters but late, that ye should deliver to Gomys Desore or to his attorney, all

[71] *C.L.* 242.   [72] *C.L.* 243.

our wool in Calais, which is an 16 sarplers 2 pokes. Ye know it was promised him twelve month agone.[73]

Maximilian signed a peace treaty with Bruges on 16 May 1488, and in May 1489, shortly before his death, George delivered Richard a letter of payment of De Lopez for £593 3s stg., part of which was still outstanding.[74] Although the Celys' shipment of fleece-wool in July 1487 was the last that they made jointly, De Lopez continued to buy from other merchants, and continued to be hampered by governmental policies. In October 1490, 'John Lopes and Gomes De Soria, merchants of Spain residing at Bruges', obtained special protection and licence to enter and leave the dominions of Henry VII, importing and exporting goods and merchandise. Without it, they feared 'to enter for purposes of com-merce...the town and marches of Calais, from an apprehension that the truce between the king [of England] and the county of Flanders and its Members is not of such virtue and strength that they may venture to do so'.[75] The treaty between England and the Archduke, which Francis Bacon later termed, with singular infelicity, the 'Magnus Intercursus', was signed in February 1496. It was ineffective, and soon fell victim to renewed wrangling. A number of pressing commercial questions were left unsettled in 1496, agreement being formalized only in May 1499.

Yet another regrettable loss from the Cely papers is the letters which William Cely must have written between March 1488 and his death in 1489. The last we hear of him – a sorry sort of epitaph for such a faithful servant – is the entry in the auditors' accounts, 'item, the said Richard [Cely] paid for his costs to and from Calais in May and June anno 1489 after the decease of William Cely – £3'.[76] George himself died a month or so later, on or about 24 June 1489.[77] He may have visited Calais in May, since there is a note among his memoranda that on 15 May 1489 he left his wife £8 to keep house with.[78] It seems that he was back in England by 1 June, when he delivered £4 to Richard's wife, and he died at London.[79] Had he caught the same fatal illness as William?

[73] File 20 no. 31, dorse.
[75] Campbell, *Materials*, II, 516.
[77] File 10 fos. 7v, 10v.
[79] File 10 fo. 3; C.I 300/15.

[74] File 20 no. 30, dorse.
[76] File 10 fo. 26.
[78] File 20 no. 30, dorse.

THE 'MARGARET CELY OF LONDON'

By 1486 the customary pattern of the Celys' trade in wool – selling to netherlanders and making home their receipts by exchange loans to English merchants – had become liable to so much disruption by civil commotion in Flanders and by embargos on the trade of merchant adventurers, that they had decided on some diversification. Involvement in the shipping business was the most obvious course. This was not an activity restricted to the members of a particular Company, nor to trade with a politically disturbed area like the netherlands, and the Celys would be free to pursue a variety of commodities and markets. For a small ship, operated by a partnership of two or three people, the initial capital requirement was not very great, and one advantage which may have appealed to them was that many of the returns would come to them directly in England and in sterling. The returns themselves were of two kinds. They could expect to carry freight for other merchants and even, on certain routes, could offer the ship's officers cargo-room in lieu of part of their wages.[1] In addition, worthwhile profit could be made on their own export of such commodities as grain and on the import of cloth, wine and salt. The risks were high, and the Celys for one do not seem to have taken out marine insurance. But by the late fifteenth century increasing numbers of English merchants were finding that investment in shipping offered a sufficiently lucrative prospect, especially when, after 1485, Henry VII's navigation acts sought to give them a monopoly of carriage to England.

Accordingly, Richard and George entered into partnership with William Maryon, and early in March 1486 they purchased 'a ship late called the *Margaret of Penmarcke*' from 'John Burdeycke [alias Bordeycke or Bordeecke], mariner [alias 'fisher'] of Penmarcke in Bretagne'.[2]

---

[1] Known as 'portages'. Sometimes a man simply sold his cargo space to one of the merchant shippers.
[2] File 13 fo. 2, etc.

Richard paid £28 for the vessel, together with a preliminary 4d for earnest at the bargain-making and the present of a yard of scarlet cloth, costing 12s. Apparently the ship was then at Dover. Very likely she had been the victim of one of the piratical attacks on Breton fisher-boats by English seamen, and was subsequently restored to her owner, 'as is, where is'. She may well have resembled the Breton ship seized at Southampton on 15 March 1485, which had a portage of 60 tons and was laden with wines, salt, cloth and other merchandise.[3] She apparently had three masts, and the maximum amount that she is recorded as carrying is 58½ wine tons.[4] Including supercargos, her crew, during her operation by the Celys, numbered between 14 and 18.

Richard Cely and William Maryon travelled down to Sandwich to buy the *Margaret*, which was rechristened the *Margaret Cely*, usually spelled and presumably pronounced 'Marget'. The progress of their journey can be traced in Richard's payments, starting with 8d for the ferry at Gravesend on 4 March 1486.[5] Dinner and horsemeat at Rochester cost 12d, and at Ospring supper and wine came to 21d and 'horsemeat that night' 9d. The next day dinner and horsemeat at Canterbury cost 2s 3d. At Sandwich, 'mine host Gyllam De La Towr' was paid 6s 8d 'for our mealtides from Sunday till Friday'. Horsemeat for four horses cost 5s, and 6s 1d was spent on wine for the party over the five days. The beds cost them 12d, and Richard gave a tip of 10d 'to childer and servants'. There were at least four people in the group: Maryon had paid 18d to hire a horse for 'John Garwes', and there was also his servant Thomas Wade. William Aldridge, the former servant of Richard Cely senior and purser-designate of the ship, was given 2s 6d 'to bring him to Sandwich' and apparently travelled separately. Maryon and Guillaume De La Towr, their host, witnessed the sale itself, which may have taken place at Dover, where Richard spent 22d 'in horsemeat and man's meat'. A breakfast for the mayor cost Richard 9d, and 'writing and sealing the testimonial under the town seal' meant expenditure of 6s 8d.

Richard then gave William Aldridge 3s 4d 'to get men to have [the ship] afloat', and there was some essential provisioning: a barrel of beer, bread and salt fish for the temporary crew. 'Two Spaniards that holp to weigh our anchor' got 20d, and 'three mariners that holp us four days' another 20d. In addition to 12 tons of ballast, the ship required pulleys, including a brazen double pulley and brazen 'schyver', the collar of a pulley bound with iron and two hawsers, one costing 3s 11d, the other, bought from

[3] *C.P.R. 1476–85*, p. 545. This was *La Seynt Marie* of 'Portaly'.
[4] Her third mast was deduced by Dorothy Burwash, *English Merchant Shipping, 1460–1540* (Toronto, 1947, repr. Newton Abbot, 1969), p. 87.
[5] Richard's chronologically confused account for the trip is File 13 fos. 1–5.

Guillaume De La Towr, costing 23s 4d. Patrick Mychellson, who also helped crew the *Margaret*, provided a yard for the foresail and replacement of a lost oar. 'Patrick' was an uncommon name in England at the time, and this is probably the man who regularly appears as master of the *Christopher of London* in London wool-fleets in 1478–9.[6]

From William Hallyngberry, roper of Sandwich, Richard bought a cable weighing 520 lb and a lead-line weighing 5 lb, for 59s. Richard Purssar of Southampton provided a miscellaneous stock consisting of

an cable, two kettles, a bonnet of an foresail, two harness barrels locked, a glass, a compass, a firkin with gunstones, a harness, forlocks, an end of a cable, with other things.[7]

These cost in all 40s. £4 bought armaments and other goods from John Parcar of Dover:

Four small serpentines [cannon] with seven chambers of one making, two greater serpentines with six chambers, three 'hacke boschys' [arquebus], two hand guns, six long bows, thirty sheaf of arrows, an anchor, forty-four pellets of lead, a mould of stone to cast lead in, a great compass, a lodestone, an horn for gunpowder.[8]

Among the possessions of Sir John Fastolf, inventoried in 1462, were a number of guns and serpentines with between three and eight chambers, to shoot stones up to seven inches thick and 20 inches in compass, 'two short guns for ships with six chambers, and three small serpentines' to shoot pellets of lead.[9] If the *Margaret* had in fact been captured by pirates before, her new owners were taking precautions against any repetition. A further two guns were bought from Patrick Mychellson for 13s 4d, and 14 lb of gunpowder cost 4s 8d.[10] The ship was also well provided with navigational aids, having a lodestone as well as two of the newer-fangled compasses.

On the way home, the land party again stopped at Canterbury, paying 18d 'for drink, fire, candle and horsemeat'.[11] At Sittingbourne, breakfast and horsemeat cost 8d. Thomas Wade and John Garwes had 18d 'for their dinner, baiting [fodder for the horses] and ferry' at Gravesend, and Garwes had to pay 7d for mending saddles and shoeing the horses. Maryon and Thomas Wade completed their journey home by taking a boat to Purfleet, where their dinner cost them 7½d. Maryon then went over to Erith to pay the 'shipmen 'at brought the ship from Sandwich'. A boat back to Purfleet cost him 1d, and so did 'fish for their supper'. Bread and mussels for the ship cost 4d.

[6] E.122 73/40.   [7] File 13 fo. 3.   [8] Ibid.
[9] *Paston L.*, no. 64, p. 113.
[10] File 13 fo. 4. In 1416 gunpowder for the royal ships had cost much more, 12d per lb: Susan Rose, *The Navy of the Lancastrian Kings...1422–1427* (Navy Records Soc., 1982), App. II, p. 219.   [11] File 13 fo. 3v.

It seems to have cost 6s 8d 'for boat hire and men to bring the boat to Sandwich' [round the coast from Dover, or from Erith?], and a total of perhaps 40s to a crew of 11 who took the *Margaret* on to London. The ordinary mariners, John of Bristow (Bristol), John Thomas, Robert Dawhe and Richard Salisbury, were paid 3s 4d each.[12] William Crepayge or Kyrpayge had 5s in all,[13] John Tayllar the cook 6s 8d, while William Code the carpenter and Gabriel Storcke the bosun were each paid 4s 4d 'for coming about', but possibly the payment of 2s at Sandwich to the bosun and his mate (Crepayge?) would bring up their total wage.[14] Piers Morres had 2s and 'the boy's hire' cost 1s. Patrick Mychellson, who perhaps acted as master's mate, was paid 6s 8d, like the cook. William Aldridge himself had 10s 'for bringing the ship about from Sandwich'. The carpenter at least may have continued with the ship once she reached London, as he was given a further 3s 4d 'to send to his wife to Sandwich', and on 25 March the same man, perhaps, was advanced 2s 6d against his wages for the next voyage.[15]

At this point a quantity of timber may have been bought for repairs, together with an appropriate amount of nail; *inter alia* 300 threepenny nail and 200 scupper nail.[16] There were 103 quarters of oaken board and ten 'oaken quarters' at 4s 4d. A quarter seems to have been 18 feet of what is commonly called 'four by two'. In addition nine elm boards cost 4s. The ship was also caulked, which involved purchases of oakum and rosin, barrels of pitch and tar at 5s a barrel. And

Item, I paid to a Dutchman for caulking – 12d. Item, I paid to John Chapman for three [days] caulking – 2s. Item, I paid to his fellow for three days caulking, the day 8d. – 2s. And for lending of his pitch kettle – 2s 6d. Item, for another caulker, the day 8s – 16d.[17]

Besides victuals for this first voyage, to Zealand, essential pulleys, blocks, dishes and platters were bought from a wood-turner. An undated account for such goods runs:

These been the parcels that be longing unto the Marget Cely.

Item, paid for twenty-two scythes	9s 2d
Item, paid for four shovels and a scoop	18d
Item, paid for four new sheaves and four pins thereto	4d
Item, for two new pulleys	4d
Item, for three new pulleys	7d
Item, for one dozen dishes	3d
Item, for half dozen saucer [sauce-dishes]	1d

---

[12] File 13 fos. 3v–4.   [13] 3s 4d and 20d 'for bringing the *Margett* to London'.
[14] File 13 fo. 3.   [15] File 13 fo. 4v.
[16] File 13 fo. 4.   [17] File 13 fo. 4v.

Item, for a dozen spoons 1d
Item, for a tankard . . . . 4d.[18]

Unfortunately, there is no detailed record of the *Margaret*'s Zealand voyage in April 1486. We know, however, that Richard and George shipped grain which Richard's apprentice, Giles Beckingham, was sent to sell for them. Each brother was trading on his own account, and Giles's report to George has recently been found.[19] George's share of the cargo consisted of 17 qtr wheat, 24 qtr oats, 5 qtr 2 bushels rye, and 6 qtr 2 bushels barley, all Essex measure – 10½ tons in all. Total buying price was £7 12s 6d stg. It was shipped on 1 April, and Giles was to take out as much wheat as was needed for the ship's store, five bushels in the event. George's instructions were to 'sell this corn when ye come into the parts of Zealand as well as ye can, and do with mine money as ye do with my brother's. Ye may deliver to Richard, Robert Herrick's [Eyryk's] servant, our money to keep, or to deliver it to some sure man by exchange if William Cely be not there [at the mart].'

On 11 April Giles paid 4s Flem. for 'premech and lodmannach', i.e. primage and lodemanage, fees for unloading and piloting. Measuring the grain cost 23d Flem. He sold almost all of it the same day to 'a frow of Owland', i.e. a woman of Holland, with one further sale of some wheat on 20 April. He reckoned the grain by a local measure, the *hoet* or *hoed*, which he termed a 'hwd', and which evidently contained 32 local bushels.[20] Most of the wheat sold at 48s Flem. the 'hwd', and the rest at 49s 8d. The oats were sold at 15s the 'hwd', the barley at 22s and the rye at 30s. The total received was £16 2s 10d Flem. One further sample of Giles's spelling ought to be given: 'Item, the scaym [same] day and tym Y scowld [sold] to the scaym frow of Owland v hwd and a qwartar of wottys [oats], le hwd xvs. Sum – iij *li* xviijs ixd Fl.'

Less costs of 5s 11d Flem., Giles delivered the money to Robert Eyryk, and took in return Eyryk's bill of exchange for £15 16s 11d Flem. Depending on the exchange rate at which the loan was made, George might have received about £10 16s stg. in England, making a possible profit of 41.6 percent. But this excludes customs dues and any costs of carriage in England, which are not stated. The profit was good in percentage terms, but the quantity involved was too small to net George more than a few pounds. This seems to be true of all his personal trading as a ship-owner.

[18] File 16 fo. 7.
[19] File 20 no. 16; File 13 fo. 21.
[20] *Dictionary of the Older Scottish Tongue*, s.v. Hude n.[2]. The *hoet* was not apparently the same as the *mudde* or *muid*, which held only three *viertels*: Van der Wee, *Antwerp Market*, I, 97.

The *Margaret*'s next voyage was to the familiar ground of Calais with the wool-fleet in July 1486. Accounts of expenditure by William Maryon and George Cely itemized purchases for her fitting out,[21] and there is a further set of accounts drawn up weekly by the purser, William Aldridge, between 1 May and about 5 July.[22] Aldridge spent a total of £7 15s 2d. His initial stock of money, which came to £7 4s 10d, consisted of £2 from George, £3 from Maryon, 10s received from a Spaniard as compensation for some damage which had been done to the ship, and 34s 10d which remained in his hands from freight charges on the Zealand voyage, no doubt for goods carried from the mart for other merchants.

While the ship was rigging, Aldridge paid a weekly average of 2s 9d for victuals, characterized simply as fish, bread and flesh. This was much less than the weekly food bill for a whole crew, and suggests that a reduced crew was kept on while she was in her home port. Their habitual duties apparently included sail-making, since the Celys provided canvas, needles and thread for the purpose, but no payment to a sail-maker is recorded. Aldridge bought four bolts of canvas, at 15s each, which were presumably for sails. Various hired carpenters were employed, usually at 6d per day, but the rate increased for specialized work: Thomas Browne was paid 7d a day for six days 'laying of the hatches', and two carpenters had 8d a day for four days' work striking the poop. In addition they had suppers on one day, at a cost of 4d. A new capstan was bought for 2s, and on 22 June Maryon provided a plank for the capstan stool, for 4s. Sawing it cost 4d. A 'whope' (hoop) of six chains for the capstan was also bought. The blacksmith who provided it also supplied a 'mothe' and six plates weighing 20 lb at 1½d a lb, and two 'gun pikes' (iron bolts?) weighing 9 lb, for which he was given 6 lb of old metal in part exchange.[23] One hundred feet of board was bought for the 'foxle', at 3s. More caulking was done while the ship lay up. One of the caulkers was paid 11d 'two tides [times], being aground', and Aldridge paid 8d for two heatings of a pitch kettle.

Miscellaneous purchases by the purser included a sheepskin at 4d, reed, horning a lantern (4d), 1 lb of twine (5d), five pints of oil, 2 lb each of 'werdgras' (verdigris), red lead and white lead and a quarter of tallow at 2s 6d.[24] Half a hundred of 'toserd' cost 9d. The best the *Oxford English Dictionary* could do with 'tosard' is 'some kind of firewood'. While negotiating with the Spaniard over 'the hurts that he did to the ship' Aldridge spent 4d at a tavern.

---

[21] File 13 fos. 5–6v.	[22] File 13 fos. 10v–15.

[23] The 'mothe' appears to be *O.E.D.* Moot sb. 2, described in 1815 as a piece of hardwood hooped with iron for block-making, or a ring-gauge for shaping tree-nails.

[24] Sheepskin was used to make mops for applying tar, pitch and tallow in caulking: *Navy of the Lancastrian Kings*, p. 96.

While the ship was moored in the channel a wherry had to be used to board her, but about 11 June 8d was paid 'for a boat to bring the ship to Blackwall', and Aldridge seems to have reckoned that the 'voyage' started when she came up to the quay. She was then 'entered into the custom' for 4d, and provisioning started for the trip the following month, with the grinding of two bushels of wheat for meal. This was later baked into bread at a cost of 2d, and another three dozen of bread was bought for 3s. A quartern of salt fish cost 9s, and William Maryon contributed, on 27 June, a barrel of beef at 13s 4d and, on 29 June, an ox at 12s 8d and two bushels of Bay salt to preserve the meat, at 2s. On 5 July he bought more bread, for 10s 6d, from Townsend, baker. A later note indicates that beer for this voyage cost 56s 8d.[25] This sum would buy almost 28 barrels (1,000 gallons), but there were at least 45 people aboard on the trip to Calais. And a good deal of beer must have been needed to wash down the bread, which was not lubricated with either butter or dripping, as well as to counteract the salt meat. A rather surprising absence from all the victualling accounts is cheese. Was this regarded mainly as a substitute for meat and fish when the latter were unavailable? Two cheeses, however, were among the provisions for another ship, the *Sunday of Porchester*, on a voyage to the Isle of Man and Carlingford in 1532.[26] Bacon is missing from the Celys' shipping accounts just as it is from their domestic provisions.

George's contribution to the voyage included another anchor and two stools (stands), costing 14s 4d. He also paid, possibly before the first voyage to Zealand, half the cost of the £2 paid 'to master Foskewe [Fortescue] to clear the *Marget* and for an quittance of him'. Before the ship left for Calais George gave the master 2s 4d 'for cokeselvyr', i.e. cocket silver, the fee for the certificate of wools carried, and paid 5s 4d to John Paynter, 'for painting of pavises', or screens against missile attack. Two and a half yards of red cloth and one of white for the top armour cost 5s 7d.[27] George also took charge of buying further armaments for the ship and her crew, which consisted of 74 lb of gunpowder at 4d a lb and a firkin to hold it, 300 tampons (12d), 66 lb of lead pellets, together with an iron dish (5s), a pair of corslets and a stool (4s), a red 'coat of fence' (4s), a long spear, three iron 'hagbushes' (another spelling for arquebus), two red and one green, and 'a rod of iron to charge withal', costing 24s in all. On 29 June he added six hedge bills (5s) and five dozen darts (4s 2d). Maryon also provided six black bills for 3s.

These extra war-like preparations were required because the *Margaret* was officially appointed to help provide the armed escort for the wool-fleet

[25] File 13 fo. 8.   [26] *Lisle Letters*, I, pp. 340–1.
[27] File 13 fo. 6v; File 21 no. 3.

to Calais, and her owners were paid £23 stg. for 'wafting' or providing this service.[28] Accordingly, she carried 28 soldiers, who were paid 6s 8d apiece. This seems to have been the standard wage for a soldier engaged in convoy duty between London and Calais. In March 1476 William Fetherston drew that amount for the wages of each of the 200 men in the king's carrick and the 50 men in the *Burnet*. There was also an allowance for their victualling of 12½d per man per week, and on that occasion the convoy was away for two weeks.[29] It would seem that the £23 stg. which the Celys received was intended to cover wages and food for the whole complement, both soldiers and seamen, but the precise basis on which the calculation was made cannot be ascertained from George's account. Besides the soldiers, the *Margaret* carried a crew of 17, including Aldridge as purser, the officers and two boys. The recorded wage bill for the whole complement came to £19 6s 8d. George calculated dues to the crew on the basis of 10s a man, which may represent the wage for the whole voyage for the ordinary mariner, who was customarily paid 5s Flem. for the outward trip between London and Calais.[30] On top of this 10s the master received 'two men's rights', giving him 30s in all. The other additional payments were 'the cook and the boatswain, 5s, the carpenter 5s, William Alldereche 10s'.

Aldridge had been given £15 12s 8d Flem. for the ship's expenses, and at Calais William Cely gave him £4 19s 4d more. Total costs apparently came to £24 6s Flem. Receipts came to £43 9s Flem., made up of the payment for wafting (£34 10s. Flem. at Calais exchange rate of 30s Flem. per £), 'freight of certain folk' at £4 6s 6d Flem., freight of chests (George's own goods being sent back to London?) at 7s 6d, freight of the Celys' fells at 45s and of Maryon's at 40s.

On these figures, the owners made a profit of £18 3s Flem. With an inconsistency typical of these shipping accounts, George elsewhere estimated the gain at £18 16s 1d Flem., which he distributed among the partners as £6 2s 11d to Richard, £6 11s 1d to Maryon and £6 2s 1d to himself.[31] Apart from the discrepancy in amount, his accounting illustrates one feature of his book-keeping. In balancing receipts from freight and the like against the purser's expenditure on the voyage, he ignored costs of the preliminary rigging of the ship. The concern was to share out all returns as soon as they were received, and to treat expenditure on fitting the ship as capital investment.

The chief expedition each year would be the voyage to Bordeaux for

---

[28] File 21 no. 3.
[29] *English Historical Documents*, IV, no. 589, misdated 1475.
[30] Burwash, *English Merchant Shipping*, p. 47.
[31] File 21 no. 2.

wine. This had recently become possible again for the English, who had made it so frequently in past centuries when Gascony had been a territory of the English crown. Their taste for Gascon wine had not been lost with the final collapse of their pretensions to sovereignty over that area. In 1486 the *Margaret* set out for Bordeaux in late August or early September. In August George paid 13*s* 4*d* to 'an mariner in Thames St. for an cable of 80 fathom of John Constantyne', and also bought a boat for the ship from Myllar of Erith, paying him £3 3*s* 9*d*.³² Maryon may have paid a further £1, and seven oars been bought as well. It may, too, have been on 21 August of that year that Richard bought 'two ropes weighing 1¾ cwt. 23 lb.' at 10*s* 6*d* per cwt, 'two tow lines of 18 threads' at 3*s* 4*d* and seven lb of marline (thin rope of two strands).³³ The individual accounts for rigging this year are confused and mostly undated, but it seems likely that purchases by Maryon of two oxen, a quarter and a half of fish, four dozen candle, ten dozen bread, a quarter and 20 lb of biscuit (4*s*), and a thousand billet (5*s*), were also for the relatively long voyage to Bordeaux.³⁴ George provided another ox, costing 20*s* plus 4*d* for killing it at Mallins and 8*d* for carriage to Blackwall, where the ship was tied up. He also paid Byrde the carpenter 4*s* 1*d* for 'hovyr loffe [orlop] borde'.³⁵ On St Bartholomew's Day he gave Aldridge 24*s* 4½*d*, and 'at the departing of the ships to Bordeaux' (evidently in a fleet) the searcher at Gravesend was paid 3*s* 4*d*.³⁶

In all, George's own claimed payments towards the rigging for this voyage came to £7 0*s* 5½*d*, and he noted, 'item, the ship has gotten toward the contentation of this again, whereof partition must be made, £25 18*s* Flem.'. He then recorded the total payments so far: 'sum total laid out upon the *Margaret* by us from [when] we had her to her voyage to Bordeaux – £91 18*s* ½*d*'. This broke down to £15 18*s* 5½*d* from George, £29 19*s* 7*d* from Maryon, and £46 from Richard, which included the purchase price of the ship.³⁷

William Aldridge's rather meagre purser's account³⁸ covers only the actual voyage to Bordeaux and back, apart from a claim for 6*s* 9*d* stg. consisting of 4*s* for his costs 'while the ship i-rigged, two weeks', and small amounts for two elm boards bought at Gravesend, 4*d* for a carpenter for half a day, pump leather, and 11*d* worth of fish bought at Plymouth. His receipts consisted of sums which Giles Beckingham and John Speryng, who travelled as merchants' factors for Richard and George, delivered to him in France, to a total of 132 francs (£13 4*s* stg.

---

³² File 13 fo. 7.
³⁴ File 13 fo. 5v.
³⁶ File 13 fo. 7.
³⁸ File 13 fos. 54–60.

³³ File 16 fo. 10.
³⁵ File 13 fo. 58v.
³⁷ Ibid.

at the exchange rate of ten francs to the £). The accounts in France are kept in francs, sous (at 15 to the franc) and hardits (at 60 to the franc).

At Bordeaux, 67 francs went to pay the crew, as follows:

William Parker, master under God	12 fr.
William Ayelryche, purser	8 fr.
Peleger Larderys	5 fr.
John Chener, cook	5 fr.
Robert Lynkholl [Lincoln, the bosun]	5 fr.
William Jacson	4 fr.
James Walysshe	4 fr.
Thomas Cardon	4 fr.
Thomas Medycrofte	4 fr.
Richard Bocher	4 fr.
Davy Wyllyamson	3 fr.
Thomas Bawen	3 fr.
James Tayler	3 fr.
Piers Parker	3 fr.[39]

A further 64 francs 47 hardits were spent at La Rochelle, the Ile de Rê ('Rethe'), Bordeaux and Blaye ('Bloy'). Provisions, particularly bread, three and a half sheep and three and half pipes (441 gallons) of 'beverage' – doubtless wine – cost 29½ fr. A carpenter had to be employed for one and a half days, at six sous, to effect repairs for which timber was bought, and two new waist-boards were put in. Two new anchor-stocks had to be sawn, and other purchases included 300 lead-nail, a pulley-pin of box-wood, 'straw to burn the ship', and a gimlet. Two water barrels were bound, and bread was baked at a cost of 10½ sous. Twenty-one ells of canvas were also purchased, with 1 lb sail twine, and Aldridge paid 2 sous 'to the fellowship when they sewed the sail'. Three more lb of marline cost 9 sous. Incidental expenses were Aldridge's costs of 6 fr. at Bordeaux and the costs of the master going to Bordeaux from Blaye, at ½ fr. and 2 sous 'for his passage up and down' the Géronde. At Blaye, where arms had to be unloaded before they proceeded up the river, Aldridge paid 2½ fr. 'for laying a-land of the ordnance', and unloading the ballast cost 1 fr. 50 hardits, plus 'a billet [certificate of permission] for to lay the ballast a-land', at 6 sous.

On the homeward voyage the ship was detained at Plymouth for 11 weeks. Some of her cargo of wine was unloaded there, but the prolonged stay was unscheduled. In January William Cely wrote from Calais, 'I have showed unto Tibbot, according to your commandment, that the *Margett* is still at Plymouth. With the which he is not well content that

---

[39] File 13 fo. 55v. The master, William Parker, was perhaps the man who had served as master of *La Governore* in Feb. 1484: *C.P.R. 1476–85*, p. 426.

she tarrieth so long', since he had a good deal of wine in her.[40] The fact that a new mizzen mast had to be provided may suggest that the ship had been caught in a storm. She also needed a new streamer (long pennon), which took three yards of linen cloth and two yards of buckram. The mast cost 14s 4½d and the streamer 2s 2½d. At Plymouth, on 19 December, Aldridge took up a loan from Roger Cotyn of London of the kind technically called a sea-loan or loan on bottomry. His letter of payment runs:

Be it known to all men that I, William Aldryge, purser of the *Marget Cele of London*, owe to Roger Cotyn of London, 25s 8d, to pay to the foresaid Roger or to [the] bringer of this bill at the sight hereof, withouten any longer delay.

In witness whereof I, the said William, bind me and the ship called the *Marget*, and have put my seal. Written at Plymouth the 19 day of December the reign of King Harry the VIIth the 2 year.

Per William Ayelryche.[41]

A subsequent note by William Maryon records that he paid 8s 8d stg. on this bill. The equivalent of 53s 4d had earlier been taken up by Speryng at Bordeaux from 'master Tate's purser', which George repaid at London.[42] There is no discernible interest charge involved in these loans, though master Tate's man got a rundlet of wine by way of *pour-boire*.

The amount taken up from Cotyn was insufficient to replenish Aldridge's empty purse, and he must have gone to London to obtain more money: both George and Maryon delivered him cash on 2 or 3 January 1487.[43] With sums that John Speryng gave him at Plymouth, he had in all a further £6 4s 4d stg. Of this, £3 16s 9d went on the expenses of the ship for the 11 weeks at Plymouth, and a further week at London while the ship delivered. Most of the expenditure was on food and drink: a total of 34s 7d on meat, 10s 7d on fish, 24s 6d on bread, and 33s 4d on five pipes of beer (630 gallons). Other payments at Plymouth were for two bushels of salt, nail and the grinding of an axe and an adze.

On the *Margaret*'s eventual return to London the crew were paid off.[44] Nominally, the master received 54s stg., the purser 36s, the cook and bosun 22s 6d, and 'Pellygger Calker', alias Larderys, 20s. Jackson, Walsh, Cardon, Medecroft and Butcher were paid the basic 'one man's right' of 18s, and four other men had 13s 6d. Against the name of Davy Williamson is the laconic entry 'dead', and part of the wages of 13s 6d which should have been due to him were split between Aldridge (9s 6d) and Speryng (2s 8d). The record is entirely silent about his fate. If the ship lost her mizzen in a storm, did Davy perish at the same time, or did he fall ill, less dramatically, in France? Possibly as a replacement,

[40] C.L. 226.   [41] File 13 fo. 32.   [42] File 13 fo. 37v.
[43] File 13 fos. 35v, 61.   [44] File 13 fo. 7v.

two more men, Robert Trewtall and Thomas Samson, had been taken on at Bordeaux and were paid 6s 8d each.

It is difficult to work out any clear relationship between the wages paid at Bordeaux, which were the same on all three of the *Margaret*'s trips there and based on one man's right of four francs, and the sums paid in England, where a basic 18s was paid in 1488, and 19s in 1489. Wages were normally paid at a standard rate for the voyage, regardless of duration, and the only obvious explanation for the higher sum in 1489 is that the ship had made an unusually large number of calls at English ports on the outward voyage. But in February 1490 the London adventurers paid a 'reward' of an extra 2s stg. apiece to 'the poor mariners of the ships [who] have long continued and lain on this "reace" [the voyage to the Bammis and Cold marts] and spent all their wages and more'.[45]

There were, in any case, deductions from the nominal amount due to several of the crew members. In 1487 William Aldridge was charged 2s for the 'red coat of fence' (half its purchase price), and Richard Butcher had 2s deducted for 'harness' given to him. Thomas Cardon had the portage of a pipe of wine, worth 9s, in place of half his wage of 18s, and Aldridge and the master each took a portage of a ton of wine, at 18s each.[46] There was a dispute over the amount due to Aldridge because of the time spent at Plymouth. George noted that on 28 January 1487, when he drew up the final account of the voyage, Aldridge had still in hand 8s 3½d and harness worth 4s (there was a 'jack' or protective jerkin as well as the red coat). 'Item, [it] is agreed amongst us that and it be found that he ought to have 2s for every week upon the voyage [homeward], he must have 11s 8½d more, or else he must restore the rest.'[47] Apparently Aldridge was claiming costs for the time spent in port, at the same rate as his 2s a week in London before the ship sailed, on top of his 'two men's rights' of 36s. It is hard to be sure what the master received on this occasion, since he was given various sums by different people, including 5s 8d which Richard 'paid in the Guildhall for William Parker' on 16 February.[48]

On the return voyage, the *Margaret* carried a cargo of 55¾ tons of wine, including 50 tons for Tibbot Oliver, marked with his initial T.[49] Most of the rest belonged to the Celys or members of the crew, but there was one ton for Peter Joye. Stockfish of 'Petty John' was freighted for 6s 8d.

---

[45] *A.C.M.*, p. 201.
[46] File 13 fo. 58. Burwash (p. 47) was puzzled by the fact that not all the mariners of the *Margaret* were credited with portages, but it is evident that it was chiefly the ship's officers who took them.
[47] File 13 fo. 58v.   [48] File 13 fo. 8.   [49] File 13 fos. 58–9.

The master's wine may have been carried in the *Carvel à Dieu*. While owners and crew were assessed at 18s per ton for freight, Peter Joye had to pay 19s, which was allotted to Aldridge as part of his wages. Tibbot was charged 19s 9d, but he got some discount because his 50 tons were counted as only 48, '21 for 20'. His total bill for freight and costs was £56 13s 10d, for which he agreed to pay £55 8s 10d, 'and a hogshead [63 gallons] of wine upon a due reckoning at our next meeting'.[50]

George reckoned the total money from the freight payments available for distribution at £49 19s 6d stg., or £16 13s 2d for each partner.[51] At the same time there was an evening-up of the payments each had made towards the ship's expenses. George calculated that Richard had contributed £8 16s 3¼, William Maryon £9 1s 4d, and George £5 4s ½d. On this basis (which does not square very well with figures in individual accounts), he proceeded to make an elaborate redistribution:

Tibbot's freight is for 48 ton, so is 21 for 20 abated	£47 10s
Item, average at Bordeaux	[blank]
Item, George Cely 5 hogsheads 3 tierce [a hogshead held ½ a pipe or ¼ ton or 63 gallons, the tierce ⅓ pipe or ⅙ ton – 42 wine gallons].	27s
Item, Richard Cely an hogshead	4s 6d
Item, John Speryng at Plymouth, 3 hogsheads . . .	13s 6d
Item, Petty John at Plymouth, 1 hogshead	4s 6d
Sum	£49 19s 6d.
Item, hereof received of Tybot the 16 day of March anno '86 [o.s.]	£20
Whereof delivered to my brother	£6 13s 4d
To myself.	£6 13s 4d
To William Maryon	£6 13s 4d.[52]

On 20 March 1487 'the clear reckoning of this Bordeaux voyage' was drawn up thus:

First, the whole of our freight amounts unto . . .	£49 19s 6d
William Maryon has laid out upon this voyage . . .	£9 16d
Item, my brother has laid out also upon rigging . .	£8 16s 3d
Item, myself has laid out for my part also . . .	£5 4s 7d
Item, my brother delivered to William Maryon . .	20d 5s 1d
Item, 'a delivered him for me that I lacked in laying out of so much	25s 6d
This being bated of £9 16d, so he laid out now . .	£7 14s
Item, my brother must have of me, for that I laid not out so much as he did, per	23s 11d
This being bated of £8 16s 3d, so it is . . .	£7 14s
Item, I pay to William Maryon	25s 6d

[50] File 13 fo. 52.   [51] File 13 fo. 59.   [52] Ibid.

Item, to my brother Richard Cely	23s 11d
This being added to my laying out makes	£7 14s
Every man's part comes unto	£16 13s 2d[53]

Or, in another set of workings,

£7 14s an man of us.

Laid out per W. Maryon	£9 16d
My brother	£8 16s 3¼d
Myself	£5 4s 7½d
[Total	£23 2s 2¾d]

The 3rd part of W. Maryon	£3 5s 0[⅓d]
The 3rd part of my brother	58s 9d
The 3rd part of mine is	34s 10½d

Pro me to William Maryon	25s 6½d
To my brother	23s 10½d
Sum	£7 14s

Per W. Maryon paid	£9 16d
Wherefore my brother delivered him	20d
And I delivered him	25s 6½d
Sum of these two parcels	£7 8½d
So you have paid	£7 14s

Item, my brother laid out	£8 16s 3¼d
Wherefore I delivered to my brother	23s 10½d
And he paid to William Maryon	20d
Sum	£7 14s.

Item, paid by me	£5 4s 7½d
Paid to William Maryon pro me	25s 6½d
Paid to my brother by me	23s 10½d
Sum	£7 14s.[54]

Which was all very satisfactory, provided there had been no errors in the original estimation of costs.

Richard and George had in fact had, by 16 March, respectively £14 10s 8d and £15 7s 2d from their £16 13s 4d profits. Richard was credited with 9s for his freight, and out of an instalment of £25 8s 10d paid by Tibbot, he paid Maryon £10 and a further £1 7s 2d which Maryon had expended, leaving himself £14 odd. George similarly had a credit of 27s for his own freight and 13s 6d for Speryng's. He had received £20 from Tibbot, and paid £6 13s 4d to Maryon.[55]

Maryon does not appear to have imported any wine on his own account, and Richard had only the small quantity of one pipe (126

[53] File 13 fo. 59v.　　　[54] File 13 fo. 61v.　　　[55] File 13 fo. 60.

gallons). George, however, had sent Speryng to France for the purpose of investing £15 11s Flemish in wine. Of this amount, given Speryng on 26 August, £5 stg. was adventured by George's wife Margery 'for her children'.[56] George had listed the more important English and other coins with a value in francs.

The value of coins at Bordeaux

First the rial [10s stg.]	6 francs
The half rial	.3 fr.
The angel [6s 8s stg.].	.4 fr.
The old noble [8s 4d stg.] .	5 fr. 20 hard.
The ducat, the half old noble, the salute	.2 fr. 40 hardits
The new crown [4s stg., 6s Flem.]	2½ fr.
The old crown .	2 fr. 24 hard.
The Savoy crown	.3 fr.
The Andreus gulden [5s 4d Flem.]	.2 fr.
The Rhenish gulden .	.2 fr.
The Utrecht gulden [4s 6d Flem.] is 27½ sous	[1 fr. 50 hard.]
The leeuw [lion]	3 fr. 10 hard.
The old [Flemish] groat	10 hard.
The new groat .	[blank]
The 'Nynhegyn' groat	8 hard.[57]

In his list, George contemplated an exchange rate of 1 franc = 2s 6d Flemish = 1s 8d stg., based on the Calais exchange rate of 30s Flemish to 20s stg. But, as mentioned, the rate at Bordeaux was 10 fr. to the £ stg., not 12 fr. Speryng's stock of crowns, Utrecht gulden, Andrews and groats, valued at 123 fr. 40 hard., was therefore the equivalent of only £12 7s 4d stg.

Some of this money went towards the ship's store.[58] With the remainder, Speryng bought a barrel of sturgeon heads for 6 fr. (12s stg.), a gross of 'points' or fastenings for clothing for 40 hardits, and a ton, three hogsheads and two tierces of wine. The wine cost 87 fr. or £8 14s stg. Incidental expenses for the royal custom duty in France and the town custom of Bordeaux, rummaging (the payment for arranging casks in the cargo space), average for one ton carried in the *Carvel à Dieu*, and the purchase of a gimlet and marking iron, came to 4 fr. 21 hard., or 8s 8d stg. At London, George paid a total of £2 2s for custom (3s, his total of over 1¾ tons being allowed for one ton), certificates, lighterage, cranage, carriage, and freight-charge (of £1 16s).[59] He also bought a further two hogsheads which were the 'portage' of one of the mariners, and two

[56] File 13 fo. 35.
[57] File 13 fo. 64. Flemish values, at Calais tariff, from File 13 fo. 35 and File 21 no. 4.
[58] File 13 fos. 36, 64.   [59] File 13 fo. 37.

hogsheads and a tierce which Speryng had bought himself, and took allowance of Speryng's freight. The total cost of his 13 hogsheads (3¼ tons) of wine came to £17 4s 10d or £5 6s per ton. Freight, at a preferential rate of 18s per ton, amounted to about 17 percent of the price at shipment at Bordeaux, or 11.25 percent of a selling price in England of £8 per ton.[60]

On 13 March George sold to Sir Thomas Tyrrell, an important person whose favour was desirable, a pipe of red wine and two hogsheads of claret, making in all a ton, at a price of £7.[61] On 24 August he sold the same quantities to Harry Brazier for £8. He thus made a profit of £4 8s on two-thirds of his import, representing a net profit on the amount sold of 41.5 percent. The rest was perhaps Margery's share in return for her £5 investment. The intricacies of the Celys' transactions are illustrated by George's dealings with Harry Brazier. The wine was in fact given in part payment for six millstones (no doubt for George's mill), which cost £24. George made Brazier a bill for the balance of £16, payable to John 'Stodell' or 'Todell', Spaniard, at London, on 10 December 1487. On 8 January 1488 he paid this amount 'to Percyvalle for John Todell'.[62]

In his new capacity of ship-owner and small-scale wine merchant, George had now invented himself a second merchant's mark. Unlike his stapler's mark, which was his father's old quartered shield with a bar in the top right quarter and a circle in the bottom right, the new mark incorporated the initials G.C. with a cross flourished with the usual flags in a W-shape. This (perhaps accidentally) appears to form the mast of an outlined ship at the base.[63]

In the second year of her operation, the *Margaret* made only two voyages, to Zealand and to Bordeaux. Her new purser was George's servant John Speryng, who had been learning the ropes when he travelled with Aldridge the previous season. He now combined the two functions of ship's purser and merchant's factor. Some versatility was required of him. Besides keeping his accounts, in several currencies, and supervising all expenditure for the ship during her voyages, he had to be able to speak both Dutch and French. He must also have needed considerable stamina to endure the uncomfortable conditions aboard a small medieval vessel, especially in winter, though during her voyages the *Margaret* spent longer in port than at sea. A ship which contracted to take goods to and from one of the marts would be expected to wait until the selling

---

[60] M. M. Postan (*Medieval Trade and Finance*, p. 123), estimated that costs of shipping a ton of Gascon wine to Hull or Ireland at the end of the thirteenth century were about 8s, rather less than 10 percent of its f.o.b. price in Bordeaux, and that they were even lower in the fifteenth century.

[61] File 13 fo. 38.   [62] File 13 fo. 42.   [63] File 21 no. 4.

concluded. In 1472 Lord Howard's charterparty constrained his two ships to remain in Zealand for 30 working days, excluding Sundays and major saints' days. They in fact departed on 20 October, nine days before the agreed date.[64]

Neither Speryng nor Nicholas Best, who took over the duties of purser in 1488, figures in the lists of 'men's hires' paid to the *Margaret*'s crews. Evidently as servants of the owners they did not receive the usual purser's wage, and one hopes their remuneration was generous. Certainly Speryng received £3 3s stg. as part of his wages after the Bordeaux voyage of 1487–8.[65]

On the ship's return from Bordeaux in January 1487, she had lain idle for about three months. There was no question of a series of quick turn-arounds with new cargos, and this greatly restricted her owners' chances of profit from her operation. In 1532 the *Mary Plantagenet* did much better, on paper at least.[66] In June her charterparty specified that she was to proceed, laded, from Topsham to La Rochelle, where she had 12 days in which to discharge and reload with salt. She would then return to Barnstable to victual, which should take no more than four days. Then, as soon as weather permitted, she should sail to the Isle of Man or Ireland for fish. She was to remain in those parts for 40 days, and then proceed to Bordeaux (for wine). Twenty days were allowed for the ship to discharge and take in wine at Bordeaux, after which she was to take her current cargo to Bristol.

In the Thames, the *Margaret*'s 'harness' was padlocked away, and one of the crew – first Richard Butcher and then James Taylor – was paid to remain on board to keep the ship.[67] On 3 March Taylor was paid 12d 'for a week, and he find himself', i.e. provide his own food. On 2 March Maryon gave him 6d to buy fish for the caulkers for the annual major work. Five men, including a Spaniard and Peleger Larderys, by-named 'Caulker', who had been in the crew to Bordeaux, worked for a total of 21½ days between them, up to 15 March. Maryon provided 13 stone of oakum and a barrel of pitch. Three quarters and 12 lb of tallow at 8s and 200 quarters of reed at 2s 3d were also used, and part of the large quantity of billet bought would be needed for heating the pitch. The ship also required three-quarters of a hundredweight of spikings at 40d the cwt, and the master was given 3s 6d to buy 'board and quarters', while Maryon paid 3d for 'sawing of a tree for the waist of the ship'. Small

[64] *A.C.M.*, pp. 63–4.
[65] File 14 fo. 23v. Unfortunately, the space for sums is left blank in his note of 'costs at Bordeaux, 5 weeks', 'my service Bordeaux voyage', 'my costs in Flanders for a month', 'my service of the Flanders voyage': File 14 fo. 39v.
[66] *Lisle Letters*, I, pp. 397–8.
[67] File 14 fos. 1–6: William Maryon's account for rigging.

purchases for her included brooms, 100 small ropes bought from William Remington, 'lacheline' (cord for latchets), 12 bowstrings, a new compass and a running-glass for navigation, four shovels, a socket for the pump-staff, a snatch-pulley (for the quick attachment of a rope) and two catheads, a pair of pot-hooks, a salmon barrel, a tankard, two scoops, half a dozen platters and the same number of dishes, and two drinking bowls. Two lanterns were 'new horned' at a cost of 8d.

John Speryng himself paid, according to his account,[68] for a casting-lead, two oars which, with the making, cost 2s 10d, three forlocks (wedges for bolts) and the pin for a gun, brimstone, taps, three pulleys, 'for the mizzen mast and the parrel', a plank for the orlop, 300 tampons, an axe, six more oars, the mending of the kettle, and 2s for striking the mast. He also 'paid unto the lighterman for his lighter for to lay in the wheat when the mast was a-striking', and in the week beginning Monday 14 May he paid 5s to the searchers before the ship's departure.

While the ship was in port the diet provided was naturally more varied than that at sea. Besides the regular supplies of bread, bought by the dozen at 1s per dozen, fish, and meat after Lent was over, Speryng bought butter and eggs on six occasions between Easter and 23 April. There was one purchase of 3d worth of oatmeal, and Maryon provided at different times a hundred red (smoked) herring at 13d, six rochets, two salt fish, mustard and mussels for 15½d, a stockfish for 5d, two half-barrels of white (salted) shotten herring for 11s and a cade of red herring for 6s. He also 'paid to my gossip Sepam for fourteen couple of "aberdenys" [dried fish], the couple 9d', and later bought 15 cast of fish for 5s 8d from 'John Fepam'. (Maryon was often careless about distinguishing between *f* and long-tailed *s*.) A cast or warp of fish, theoretically a handful, contained between two and four, depending on size. Between 17 and 26 March Maryon also bought three lb of figs, one lb of raisins, unspecified quantities of leeks and mussels, and three bushels of green peas (i.e. field peas) costing 7d a bushel. The unlikely medlars with which Dorothy Burwash sought to endow the crew derived from a misreading of (sail) needles in one entry.[69] In preparation for the voyage itself, Speryng paid for the grinding of three-quarters of wheat, at 20d, bolting the meal (12d), and 'a hogshead and a barrel for to put in the flour' (15d). Two oxen cost 35s, and three barrels 'for to put in the flesh' cost 14d. Eight large fishes cost 4s. In all, Maryon paid for the rigging for the Zealand voyage this year £7 18s 11d stg., including money delivered to Speryng towards costs on the voyage. In England before it started, Speryng paid out £6 18s 2d stg.

[68] File 14 fos. 7–12.
[69] Burwash, *English Merchant Shipping*, p. 73; File 14 fo. 2.

The *Margaret* reached Arnemuiden on 24 May. She went on to Antwerp, an extension for which the crew were all paid 2s Flem. extra, and returned to London about a month later. A variety of payments had to be made in the netherlands: for 25 needles, eight stics of canvas at 4d Flem. the stic, grommets, a cable and two hawsers, and two hooks 'for the packs'. The 'lodesman' charged 6s 4d for pilotage, and the mast required mending, which cost, with timber and workmanship, 14s Flem. Supplies were replenished with 2s worth of fish at Antwerp, and another 14 for 7s, baking of bread cost 3s 3d, and on 11 June one barrel of beer was bought for 3s 4d Flem. (Unless it was a special brew, it was the equivalent of a barrel for about 20d stg. in England.) A further 10s Flemish worth of beer was bought before the ship returned home.

There is a complete record of the crew's wages for this Zealand voyage.[70] It was not customary to pay portages on this run.

	Paid in Zealand		Paid at London
Robert Smythe, master		30s Flem.	15s stg.
Raffe Stamyr		10s	5s
Harry Halle		10s	5s
Crawschanke		10s	5s
Thomas Hylle	bosun	12s 6d	—
Gyllyam		10s	5s
Thomas A'Sanwic		10s	bosun 6s 3d
Garard		10s	5s
Lawrans		10s	5s
James Taylor		10s	5s
Richard Bocher, cook		12s 6d	6s 3d
Adrian the Dutchman		10s	5s
Harry		7s 6d	3s 9d
Peper			5s
The boy			2s 6d

Sum – £7 12s 6d Flem.
    £3 18s 9d stg.

At the Calais exchange rate of 30s Flem., per £ stg., the basic rate for the round trip that year was 17s 6d Flem. or 11s 8d stg. It seems, however, that there was a fixed wage of 10s Flem. from London to Zealand and 5s stg. from Zealand to London, and that this customary amount bore no relationship to fluctuating exchange rates. The wage may have been the same in 1536.[71]

Evidently, from Speryng's reference to laying in the grain in England, the *Margaret* had again taken a cargo of grain to Zealand, but there is no record of sale. On 4 January Speryng bought from the priest of

[70] File 14 fo. 9r–v.   [71] Burwash, p. 53.

Stifford 10 qtr of wheat at 5s 2d per qtr, 10 qtr of rye at 3s 2d, 10 qtr of oats at 1s 5d, and 5 qtr of barley at 2s 6d, and a further 10 qtr of oats from Peacock's wife at 1s 4½d, making in all nine tons of grain at a buying price of £6 3s 9d.[72] This was probably destined for export. The £17 which the purser received 'from the merchants at Antwerp' was perhaps for cloth or other goods being carried to the mart.

The interesting feature of Speryng's account for this year's Zealand voyage is the detailed description of the freight carried on the return trip from Antwerp, evidently of goods purchased at the mart. One or more of the owners may have accompanied the goods in the ship, because Speryng 'received of the merchant[s?] for lying upon the voyage, £4 4s stg.' In his list of freight, many of the items have the owner's mark depicted alongside, usually a simple device based on the initial of his surname.

John Dawson a last of treen [wooden goods], freight		5s
John Gravyro	6 bales of madder ·	12s
	2 pipes of wire	8s
Water More	1 fardel ·	12s
William Hide being with Thomas Abraam, ⎰		
	1 barrel ·	1s
	1 long settle ·	12s
	1 dry fat	4s
	1 maund [basket] and 3 barrels of nails ·	6s 2d
Master Welbeke	1 fardel	4s
John Armynar	4 last of wood ashes	16s
	6 cradles of glass ·	8s
Roger Grove	1 pipe and a dry fat	6s
Godfrey Hellow	1 dry fat with harness	4s
Robert Dyrke	1 barrel of nails & 12 hides ·	1s 4d
Jacob Valke	5 cradles of glass ·	6s 8d
John Keell	2 pipes ·	8s
	2 straws of wire and 2 dry fats	16s
	2 fats of woad	6s
	1 straw of wax	6s
	2 lasts of tree	10s
	1 peyse [wey] of wax	4s
Angel Domid	1 fardel ·	3s
Paul the brewer	4 sacks of hops	13s 4d
John Spenser	1 cupboard and 3 pans and 3 kettles	5s
William Wordyngton	1 pack ·	8s
Steven Everton, haberdasher without Temple Bar,		
	2 dry fats, 1 chest with combs, 4 dozen bottles	12s

Sum – £9 17s 6d.[73]

[72] File 20 no. 35.
[73] File 14 fos. 11–12. A dry fat was a barrel or other container for dry goods.

For this voyage, it is possible to make some comparison between receipts and total recorded expenditure, including rigging and the full wage-bill. As far as it is recorded (but the provision of beer in England is excluded for a start), total expenditure was £31 4s 11d, and the receipts were only £24 7s 8d stg. Regarded in this way, the ship made a loss on her carrying activities. Even ignoring Maryon's outlay on rigging and taking the purser's expenditure alone, as George normally did when dividing the 'gains', there was only a small profit (£2 or 8.9 percent) from freight and fares. If Richard and George also sold grain on their personal account, the records of the transaction are lost.

In point of fact, George seems to have deferred any complete balancing of the accounts for this year until May 1489, when the *Margaret* had returned from her last voyage to Bordeaux for wine.[74] The relative unprofitability of the Zealand voyage of 1487 could have persuaded the partners to switch their attention to Brittany and the salt trade in 1488.

The Bordeaux voyage of 1487–8 produced better receipts, but the accounts are somewhat confused and George's book-keeping methods are further complicated by arithmetical errors. Speryng's account as purser begins on 27 September, with the receipt of a total of £15 stg. on behalf of the partners.[75] Miscellaneous purchases included two gunwales (2s), two augers, a chisel and a round chisel, another sounding-lead, a cable of 4 cwt and a second-hand cable 'that was the Frenchman's', a hammer, pins and cheeks for the guns (but no more gunpowder is mentioned), a bow, 14 ells of canvas, and a rope weighing 34 lb for the mizzen. Speryng also paid 8d for hooping the flesh barrels, steeping tubs and bucket, presumably to hold the three oxen and three and a half 'beefs' bought to provide salt meat. The ship went on to Sandwich before 14 October, and by 4 December was at Southampton. In the meantime she had taken on 23½ dozen bread, 7½ cwt fresh herring, a cade and half-a-barrel of other herring, 3 cwt and 35 lb of biscuit, at 3s the cwt, five bushels of salt (for the meat), eight pipes of beer and two barrels of 'new beer'. The new beer cost 3s a barrel of 36 gallons, the pipes cost as usual 6s 8d for 126 gallons. Speryng's total expenditure on this leg of the voyage was £14 16s 6d stg., which George misrepresented in auditing the account because he overlooked one sub-total of £5 1s 9d.[76]

The progress of the ship can be followed in Speryng's subsequent accounts. She was at Le Conquet on 14 December, near her original port of Penmarch, and Speryng bought a roll of 'poldavit' (Breton canvas).

---

[74] File 14 fos. 19–33 purports to deal with expenditure in 1487, but no balance is struck between expenditure and receipts for that year.
[75] His account is File 14 fos. 35–40.
[76] File 14 fos. 36, 38v.

At Bordeaux, which the *Margaret* had reached by 24 December, his costs included 90 aunes of canvas at 16 hardits the aune (ell), timber for the rails, and wages to a carpenter for making the rails and bowsprit, 'a ring of iron for the Breton tackle', and a new hawser weighing 110 lb for the winding-tackle, reed 'for to tallowing of the ship', making (i.e. repairing) the hearth in the cook-room, small ropes for the lifts (the ropes running from mast-head to yard-arms), weighing 89 lb, a 'shever' (shiver, a small grooved component) for the pulley, three boards for the pavis, and two new lanterns. Hire of a 'gabyr [lighter] for to have out the ballast' also called for a small fee. At Blaye on 28 January Speryng 'paid for keeping of the [unloaded] harness 2½ francs', and for three wimble irons 'and for filing of the same and mending of the ship tools'. On 4 February they were at Notre Dame (Notre-Dame-de-Monts, Vendée, between the Ile d'Yeu and the Ile de Noirmoutier),[77] and by 14 February back at Le Conquet, where more provisions were bought for the voyage home. At Plymouth on 19 February bread, fresh fish and a barrel of beer for 3s 4d replenished the stores, while a hogshead was also filled with beer for 4s. The wine bought in France, including a hogshead of 'marchand wine' at Le Conquet, together with the beer, provided an average of 0.7 gallons per man per day. If the total voyage, from the time the ship started rigging in London, took 21 weeks, the victualling allowance approximated quite closely to the 12½d per man per week allocated on convoy duty in 1476. Like most people, they could expect only one hot meal a day.[78]

The crew and their hires in France were as follows:

Robert Smythe, master	.12 fr.
Perys Randall	. 6 fr.
William Wynter	. 4 fr.
John A'Kaen [Caen]	. 4 fr.
John Hawkyns	. 4 fr.
John Feays	. 4 fr.
Simon Harys	. 4 fr.
Perys [Hoke]	. 4 fr.
Tyllar	. 4 fr.
Thomas Merycroft [Medecroft]	. 4 fr.
James Tayllar	. 4 fr.
Thomas Makow	5 fr.[altered from 4 fr.]
Clays	. 3 fr.
Robin Harys	.3½ fr.
Harman the boy	. 2 fr.
Total	. 65 francs [*sic*, correctly 67½ francs].[79]

[77] This is more probable than Notre Dame de Trescoet, Morbihan: Margery K. James, *Studies in the Medieval Wine Trade*, ed. Elspeth M. Veale (Oxford, 1971), p. 123 n. 3.   [78] Burwash, p. 75.   [79] File 14 fo. 40.

To this George appended a note that at seven groats (stg.) to the franc, it amounted to £7 11s 8d stg.

To judge by their names, this crew were a mixed lot by nationality. Several of them were sufficiently satisfied with the conditions aboard the *Margaret* to sign on for two or more voyages with her, but there was a frequent change of master.

Speryng's expenditure in France came to £10 15s stg., by George's calculation. He paid 12s 2d stg. at Plymouth on the return journey, and was also charged with £6 8s 3d spent earlier on the rigging and itemized on a page among accounts for the previous voyage to Zealand.[80] His total disbursements for the voyage came to £34 8s 4d stg., plus unstated personal costs for five weeks at Bordeaux. George's stated total of £35 5s 3d may include these costs, but his book-keeping seems unreliable. Most of the expenses in France were met with a loan of £9 6s 8d, taken up from a London fishmonger. 'Moun Jenyn' (Mundus Jenyn, cheesemonger of St Dunstan in the East, and perhaps the same as Mount Jenyn de Melat, merchant of Bordeaux),[81] shipped 12 tons of wine in the *Margaret* and withheld 23s 4d stg. from his freight-payment at London because his man had paid so much to Speryng at Bordeaux.[82] William Wordington had been expected to pay £4 2s 10d stg. at Bordeaux, as freight for the cloth which the *Margaret* had carried for sale there, but he failed to do so and Speryng had to take out some of the money entrusted to him on George's private account.[83]

Apparently the only freight carried on the outward voyage was two weys of cheese belonging to George, valued at 18s stg., and the 97 cloths belonging to William Wordington, which consisted of 59 kerseys, four broad cloths, 82 dozens (cloths of half-length, measuring 12 yards by 1½–2 yards), two short cloths and 59 pieces of cotton russet.[84] The ship's freight on her return was 53 tons and three hogsheads of wine and two tons of woad, from which the total receipts came to £54 3s stg.[85] In London, Richard bought for 30s one hogshead of wine from the ten tons shipped for Harry 'Vavyser', alias Brazier.[86] But George seems the only member of the partnership to have purchased any wine at Bordeaux on his own account that season. Speryng bought him two tons and one pipe, total price 80 francs.[87] Petty costs for average of one ton in another ship, housing and custom of a ton brought the total to 85 francs. George notes

[80] File 14 fo. 10.
[81] *C.C.R. 1476–85*, no. 1164; *C.P.R. 1476–85*, p. 145.
[82] File 14 fo. 23.
[83] Wordington, a London draper who was now exporting cloth to Bordeaux, had previously imported a pack of cloth from Antwerp: p. 380.
[84] File 14 fo. 39.   [85] File 14 fo. 23r–v.   [86] File 14 fo. 24.
[87] File 13 fo. 41.

simply that the wine was sold by Speryng (at Bordeaux as part of a consignment for another merchant?) for £14 3s 4d stg.

Part of the difficulty about accounts for voyages to France lies in the fact that much of the purser's stock of money was in 'Flemish' coin, obtained by William Cely from sales of wool at Calais. George in effect converted into Flemish valuation any additional sums in sterling which the purser received for disbursement in France, so that his stock was expressed in French francs at 30d Flemish or 20d stg. This, however, represented an overvaluation of sterling: on the French market the rate hardened from ten francs to the £ stg. in late 1486–7 (24d stg. per franc) to 8.57 francs (28d stg. per franc) in late 1487–8 – the seven groats of 4d stg. for a franc in George's conversion of the wage bill. Consequently, the profit that George made on his purchase of wine in 1487 depends on what proportion of the purchase price was paid in Flemish coin (no more than 48 fr. 20 hard.), and how much was in sterling. He possibly made something under £4 stg. on an expenditure of about £10 5s 6d stg., or about 38 percent. Unlike the rate for sterling, the French exchange for Flemish money seems to have remained constant, at eight francs to the £ Flem. Some of the Flemish coins employed by William Rogers in April–May 1488 even made more than he expected in Brittany.

Perhaps it was disagreement between George's account for the Bordeaux voyage and John Speryng's account which caused Speryng to be summoned back from Calais in February 1488. On 29 February William Cely wrote to George, 'Sir, as for Speryng, I have showed him the intent of your letter, for the which he cometh over to your mastership at this same passage to clear himself.'[88] 'Clear' in this context usually meant to settle up an account.

The various accounts concerning the Bordeaux voyage of 1487–8 are so confused and full of contradictions that it is perhaps a mercy that there are no similarly detailed records for the *Margaret*'s voyage to the Bay of Bourgneuf between 30 March and 14 June 1488. One would, however, like to know what wages were paid. Possibly the second instalment, at London, came to £8 7s 10d, but we are not told the size of the crew. Speryng may again have acted as purser, but this time a new entrant on the scene, William Rogers, served as George's factor. One surviving account covers Rogers' purchases on George's behalf.[89] These were chiefly of cloth, from that region of Brittany whose place-names formerly made the fabrics 'lockram' and 'dowlas' household words in England. Entries elsewhere in George's accounts for the ship describe the sale of part of her cargo of salt, bought jointly by Richard and George, and the costs incurred on it at London.[90]

[88] *C.L.* 242.   [89] File 10 fo. 33.   [90] File 14 fos. 25–6.

George listed the payments of money to Rogers thus:

Jesu 1488

Item, the 30 day of March anno ut supra the *Marget Cely* departed from Gravesend toward the Bay for salt, at our three adventures, God speed her.

Item, that same time I delivered to William Rogers, mine attorney, for me in Flemish pence and in 'Hewttrytus gylldorns' [i.e. Utrecht gulden] – £26 Flemish.

Of the £40 Flemish that William Cely delivered us, my brother takes out for him for freight for his men £6 Flem. [Richard had a ship of his own], and I take to me as much. Sum of both – £12. Rest, £28 Flem.

Item, William Rogers has of my brother's and mine that is parteable between us at this voyage – £28 Flem.

Item, William Rogers has of me, as anfore rehearsed, of Flemish money	£6 Flem.
Item, of Speryng for me that he must deliver	£3 6s 8d stg.
Item, of Flemish groats of 8d le piece, 28. Sum	18s 4d
Item, 4 Mylen groats [groats of Malines]	8s Flem.
Item, an groat	9d Flem.
Item, 4 nymeryn groats	20d Flem.
Item, an piece of	4d Flem.
Sum total of mine money above	£13 10s Flem.
Sum total	£41 4s 1d Flem.[91]

The £26 Flem. first mentioned seems to be quite separate from the rest of the account, in which the addition is wildly wrong. The subtotal of George's own money should read £12 9s 1d Flem., but George gave Rogers a further 5s, mentioned in another memorandum as well as by Rogers in his own meticulous account:

Jesus Maria. Asset principio Sancta Maria meo.

Here following are the parcels of receipts and payments of me, William Roggers, to the use of my master George Cely, merchant of the Staple of Calais, in the months of March, April and May in the year of Our Lord God 1488, the third year of the reign of King Henry the 7th. That is to say,

First, I received of my said master in diverse coins, as it appeareth as well by a bill of my said master's own hand as by my book of parcels	29s 1d Flem.
Also, I received of my said master 3s 4d in sterling money for mine expenses	5s Flem.
Also, I received of my said master within the sum of £40 delivered to me for himself and my master his brother, as parcel of the said £40 by his commandment taken to his own use	£6 Flem.

Also, I received of increase in the change of 3 Mylleyn groats and 2 half-groats, every groat delivered to me for 2s Flem., for as much as I put them away in the exchange of them, every piece for 2s 1d Flem., more in all by ½d Flem. . . . . . 4½d Flem.
[That is, there was a further increment of ½d on the total sum.]

Also, I received of increase in 4 Lymmyn groats [George's 'nymeryn' groats], delivered to me for 5d Flem. every piece, for as much as I put them away every piece for 6d Flem. . . 4d Flem.

Also, I received of increase in 39s 2d of Flemish pence, in every 12d Flemish, 2d Flemish [and] 2d Breton . . . 6s 6d Flem.
 Total – 7s 2½d Flemish and 2d of British money.

Also I received [*sic*] of John Speryng, as in money retained in his own hands for part of the price of 6 bolts of Elron canvas bought of him for a new sail for the *Margaret Cely*, price of every piece 12 francs, which is 40s Flem., which money he should have delivered to me at the Bay. That is to say, 66s 8d stg. . . . . 100s Flem.
[In other words, Speryng failed to hand over the expected £3 6s 8d stg. at the Bay, because he had to devote the money to the purchase of a new sail.]

Sum of all the receipts abovesaid is £13 15½d Flem. and 2d of Briton money.[92]

A second account by William Rogers, partly in accountant's Latin, shows that as well as the £3 6s 8d stg. or £5 Flem. which Speryng retained for his canvas, Rogers gave him £3 17s 8d Flem., made up of 11 'Utrit gildrons' at 5s 6d Flem. each, 22 groats of 8d Flem., and six 'targes' at 5d Flem. apiece.[93] These last are double briquets under yet another name to add to the Celys' 'neming', 'nimhegin', 'nimerin' or 'limon' groats. The 22 groats at 8d Flem. are described on the dorse of the document as 'grotys Regis Romanorum', i.e. new groats of Maximilian as King of the Romans and Duke of Burgundy. The sum included 11s 6d towards the expenses of the ship and 2s Flem. owed to Speryng for 12 lampreys. There was also the freight of two pipes of beer (or 'beverage'?) of Speryng's, to be balanced against the (unspecified) freight of the linen which Rogers bought for George.

With the remaining £8 1s 3½d Flem. Rogers bought 104¾ aunes of Breton cloth at Bourgneuf and 'Mascoo' (Machecoul, inland from Bourgneuf) for a total of £6 2s 9¼d Flem.[94] This was all linen cloth, bought in 'remnants' of between 4¼ and 28¾ ells, and priced variously at 10d, 13d, 15d Flem. or 14d Flem. and 2d Breton per ell. In addition, Rogers paid 14d 'for mine expenses and one other man's that help me to buy the said cloth', and 2*d* Flem. 'for washing of three pieces which were wet in salt water'. He paid further for

5¼ aunes of British [Breton] russet woollen cloth, bought at Mascoo, price of every alne 6*s* 8*d* of British money, more in all by 1½*d* of Breton money . . . .   5*s* 10*d* Flem.

Also, for a paring shovel of iron for gardens, bought at Mascoo . . . .   4*d* Flem.

Also, for my dinner and drinking at Mascoo upon Saturday the 10th day of May . . . .   9½*d* Flem.

Also, paid to a man of 'Conket' for 15 lings, price of every piece 6*d* Flem. . . . .   7*s* 6*d* Flem.

Also, for a piece of powdered ['spiced'] fish called [blank] . . 3½*d* Flem.

And finally, there were costs 'upon Martin Gye':

Also, paid for new making of a coat and for the collar and vents of the same, for Martin Gye, the British child . . . .   5*d* Flem.

Also, for a new cap (4*d*), a pair of shoes (4*d*) and laces (½*d*), and for shaving (½*d*) and washing (½*d*) of Martin's shirts. . .   9½*d* Flem.

Also, for his meat and drink at mine host's house at Bourgneuf after he was arrayed . . . .   3*d* Flem.

Also, paid for 6 aunes 3 quarters of linen cloth in three remnants bought at Conket, price of every aune 6*d* Flem. .   3*s* 4½*d*.

There was left over to pay back to George, the sum of 5*s* 4¼*d* Flem. and 2*d* Breton, made up of four groats of 8*d*, four Flemish pence, 'a piece of silver delivered to me for 4*d*', 'a piece of Breton money of 2*d* Breton', and 16¼*d* in sterling money. There is no account for resale of the cloth in England. Nor is anything more said about 'Martin Gye the British child', who cannot have been very young if the shaving was for him.

The *Margaret* returned to London on 6 June according to the customs accounts and 14 June according to the Celys,[95] with a cargo of 55 wey and six bushels of salt (55 tons odd), 'at the adventure of Richard Cely, George Cely and William Maryon'. Of this, 44 wey was 'laid up in an house at the "wowllde wolkay"', i.e. the old wool-quay in London. Nine loads were apparently sent later by barge to Stratford.[96] The remaining 11 wey six bushels were sold, one wey to 'a man of Kent' for 20*s* 20*d*, and at Billingsgate the other ten wey and 6 bu. 'the most part 23*s* 4*d* le wey, and some less', for a total of £11 16*s* 10*d*. Petty costs on the salt amounted to 17½*d* per wey, and are recorded by George as follows:

Paid to the porters for bearing of 44 wey of salt, 5*d* le wey . .   18*s* 4*d*

Item, spent at Billingsgate 4*d*, and spent upon an sergeant at the wool-quay 4*d* 8*d*

[95] File 14 fo. 25; E.122 78/7, quoted A. R. Bridbury, *England and the Salt Trade in the Later Middle Ages* (Oxford, 1955), p. 128.   [96] File 21 no. 8.

Item, paid to the mayor's yeoman [For pricing the salt for resale.]   .   12*d*
Item, paid to the meter for the meting [measuring] of 54 wey salt,
4*d* le wey 18*s*
Item, paid for a plank there 4*d*

. . .

The 10 day of September, Item, paid by me to Cortesse of the
custom house for the custom of 55 wey salt, 8*d* le wey   .   .   .   36*s* 8*d*.[97]

In addition, on the same 10 September George paid on Richard's behalf
'for the custom of the *Anne*'s salt' a total of 48*s* on 66 weys, 58 wey of
Richard's and eight wey of the mariners. An account of the Chancery
auditors names the *Anne* in full as the *Anne Cely*.[98] These are the only
indications in the papers themselves that Richard had an interest in a
second vessel, but one reference in the *Acts of Court of the Mercers'
Company* to a ship named the *Anne Cely*, paid 'conduct money' of £11
13*s* 4*d* in February 1490, suggests that he was owner of or partner in this
other ship, named perhaps for his wife.[99] She almost certainly appears
again in the guise of the *Anne of London* carrying fells of Richard Cely
in the London wool-fleet of August 1488, with as master Robert Smythe,
the man who had captained the *Margaret Cely* in 1487–8.[100]

For customs purposes, the purchase price of the salt in Brittany was
set at 2*s* 8*d* per quarter.[101] If this is accurate, and adding petty costs in
England of 3.5*d* per quarter, George's average selling price of 4.5*s* per
quarter would give him a profit of 52 percent, excluding other costs at
the Bay. At 2*s* 8*d* per quarter, the *Margaret*'s total cargo would have a
nominal value of £36 15*s* 4*d*, rather than the average value of under £20
imported to London by individual merchants.[102] But the discrepancy
between the amount recorded in the enrolled customs account and
George's record is noteworthy. The customers apparently entered her
cargo as 250 quarters. George says she carried 275¾ quarters, and records
the actual payment of duty on 275 quarters.

George added the '£12 18*s* 1*d*' (recte £12 18*s* 6*d*) received from the
sale of part of the salt to the £30 13*s* 4*d* which he claimed to have received,
'with my freight and all receipts beside', from the previous voyage to
Bordeaux.[103] (This second figure should perhaps be £29 13*s* 0*d* on the
various sums given in the accounts for that voyage.) His total of £43 11*s*
5*d* will occur later in his accounting of the entire series of ventures in
1487–9.[104]

[97] File 14 fos. 25v–26.   [98] File 16 fo. 44.   [99] *A.C.M.*, p. 202.
[100] E.122 78/5 fo. 26v.
[101] Bridbury, *Salt Trade*, p. 134 n. 1. (This was probably an understatement.) The wey
contained 5 quarters of 8 bushels.
[102] Bridbury, *Salt Trade*, p. 127.   [103] File 14 fos. 24, 25.   [104] See pp. 394, 395.

Soon after the *Margaret*'s return from the Bay, preparations started for
what was to be her last voyage during George's lifetime, the regular trip
to Bordeaux for wine. In the middle of his account of payments for the
salt he noted that on 21 July 1488 Nicholas Best had 'laid out upon the
Margaret's rigging' 22s 4½d, and that, out of money received from Peter
'Walle Delett', i.e. Valladolid, £4 was expended on paying the cutler for
the *Margaret*'s mast.[105] On 15 September he paid the baker of Radcliffe
for 20½ dozen bread, and 'the goodman of the "Armyttayge" [Hermitage]'
was given 6s 6d for seven kilderkins (or one pipe) of beer. Two cows for
the ship cost 12s each, and the wife of Robert Wodelas, the new master,
sold 1½ cwt of reed for 18d and some meat for 16d.[106] John Amore's wife
supplied 7 cwt of biscuit at 32s 8d, Remington, the roper, was paid £6
17s 5½d, and Robert Welle 20s 7d for 130 lb of tallow and seven dozen
candle, while Byrd the carpenter had 6s 4d for timber. Twenty-four tons
of ballast cost 7s 4d.[107] A surviving bill was furnished by Thomas
Hamlen, turner:

First for 6 sheaves, price	6d
Item, a bow line pulley for the sail	4d
Item, 5 pulleys	10d
Item, a dozen dishes	3d
Item, 3 cups	2d
Item, a dozen and a half of spoons	1½d
Item, a ladle	½d
Item, a dozen trenchers	1d
Item, a scoop	2d
Item, 2 trays	3½d
Item, 2 platters	1d
Item, 2 tankards	7d
Item, 6 deadmen's eyes	9d
Item, 4 scoops	8d
Item, 2 small pulleys	4d
Item, 2 dozen spare trenchers	8d.[108]

The crew seem to have used up eating utensils with some regularity. An
intriguing note in George's account of the rigging, which has been
cancelled, runs, 'Item, paid for boat-hire while my cousin Maryon and
I yeed to warn Nicholas of Charles's sayings – 3d.'[109] From this account
it also emerges that a long bill for beer supplied to the ship had been run
up with Paul the brewer, which means that more beer was consumed on
some of the outward voyages than always appears in particular accounts.

[105] File 14 fo. 25v.   [106] File 14 fo. 26.
[107] File 14 fos. 26v–27.   [108] File 16 fo. 8.   [109] File 14 fo. 26v.

Item, reckoned with Paul Beerman for 7 voyages for beer, beside the pipes, as his reckoning appeareth at long. Sum.   .£24 16d.

Hereof paid...per me at diverse times, £12, and the freight of 4 sacks hops [from Zealand in 1487], 13s 4d. So rest to pay.   .£11 8s.

£11 of this was paid in instalments, to Paul or his wife or servant, between 12 February and 4 May 1489.[110]

By the time the ship left, Nicholas Best had spent a further £7 7s 3½d on her rigging. His 'Book of Bordeaux Reckoning, Anno 1488'[111] starts on 12 September with a list of the moneys received for the voyage: 7s 10d from George, from Maryon £3 'in gold and groats', and £3 3s 8d comprising 21 'Raynnes gylldorns' (Rhenish gulden, reckoned at 3s stg. each) and two groats. From 'John Smith at Bordeaux, attorney for his father William Smith, merchant of Stratford in the county of Suffolk', Best was to receive 100 francs, making £11 13s 4d stg. at seven groats the franc, and other receipts at Bordeaux were another 100 francs from 'John Fox, attorney for master Thomas Nycalson, dyer, of London', and 20 francs from Giles Beckingham.

Best, whom we have previously seen acting as the steward of George's household, kept exceptionally careful accounts as purser. The voyage itself can be said to have started with his barge hire of 2d on 14 September and the 2d he paid at Gravesend that night. There were last-minute purchases of half a hundred 'blanch board' and the sawing of an anchor-stock, a meal of bread, butter and oysters for the crew, and then 2s 4d was paid to the searchers at Gravesend and 4d given in offerings at the chapel, at 'St Anne's light', to judge by an entry in one account for 1486.[112]

The ship put in briefly at Queenborough and then Dartmouth, and by 28 September was at Falmouth. Here a line and hooks were among the small purchases, perhaps for fishing for fresh additions to the diet at sea. The *Margaret* was at Plymouth by 5 October, and remained there for five weeks. An item no other purser had mentioned was laundry. Best paid 4d in the first week at Plymouth 'for washing of the ship cloths and my shirts'. He bought a great deal of nail at Plymouth, but the greatest part of his purchases were bread, fish and meat. The ship required 'iron work for the rudder and for the helm-head' at 12d, two hoses for the pump, and 'nosing' for the lanterns. Best's personal costs over these five weeks came to 8s. He was paying his charges in the Flemish coin provided by Maryon, and accounts for 16d 'lost in [the exchange on] four pieces of gold'. Similarly, he lost 20d on five pieces of gold during the two-week stop at Fowey between 30 October and about 13 November. Apparently

[110] File 14 fos. 26v–27, 46.   [111] File 14 fos. 49–58.   [112] File 13 fo. 7v.

the Rhenish gulden were taken for only 2s 8d stg. At Fowey he made, among other purchases, one of 'yerbes' (vegetables) for 3d and stocked up with 3s worth of bread before they left. His own costs here were 4s: previous accounts have made it clear that the purser took lodgings in the town when the ship stayed in port for any length of time. Total costs for this leg of the voyage were £4 5s 5d 'that I have laid out for the *Marget Cely of London*, of master Maryon's money'.[113]

Blaye was reached by Sunday 16 November. The ship already needed a hogshead of beverage, and on the following Saturday 'herbs' and mustard were bought at Bordeaux. Next week Best paid 2 fr. for wheat, and had it ground and baked. More 'herbs', mustard and oil were bought for the weekend, to go with some fresh meat costing 1 fr. six hardits, and a pipe of beverage was laid in. In the week beginning 30 November there was a payment of 14 sous 'to the customers and controller to have licence for to have out our ballast and for entering and grounding of the ship', and along with meat, fish, herbs, eggs and two more hogsheads of wine, reed was bought and six sous were paid 'to the clerks for bringing of holy water'. This is the first reference to such a practice, as well. Best, or the master, must have been outstanding for both cleanliness and godliness. The ballast was landed by 'the gabbard man' the following week, when 'a iron for to smite fire withal' was bought, as a replacement one supposes, as the ship could hardly have done without such a thing. Further replacements were 13 oars (objects which the ship was forever losing), a chest, and timber to bind the poop, while stores of meat and drink were augmented with another two hogsheads and one tierce of wine, half a hundred hake, bread, an ox, and a quarter of mutton. It is interesting that mutton (or 'sheep') is specified only in accounts in France, like 'a pork', bought at Notre Dame. In the last week at Bordeaux Best paid 12 hardits 'for my chamber at Bordeaux', and he apparently rejoined the ship at Blaye, since his passage there cost two sous and he 'spent that night 1 sou'. He charged 11 fr. for his costs at Bordeaux for 'six weeks and odd days'. Washing the ship's cloths before her departure cost six hardits.

A stay was made at Notre Dame on the way home, about 4 January, and besides the 'pork' at 3 fr. Best bought half an ox, a boat-hook, and one pipe and a hogshead of wine. With another pipe bought at Bordeaux this made a total of wine bought for consumption by the crew of 798 gallons, which once more provided each man with 0.7 gallons per day until the ship reached London. Besides Best, Speryng and Giles Beckingham, the ship had a crew of 15 on this voyage. They were paid a total of 72 francs at Bordeaux, which, with a total of 128 fr. 51 hard.

[113] File 14 fo. 53v.

disbursed by Best, made 200 fr. 51 hard. or £23 8s 8d. Hires in France were paid as follows:

Robert Wodellas, master	12 francs
Richard Tode, his mate	. 6 fr.
'Father' Geffrey	. 4 fr.
Richard Carpenter	. 6 fr.
John Ball, the boatswain	. 6 fr.
Thomas Makso	. 4 fr.
Thomas Kyng	. 4 fr.
Allen the Bretten	. 4 fr.
Robert Torner	. 4 fr.
Gyllam Bretten	. 4 fr.
Thomas Car	. 4 fr.
Robert Carvar	. 3 fr.
Nicholas Dowell	. 6 fr.
Thomas Edward	. 3 fr.
Walter Nores	2 fr.[114]

The 'father' in Geffrey's name was a soubriquet, for the *Margaret* would not carry her own chaplain, and a priest would be called 'Sir Geffrey', not 'Father'. The master on this voyage was a man of long experience, who had commanded the *Anthony of London* to foreign parts (probably through the Straits of Gibraltar) in June 1479.[115]

The ship reached London on 16 January 1489, but Best continued to keep accounts until 1 March. Further disbursements here amounted to 23s 3d, including payment of 12d a week to Guillaume 'to keep the ship'. 'Scouring and mending of the ship harness' cost 20d, and 'Father Baker' (i.e. Geffrey) was given 4d 'for to buy his victuals withal in the ship', perhaps when he took over from Guillaume at the beginning of March. The hires paid at London by George were

Robert Wodeless, master: three men's right	£3
Richard Tode: a man's right and a half; one hogshead portage – 5s.	
Rest	. 25s
Jeffere	. 20s
Richard Carpenter: a man's right and a half, he had one hogshead portage – 4s 9d. Rest	23s 9d
John Ball, boatswain: a man's right and a half, 3 hogsheads . .	. 15s
Thomas 'Makko': a pipe. Rest	. 10s
Thomas Kyng	. 19s
Allen 'Bedron'	. 19s
Robert Pasyngborn [alias Torner]	. 19s
Gyllam	. 19s
Thomas Car [Cardon?]	. 17s

[114] File 14 fo. 56.　　　　[115] E.122 73/40 fo. 48v.

Robert Carver .	14s 3d
Nicholas Dowell	25s
Thomas Edeward	14s 3d
The boy .	9s 6d

Total – £15 9s 9d.[116]

Portages seem to have been costed variously at 18s, 19s or 20s per ton. And although 'three men's right' was 60s, the ordinary mariner got only 19s, not 20s.

The *Margaret* carried 58 tons and a pipe of wine on this occasion. In addition to the crew's portages, Nicholas accounted for part of the freight as follows:

Five tons of John Salford, carried at 22s a ton; primage and average 4d a ton. Sum	£5 11s 8d
Five tons of Thomas Nicholson, dyer, at 20s a ton, primage and average 4d a ton. Sum	£5 0s 10d
Three tons of Nicholas Best, at 19s a ton [No primage or average, since he was purser.]	57s
One ton of John Smith, at 24s. Primage and average 4d. Sum	24s 4d
One pipe of George Cely, at 9s 6d	9s 6d
Three hogsheads of William Maryon	14s 3d.[117]

The rest of the wine must have been carried for other merchants, whose accounts have not survived. Both Best and George made total receipts for freight to be £56 0s 2d. Out of this, George repaid £11 13s 4d to 'Botshead's man for money taken up by exchange' of John Smith, and the same amount to Thomas Nicholson. This left, by his calculations, £32 13s 4d.[118] It is another example of Cely finances that the dyer's payment was made up of £5 'which Nicholas received of Alvard' (De Cisneros), probably for wool sold to De Lopez, of an allowance of £5 1s 8d for his freight, and £1 11s 8d 'paid by Nicholas', from an unstated source.[119]

Before examining George's final reckoning of dues, his own purchase of wine can be briefly dealt with. At his request, William Cely had given Speryng £8 Flem., out of which Speryng bought a pipe of red wine at Bordeaux. Wine stocks in London were particularly high that year: 5,008 tons of non-sweet wine were imported in 1488–9, against 2,588 tons in the previous customs year.[120] The rest of George's purchases were made in England. On Christmas Eve he bought a hogshead of wine from his old associate Pedro Valladolid for 23s 4d, and on 4 February 1489 Valladolid supplied a further six tons at £4 10s per ton, for which George

---

[116] File 14 fo. 33. [117] File 14 fo. 58 (summarized). [118] File 14 fo. 58v.
[119] File 14 fo. 27v. [120] James, *Studies in the Medieval Wine Trade*, p. 115.

gave him a letter of payment for £27, payable on 10 January 1490. Petty costs amounted to only 6s to the porters 'for bringing home to my place, 12d le ton'.[121]

On 11 February 1489 he sold the pipe of red wine to Sir Ralph Hastings at 50s. This was only 5s more than the price paid to Valladolid, and was no doubt a favourable one to a useful patron. On 13 May he made a more profitable bargain with Thomas 'Sholldam' of Marham in Norfolk, squire, selling him five tons of Gascon wine at £6 a ton. His gain, on paper, was £7 5s, or just under 32 percent over total costs. But he had to wait for payment in both sales. Shouldham was to pay £15 at 'the Annunciation of Our Lady before Christmas', i.e. the Feast of the Conception, 8 December, and a further £15 at St John's Day at Midsummer, 1490. 'Specialities of statute merchant' were drawn up and George's share of the payment to the broker was 7s 6d, which reduced his profit slightly.[122]

About 13 May 1489 George drew up an account which apparently covered receipts and expenditure for the four previous voyages, to Zealand and Bordeaux in 1487, and to Brittany and Bordeaux in 1488.[123] In one account he gave the 'sum total laid out per me G. Cely' as £111 11s 9½d stg. With £43 11s 5d received by him from the Bordeaux and Bay voyages in 1487–8, and 9s 6d debited for the freight of his pipe of wine, this meant that he still had a credit or 'discharge' of £67 10s 10d.[124]

The total of unrequited expenditure by the three partners was estimated to stand at £111 18s 4d: £3 7s 6d still due to Richard, who had laid out £21 7s 6d and been repaid £18, perhaps as his share of the £54 freight-money from Bordeaux in 1487–8, George's outstanding £67 10s 10d, and £41 still due to Maryon, who had laid out £44 12s 10½d, but received £3 12s 11d from various freight dues.[125] The costs therefore shared out at £37 6s per person, to be offset by disposable receipts for freight on the final Bordeaux voyages of 1488–9, which amounted to £32 13s 3d or £10 17s 9d each. Individual accounts were calculated as:

RICHARD CELY	Credit			Debit		
	3	7	6	37	6	0
	10	17	9			
	14	5	3	23	0	9

---

[121] File 13 fo. 43v.
[123] File 14 fos. 19–33.
[125] File 14 fos. 29, 46.

[122] File 13 fo. 44.
[124] File 14 fo. 27.

GEORGE CELY

67	10	10	37	6	0
10	17	9			

78	8	7	37	6	0

41	2	7

WILLIAM MARYON

41	0	0	37	6	0
10	17	9			

51	17	9	37	6	0

14	11	9

At the same time it is casually revealed that Richard and George still owed William Maryon 53s 4d for the sum of four marks bequeathed to him by their mother in 1483.[126]

A different account of the state of affairs between George and Richard was furnished by George, also on 13 May 1489.[127] It does not, however, say whether Richard was creditor or debtor in their joint finances.

Memorandum that I have laid out upon the *Marget* from Zealand voyage to this day [the 13 day of *cancelled*] of reckoning between us Richard Cely, G. Cely and William Maryon, as by our book appeareth £111 19s 3d

Received by me . . £43 11s 5d

Delivered my brother of the sale of the salt that was sold at the coming home of the ship . . . £8

Rest to me . . . £35 11s 5d

Sum clear paid by me as per book £76 7s 10d

Freight of the *Margaret* now last from Bordeaux, as by my book of Nicholas makes mention . . . £56

Paid by me to Botshead's man for money taken up . . £11 13s 4d
Paid to Thomas Nicholson, dyer, for money taken up . . £11 13s 4d

[126] File 14 fo. 29, rearranged.

[127] File 20 no. 32, rearranged.

Paid to Mistress Rasson [Rawson] of
this money. £12
    Sum £35 6s 8d

Rest due by me   .   .   £20 13s 4d
[Less his own share of freight money.]

Paid by me clear of the charge between
my brother and me   .   . £56 7s 9d
   [*sic, recte* £55 14s 6d].[128]

Professor Postan has stated that 'a boat was not an undertaking to be run by joint management'.[129] The Cely–Maryon partnership undoubtedly did run the *Margaret* in this way. Whether they were wise to do so is another matter. It has been argued that there was a shortage of available shipping for English merchants in the later fifteenth century, with consequent high freight charges, 'and no doubt men of the standing of the Celys found it very profitable to invest in shipping services, at a time when they must have been in great demand'.[130] How well did the *Margaret Cely* pay, in fact?

Given the incomplete and sometimes chaotic state of the accounts, there is no way of knowing whether the partners' recorded expenditure of £115 in the first year of trading had been recouped by the time that George's last balances were struck. The resale value of the vessel ought to be deducted from expenditure, as representing capital investment (George willed his share of her to Richard in his testament). Taking the entirely arbitrary figure of £35 for capital value would allow the partners to break even with the receipts recorded for two of their voyages in 1486, those to Calais and Bordeaux. No figures are available for the Zealand trip. But George's accounts for the further four voyages between March 1487 and January 1489 suggest that if the *Margaret* in fact gave them a net profit, this can only have come from her owners' individual export and import activities. The money received from freight charges was insufficient to cover her running costs. Certainly ship-owning on this scale and as operated by the Celys and Maryon would not compare in profitability with the wool trade, or with the Celys' sales of grain to Alvaro in 1487, both of which gave returns which represented a net profit in the region of 20 percent. It will be calculated later that, taking good and bad years together, Richard and George could each have expected about £111 annually from their normal trade in wool.[131] All figures at this point are highly conjectural, but if we took it that each partner contributed a yearly average of £25 5s to the *Margaret*'s expenses,

[128] The sum of £56 7s 8d is copied in the auditor's account, File 10 fo. 7.
[129] *Medieval Trade and Finance*, p. 87.
[130] James, *Medieval Wine Trade*, p. 146.

Richard and George would have expended on her about 23 percent of their estimated income from wool, and made little if any addition to their net earnings.[132] If George's figures for 1487–9 can be accepted, over the last two seasons the partners had spent £177 12s 2d and received only £98 7s 1d to their common account, with a little more to come from further sales of their salt.

A bigger ship might have meant better profits, but the Celys could not afford a greater capital outlay, and large ships were not common among the English vessels trading to Bordeaux at this period.[133] Clearly, too, the Celys were unwilling to invest much of their money in any large-scale importing, and usually preferred to carry freight for other merchants. Since ship-owners notoriously faced high risks, it is ironical that the brothers' major loss in these years occurred, not in connection with the *Margaret*, but from the shipwreck of their cargo of fells in the *Clement* in 1488.

During the Chancery suit after George's death there was little reference to the *Margaret*, and apparently no suggestion that her operations had contributed materially to the difficulties that beset Richard after 1489. The Chancery auditors or their clerks carefully annotated the various shipping accounts (but did not correct the arithmetic), but this aspect of the brothers' joint affairs is virtually ignored in the extant summaries of indebtedness.

The *Margaret* may have represented a hidden liability. Operating her required a considerable investment in time and the concentration of the owners and their servants, and also meant a constant need to find money for her fitting, provisioning and wage bills. The complexity of the Celys' finances at this period suggests that they may have over-diversified their business activities without enjoying sufficient capital backing to support them adequately. The *Margaret*'s finances constituted only one part of a series of tightly interlocking loans, receipts and disbursements, but there were long periods in the year when she must have added to the brothers' liquidity problems.

[131] See Ch. 15, p. 421.
[132] It must be stressed that the brothers had other sources of income than their dealings in wool.
[133] James, *Medieval Wine Trade*, p. 49.

CHARGE AND DISCHARGE:
THE CELYS' FINANCES,
1482–9

A welter of rather confused accounts and memoranda bears witness to the intricacies of the Celys' financial affairs in the years 1486 to 1489. Pressing bills would often be met by advances from the ever-obliging 'Alvard', but the very availability of loan-money may have helped conceal from the brothers that their position was becoming precarious.

Their transactions with Alvaro De Cisneros took several forms. He was responsible for paying money due from De Lopez and De Soria for their purchases of wool, for which he sometimes used intermediaries like Fernando (or Farand) Caryan, or 'Laurence Garm, Fryske abaldy's [i.e. Frescobaldi's] clerk'.[1] As sums were paid they would be 'written upon', i.e. deducted from, one of De Lopez' current bills. One undatable memorandum, labelled by a clerk 'The reckonings of money received of John De Loopys by the hands of his attorneys', lists letters of payment payable at future date:

At St Helen's [Day, 18 August]

Item, of John Ambrosse Dene Grone (i.e. De Nigrone) [payable] the 19 day of May.	£62 3s 1d

St Bartholomew's [24 August]

Item, Benet Boneffyse to pay the 18 day of May	£62 3s 1d
Item, John and Jerome Penell, 18 day of May	£22 9s 4d
Item, Dego Decastrone with Grafton, payable 19 day of May . .	£41 20d
Item, in ready money	£19 6s 8d

Sum – £207 3s 10d

Item, there is writ upon the first bill	£100
Item, upon the second bill	£107 3s 10d.[2]

The temptation was to obtain advances in ready cash against bills of future date. At least one loan from Alvaro was 'repaid by George Cely

---

[1] File 10 fos. 7v, 8.   [2] File 15 fo. 35.

by a letter missive direct[ed] to John De Loopys and Gomys De Sore', to be deducted directly from their next account.[3] On other occasions, Alvaro's advances took the form of exchange loans, which might be fictional in so far as they were repaid in England and not abroad. It has been seen that one such loan was repaid, with interest, by a deduction from Alvaro's debt for his wheat.[4] In September 1486 George paid off part of another loan by paying 54s 8d stg. 'for the shipping of forty cloths of Alvard'.[5] 'Cloth' could mean a sarpler of wool, but more probably it here bears its common sense. Alvaro may have bought English cloth for sale abroad.

A further twist to the tale of Alvaro's wheat is given by the fact that in one list of George's borrowings the £60 which was repaid with 'loss of money in the same' by means of a deduction of £62 10s stg. on Alvaro's bill (an increase of 4.166 percent), is described as 'taken up' from him on 8 March 1487 at an exchange rate of 10s 9d Flem. per noble sterling (32s 3d Flem. per £).[6] The exchange rate at par was being calculated at 30s Flem. per £ stg., so that if repayment had in fact been made abroad interest would have amounted to £6 15s Flem. on £90 Flem. – a 7.5 percent surcharge. The saving of £4 10s stg. adds to the profitability of their venture into the grain market.

Some other loans from Alvaro were also, apparently, paid back in England in sterling. £60 was taken up from him in April 1486, and the return payment was made on 5 June as £63 8s 2d.[7] On 12 June Richard and George then took up £50 stg., nominally at 10s 3½d Flem. per noble (30s 10½d Flem. per £), which was repaid 'with return of the same' as £52 9s 6d stg., making an increment of 4.9 percent.[8] In this case, if the transaction had been treated as a straightforward exchange loan the principal would have attracted interest of only 2.9 percent. Rechange, at 29s 5d Flem. per £, may have been involved. It is not explained why George repaid one loan and almost immediately took out another, but the implication must be that although wool sales to De Lopez ran at a satisfactorily high level, the payments were not keeping pace with the Celys' need of cash.

During their father's time, a working balance seems to have been maintained between the three operations of purchasing wool at home, collecting receipts from customers at Calais and the marts, and negotiating agreements with the mercers and other English adventurers to whom the Celys delivered their surplus money at the mart for eventual repayment in London. The whole system worked on extended credit, which might run for a year or more. Old Richard was very chary of

[3] File 10 fo. 7.   [4] Ch. 13, p. 348.   [5] File 10 fos. 9, 37.
[6] File 10 fo. 37.   [7] File 16 fo. 42.   [8] File 10 fo. 37.

borrowing at an unfavourable rate. For instance, in May 1481 when George had reported that the exchange rate for loans at the mart was too close to parity to be profitable, and advised his father 'to speak at London to some man' in order to obtain cash there, the rate for loans between London and Brabant would be correspondingly dear, and Richard replied trenchantly, 'that were not good. For the which I have spoke to no man for that matter.'[9]

By 1486, as we have seen, it had often become extremely difficult to find any English merchants who were willing to be takers of the Celys' money in the low countries, and falling values of Flemish money against sterling exacerbated the situation. When he did not rely on the forbidden arrangement by which De Lopez transferred money to London, William Cely was once more forced to send coin across the channel with a reliable courier, and the memoranda refer on a number of occasions to bags of money which were so received. Now, in place of 'making over' sums at long term but some profit, George more often took up loans at London, at short term and frequently at a high rate of interest.

Against payment of the £1,153 15s 6d stg. (£1,729 8s 6d Flem.) owed by De Lopez for 30 sarplers sold him in November 1486, George listed the following loans from Alvaro:

Item, at London in December [1486]　.　　.　　.　　.　　.　£100 stg.
　　It was taken up at 10s 10d [making £162 10s Flem.] Lost £12 10s Flem.
Item, in February [1487] we had of Alvard £200 stg.　　.　　.　£200 stg.
　　at 10s 9d the noble.
　　I lost in this £200 stg., £33 10s Flem.
Item, Alvard took up by exchange for us in April last also　.　.　£50 stg.
　　At 10s 9d, lost £5 12s 6d Flem.
Item, the brokage is 14s 7d stg. yet also.[10]

Brokerage on loans by Alvaro regularly cost ½d in the £ stg.

Alvaro was not the only lender in April 1487:

Item, of Thomas Blaynche, mercer of London, £20 at 10s 10d, payable
　　3 May next. Whereof he has two bills, one directed to Thomas
　　Wyght, and the second, if he will not have it at Passe mart nor at
　　Sinxen, I must pay it him again at Whitsuntide next at London,
　　£20　.　.　.　.　.　.　.　.　.　.　.　.　£20
Item, taken up of Thomas Riche, mercer of London, £50 at 10s 10d,
　　payable 10 May next　.　.　.　.　.　.　.　.　£50.[11]

By July 1487 the exchange rate for loans at London (made at a rate above parity) had risen (in favour of sterling and in terms of Flemish currency) to 33s 9d Flem. per £ stg., and the rate had climbed further

[9] *C.L.* 116.　　　　[10] File 20 no. 38 fo. IV.　　　　[11] File 20 no. 22.

from 34s or 34s 3d in August to 34s 7½d or 35s in September–October. Most of these loans to the Celys were made 'at usance' for 30 days. While, on 12 October, George noted that £1 stg. worth of bullion would cost 33s 4d Flem. at Bruges,[12] the effective exchange rate for money of account there was probably about 34s Flem. per £ stg. This although a ducal proclamation in September had valued the rial at 15s 6d stg., making only 31s Flem. per £ stg.

On 12 September, shortly before George's visit to Bruges, William Cely had indeed reported that 'money goeth now upon the Burse [at Bruges] at a 11s 3½d the noble' or 33s 10½d Flem. per £.[13] At the same time he managed to make over a proportion of the £300 Flem. which he had by him, at a small discount, paying Benigne Decason, Lombard, £100 17s 6d returnable as £60 stg. at an exchange rate of 11s 2½d per noble or 33s 7½d per £. The correspondents were Gabriel Desuyr and Peter Sauly, Genoese, in London. Jacob Van De Base, a 'Lombard' only in the sense that he dealt in the money-market, took, according to William, £50 Flemish at 33s 6d Flem. per £, which made £29 19s 4d stg.[14] His letter of payment was directed 'to Anthony Corsy and Marcus Strossy, Spaniard [read Florentine]. In Lombard Street [London] ye shall hear of them.' The deal with Van De Base apparently allowed the Celys 1.5 percent profit on their loan (which nevertheless is the equivalent of 18 percent per annum, to be compared with a probable annualized interest rate of between 30 and 40 percent on their own borrowings).

On 29 October William Cely had arranged to make over a further £30 stg., at only 33s Flem. and three months, with John Etwell, but Etwell subsequently reneged on the deal, owing to the 'trouble' in Flanders.[15] In December William found some other English merchants, Roger 'Bouser' [Bourchier], mercer, and John Flewelen [Llewellyn], mercer and William Warner, armourer, who were willing to borrow small sums equivalent to £18 stg. at 33s Flem., for 90 days and £27 stg. at 34s Flem. for a month or less.[16] By then the regular rate at Bruges was above 12s 8d Flem. per noble at usance (38s Flem. per £ stg.), and the rial was valued at 20s in Flanders, making an effective exchange rate of 40s Flem. per £.[17] The rate may have dropped slightly in early February 1488, when George borrowed £40 stg. from Thomas Blanch at 40s Flem.[18]

Richard and George were not so ill-provided with money that they were unable to repay their loans on time, even if they had to borrow from

---

[12] File 13 fo. 30v. [13] *C.L.* 234.

[14] The arithmetic of this loan, as stated by William, makes no sense. But on the basis of the current rate on the Burse, the Celys' £29 19s 4d received in England cost them 1.5 percent below market price at Bruges. [15] *C.L.* 236, 239.

[16] *C.L.* 238. [17] *C.L.* 239. [18] File 20 no. 11 fo. 1.

someone else in order to do so. There is a list of loans taken up in the autumn of 1486, all marked 'soll.' ('paid'), and another memorandum shows that two at least were repaid before the due date.[19]

First we took up by exchange at London of Alvord De Sesseneros, £120 stg. at 10s 7d le noble, payable the 24 day of September next – £190 8s 3d Flem.

Item, the 4th day of September we took up of William Borwell, mercer of London, £20 stg. at 10s 3d le noble, payable the 4th day of October next – £30 15s Flem.

Item, the 20 day of September we took up by exchange of Richard Crisp, mercer of London, £40 stg. at 10s 6d Flem. le noble, sum – [£63 Flem.]

Item, the 25 day of September anno 86 my brother and I took up by exchange of John Raynold mercer of London, £50 stg. at 10s 10d le noble, payable the 10 day of December next – [£81] 5s Flem.

Item, on St Catherine's Day the 25 Day of November I paid to John Peper at Bruges for John Raynold mercer of London...£50 12s Flem. in [groats of] 5½d le piece. And 69 Andreus at 5s 6d – £18 19s 6d Flem. [And] 47 Utrechts at 5s – £11 15s. Premium 8d abated. £81 [5s 10d?].

John Peper must send me my letter by the next sure man. I have an quittance of Peper.

Item, the first day of October we took up by exchange of Roger Hongate and Richard Pyghellys, fishmongers of London, £90 stg. at 10s 8d le noble, payable the 6 day of December next – £144 Flem.

Item, 22 November I paid to Roger Hongat for my brother Richard and me for this letter of payment here against, £44 Flem. and an letter of payment of Gomez Dessore payable at the pleasure at Barrow [Bergen-op-Zoom], of £100 Flem. Sum – £144 Flem.

I have made Roger Hongat an bill of my hand that and Gomez pay not his bill, that William Cely shall pay him the 6 day of December next – £100 Flem.

[19] Receipts from File 13 fo. 34r–v; payments File 20 no. 38.

The arrangement to pay Hongate with a bill on Gomez is interesting, because it was not simply a matter of assigning a debt by means of a negotiable instrument. Gomez deducted £100 Flem. from a bill due to the Celys for wool bought, and gave George, on 22 November, a specific bill of payment 'to Peter Castell at Barrow, payable to Roger Hongatt, fishmonger, at the sight'.[20]

Plainly, much of the Celys' difficulty lay in the fact that they had heavy expenditure in England while their profits were likely to be frozen in Calais or Bruges. Consequently, money received from any source was quickly paid out again, whether 'put in the purse' of George or Richard, spent on the *Margaret*, or used to meet the requests of the crown for loans, the demands of the Staple solicitor for instalments of custom and subsidy, debts to William Midwinter for wool and fell previously supplied, or the repayment of friends and relatives who had themselves lent small amounts to meet earlier emergencies. One account of expenditure in 1487 which George produced for Richard may be cited.[21]

'A remembrance of money taken up by exchange [since 24 July 1487], and how it is paid.'

24 July. 'We took up of Lewes More [Lodovico Moro?] £50 stg., 11s 3d Flem., payable "at the hewssans" [usance]'	£50 stg.
20 Aug. Taken up of 'John Raynowllde' mercer, £60 stg. at 11s 4d, payable 'at the hesans'	£60
25 Aug. Taken up of Avery Rawson, first £40, 'and then you in Essex £20, and then next per me at London, £40. Sum – £100 stg. at an 11s 5d Flem.'	£100
1 Sept. 'We took of Dego Decastron, Spaniard, £60 payable at the 26 day of the said month, at 11s 6½d Flem.'.	£60
19 Sept. 'We took of Lewes Mowre also £50 payable at the usance at 11s 8d Flem.'.	£50
Sum – £320 stg.	

'The payments of the said money'

Paid to John Dorsett for William Midwinter	£7
27 July. 'Delivered by me to Thomas Boshe, servant with William Midwinter'	£33
7 Aug. 'Delivered to Lontley to bear to my brother to Berttis [Bretts]'	£1 10s
Paid to William Cely 'as by his bill of costs appeareth, and laid per me since to the porters' .	£4 2s
'The said season delivered to John Hawkyns [churchwarden of St Olave's] for us'	£3

---

[20] File 20 no. 20 fo. IV.
[21] File 20 no. 24 fos. I–2v.

To the beerman in part payment of beer for the *Margaret* . . . £2
To Speryng 'for certain costs longing to the *Margaret*' . . . £1 10s
Paid [22 August] to John Harfford [churchwarden] 'for full
    payment of our promise to the steeple'. £3 6s 8d
24 August. To William Midwinter £50
31 Aug. 'To diverse men in London for William Midwinter
    as by my book' £59 12s
For brokerage to 'Aran Borsse'. 4s 7d
20 Sept. To 'John my brother's child' £3
Received by George as his share of money lent by Avery
    Rawson £50
20 Sept. Paid to 'Alvard De Sessoneros' for £12 borrowed in
    July £12
To John Smith, mercer of London, in part payment for wool
    bought of him £39 11s
20 Sept. 'Paid to Sir William our chaplain for an year's salary
    [as chantry priest], at Midsummer last past', 10 marks . . [£6 13s 4d]
To Sir William 'which he lent me at Easter' £5
22 Sept. To the solicitor of the Staple, for the mark of the
    sarpler £22 10s
23 Sept. 'Delivered to my brother in Essex at my departing
    over the sea'. £1
Sum – £304 18s 7d
'Memorandum that we owe now at Michaelmas to William
    Midwinter £95 8s
Item, I leave with you to pay the said charge withal, two letters
    of payment that William Cely has made to us, payable at the
    usance which runs upon that day':
Due 6 Oct. A letter of Benyg Decason, for 180 nobles at
    11s 2½d Flem. per noble . . . . £60 stg.
Due 7 Oct. With Jacob Van De Basse, 89 nobles 6s at 11s 2d
    Flem., at usance . . . . £29 19s 4d stg.
Sum – £89 19s 4d stg.

On 8 February 1487(?) George had noted his personal debts, including
£4 owed to his wife, and £3 borrowed on that day from William
Maryon.[22] Having repaid the £4, he again borrowed from Margery on
20 February: 'in gold, eleven nobles and forty pence' (£3 16s 8d). He
had previously detailed 'what money I have by me of Sir William's our
priest's', namely seven old nobles, a rial, 11 half rials and a quarter of
a rial at 2s 6d, five angels and an angelet, and £3 4s 6d in groats. On 16
January he had 'delivered Sir William our priest his seven old nobles,
a rial and quarter of a rial, and five angels and half an angel. The rest

<hr>

[22] File 20 no. 35.

I owe him. Sum that I owe him: £5 19s 6d.' And later, 'on Easter Even I delivered Sir William in angels, eighteen: £6'. Poor Sir William Stephenson seems to have lent his salary back to George as often as he received it. Another memorandum records that on 8 November 1487 George borrowed £5 from Sir William in nobles.[23] This was handed over to Richard, 'and my said brother must content me'. George also borrowed £2 in nobles from his wife, 'so I owe in all £7 the 6 day of December, anno '87'. But later:

Item, I had of my wife since in Essex £1
Item, borrowed of Sir William on New Year's Even also . . . . £5.

Of these amounts, £4 was again lent to Richard, with a further 4s 8d 'to pay the Prior of St Mary Spital's rent-gatherer'.

It is good to report that George still had enough money to clothe himself. Among a series of payments he notes that on 1 March 1488 he delivered 10s 'to Jenyn my tailor for two yards fine damask', together with 3s 6d for a doublet cloth of English saye, and 2s 8d for a 'performing [trimming] of damask for sleeves'.[24] But a shortage of coin is indicated by George's note next month that on Tuesday 20 April he 'delivered to Bartholomew Rede's man...as much gold of my flat cup as amounts unto 4 mark [worth], price [for] 2 ounces, 5 dwt. less, [at] 20d le pennyweight – 58s 4d. He must bring me money for it.'[25] And on 5 November 1487 he 'bore to Bartholomew Rede his man in Lombard Street, five ounces quarter of fine gold, and he delivered to me in ready money there for, sum – £10 5s. That is after 12d le ounce for coinage.'[26] George noted later that fine silver at 3s 3d per ounce, 'will make even in the Tower if it be as good as Paris touch'.

Both Anne and Margery Cely lent their husbands small sums from time to time, and Margery also had money to 'venture' for her children. Did they enjoy incomes of their own, or save 'out of the housekeeping', or were they given a personal allowance? The men who kept the accounts are silent on the matter. The wives sometimes appear, dealing with business when their husbands were absent. Thus, in September 1488 Anne Cely gave George £20 to pay William Midwinter, and when George was in Calais in November 1486, Margery received £10 from a Robert Goodwyn, which she delivered to Richard.[27] Margery clearly dictated some items in household accounts to Nicholas Best, and probably made one or two entries in her own hand.[28]

[23] File 20 no. 25.
[24] File 20 no. 11.
[25] File 20 no. 27.
[26] File 13 fo. 30v.
[27] File 16 fo. 44v; File 10 fo. 1v.
[28] File 14 fo. 61r–v.

The impression gained from George's accounts is that in the last years of his partnership with Richard they kept the wheel of fortune from turning sharply downwards only by holding a precarious equilibrium between borrowings and receipts. Heavy investment in wools in 1486 and 1487 should have brought good returns, but also saddled them with the problem of repayment to suppliers, and they failed to keep up the same level of investment in wool in 1488, relying instead on their shipping ventures. That Richard should fall into debt after George's death need cause little surprise. He blamed part of his troubles on George, and since his claims against George's estate were investigated by four senior staplers appointed (presumably) as arbiters for the Court of Chancery, and the extensive notes drawn up for them survive with the rest of the Cely papers, it should be a simple matter to draw up a balance sheet to show the state of affairs between the two partners at George's death.

In fact, nothing could be more difficult. No balance is struck in the extant auditors' accounts, and none can be deduced from them because the documents are merely interim drafts and a number of crucial totals are blank. In his will, made after the preliminary drafts had been written, Richard alleged that George had owed him £280(?) towards the payment of their joint debts, and a further £1,000 'or thereabouts'. If George was indeed indebted to Richard to this extent, he ignored the fact in all the statements of account which he drew up. The last such statement that survives was made on 17 May 1489, just over a month before his death.[29] Two years previously, on 31 May 1487, finances, by George's account, had been in a reasonably healthy state: 'all the debt that my brother and I owe now at this day' amounted to £189 11s (£39 11s owed for Smith's wool, payable at Easter, £100 to Midwinter, and £50 to Avery Rawson for his exchange loan). Their good debts came to £310 (£250 stg. due from De Lopez and De Soria at Whitsun, £30 which was owing from Thomas Crayford from last Christmas, and £30 from Thomas Hondes or Handes, mercer).[30] 'At this day' might, however, mean merely 'due at this term', and some £380 may have been further due to Midwinter, payable in 1488.[31]

In May 1489 George was concerned with the state of account between Richard and himself rather than with their joint dealings. He stated his own receipts and expenditures since 8 November 1488 according to the following summary:[32]

[29] File 20 no. 30.
[30] File 20 no. 22 fo. 2v.
[31] And fells costing £115 18s 8d were bought from him in June 1488.
[32] Arranged from File 20 no. 30.

Receipts				*Expenditure*			
Gomez De Soria	10	o	o	Mayor of London for			
Harry Joye (for				Richard Cely	2	o	o
freight)	13	19	o	To Richard at various			
From Alvaro	137	4	6	times	21	10	8
W. Norborow	40	o	o	W. Midwinter	129	o	o
Freight money etc.	40	o	o	Custom and subsidy	24	o	o
Thomas Blanch	30	o	o	Lent the king	16	o	o
				Mrs Rawson	12	o	o
	£271	3	6	Paid for the ship	41	6	8
				Paid to Botshead			
				for sea-loan	11	13	4
Due by George	£13	12	10[33]		£257	10	8

At the same time (just a month before he was to make his will in the face of death) George gave Richard an account which apparently covered a longer period:

Memorandum that 15 May '89 delivered to my brother an copy of my receipts of money to the said day, which mounts sum . . . . £457 3s 6d.

Memo. My discharge beside old reckonings of le *Margaret* is £400.

Item, I delivered my brother the letter of payment of John De Lopez . . . . £593 [10s 1d?]

Item, the debenture of the fell [...] £26

I delivered the bill of payment of the money lent the mayor for my lord Dowbney [Daubeney] £10

I delivered an remembrance what money is paid upon the letter of payment [from De Lopez].[34]

What these accounts do not include are items such as the repayments of the exchange loans from Norborow and Blanch (and of one for £60 included in the receipts from Alvaro), nor further loans taken up about April 1489 for £36 stg. from Alvaro, £20 from Thomas Blysset 'upholster', and £60 from John Style or Steel.[35] It is merely one among many peculiarities of the arbiters' investigation that they too ignore this question in the extant accounts, which derive exclusively from the Celys' papers and therefore share their inadequacies.

[33] 'Which is laid [out] upon the *Marget*, and much more, as by my reckoning shall appear.'

[34] File 20 no. 30. George also left his wife £8 'to keep house' and an obligation for 20 marks to be received from William Wordington. The amount of De Lopez's letter of payment is supplied from File 10 fo. 28. The debenture was apparently for money lent the king: File 10 fo. 3.   [35] File 10 fos. 3, 21.

Already during Richard's lifetime the four 'viewers' or 'directors' had been appointed to collect and collate evidence in his suit against George's widow. These were Hugh Brown, Christopher Hawes, Roger Grantoft and Thomas Granger, all substantial merchants of the Staple, and Granger, for one, a family friend and former host at Calais.[36] Accounts were drawn up for them, by the factor William Rogers among others. The system was the usual one, employed for example in churchwardens' or bailiffs' accounts, and much the same as that adopted by George in his own accounts. Each party 'asked allowance' for sums disbursed and was 'discharged' of the total, while he was 'charged' with sums received. Thus 'Billa Willelmi Roggers de A' is a statement of discharge, listing George's payments,[37] and 'Billa Willelmi Roggers de B' is an addendum containing certain items 'as yet not allowed to George Cely, whereof part are put in respite'.[38] In the latter, for instance, is included £13 paid to William Midwinter out of £18 received from 'Peter Vale De Leet' (Valladolid, acting for De Lopez). Further records of George's payments were extracted from Richard's books: 'Item, borrowed of my brother George Cely for Busshe [for supplying wool], 20s [and] 10s',[39] or 'Richard Cely received of George Cely when going on pilgrimage [*peregrinando* – this was to 'Our Lady of Camberwell'] – 40s'.[40] A more coherent but unfinished 'Copy of the demand general last engrossed' contains claimed discharges for Richard and George.[41] The only statement of any 'charge' for George consists of sums in ready money or letters of payment 'delivered and sent into England by William Cely... in the time when [George] kept the reckoning in England', which were extracted without details from 'a book marked "Calais"' and 'set to the charge of George Cely'.[42] The total comes to £5,407 6s 10d, much of it offset by sums paid out and (with luck) included in George's corresponding 'discharge'.

Richard's charge is, by implication, included in George's discharge. His own discharges are listed in detail in a preliminary draft, preceding the writing of the 'Demand General'.[43] A damaged supporting document details Richard's expenditure for petty costs on wool and fell in England.[44] There are further rough notes,[45] and finally schedules made by William Rogers of shipments of wool and fell to Calais between July 1482 and August 1488 (with some mistakes in date), the numbers of fells sold at Calais at dates between 8 March 1483 and 10 September 1487, and the sales made by William Cely between 8 March 1483 and August 1485.[46]

36 File 10 fos. 12, 14.   37 File 10 fos. 1–3.   38 File 10 fo. 7.
39 File 10 fo. 8.   40 File 10 fos. 2v, 8.   41 File 10 fos. 34–7.
42 File 10 fo. 28.   43 File 10 fos. 12–26.   44 File 10 fo. 29.
45 File 16 fos. 41, 43, 44.   46 File 10 fos. 30–31v.

This last was taken from George's concocted book of sales, with corrections based on William Cely's authentic record book.

The information for these draft summaries came from two sources. One was the mass of letters, accounts and memoranda which still exist, for the most part, in the Public Record Office collection. Some of this material bears reference numbers and annotations made for the arbiters. Some of George's papers, for instance, were placed in the two series of 'bills' labelled 'A' and 'B'; thus File 20 no. 4 was classified as 'G[eorge] A.xi', and File 20 no. 10 was 'B.29', while File 20 no. 27 was 'B.8.xvij'. Forty-seven of the letters (now S.C.1 vol. 59) were bundled together and numbered consecutively. A further two series of documents, labelled 'C' and 'D', dealing with expenditure by Richard, were either returned, remain hidden among unsorted papers in the Public Record Office, or perished long ago in the Tower of London through damp or in the digestive systems of rodents. Some bills were in the keeping of William Rogers at the time when the arbiters' accounts were drawn up. For example, there is a list of Richard's payments to Maryon for 'costs of household', taken from folio 86 of his black book and 'a quire of the particulars of payments...remaining in the keeping of William Rogers'.[47] There are few references to the correspondence in the notes, but one example is a citation of Richard's letter of 22 May 1482 'in a bundle of letters'.[48]

The other source of information was a collection of ledgers and other account books, which were no doubt returned to their owners.[49] There is mention of Richard's 'coucher', a great loss to us because it contained in its first 37 folios a consistent account of expenditure on wool and fell.[50] There was also his 'great black book', his little tawny book, and his 'russet book marked B.', which apparently started in July 1485. George also had a black book, books marked 'B.' 'C.' 'D.' and 'G.', and a 'narrow thick book covered with tanned leather', besides 'the book of Calais'.

The clerks made a diligent search through all this, and coped valiantly with such findings as 'Item, upon St Andrew Even the said George Cely delivered of his own money to the said Richard Cely, 70s, whereof the same Richard paid to him again in Barking church, 13s 4d, and the rest is 56s 8d'.[51] Or payments to William Midwinter for wool bought in 1487, of which three sums were 'entered in the black book labelled D., folio 7', and a further five in 'George Cely's black book, folio 10', or that

[47] File 10 fo. 22v.
[48] File 10 fo. 3v; *C.L.* 168. The letter (S.C.1 53/122) is annotated by a clerk.
[49] Examples of surviving, unbound, pamphlets of expenditure are File 11 fos. 1–7 (1473–5), and File 13 fos. 26–31 (1486–7).
[50] File 10 fo. 34.   [51] File 10 fo. 2v.

shortly before George's death, 20 ells of canvas were bought from Alvaro, which appear in the inventory of George's goods, priced at 4*d* the ell, and remain in Margery's hands.[52] They cross-checked carefully. One original document has been annotated 'ideo non allocatur per hanc billam, sed per librum B. folio lij^do',[53] and they wrote notes to themselves: among sums claimed as credits for George was £100 taken up by exchange from Alvaro, of which £64 was delivered to Midwinter by Richard Cely, 'ut patet per librum C. inter solutiones, folio 7. Et ibidem positum in allocatione ad usum Ricardi Cely contra rationem, ut videtur. Unde fiat examinatio'.[54] And, 'Item, to know how the money delivered to Richard Cely the 18 day of October anno '84 to [pay] Rede, mason, is allowed in the bill of the four directors, because it is cancelled in the bill written by William Roggers' – to which a note is added in Latin that this sum was allowed in Book C. as a bequest of Richard Cely senior.[55]

It is no wonder that the draft accounts are very closely written and contain innumerable cancellations and obliterations. Sometimes the clerks made mistakes, as when they mistook an entry in George's accounts for a loan to Richard when it was really to Robert, and sometimes items appear to be 'contra rationem', as when Richard is allowed to claim £10 given him by George to pay Midwinter.[56] But perhaps this was intended to balance some corresponding claim to credit by George. Richard had to be specifically 'discharged' of the £28 paid for the *Margaret* 'because he is charged therewith in George's book marked C., folio 9', meaning that George had given him the money.[57] Some entries are less than illuminating: 'Item, the said George received of the said Richard from the [   ] as in the book of the said George marked B. in the second quire may appear, that is to say folios 28, 29, 30 [a total of] £128 11*d*.'[58] There was some confusion over whether an unredeemed obligation from Sir John Weston should be charged to George or Richard, and it was finally decided that George had received it, 'as appeareth as well among receipts...of the book C. as by the lord's books of St John's and in folio 173 of the said Richard's book'.[59]

In doubt, the clerks tried to consult the persons concerned, including at times one of the arbiters themselves:

Loquendum Thomas Graunger pro 16*s* residiis £4 16*s* Flem. pro precio 1 equi badij coloris eidem Thome venditi pro G. Cely in feste Sancti Andree Apostoli

[52] File 10 fo. 21.   [53] File 20 no. 15.
[54] File 10 fo. 7. When someone first noted the peculiarities in George's book of wool sales for 1483–5 he wrote 'Fiat examinatio discrete de parcellis sequentibus de venditio lane': File 10 fo. 31.   [55] File 10 fo. 10v.
[56] File 10 fo. 19v. Supposed loan to Richard, fo. 3v, based on File 11 fo. 54 (19 March 1479).
[57] File 10 fo. 19v.   [58] File 10 fo. 18v.   [59] File 10 fo. 19v.

anno '87, quosquidem 16s Flem. Willelmus Cely reciperet pro dicto Georgio ut patet per librum G folio 6to[60]

The sale to Granger of this bay horse is recorded in File 20 no. 21. On another occasion Granger's memory was taxed to say

whether the 60s delivered to the same Thomas by George Cely as money given to the king, as it appeareth in the margin of C. book, whether it were for Richard Cely and George Cely or else for George Cely only, etc.[61]

John Speryng 'can show more at large' why he was given costs of 30s, and Nicholas Best was to be asked whether the 40s claimed for Richard as freight money of the *Anne Cely* was owed to Richard by George.[62] Mistress [Margery] Cely for her part was to be consulted as to whether the £10 which she had delivered to Richard while George was overseas was part of the money taken up from Roger Hongate, or George's own.[63]

Some claims were disallowed after consideration by the arbiters. An item in 'Billa A.5' of 20s 2d 'to my cousin Maryon for our dinner Saturday and Monday' was not admitted as a legitimate business expense, nor was George's receipt of 53s 4d 'from his cousin of Northampton for a book of law bought'.[64] On the other hand, a substantial proportion of Richard's permitted claims consisted of sums laid out as executor of his father and mother, payments on behalf of his brother Robert after their father's death, and costs of household between that time and George's marriage in May 1484.[65] These are totalled to £660 8s 8¾d, updated later to £758 13s 4d, among his payments

as well for all manner costs...for the bequests of his father and mother as for other diverse costs and expense for all manner of occupyings had between the said Richard and George Cely his brother from the 14 day of January anno [1482] at the time of their father's decease, unto the 20 day of March anno [1490].[66]

George's smaller number of executor's payments, for the building of the church steeple and the salary of the 'soul priest', and for a legacy under Robert's will, are similarly claimed as credits in his account.[67] But Richard also claimed (curiously) £45 odd, being the value of the contents of the house in Mark Lane which formed part of his marriage settlement, and an unstated amount for

---

[60] File 10 fo. 7v.
[61] File 10 fo. 10v.
[62] File 10 fo. 37; File 16 fo. 44.
[63] File 16 fo. 44.
[64] File 10 fos. 7, 8.
[65] File 10 fos. 14–24, among 'sums allowed and discharged by [the] viewers'.
[66] File 10 fo. 34, which gives the amounts which Richard 'asketh to be allowed of' up to 20 March 1490. Payments for his father's legacies, etc., have been changed to £527 19s 4d in place of the £384 18s 10½d previously allowed.
[67] File 10 fo. 9.

all such [h]ustilments of household, plate, jewels and ready money, wools and wool fells that were at Calais at the time of their father's decease, and of all such debts of his father's that George his brother received of diverse persons, as well by diverse debentures specified in their father's inventory, as of the farms and tenants of Malyns.[68]

What we have here is evidently a claim for sums to be deducted before assessing the residual value of the heritable 'stock', sums themselves to be offset by receipts and assets of the deceased's estate. But since no statement of the gross value of the estate survives, a partial list of deductions is no use in estimating how much Richard and George were left to share.

The extant auditors' notes were compiled over a period of time. Initially at least Richard was still alive: he 'asketh allowance' of certain sums, and 'promised the arbiters to pay' his share of expenses over the execution of felons.[69] The accounts may therefore have been compiled between 20 March 1490, the terminal date mentioned above, and Richard's death in July 1493. In the interim Margery Cely had remarried, because while 'Mistress Cely' was to be consulted at one point, at another one of the clerks 'spake to my lady Haleghwell' about the same matter.[70] It is unlikely that any decision had been reached on the central question of George's indebtedness before Richard died.

George's will, dated 18 June 1489, was not admitted to probate until 1496, when administration of all debts and goods not specifically reserved to his widow was granted to John Cutte, gent. (later Under-Treasurer of England), and Avery Rawson, merchant of the Staple – and brother-in-law of Richard Cely junior.[71] Unbusinesslike to the last, George had appointed Margery sole executrix 'for the substance that I have comen by her'. This ambiguous wording could have caused legal argument about whether he meant 'executrix of all that she brought me in marriage', or 'executrix because she brought me so much'. He probably meant the second. But probate was doubtless held up chiefly because Richard prosecuted his claims against the estate, and the appointment of Avery as an executor suggests that some part at least of Richard's case was eventually upheld.

George's chief concern had been to make provision for his family. He left £50 apiece to his four children and 'the fifth in the mother belly'. Margery was to have for her life the lands assigned for her jointure, which are not identified. To his son Richard, George left his lands and tenements called 'Malyns and Sacokkys' in Little Thurrock, to his son Avery the lands and tenements in Essex late purchased of the widow

[68] File 10 fo. 34.   [69] File 10 fo. 7.
[70] File 16 fo. 44; File 10 fo. 8.   [71] P.C.C. 8 Horne.

Hungerford, to George his house in Mark Lane, 'with half the garden late purchased', and to John the other half of the same garden, together with the house and tenements in Mincing Lane. The reversion of two messuages and two gardens in Mincing Lane, in the parish of St Dunstan, had been granted to George by Hugh Bramanger, clerk, in June 1488.[72] They lay to the south of the abbot of Colchester's tenements, and on the east abutted upon property 'lately' belonging to Richard Cely (in Mark Lane). The unborn child was to have all his father's lands and tenements in Wennington and Aveley. During the children's nonage the profits from these properties went to Margery.

To his brother Richard, George bequeathed 'the jewel which I had of King Richard and the third part of the ship called *Margaret Cely*, forener' (i.e. vessel engaged in overseas trade). The witnesses were John Reed, notary public, and William Cutlerd or Cottillard, the 'cousin' who was the lawyer entrusted with much of the Celys' legal business.

Richard's comments are in his own will of 3 July 1493.[73]

Item, whereas there belongeth to me of right, by the bequest of my brother George Cely, a jewel with a balas and five pearls hanging thereby, and also as much plate as should amount unto the sum of £180 sterling, toward the payment of such debts as we were jointly bound for, and I by survivorship stand yet charged for – of the which jewel and plate, nor also of the sum of £1,000 or thereabouts, which as God knoweth the said George my brother truly owed unto me, I could never sith the death of the said George have recovery of the same or of any part thereof – I give and bequeath the said jewel and plate to mine executors...to th'intent that they with the same plate and jewel content and pay such debts as I and the said George stood jointly charged in to any manner person or persons, as far as the said jewel and plate will extend to.

In fact, the enrolled copy of George's will makes no mention of any plate. The jewel 'had of King Richard' in 1484 was valued at £100.[74]

Richard was himself deeply in debt to his wife's family by the time of his death. Avery and Isabel Rawson, Richard's mother-in-law, had already been lending money during George's lifetime, but the two recorded loans (a total of £100 from Avery and £60 from Isabel) were repaid at due date. But about 18 months before his death, in February 1492, Richard had enfeoffed all his lands and tenements in Mark Lane and in Aveley, Upminster, Rainham and elsewhere in Essex to a group including Christopher Rawson and John Rawson, 'to the use of Isabel Rawson, widow, and Avery Rawson, mercer of London' and their executors until they had received satisfaction from the issues for all Richard's debts to them, including bonds made by them to William

[72] Hustings Roll 217 (27).   [73] P.C.C. 25 Dogett; E.R.O. D/DL T1 528.
[74] File 10 fo. 9v.

Midwinter of Northleach.[75] Richard's executors – Anne Cely, her mother and her brothers Avery and Christopher Rawson – were also instructed in his will to sell his lands and tenements in the counties of Oxford and Northampton to meet his debts and the various bequests for funeral expenses and tithes.

Isabel Rawson died in 1497. Avery, as her executor, accounted with Anne Cely on 4 June 1498 and it was established that she still owed him £432 6s 1d on his own account and £270 5s 1d which had been due to their mother. A certificate was then issued to Richard Cely's former tenants and farmers in Essex that they should now become tenants to Avery or his executors until the total debt of £702 11s 2d had been paid.[76] The final amount was eventually discharged in 1509.[77]

Whereas our only knowledge of Richard's own claims against George is his vague statement about joint debts (amounting to at least £560?)[78] and a further £1,000 owing for unstated reasons, Anne Cely's subsequent petition to Chancery is specific about the nature and amount of George's debt, the amount of stock held in common, and the income realized from it.[79] It is therefore disconcerting to find that there is nothing in the auditors' accounts, or the Celys' own papers, which can substantiate or even elucidate most of her claims.

Anne petitioned as widow and executrix of Richard Cely junior, executor of his father. She stated that Richard and his brother George 'had and occupied in common a stock of wares and merchandises of their own proper goods to the va[lue of] £1,805 7s [4]d [t]he space of eight [years]'. Half the value of this trading stock, 'and the moiety of the gain of the same by all the said time, which amounteth to the sum of £900 53s 8d, belongeth of righ[t and owe]th to belong to the said [Richard Cely] the son'.

In addition, Anne had brought Richard 500 marks in marriage, 'which he put to the said stock', and she now claimed the 500 marks and the profit made on it.

And over and beside that, the same Richard the son and George occupied a stock of the said Richard the father amounting to the sum of £959 2s ¾d. Whose executor the said [Richard was, so that the?] whole stock and gain of the same belongeth to the same Anne as executrix of executor.

Out of the which stocks the same George, having none other goods, chattels or money but of the [said common stock, spent upon?] [je]wels diverse and many

75 D/DL T1 526 and *C.C.R. 1500–1509*, no. 883.
76 *C.C.R. 1500–1509*, no. 883.   77 D/DL T1 589.
78 £560 if the value of King Richard's jewel is included in George's share of the debts.
79 C.1 194/17.

rich gifts and pleasures given to one Margery Rygon, then widow, and other her friends, time of his wooing, expenses of his marriage and household, and in lands b[ought to] have th'expedition of his said marriage, as much as amounted to his portion of the same stock. And also purchased as many lands and tenements as cost £483 13s 4d. And in reparation...spent £100 and above. Whereby the said common stock was adminished by the said George to [i.e. diminished by] the sum of £1,486 7s.

Apparently this means that George spent his half share of the brothers' alleged own stock of £1,805 odd and a further £583 13s 4d or more, which he diverted into the purchase of real estate.

Further, at George's death the partners were 'indebted to diverse several creditors £592 11s 8d', of which Richard paid 'diverse and many sums, and the said Margery nothing paying', although George's lands and £692 odd came into the hands of Margery, as George's executor, and of her new husband, Sir John Haleghwell.

Wherefore the s[aid] Richard in his life and the same Anne [after his dea]th have diverse and many times required, as well the same Margery the time of her widowhood as the same Sir John and Margery since th'espousals betwix them [a sum amounting to the value of the said?] tenements, the stock and gain of their own proper goods and entire stock and gain of such goods as were the said Rich[ard's] the father, and of the 500 mark of the marriage [portion a]bovesaid, for their occupation in common due. Which they to do at all times have refused, and yet do, contrary to law, reason and good [conscience].

The petitioner therefore requested a writ of subpoena to Sir John and his wife to answer her case in Chancery.

This rather confusing document appears to allege, inter alia, that Richard and George originally had a common stock of £1,805 7s 4d invested in wool and fell before their father's death in January 1482, and that, although George diverted over half their trading capital to his own use, over the eight years (in actuality seven years five months) of their partnership after their father's death, they made a total profit of 100 percent on their stock of £1,800 odd, or an average of about £112 each per annum.

There is no way of knowing how much George spent on the purchase of property (though the alleged amount seems very high), or how he obtained this money. The first allegation, if the petition really meant to imply that Richard and George had their own capital of £1,800 before January 1482, is easily disproved. In late 1481 they had shipped 1,641 fells, with a sale value of perhaps £75 stg. A recent sale of North Holland wool had been made for £82 13s Flem.[80] They must in fact have been

[80] File 12 fos. 33, 38.

subsidized almost entirely by their father until his death: George's annual fee as factor at Calais was £22 10s Flem. in 1477–8.[81]

While it seems unlikely that the partners jointly owed as much as £592, it is not clear how much remained due to Midwinter by June 1489. The bonds given to him by Isabel and Avery Rawson might have been issued before then, but they could equally well have been given subsequently for the purchases of wool made by Richard on his sole account. Already in 1488 he shipped some fell for himself and not in partnership with George.[82]

How large was the residue of their father's estate, and what proportion of it furnished Richard and George with a trading capital? The arbiters do not seem to have made any attempt to establish this. In April 1482 receipts and assets for Richard senior, including the value of unsold fells and letters of payment due at future date, might have amounted to £1,208 18s stg.[83] The receipts came mainly from sales made in 1481, which had totalled at least £1,489 9s stg. gross. (For comparison, in late 1478, after an exceptionally good trading year, George's current 'charge' from sales for his father amounted to about £2,876 10s stg. table.)[84] At a guess, in 1481–2 old Richard may have had a current capital investment in stock of about £1,250 stg. After January 1482 Richard junior spent £1,047 on purchases of wool and fell, in addition to £310 already paid by his father in deposits.[85] Further costs might bring total expenditure on stock up to about £1,690 in that year. In the absence of the inventory *post mortem* of Richard senior, it is quite unclear how Anne and her advisers arrived at the figure of £959 odd for the trading capital inherited by Richard and George. There is no reason to doubt that Anne's 500 marks were added to the stock after Richard's marriage, to give the brothers the total capital of £1,690 which they may have enjoyed by the end of 1482. But if they expended this amount in 1482, it can be shown that, with fluctuations in their annual purchases, their average expenditure on Staple ware was much below their outlay in that particular year.

The estimate of profit in Anne's petition, of 100 percent over eight years, may involve a purely conventional calculation at the rate of 12.5 percent per annum (or, of course, more on a diminishing capital). Whatever the accuracy of the basis, the resulting estimate of £112 each from the wool-trade may be nearly true of all but the last few months of the partnership.

It is entirely possible that George bought some of his lands with money

---

[81] File 21 no. 1 (fo. 2).
[82] E.122 78/5 fo. 26v (836 fells).
[83] File 12 fo. 38; File 20 no. 5.
[84] File 15 fo. 23: £3,643 10s Flem., converted at the current Calais rate of 25s 4d Flem. per £ stg. table.
[85] File 10 fo. 12.

which would otherwise have been devoted to the trade he shared with Richard. But if so it was careless of Richard not to keep proper accounts, and in general Anne Cely's claims on George's estate seem highly exaggerated. In particular, the demand for repayment of the entire capital inherited from Richard senior together with all the income earned from it must, one would hope, have been put forward in full expectation that it would be contested by the opposing lawyers, and on the principle that in a court of 'equity' one asked for everything conceivable in the hope of obtaining something reasonable in the final settlement.

It would be very interesting to have the rejoinder of Margery and Sir John Haleghwell to Anne's petition. It might well have given the missing side of the story, namely how Richard came to owe so much to the Rawsons, what purchases of land he had made himself, and what sums he had expended on the ship *Anne Cely* or on other trading ventures outside his partnership with George. What fortune, moreover, did Margery bring George in return for the expenses of obtaining her? In short, the case should have proved an accountant's nightmare and a lawyer's dream, capable, in expert hands, of outlasting *Jarndyce* v. *Jarndyce*. Although, in a sense, the associated documents have remained 'in chancery' to this day, the absence of recorded decision does not mean that none was reached, or the case not compromised.

Can anything be deduced from the Cely papers about the average value of the brothers' trade in wool and fell in the period 1482–9? This simple question proves an inappropriate one to ask of the material. But some tentative answers can be proposed in conjunction with some rather complicated investigations of the evidence.

One calculation can be made from various entries in the arbiters' notes. Richard's total contribution to the 'common stock' in payment to suppliers, customs dues, petty costs and the like, is totalled to £3,281 7s 4d.[86] George's corresponding disbursements come to £3,183 5s 3¼d.[87] According to other statements in the same accounts, William Cely sent over letters of payment and ready money to a total of £7,605 4s stg.[88] To these receipts one must add money obtained from the sale of wool in England to Pardo and Crayford in 1486, perhaps £415 stg., making an estimated total of £8,020 4s in receipts.[89] In themselves these figures would indicate a total gain (balance of receipts over expenditure) of £1,555 11s 5d stg. rather than the £1,805 7s 4d postulated in Anne Cely's petition, or £103 14s as average net annual income for each brother over the full seven and a half years.

---

[86] File 10 fos. 12–13v.
[88] File 10 fos. 21, 28.

[87] File 10 fo. 35.
[89] Ch. 13, p. 341.

This calculation, imprecise as the basis is, has the merit of comparing expenditure with ultimate receipts in England. But at least one caveat must be entered. Almost all the income between February 1482 and March 1483 derived from stocks already sold in 1481, or from the sale of fells shipped by Richard Cely senior before his death. That is, this income derived from investment which does not figure in the auditors' accounts. Perhaps, however, in calculating an average this period can be taken to balance the calendar year 1488, when receipts were again derived from stocks shipped in previous years, and there was a nil return on the current year's export of 5,250 fells which were lost at sea. For the six months of 1489 up to George's death no exports at all are recorded.

The expenditure of £6,464 12s 7d which was taken as a basis in the above estimate of income does not represent total investment, because returns from William Cely were net, representing the surplus after William had met a variety of costs on the continent. These would include his own salary (of unknown amount), his board at Calais, miscellaneous overheads, cost of travel, petty costs, and a variable proportion of custom and subsidy dues to be paid at Calais. If a conventional figure is taken for the petty costs and custom and subsidy met at Calais on the 22,555 fells and 198.7 sarplers exported by Richard and George between July 1482 and July 1487 inclusive, total investment can be estimated at £7,578 19s 3d, or £1,010 10s per annum on average, and gross receipts would be £9,134 10s 8d, or £1,218 per annum, suggesting an average annual profit of 20.5 percent. This compares with the stock of £1,160 employed by Thomas Betson and William Stonor in partnership in the 18 months up to September 1479.[90] Over that period they shipped a total of 142.7 sack-weights (by customs estimate) of wool and fell.[91] Betson was ready to answer to Stonor 'for the occupation of [their capital] between God and the devil', and could produce 'the book that he bought [the wool] by' and 'the book that he sold by'. Would that they survived.

These general estimates of the Celys' investment and income can be tested by examining some records of specific sales, but in these cases only the selling price of the goods is recorded, expressed in the sterling of Calais. Eventual receipts for any wool not sold to De Lopez and paid for in England would depend upon the exchange rate and upon the interest obtained if receipts at the mart were made over by exchange loans. On the basis of nominal receipts, an estimate can be made of the value of the Celys' trade over the two and a half years between March 1483 and August 1485, by comparing payments to suppliers, as recorded among Richard's 'discharges' in the auditors' accounts, and sales listed in William Rogers's extracts from books kept by George and William

[90] *Stonor L.*, no. 249.   [91] E.122 73/40.

Cely.[92] All the wools and fells shipped between July 1482 and March 1484 were sold during the period March 1483 to August 1485, except possibly for a few refuse fells. Total sales came to £3,589 2s 8d Calais, or a nominal annual average of £1,435 13s in the same money of account.[93]

The whole series of transactions may have involved an investment of £2,998 16s 7d over two and a half years, which would produce a profit of £590 3s, or 19.7 percent, plus or minus any advantage or loss incurred through variation in exchange rates and interest on exchange loans. At that rate, to obtain an annual receipt of £1,435 12s Calais, average annual investment of £1,199 13s stg. was required. From this, each partner might expect to receive a net annual return in the region of £118. To achieve an income of this order, it was necessary to sell about 113 sacks of wool and fell a year. But between 1484 and 1487 the Celys' average annual export was only 99.65 sacks, and no stocks reached Calais in 1488 or the first six months of 1489.[94]

Costs and profits cannot be usefully estimated for the years 1485–6 in any detail, although it may be noted that in 1486 the Celys paid £1,285 as the purchase price of fleece-wool alone.[95] Information about shipments in 1487 is a little more complete. Total investment in both fells and fleece-wool may be estimated at £987 8s, and total receipts at a nominal £1,193 Calais, giving an overall profit of 20.8 percent and a possible net return of £102 16s to each brother.[96] In 1487 they also invested £181 odd in grain sold to Alvaro de Cisneros, as well as their expenditure on the *Margaret Cely*.[97]

Was Anne Cely correct in alleging that the trading capital available to the brothers diminished between 1484 and 1489? The best way of testing this claim is to examine the amounts of wool and fell shipped, first by Richard Cely senior and then by Richard and George after his death. The results are set out in Table 8. Since Richard senior died in January, it was more convenient to calculate shipments by calendar year, rather than the customs year from Michaelmas. This also obviated the difficulty of deciding where to place shipments like that dated 4 October 1483 in the Celys' records, which was customed on 26 September.[98] Where accurate

---

[92] File 10 fo. 31.

[93] 15,300 fells sold for £715. The original total of 15,467 had been bought for £390 6s 9½d stg.; total cost price was perhaps £578 16s 7d. There were 87.65 sarplers of fleece-wool, comprising 64 percent good Cots., 24.5 percent middle Cots., 7.5 percent good Kesteven and 2 percent each of middle young Cots. and refuse Cots. Purchase price came to £1,888 9s 5d stg., and total estimated cost price might be £2,420 stg.

[94] Table 8, p. 420.

[95] File 20 no. 14. Not all of this went for export.

[96] Fells may have produced a profit of only 9 percent on 777 eventually shipped. If all the fleece-wool was mature Cotswold, profit could have amounted to 21.3 percent.

[97] Ch. 13, p. 348.   [98] File 10 fo. 30; E.122 78/2.

Table 8. *Volume of Celys' trade, 1478–88, according to shipments by calendar year (new style)*

Year	Fleece-wool		Fells		Total in English Sack-weights
	Sarplers	Sacks	No.	Sacks	
1478	47.68	119.2	5,568	23.2	142.4
1479[a]	0	0	0	0	0
1480	54.68	136.7	8,400	35.0	171.7
1481	16.68	41.7	11,464	47.8	89.5
average per annum		74.4		26.5	100.9
1482	24.29	59.2	5,400	22.5	81.7
1483	31.68	78.6	10,250	42.7	121.3
1484	55.72	142.65	1,099	4.6	147.2
1485[b]	17.68	46.25	0	0	46.2
1486	36.65[c]	98.75	5,029	20.9	119.7
1487	32.68	82.26	777	3.2	85.5
1488	0	0	5,250[d]	21.9	21.9
average per annum		72.5		16.5	89.0

[a] 27 sarplers bought, but not shipped until March 1480.
[b] Includes shipment misdated 1484.
[c] A further 15 sarplers sold in England.
[d] Lost at sea.

weights were not given for Richard senior's shipments, sarplers were averaged at 2.5 sacks, pokes at 0.68 sarpler, and pockets at 0.29 sarpler.

At both periods there was considerable variation in annual shipments. If figures for shipments by Richard senior, gleaned from a few shipping lists and from references in the letters and memoranda, are reliable, his sons exported a little less fleece-wool and substantially fewer of the less valuable fells. It is true that after 1484 their exports suffered a marked decline. But George's extravagance is not the necessary explanation. The drop in wool exports in 1485 was general, and in 1486 some of the Celys' wool was sold on the domestic market. As well, rising prices at home might mean that Richard and George spent much the same amount as their father, but obtained less for their money. And from early 1486 they extended their trading activities into other spheres. If their decision was unwise, it was made by joint agreement.

Up to 1489 the brothers' annual income from wool fluctuated, like their father's before them, but may have averaged £111 each. The inclusion of six months in 1489 when, owing to several disasters, their only income from the wool-trade derived from shipments made in 1487, reduces this estimate to about £103. The higher figure is the more realistic indication of the income which they could expect to enjoy under normal trading conditions.[99] For a comparison with a joint average income from wool of between £207 and £222 per annum, one can cite the £115 p.a. which Sir Geoffrey Boleyn (died 1463) is said to have derived from an investment of over £2,000 in land – a return of 5.75 percent.[100] Nevertheless, despite their lower return, landed estates represented social status and a degree of security, and if Richard and George diverted capital into this less profitable area of investment, they were following a firmly established practice. Their father had doubtless done the same. It is noteworthy that they do not seem to have reinvested any significant part of their income from rents in their trading ventures, even when they were facing a severe liquidity problem towards the end of their partnership.

The Celys' failure to export any wool to Calais in 1488 or early 1489 meant a loss of profit at a time when they could ill afford to forgo it. Unwisely, perhaps, they were selling a large part of their wool (probably all of their best quality) to the single partnership of De Lopez and De Soria, and for over 12 months in 1487–8 these residents of Bruges were unable to collect a promised consignment of wool which William Cely was holding for them in Calais. The *Margaret*'s earnings were no substitute for the delayed returns, and the shipwreck of 5,250 fells in August 1488 came as a further blow to the Celys' finances. William Maryon also had 884 fells in the ill-starred *Clement*, but luckily for him he had shipped another 1,803 in the *Fortune of Alburgh*.[101] Richard and George made strenuous efforts to salvage their fells, spending £32 9s 2½d 'about recovery and landing of a ship and fells drowned',[102] and obtaining rights of lagan from the Earl of Oxford, Admiral of England, in a document dated 30 August 1488.[103] It does not appear that they were successful, and at George's death only 553 fells, one poke and one pocket of wool remained unsold at Calais.[104]

Coupled with the shipwreck of the fells and their temporary loss of a market in Bruges during the civil disturbances there, other factors such as the high cost of borrowed money, the repeated need to pay out cash for the *Margaret*, and possibly a growing reluctance by Midwinter to

---

[99] From trade in wool only, not total income.
[100] Thrupp, *Merchant Class*, p. 128; Bolton, *Medieval English Economy*, p. 285.
[101] E.122 78/5.   [102] File 10 fo. 10.
[103] File 14 fo. 15.   [104] File 10 fo. 31v.

extend unsecured credit, had all put the partnership in a precarious situation. The record of sums paid to people such as 'a man in Fleet Street', 'a bill-bearer', 'a haberdasher in Bow church-yard', almost gives the impression that Richard and George could scarcely venture out into the streets without being accosted by some emissary of William Midwinter, 'God rid us of him'.[105] When William Cely and then George died suddenly in 1489, Richard was additionally left to shoulder the burden of carrying on a complicated business on his own, a task in which he cannot have been greatly assisted by George's book-keeping methods.

Undoubtedly, George's widow, and in course of time her new husband, Sir John Haleghwell, were reluctant to meet their obligations to Richard. This fact must have increased Richard's natural inclination to blame his difficulties on his dead partner, and inflamed his resentment at being forced to sell or mortgage his own landed property to content his creditors. Any currency of the allegation, produced later by Margery's woman Jane, that George had been worth £2,000 at his death, would have created more antagonism between the two families.[106] After Richard's death, his widow, with three young daughters to support and looking to make a good marriage for herself, had every incentive to claim as much as possible from George's estate. More specific evidence must have been produced in support of her claims than we know about, since her brother Avery obtained a share in the administration. But as far as the surviving documents go to show, the bulk of Richard Cely's debts to the Rawson family were not, in reality, any direct responsibility of George's.

[105] E.g. File 16 fo. 44v.   [106] C.1 368/86.

POSTSCRIPT ON LATER
FAMILY HISTORY

We learn more about William Maryon's material circumstances from his will than ever emerged from references to him in the papers of his close friends, the Celys. He drew it up on 7 May 1493, about two months before his godson Richard Cely made his own will, but died later than Richard, and probate was not obtained until 6 February 1494.[1] Maryon's executors were Richard's wife Anne and his own nephew, Robert Eyryk, who were left the residue of the estate and all moveables not otherwise disposed of. Some of his properties, 'lands freehold and copyhold', tenements, meadows and pastures in Watford and Bushey, were to go to Richard Cely for his life and then to his daughter 'Barbara', Maryon's god-daughter, and to her elder sisters and their heirs if she died before marriage. Robert Eyryk and his wife Elizabeth were to have property in Great Billing, five miles north-east of Northampton, and also two tenements in Watford; one, formerly Grafton's, in which Maryon's 'mother-in-law' was living, and the other, at the furthest end of the town, which had been bought from John Waleys, with three acres of meadow lying in the West Mead against 'Wegyn halle brigge', i.e. Wiggen Hall bridge. A charge on the Watford properties last mentioned was an 'obit' to be kept in the church of his burial for 60 years at 10s a year for priests and clerks and for ale and cheese to poor men. At his death two trentals were to be sung, one at St Olave's, Hart St, where he was to be buried if he died in London, the other at the Crossed Friars, the priests to 'sing two and two together, *Placebo* and *Dirige*'. The poor householders of the parish where he was buried were bequeathed £5, and £12 was to be spent on bread, ale and 'meat' on the day of his burying. Four men who carried his body to the church were to have 12d, and 20s each was left to the church of Watford and the Fellowship of Grocers.

If Robert and Elizabeth Eyryk died without issue (their daughter Agnes, named for Agnes Cely, was evidently now dead),[2] the properties

[1] P.C.C. 19 Vox.   [2] Will of Agnes Cely, P.C.C. 8 Logge.

bequeathed to them were to revert to 'my brother son, John Waleys'. John was to have £5 in money and a livery gown and hood and a little feather bed at Watford 'and all manner of things that longeth to a bed'. 'My mistress Anne Cely' was left a chased gilt cup, with £3 in money and another 40s (for acting as executor?). Her daughter Margaret had a mazer and six spoons with round knops and £5, her daughter 'Elizabeth' (Isabel) a plain white (silver) piece, a great flat basin of latten and £5, and Barbara a flat gilt cup with covering, Maryon's best towel of diaper, and £10. Elizabeth Eyryk had a standing cup gilt with covering, a mazer with a foot, a gold ring 'with a spur of pearls', and £10. 'William Clerk my child' was generously remembered with 'my worst mazer', eight silver spoons, a chest at Watford, the hanging bed with the chest in the meal-house and one of the feather beds with bolster 'that I lay in', with the blankets, pillow, coverlet and pair of sheets, a pair of brigandines and sallet, one of his livery gowns with hood, and £5. Maryon was precise enough about the details of his bequests: had he confused the names of two of Richard's daughters, or were they known at home by other than their baptismal names? A decisive family estrangement seems to lie behind the total absence of reference to Margery, or to any of George Cely's young sons.

Although the later history of Margery and Anne Cely and their children has not been investigated in detail for this study, the outlines can be traced through records of law-suits and property-transfers, wills and funeral monuments and so on. Both widows remarried, as widows commonly did. There was good reason for this in the case of women like Anne, who had another 34 years to live. Both wives advanced socially, as women doubtless hoped to do. Anne Cely took as her second husband Walter Frost, esquire, of West Ham, who was a commissioner of the peace for Essex in 1502–8 and held, according to his monumental inscription, a minor royal appointment as 'sewer' to Henry VIII.[3] Anne died on 23 October 1527 and was buried with her second husband in the church of West Ham.[4] Until Richard's remaining properties were clear of debt she had enjoyed her jointure in the properties in Mark Lane and a tenement in Aveley called the 'Swan', which her brother Avery Rawson had been forbidden to touch under the terms of the agreement of 1498.[5]

---

[3] *C.P.R. 1494–1509*, p. 639; John Weever, *Antient Funeral Monuments* (1767), p. 359. According to Povah, *Annals of…St Olave Hart St*, p. 250, Walter Frost, armiger, presented Richard Rawson as Rector of St Olave's in Oct. 1510, and his successor in June 1518. Hennessy, *Novum Repertorium*, pp. 355–6, appears to have very inaccurate dates in his list of patrons for this period.

[4] Weever, loc. cit.

[5] *C.C.R. 1500–1509*, p. 330.

The three daughters of Anne and Richard who survived their father had been born quite late in his ten years of marriage: Margaret about 1489, Elizabeth (Isabel) in 1490 and Anne or Barbara in 1492 or early 1493.[6] The child for whom Richard had cradle clothes in 1487 must have died, along with any others born earlier.[7] Margaret and Isabel were married by 12 July 1509 when, by an indenture tripartite, Richard [Foxe], bishop of Winchester, John Foxe and Thomas Semer, as feoffees, transferred properties in Aveley, Upminster and Rainham to John Ketylby, armiger, and his wife Margaret, Robert Wareham, gent., and his wife Isabel, and Anne Cely, sister of Margaret and Isabel.[8] Avery Rawson issued a quitclaim on these properties, and was paid the final 100 marks of his debt from the girls' father, out of the sale of a place called 'Blaches' in Aveley, bought by John Barrett.[9]

Margaret Cely's husband, John Ketylby, was probably from Cotheridge, Worcestershire.[10] Margaret herself was buried near her mother in the parish church of West Ham, and near a Henry Ketylby, one time servant of Prince Henry, who had died in August 1508.[11] The date of Margaret's death was not legible when the inscription was copied *c.* 1767. Anne, the youngest of Richard's daughters, disappears from the records and may have died young and unmarried. Isabel's first husband, Robert Wareham, was dead by August 1530, when Isabel had taken as her second husband Anthony Coke or Cook, senior.[12] She was apparently still living in June 1560, when a covenant describes her (by then aged 70) as 'Isabel Cooke, widow, of Aveley'.[13] Twenty-eight years earlier, on 1 January 1532, Anthony Coke, senior, gent., and his wife Isabel, daughter and heir of Richard Cely, 'gent.', sold the manor of Bretts and many other properties to John Baker, Recorder of the city of London, with use reserved to them for their lives.[14] It was through [Sir] John Baker, the Recorder, that Bretts Place descended to the Barrett-Lennard family of Aveley, whose deeds are now in the Essex Record Office. In 1936 'Bretts Farm' was bought by the Essex County Council, to be kept up as a farm.

[6] *Calendar of Inquisitions Post Mortem, Henry VII*, I, 379.
[7] Unless Margaret's age was seriously underestimated for her father's inquisition post mortem.
[8] E.R.O. D/DL T1 586.
[9] Ibid., 588–9.
[10] *Victoria County History of Worcestershire*, III (1926), 552, 563; Weever, p. 359. According to Povah, John Ketylby 'fil. "Annae" filiae et haer. Ric. Cely' presented to St Olave's in 1528. Was this the husband, or a son, of Margaret?
[11] Weever, loc. cit.
[12] The next presentation to St Olave's was made on 8 Aug. 1530 by Anthony Coke and 'Elizabeth' his wife, second daughter of Richard Cely: Povah, *Annals*, p. 250, from Newcourt, *Repertorium*.
[13] D/DL T1 653.
[14] D/DL T1 616. They also sold the third part of the advowson of St Olave's.

Before leaving Richard Cely's family, something should be said of his brother-in-law Avery Rawson, who experienced the caprices of fortune in full measure. He rose to be a warden of the Mercers' Company in 1501–2.[15] In 1502 he paid £340 for the manor and lordship of Aveley, which was then in the hands of Adrian Fortescue and Anne his wife, daughter and heir of Sir William Stonor.[16] The purchase included

all and singular advowsons, lands, tenements, woods, lesows, pastures, meadows, fields, rents, reversions, services, commons, ways, paths, free chase, fishing, waifs, strays, wracks, courts and the profits of the same, bondmen and nefs [natives] with all their blood and sequelae and with all their lands, tenements, goods and chattels, with all other issues, profits, customs, liberties and commodities whatsoever they be, to the said manor pertaining or in any wise belonging, in Aveley, Rainham, 'Wokingdon', Stifford and Little Thurrock.

Its possession gave Avery additional standing in the area where he had been drawing revenues from his late brother-in-law's estates. But 11 years later, when Avery's fortunes were ebbing, John Colet, dean of St Paul's, Christopher Rawson and George Cely junior obtained a recovery of the manor.[17]

In 1515 Christopher Rawson, who was nearing the end of his own term as warden of the Mercers' Company, must have been greatly embarrassed when his elder brother Avery requested the return of three pieces of arras, which he said he had lent the company to hang in their hall when he himself was a warden.[18] On investigation, the company found that the tapestries, which depicted the history of 'Aman and Mardochus', alias the Old Testament characters Hamon and Mordecai, had in fact been solemnly presented to them as a memorial to Avery's parents, together with certain 'scochyns' (escutcheons) of their arms which were still set about the hall. But the company charitably considered that Avery had 'lately sustained many great losses, whereby he is grown much in poverty and necessity', and granted him £20 'for his relief in his said necessity', upon condition that he confirmed his gift of the arras and promised that no further claim would be made for its return. The mercers also assisted him by giving him the coveted position of weigher of silk in the City, only to be informed in July 1520 that Avery had now 'deceitfully, rebukefully and shamefully withdrawn himself from this city of London', so leaving the office vacant.[19] Among the contenders for it, incidentally, was William Burwell, the Celys' old partner in many exchange loans, now also fallen on hard times.[20] To the mercers' disgust,

---

[15] *A.C.M.*, pp. 248–54.   [16] *C.C.R. 1500–1509*, no. 199.
[17] D/DL T1 598 (Easter 1513).   [18] *A.C.M.*, pp. 428, 431–2.
[19] Ibid., p. 499.
[20] Ibid., pp. 499–500. By 1526 he was 'in great decay': p. 743.

they had subsequently to dismiss Avery's deputy weigher, Avery Skampion, and deprived Skampion of the freedom of the company, declaring that henceforth he was to be regarded 'as a man false, perjured and untrue', for having

utterly misordered and misdemeaned himself, in weighing of silks between merchants buyers and sellers of the same, contrary to his oath by him here in this our hall sworn. Not only to the great displeasure of God [and] hurt and damage of the said merchants, but also to the great slander and disworship [of] this fellowship.[21]

It may not have been entirely Skampion's fault. Avery Rawson had quitted the City in order to go into sanctuary to escape his creditors, among them 'master Hynage' (Heneage), servant of Cardinal Wolsey, under whom Rawson had enjoyed another office in the king's customhouse. Heneage had confiscated the beams, scales and weights necessary for weighing silk, against 100 marks owed him. Skampion's successor as weigher had to buy them back.[22]

Despite these scandals, in December 1524 Avery was sufficiently optimistic, or desperate, to petition the Mercers' Company for a 'benevolence', which they refused on the grounds that it was contrary to their policy to give such assistance to 'a sentwary [sanctuary] man'.[23]

Margery Cely, née Punt, George's widow, married as her third husband Sir John Halwell or Haleghwell, the representative of a Devon family who were busily amassing lands and offices. John, who had previously been married to Isabel, widow of Sir Thomas Beaumont,[24] had profited through his support of Henry Tudor, being knighted at Henry's landing in England in 1485, and appointed steward of the Duchy of Cornwall after Henry's accession to the throne. Among other pickings he obtained a grant of some lands in Northamptonshire, formerly held by William Catesby, the executed 'Cat' of Richard III's reign.[25] Sir John, a widower once more, died before August 1500 and was buried between his two wives.[26]

At different times between 1503 and 1515 two petitions to Chancery put forward claims against Haleghwell's grand-daughter, Jane Haleghwell, and her husband Edmund Bray.[27] One was from a William Upton and his wife Jane.[28] Jane Upton, who had been 'long and true servant at will' to George Cely and to Margery, whose 'nigh kinswoman' she

---

[21] *A.C.M.*, p. 517. [22] Ibid., pp. 512–13. [23] Ibid., p. 690.
[24] C.1 61/212. [25] *C.P.R. 1494–1509*, p. 11.
[26] Ibid., p. 206, and J. C. Wedgwood and Anne D. Holt, eds., *History of Parliament. Biographies of the Members of the Commons House, 1439–1509* (1936).
[27] Edmund was the nephew of the notorious Reynold Bray. [28] C.1 368/86–7.

was, claimed payment of £20 bequeathed to her by Margery, at George's request, as a 'special act and deed of charity' and for the provision of her marriage. She made the incidental allegation that George had died possessed of goods worth upwards of £2,000. According to Edmund Bray's answer to the petition, Margery's testament, if any, was void, but after her death Sir John Haleghwell, 'for very zeal and love that he bore and owed to the said Dame Margery', left £300 to her kinsfolk and friends. Any remaining claim upon himself, Edmund said, was falsely alleged and 'surmised by coven and craft' of one of the feoffees of his late father-in-law, Richard Haleghwell.

In a different Chancery suit, Margery's only surviving son, George Cely, advanced claims, not only for the £50 left to him under his father's will, but also the £200 there bequeathed to his four dead brothers, to which he was now entitled 'by the honourable custom of the City of London', of which his father had been a citizen, and where he had died.[29] The debt, according to George, was passed from Margery to Sir John Haleghwell, from Sir John to his son Richard, and thence to Edmund Bray as Richard Haleghwell's executor. This suit may have been instituted shortly before 1513, when George was busy tidying up his inheritance. He had also had to sue one of his mother's connexions by marriage, Elizabeth Punt, widow, over her detention of deeds relating to three messuages and gardens in London.[30] In February 1513 he and his wife Isabel sold properties in Mincing Lane and the garden in Mark Lane to Sir John Dance, who had already bought George's house in Mark Lane.[31] The Mincing Lane properties were held 'of the gift and concession of Avery and Nicholas Rawson'.[32] At Easter that year, as mentioned above, George recovered the manor of Aveley from Avery Rawson, but the family seem to have moved to another part of Essex. In the 1520s he and Isabel also had property in Stratford, Stepney and Holborn.[33]

George's will was dated 23 December 1545.[34] By then Isabel was dead, and to his second wife Christabel George gave, 'for her gentle ordering of me in mine extreme sickness', the lease of his house in Ivy Lane for her lifetime, together with its contents. Ivy Lane runs between Paternoster Row and Newgate Street, north-west of St Paul's Cathedral, In case her existing jointure of 'Pynchebexe' in the parish of Stapleford Abbots, Essex, would not 'stand by law nor conscience', he formally

---

[29] C.1 300/15.   [30] C.1 129/12.
[31] Hustings Roll 236 (11, 12).   [32] Ibid. 236 (12).
[33] Including premises with a mill at Stratford at Bow and Bromley: W. J. Hardy and W. Page, *Calendar to the Feet of Fines for London and Middlesex*, II (1893), 14 Henry VIII.   [34] Guildhall MS. 9171/11 fos. 177v–178.

bequeathed that as well.[35] His eldest son Walter was to have 'all my interest of farms and leases' in the parish of Stapleford Abbots, paying out of 'Skege['s] farm' 20*s* annually to each of his younger brothers Richard and Alexander for their lifetimes. Other bequests were 'the standing bed with all that pertains to it in my bedchamber at Stapleford Hall' to his daughter Mary, to Richard his black gown and russet worsted coat, to Alexander his tawny satin doublet, and to William his servant his black cloak and jacket and 'my little black nag'. The rest of his goods went to Walter,

and I shall pray him and heartily desire him to be good unto my wife, as he would have been unto the mother that bare him. For I have found as much gentleness in her as ever any man have found in a woman, in mine extreme troubles which hath been chargeable ['burdensome'] unto her and me – my long sickness.

The long and burdensome sickness had not much farther to run: the will was proved on 12 February 1546. In George's touching references to his wife, there is something very reminiscent of that other George, the father who had died before he was old enough to remember him.

The eldest son, Walter Cely 'esquire', died less than four years after his father. In his will of 21 August 1549 he gave business-like instructions for the disposal of his estate, listing his main debts and detailing the succession of his property, which included leases of Stapleford and 'Suttons' and a house in London.[36] These were to go to his brothers in the case of failure of his immediate heirs. His son George 3 and unnamed daughters were still young and may have died, because in 1561 his will was declared void and administration of the estate was granted to his brother Alexander, the eventual legatee if the other brother, Richard, died without issue. One of Walter's chief concerns had been that his wife Elizabeth should complete the building of his new place, called 'Albyons', and part of his bequest to her was contingent upon its completion.[37] One of the overseers of the will was 'the right worshipful John Rither, esq., my old good master'.[38]

Elizabeth subsequently married Thomas Smythe, alias Clark, 'clerk in the skollage' [school] of the household of Edward VI, and later, under

---

[35] The name 'Pynchebexe' survives in Pinchback Bridge: Reaney, *Place Names of Essex*, p. 80.

[36] P.C.C. 44 Populwell.

[37] Albyns and Suttons are estates near Stapleford Abbots, both shown as gentlemen's seats in later maps of Essex.

[38] Probably John Ryther, M.P. for Colchester 1547, who had a successful career in royal service: S. T. Bindoff, *The House of Commons, 1509–1558* (History of Parliament, 1982), III, 240–1.

Mary, 'clerk of the queen's bakehouse'.[39] She thus followed a precedent among other Cely widows who took husbands in royal service. Smythe is probably the man to whom Walter owed £89 at the time of his death, and to whom he bequeathed 'my gown of tafitay'. Under Philip and Mary, Richard and Alexander Cely sued Smythe over an annuity due from the manor of Stapleford Hall, presumably that assigned to them by their father in 1545. So we end as we began, with a remarried widow and a lawsuit to recover money.

[39] Court of Requests Proc. Req. 2 Bundle 19 no. 23; Bdle 23 no. 49. This was evidently the Thomas Smith, gent., of Mitcham, Surrey, clerk of the Green Cloth, who died in 1576: Bindoff, *House of Commons*, III, p. 341.

SELECT BIBLIOGRAPHY

Arnold, Richard, *The Customs of London, otherwise called Arnold's Chronicle*, ed.
  F. Douce, 1811. Original edns 1503, 1521.
Balliol College, Oxford, MS. 354: the Commonplace Book of Richard Hill.
Bolton, J. L., *The Medieval English Economy, 1150–1500*, London and Totowa,
  1980.
Bridbury, A. R., *England and the Salt Trade in the Later Middle Ages*, Oxford,
  1955.
Bronnen tot de Geschiedenis van de Leidsche Textielnijverheid, ed. N. W. Posthu-
  mus, 2 vols., The Hague, 1910–11.
Bronnen tot de Geschiedenis van den Handel met Engeland, Schotland en Ierland,
  ed. H. J. Smit, vols. 1 & 2, The Hague, 1928–42.
Brown, E. H. Phelps and Hopkins, Sheila V., *A Perspective of Wages and Prices*,
  1981.
Burwash, Dorothy, *English Merchant Shipping, 1460–1540*, 1947, repr. Newton
  Abbot, 1969.
Calendar of Inquisitions Post Mortem, Henry VII.
*Calendar of Letter-Books Preserved among the Archives of the Corporation of the
  City of London at the Guildhall: Letter-Book L*, ed. R. Sharpe, 1912.
Calendar of Plea and Memoranda Rolls, 1437–1457, ed. Philip E. Jones,
  Cambridge, 1954.
Calendar of Plea and Memoranda Rolls, 1458–1482, ed. Philip E. Jones,
  Cambridge, 1961.
Cartulaire de l'ancien Consulat d'Espagne à Bruges, ed. L. Gilliodts-van Severen,
  Bruges, 1901.
Cartulaire de l'ancienne Estaple de Bruges, ed. L. Gilliodts-van Severen, Bruges,
  1904.
Carus-Wilson, E. M. and Coleman, Olive, *England's Export Trade, 1275–1545*,
  Oxford, 1963.
Carus-Wilson, E. M., *Medieval Merchant Venturers: Collected Studies*, 2nd edn,
  1967.
Caxton's Dialogues in French and English, ed. Henry Bradley, Early English Text
  Society, e.s. LXXIX, 1900.

Childs, Wendy, *Anglo-Castilian Trade in the Later Middle Ages*, Manchester, 1978.

A Chronicle of Calais in the Reigns of Henry VII and Henry VIII to the year 1540, ed. J. G. Nichols, Camden Soc., 1846.

A Chronicle of London from 1089–1483, ed. N. H. Nicolas and Edward Tyrrell, 1827.

A Dictionary of English Weights and Measures from Anglo-Saxon Times to the Nineteenth Century, ed. Ronald Edward Zupko, Madison, Milwaukee and London, 1968.

A Dictionary of the Older Scottish Tongue, ed. W. A. Craigie and A. J. Aitken, 1937–.

Dillon, Hon. H. A., 'Calais and the Pale', *Archaeologia*, LIII (1893), 289–388.

Dyer, Christopher, 'English Diet in the Later Middle Ages', *Social Relations and Ideas: Essays in Honour of R. H. Hilton*, ed. T. H. Aston and others, Cambridge, 1983.

Emden, A. B., *A Biographical Register of the University of Oxford to A.D. 1500*, Oxford, 1957.

Englische Handelspolitik gegen Ende des Mittelalters, ed. Georg Schanz, 2 vols., Leipzig, 1881.

Espinas, G., *La draperie dans la Flandre française au moyen âge*, Paris, 1923.

Gottfried, Robert S., *Bury St Edmunds and the Urban Crisis, 1290–1539*, Princeton, N.J., 1982.

 Epidemic Disease in Fifteenth-Century England: The Medical Response and the Demographic Consequences, New Brunswick, N.J., 1978.

 'Population, Plague and the Sweating Sickness: Demographic Movements in late Fifteenth-Century England', *Journal of British Studies*, Fall 1977, 12–37.

Grierson, Philip, 'Coinage in the Cely Papers', *Later Medieval Numismatics (11th–16th Centuries), Selected Studies*, 1979.

Hanham, Alison, 'Foreign Exchange and the English Wool Merchant in the Late Fifteenth Century', *Bulletin of the Institute of Historical Research*, XLVI (1973), 160–75.

 'Profits on English Wool Exports, 1472 to 1544', *B.I.H.R.*, LV (1982), 139–47.

Henisch, Bridget Ann, *Fast and Feast in Medieval Society*, University Park, Pa., 1976.

The Historical Collections of a Citizen of London in the Fifteenth Century, ed. James Gairdner, Camden Soc., 1876.

Hoskins, W. G., *The Midland Peasant: The Economic and Social History of a Leicestershire Village*, 1957.

Hustings Rolls, Corporation of London Records Office.

Inventaire des archives de la ville de Bruges: Inventaire des chartes, ed. L. Gilliodts-van Severen, Bruges, 1871–85.

James, Margery K., *Studies in the Medieval Wine Trade*, ed. Elspeth M. Veale, Oxford, 1971.

'The Johnson Letters, 1542–1552', ed. Barbara Winchester, unpub. Ph.D. thesis, University of London, 1953.

Kingsford, C. L., *Prejudice and Promise in Fifteenth-Century England*, Oxford, 1925.

The Ledger of Andrew Halyburton, Conservator of the Privileges of the Scotch Nation in the Netherlands, 1492–1503, ed. Cosmo Innes, Edinburgh, 1867.

The Lisle Letters, ed. Muriel St Clare Byrne, 6 vols., Chicago and London, 1981.

Lloyd, T. H., *The English Wool Trade in the Middle Ages*, Cambridge, 1977.

The Movement of Wool Prices in Medieval England, Economic History Review Supplement, Cambridge, 1973.

A Mediæval Post-Bag, ed. Laetitia Lyell, 1934.

Le Menagier de Paris, ed. Georgina E. Brereton and Janet M. Ferrier, Oxford, 1981.

Middelnederlandsch Woordenboek, ed. E. Verwijs and J. Verdam, The Hague, 1885–1952.

Middle English Dictionary, Ann Arbor, 1952–.

Morant, Philip, *The History and Antiquities of the County of Essex*, 1768.

Munro, J. H., 'Wool-Price Schedules and the Qualities of English Wools in the Later Middle Ages, *c.* 1270–1499', *Textile History*, IX (1978), 118–69.

The Navy of the Lancastrian Kings...1422–1427, ed. Susan Rose, Navy Records Soc., 1982.

Novum Repertorium Ecclesiasticum Parochiale Londinense, ed. G. L. Hennessy, 1898.

The Ordinance Book of the Merchants of the Staple, ed. E. E. Rich, Cambridge, 1937.

Paston Letters and Papers of the Fifteenth Century, ed. Norman Davis, 2 vols., Oxford, 1971–6.

Pirenne, Henri, *Histoire de Belgique*, 4 vols., Brussels, 1902–11.

The Plumpton Correspondence, ed. T. Stapleton, Camden Soc., 1839.

Poerck, G. de, *La draperie médiévale en Flandre et en Artois*, 3 vols., Bruges, 1951.

Postan, M. M., *Medieval Trade and Finance*, Cambridge, 1973.

Povah, Alfred, *The Annals of the Parishes of St Olave Hart St and Allhallows Staining in the City of London*, 1894.

Power, Eileen, *Medieval People*, 1924.

The Wool Trade in English Medieval History, Oxford, 1941.

'The Wool Trade in the Fifteenth Century', *Studies in English Trade in the Fifteenth Century*, ed. E. Power and M. Postan, 1933.

Reaney, P. H., *The Place Names of Essex*, Cambridge, 1935.

Recueil des documents relatifs à l'histoire de l'industrie drapière en Flandre, ed. H. Pirenne and G. Espinas, 1906–24.

Repertorium Ecclesiasticum Parochiale Londinense, ed. Richard Newcourt, 1708–10.

Rerum Anglicarum Scriptorum Veterum, tom. 1, ed. W. Fulman, Oxford, 1684 (Chronicles of Crowland Abbey).

Roover, Raymond de, *Money, Banking and Credit in Mediaeval Bruges*, Cambridge, Mass., 1948.

Ross, Charles, *Edward IV*, 1974.

Richard III, 1981.

Scofield, Cora L., *The Life and Reign of Edward the Fourth*, 2 vols., 1923.
Spufford, Peter, 'Calais and its Mint', *Coinage in the Low Countries (880–1500)*, ed. N. J. Mayhew, BAR International Ser. 54, Oxford, 1979.
  Monetary Problems and Policies in the Burgundian Netherlands, 1433–1496, Leiden, 1970.
The Stonor Letters and Papers, ed. C. L. Kingsford, Camden Soc. 3rd ser., 2 vols., 1919, and 'Supplementary Stonor Letters and Papers (1314–1482)', *Camden Miscellany*, XIII, 1924.
Stow, John, *The Survey of London*, ed. C. L. Kingsford, 2 vols., Oxford, 1908.
Studies in English Trade in the Fifteenth Century, ed. Eileen Power and M. Postan, 1933.
Talbot, C. H. and Hammond, E. A., *The Medical Practitioners in Medieval England*, 1965.
Testamenta Eboracensia, III, ed. J. Raine, Surtees Soc., XLV, 1865.
Thrupp, Sylvia, *The Merchant Class of Medieval London*, Michigan, 1948.
Tudor Economic Documents, ed. R. H. Tawney and Eileen Power, 3 vols., 1924.
Tudor Royal Proclamations, I, ed. Paul L. Hughes and James F. Larkin, New Haven and London, 1964.
Veale, Elspeth M., *The English Fur Trade in the Later Middle Ages*, Oxford, 1966.
Wee, H. Van der, *The Growth of the Antwerp Market and the European Economy, Fourteenth–Sixteenth Centuries*, 3 vols., The Hague, 1963.
Winchester, Barbara, *Tudor Family Portrait*, 1955.
Wood-Legh, K. L., *A Small Household of the Fifteenth Century*, Manchester, 1956.

INDEX

Printed in the United...
... Books Ltd

Printed in the United States
By Bookmasters